The Origins of Human Language
The Shape *of* Sound

BY
B. Redzisz Hammerstein

Sarasota, Florida

Copyright © B. Redzisz Hammerstein, 2021

All rights reserved. Published by the Peppertree Press, LLC.
The Peppertree Press and associated logos are trademarks of
the Peppertree Press, LLC.

No part of this publication may be reproduced, stored in a retrieval system, transmitted in any form or by any means, electronic, mechanical, photocopying, recording, or otherwise, without prior written permission of the publisher and author/illustrator. Graphic design by Rebecca Barbier.

For information regarding permission,
call 941-922-2662 or contact us at our website:
www.peppertreepublishing.com or write to:
the Peppertree Press, LLC.
Attention: Publisher
1269 First Street, Suite 7
Sarasota, Florida 34236

ISBN: 978-1-61493-731-9

Library of Congress Number: 2021917953

Printed October 2021

The SHAPE *of* SOUND

"It's from something inside of you, you don't turn back, you

don't look back, you don't look at the pain behind you,

you walk toward the light. Do what you have to do,

let the flowers fall. Do you understand me?

And you walk straight."

∞

Ma Jaya Sati Bhagavati

The Shape of Sould is dedicated to all of the
disrespected, abused and exploited women
who often silently wondered how and why they
universally became treated like second class
citizens after they created and maintained human
life of the body of Mother Earth.

Ambushed by Deity

May 22, 1977

In the past while mediating and telling myself to go deeper, I felt a small drop and sometimes experienced a full relaxation. Now after hearing the command from Joya to 'go keeper', I felt as if I had stepped into an elevator and plunged from the top of the Empire State Building down to the center of the earth. I catapulted deep into myself and felt as if the wind that whistled past my body was leaving my aches and pains behind. As she gave directions to breathe deeply into a heart, with the haunting music behind her, I felt as if I were being pulled gently back, as if some unseen force, a magnet, drew me straight up and back, forcing me to sit very tall. I found myself as stiff as a ram-rod, and then my breathing started to accelerate becoming faster and faster, louder and louder. The hair on my body, on my arms and my legs, stood up and my clothes moved imperceptibly, as I became completely still, and waves of goose pimples swept over me. The sensation started somewhere in back of my knees, moved up and around in waves around my body, around my spine. They came closer and closer together, until my body became a pulsation. Then all of a sudden an explosion of heart, light and ecstasy, again in expanding, ever widening circles, light and ecstasy, again in expanding, ever widening circles, occurred somewhere near the base of my spine and rose like a volcanic eruption of great pleasure up through my body. I began to rock back and forth. A roaring filled my ears. Heat and ecstasy rose and cascaded upward, intermingling with light that seemed to spark on and off inside my hear, reflecting fragments of multi-colored crystals. I had the momentary image from some great height of watching an atomic bomb explosion, a pushing up from the center and then rising, gathering heat, light, and with a great roaring sound exploding in its own center somewhere below me.

Then at a point, I realized that my breathing accelerating louder and faster was breathing me! I had no control over it. The waves of goose pimples were coming in an expanding spiral. As the ecstasy poured through me I felt as if I were sitting in the center of a great flaming pyre. I could almost see the flames going straight above me, and wondered if it was visible to others. Over the roaring that filled my ears I could hear the frantic pace of my own breath and felt no desire to stop it. Some part of me was like a bystander, a witness to the ecstasy that racked my body. My palate arched up high inside my mouth. Popping noises filled my nasal cavity and lights splintered in my head behind my eyes, as a roaring filled my ears splintered in my head behind my eyes, as a roaring filled my ears.

Through all this churning and the eruption of pleasure that was using my body as vehicle, I heard Joya's voice above the music, yell out as if it me.

"Rise above the breath, rise above the breath." With great effort and with only the image of her voice to guide me, I rose above The heat and light that pulsed in my brain subsided. Only the goose pimples continued to erupt across my body. Then a spasm wretched me forward, and I was sobbing uncontrollably. Except I wasn't sobbing. It was sobbing me. There was a part of me that stood aside and watched another part of me that I had been aware of before, but only in my dreams.

Somewhere in all that activity the something in me became aware that I had stopped breathing, I had not taken a breath since the last sob. The group was still chanting. Many verses later, a long space of time barely felt through the fog of my ecstasy, I took my first breath, more out of fear than of need. When my breathing returned, I became aware that splinter of light still pulsed in my brain. Along with the rapture, a throbbing ache was spreading at the base of my spine. As I opened my eyes, I also realized that I was drenched, my body was wet, and my blouse clung to me. Looking up I realized that Joya was staring at me.

"Are there any questions?" She looked straight at me. I was speechless. Blissed out, I was later to learn.

"Gunga Priya stand up." That was me, my new name, she was ordering me to stand.

I sat there in my soft pillows fumbling to make a move. The others around me pushed me up into a standing position. I reeled as I held on to their shoulders.

"Tell me what happened to you Gunga Priya."

Mixed emotions careened inside of me. One side of me felt a great desire to remain anonymous with my new joy, cradle it in my arms. Another part of me was jumping up and down like a demented child, screaming, I did it! I did it! I touched it! I touched something fantastic! I looked around me. The outside world looked the same. Back of heads were turning to look at me revealing inquisitive eyes. The room was the same. The sun shone outside. Musicians were strumming their guitars. My body subsiding and gathering strength was becoming a bit more settled and limp. Inside of me a great upheaval had taken place.

"Tell them." Joya's voice coaxed me.

I didn't know what to say, how to explain it. If I said too much, would it go away and never come back? I looked around again feeling that something was expected of me.

"Teach them, teach them, Gunga Priya."

"I...I, just had this experience that I can't describe," I stumbled through the words, my tongue heavy, my mouth dry. "you don't have to describe it, everyone look at her, look at her face. You are looking at someone who has just been Raped by God."

I swayed and reached out for the shoulders around me to steady myself. Raped by God? So much for under statements. Should I tell them that it seemed to me that my skin that exploded.

THE STORY OF
SHAPE *of* SOUND

The search inherent in The SHAPE of SOUND deals with the origins of the universal abuse of women and the exploitative practices upon the body of Mother Earth and how those abominable practices came to be. The search has to travel far back in time before the evolution of male centrality or make history (HIS STORY) came into being. The only certifiable artifact out of that ancient time has been the SOUND that humanoid and then humanitys ancestors carried with them as they dispersed off the climactically beleaguered continent of Africa.

THE SHAPE of SOUND (SOS) deals with the original codification of human language using the capital consonants of the Western Alphabet as major linguistic tools for the search. It becomes apparent that the SOUNDS associated with the SHAPE of the consonants of the Western Alphabet had their origins out of the INDIVIDUAL MOTHER'S FACE and the metaphoric round flat surFACE of MOTHER EARTH. It also becomes apparent that the SOUNDS of language and the SHAPES that became the subsequent capital letters of the Western Alphabet had their origins out of humanitys ancient heritage (HER IT AGE), out of a much more distant time of hemispherically balanced mother centrality before the most recent emergence of segmented left hemispheric male history (HIS STORY).

The SHAPE of SOUND also documents how the shift from the ancient mother based circular cooperative heritage of the right hemisphere of the human brain separated from that ancient hemispheric balance due to a shift from the left hand of the mothers to the right hand of the fathers, from the right hemisphere of the mothers to the linear male single focused repetitive flow of music, speech and writing itself using half of the male brain leaving behind feelings, care, kindness and compassion. The resulting single linear focus of left hemisphricc men of overdeveloped hierarchy, technology minded reason, power. war, violence and unbridled sexuality saddled the world with impending chaos and disaster. Not to be left behind has to be added the universal and expansive eunuch priesthood, other living creatures, elongated human skulls and what the transformative trance of Mother Earth's electro-magnetic prana of the Kundalini shakti energy played upon humanity through the use of the RULES of the ORIGINAL SOUND DISCOVERY (ROSD) in SECTION TWO in that massive, little understood, *universally suppressed* and pragmatically dealt with multifaceted 'spiritual' transformative shift.

SOURCE: *Stampede of the Natives* by B Redzisz Hammerstein

TABLE of CONTENTS

Ambushed by Deity	v
The Story of SHAPE of SOUND	viii
The Three Sections—	
Table of Contents in SECTION ONE	3
Table of Contents in SECTION TWO	117
Table of Contents in SECTION THREE	421

THE THREE SECTIONS
SHAPE of SOUND exists in THREE extended SECTIONS,

SECTION ONE contains many aspects of ancient reality based on the prehistoric time of mother centrality with Mother Earth, a flat round African plane containing all aspects of creation along Her lea lines, plus individual mothers as leaders and rule makers of migrating humans. Original specific paternity unknown, rape and violence common, first born son castrated to act as protector of human family. Blood descent through mother and baby girl as in hyena clan and mir cats.

SECTION TWO deals with the twenty five RULES of ORIGINAL SOUND DISCOVERY (ROSD), and how to find the original linguistic SOUNDS that had been codified into the capital letters of the Western Alphabet out of the individual mothers face and the metaphoric surFACE of Mother Earth which evolved into the subsequent mother created original universal language.

SECTION THREE explains the meaning locked in the individual consonants of the Western Alphabet, their source and evolution.

SECTION ONE
SHAPE *of* SOUND

SECTION ONE EXISTS IN THREE PHASES.

PHASE ONE deals with *mother central0ity*, worship of Mother Earth's rising Kundalini lea energy as the singular original and primal creator deity, and many aspects of ancient prehistoric reality based on the *worship of the natural world*. Blood line power descent through mother and daughter as in hyenas and mir cats.

PHASE TWO deals with the *transitional state* of male awareness of their role in specific paternity and a search for the male personal and existential father. Most of the mother centered concepts and rules redefined, destroyed, pilfered, purloined and suppressed. Shift from the left handed cooperative mothers to the right handed competitive fathers based on the change from the left hand to the right hand due to the evolution of *visual perception linear music, language and writing*. Male heroes enter the scene, followed by kings and male dictators reeking with violence, war and sexual license. Dehumanizing convoluted technology follows in their wake. Blood line power descent through mother and son.

PHASE THREE is the contemporary global scene of *father centrality* based on a shift in the human brain from the mother's holistic cooperative right hemisphere of the brain to the singular, linear lacking in compassion left male hemisphere. Blood line power descent through father and son in the hidden cosmos.

STAGES, SECTION ONE, PHASE ONE
contains five sequential linguistic STAGES.

STAGE ONE; letters sourced out of the individual *mothers face*
STAGE TWO letters out of the metaphoric *surFACE of Mother Earth*.
STAGE THREE letters sourced out of the individual *mother's body*
STAGE FOUR letters out of the metaphoric *body of Mother Earth*.
STAGE FIVE letters dealing with *other aspects and creatures*.

SHAPE of SOUND

SECTION ONE
TABLE of CONTENTS

Introduction; Female centrality, origins of language	6
The warring hemispheres of the human brain	11
The elongated skulls	15
SHAPE of individual letters	19
Dream; Robert Oppenheimer, July 14, 1981	28
Garage sale; Serendipity	31
WARP and WOOF; Mosaic, Hologram	32
PHASE ONE in SECTION ONE; mother centrality	35
PHASE TWO in SECTION ONE; transition	39
PHASE THREE in SECTION ONE; father centrality	42
The RULES of ORIGINAL SOUND DISCOVERY (ROSD)	45
The Tri-Parted Ancient Reality; the sun above, upon, under	47
PART ONE: **above** as the universe, (**at one**=atone)	47
PART TWO: Bi-Parted Reality	48
PART THREE: A Tri-Parted Reality (**below** Her surface)	50
PROCESS, linguistic origins of the sun (IS HANA);	55
The Origins of Flat World Phenomenon	57
The Perception of Balance and Immortality	60
UNIVERSALITY OF ANCIENT PERCEPTION	70
Mother's Face; look at me mommie syndrome	70
Migrations; semi-annual trek	71
Seven; (IS EVEN) or (HAVANA) lunar year fulcrum	74
Transformative journey of the sun (ate, eight, 8)	77
Menstruation, coagulation, maintenance	78
Liver, intestines	83
Mother Earths relationship to the sun, Elegy	94
Eunuch uncle, Heterosexual males,	94
Hierarchy, test, male line up; Curse of the alpha male	100
Female sexuality	106
The nose knows, the eyes have it, clitoris	108
Orgasm, orga(ni)sm	111
Passion, rape	113

INTRODUCTION to SECTION ONE

The capital letters of the Western Alphabet their SHAPE and SOUND surface like a Rosetta stone to the origins of human linguistic communication. Their magical contemporary existence bear witness to the ancient ultimately not so obvious fact that they emerged out of prehistory (-HIS STORY), out of a time that expressed itself through female centrality based on the personal mother as the individual source of creation expanding to include the more inclusive, all encompassing metaphoric body of Mother Earth through whom individual mothers of the specie had been perceived to act as surrogates in the creation of small replicas out of their bodies.

Except as seen through often mysterious myth, legend and poetry, mother centrality had been the time of humanity's almost forgotten, obliterated, suppressed, rewritten, often purloined and universally ignored ancient mother based heritage (HER IT AGE), the AGE that belonged to HER. How did the ancient clusters of ruling mothers lose their centrality to become abused second class citizens, considered intellectually inferior, denied basic education, used as brood sows for male offspring, enslaved in harems, subject to honor murder, arranged and child marriage, loss of their identity and brutally clitorectomized.

Since the human species had its genetic origins out of the African natural world, then it was primarily to Africa and the natural world that the origins of linguistic evolution had to be prodded loose in order to rediscover humanity's linguistic roots.

Due to massive cataclysmic climactic changes and humanity's recurrent systematic ancient dispersals by land and by sea off the besieged continent of Africa, there have surFACED upon the body of Mother Earth shamanistic practices that display discernible lea lines including long forgotten power centered pyramids and mounds, echoes of an ancient universal global grid, elongated and crystal skulls, mysterious monolithic structures, names in secret symbols and codes. Few cherished potsherds have surfaced from that most ancient mother centered time. The only and singularly verifiable clues that do surface and throw some light upon humanity's dim and ancient reality desperately trying to push their way up to the surface exist on another, not so easily verifiable level.

The tell tale signs to that ephemeral ancient reality exist floating upon the airy breath as the multi ethnic cacophonic SOUND of language itself made by many of the same organs on the human face as they originally had been made over more than two hundred thousand years ago on the faces of ancient humanoid and Homo Sapiens human mothers. The original SOUND of language like love itself leaves few actual traces upon the physical, verifiable archeological map.

The linguistic journey in The SHAPE of SOUND dipping into humanity's mother centered pre history at the time of humanity's ancient heritage out of Africa and then around the world, documents aspects that can only be discerned from the relative and recurrent constancy of the consonant SOUNDS that still exist in ALL of the languages of the world. *They can be deciphered singularly through the original SHAPES and SOUNDS locked in the capital letters of the Western Alphabet.* That unique exercise can be discerned through the use of the following twenty-five RULES of ORIGINAL SOUND DISCOVERY (ROSD) in SECTION TWO.

The SHAPE of SOUND also uses the origins of language to document the shift away from mother centrality, from the preoccupation with the individual mothers face, the worship of the metaphoric round flat surFACE and body of Mother Earth as the dual sources of singular creation, to the massive evolutionary shift from the left hand to the right hand and into the linear fear driven left hemisphere of the human brain of male centered rationalized power, unrelenting sexuality and violence. In the process of the shift out of PHASE ONE into PHASE TWO creating a host of fantasy based celestial Gods and ultimately a 'hidden' religion based father God in the ethers *away* and *above* the body of Mother Earth and *outside* of Mother Nature. It resulted in all of the massive individual and planetary disruptions that this over evolved rational fear driven, fantasy besotted linear left hemispheric male brain gave birth to.

How did it happen that women have been so universally abused and vilified? Mothers have been and most still are at the center of most of animal configurations. How did human mothers become so peripheral and universally abused ? And how did the father assume his role as not only the boss in the familial context but also the bossy heavenly father on the level of all of creation?

It wasn't until I had a Mother Earth sourced transformational 'spiritual' Kundalini experience at the feet of a female guru named Ma Jaya Sati Bhagavati that the journey to the answers began to unfold in my life. It took many years but an opening into the possibility of answers started an avalanche that almost overwhelmed my ability to make coherent sense out of it. I recount that specific

Mother Earth sourced 'spiritual' Kundalini experience in my book STAMPEDE OF THE NATIVES. It led me down many uncharted corridors, many doors that held empty rooms but eventually a linguistic pattern began to discern itself. A question proceeded to spin itself though my questing brain and it dealt with a phrase out of the Hebrew Bible. "In the beginning was the word."

How could 'the beginning' establish itself in 'the word'? Who spoke the word? If the word was spoken then someone came before and gave voice to it. But who was it? There must have been people who came before 'the word' in order to create such specific meanings dealing with often subtle multilayered concepts. The Hebrews blamed it on a visionary celestial deity, the Sumerians on the winged Anunnaki. Something down to Earth was needed. Then slowly the skein of linguistic possibility that had been so tightly and often so secretly woven began to unravel.

The possibility is that human beings have existed on this planet for over two hundred thousand years. Except for the elongated skulls, apparently for all of those years the brains of the emerging Homo Sapiens had been relatively the same size as contemporary humanity. Did they somehow come up with 'the word'? Who were they? Research into spirituality, anthropology, sexuality, theology, archeology, mythology, history, linguistics even religion slowly began to sow the seeds that began to bear some fruit.

There was an ancient prolonged human prehistory before 'the Biblical word' announced itself as 'the beginning'. It was a time before what came to be known as contemporary male centered, fantasy based linear 'rational' left hemispheric history (his story). There was a cornucopia of existence that spilled across the pages of humanity's ancient heritage before 'the word' spoken by the left hemispheric linear rational male mind had its 'beginning'. It dealt with mother centrality and established what became an ancient heritage (her it age).

It also became apparent that Mother Earth, specifically the climactically beleaguered continent of Africa went through recurrent violent catastrophes; massive climate changes, volcanic eruptions, floods, earthquakes, fires, asteroid strikes and ice ages that wiped out much of what came before. There has been a paucity of potsherds out of those ancient times.

What happened when one of those recurrent disasters struck the huddled groups of foraging migrating human ancestors? Apparently they had to flee in panic with only their clinging infants, their tattoos and the stories that often in song accompanied them. They could carry little else. It was to the SOUNDS that accompanied them at the time of their many dispersals that had to be turned to in order to discern the answers. How did they originate?

What gave birth to them?

Some things became apparent very early on. The major and overwhelming fact was that at the time of humanity's heritage, as language was becoming codified, mothers not only ruled from the center creating not only many civilized societies but what became the core of humanity's subsequent single universal multi-phonic language, the subsequently defined babble of Babel phenomenon.

Clusters of human beings followed not only the migrating herbivore herds across the savannahs of Africa but also dealt with massive climactic changes that over a span of thousands of years came out of multiple areas of Africa. Some most ancient, like the Saan, or Bushmen of the Kalahari Desert emerged out of the Southern reaches of Africa. Still others like the Hadza had their development out of the Rift Valley along with the Ethiopian highlanders. Then the most recent massive climactic change may have left its mark on the Berbers of North Africa and the Equatorial Sahel South of the Sahara Desert.

When the catastrophic cataclysms sent clusters of ancient ancestors scurrying to other areas of the world they took with them their SOUND based stories. There must have been a 'beginning'. It may very well have been in 'the word'. But 'the word' emerged originally out of the naming of things and processes separating them from their background, out of a much more distant mother based pre six thousand year Sumerian, cum Biblical past.

As a child learning my alphabet in Poland, the SHAPE of the capital letters of the Western Alphabet seemed to have hidden messages locked in them. Why were most of them marching to the right? What was it that made them so specifically and uniformly different? Where did they come from? What was it that over the landscape of SOUND the consonants stayed relatively constant and the vowels did their SHAPE shifting dance?

The turn had to be made to the relative constancy of the consonant SOUNDS that turned out to be wedded to the SHAPE of the capital letters of the Western Alphabet. How was that ancient coupling of SHAPE and SOUND accomplished? The source of the actual capital letters that emerged representing a multitude of SOUNDS was not only originally specifically codified but is still alive. Like the double spinning spiral of the DNA molecule existed at the very beginning of time and could be found in contemporary life on the planet, so the molecular DNA of SOUND originally created by humanity's ancient mothers still exists floating upon the airy breath.

The SHAPE of the capital letters of the Western Alphabet revealing their ancient origins, development and meaning, became the maps for the subsequent linguistic journey. Contemporary archeological digs have been reluctantly giving up their secrets. Ancient monolithic humongous stone structures in Machu Picchu, Gobekli Tepi, Pumapunku, Malta, Arkaeen, Petra, Henki, Tihuanako Bolivia have come to light. Stone circles more or less like Stonehenge have been surfacing all over the world. Pyramids following prescribed patterns along lea lines, mounds and serpentine configurations have been discovered in desolate reaches of China, Africa, Central and South America, Indonesia even in the United States. For the Maya precise celestial alignments have become apparent. Some ancient structures in Gobekli Tepi Turkey have animal and bird sculptures prominently carved upon their surfaces. Others still more ancient in Pumapunku flower with the races of humanity etched on their stone facades. By exploring the oceans archeologists and geologists have found many submerged cities off the coasts of Greece, India, England and Spain. Others wait to be discovered.

Then what happened to the much maligned larger brained, kind and relatively peaceful Neanderthal who shared humanity's heritage for approximately eight thousand years from twenty seven to thirty five thousand years ago, perhaps much, much longer? All this happening in the cold and rarified 'Stone Age'? Perhaps not, perhaps human history has to be rewritten. Perhaps all of human heritage including the balanced cooperative right hemisphere of the female based human brain, not only the subsequent competitive left hemispheric rational male brain, has to be taken into account.

Geologic accounts refer to civilizations that may have existed before what has come to be accepted as the contemporary spread of human history. The asteroid strike passing over Sumer and North Africa seventy two thousand years ago may have wiped out the verdant Sahara. The Black Sea flood, eight thousand years ago sent ancient ancestors scrambling to higher ground. Then there was the Clovis comet that thirteen thousand years ago decimated North America and sent a cloud of nuclear winter around the world. Every twelve thousand years or so the glacier moved its way down and entombed ancient groupings of humanity forcing them to live in caves. The twenty six thousand year cosmic alignment that periodically played havoc with Mother Earth cannot be left out. Just to name a few.

Since multitudes of humanoid and human creatures somehow survived and evolved, becoming the much touted bi-pedal, upright Homo Sapiens who have been around for at least two hundred thousand years, then they lived through and somehow surmounted all of those repetitive disasters. The stories as SOUNDS that they carried with them and the specific SHAPES that created them as they dispersed far from their ancestral African nest still exist. Linguists, including women, have to look at their evolution through a different set of long distance lens of both hemispheres of the brain and set aside the singular linear vision created by the rational violence focused misalignment of the contemporary left hemispheric male centered single focused fantasy prone, linear world.

There came to be a cluster of SOUNDS that left linguistic tracks acting like maps to an ancient universal past. They became wedded to specific SHAPES that still exist as the capital letters of the Western Alphabet.

The Warring Hemispheres of the Human Brain

Most of humanity's ancient and contemporary confrontations although having many different symbolic configurations have been understood at the time of ancient mother centered reality to have had their origins out of the two hemispheres of the human brain at war with each other. The two hemispheres emerged with very specific and very different functions. The right hemisphere of the human brain had been perceived to govern the left side of the human body and dealt originally with the creation of female creatures that shared their creative aspect on the multi-faceted body of Mother Earth. Over millennia it was the right hemisphere that dealt with the left hand and has remained relatively constant in its creative aspect.

The left hemisphere of the human brain which governed the right side of the human body had been singularly considered to belong to the male creating only male off spring and had been prone to massive evolutionary changes.

Scientists claim that the universe has been expanding. Sexual fusion between female and male creates smaller aspects of that fusion. The universe at its most basic does not expand from that sexual fusion. It creates more individual creatures but the universe itself does not get larger. For the universe to expand it has to deal with the constancy of the mother molecule splitting into exactly the same two daughter molecules who in turn split further into four more and so on down the line in a geometric progression. So the tumbling universe as such is basically based on the mother essence. What happens if the mother molecule finds itself on the planetary plane of Mother Earth with its changing climactic conditions? If it doesn't succumb to the climactic changes, asteroid strikes, ice ages and floods, for it to survive it has to find a way to somehow adapt. That's when a male molecule pops up as an aspect of possibility. It attaches itself to the mother molecule and begins the journey into growth and adaptive survival. In time with the evolution of polarity and balance it emerges as part of the human brain with two sided aspects of hemispheric survival. The mother molecule continues her journey of splitting into two daughters but within the two emerging daughters there begins to occur the possibility of adaptive survival. The mother molecule creates and maintains the offspring. The emerging male molecule brings not only change but specific characteristics dealing with the adaptive changes that it causes.

The right hemispheric mother molecule creates only female fetuses at conception housing the clitoris, ovaries and vulva creating the expanding universe. As a process of survival right after conception the male side of the brain releases some molecular testosterone hormones into the newly created female embryo in the process creating another female body but with male organs. The original female body stays constant but splits in half into another female body that shifts its genus into a male entity surfacing with the penis and testicles that drop down needing a cooler environment to develop but retains the female body and the vestigial breasts. That is why there are so many relative aspects to male sexuality. It depends on how many male molecular testosterone hormones that the left hemispheric father is host to. If there are many that flow into the newly created conception then heterosexual male babies see the light of day in a male body. If he has a few male testosterone hormones then the birth of the subsequent fetus is either homosexual, intersexual or eunuch. Possibilities for survival have to be taken for consideration. Mother Nature as the most creative artist experiments without stop. Those that can reproduce and find food are usually the most successful. Some females seem to evolve with more testosterone than males. In most females who become the matriarchs, the testosterone level rises as they become leaders. Aging males on the other hand begin to lose the level of their testosterone often becoming kinder and gentler as they age becoming more like the mothers. It has been postulated that often the last born male child often is gay due to the fact that the father had used up his male testosterone input and creates a gay son. The Biblical madness postulates that there are only two sexes with Adam and Eve. There are at least seven that can be acknowledged; heterosexual female-heterosexual male, lesbian female-gay male, female in male body-male in female body, both in either body.

In the Oxford Universal Dictionary on page 325 there exists an upside down definition of the clitoris as quote 'A homologue of the male penis present in the female of many of the higher vertebrates'. The original construct of the potential fetus is female at birth with female organs. When it splits into two equal halves, half the female part stays constant but the split off part becomes male in the other female body. It is not the female emerging out of the male but the other way around, the male fetus emerging out of the female. It is a vivid example of how the reality of human evolution by the evolving male patriarchy in PHASE THREE has redefined and obfuscated what is basic reality.

The male molecule housed in the left hemisphere of the human brain can only reproduce male children, who in turn do not singularly reproduce themselves. The human mother with her right hemisphere creates female offspring. The human creature called the Homo Sapiens based on the size of the brain of the mother and the myocardial DNA has been postulated by scientists to be 200.000 years old and has had many aspects associated with the North Congo River Basin chimpanzees. The males of both the male Homo Sapiens and the male chimpanzee of the North Congo River chimpanzees upon reaching hormonal puberty becoming testy and violent fought the Alpha males for turf and mating rights. As in all male creatures at the time of their puberty, violence and sexuality has been housed in the same area of the male brain. They formed scheming male groups, raging and killing males from other groups and systematically raping and abusing the females and their children. Specific paternity in PHASE ONE was unknown. Protection of the children was also unknown. The female groups as they evolved into humanoid and then subsequently human beings, for the protection of their families universally castrated their first born male child to become a eunuch uncle protector of the family.

All young females had to do was to sit and wait for their menstrual blood to flow to be ready to mate. There had been and still is no inherent violence in that patient waiting as they reached the time of their quintessence. Mothers who begot daughters did not have to go through all the confusion that exists with the birth of boys and their often perilous future.

When did the passage out of primate, humanoid evolution did SOUND become codified into words and then into more expansive communication. It apparently came out of mother centrality before the left hemisphere of the human brain became bifurcated, before the left hemisphere of the male brain had been set adrift on the sea of exclusive linear reason, selfishness, narcissism, creativity, rationality, imagination, fantasy, lying, secrecy, violence, competition, war, convoluted technology and madness leaving behind the female with her mucilage of compassion, kindness, maintenance, inclusive cooperation, all aspects of the right hemispheric mother brain.

History is his story not our story, not the human story or female story. It is singularly a male story created by the bifurcated left hemispheric male brain. All that contemporary humanity considers to be their past has been written by the left hemisphere of the male brain. Using only half of their brains male historians tell only half of the human story. Not only women have been left out but homosexual men have had to hide their sexuality in closets. Compassion and kindness had been left out of the left hemispheric male genus and animals became 'instinctive', not thinking and feeling creatures to be often used only as game. Creatures are limited by their bodies and not by their brains.

The left male hemisphere of the human brain became bifurcated and had been set adrift on a sea of possibility. The hemispheric balance that had been the gift of creature evolution had been thrown askew. Due to the helplessness of human creatures, not only at birth but throughout their lives, having no fangs, no claws, limited running skills, no climbing of trees, not even the ability of flying, at the mercy of bacteria and accidents, they had to rely on their brains to continue to exist. To that end their opposable thumb came to their rescue as it had for the primates. To create tools, weapons, fabrics, they had to rely on concentration, on focusing the mind to find answers. To focus the mind possibilities have to be lined up in a straight line in the brain. The mind had to stay focused. The left hemisphere of the brain, with its very specific linear image accumulation, one frame after another, came to their rescue. As the focus of the left hemisphere gained in taking over the human brain, the left hemisphere controlling the right side of the body with the right hand gained momentum. The primacy of the left handed mothers had been evolutionarily replaced by the right handed fathers. The focusing of the mind also has links with the process of linear codification of SOUND, of writing and the transformative state.

The making of individual SOUND of communication had been the legacy of the mothers teaching their offspring how to survive. Most creatures including human beings had been raised and taught the lessons of survival by their mothers. The first important lesson had been to stick to her like glue. The next was how to suckle to still their hunger and express the pleasure in suckling. Then she had to teach them which foods were safe and which were dangerous. As they grew older they had to learn their range of foraging or territory.

All creatures have body language, some aspect of tonal communication and a mysterious mental connection with their offspring. It came to human beings to associate the SOUND of communication with the organs on the mothers face in stage one and in time metaphorically on the round flat surFACE of Mother Earth in stage two.

The Elongated Skull

There exists upon the body of Mother Earth a mysterious and puzzling phenomenon, the humanoid looking elongated skull. The bony facial holes are there as are the teeth and a lower jaw. But above the brow the skull does not end into a round orb but continues in the back into ten or more inches rounding into an elongated curve with no hemispheric fissures fusing at the top. The elongated skull has 25% more brain power than its regular human cousin. It seems that this phenomenon has been a common occurrence all around the world in a very ancient past, concurrent with the time of mother centrality in PHASE ONE. It might explain gifts in that elongated skull that surface in the transformative trance, the massive stone monuments, power centered pyramids, levitation, communication with animals, super awareness and the use of the ancient lea lined electro-magnetic Mother Earth centered Kundalini grid.

With the discovery of these elongated skulls and their lingering remains in Egyptian royalty there exists the possibility of answering a variety of perplexing questions. In one direction it is, how did these strange elongated skulls emerge and how had they become lost. Was it a natural phenomenon? Or had it been created by human mothers? And what might have been their purpose?

What the science of the day knows about the skull. It had been found around the Nazca lines and in three hundred more caves in Peru but others have surfaced all around the world. One surfaced in a small forgotten tomb in Egypt, hidden from sight. Another had been found in Arkaeen Kazakistan on the same latitude as Stonehenge going back to the prehistoric Kundalini grid. DNA tests reveal that the Tihuanako Bolivian skull had its origins out of Europe. Some have been found in Hungary. Another astounding aspect is that it contains no Y male creative chromosome. How did it reproduce itself? Did it lay eggs, like the Anaconda? Like the Virgin Mother Earth out of PHASE ONE it had been perceived to be self perpetuating like the Anaconda snake in South America. Because it has no fissures melding the two hemispheres together as exists in normal human and most other terrestrial animal skulls, it must be from a time when evolving creatures didn't have two hemispheres. That must go back to a more ancient aquatic world primarily populated by the eight armed octopus with a head the same SHAPE as the elongated skulls or a variety of scientists have postulatd that some dinosaurs may have had an extension of their skulls.

There have been known and unknown evolutionary throw backs that surface in the human specie. Stalin had webbed feet like a frog. *I have personally known a young man who had a vestigial tail.* In Mexico there lives a hirsute family who give birth to children who are covered from top to toe in short nappy hair. There are many others. Perhaps the humans with elongated skulls are a throw-back to a time when human beings with elongated skulls had been decimated because their elongated skulls gave them powers that could not be controlled by the emerging left hemispheric power and control hungry bifurcated male brains.

The elongated skulls must have had a desired and sought after hemispheric condition. Many mothers in 'native' societies the world over have wrapped tightly and still wrap the skulls of their children at birth for the skull to become elongated. Something desirable must have become associated with those ancient elongated skulls for 'native' mothers to still carry on the tradition. That elongation must have been very desirable for royalty, the pharaohs of Egypt sport head gear in the back of their heads reminiscent of the elongated skulls.

Original rulers in PHASE ONE had been the mothers whose dominant right hemisphere contained the female essence. Perhaps also in PHASE ONE some human babies with elongated heads emerged as a throwback to a time when single hemispheric octopus patrolled the ancient seas carrying in their DNA all the future possibilities of mind enriched survival and the dinosaurs hopped along with their long brains following behind. With an elongated carapace their brains often had to be balanced hemispherically with both sides of the brain working in concert, without the central fissure becoming apparently fused bringing with it great wisdom, prophecy, healing, mind reading, and even the levitation of all of those massive ancient megaliths long buried under and presently becoming exposed out of the body of Mother Earth.

Among animal mothers specifically the carnivores there exists some kind of communication without outward signals. Without uttering a word carnivore cubs will hit the dirt without hearing a word from their mother. It seems like the 'walk about' of Australian Aborigenies who in their 'dream time' communicate over long distances without uttering a word. Perhaps its those electro magnetic Mother Earth sourced lea lines of the Kundalini energy that the Aboriginies and carnivore mothers have had access to. That may be why animals the world over and especially in Egypt have been buried not only with royalty and pharaohs but with ordinary human beings. Perhaps they understood the role that their fellow creatures played in that ultimate passage into immortality.

When my sister Jane was in the hospital a few weeks before her death. With our family around her she pointed to the corner of the hospital room and informed us. Look, I didn't know that they allowed cats into the hospital rooms. We all turned to the empty corner and tried to reason with her that there was no cat sitting in the corner.She continued to insist that she saw a cat sitting in the corner of the hospital room. A few days before she passed on she advied us not to sit on the corner of her hospital bed for the cat was now sitting much closed to her.

It explains the reson that the ancient Egyptians mummified and buried cats with the deceased. They knew something that has long been suppressed by the left hemispheric rational male brain. The role of animals as creatures of passage along with the lea lines upon the surFACE of Mother Earth has been lost to humanity due to the over evolution of left hemispheric rational male brain.

Speaking of lea lines. The surfacing of lea lines as a physical reality is the acknowledgment that itself is a throwback that is being rediscovered. Surreptitiously it surfaced in the inventive spirit of Nicola Tesla. In Yoga it is cautiously becoming known as the energy of Mother Earth. At a very ancient mother centered time with the help of their elongated brained children the understanding of Mother Earth's power grid surfaced in ancient civilizations and had been focused as containers of power in pyramids. Shamans, animal whisperers, birthing mothers and transformed human beings felt this power of joyful transformation rising up from the lea grid on the body of Mother Earth as they traversed back and forth across the ancient savannas. They often followed tracks that had been established as 'animal crossings' that had been used by animals for thousands of years as they too migrated in search of food and water following tracks upon the body of Mother Earth that guided them with a surge of pleasure. For a time and periodically it seemed to have been lost then it surfaced again in the giant pyramidal structures in Egypt and the world over as elongated brain power source.

Male scientists do not deal with this Mother Earth sourced energy as a reality. They call it electro-magnetic solar wind, if they deal with it at all, *never calling it the magical creative energy of Mother Earth as the original God*. When in PHASE TWO they shifted to the sky *away* and *above* the body of Mother Earth they began to call the celestial energies as gods and then the Father God up in the ethers with the magical energy of creation falling down from the sky. Never has the creative energy rising up from the body of the planet called the sacred rising energy of Mother Earth. Awareness of the Mother Earth as the major source of transformation periodically raises its hopeful head. But the emerging left hemispheric male power bases push it down again to be resuscitated in the constant future. It rose in megalithic finely chiseled stone structures, giant stone heads, pyramidal power sources, all sorts of healers, whisperers. Mother Earth as a living creative source tries to communicate with human beings as She communicates with all of Her other creatures. Because the human race is in rational peril Mother Earth has tried to communicate with human beings by creating Crop Circles and whisperers. There are no extra terrestrials falling down from the sky as the left hemispheric males try to create their source in the expansive cosmos on other perhaps male centered planets *away* and *above* the body of Mother Earth and *outside* of Mother Nature.

There very well might have been an Atlantis and other distant civilizations that have been engulfed under the waves. Some of their citizens might have escaped the massive destruction that Plato wrote about. The Atlantians were sailors as more and more discoveries will attest to their aquatic wanderings. Among many native ancient civilizations there are god like usually males that 'fell from the sky' became great leaders and teachers sporting beards and mustaches` which surface in Pumapunku which were not common to the local native populations. There have also been many women that appeared from nowhere and with great wisdom led ancient peoples as the Goddess Amaterasu in Japan. They may have had the elongated skulls that began to pepper the ancient landscape. Plato also states that not only were they sailors but that their civilization had been amazingly advanced and ahead of their neighbors.

SECTION ONE

SHAPE AND SOUND OF THE INDIVIDUAL LETTERS

These ancient SHAPES dealing with mother centrality in PHASE ONE may have been lost and obliterated due to male awareness of their paternity in STAGE TWO and a great catastrophe that befell Mother Earth either as a massive flood or an asteroid strike. Their SHAPES and SOUNDS in PHASE ONE became codified out of the individual mothers face and the surFACE of Mother Earth.

The letter A (ah); first breath, volcanic SHAPE, alpha of beginnings

The letter H, of air, breath out of the letter A, open on top, AH-HA

The letter M (mm); hum, mothers top lip, yes to food, Mountains on Mother Earth

The letter N (no); angle of nose in profile, nasal rejection of food, breath

The letter L (la); tongue, Lengua in Latin, <u>angle</u> on floor of oral cavity.

The letter B (be); both bulbous lips in profile

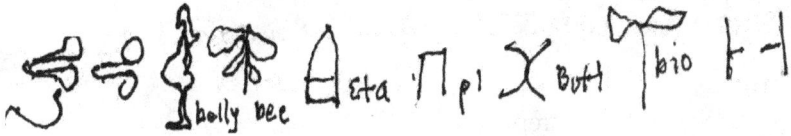

Shape of Sound

The letter P (pee); movement of air out of top lip, paw, passage of piss

The letter W (double U, V (vee); water, waves, woda (voda) in Polish, reflected letter M of top lip, or mountains.

The letter V (vee); voice, vision, vulva, vagina, volcano, valve of passage

The letter F (ef); fingers of individual mother, Mother Earths rays of light at dawn

The letter D (dee); open hand, 'gift of', dam, dom, dame, dome, abdomen, Democracy

The letter T (tee); upon the top, tip, edge, teeth, toes, trees,

The letter S (es, sa); est, blood, spiral, spring

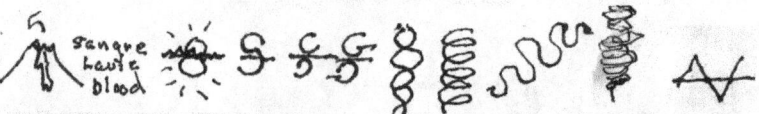

The letter C (see, kh); seeing above in life, (KH) of corpse in death

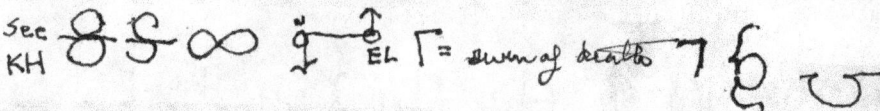

The letter X (eks. ks) buttox from back

20

SECTION ONE

The letter K (kay); Letter X halved vertically, smallness, bird SOUND coos

The letter Q (cue); one legged sun, questing why of male periphery

The letters CH (chee); chicks chirping out of cheek and chin, children, change

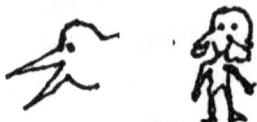

The letter G (gee, gh); ground (gh) of generation (gee) and be getting (gh)

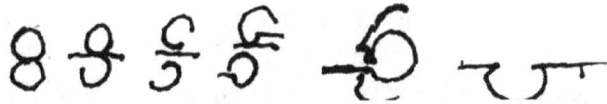

The letter J (jay, jee, h, y;) jaw, joven young Spanish,

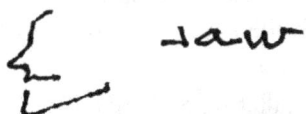

The letter Y (why); pubis, bifurcated brain asking why of male periphery

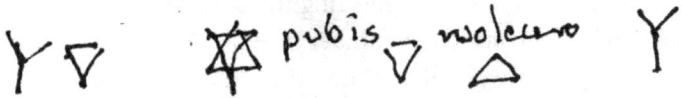

The letter R (are); top male sun, bottom Mother Earth volcano

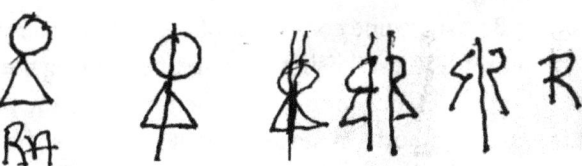

A- The SHAPE of the letter A (ah) came out of the triangular volcanic cone on the surFACE of Mother Earth in stage three. The SOUND associated with the letter A (ah) had been considered to be the SOUND taken by a baby with its first breath. The letter A (ah) as Alpha deals with beginnings of out of volcanic land and the first breath of life.

M- On the individual mother's face the SHAPE of the letter M represents the top lip of her mouth in stage one. Its SOUND is associated with the HUM of acceptance that the food is safe and edible. On the body of Mother Earth the SHAPE of the mountains on the flat round ground of Her horizontal rim represented the many mountainous mouths out of which She regurgitated the solar disc in the East and swallowed it at twilight in the Western sea. The letter M deals with the mothers assent, or yes saying.

N- The letter N on the individual mother's face in stage one deals with the angular SHAPE of the nose as seen in profile. It deals with negation and change. It also deals with scent and of breathing in and out. On the body of Mother Earth it deals with the SHAPE of islands poking their way up to the light as they spew volumes of air up to Her surFACE.

L- The SHAPE of the letter L comes out of the tongue in the mothers mouth in stage one . It is the flap that lies on the floor of the oral cavity and angles down into her throat. Its SOUND is associated with the flapping of its loose frontal part making its specific lallating SOUND. On the surFACE and body of Mother Earth the letter L creates the angle of ascent of the sun out of Her Eastern rim at dawn reflecting the descent of the solar disc in the Western horizon creating the number seven.
Its ascent deals with the (L) of light and life, and descent deals with the SHAPE of the number seven and the death of the sun. It also codifies the daily passage of time.

B- The SHAPE of the letter B in stage one comes out of the individual mothers mouth as it is seen in profile. It establishes the two lips creating the one mouth and the concept of 'two in one', or both. It also embraces the brow. Out of the individual mother's body in stage three it embraces the two breasts, the two buttocks, the two Spanish brazos, or arms and morphs into the number eight as the reflective passage of the sun at twilight into the Western waters. On the bountiful body of Mother Earth in stage four it brings forth the bio of life as it buds into beautiful being.

P- The SHAPE of the letter P in stage one deals with sequential movement of plosive SOUND out of the top lip on the individual mothers face specifically out of her mouth. It deals with passage, or one thing after another being pushed along by the breath. On the bodies of carnivores it deals with movement created by their angled paws of power as it does with the pads on human feet. On the body of Mother Earth in stage four it deals with the ex plosion out of the volcanic vent on Her surFACE and the concept of passage itself.

W- On the individual mothers face in stage one the SHAPE of the letter W is the bottom lip, or the reflection of the top lip that creates the two parts of the mothers mouth. On the surFACE and body of Mother Earth the letter W deals with the reflective surFACE of water and the mysterious darkness that it holds under its wavy aqueus mirror. Puckered up it deals with woe, war, worry and wonder. Its SOUND is often interchangeable with the letter V.

V- The SHAPE of the letter V establishes its life as an angle of ultimate creation. Its SOUND in stage one deals with air being pushed out of the vocal cords through the bottom lip becoming the voiced (Vee) as opposed to being the unvoiced (F). In PHASE ONE and stage three It began its life as the triangular vulvic patch on the mothers body. In PHASE TWO also in stage three it merged into the Y of the female pubis. In PHASE THREE it became redefined as the trident of the male sea god Poseidon. Because the human creature had been perceived as eminently visual, the angle of vision as the eye of the I also came to define it. On the body of Mother Earth in stage four it surFACES as the three sided volcano performing the same creative lavic bloody function as the female vulva on the individual mothers body, a turn-around of the volcanic magmic blood that returns to the surFACE to create land.

F- The SHAPE of the letter F in PHASE ONE and stage three comes out of the five fingers of the individual mother who did most of the work of maintaining and teaching her offspring how to survive their perilous infancy. The SOUND of fillibration has been made by the same configuration of the lips as the letter V, except that it is unvoiced. On the round, flat surFACE of Mother Earth it deals with the five fingers of fire of the mother or the four fingers of the father that as the helping rays of the sun light up the firmament of the Eastern sky at dawn.

D- The SHAPE of the letter D in one direction deals with 'the gift of' the closed fist in stage three before it opens to reveal the gift that hides inside. In another direction it is the circle of constant returns that exists halved vertically in the individual mothers abdomen or laterally in the belly of Mother Earth. It extends to contain the bulging abdomen in the individual mothers body that contains the 'gift of' the fetus inside. The SOUND of D deals with the voiced SOUND of T created by the tip of the tongue. Also it deals with not only with giving in PHASE ONE, but the aspect of doing in PHASE TWO on many subsequent levels and in many subsequent languages. On the body of Mother Earth it is the dirt underfoot that underlies all aspects of survival, the soil, the land that offers up crops as food, the trees as leaves and fruit, grass for foraging animals, caves for shelter, water for travel, the appeasement of thirst and source of Mother Earths electro magnetic Kundalini energy. Without dirt (D) as the gift giver on the surFACE and body of Mother Earth there would have been no perceived possibility of terrestrial life.

T- The SHAPE of the letter T deals with the tip top or tail end. On the individual mothers body it deals with the tip of the tongue, the tip of the gums that claim the teeth, the toes that sprout on the tips of the feet. On the body of the individual mother and the body of Mother Earth it deals with Her titties Her mountainous summits covered with snowy milk as the majestic Tetons. Trees round out this picture. Its SOUND is the unvoiced D of potential creation at the tale end of an activity.

S- The SHAPE of the letter S consists of two broken circles, one above the line as the letter C (see) the upper circle in life and the letter C (hk) below the circle in death. The SOUND associated with the letter S in stage one deals with the hiss or siss out of the mother's mouth as air is pushed out through approximated teeth and tongue. On the surFACE and body of Mother Earth in stage two the SOUND of the hiss comes out of volcanic vents and steaming calderas. The SHAPE of the electro-magnetic Kundalini energy of creation on the body of Mother Earth had been perceived as a double spiral, encoded in hurricanes, tornadoes, water spouts and whirlpools . It deals with the concept of being or isness. Because a snake makes a hissing or sissing SOUND it had been one of the reasons that it became a metaphoric symbol for the energy of isness expanding to cover the actual SHAPE of the lea line emergence of the Kundalini energy of Mother Earth. As the concept of isness, the metaphoric snake also slithered in a sinuous pattern across land, water and trees. In the human body the serpentine Kundalini energy rose pragmatically up the spine in a double pattern exiting through the top of the head. The newly discovered DNA sequence

SECTION ONE

mirrors the same pattern . It was the blood (SA) that had been considered the main carrier or isness and being both as menstrual blood out of the body of the individual mother and as lavic blood out of the more expansive surFACE and body of Mother Earth. The SASA construct in miss and lass covers that linguistic pattern.

C- (see) The SHAPE associated with the letter C emerges partly out of the top half of the letter S. On the human face in stage one it is associated with the eye and deals with SEE-ing, or the activity of reflection. On the surFACE of Mother Earth it deals with the SEA as the great aqueus eye that reflects the sky. The sassing or hissing SOUND associated with the letter C takes it back to its source and the letter S. The top part of the letter S as the letter C deals with life and isness. It has a reflected companion that plays a double role.

C- (KH) The SHAPE associated with the letter C as the KH or the cough (KH) of death deals with the other aspect of existence or the underground cavity of death under the surFACE. It is the bottom part of the letter S that deals with the corpse (KH), cadaver (KH), carapace (KH), cave (KH), caldera (KH) or containment (KH) after death.

K- (KH) The SHAPE of the letter K (kh) covers a variety of bases. One of the most ancient out of the time of mother centrality in PHASE ONE deals with the letter X of the buttox in stage three as seen from the back halved vertically to emerge as the SHAPE of the letter K. Because 'X marks the spot', the spot has been perceived to be the bloody discharge of either estral or menstrual blood at the buttox. The buttox had been perceived to be the source of creative (kh) activity and the definition of subsequent creation of smallness (KA). Another aspect deals with the emergence of feces or KAKA out of that same buttox. The transformative aspect of a butterfly or moth had been the making of a cacoon (KAKA-) its anal effulgence on its way to becoming a creature of the air. Also as a relationship to the creatures of flight, the SHAPE of the letter K emerged as an open bird's beak cooing (kh) its way into onomatopoéic SOUND out of its oral cavity.

X- (KS (KASA)) The SHAPE of the letter X also covers a variety of ancient symbolic perceptions. Not only it reflects the buttox as seen from the back halved vertically into the letter K (kh) of smaller creations (kh) of the fetus and feces (KAKA). The (ks) as casa deals with the coos (KASA) the actual place of emergence of the fetus in the front and out of the buttox in the back of the feces as KAKA.

Halved laterally it emerges with a V of the vulva on top and the A, the Alpha of the V of the vulva reflected on the bottom. Also the letter X (ks) had been an ancient definition of time. It dealt with the sun and moon crisscrossing the sky from East to West daily and the birds crisscrossing the sky North South seasonally creating the ancient celestial cross that morphed out of the SHAPE of the letter X. It was an ancient universal PHASE ONE calendar predating the swastika. Along the way putting the two V's as the two five fingered hands together it surfaced as the number ten (X) in Latin. Ten is the number that not only defines the ten fingers that do the holding and helping but also the ten lunar months of gestation of a human fetus having links with that ancient spotted buttox. The Runic hooked X deals with ten months of human fetal gestation to which the male aspect of the erect penis had been added. It establishes its transitional reality out of PHASE TWO when females and males cocreated as they cohabited.

Q- (KUE) The SHAPE of the letter Q comes out of the circle of the male solar disc dragging its one snake like leg across the sky. It emerges out of the time of questing, of asking why (Y) of male periphery. In PHASE TWO the bifurcation of the two brain hemispheres and the eunachization along with mutilation of one leg to force the metal worker to remain at the forge making metal tools and weapons and for the shepherd tending to his flocks of domesticated animals. It also shares links with the trance state of transformation with the one remaining leg after the first born sons had been castrated and mutilated that looks like the solar disc of the metaphoric Kundalini snake trailing its one remaining leg across the sky.

CH- The SOUND associated with the cluster of (CH) deals with the chirping (ch) of young chicks (ch) created by their cheeks (ch) and chins (ch) or upper and lower mandibles of young chickens (ch). It has punning links with the coos of the mothers. It also deals with avian change (ch) and their coming and going North and South across the sky creating part of the seasonal monsoon water laden African clock.

G- The SOUND associated with the letter G contains ancient links with the letter C. Both deal with aspects of creation out of internal caves, cavities and containments. The SHAPE of the letter G is the letter C(kh) of the oral cavity with the tongue sticking out, pushing life of generation (JEE) and be*get*ting (gh) of matter out of internal cavities as it does of Mother Earths ground (gh) of being.

Section One

J- The letter J (JEE) is the SHAPE of the jaw, or the lower mandible. It is the voiced SOUND of chewing food. It is also the hook that hacks food apart; leaves and fruit from trees and life from prey.

I- The SHAPE of the letter I is not only a vowel but also the number one. It has a varied history. Originally it defined a new born baby boy as 'one more' based on the finger like SHAPE of his penis. A little girl had been defined by the triangular SHAPE of her vulva. A little boy without the vulva became defined by the SHAPE of his penis as 'one more' and the 'one more' moved from his unknown state dealing with his lack of subsequent paternity, to the I of the individual self and then to the first one and then the most important one in Linear PHASE. In English the I SOUNDS like the eye or the aspect of seeing (C) that defined the visual source of male sexuality.

Y- In different PHASES the letter Y takes on different meanings. The most ancient at the time of mother centrality in PHASE ONE dealt with the individual mother's body and the SHAPE of her vulvic patch. With male children asking the WHY of their periphery it came to define the bifurcated brain asking WHY (Y). In time the WHY of their peripheral state of questing dealing with their permanently empty belly and castration along with music, words and writing it fed into the primacy of the left hemisphere of the brain. As human beings dispersed across the seas following the many catastrophes that befell their African continent, their maritime symbol of Mother Earth as the vulvic sea became the god Poseidon of the triple trident. like the Goddess Amaterasu of the Japanese both had been originally female.

R- the letter R contains a very secret ancient PHASE ONE beginning. The SHAPE of the letter R originally dealt with a transitional balance between the body of Mother Earth as the volcanic triangle on the bottom and the male orb of the solar disc on top creating the balanced symbol of passage . Along the way as the brain became bifurcated so did some of the letters such as the letter X halved verically into the letter K and laterally into the two Vs. The symbol of the sun on top and the volcano on the bottom become the letter R. The sun volcano configuration became vertically halved to become the subsequent letter R. It surfaces in PHASE THREE as the Egyptian male solar deity RA.

Thrashing around in a sea of SOUND I had one of my lucid dreams.

DREAM OF J. ROBERT OPPENHEIMER,
July 14, 1981

"Now I am become death, the destroyer of worlds"—Bhavagad-Gita

Four years after my Mother Earth sourced 'spiritual' Kundalini experience, in May 22, 1977 at the feet of a female guru Ma Jaya Sati Bhagavati, as my usually well crafted life was disintegrating into a chaos of loss and reorganizing frenzy, I woke up from the following dream. In the dream I knew that I had gone through a very difficult time and sat facing the haggard face of Robert Oppenheimer the American physicist who was instrumental for bringing into fruition the first successful explosion of the atomic bomb. He had been called 'the father' of that awesome left hemispheric technologically destructive force that spread massive destruction and lingering radiation all over the world.

He was leaning forward toward me across the small kitchen table. The anguish in his stricken eyes held me in place, for I knew that he was desperately trying to say something very important to me. It was something that he wanted for me to understand. I leaned forward trying urgently to hear what his stricken eyes, riveting me to his anguished face were trying to say. There were many words that flew by me before I was able to transfer the meaning in his eyes into audible SOUND. I asked him to repeat what he was saying to me, for it went by so quickly. He seemed impatient with my obtuseness, but made a concentrated effort to be more clearly understood.

He gazed levelly at me and shared with me that,

'I HAD MOVED MY WAY IN', and after a pause, 'WE HAVE TO BECOME AWARE OF WHAT COMES TO US, NOT ONLY WHAT WE PUT OUT'.

He went on to say, that I had been given the opportunity to understand what he, and others like him were saying, because I had grasped the implications of the STAMPEDE OF THE NATIVES that night. By understanding the implications of that flight, something had opened up in me and I would be able to get the information I was seeking from him and from others like him. What he said to me was difficult for me to grasp and I strained forward trying to remember as much as I could, for he said a great deal and I knew that what he was trying to make me understand was very important.

AHA! Then, as he continued to speak and his lips continued to move on his anguished face, I realized that I could no longer catch what he was trying to say to me no matter how much I strained across the kitchen table to hear him. Both his anguished face and his voice filled with desperation receded into the middle distance and I began to wake up. The dictionary defined STAMPEDE as that which was put to flight in a panic, that which broke away fuelled by a common fear driven impulse. NATIVES defined a state, or characteristics that came with the package, were natural, emerged out of nature, were indigenous to the place and were not acquired. NATIVES were at home on the planet, be they plant, animal or human. Trying to understand my Mother Earth sourced Kundalini experience, STAMPEDE OF THE NATIVES became the name of my fourth book.

What emerged from my dream and what Robert Oppenheimer was trying to share with me, was that what he and his left hemispheric technologically oriented fellow physicists created may very well bring the end of life on Mother Earth as we know it. I also began to grasp that he was trying to give me some kind of information that would help me to understand what had created the possibility of the oncoming catastrophe. What he did actually say was how everything that was real, natural and NATIVE to planet Earth had become panicked into a stricken STAMPEDE toward oblivion. He did not give me any actual clues that led into that head long descent into the possible extinction of plants, animals, human beings and the planet Herself. That I had to figure out for myself.

I also wondered where he was coming from. Where were he and others like him hanging out. Was it only a fantasy conjured up by my dream state of mind? Or was there a reality that we had no access to our waking consciousness, a reality beyond our grasping? And since I had been asking the eternal questions not only about life and death but about the universal abuse of women, I wondered what answers lay at my feet.

I realized that it was the question that I had been asking most of my life. How did women lose their cooperative clusters of peaceful centrality and how did men competitively take over the planet, tormenting all living creatures, enslaving women, abusing them and their children, making them into slaves, sequestering them in harems, subjugating them into unrelenting universal sexual servitude, extending the same exploitative harassment to the body of Mother Earth.

Since the current human madness apparently became petrified in 'the word', it was to 'the word' that as language itself that I had to turn to find the answers to the questions that churned their way through my brain. I had also asked for the roots of organized religion that had become sanctified in 'the word'. I realized that the much misunderstood Mother Earth sourced Kundalini experience was given to me as an answer to that overwhelming question. As Robert Oppenheimer tried to share with me in the dream;

'WE HAVE TO BECOME AWARE OF WHAT COMES TO US, NOT ONLY WHAT WE PUT OUT'.

When I was on staff with EST in 1975, Werner Erhard admonished us to be responsible for all that we had created and that we were responsible for it all. I realized that I had gotten a change of perceptive direction in my dream with Robert Oppenheimer.

Many years later after much searching I became aware how serendipitously ironic it was that the famous physicist came to me in my dream. I had been blessed with a beautiful voice and a gift of musicianship that came with the package. All I wanted to do was to sing and to share my feelings with the rest of the world. Somehow it was not to be. After I sang, I either got hoarse or lost my voice. Doctors, psychiatrists, nutritionists even dipping into 'spirituality' did no good. After many years of trying to find an answer why I had been given such a marvelous gift and why I wasn't able to use it, in never ending despair I gave up. Then my mother died, not only had a light gone out of my life never to be lit again in the empty hole that remained, but the doctor to whom I went for my entombing depression couldn't find my pulse. I had gotten so close to that terminal passage. He had me go through a series of tests and shared solemnly with me that my thyroid gland was so low that he couldn't understand why I was still alive. He put me on thyroid supplements and I slowly recovered. Again I wanted to know how was it that my thyroid had become so low. I had been a relentless nutrition minded health nut. Then Chernobyl happened and many of the Polish women who came to this country on work visas, many came with goiter problems. It was also at the time that my dear college friend Nancy Merritt had her goiter removed. Slowly the answers began their journey through my brain. It seems that there exists a gland next to the thyroid gland that squirts a fluid across our two vocal chords every time we phonate or make a SOUND. If the thyroid gland is too low then there is no fluid wetting the two vocal chords they knock together causing hoarseness even polyps. What caused the loss of power in the thyroid gland for women my age, the Polish women who came to work in this country after Chernobyl and my friend Nancy was the massive radiation that had been visited upon our Mother Earth in the forties, fifties, sixties and on and on as the United States, Russia, France and England exploded countless nuclear bombs in the islands, deserts and every place that could not be easily detected. Nuclear radiation causes diminution of the efficacy of the thyroid gland and the squirting smaller gland that lies next to it. Ergo goiter, hoarseness, vocal *polyps and as in Chernobyl even death.* Since Robert Oppenheimer had been so responsible in the creation of the nuclear weapon of massive destructive radiation, could it be that is why he came to me in a dream, not only to atone for the left hemispheric madness that he helped to create but to give me an answer why I had been burdened with my vocal failure. Who knows, it could be serendipity, or maybe he exists somewhere out there and wanted to atone for the massive destructive global catastrophe that he helped to unleash.

Garage Sale

The SHAPE of SOUND as the study of the origins of language came out of a serendipitous experience. It's as if you went to a garage sale and found a pretty landscape painting alone in a corner that matched your living room and that everyone seemed to have overlooked. After paying a few dollars for it and marveling that the gorgeous frame was probably worth more than the painting itself, with growing self satisfaction you cavalierly shoved it into the back of your car.

As you began cleaning it, you began to realize that under the rather pretty but banal landscape there seemed to be something hidden. Some other painting was trying to push its way up to the surface. With pounding heart you leaped into the land of possibility and hoped for a lost treasure, perhaps a Leonardo or even a Picasso.

The spot that you had again cavalierly cleaned with some wet cotton cue tips glowed with brilliant color. If it was a hidden treasure then you had to do the job of revealing it very carefully. You had to study the science of exposition. You had to clear off the top overlaid layer without obliterating the basic painting underneath. Much research entered the scene.

After accruing as much knowledge as the subject seemed to demand you plunged into cleaning out the debris filled top layer. What started to shine through was not only a magnificent masterpiece but a mysterious creation out of a different time and place and apparently out of a different perception of reality. Not a Leonardo or even a Picasso began to lay down its tracks. What seemed to desperately want to push its way up to the clarifying surface was apparently a long forgotten story from an ancient prehistoric time of mother centrality, of female rulers, queens, sagas, the long forgotten and obliterated story of universal matriarchy.

And so it was after I began to plummet the depths of our linguistic heritage that it became apparent to me that our universal contemporary language is like a cacophonic overlay hiding in its linguistic folds something that existed before, *something that was constant, that was humanity's linguistic mother based construct and that its origins seems to have been lost. I realized that I had been given the job of finding those deeply entrenched and universally obliterated roots.*

WARP and WOOF

As facts in the SHAPE of phonemes began to spill around me I began to fill ever-expanding color-coded notebooks. The phonemes themselves were not enough, so in trying to understand what they were trying to tell me I turned to myths and legends and then to different language dictionaries to further get a hook on what I had been uncovering. The lists grew and I despaired at ever being able to organize the information for which I had been asking and which was being given me.

Maybe a Mosaic

At first I thought that I could somehow make the growing mass of information coherent by organizing it into a kind of a mosaic. Maybe I could take the growing shreds of apparently disparate tonal facts and beginning randomly on a flat plane, make them fit into a picture driven story that was coming alive in my mind. But to create a mosaic, like in a picture puzzle you have to have a plot, a plan, something that came before, something that you are able to look at and to copy. I had none of that.

Maybe a Hologram

I needed something that allowed me more complexity, something like a hologram. The construction of a hologram through the use of SOUND and then words was beyond me. I needed two disparate and distinct processes that I could work on simultaneously. One dealt with the perception of ancient reality at the time that language was becoming codified and the other dealt with the origin and evolution of meaningful SOUND and then the words themselves. So I settled on the next best thing and the weaving of a fabric came to mind. Through the miasma of complexity I began to see the seeds of possibility take root and poke their way up to the light.

The weaving of a linguistic fabric involved two distinct inputs, a WARP and a WOOF. The WARP would be the vertical threads running up and down as ancient reality and the WOOF would be the lateral threads that as SOUND would weave their way through that same ancient construct. If I needed more complexity I could always turn to the added discipline of embroidery. Embroidering the facts is not too rarified a tactic to use in the telling of a story.

All of those phoneme driven facts and pictures were beginning to make a great deal of sense to me, but as I tried to explain them to wary friends, I was met with incredulous skepticism. I tried to explain to them that the SOUNDS that exist in all of the languages of the world, in spite of some linguistic theories denying the fact, came from a single source out of the continent of Africa and are the only potsherds that remain from a very ancient past when humanoid SOUNDS that evolved into human language were becoming codified.

That wasn't all. That ancient past was not only pre-historic but emerged at the dawn of humanity's heritage at the time when reality had been perceived not only through the left hemispheric linear reason lacking compassion and relationship but through both the linear reason and the right hemisphere of the human brain, through the physical body, through emotion, the state of trance and through the lens of mother centrality. The elongated skulls of ancient humanity constantly insisted on being dealt with as did the magnificent crystal skulls and similar rites of mother worship practiced around the world.

The semi-annual coming and going of birds from the Northern and Southern reaches out of the body of Mother Earth rounded out the holistic picture in sync with the migratory treks of herbivores who also semi-annually crisscrossed the continent of Africa.

Since the female as mother exists at the center of all living families, then how in the torrential rush of human experience were human mothers pushed out of that ancient pre-historic center to exist on the periphery as second class citizens if that, in almost all of the societies in the modern world?. The letter (M) is an anlaut defining the mother, exists in all of the languages of the world except for the Japanese. Linguistically (M) extends into MA the first consonant (M), vowel (A) combination to be codified. Through the repetition of the MA SOUND into MAMA a tentative journey into words began.

How could the (M) SOUND define the mother in all of the languages of the world, except in Japanese, if the definition of motherhood as claimed by some linguists, like spontaneous combustion burst fully upon the scene in different places, savannahs, jungles, deserts and subsequently continents and at different times? The (M) SOUND for the mother is universal and therefore it had to have sprung from an original *single* African source.

The SHAPE of the capital letters of the Western Alphabet and the SOUNDS that they represent at the time of female centrality also cast a light on the multi-layered relationships between women, their relatives and children, and their most important relationship of all, with the all encompassing flat round surFACE and body of Mother Earth. Expanding their understanding of their complex reality they endowed Mother Earth with the same organs, processes, qualities and functions that reflected their own familial configurations. All mothers were the daughters of Mother Earth in the creation of smaller aspects of reflective reality out of their bodies.

On all levels in the very beginning when shreds of language were becoming codified, the whole cycle of existence was considered to be one familial mother centered unit. Language also bears witness to the then misunderstood and absent role of males in the specific procreative process. *There had been little or no pair bonding and no marriage. All of the females either mated with the alpha male or with all of the male members of the whole group.* There had been little or no care of the children from the specific male members of the group. Mothers and babies had been on their own.

Mother Earth out of Her volcanic eruptions not only created the emerging land upon Her surFACE, but the belly of air above Her mantle blasted forth by the sissing volcanic vents breathing their way up to Her surFACE. The heavenly bodies that were originally perceived to emerge out of Her flat circular surFACE, out of Her side at the Eastern horizontal rim, had been considered to be like the matriarchal elephant herd, one interrelated protective mother based unit. All aspects of creation were at one with Her.

What the ancient SOUNDS, cum letters, cum phonemes, cum words also share with humanity at the time that the SHAPES of the human language were becoming codified, is a glimpse into an age that had a very different perception of reality. They illuminate an ancient time that has been lost to us through suppression, obliteration and the redefinition of ancient data, a shift from left handedness to right handedness, from female to male centrality, from the primacy of the mother and child to the primacy of the father and his sexuality, from inclusion to exclusion, from cooperation to competition, from communal compassion to individual selfish greed, from Goddesses to Gods, from the physical maternal female surFACE and body of Mother Earth as the source of all creation, to the left hemispheric linear mind of a hidden father God as the intelligent designer not only of the world, but subsequently of the whole universe.

Section One

> In the SHAPE OF SOUND for the sake of clarity there exist three SECTIONS. SECTION ONE breaks down into THREE PHASES, and then the three PHASES in SECTION ONE break down into five STAGES;
>
> The WARP dealing with ancient reality begins its life in SECTION ONE, PHASE ONE

Phase One in Section One:

MOTHER CENTRALITY;

In PHASE ONE Mother Earth and the individual mother emerge as the total sources of creation with complete and total worship of all aspects of Mother Earth. Using three linguistically related activities beginning with the codified phoneme in the Hindu KU dealing with the female as mother deliverer of small (K) objects and the contents of her right hemisphericly balanced sKUll. It will become apparent that they historically represent the THREE major PHASES of linguistic evolution; mother centrality in PHASE ONE, transition from mother centrality to father centrality in PHASE TWO and father centrality in PHASE THREE.

The three distinct processes inherent in the words beginning with KU as an example cover not only PHASE ONE but linguistically overlap into the following male centered PHASES of TWO and THREE. Human beings at all times travelled, migrated, sailed and wandered all over the surFACE and body of Mother Earth to a greater degree than has been postulated by historians. Evolving out of a migratory life following the herbivore herds across the African savannah they did not stay put in one place. It becomes apparent that the phoneme KU has its origin associated with the human brain that is housed in the female sKUll.

KU, KUN, KUNDA, KUNDALI, KUNDALINI

The words dealing with mother centrality after human beings began to spread out of their African nest North to the continent of Asia bear witness to one of the most ancient linguistic codifications of language. Ironically the syllable KU in the sKUll standing for the female as mother creating smaller aspects of herself in PHASE ONE surfaces linguistically in all three PHASES even as they shift into male centrality. The SHAPE of the letter (K) dealing with the creative aspect of 'smallness' emerged out of the letter(X) halved vertically. The letter (X) had survived to this day with the idiomatic observation that 'X marks the spot. What 'spot'? And what did the letter (X) 'mark'? It goes back to the body of the individual mother, be she animal or human and the SHAPE of her buttox as seen from the back, running through the undergrowth with the ruddy e*stral* or men*strual* spots of bloody sexual receptivity emerging out of her(X) SHAPED bottom.

When the (X) SHAPE marked her buttox with red or ruddy bloody spots it announced to the rutting males in the group that she could be read as ready to be mounted. With the passage of lunar time she had been perceived to break in half at her buttoxs, as half of her emerged out of that (X) configuration and a small replica of her, or half of her plunged itself into new life. She created a smaller version of herself, ergo the letter (K), half of the letter (X) and perceived symbolically as half of the larger context. In time the letter (X) became the number ten dealing with a disTENded belly and with the ten lunar months of gestation in the individual human mother. The letter (U) in KU deals with that which was *u*nder and then came *u*p to the surface.

KU out of Asian Hinduism deals with the individual mother, the one who created the smaller version of herself (K), as part of her not only halved but separated itself from her buttox (X).

KUN (KANA) will become known as the creative body of Mother Earth and Her triangular volcanic cone (KANA) of creation as She sprouted with magma and lavic sourced land upon Her surFACE. The letter (N) deals with 'change from a former state' or 'emergence on the surface' of land out of the body of Mother Earth.

KUNDA (KANADA) becomes the Earth Goddess the 'gift of' (DA) of the Mother Earths cone (KANA) of creation. It reflects the triangular SHAPE of the volcanic cone and the SHAPE of the triangular hairy vulvic patch on the individual mother's body. In time the source of creation on the individual mothers body encoded in the letter (X) shifts from the buttocks as seen from the back to the triangular SHAPE (V) of the vulvic patch as seen from the front.

KUNDALI (KANADALA) The (LA) establishes the female as mother and becomes associated with both the body of Mother Earth as source and Her daughters as co-creators of smaller aspects of themselves. It also deals with the angle of movement and has its roots out of the SHAPE of the sun emerging out of the circular Eastern rim, out of the flat round surFACE on the body of Mother Earth creating the light of day and illuminating the land upon Her surFACE.

KUNDALINI (KANADALANA) The (NA) at the end reiterates the concept that the electro-magnetic Kundalini energy of creation out of the body of Mother Earth rose up to the surFACE out of Her underground chambers. As (-LANA) it emerges out of luna (LANA) the Roman moon and the dark night of its source. The Kundalini energy rising out of the body of Mother Earth as electro-magnetic power of singular global lea line creation is symbolized not only by the moon but also by the sun emerging vertically at an angle out of Her flat, round horizontal body at dawn. As the Ida-Pingali of Hinduism it has been expressed as a double serpentine coil of potential that had been experienced to be compressed out of the body of Mother Earth along Her lea lines and up the spine of human beings.

The SHAPE of the electro-magnetic Kundalini energy rising up from the body of Mother Earth has been represented by the metaphorically symbolic *double spiraling snake, serpent, dragon, Leviathon or worm*. In PHASE ONE the universal worship had been of Mother Earth as the crucible of singular creation. Since in PHASE ONE specific paternity had been unknown there as yet had been no father God floating in the sky orchestrating His awesome power.

There are many other aspects that belong in PHASE ONE. Originally on the prehistoric body of Mother Earth there existed a perception that the body of Mother Earth upon which they had their being had been a spheric globe out of which emerged an energy that was not only ecstatic, prophetic, healing and the source of great power but that it could be experienced not only along grid like lea lines out of Her body along Her surFACE but also through Her surrogate individual mother's panting breath in the last stages of labor orgasming human life up to the light and through castrated first born sons.

It all began with the individual mother, her face, the processes inherent in her body, her blood that singularly created the offspring and the SOUNDS that she made out of the lateral slit on the bottom of her face that led to infant survival and subsequently to the codification of language. The process of the Kundalini electro magnetic energy coiling its way to the surFACE of Mother Earth along Her lea lines became symbolized by the twisting turning SHAPE of the metaphorical snake, serpent, dragon Leviathon and even worm.

Emerging out of a primate background especially out of the North Congo

River violent patriarchal male hierarchal chimpanzees, the individual mother had been at the mercy of the 'old boy' network, systematically brutalized along with her small children and on the lowest rung of the social totem pole. Specific paternity had been unknown. The females mated either with the alpha male or often secretly with other male members of the group. Because specific paternity had been unknown the males were not involved with caring for their offspring. Often facing violence, brutality incest and rape mothers and children were on their own. Along the way, she as an evolving humanoid creature split from the violence of her male counterparts and their unrelenting territoriality began to follow the herbivore herds across the savannahs of Africa originally primarily for an alternate milk supply.

To stem adolescent male violence individual mothers also began to castrate her first born sons to become the eunuch uncles and protectors of their subsequent sisters. This led to the suppression of the testosterone hormones and the evolution of the hemi spherically balanced trance state of the awakened electro-magnetic Kundalini energy that emerged in shamanism which echoed the individual experience of the ecstatic birthing breath and the subsequent power base of the birthing mothers. The uncastrated heterosexual males had been pushed out of the herd at the time when their pubescent hormones turned them into violent sexual marauders forced to wander around the periphery of the mother centered unit, the 'band of brothers' scenario. Most native societies separate their sons from their mothers at puberty to live with the male groups.

At around this time both set of males, the castrated eunuch uncles and their cast out heterosexual brothers began to ask why about their peripheral state. Why did not babies use their bodies as a vehicle of passage and why they had no part of the ecstatic breath and the inherent power of the birthing mothers? The asking of why of their peripheral state bifurcated the human brain thinning the corpus callosum and sent the left hemisphere adrift into the state of fantasy and answers to the why (Y) of their periphery. It all dealt with having babies or not. Why did their bodies refuse to give birth? That has been the eternal question for males leading to cloning and the creation of human robots, their technological babies way down into PHASE THREE.

It will become apparent in the subsequent PHASES that most of the early human beings, especially the mothers had been left handed and governed by both hemispheres of the human brain. It will also become apparent that animals with their specific characteristics played a major role in defining the vertical WARP of ancient reality.

Mother Earth had been considered their singular all encompassing creatress and they Her daughters, who had been Her surrogates in the creation of life on Her very skin. The laws that they followed had been based on natural law and not on pronouncements of a celestial male deity. For that reason they sought Her out along Her ecstatic lea lines, in Her grottoes and caves, Her mounds and volcanoes and the symbols that they created to express their perceptions. Those experiences were to make a break in PHASE TWO and to become totally obliterated, suppressed redefined, and with the growth of religious systems turned upside down as fantasy replaced reality in the following PHASES.

Phase Two in Section One:

TRANSITION, MOTHER CENTRALITY AND THE DEXTRAL SHIFT TO FATHER CENTRALITY

KU KUL KAN; The Feathed Serpent, Maya of Central America, Northern South America and Mexico

The concept of KU in Hinduism out of the English skull defining one of the major aspects of the individual mother as the creatress of smaller aspects of herself surFACES on the other side of the world among the Maya and the Americas beginning with their major deity of creation as KU KUL KAN the 'Feathered Serpent'. In PHASE TWO as the peripheral human males were becoming aware of their role in specific paternity there began a search for the individual father and an existential father replacing the mother on the throne in the creation of all of reality. Since the body of Mother Earth had been taken by the individual mothers, males had to create their father deities *away* from the body of Mother Earth and *above* Her in the air which the heavenly bodies, birds and insects used as a vehicle of passage. For the Tibetans the Bardo defined an 'intermediate state'. It covered the state between death and reincarnation as the disembodied spirit waited to be reborn. The concept of the 'intermediate state' expanded to include other possibilities, one of which had been the breath of air between the surFACE of Mother Earth and the inverted bowl of the sky above. It was through that intermediate current of air that birds and insects made their journeys back and forth across the continent of Africa.

On the other side of the planet the Maya kept the metaphorical serpent Kundelini energy of the mother of the Hindus and added the feathers of birds and birds themselves as male deities calling their new evolved deity, KU KUL KAN the 'Feathered Serpent'. They also used the elements of the sky *above* and *away* from them as a source of their astronomical wisdom. Along the way the reflective sea and its upside down reflected reality had also been used as a metaphor for male source of worship.

There begins a shift from the left handed reality of the mothers to the left hemispheric right handed fantasy of the fathers. The word dextral is the (DA) 'gift of' the extra hand. The left hand as the primary hand belonged to the ancient mothers. There evolves a shift in the hemispheric balance of the human brain. Mother Earth creating all, both females and males, shifts in PHASE TWO. Males begin to occupy the bifurcated linear, rational, fantasy prone left hemisphere of the human brain, leaving behind common sense and compassion of the balanced mother based right hemisphere.

The bifurcated linear left hemisphere of the male brain leaving behind relationship, compassion, maintenance and kindness plunged humanity into a morass of sexual violence, torment and war. There also began in PHASE TWO battles for power between the emerging males and the established mothers with their eunuch sons.

The letter (R) tells its own story similar to the letter(X). It bridges the gap but not completely. For the letter (R) began its life out of the body of the volcanic triangle of Mother Earth on the bottom and the circle of the male sun (O) on top halved vertically not unlike the letter (X).

With the male circle of the sun *above* the volcanic triangle of the mother on the bottom we are heading into male centrality, for the male sun is *above* the body of Mother Earth. She lies under him. Assuming that Asian India is the older civilization, perhaps not, the letter (K) in KU KUL KAN as the 'Feathered Serpent' somehow travels to the Maya of the 'New World' way before historians have defined the passage and uses the same SHAPE letters of the ancient mother as total source in the creation of smaller objects to tell its story but now with a twist.

In PHASE ONE not having the knowledge of specific male role in paternity, it had been considered that a woman's blood had been the sole creation of a baby. At puberty it began to flow monthly out of the female body. Then it stopped flowing and ten (X) lunar months later a small replica of the mother broke its way to the surface. It must have seemed like magic. Since males did not go through the same generative process, among the Maya they used to stab the penis to make it flow with the sacred blood of creation. The Hebrews on the other side of the world also considered blood sacred and they koshered their animals, drained them of the sacred blood before they ate the frontal quarters of the butchered meat.

With the realization of specific paternity and the male search for the father there exists a transitional shift with the keeping of the metaphoric snakes (Mother Earth and individual mothers as source) with wings (sacred role of birds as male source) sailing into the heavens *away* and *above* the body of Mother Earth into the sun, stars, comets and the sky itself. In the Maya as the symbolic KU KUL KAN the Mother Earth snake creation deity of the electro magnetic Kundalini energy emerges with male wings, the Sumerian Anunnaki males also emerge with wings, the Christian angels had originally been males with wings. The Arc of the Covenant sports two angels with extended wings. Birds with their wings and feathers surface at the time of the shift into male centrality. Feather (without the (e) of emergence at the center) and father have close linguistic links.

In PHASE TWO metaphoric battles between Mother Earth and the male sun gain momentum. Since the sun had been perceived to have been swallowed in the Western waters of Mother Earth at twilight it had to fight its way back to be reborn in the Eastern sky at dawn. The metaphoric battles between the body of Mother Earth and the male sun reflected the battles that had been occurring between the power bases of the mothers and the emerging fathers. What also surfaces in PHASE TWO reflecting the changes between the mothers and the emerging fathers is the role of the sun as it shifted from the helping hands of the son in PHASE ONE, to the shackles of the solar master in PHASES TWO and THREE. It ushers in the beginning of obliteration, suppression of power and centrality through the ancient practice of clitorectomies and the denial of the individual mother's pleasure filled birthing breath and her sexual joy filled freedom. The same occurs with the body of Mother Earth who shifts from being the *source*, to becoming the *resource* and the power base for left hemispheric male greed as she becomes mined, gouged and Her creatures become systematically exploited. It also deals with the negation of a protective uncle eunuch hierarchy that spread its mysterious often brilliant influence and perceived hemispheric balance of the brain across the ancient prehistoric world.

Phase Three in Section One:
FATHER CENTRALITY, OBLITERATION OF THE MOTHER POWER BASE ON ALL LEVELS.

KU KLUX KLAN, Contemporary human male madness. The KU of the Mother as the creatress of smaller aspects out of the (X) SHAPE of her buttox halved vertically, as seen from the back, somehow refuses to surrender its linguistic source. She somehow emerges with pristine clarity in the title in the United States of America as part of the most hateful organization to enhabit the body of Mother Earth having links with left hemispheric Nazi Germany and its murderous Second World War past. FATHER CENTRALITY as the PHASE THREE eventual monotheistic patriarchal despotic hierarchy and competition from the top down of the father, replaced the cooperation from the bottom up of the mother, deals with the over evolution of the left hemisphere of the human brain and the preponderance of single focused reason and reliance singularly on the rational. For many, especially Nazi males as part of that continuum, compassion had been jettisoned as the single focused left hemispheric linear male brain sailed into the morass of power, greed, control, rape, destruction, murder, human experimentation, irresponsible science, technology, unbridled sexuality, violence and war that has had its resurgence in the American KU KLUX KLAN.

Not only had the battle between the ancient mothers and the emerging fathers reach Biblical proportions but in the malignant PHASE THREE another war had slowly come into full fruition. It has been a battle between the armies of the heterosexual males and the growing shamanistic eunuch priesthood that had been emerging into universal secretive religious systems.

Mothers had been and are squeezed out of the picture altogether perpetuating their almost singular evolutionary origins out of the Northern Congo River brutal male centered chimpanzees leading to the occupation of North Africa and then spreading Northward into the rest of the world. The father replaced the eunuch uncle becoming the husband and master to both the individual mother and the Motherhood of Mother Earth as the 'hidden' Father God began his reign in the sky. There intensifies the obliteration not only of the female power based in her birthing breath but her sexual pleasure through stoning, arranged marriage, clitorectomies, sexual slavery, witch hunts, nuclear family, the list goes on is universal and endless.

The abdomen of the potential mother swelled with the growth of the fetus inside of her belly. She was the apparent parent. As male role in procreation

Section One

was becoming known, since his body did not swell with the bulge of a baby inside his belly, then it must have had its source from somewhere else. In many who aspired for greatness and control, the human mind became the male source of creation, specifically the bifurcated left hemisphere. As expressed through the contemporary American KU KLUX KLAN their rationale has been a single focus on hate for the other; racism, sexism, single male power and control from the top down, dictatorship and all the madness that came into fruition in the current PHASE THREE male centered world. The KU KLUX KLAN embodies all that has become abhorrent to gentle right hemispheric males, mothers and their children and all the creatures who scurry away in panic at the sight of man.

Stages

There have existed FIVE relatively fluid STAGES within PHASE ONE as the spreading codification of the capital letters of the Western Alphabet had their beginning. Originally linguistic origins as the vertical WARP began out of STAGE ONE; the INDIVIDUAL MOTHERS FACE, STAGE TWO; the metaphoric round, flat surFACE of MOTHER EARTH, STAGE THREE; the INDIVIDUAL MOTHERS BODY, as process, quality and function, STAGE FOUR; the BODY OF MOTHER EARTH, STAGE FIVE; the qualities inherent in OTHER CREATIONS; insects, birds, animals, trees, springs, stones.

STAGE ONE; THE INDIVIDUAL MOTHERS FACE

In STAGE ONE it had been the SHAPE of the features on the face of the mother that defined many of the letters, the WARP of ancient reality. The WOOF as SOUND became associated with those organs to emerge as many of the capital letters of the Western Alphabet. The mouth on her face came to define the (M) for the HUM of the mother and then subsequent HUManity. The SHAPE of her nose as seen in profile came to symbolize the concept of negation and change. Her two eyes not only dealt with reflection but with balance. Her forehead became the temple of inner vision during the state of trance. Her cheeks and chin echoed the chirping of birds.

STAGE TWO IN PHASE ONE;

The metaphoric round flat surFACE of MOTHER EARTH; All mothers had been considered to be sisters, surrogates in the creation of life upon the body of Mother Earth. Since She had been considered to be their Mother, their overwhelming context, then She too must have had the same organs as all mothers did upon Her majestic surFACE and body. If the individual mother had lips then Mother Earth also had lips. It had been perceived that there had been two openings on either side of the rim of Her round flat surFACE out of which She regurgitated the sun at dawn in the Eastern sky and swallowed it at twilight in the Western waters. She also had eyes that Her expansive waters could see as they reflected the sea.

STAGE THREE IN PHASE ONE

The Individual Mothers Body;
After they established the face of the INDIVIDUAL MOTHER they expanded their perceptions to include her whole body as process, quality and function. She created life out of her swelling belly as she gave birth to a small replica of herself. She then maintained her offspring with milk out of her mammaries. She taught them how to survive by mimicking her. The INDIVIDUAL MOTHER had perceived to be their greatest mentor and teacher.

STAGE FOUR IN PHASE ONE

The metaphoric BODY of MOTHER EARTH; All that existed emerged upon the surFACE of Mother Earth out of Her magnificent body. She gave birth to Herself, out of Herself, by Herself out of Her fulminating volcanoes having been considered the original virgin in PHASE ONE. The magma within Her body became the lavic land upon Her surFACE where all terrestrials had their being. After they lived their lives and died, be they creatures or plants, they sank back into her waiting arms. In the very beginning She and the sun had been considered to be a single balanced unit. They had been at one with each other but She, as the mother, had been considered to be the overwhelming context and he the sun, Her son, Her helping hands.

STAGE FIVE IN PHASE ONE

Other aspects of creation. The snake, serpent, dragon, Leviathon, worm became metaphors for the rising, twisting Kundalini energy rising up from the body of Mother Earth and the human mother during the process of birthing. The bee in her six sided nest with her hierarchy of jobs became a symbol for Mother Earth as the universal all creative mother. The ant became another metaphor for all the laboring sisters or aunts. Termite mounds with their magnificent cities became symbols of industry. Birds with their migratory habits mimicked the back and forth journey not only of the flocks that darkened the sky, but the herbivores who following the monsoon rains as they trekked their way into the promised land of newly sprouting grass. Because they flew in that 'intermediate state' between the body of Mother Earth and the inverted bowl of the sky they became in PHASE TWO male symbols of flight *away* and *above* the body of Mother Earth.

SYNTHESIS OF THE RULES OF ORIGINAL SOUND DISCOVERY (ROSD),

In PHASE ONE the lateral threads as the lateral WOOF of the linguistic fabric weaving their way as SOUND through the vertical WARP of ancient time, the synthesis of the following twenty-five rules will facilitate the discovery of the *original* SOUNDS that became associated with the SHAPES of the capital letters of the Western Alphabet.

To rediscover the original SOUNDS and SHAPES that created them these rules can be used in any ancient or contemporary language. Not all phonemic structures or words will respond to the prodding of the following rules but enough will comply and will begin to reveal the roots of an ancient linguistic mystery. The twenty-five RULES OF ORIGINAL SOUND DISCOVERY (ROSD) are like a Rosetta stone to discern how the SHAPES and SOUNDS of language as codified in many of the capital letters of the Western Alphabet came into being.

RULE ONE; MONOGENESIS is the single source of language originally out of Africa. There are no actual boundries between languages.

RULE TWO; There exist five progressive STAGES delineating the SHAPE and SOUND of the capital letters of the Western Alphabet out of the individual mothers facial organs including the metaphoric surFACE of Mother Earth.

RULE THREE; CONSONANTS are constant and carry the meaning. Deal with the SOUND of the consonants, not in the way that the words may have been written.

RULE FOUR; Work back from the original codified SOUNDS locked in both obsolete and contemporary languages. Hara is belly Hebrew and belly in Japanese.

RULE FIVE; NATURAL PHENOMENA. Rely on the names of native phenomena, especially but not singularly out of Africa; Mara river.

RULE SIX; PHONOLOGICAL CORRESPONDENCE. Become aware of the interchangeable SOUNDS made in the same area of the mouth. Some are unvoiced and others are voiced, thin<u>k</u> (unvoiced), thing (voiced).

RULE SEVEN; ANLAUT, the first SOUND as a consonant often establishes the meaning of the following word, mouth (MATA), mother (MATARA).

RULE EIGHT; ANASTROPHE, PALENDROME, REFLECTION, MIRRORING or inversion of words; read phonemes forwards and backwards. (MARA/RAMA), (MAYA/YAMA)

RULE NINE; A (ah) SOUND. After every consonant replace the existing vowel with the most ancient A (ah) vowel SOUND, Her (HARA). RULE TEN; H (huh) SOUND; Replace the H (huh) SOUND before most words beginning with vowels, erb=herb (HARABA).

RULE ELEVEN; EMPHATIC. The letter S, is an EMPHATIC standing for 'it is'. Remove the letter S from words beginning with the SOUND of S. SEVEN (IS EVEN or HAVANA), snake (IS NAKA), skin (IS KIN).

RULE TWELVE; Find A (ah) based single syllables. They are the most ancient SOUND clusters, ma, ka, na, la, ba, ra, sa.

RULE THIRTEEN; Repetition of DYADS (double syllables) based on the A (ah) SOUND using the same consonant; baba, mama, lala.

RULE FOURTEEN; Find DYADIC constructs based on the A (ah) SOUND with different consonants; mata, rama, casa, hana, naka.

RULE FIFTEEN; Deal with the REPETITION of words; (N'Goro N'Goro), East African mountain, (gal gal), Hebrew wheel.

RULE SIXTEEN; Find OVERLAPPING DYADS (two syllables) twice and OVERLAPPING TRYADS (two syllables) three times. OVERLAPPING DYADS; future (FATARA) (FATA/TARA) OVERLAPPING TRYADS; migrate (MAGARATA) (MAGA/GARA/RATA).

RULE SEVENTEEN; HOMONYMS, find puns within a language (English write, right, rite).(Polish rana wound, rana dawn)

RULE EIGHTEEN; HOMOPHONES, find puns across languages; chmura (HAMARA)=cloud Polish, chimera (HAMARA)=monster Greek.

RULE NINETEEN; METAPLASM, the transposition of letters. Hebrew

(HA*BARA*), Arab (HA*RABA*)

RULE TWENTY; DEROGATORY words for female processes; cunt, coos,

RULE TWENTY-ONE; MYTHS, LEGENDS and GODDESSES. Artemis, Deborah, Maat, Kunda

RULE TWENTY-TWO; CREATURES that became metaphoric examples; snake, bee, ant, cat, termite, goose, elephant, lioness, owl, stork, sow. beetle, bat, octopus..

RULE TWENTY-THREE; SYMBOLS; Uncover original meanings locked in ancient 'mysterious' symbols; Yin Yang, Star of David, Tibetan wheel, cross, swastika, the ankh, 666, labrys.

RULE TWENTY-FOUR; NUMBERS; their original ancient source. Seven (IS EVEN), even (HAVANA), eight, ate

RULE TWENTY-FIVE; VOWELS; carriers of extended SOUND.

THE TRI-PARTED ANCIENT REALITY

The vertical WARP in PHASE ONE deals with a tri-parted ancient reality dealing not only with the individual mothers face in the SHAPING of the capital letters of the Western Alphabet in stage one but with Mother Earth's stage two majestic surFACE and in stage four out of Her nurturing, magnificent body.
THE ANCIENT UNIVERSE; the sun *above, upon, below* the surFACE and body of Mother Earth.

PART ONE; Passage of the sun in an arc *above* Mother Earth's surFACE.

PART TWO; Passage of the sun *upon* Mother Earth's surFACE and body.

PART THREE; Passage of the sun *below* Mother Earth's plane.

PART ONE;
ABOVE AS THE UNIVERSE, (*AT ONE*=ATONE)

In PHASE ONE the universe began as one of the earliest perceptions of Mother Earth being at one with the sun and other celestial bodies. It all began with the flat circular visage that had been perceived as the encompassing surFACE of Mother Earth, the original *universe* as the all embracing, all-inclusive creative maternal context. All that existed in one way or another emerged *above, upon and below* Her flat circular surFACE and magnificent expansive, nurturing body.

Sometimes it was out of the mountains at Her Eastern horizontal rim acting like regurgitating mouths that they all believed to have had their being. At other times it was out of Her planetary skin. It was out of the holes, caves, and burrows that She threw up Her small scurrying offspring. Out of Her calderic bloody womb She created Herself out of Herself, as magmic menstrual lava coagulated into land, as mountainous mouths rose out of Her horizontal surFACE and smoke spewing islands like exposed noses searching for air, rose out of the depths of Her reflective waters.

The universe, life *above* Mother Earths surFACE.

Out of Her side at the horizontsl line in the East, heavy with the burden of night, She heaved forth into Her belly of air, into the heavens, Her most impressive celestial creations, the sun and the moon. At the end of their passage *above* and across Her great belly of air She swallowed them back into Herself in the West for them to begin their trans-formative journey of rebirth *below* Her flat round surFACE, through Her underground intestinal maze, Her transformative womb of re-creation. At that moment in time in PHASE ONE the sun, the moon and the heavenly bodies had been considered to be a single unit *at one* with Her.

PART TWO
BI-PARTED REALITY,

Life *upon* Mother Earth extended Her bounty with Her surrogates in the creation of matter *upon* Her surFACE. Her female offspring that as stationary plants and perambulatory creatures through their bodies helped Her in the perpetuation of life *upon* Her expansive body. On all levels in the very beginning the whole cycle of existence was considered to be one familial female unit. They considered Her their beloved Mother. Treading gently upon Her surFACE they worshipped Her and all of Her creations as they migrated originally back and forth across Her planetary skin, across the great savannahs of Africa. *There had been no private ownership of land*. Mother Earths body belonged to all.

Reality was based on a series of apparently observable facts. Their Great Mother was a flat round female surFACE, that not only gave birth to everything that existed but ended in a great circle around them as far as their eyes could see at the horizontal rim. They stood at the center, the cog of that great wheel. When they moved, no matter in which direction they ventured, the

Section One

circle ending at the horizon line always went with them. It was as if a great belly of airy breath above them and *upon* the surFACE of Mother Earth contained them at all times at its very hub. Since they considered themselves to be Her children, the air, the sky, the very heavens cradled them in the arms of life supporting air.

Sometimes the peaks of distant hills rose *upon* Her surFACE as they migrated toward them. They seemed to grow larger and larger, more and more impressive towering above them, often glistening with caps of milky white snow. It was as if Mother Earth also gave birth to the mountains, slowly pushing their growing peaks up and *upon* Her flat, ever creative surFACE and body.

Her most vulnerable creatures huddled together weaving their way through the dangerous savannahs seeking shelter within the arboreal embrace of the towering hills. Often the mountains acted as great impassable walls. At other times it was the wide expanse of standing water spreading out before them that halted their semi-annual migratory trek. Deserts and swamps also had to be traversed. Carnivores had to be avoided. The passage of time had to be dealt with. They lived in a dangerous world surrounded by a constancy of perilous change.

One of those constancies above and *upon* Her surFACE was the belly of air surrounding them that as breath entered and left their bodies at will, bringing with it movement, warmth and a constant pulsation under the skin. The pulsation seemed to have its roots at their core, in their very hearts, radiating outward filling their moving parts with life. When the air left them, with the air also departed the warmth, movement and the pulsation under the skin as the heart withdrew its rhythm and the body grew still and cold.

The air through which they moved and which they breathed supported and animated their lives. Every living thing around them existed in that great inverted blue bowl of the sky that contained the air under it. Therefore everything that had it's being in that great belly of air under that inverted bowl of the sky above and *upon* the body of their Great Mother shared the air as a support system. To exist was not only to move through that ever constant air, but to breathe, to have it enter the nostrils, let it fill the lungs, push out the belly and just as mysteriously, without asking permission, to exit, to leave.

All living creations on the body of Mother Earth shared the air. All living creations, plants and trees, even rocks, were perceived to breathe, for they had their being in that great belly of air above and *upon* Her generous round flat surFACE.

Humanity's ancient ancestors believed that it was the breath that sustained life. They believed that the breath was not only universally shared, but because it was part of the body of Mother Earth, it was sacred. To have been born, to have had the air enter the lungs was to have been filled not only with the breath of life, but with the spirit of existence. In Latin the word spirare gives us a clue, for it means 'to breathe'. It shares with us in English the original phonemic construct for the word 'spirit'. To have been born, with the intake of the first breath was to have been blessed with the sacred spirit of life.

In PHASE ONE it all began with the voluminous body of Mother Earth and everything that emerged above Her as the original UNI-VERSE, the single source of being. Then, for an extended period of time the belly of air *upon* Her surFACE with all the heavenly bodies and even birds entering the picture defined their ancient reality as a BI-PARTED construct.

PART THREE
A TRI-PARTED REALITY *BELOW* HER SURFACE

After the BI-PARTED reality that had been perceived to be the flat round surFACE and the body of Mother Earth with the belly of air upon Her, the great arc that created the inverted bowl of the sky and plane upon Her surFACE, a TRI-PARTED reality began to emerge.

They perceived themselves to be extensions of the flat plane of the round surFACE of Mother Earth. It was an early given that they were part of Her. They were not apart from Her. They also knew that they moved through and breathed the air that curved into a great vault of sky above them.

Along with the flat plane that was the female surFACE and body of Mother Earth and the inverted bowl, the belly of air that sustained life above Her surFACE, there was also a third reality which was no less real to humanity's ancient maternal ancestors. It was the womb of re-creative transformation that existed *below* the surFACE of Mother Earths skin in the subterranean intestinal recesses within Her body. They reasoned that everything that lived either came up to Her surFACE out of Her body, or out of the bodies of Her surrogates, the individual mothers of the specie.

Since women had wombs within their bodies that created small replicas of the mother as they popped babies up to the surface, not only did Mother Earth also have a great internal womb but everything that popped up onto Her surFACE was a miniature replica, a smaller individualized version of Her. She was the biggest context. There was nothing bigger than She was. Everything was a minute aspect of Her. Everything therefore was related. In the very beginning there were no outsiders. The creation of the 'other' came later on but still very early on in humanity's story.

The workings under the skin, any skin, were a mystery. That is why the noun 'hide' as animal skin also means 'to hide', to conceal as a verb. The skin concealed the life that existed under it. Dead bodies revealed only organs. They didn't reveal how the body worked. There emerged many deeply observable and often fanciful conclusions to explain some of the internal workings.

Food went in the top hole on the body of a biped, a bird, an insect and on the snout end in a quadruped. It came out on the other end as feces or urine. Often there was also gas. As it moved through the body a transformation of the ingested morsels took place. The pieces of food that went into the hole on one end went through a process that was perceived to have some link with the heat associated with cooking. It may be that language came to be codified around the time when human beings began to learn how to control fire. Or it may have come to them when they saw hens warming their eggs into life under their downy breasts.

When the feces or urine emerged from the bottom or end hole, both created a curl of steam in the morning sun that led to the conclusion that some kind of heat changed the intestinal contents from one state to another. It transformed them.

The process of feces, urine and gas production was universal in all creatures, but the females of the specie also periodically passed blood. When the blood stopped flowing, more often than not the belly of the mother distended, like a hill or circular mound on the body of Mother Earth. In a very specific period of time, ten lunar months later, she pushed a small replica of herself up to the surface, i.e. she gave birth.

Since some kind of transformation took place to change morsels of food into solid feces and liquid urine, then a similar transformation must have occurred when the blood in a female body stopped flowing. It only took a longer time for it to emerge as a solid baby. Specific male role in pro-creation was not known at this most ancient time in PHASE ONE when the basic SOUNDS of language were becoming codified. Along with the Northern Congo male chimpanzees they did not understand that male sperm was part of the input that created a baby. Lunar then seasonal, then year round mating didn't seem to have anything to do with a human baby born ten lunar months later.

Since food went through a trans-formative process within the female body to become feces, so it was reasoned, the blood went through a similar transformation to become a fetus. The small fetus, a budding replica of the mother also went through some kind of a trans-formative cooking process, a sort of parboiling and coagulation as it grew in the mother's belly, for the baby emerged not only as a sold reflective unit but steaming out of her distended belly.

What went on inside to create the hidden internal transformations was a mystery to them. The two words for the internal cooking present a clue. Ingestion and digestion for the processing of food are not that far away from gestation linked to the process of making a baby. They also observed that often liquids turned into solids. Milk curdled into cheese. Blood clotted. Oozing tree sap turned into thick resin. Molten magma solidified into land. High up in the gestating mountains water turned into ice. Sea water drying in the heat of the sun turned to salt. Puffy white clouds high up in the sky turned into solid drops of rain.

The liquid blood inside of a mother's body must have gone through a similar trans-formative process. It emerged not only steaming but solidified, coagulated inside of the mother creating a baby. That is why they reasoned for ten lunar months the blood couldn't be spotted to flow on the outside. The spots of blood were hiding inside, percolating along making a baby. The process of baby production was 'hidden'. What could be simpler? What could be more obvious? The ancient Egyptians called SA the 'wise blood' of the mother. It knew all by itself how to coagulate and how to make a baby. These original eminently innocent perceptions in PHASE ONE led to many subsequent social and psychological dislocations.

Another mystery surfaced after a baby emerged out of the mother's body. Her belly may have gone down, but the swelling breasts swelled further, flowing with nourishing milk as the blood resumed its periodic external flow. The mother's blood had been considered the sole source of creation, therefore it had been considered sacred.

Since all female creatures were made in the image of Mother Earth as Her surrogates in the creation of life, then She too must have shared with them the same organs, processes, qualities and functions that they as females of the specie, Her surrogates were experiencing.

In stages two and four all that Mother Earth created through a variety of holes upon Her surFACE and at Her circular horizontal rim, after they rose into life above Her surFACE, went through the journey of their lives and then died. Once they died they decayed (DK) and became reabsorbed by Her patiently waiting ground of being. They became *at one* with Her in death. The sooner they became reabsorbed into Her restless heart, the sooner they could be reborn to a new life. Reincarnation was based primarily on the journey of the sun through the belly of air above the body of Mother Earth to which the human soul had become attached. It was a belief that emerged in Africa and spread with human dispersal to many corners of the ancient world.

Scavengers in many forms became facilitators in the ingestion and digestion of dead carrion. In the heat of the tropical sun deposits of feces left upon the surFACE of Mother Earth became re-absorbed quicker than even a dead corpse. The creatures that assisted the fecal remains to unite with the body of Mother Earth, the condors, vultures, dogs, cats, jackals, beetles often became sacred totemic animals, worshipped for the fecal recycling service that they performed.

After the semi-annual burst of the monsoon rains, patiently sleeping plants with their bent knuckles of possibility pushing their way up to the surFACE created their own small wombs of creation under Her skin. Then the sprouts unfurled their shoots, broke through Her surFACE, making their own holes of creation to live out their lives in the sun. All of these processes seemed to converge. Female mothers gave birth to small replicas of themselves though the bottom holes that led to the wombs in their bodies. Plants slumbering under Mother Earth's surFACE creating their own small wombs of creation broke free poking holes of their own, like baby chicks poked their way out of their shells through which they could facilitate their journey out of the dark night of potential, into the light of realization of a new day.

The same process that brought forth all living creatures and plants that existed within the body of Mother Earth up to Her surFACE must have expanded to include Her two major creations that She gave birth to, or regurgitated out of Her horizontal Eastern rim; the sun and the moon. At the end of their journeys through their lives of light above Her surFACE, they became reabsorbed back into Her body into the dark convoluted intestinal chambers *below* Her skin. She apparently swallowed them back into Her body into the apparent holes in the Western rim as she swallowed the creatures that died and decayed upon Her surFACE. Except the sun and the moon did not apparently die and decay. Both the sun and the moon disappeared into the body of Mother Earth at the edge, at Her horizontal rim, pulling their light behind them. After going through some kind of subterranean transformative journey *below* Her dermal surFACE, through Her intestines, the sun at night and the moon during the day, they emerged triumphant to the dawn of their new lives, the sun more consistently than the moon. This led to many speculations and even more creative conclusions.

In the TRI-PARTED reality both the sun and the moon went through a kind of mysterious trans-formative journey once they fell off Her circular horizontal edge, became swallowed in the great maw, were killed to the life of their light, or set into the watery wound of the Western waters. Because it was believed that flowing menstrual blood coagulated within the mother to create a baby, the same process must have existed within the body of Mother Earth. The sun became associated not only with the red lavic blood that coagulated within the body of Mother Earth to create Her variety of offspring; the transformed coagulated disc of the sun, the SHAPE shifting moon and not to be left out the solidified lavic menstrual blood that hardened into land upon Her surFACE.

The sun using its bloody demise in the gore filled Western waters after Mother Earth ate it, coagulated and cooked its way through Her body. The moon because of its eerie whiteness associated with white milk curdled its way through to emerge as the solid block of cheese tumbling its way through the night sky. The nursery rhymes that the moon is a block of cheese still exist as nursery rhymes. Both the sun and the moon transformed themselves from a solid to a liquid and then into a solid again. All of this happened *below* the mantle, the skin within Her body, *below* the hidden round flat surFACE of Mother Earth.

As an addendum. The sun became associated with gold because of its color and constancy. The moon became associated with silver because it darkened when exposed to air and periodically lost its brilliant white glow. Gold because it never changed its essential character, never decayed, rusted or disintegrated, like the sun it had been considered to be immortal. The sun pale and yellow echoing its immortality always returned at dawn. The same could be said about gold that always remained with the same color and consistency. Because it never decayed, tarnished or rusted had been considered immortal. Both the sun and gold could be relied on.

Gold as a conductor of electricity establishes its links with Mother Earth's electro- magnetic Kundalini energy of prana rising up out of the lea lines on Her body and as the metaphoric double serpent spiral curled up at the base of the human spine. During the birthing breath of the mothers the electro-magnetic Kundalini energy of prana bursts forth awakened, filling the birthing mother with power and blissful ecstasy. The prana (PARANA) of electro-magnetic power rose in the birthing mother at the time of partition. Also at the time of birthing in PHASE ONE she became the princess (PARANAsasa) the potential mother based leader out of the same familial configuration that had existed in the lioness, the mir cats and the hyena clan. In Greece the

SECTION ONE

sacred mount Parnassus (PARANAsasa) surfaces with the same linguistic construct.

Because of the universal belief in reincarnation in PHASE ONE at the time of death that same conducting electro-magnetic Kundalini energy associated with the birthing breath of the mother's had been perceived to accompany the corpse on its journey of death and then rebirth. It had been believed that gold as a conductor of electricity guaranteed the dying person with immortality. It may be why the Egyptian pharaohs were encased in gold after they died. The electro-magnetic Kundalini energy conducted through their gold sarcophagus would guarantee them eternal life. It may also be why the Arc of the Covenant is also encased in gold and dispatches all who touch it. It is probably why as the major aspect of immortality that gold has grown to be so priceless. Individuals must have worn it for its transformative electro-magnetic properties. Otherwise it boggles the mind why as a glistening yellow metal it would have such enduring value.

The three major perceptions dealing with humanity's most ancient reality and Mother Earths relationship to the heavenly bodies in PHASE ONE was originally the UNI-VERSE or a single all inclusive maternal matrix *above* Her flat maternal surFACE. Then life *upon* Her surFACE became the bio of a BI-PARTED reality. With questions of meaning and the emergence of answers dealing with the journey of the heavenly bodies *below* Her skin, through Her intestines still in PHASE ONE, a TRI-PARTED reality came into being.

PROCESS

A short version of the PROCESS in the WOOF of SOUND moving laterally through the vertical WARP of ancient time to find the roots of language using some of the Twenty-five RULES OF ORIGINAL SOUND DISCOVERY (ROSD).

It becomes apparent that the sun was considered not only *at one*, but a major player with the flat round surFACE and body of Mother Earth. Using a multitude of rules to rediscover the sun's ancient linguistic source and ancient meaning, the dissection of one of the words for the SUN follows. There are others; HALA, HAMA, HADA, HABA etc. SUN (IS HANA)

RULE ELEVEN; The SOUND of the letter (S) is an emphatic dealing with 'it is'. Remove it from the beginning of the words. SUN becomes (IS UN).

RULE TEN; Place the letter H (huh) before a word that begins with a vowel,

(IS UN) becomes (IS HUN). Because the Sound of H is unvoiced many of the words beginning with a vowel dropped off the letter (H).

RULE NINE; Place the A (ah) SOUND behind every consonant. (IS HUN) becomes (IS HANA). The A (ah) SOUND became the first codified both vowel and consonant SOUND. It establishes the Alpha of beginnings out of the triangular SHAPE of the volcanic cone in the creation of land upon the surFACE of Mother Earth and the SOUND of a human baby's intake of the first breath.

RULE FOURTEEN: Find dyads based on the A (ah) SOUND using different consonants. The sun (IS HANA) becomes the dyad for one of the names of the sun. (HA) is the belly of air above the body of Mother Earth through which the sun travels. (NA) originally as the nose seen in profile on the mothers face in stage one deals with 'emergence on the surFACE' and 'a change from a former state'.

HAND; (HANADA) is the (DA) 'gift of' the sun (IS HANA) in its activity as being at one with Mother Earth the sun creates a double process daily rising and setting, at its specific time one hand pulls the sun out of its nocturnal sleep in the East at dawn and the other hand either pushes, or with its stiletto like fingers pierces the fabric of the firmament creating a wound on its Western horizontal rim for it to be swallowed or to disappear for the night.

SAND (IS HANADA) The activity of the sun (IS HANA) as a blistering, desiccating solar helping hand (HANADA) often turns the verdant savannah into a sandy (IS HANADA) desert, (DA) deals with the gift of.

SOUND (IS HANADA) is the (DA) 'gift of' the sun (IS HANA). It was in the Eastern sky when the birds rose before dawn singing their rapturous song to awaken the sun. Animals screeched and bellowed their welcome as did human beings with their aves and hallelujahs.

RULE NINETEEN; ANASTROPHE, PALENDROME, REFLECTION; The linguistic dyad of the sun (IS HANA) reflected becomes (NAHA), (HANA/NAHA). The ancient reality dealt with that which was above as the sun (HANA) during the day and what was below (NAHA) as a reflection in the still waters as that which dealt with nothingness and death. (NAHA) deals with the disappearance of the sun in the watery Western horizontal rim fading into the nothingness of night. In Latin nihil (NAHA-) means nothing.

Section One

RULE SIXTEEN; OVERLAPPING DYADS; Nihil (NAHALA) (NAHA/HALA) contains not only the dyad (NAHA) of nothingness but with (HALA) embraces one of the other names for the sun in Spanish as the sol (IS HALA).

RULE EIGHTEEN; HOMOPHONES; Puns across language 'barriers', Sol (IS HALA) and soul (IS HALA) both deal with the sun. Like gold, all three along with honey (HANA) had been considered to be immortal. With the belief in reincarnation the soul (IS HALA) was recycled like the solar (IS HALA-) disc. In one way or another they always returned, or had been reincarnated.

RULE SEVENTEEN; HOMONYMS puns within a language (son-sun), the sun (IS HANA) of Mother Earth in PHASE ONE had been considered to be at one with Her, as Her son (IS HANA).

All twenty-five RULES OF ORIGINAL SOUND DISCOVERY (ROSD) are presented and expanded in SECTION TWO of The SHAPE of SOUND.

THE ORIGINS OF THE FLAT WORLD PHENOMENON

The belly of air above the flat circular surFACE of Mother Earth through which birds, insects, sun, moon, stars and clouds passed overhead, Her bountiful surFACE out of which plants emerged and upon which all creatures traveled, Her skin into which many others burrowed, others who swam in Her mysterious watery depths, and the underground intestinal tunnels through which they had to pass to become transformed and reborn, were considered to be one unit. She was a flat maternal surFACE that ended at the horizontal rim in a great round flat circle around them. No matter in which direction they moved they were in the center of that great circular sweep, which in one way or another always ended as far as their eyes could see at the rim of the horizon. The anient circles upon the body of Mother Eearth attest to that perception.

Sometimes the line ended at the walls of murderous mosquito ridden swamps, at others into reflecting pools of quiescent standing water. The tightly knit mother led family plowed on, following the herbivore herds through unforgiving deserts, crocodile infested rivers into the welcoming verdant blessed savannahs. No matter which way they turned, they were always aware that they were at the center of a great circular sweep around them, that they were cradled in the center of a great maternal airy womb, the flat maternal body upon which they had their being. They were at the hub of the circular expanse that moved with them all their lives and that always seemed to end at the horizontal rim.

Everything that lived upon and above Mother Earth's surFACE, in that great vault of space above Her, in that expansive belly of air, flying or passing through it, breathed the air that She apparently created out of Her very internal volcanic essence.

They could see and hear it, as it sissed and hissed its way up to Her surFACE, out Her fiery vents and fulminating calderas. She also created a bonus of breathable air, when out of Her belching volcanic cones, ash, rocks, lava and other debris blasted its way up to Her surFACE. It seemed to be carried by a massive explosion, an exhalation of air that stained the sky above them with plumes of purple smoke while blanketing the plane below with coagulating lavic menstrual blood that turned into solid land.

At the time that these perceptions began to emerge, out of Her side at Her horizontal rim, semi-annually She gave birth to banks of rain laden clouds that swept across Her parched African savannah turning the drought stricken pastures into grassy marshlands. She created it all. It all emerged out of Her flat circular surFACE and all encompassing body; the air that creatures breathed, the land and water upon Her surFACE, the plants that sprung forth out of Her very skin, the sun, moon, stars, clouds and birds that rose at an angle out of Her flat maternal plane at Her Eastern horizontal rim, vaulting across Her great belly of air above Her surFACE, to disappear on the other side back into Her waiting heart were all Her creations. She was the Mother of them all and the original universally deified God.

All the many learned arguments notwithstanding, all the tomes agonizing whether or not there was a beginning and when it occurred, could be dispelled with a smidgeon of common sense. Forget about worrying about what came out of space and the *big bang theory of the male orgasm in PHASE THREE*. There could not have been any beginning of life without the planetary plane of land and water that has been the body of Mother Earth. It was Mother Earth who came first. Without Mother Earth there could not have been any life. All life needs is the body of Mother Earth to exist. All life needs the maternal surFACE and body upon which, within which, above which, through which it can make its home in order to subsist and to survive. It needs the maternal matrix of Mother Earth as its planetary nest.

Where did land come from? It is not a rhetorical question. For land obviously came from only one place. It burst up to the surFACE through the planetary skin of the great Mother, belching smoke, dust, ashes, rocks with

Section One

the volcanic eruptions that quaked and exploded upon Her spasming, orgasmic surFACE, spreading lava and rubble kicked up from the deep inner recesses within Her fiery, restless body. As the effulgence spread across Her top engulfing Her like a cape, or as islands emerged like noses out of Her great oceans, they covered her with a new skin, a new ground of being.

The wind and rain pummeled Her, creating chinks in that tough lavic hide. Waves of hot and cold air blasted across Her open terrain creating fissures in which seeds snuggling against the wind could take refuge. Insects spread pollen. Birds descended upon the insects. Herbivores evolved. Predators adapted. Human beings survived.

It all began as the womb of creation, the surFACE that begat the possibility of life to form on the body of Mother Earth, with Her cone of creation, the triangular volcanic SHAPE that pushed itself up from the center, emerging out of Her skin, becoming the source of the cataclysmic eruptions that spread across Her round relatively flat surFACE in stage one and the source of all terrestrial life that took root upon that great and awesome nurturing body in stage three.

The most important relationship that human mothers shared beyond their familial relatives had been the relationship that they had with the surFACE and body of Mother Earth whom they considered to be their extended matriarchal family. As babies, small replicas of themselves emerged from their bodies, so all kinds of babies also emerged out of the body of Mother Earth. Everything that She gave birth to was in one way or another Her baby, was Her smaller offspring (KA). She was the large, all encompassing context. Individual mothers were Her surrogates, Her helpers in the creation of smaller replicas out of their bodies.

Out of Her flat surFACE, Her circular top, She gave birth to land as lava poured down Her flanks and hardened into land. As the original virgin in PHASE ONE She made Herself, out of Herself, as Herself, by Herself, parthogenesis in action. She also gave birth to the air above Her surFACE as She breathed in and out of the volcanic calderas and vents. Plants, trees, burrowing animals and insects pushed their way up to Her top to expand in the light of day.

Out of Her mouth or side at the horizon line She either regurgitated, handled or gave birth to the sun, moon, clouds, stars and even birds as they emerged to share the bounty, sailed across Her belly of air above Her surFACE and set back into Her waiting arms on the other side, passing through Her transformative underground intestinal maze to repeat that endless cycle of becoming.

To that end the reflective plane of water presented a never ending mystery under its often glassy surFACE. If the life of reality was above the plane on the body of Mother Earth then the reflection in the still standing waters below the plane was the realm of death. It was that watery divide that had to be crossed to be reborn, reincarnated like the sun that sank out of sight into that glassy surFACE in the West was reborn again into the light of a new day in the East. They too would follow that same journey.

THE PERCEPTION OF BALANCE AND IMMORTALITY

One of the most persistent ancient beliefs in PHASE ONE which emerged in many forms was a belief that an *even* balance existed in the universal system that surrounded them in Mother Earth, with Mother Nature and in the process that defined life and death. One of the simplest and most ancient universal expressions of balance dealt with the following two letters that reflected each other. Some came out of the face of the individual mother then expanded to include the surFACE of Mother Earth and then into other less specific categories.

Out of the face of the individual mother evolved the SHAPE of the letters laterally reflecting each other in the construct of the EYE. The two E vowels create a reflection, an evenly balanced linguistic distribution on either side of the letter (Y) as they do on the individual human face. The same construct emerges as the eye, or OKO in Polish. The vowel (O) on either side of the letter (K) creates the same lateral reflection and even balance on the human face as is reflected in the sequence of the letters. It is the EYEs, and the Polish OKOs that with the blessings of light begin their journey into awareness.

Moving to the surFACE of Mother Earth there emerges the three letter construct of AYA which means light in Persian and dawn in Assyrian. The letter (Y) of vulvic creation at the center of AYA in PHASE ONE is flanked by the vowel A (ah) on either side. The vowel or consonant letter A(ah) deals with the three sided volcanic cone that creates the beginning of life with the creation of land and the Alpha of beginnings extending to the first shafts of dawn as the beginning of daylight. In Swahili Alfa Giri deals with the moment before the birth of the sun in the Eastern sky and its rosy glow stirring the birds with their rapturous song to assist Mother Earth on Her journey into the light of life. The AYA linguistic creation on the surFACE of Mother Earth reflects the same construction as the EYE on the human face.

As a verbal construct following the same pattern of EVEn balance, EVE enters the picture. At the equator and the African Sahel the balance and even distribution occurred with the days and nights being of equal duration. The vowel E (ee) on the left side of the letter (V), Mother Earth's vulvic aperture in the East (Eee), dealt with the emergence (Eee) of daylight out of Her body in stage four. The vowel E(ee) on the right side of the letter (V) dealt with the emergence (Eee) of the darkness of night, or the exit (Eh) of the light of day. The SHAPE of the letter (V) stands for the letter (W). In Polish they are interchangeable and water is written as woda and pronounced as voda. As a system of beginnings and balance a creature enters the picture out of stage five. EWE is a baby sheep (SHE-) or lamb (LA-), extending the concept of beginnings, balance and motherhood to the herbivore herds that often accompanied the ancient migrations.

It also must have been that the balance occurred at the emergence of water or the monsoon rains halving the ancient year into two equal parts creating an even passage into the wet and dry seasons.

It was the mountains at dawn, the Swahili giri (GARA), reflecting the same consonant construct as the Polish gora (GARA) that surfaces in the SHAPE of the AYA, or EYE on the body of Mother Earth establishing the two mountainous peaks A(ah) or (Y) between which the sun was born at dawn. The (GA) deals with begetting the sun and (RA) deals with the sun having been begotten. In PHASE ONE the linguistic construct of AYA with the (Y) at the center stands for the mons veneris, the birthing area of the sun rising at dawn in the East between two mountain peaks on the body of Mother Earth.

Not to be left out and linking it to the concept of even balance and immortality is the Spanish ORO which is the name for gold. The sun emerging at dawn had been considered to be immortal because it always returned in the Eastern sky, never varied in its form, SHAPE and substance, never died to its light. Pale and wan but warm, emerging from the Eastern waters at dawn it had always been considered as a dependable helper at one with Mother Earth. The same could be said for gold. It never lost its golden glow, never rusted, tarnished or decayed. It had also been considered to be immortal.

They also expanded the concept of even balance not only dealing with the eyes, light and gold but into the two sides of the body and specifically the two hemispheres of the human brain. Since a balance existed linking the two sides of the body together on the surface of the skin, it also must have existed as a balance internally under the skin inside the skull.

They somehow understood that human beings were governed by two distinct hemispheres that balanced each other in the human brain. Each hemisphere was given to perform specific functions. The left image linked linear hemisphere dealt with individual competitive logical rational thought, exclusion and was subsequently associated with most males. The right holistic hemisphere dealt with relationships; compassion, cooperation, maintenance and had been associated with most mothers. The hemispheres of the brain crisscrossed in the skull at the area between the two eyes. The left hemisphere controlled the right side of the body. The right hemisphere controlled the left side of the body. The only sense that did not crisscross to be balanced in the brain was the sense of smell. The two nostrils of the nose went straight up into the olfactory bulb. They did not crisscross. Therefore the sense of smell may be the oldest contact with the universal reality. The cosmos may be based on the portal of the nose and the sense of smell.

To become balanced as a human being the two hemispheres of the human brain had to work in tandem for the universe to continue on its balanced way. They had to have been even. They had to balance each other. The word for even is encoded in the Persian word hattah which linguistically reflects itself (HAT/TAH) or (AT/TA) is balanced and actually stands for the word even.

The English word even (HAVANA) begins to establish links with an ancient perception of balance. For even (HAVANA) morphs into a variety of concepts specifically into the number seven (IS EVEN) or (IS HAVANA) that not only deals with an even balance in the human brain but with life and death.

As the linguistic construct of EVE of EVEning dealt with an even (HAVANA) distribution of day and night and the dread of darkness at the Sahel and the Equator, so on the continent of Africa the same distribution had been perceived to exist in the more expansive cycle of the migratory year.

The African continent was privy to two major seasonal climactic events (HAVANA-) that balanced each other. One dealt with the coming monsoons that drenched the parched savannah (IS HAVANA) with the welcome rain that emerged from the distant horizontal rim out of the body of Mother Earth. The other dealt with the parched spell of waiting that lasted the other half of the year.

Based on the vagaries of climactic change the herbivore herds in need of new grass followed the falling rains to the distant verdant savannahs (IS HAVANA) and they too were based on the dual activity of foaling. The ancient herbivore migrations based on the annual cycles of rainfall not only followed the falling rains in the far distance but also mated and gave birth in tandem with those dual, even cycles that depended on the falling rain.

The ancient mother led migrations following the herds to the distant savannahs (IS HAVANA) came upon pools of quietly standing waters at the

Okavango River Delta, Mara River and many other African lakes, rivers and mashes. They must have observed that the quietly standing pools of water at the savannah (IS HAVANA) created an illusion of duality and balance. One dealt with the solid soil or dirt under their feet on which they were standing. The other was the temporary illusion of an upside down reflection in the waters before them. The upside down reflection of reality in the waters below was an even (HAVANA), if temporary picture of that which existed above in the quiet waters of the savannah (IS HAVANA). For the Hadza people of the Olduvai Gorge one of their ancient myths claimed that 'the sky used to locate under the Earth' which seems to deal with the reflection in the standing waters that was perceived to be part of their very ancient mother centered reality.

In time and many changes later the number seven which originally came to represent the illusion of evenness and balance at the water's edge emerged as an odd number and the number dealing with death. It was at the soggy savannah (IS HAVANA) that the number seven came into being. It was also at the savannah that the ancient migration broke the migratory year into two even (HAVANA) halves. There exists an 'mystical' throwback to mother centrality when the Christian Saint Peter had been deliberately crucified upside down and the not so 'mystical' Mussolini and his mistress had also been hung up-sie down. The only creature hanging up-side down is the bat in its nocturnal cave.

As the EYE sees reality upside down, so the mirrored surFACE of water on the body of Mother Earth also drew the picture of reality upside down.

An ancient Mother Earth Goddess Accat defined as a 'water drawer' did not draw water with a bucket out of a well. What the Mother Goddess represented was that she fashioned or *drew* a picture, a reflection of evenness on Her surFACE. As above so below. It was the Saan Bushmen of the Kalahari who are not only one of the oldest group of people as defined by their DNA but also had been considered to be great and productive artists. Their caves in Africa have been filled with thousands of *drawn* pictures.

The even distribution of the ancient thirteen month migratory lunar year dealt with movement for six months in one direction, resting, foaling and mating, then following the monsoon rains returning for the other six months in the other direction. The ancient migratory march began in late March or early April, Aries A (ah) the Alpha of beginnings at the time of the Spring Equinox. The return back to their beloved mountains began in the seventh month, the sept of September at the time of the Autumnal Equinox, if you count from March as the first lunar month. The two Equinoxes created the balance, an equal, even (HAVANA) distribution of time on the level of the ancient thirteen month lunar year.

The number seven (IS HAVANA) of the return to the verdant savannah (IS HAVANA) as a number not as a letter comes to define the SHAPE of the even (HAVANA) journey of the sun, delineating the light of day in the Eastern sky and the darkness of night in the Western waters reflecting its even distribution of light (L) and night, the (N) of night creating the negation of light at the equator. As the angular solar disc rose in the Eastern horizontal rim out of the flat round surFACE of Mother Earth it symbolically created the SHAPE of the letter (L) of light, and life and the beginning of day. After it passed through the inverted belly of air above the body of Mother Earth it set back down into Her Western waters in the angle encoded in the SHAPE of the number seven. The SHAPE of that angular fall off the edge became associated with the death of the sun as it died to its light. Because the processes inherent in the human condition had been shared by Mother Earth and the sun, the number seven embraced the concept of death on other levels.

Then a shift occurred. As human beings were beginning to name things and of males began the asking of why of their peripheral state in PHASE TWO they created the first separation. The naming of things used the left hemisphere of the human brain and its single focused linear linguistic configuration. As the naming of things became a categorical imperative, the left hemisphere of the human brain took on the extra burden becoming over evolved. It began to dwarf the holistic responsibility of the right hemisphere. In time along with the naming of things came the codification into words and the secretive evolution of writing.

Because it was the mother, the lady (LADA), that had been the leader ((LADA-) of the ancient migrations and defined reality in PHASE ONE based on the caring of the young, responsibility and enduring familial relationships she had been right hemispheric and usually left handed. With the advent of naming of things and then linear writing a shift became apparent as the primacy of the balanced right hemisphere of the mothers became replaced by the left hemisphere of the fathers as the left hand of the mothers became replaced by the right hand of the emerging fathers in PHASES TWO and THREE. But the balance demanded by their ancient perception of reality had to be served.

There existed a massive imbalance in the human family at the time that young males reached puberty. They became testy and unrelentingly sexual like the male elephants and male lions. To protect the family they had to be

Section One

shoved out of the familial unit. Circling the periphery they not only established turfs that had to be defended causing nothing but trouble. The ancient mothers knew that male animals when they reached puberty and became sexual, also became violent. To still the violence and maintain the balance of peace they castrated the male animals making them into docile beasts of burden. A steer is a castrated oxen creature that can be steered.

Based on those perceptions because the humanoid and then human females mated with the Alpha male and *all* of the peripheral circling males as they had done in the North Congo River chimpanzees, there was no specific father to protect the mothrys and their off spring. Kidnapping, incest and rape, beginning among the violent male chimpanzees followed an evolutionary track into the humanoid and then human creature.

Because of the violence visited by the marauding territorial shoved out at puberty males upon the migrating put upon mothers, the mothers created their own specific families and tribal clans. Along the way extending the act of castration of animals to their violent sons, they castrated their first born sons to become the avuncular uncles protecting the human family. *The castration creating a cessation of male testosterone flowing into his male body created not only peace but a balance in the male brain.* It rid him of his violent sexuality becoming the protector of his mother's family. The word LIB (LABA) deals with castration. The syllable (LA) deals with the mother as Mother Earth the pLAnet extending to Her daughters the LAdies as the leaders on the LAnd. The (BA) surfaces as the concept of two in one which in Lib (LABA) comes to deal with the female and male alive in one male body. The LABIOS as lips also deal with two in one as the complete mouth in stage one. Had castration been done by the two lips of the mohel as it subsequently surfaces in the Hebrew sourced male history. What about the secretive LABRYS, the two headed triangular axe hidden on the back of stone walls in Malta? Does the BRIS at the end of LABRYS surface with another clue that circumcision had been a result of the ancient practice of castration, if thinly veiled. It also deals with LIBRA holding the scales of balance dealing with LIBERATION from the son's violent self. The 'word' has its entrance here for it also includes LIBRA not only in the naming of things but with the accumulation of knowledge as in a LIBRARY. Along with castration, LIB also defines the activity of maiming of the smith and shepherd to keep them tied to their LABors.

Ironically The Statue of LIBerty in New York harbor with her shackled feet is the personification of the ancient body of Mother Earth as the *castrated* Goddess of Light in PHASE THREE of male centrality holding the light of freedom in her right hand extended into the heavens *away* from her body. She contains seven (IS HAVANA) spokes of sun light emanating from her crown.

Castration of the first born son opened the doors into the state akin to the mothers birthing breath and the experience of the Kundalini energy rising up from the body of Mother Earth, and in a double helixical pattern shafting through the body giving birth to shamanism. The shift into male shamanism dealt with the neutralization of fear and the death of his male essence.

Another factor enters the overburdened collage. As heterosexual males began to understand their role in specific paternity, at the beginning of PHASE TWO they needed their own concept of source, procreation and fatherhood. One ancient direction that they went to in the latter part of PHASE ONE was to the standing waters on the body of Mother Earth searching for an answer. If the reality above the surFACE, the ground under their feet dealt with Mother Earth and life, then the even (HAVANA) reflection in the still waters became the domain of male source and death. The balance between life and death had to be maintained. Since the reflection in the still waters dealt with the death of the light and a plunge into the darkness of night, males began to worship the celestial bodies of the night. For a very short period of ancient time they had links with the moon but the moon had been the single source of menstruation in quintessent girls, so they turned to the stars to be their primary source of creation before in PHASE TWO they rose into daylight with their encampment in the sun. When they turned into the stars of night associated with the darkness of death *away* and *above* the body of Mother Earth they went through a series of evolutionary progressions.

Both the shoved out at puberty heterosexual males and the castrated uncles yearned for the powerful ecstasy and courage inherent in the birthing breath of the mothers. They came to that experience not only through castration but through ritual using many activities and herbs to divine that desired state which surfaced as the state of trance, an entrance into the balanced center at the third eye. One very early activity in Hebrew dealt with the activity of rocking back and forth called to d'aven (DA' HAVANA) gift of (DA) (HAVANA). As they rocked back and forth entoning their written words they moved into the desired state of trance. The state of trance created an entrance into the Akashik Record or the universal consciousness of all that exists in the NOW moment. The state of trance brought with it the possibility of great power, healing, prophecy and the manipulation of matter. It also moved them into the conscious dream state still experienced by the Australian Aborigines as they 'walk about'. It is a state that has been systematically suppressed by the

Section One

over evolved left male hemisphere of the human brain because *IT CANNOT BE CONTROLLED*. All that is, exists in the dream state, in the Akashic record. There are no rules. Everything is possible. Combinations which are impossible in the state of awakened awareness come up for consideration in the dream state. The dream state is the state of creative activity. Plants grow at night. Animals can emerge with human heads. Human beings can emerge with animal heads. Some humans, horses, even pigs can grow wings and fly. There are no extra terrestrials. Extra terrestrials as a reality exist as realms of fantasy in the human brain that has become overwhelmed by the over evolved fear driven left male hemisphere.

As Africa became host to climatic change, floods, earthquakes, ice ages and volcanic eruptions, the migrating mother clusters moved off the beleaguered continent of Africa passing through many linguistic configurations that contained the HAVANA dyad in them. One was in France and the place called the city of Avignon (HAVANA-). On the Western shore toward the setting sun they encountered 'lands end' in Anglia or England. There they set up one of their major mysteries in the round circle of vibrating stones called Stonehenge. Next to Stonehenge flowed the river Avon (HAVANA) that could be reached by a wide avenue (HAVANA) a place of ecstatic healing, transformation, trade and community. That was only the beginning of their journey toward immortality. For after they drummed their way into states of trance within the vibrating stones sitting upon Mother Earths lea lines, they sailed their dead across the wide expanse of the Atlantic Ocean into the Cuban Island and the place of Havana as a haven (HAVANA), a stop over on their way to their starry heavenly (HAVANA-) source *away* and *above* the body of Mother Earth into the Pleiades Constellation of the Seven (IS HAVANA) Sisters. Since we are dealing with sisters and not with brothers then we are on the cusp between PHASE ONE of female centrality and PHASE TWO moving into the transition into male centrality. The Seven Starry Sisters created the balance inherent in the number seven (IS HAVANA).

A similar myth surfaces among the Lakota Indians of Wyoming. Stonehenge is a massive circle of stones that vibrate when drumming. The Lakota Indians of Wyoming have their own place of sacred vibratory ecstasy and transformation, the Devils Tower, a majestic stone butte with vertical parallel tracks etched upon its surFACE. The myth declares that seven (IS HAVANA) sisters ran from a bear (BARA) up the stone tower. The bear chased them but they got away. He left vertical parallel claw marks on the face of the rock. The seven sisters sailed away into the starry constellation of the Pleiades. So it seems that the savannah (IS HAVANA) out of Africa found its way across the great expanse of the Atlantic Ocean not only surfacing linguistically in Havana Cuba but also reappearing in the Lakota myth of the seven (IS HAVANA) sisters having (HAVA-) their haven (HAVANA) up in heaven (HAVANA) in the constellation of the Pleiades.

As a process of reflection creates an even balance, so when the reflection became a linguistic process the letters in a word became mirrored. It happened in the four corners also in North America among the Navajo (NAVAHA) tribe. For Navajo(NAVAHA) reflected is (NAVAHA/HAVANA). The process leading to male centrality in PHASES TWO and THREE rears its linguistic head here. The name may be reflected and male sourced but the Navajo had been still matriarchal, the oldest brother shared leadership with the mother. The sexes had been divided into hogans. The male hogan was four sided. The female hogan was eight sided as have been the number of spokes of the Tibetan flag and arms on the octapus. The meaning of this will become apparent. In the ancient Middle East the city of Nineveh reflected as (NANAVAHA/HAVANANA) establishes its roots out of PHASE ONE and the worship of the moon the Greek Nana on the shores of a distant land. Moving further East still on the North American continent is the city of Savannah (IS HAVANA) in Georgia, not part of the African plain and there is also the Suwanne (IS HAWANA) River in Northern Florida. In the Yosemate Valley there exists the Hawana of the Neewah /HAWANA) culture. The The V and W are interchangeable.

Mother centrality constantly raises its hopeful head to balance out the unrelenting violence visited upon the human race by the over evolved male left hemisphere of the human brain. In England King Arthur with his round table and sacred *sword* gave birth to Avalon (HAVA(LA)NA). Take the LA of the LAdy of the LAnd out of the center and you have the haven (HAVANA) of the searched for mother based peaceful heaven (HAVANA) that King Arthur yearned for and lost. The sword Excalibur (hakasakaLABARA) being engulfed by the lake at the end of the myth establishes the demise of female centrality and her castrated (LIB) and maimed (LIB(LABARA) eunuch son. Similar story of Beowolf.

An ancient painting out of the Bible has Christ sitting on a horse with a *sword* in His mouth. It has been interpreted as Christ being a warrior. Perhaps not. Perhaps Christ came with the spoken *word* as a weapon to battle the unwary and transgressors. He did say, 'you better love your neighbor and turn the other cheek or you will be in a lot of trouble'. History (HIS STORY) has fulfilled His prophecy.

Section One

In spite of all the Biblical pronouncements to the contrary there are really only three sins. One is jealousy. Another is exploitation. The third is revenge. Cain and Abel cover the sins of jealous siblings fighting over the access to the mother's body on a universal level. Exploitation covers all the masks of slavery, rape, indenture, greed, manipulation, theft, pornography, murder and harassment.

The concept of revenge fits into the category of not only being a major sin but it creates the necessary balance in the universe. For rEVENge contains in its linguistic folds the process of getting even (HAVANA), of balancing the score. Revenge is as ancient as language itself. It is only in contemporary law that justice is a game of winning and losing between the left hemispheric minds of the lawyers and not a search for that ancient balance for justice that held the universe 'on its rightful way'.

It seems apparent that the Biblical admonition as an EYE for an EYE dealt with revenge (RAVANAGA) and the balancing of the scales, of getting even (HAVANA). It doesn't proclaim that instead of an EYE for an EYE, it should have been a nose for a nose, or an ear for an ear, although that may have had its run also. Since it contains in its linguistic structure the letter V (haVAna) dealing with the female vulva then the activity of revenge may have been an activity of the ancient mothers balancing the scales of justice for themselves and their kidnapped and RAVAged daughters. Rape had been a constant problem for many ancient mothers, specifically decried by the ancient Hadza people.

In PHASE THREE there is no balance upon the body of Mother Earth as the violent male competitive sexually driven left hemisphere became dominant, setting itself as superior, swamping the cooperation of the mothers right hemisphere. It also created the bifurcated human mind asking why (Y) not only of male periphery but of existence itself. Justice is that which just is. There are no answers. There are only endless tales and stories and even more endless questions dealing with the why of human existence.

The answer to why is always a lie. The answer to why is always a lie. The answer to why is always a lie.

The fundament upon which humanity teeters in its present mess is based on the illusions based in the asking of why. In PHASE ONE there existed a possibility in the languages that still exist, that some answers to existence itself during states of trance had become apparent but they had been snuffed out as not rationally controllable and therefore along with the mother's birthing breath, suppressed, obliterated, burned at the stake and discarded along with the elongated skulls. The only hope for the survival of humanity and the planet is a reconnection with the mother energy on all levels.

UNIVERSALITY OF ANCIENT PERCEPTION
'Look At Me Mommie Syndrome'
MOTHER'S FACE

Modern psychiatry out of the left hemispheric male mind only working with half of reality with HIS story has left out a variety of telling concepts. In the *fight* or *flight* scenario they left out *fright* which is as important as the other two considerations. So in *nature* and *nurture* they left out the fact that a human baby is born totally **helpless** and **conscious** of its helpless condition. The inability to do anything for itself and the realization that it is trapped in a body that doesn't work creates a situation for panic to set in. The helpless infantile victim in a jail cell that is its body searches for any object that might help it in its helpless entrapped condition. Upon opening its eyes the first thing that a baby spots is a round flat concerned object hovering above it. The concerned round flat object contains a slit on its bottom that opens and closes. It also curves up creating what becomes defined as a smile. The baby is a born mimic, so it returns the smile and realizes that it has to learn to keep on smiling to get constant unrelenting attention from that round singularly focused object above it. The infant as an attention getting machine realizes that keeping focus on that intensely interested face on itself, leads to all kinds of favorable results. *The life of habit entrenches itself through a filter of infantile helplessness following the human creature for the rest of its life.* Every time that a human being feels helpless it pulls up the helplessness it felt right after it was born. The seeds of depression, despair and suicide have been planted out of that initial sense of helplessness. It may be why many babies aware of their helpless condition cry a great deal.

As an aspect of bonding, the baby memorizes and imprints the face of the mother along with her very specific SOUND and smell. It searches for the eyes to make sure that they are watching its every move. But the eyes, along with following its every move, only blink. What seems much more interesting is the hole on the bottom of the round, flat face. For in and out of that hole all kinds of interesting activities occur. When that lateral slit separates to become the SHAPE of a round hole, pieces of morsels that have been pushed into the newly created hole succumb to being ground into smaller pieces and then with luck, being shoved out. The baby often shares in the bounty created by that moving slit on the bottom of that circular sweep of the face.

Then there are times when the hole on the bottom of the mother's face pushes out not only juicy masticated morsels but also comforting soothing

SOUNDS that float upon the air around the baby's head. The most important SOUND that the infant learns to identify that leads to its survival is the SOUND made by the mouth of the mother as she hums about the edibility of food. When a mother is masticating the food in her closed mouth, she can only make the humming SOUND, MMM it is good or edible. The next SOUND on the agenda is the nasal SOUND associated with the food being rejected indicating that it is not good, which became associated with the SHAPE of the nose as seen in profile. When the mother pushes food out of her mouth the only SOUND that she can make is the nasal SOUND of NNN or, no it is not edible. The baby relishes not only the food but also the SOUNDS that the magical hole and nasal angle on the mothers face create. Then as it intently watches, it learns that both the food and the SOUND are helped along by a darting finger like object inside the hole of her mouth that with great and lingering affection licks their parched skin and plasters down their emerging hair. It also lallates them to sleep.

The eyes on the mother's circular flat face may need to be intensely watched, but it is her mouth with all the activities within and around it that holds the greatest wonder for the baby. It is the mouth of the mother that begins the journey of definition. It is the mouth (MATA) of the mother (MATA-) that defines her. Not only the mouth defines the mother in stage one but also the rest of her face. Human beings expand the impression of the first sight of the mother's face to see faces in everything around them, in patterns of leaves on trees, in piles of rock often called rock faces, in the passing faces of changing clouds. There are faces that appear in patterns of wall-paper, in the bumps on ceilings, in the cracks on the linoleum. They all come from the first round object that a baby sees right after being born, the mothers face. It is the intense focus on the mother's face that leads to bonding and growth of intelligence and wisdom in the right hemisphere of the human brain.

MIGRATIONS

In the tropical climate of Equatorial Africa, where both humanity and language have had their origins, for all intents and purposes, there have been mostly two seasons. One season was dry, with the savannahs growing parched from the broiling sun, in time often turning to drought stricken deserts. The other time was when the rains came, announcing with their thundering presence in the far distance, the promise of greener pastures and the beginning of relief from the impending famines. It was at those semi-annual cycles of drought and monsoon that the ancient migrations of the herbivore herds began creating a great even circular sweep back and forth across the continent of Africa. Based on the vagaries of climate, the great sweep of the migrations shifted back and forth across the great expanse of savannah, jungle, desert, marsh and often raging crocodile and hippopotamus infested rivers that had to be crossed by both beast and by human beings to get to the 'greener pastures' of the 'promised lands' of the beckoning verdant savannahs.

The showers in the distance showed them the way, as they sought out sprouting new grass. Accompanying the torrential rains that semi annually swept across the parched savannahs, was the coming and going of birds. Clouds carrying rain also brought with them shoals of insects and even more clouds of birds that covered the darkening sky. They all seemed to rise vertically out of Mother Earths flat circular horizontal rim out of the side of Her body, to spend their time in the marshy swamps and then in the seventh lunar month to leave.

The reckoning of time counted by the ancient grandmothers at the time that language began to make its journey into the future in PHASE ONE was based on the thirteen-month lunar cycle that coincided with the monthly flow of menstrual blood in human females. With the shift in PHASE TWO and THREE into the male based irregular solar reckoning of monthly time it coincided with the seasonal estral flow of birthing of the herbivore mothers in the spring and fall but still coinciding with the semi-annual coming and going of birds also in the spring and fall.

The estral time in the spring and fall were periods of much bellowing and frenzy, of the butting of male heads and then of the butting of female buttocks. There was much shedding of blood on all levels. The herbivore males with their tusks, horns, antlers, teeth and hooves left gaping wounds in their adversaries responding to the pressure presented by the red flecks of blood that began flowing from the hind quarters of the females. Not to be left out, human beings shared in the frenzy. It was a time of beginnings. ESTrus in the herbivore females created the beginning of life out of their bodies. On the body of Mother Earth one of the times of beginnings was in the EAST where the sun rose out of Her horizontal rim at dawn. What remains to this day, out of the ESTral orgy is not only the Christian holiday of 'rebirth', and beginning in EASTer dealing with immortality of the 'risen' Christ, but underneath it, the time of the orgiastic ESTral Carnival.

In PHASE TWO as male role in specific procreation was becoming known (the begats of the Bible) they included Mother Earth in the mutual procreative processes with the sun acting like the male cohabitative penis during the Spring and Fall Equinoxes. All over Her expansive body, on many continents are creations of massive Earthen and stone mounds, metaphoric wombs of recreation, with a narrow tunnel, a symbolic vagina, that led to the hole where the shaft of light that broke through the darkness at exactly the time of the first sunlight of the Spring Equinox, like a penis broke through the body of the individual mother. For some it was only in the Spring at the beginning of the year. For others it embraced both the Spring and Autumnal Equinoxes. Even more expansive cohabitation had been created all four times around the ancient year with the inclusion of the two Solstices.

At the end of PHASE ONE the sun was no longer considered to be Mother Earth's son. In PHASE TWO It had become Her mate, Her soon to be in PHASE THREE Her lord and master echoing the status that came to reign for Her Earthly surrogate daughters. She lost Her royal residency as the Virgin Mother, making Herself out of Herself emerging *below* the sun in many ways. The SHAPE of the letter R came to reflect that process. The male circle of the sun on top and the triangle of the volcanic cone of the Mother under him halved vertically became the raging, roaring rapist of the lavic solar ascendency. It is a similar process echoed in the SHAPE of the Egyptian Ankh.

Mother Earth established the seasonal flow of moisture out of Her belly of air with the falling rains in the far distance beyond the parched savannahs, beckoning the ancient trekkers forward with the promise of survival and surcease from the hunger pains that echoed in their bellies the external rumblings of thunder in the far distance. It was at the time of the Spring Equinox (fall in the Southern Hemisphere), subsequently associated with either March or April, when based on the seasonal solar cycle, the estral blood of the herbivore mothers also flowed, not only marking their buttocks with red spots of blood (X), sending their scent of readiness upon the wind, announcing that they were ready to respond to the mating dance, alerting the hungry assemblage that the ancient migratory march was to begin in March (ancient Aries with the anlaut A, the Alpha of beginnings). The ancient march began with the left foot of the mothers, left-right, left-right.

As humanity spread out into the Northern reaches of Africa and into the Northern hemisphere away from the equator the seasons became reversed. Fall came in the spring and spring came in the fall. It caused a great deal of subsequent linguistic confusion.

The great surge of the herbivores; elephants, wildebeests, zebra, antelope and the accompanying gaggle of humans; women and children at the core and two sets of humanoid males, one the violent heterosexual males who circled the periphery and mated with the females often creating and fighting over their established, if temporary migratory turf, and the other avuncular hairless eunuch uncles who at the side of the mothers protected their sisters. All trudged in the direction of the falling rains and the promise of newly sprouted shoots of green grass for the herbivore mares. The mothers with their clinging infants also followed the herds for an alternative supply of milk, for meat, hides and for bones.

The other time of the great migratory march back to the foot of their beloved mountains was at the time of the Autumnal Equinox, which fell in the redefined September, the seventh month, if you count March as the beginning of the ancient lunar year; left-right, left-right,. It was a time in the fall when the migrating herbivore mothers rested and gave birth to their new foals. The dropping of new foals activated their supply of milk, which the humanoid and then human mothers following the herds needed for their often un-weaned, helpless infants.

As the wobbly herbivore foals tried out their spindly legs, the journey back began in the sept of September creating the ancient physical cycle of constant returns, the boomerang, the even (HAVANA) return upon the body of Mother Earth. Often the ragged band of human trekkers following the herds through terrible terrain filled with tawny, swaying tall grasses, had to fight their way though equally tawny crouching, waiting, hungry territorial predatory carnivores.

The ancient lunar based thirteen month year had two beginnings, one in the month of March when the march began to the marshy, verdant savannahs, the other was in September when following the herbivore herds the journey back to their beloved mountains took place.

SEVEN

In Latin 'SEPT' of SEPTember means both, 'seven' and 'separation'. As an example, the SEPTum bone in the skull evenly separates the two sides of the nose. The 'seven' of 'separation' fell on the seventh month of September if you counted from March as the beginning of the ancient mother centered PHASE ONE lunar year. Not only did the migratory march back home create a 'separation', a shift in direction from their circular journey which peaked in SEPTember, but 'SEPT' of SEPTember also defined the birthing process of the foals falling out of the bodies of their mothers in the fall (Southern hemisphere spring, as in off-spring), as they separated into the journey of their own often short and perilous lives. At the time of the Autumnal Equinox the Eastern sun beginning a new day also lit up the dark mounds of creation as in PHASE TWO a penal shaft of solar light shot through the body of Mother Earth.

Other clues surface in the word 'seven'. In one direction 'seven' breaks down into the phonemic construct of (IS EVEN). Dealing with RULE ELEVEN; at the beginning of words the letter S, or phoneme IS, deals with IT IS, and is an emphatic. How can 'seven' be 'even' when it is an odd number? You are dealing here with a very ancient mother based perception. The reckoning of time associated with the ancient migrations in PHASE ONE at the time of female centrality, had been based on the thirteen-month lunar cycle associated with female menstruation. The month of September as the seventh month, if you counted from March as the first month, existed as a fulcrum that broke the ancient year into two equal or even (HAVANA) halves. They journeyed six months in one direction toward the verdant savannah (IS HAVANA). In the month of August the sixth month they gave birth and had sex. Then in September the seventh (IS HAVANA) month they turned around, separated and trudged back for six more months to their beloved mountain home.

Another clue surfacing in the number 'seven' (IS HAVANA) shares its origins and phonemic structure with the word 'savannah' (IS HAVANA). It was in the seventh month of September as they grazed and foraged across the newly lush and verdant savannahs, that the herbivore mothers began their journey of separation.

In the Hebrew and Roman calendars, in the Northern hemisphere, the New Year began in late March or early April. In English it is known as the Spring Equinox. There seems to be a longing to remember the equal or even (HAVANA) distribution of day and night at the equator and the cycles of constant return based on the evenly spaced semi-annual migrations after the ancient migrators left Africa and scattered into the temperate and even Arctic areas of the globe.

The anlaut of A (ah), beginning the words associated with the months of April and Aries, establishes those months as falling at the time defined as the Alpha of beginnings. For the Maya in the 'new world', coincidentally the New Year is also celebrated twice. One is called the 'greater', the other is called the 'lesser', holiday of beginnings. Both fall approximately around the same times of the year as it had done in Africa. Since the Maya have not been considered as Central American migrators, but city building intensive farmers then their customs must go back to a very ancient Africa and subsequent Asia where the cycle of the year had been broken into two equal halves. They must have dispersed at the time of great cataclysmic upheavals and found new havens (HAVANA) in Havana across the great expanse of ocean, leaving their migrating habits behind but keeping intact not only their lunar based thirteen month calendar associated with menstruation but also their solar based calendar that indicated both the Spring and Fall Equinoxes. Their Feathered Serpent their main god KU KUL KAN contains both the serpent of the mother Kundalini energy rising up from the Earth and the father, the bird centered male energy circling in the Mayan air. Both surface again in the medical Cadesus of the Greeks..

The word to migrate (MAGARATA),(MAGA/GARA/RATA) shares its own secrets. The third dyad (RATA) deals with the completion of the ratio (RATA) of a circle of constant return. The sun and moon above the body of Mother Earth and the sun and moon below the body of Mother Earth created the twin distribution of cyclical time that marked the ancient year. In this case the (RA) represents the sun, as it created its own circular passage above and below the body of Mother Earth. The phoneme (TA) deals with where the journey occurred, at the tip, top, edge out of and upon Mother Earth's surFACE. The central dyad (GARA) is the word for 'mountain', the terrestrial be-getter (GA) of the sun (RA). N'goro, N'goro (NA'GARA-), is an East African mountain. In the Northern reaches of Europe gora (GARA) in Polish also means mountain. In Hebrew the pregnant mountain giving birth to the sun becomes har (HARA), the G (gh) and H (huh) are interchangeable being made in the same area of the mouth. In Hebrew the sun (RA) emerges into the neutral belly of air (HA), and is not begotten by the body of Mother Earth. The third dyad (MAGA) means great. In this case (MA) is not only the 'mother', but also embraces the concept of 'holding'. Mother Earth as the holder gives birth to the sun (RA) out of Her tip (TA-) where there are mountains, the gestating bellies that hold and then throw the sun up to Her surFACE. So the ancient migrations dealt with the passage of the sun, born out of the tips of the mountains at dawn, marking the great circle of returns across the continent of Africa, at the time of mating, foaling and begetting.

Since the second dyad (GARA) describing the mountain, also has echoes in the word gore (GARA), then the mountain in question may have dealt with the gory (GARA) lavic effulgence out of a volcanic cone, and may have had its origins out of Mount Kilimanjaro or another then active African volcano of the Rift Valley and the Ethiopian Highlands. The volcanic cone as the mountain of begetting had been the body of Mother Earth begetting Herself as land with one of Her greatest helpers, out of PHASE TWO the sun blasting forth out of Her fiery depths.

SECTION ONE

THE TRANSFORMATIVE JOURNEY OF THE SUN

A legend for the Dieri tribe of South Eastern Australia, 'the setting sun disappeared into a hole on the Western horizontal rim on the body of Mother Earth and traveled underground below Her skin to the East where in the morning it rose to a new life'.

Back home in their ancestral home in Africa, as they waited for the darkness of night to dissolve into light of day, they also must have wondered what happened to the sun after it disappeared into that Western horizontal hole, in fact what happened to all of the creations out of the body of Mother Earth. What became of the moon, stars, clouds, birds even plants after they all folded back into Her waiting arms. Where did they all go after they all sank out of sight and in one way or another became at one with Her.

Since they believed that Mother Earth was a great maternal body then like a specific individual mother she must have had all of the same organs and had been governed by the same processes, qualities and functions that governed all of Her female creations.

As the sun made its descent off the surFACE of Mother Earth into the Western horizxontal wall, sometimes into the looming mountains but more often into water (this perception is a recurring theme in many of the mythologies of the world), they believed that Mother Earth bit Her solar offspring into smaller pieces before She could swallow it. She ate it. The SHAPE of the activity of the eating of the sun in the West is the SHAPE of the number eight, (8),ate, RULE SEVENTEEN; Homonyms (puns abound), the sun reflecting itself, sliding down into the waters of its entombment.

Her daughters, mother surrogates in the creation of smaller aspects of themselves, also had to bite and chew their bloody prey before they could swallow, or share it. That is why they reasoned, sunsets were often blazing, bloody red fiery flames of the setting sun splattered like crimson droplets across the ominously darkening Western sky, mirrored in the glistening gore filled waters below.

The round solar disc of the setting sun in a liquefied state as the splattered blood in the Western sky, slid out of sight and became chewed up and swallowed by the watery body of Mother Earth giving birth to many of the letters dealing with war. Since it always emerged on the other side in the East at dawn, then somehow it had to go through the body of Mother Earth, below Her planetary surFACE to be transformed and reborn. Where else could it go they wondered, as darkness enveloped them.

There are clues in the phonemes that make up language that our human ancestors, especially mothers were great environmentalists. Every natural aspect that impinged upon their lives they somehow with time translated into tonal communication. They gave names to objects and processes that they observed around them.

Their greatest preoccupation after they codified the flat round face and body of the individual mother and the metaphoric flat round surFACE and body of Mother Earth was the codification of the sun. The tapestry now begins to glow with color and takes on new levels of meaning. There are changes in the understanding of the role of the sun through time, which deals with the vertical WARP of the linguistic tapestry.

It has one of its beginnings in the West where the sun either fell off the horizontal rim, set to the light of day, was swallowed by the great maw, slipped into the open lips creating a wounded hole and crawled in for the night. As it moved to disappear to the light of its day, it went through a process of being killed. The lights went out. Cold night descended upon the creatures of the savannah. As the solar disc was killed to the light of its day, the Western sky was set ablaze with the splattered blood in the Western waters of the setting, dying sun. Slowly it expired pulling the red flaming ribbons of blood down into the watery body of Mother Earth to begin its journey of transformative rebirth. The sun went from being a solid disc coursing through the belly of air above Her surFACE, to liquid blood that had to find its way through the nether chambers within Her body.

The blood coursing through Her underground intestines went through three distinct initially related processes.

MENSTRUATION became the lavic menstrual blood that poured out during a volcanic eruption to create land upon Her surFACE, COAGULATION solidified within Her mysterious belly into the integral disc of the sun and into solid land reborn upon Her surFACE.

MAINTENANCE after giving birth, to keep Her and Her offspring alive and powerful.

MENSTRUATION

Her surrogates in the creation of life the individual mothers of the specie were periodically enslaved to flow with either estral or menstrual blood. Mother Earth must have gone through the same process. She also flowered with a bloody maternal discharge. In Her case it was the lava that poured out of Her body out of Her three sided volcanic cone. When a volcanic eruption shuddered Her very core, She spasmed, orgasmed, flowered with the flow of

MENSTRUAL, in Her case lavic blood. As the bloody magmic lava poured down Her flanks it hardened into land upon Her surFACE. She created Herself, out of Herself, as Herself, all by Herself. Apparently even for Mother Earth in PHASE ONE there was no external solar male input. She had to do everything by Herself. *Specific paternity* even as a concept was unknown. Out of those perceptions came the subsequent religious and eminently confusing concept in PHASE THREE of virgin birth, mitosis, and pathogenesis.

When the concept of virgin birth occurs in antiquity in PHASE ONE, the ancient mothers perceived that through a mysterious dual process without any outside help Mother Earth as the Virgin Mother MENSTRUATED and with Her lavic blood of the sun that had its origins in the Western waters when it sank to its doom, She gave birth to all the smaller aspects of Herself. They could also see that habitually like clockwork every morning she gave birth to the sun at dawn. It emerged out of Her body as an aspect of the transformed coagulated blood beneath Her mantle. She was the Virgin Mother of the sun and the Virgin Mother of the land upon Her surFACE.

Many of the ancient transformed heroes; Zoroaster, Sargon, Perseus, Jason, Meletus, Zeus, Hercules and Jesus were all a throw back to having been born out of a virgin mother, out of the self perpetuating body of Mother Earth who remained the eternal virgin. For the Buddhists, the Virgin Mother of Buddha was Maya (the holder (MA) of the light. Aya is light in Persian and dawn in Assyrian. Buddha was also known as the 'enlightened one'. The Roman Catholic Church in PHASE THREE resurrected and rearranged the concept of virgin birth as dealing with Mother Mary the virgin Mother of God and her child Jesus as her celestial son.

COAGULATION

Since in PHASE ONE the knowledge of mating having links with specific paternity did not yet have its dawning, the ancient mothers perceived that there must have been some kind of mysterious culinary magic at work within a mother's body to create a baby. After a young girl started menstruating and then stopped passing blood, as her belly disTENded, for TEN lunar months, she was apparently on her way to becoming a mother. After ten lunar months of gestation, with the birth of a baby, she not only began to pass blood again, but her breasts flowed with milk. They wondered, what happened inside of her body for those ten lunar months to keep the blood from flowing on the outside and to create a new creature on the inside. It must have been that the blood inside of the young mother COAGULATED inside of her body to make a baby, like the blood in a wound COAGULATED outside, stanching its flow. That is why it stopped flowing.

The Egyptians called SA, the 'wise blood of the mother', for it knew all by itself what to do, how to solidify, how to change from a liquid into a solid, how to COAGULATE to create a baby inside of the mother's body. The English words of SAga and SAgacity as wisdom come out of that ancient linguistic anlaut of perception, as do the words for blood SAngre in Spanish and SAnguis in Latin.

The same process extended to explain the creation of the integral round disc of the sun after it was chewed and swallowed by Mother Earth's maw in the Western wall of death and then coursed under Her skin in a bloody liquefied state. They posited that it was one of the same processes of transformation, from one state to another that the fetus went through within the individual mother's body, changing liquid menstrual blood into a solid recognizable miniature replica of the mother, that the liquefied sun also went through within the body of Mother Earth. It changed from the flowing liquefied solar blood of the Western waters to the solid integral round disc of the sun on one hand and the coagulated, hardened lavic effulgence of land on the other.

MAINTENANCE

The third perception that Mother Earth needed the solar sourced blood to course through Her body to MAINTAIN Her was an understanding that She shared with all of Her creatures. The menstrual lavic blood that created land upon Her surFACE didn't affect them directly. It was a planetary event. The blood that coagulated to create the integral disc of the sun was also an activity singularly related to Mother Earth.

It was the magmic blood below Her surFACE under Her skin out of the tri-parted reality in Her underground chambers that like the breath above Her surFACE in Her belly of air supported and sustained their lives. It was the magmic blood coursing through the veins of Mother Earth moving up through Her mantle as the solar electro-magnetic shakti of the Kundalini prana energy that also rose within them on the birthing breath and entered the bottom of their feet moving up through their bodies healing their ills while bathing them in ecstasy.

They had many ways through which they could awaken this solar sourced, Mother Earth delivered energy. Originally it came alive for them in caves and underground chambers within the body of Mother Earth close to Her pulsating fiery heart. They traced veins above Her surFACE that reflected the reality of venal networks below Her surFACE. Because they could feel the fire awakening within their bodies as they traced their way across the beckoning savannahs they laid external tracks across the body of Mother Earth and within the traces of their memory. Some may have been the Nazca lines in Peru. Others surface as the dragons way in England.

They also became aware that there were times during the great circular sweep of their year that at certain times the fire and the ecstasy rooted them to the spot, to the magnificent body of Mother Earth and heaved them around in a stationary place. Some among them and all mothers during childbirth in the last stages of labor also carried and awakened the solar sourced fires within them as they panted hard and fast flipping into the mysterious state of trance. It was the body of Mother Earth at Her most intense that they worshipped as they drummed, danced or drank their way into trance. As they entered the state of trance they became privy to different states of being.

The high fast panting breath of the birthing mother created one of the original openings or portals into the trance state. The other portal had been created in the castrated first born sons when their testosterone production had been destroyed and they became fused with the female essence. The fusion created a balance between the two hemispheres of the brain and an opening into shamanism, along with the elongated skulls the powers of healing, prophecy and the manipulation of matter.

The even (HAVANA) balance in Amharic is sank (IS HANAKA) and surfaces in the castrated eunuch (HANAKA) hemispherically balanced first born son.

With the plunge in PHASE THREE into male centrality and the over evolution of the right handed left hemisphere of the brain based on the intense focus that is necessary in music, speech and writing itself, the rational system of left hemispheric male individuality came into prominence and the mysterious life of mysticism and a connection with the cosmic universe not only went underground but with the growth of religious systems became almost totally obliterated. Not only did Mother Earth supply Her creations with their needs for survival but She gave them a dose of pleasure MAINTAINING them in a state of suspended joyful living.

LIVER

LIVER and the emergence of the fetus, out of the lower hole on the bodies of human mothers, or the back holes on the bodies of mammals, must have given them pause, but not for long. If ingested food went through a process of transformation to become the feces, then so did the blood become transformed to become the fetus. The LIVER was perceived to become one of the homes of fetal, gestational life. The blood coagulated within the mothers body to create a new being, that was a given. The LIVER as the internal, solid bloody coagulate had been perceived to be the seat of the coagulated fetus.

There was ancient confusion as to exactly where the gestational life of the fetus occurred. In Russian the word for womb is utroba. A similar sounding word in Polish is wontroba, and means, the LIVER. Also in Polish a zawias is a hinge. In Russian a zaviaz is an ovary. It echoes the same concept as the vulva (vaLAVA) as the valve (vaLAVA) of constant return. Its origins go back to Mother Earths menstrual (LAVA) as it pours out of the volcanic (VA) aperture. It expands to include the linguistic SOUND of (VA) on either side of (LA) the LAdy of the Land, to establish the vulva (VALAVA) and the volcano (VA) as part of a system of linguistic evenness and balance.

The 'womb' and the LIVER were often mistaken one for the other. A formidable clue exists in the English word that has to do with 'giving birth', it surfaces in the word 'to deLIVER. It seems that the deLIVERY of a baby dealt not only with (DA) 'the gift of', or the separation of it from the mother's body, but also the separation of it from her LIVER, the internal organ that in mother centered PHASE ONE represented the coagulated bloody mass, cum fetus in her body.

The liver (LAVARA), has links with the body of Mother Earth, with LAVA, the linguistic source of natural 'law' (LAWA, LAVA), the (V) and (W) are interchangeable and with being alive (HALAVA). (LA) deals with the feminine as mother and Mother Earth and with the angular SHAPE of emergence of the blood out of (VA) of the volcanic vent or hole (HALA). At the end of the word liver (LAVARA) the RA, out of PHASE TWO, deals with the sun as the male helper of Mother Earth, 'the doer', or 'one who does', as in English the suffix (-ER), or (-OR), on the end of many words indicates.

The (HA) in the word alive (HALAVA), deals with the belly of air above Mother Earth's surFACE, the support system, through which all creatures suspended on the breath traveled. In the word deliver (DALAVARA) the only thing that is added to the word liver is the (DA) phoneme at the beginning that means not only 'separation from', but also the 'gift of'. As the bloody monthly menstrual discharge was the 'gift of' life out of the bodies of Her surrogate daughters in the creation of life under their surfaces, so lava as Mother Earths menstrual blood was the 'gift of' the liquefied sun, which also became the 'gift of' coagulated land upon Her surFACE and beneath their feet. In PHASE ONE mother's on all levels were revered for their great and unceasing labors in the creation and maintenance of life.

INTESTINES

It wasn't only the veins and arteries that carried the fiery bloody solar cargo of transformation below the surFACE and body of Mother Earth that had its solidifying end run in the liver. There were also the internal INTESTINES, for they seemed to do the major job of transportation from one state to another, whether it was perceived to be the feces or the fetus. Clarity of process was not one of the strongest points of early humanity, explanations and story telling were.

In Mother Earth's perambulating creations, Her creatures, food went into a hole on one end. Then a kind of mysterious process similar to cooking took place. It emerged as steaming feces, or in Her female creations, a slippery steaming fetus. There must have been some kind of hidden culinary magic that made ingested food turn into feces and gestated menstrual blood, once it became internally coagulated and dammed up turning into a liver based fetus.

They surmised that the same mystery happened within the body of Mother Earth. At Her Western horizontal rim She ate the sun, moon, clouds, stars even the birds. They were swallowed as they disappeared into that great maw on the Western horizontal rim and then as if by magic, in one way or another, after passing through Her great internal fiery underground furnace, they all returned back up to Her surFACE on the Eastern side.

Since Mother Earth was a flat round maternal plane that they as Her children all disappeared under after they died, then the passage of the heavenly bodies, which were also Her children, when they disappeared under Her surFACE also had to go through a similar process after they too passed from their lives.

The bloody liver may have been the seat of coagulation, but it fell to the internal INTESTINES within the body of Mother Earth to become a via of passage for the trans-formative rebirth of everything that died, especially Her most important offspring, in the latter part of PHASE ONE and the beginning of PHASE TWO, Her helper and first born son, the sun.

MOTHER EARTH and the SUN, healers and helpers
The curfew tolls the knell of parting day,
The lowing herd wind slowly o'er the LEA,
The plowman homeward plods his weary way,
And leaves the world to darkness and to me.

Elegy written In a Country Churchyard by Thomas Gray

The human creature is addicted to pleasure. It will seek out pleasure at any cost. Not only sex, liquor, fear, sugar, honey, sweetness of any kind and what became organized religion had been created out of the search for pleasure. Before religion became a profitable business based on the fear of death culminating in sanctified bribery, it had very different universal natural 'pagan' origins.

There had been many ancient civilizations that had been erected and then destroyed apparently over the two hundred thousand years that human beings evolved with the same sized brain that exists today. During all those years they didn't sit around and twiddled their thumbs. Mapping the body of Mother Earth they sailed across Her expansive aqueous surFACE and migrated across Her verdant savannahs. Their mapping dealt with LEA lines upon Her ground of being that moved within them as ecstasy and power when they ventured upon them. They knew that there were places on the body of their Great Mother that when they stepped upon a specific area a surge of mysterious power spun them into states of ecstatic trance. The trance brought with it a loss of the conscious voice over rational left hemispheric brain and shoved them into a new territory, a territory that usually they had access to only in their dreams and in a transformative state. In that subconscious state they could heal, foretell the future, warn against tragedy, manipulate matter, levitate, even bring the dead back to life, qualities they shared with the elongated skull humanoids.

But not all of the ancient people had easy access to that ecstatic subconscious transformative state. Originally in PHASE ONE it occurred at the time of birthing in the human mother. Due to the evolution of bipedal locomotion the hips of the mother did not spread wide enough for the large headed human fetus to easily push its way through. The laboring mother had to pant high and fast and work hard to help push the large headed baby out of her body. Since being Her surrogate she had the same qualities that Mother Earth possessed. She also had hidden below her surface at the base of her spine that same ecstatic power filled energy coiled like a metaphoric snake to spin forth with goose pimpled ecstasy to help bring the fetus to the surface. As she panted hard and fast, her birthing breath acting like a bellows awakened the sleeping coiled double snake Kundalini prana lying at the sacred sacrum ascending like a fire up the spine burning out her fears making her a fearless protective mother of her off-spring replacing the pregnant young girl that came before.

With the high fast panting birthing breath of the laboring mother, also came a cascade of orgasms. The head of the fetus pushing against the clitoris activated its pleasure center as it worked its way up to the surface. The head of the fetus pushing on the clitoris from the inside during the birth process became like the head of the penis pushing from the outside during cohabitation. Since all qualities had been to a greater or lesser degree shared by both sexes, in time the mother's sexual partner also began to share in the ecstatic relief that sensuality brought to the human creature sharing its links wiith the South Congo River Bonobo.

The mothers birthing breath and orgasmic power filled ecstasy laid the groundwork for what in PHASES TWO and THREE became the redefined mystical experience. It was not a mystery to the ancient mothers. Since males did not experience the birthing breath of the mothers, it became a mystical mystery to them as the ecstasy and the power had been denied them. The sacred Kundalini energy risen upward on the birthing breath became redefined in PHASES TWO and THREE as the father energy of God falling down from heaven. Mother Earth had been denied as the singular source of divinity.

Because of the violence, rape and kidnapping that had been visited upon the migrating clusters of females and their offspring as expressed by the Hadza people of the Rift Valley, they had to find ways to survive the constant barrage from the peripheral, marauding heterosexual males. They must have tried many ways to survive the onslaught. One became a major way into the future.

Children love to have pets, creatures closer to their own size. On their yearly migratory trek they dragged along not only puppies but lambs, kids and cubs of all kinds. When the male creatures grew up and reached their sexual maturity they often mounted everything in sight becoming testy and violent. Somehow along the way in PHASE ONE it became apparent to the ancient mothers that with the removal of the testes the male creatures became docile, no longer violent. As a survival factor for the rest of the clan the process of castration had been visited upon the first born son to make him as docile as all the other male creatures. There was no protection from the rest of the tribe. As among the African Northern Congo chimpanzees the females mated mostly with the alpha male and often with many others. Specific paternity was unknown and males had no stake in protecting the children. Mothers and children were on their own.

Because their sons were larger and stronger than their daughters and became dangerous when they reached puberty, it became a rite of passage for the first born sons to become castrated and protectors of their mother's daughters and their sister's offspring. They became the castrated eunuch (HANAKA) uncles (HANAKAla) joining the ranks of the docile male creatures that accompanied the trudging migrators.

The castration of the first born son brought with it an extra unanticipated gift. With the destruction of his testosterone hormones he not only became docile and a protector of his family but with the loss of the testosterone hormones he fused with the mother energy, becoming even and 'balanced'. Many began to share in her mystical powers. He didn't have to experience the birthing breath of the mother to become a shaman. The loss of his manhood often guaranteed him that status.

It was as if the coiled serpentine Kundalini energy at the base of his spine had been held locked in place by his manhood. With the removal of his testes he could join the ranks of the mothers and the mystery of her mystical breath.

As outlandish and bizarre as that may have been, the lost civilizations that have come out of the surFACE of Mother Earth with humongous monuments, massive stone circles and pyramids could only have been built by people who had gifts that were not akin to ours. Mentally we cannot manipulate matter, although scientifically we are doing it. We cannot melt massive stones and fit them exactly in place. Few can heal with their hands. Few others can foretell the future. Some have been left over from a most ancient past and when not burnt at the stake or driven into the wilderness became healing witches.

The eunuch uncle, the castrated first born son and the child with the elongated skull began to assist their priestess mother in the rites of the rising and setting sun and the rites dealing with the birth and death of subsequent members of the clan. The names of the eunuch priesthood in one way or another hidden within the folds of emerging languages using the RULES OF ORIGINAL SOUND DISCOVERY (ROSD) surface and become apparent to have existed all over the world.

Mating males with their manhood intact began to hanker for the power inherent in the birthing breath of the mothers. In PHASES TWO and THREE there began a search to find the fearlessness that the mother's possessed with their pleasure filled ecstatic birthing breath. What also accompanied the birthing breath of the mother was a transformation dealing with fear, of being a wimpy teenager to becoming a fearless mother. As the rising serpentine electromagnetic shakti of the Kundalini energy blasted its way up her spine, it not only bonded with the product of her labors but burned out her fears and anxieties.

Section One

The quest of the hero in PHASE TWO entered the pages of human mythologhical history. Young males jumped on their steeds to do battle with every possible adversary in order to prove their courage and fearlessness. There were others who turned to ritual to gain the exalted state. Somehow they understood that there occurred a *fusion* within the brain and it was the internal mystical *fusion* of balance that created the transformative state.

The *fusion* was a *focusing*, the con*cent*ration at the *cent*er that resulted in that much desired state of trance. Here lie the roots of all the different systems that awakened the pleasure filled mystical breath. Some males stopped eating knowing that in forty days and forty nights they would begin to have hallucinations, to be wrapped in pleasure and to enter the state of trance. Others chanted their way hOMe. Still others spun their way in circles. Mother Earth helped them by producing mushrooms, cactus and plants to open the doors into their freedom. They discovered fermented drinks to guide them on their way. The search for and result of 'spirits' has a double meaning.

When *focus* is created a bridge occurs between the two hemispheres of the brain. The bridge of the nose is the place to *focus* the two wandering eyes. When the focusing is deep enough, long enough and enough desire is housed in the *focusing* activity, different aspects occur in different adepts. In all, the intense *focusing* as either prayer or meditation shuts down the negative prattle in the fear image driven left hemisphere of the human brain.

Christ said "Teach all ways, all ways are mine". It is the activity of meditative *focusing*, of concentrating, of bringing the two hemispheres together creates the entrance into the center. Prayer is *focusing* out to some power out there that will come in and administer the transformation. Meditation is a *focusing* inward looking for the inherent personal power to do the job. If the desire or despair is strong enough the *focusing* will activate the electro- magnetic dual coil of shakti of the Kundalini serpent energy that lies coiled at the base of the spine and burns the adept clean. It is the habits created at birth through a filter of panic driven helplessness that have to be neutralized. Gurus who have been mostly transformed males in whom the Kundalini energy had become awakened have been known to have had all their habits burned clean and have had to learn how to eat and how to tie their shoe laces all over again.

There were other factors that fed into the results of the risen Kundalini energy which have been part of the experience. One had been the activity of trepanning. The other dealt with symbolic SHAPES that emerged defining the process. When meditation is deep enough and the left hemispheric prattling fear driven male brain becomes stilled, not only does the mind become stoned and quiet but a flush of goose-pimples announces an oncoming state of trance. Before the light at the center of the forehead starts pulsating with its own rhythm, a variety of star SHAPES begin their journey into transformation.

As the wafting breath quiets the mind body continuum diagonal shafts of light begin to shatter the blackness between the concentrated eyes. They create specific SHAPES. One at the most ancient time in PHASE ONE had been the six pointed Star of David. The other emerged as the eight pointed British Union Jack, the eight spokes on the wheel of the Tibetans and the eight arms of the octopus. When the Star of David began its journey into the future it began its life as six diagonal bursts of light on the dark landscape of the mind. As the diagonal pulsations criss-crossed each other in that dark quiescent space they fused into what emerged as the six pointed star before it fused into the circle of light that became defined as the brilliant light of the third eye.

In PHASE ONE at the time of female centrality with the worship of Mother Earth and the individual mothers as the sole creators of life, the six pointed Star of David as the fused polarities of Mother Earth and the triangular volcanic cone astride the triangular SHAPE of the female vulvic patch became the SASA dyad of transformation. The SA as the lavic blood out of the triangular volcanic cone of Mother Earth and the SA as the blood of the triangular vulvic patch of the individual mother fusing together at the center pulsating in the darkness above the nose and between the eyes both created the round light filled blazing circle of the third eye and the pathway of moving into the trance state.

In PHASE TWO as male role in specific procreation was becoming known, the Star of David along with the Biblical be-gats became redefined as Hebrew symbols. No longer did it belong as a process inherent in the lavic and bloody creative aspects of the ancient mothers. It became a male symbol deeply entrenched in the traditions of Judaism.

A similar if more expansive obfuscation happened to the eight pointed diagonal star of the British Union Jack. As meditation grew more and more profound and the darkness more promising, the six pointed Star of David expanded to include two more arms as eight shafts of starry light began their insistent pulsation in the third eye. The eight diagonal shafts of light of the Union Jack in PHASE TWO included aspects of the male as the father moving into his space of paternity and directly to the processes in*her*ent on the surFACE of Mother Earth.

One line of criss crossing passage dealt with the circle of air above Her through which the sun rose in the Eastern sky at dawn and set in the Western horizon. The other line of criss crossing passage dealt with the semiannual passing of birds North and South creating the vertical line of the cross announcing the time of the ancient migrations. The passage of the sun laterally and the birds vertically created the cross across the surFACE of Mother Earth.

But there emerged another set of diagonal lines that flooded the landscape of the mind reflecting the male aspect of creation. It had its origins in the square.

In PHASE ONE at birth little girls were defined by the triangular SHAPE of their vulvic patch and their ability to produce babies. Three became an ancient number defining the females as potential mothers. Because boy bodies did not produce babies they were defined not only by the zero (IS HARA) of the empty belly but by the number one, (I) of *one more* based on the finger like *SHAPE* of the penis. One more to the three of the Mother became the number four which began to emerge as a male symbol. The square as the four sided box not only became the tefilah of davening Jews but took its symbolic place in the sky above the body of Mother Earth. The two diagonals with their four shafts of light extending into the four corners above Her surFACE; East-West, North-South, delineated the four male directions as the emerging compass.

Placing the circle with the cross of the mothers upon the two criss-crossed diagonal lines the square of the fathers, you get the SHAPE of the Union Jack. That emergent eight pointed star of the Union Jack had its origins in the pulsating third eye during meditation. In PHASE TWO it began to create the even balance between the circular three sided polarities of the mothers with the four sided polarities of the fathers.

The eight pointed star of pulsating light in the third eye emerged with another set of symbolic meaning in Tibet. To the Tibetans their flag has a wheel with eight spokes within it. The symbolism of the flashing light in the third eye is the same, even if the given example of a circle is different. During deep meditation it is the flashing lights in the third eye either as six or as eight shafts of pulsating light that gave us the Star of David, the Union Jack and the Tibetan wheel. The eight arms of some of the Hindu Goddesses in PHASE ONE fall into that same category. Since all ancient processes and deities had their origins out of the natural world then the octopus with its eight arms has to be considered. Its name as Kraken (KARAKANA) breaks up into three overlapping dyads as (KARA,RAKA,KANA). Reading right to left as had been done originally (KANA) is the volcanic cone (KANA) of Mother Earth and Her kin (KANA). (KA) is the creation of smaller aspects out of Her body. (RAKA) is the hand in Polish having links with the sun as the helping hand of Mother Earth. (KARA) is the creative source that Mother Earth represents. The Kraken with its eight arms or hands surfaces as an apt symbol of many ancient mother based processes.

That may not be the end of the story. Around the world there are buildings with round turrets and eight arches or doors that reflect the ancient mother based traditions like the New Port Tower in the United States. Whenever eight windows or doors are set in a circle in an archway or a building you are dealing with an ancient, if disguised source out of the trance state of meditation. With the growth of the monotheistic patriarchy in PHASE THREE and the growth of persecution of the mothers and their eunuch sons, the ancient symbols dealing with the trance of transformation and mother centrality had to be disguised.

The SHAPE of the number eight surfaces also with the solar disc either emerging or dying to its light as it rises or descends into a body of water on the horizontal rim of Mother Earth creating the two solar orbs reflecting each other creating the number eight and a momentary balance at the horizontal rim. The two solar discs scending or descending into or out of the reflective waters also define the SHAPE of the letter D as half of the circle halved laterally emerging as the gift of day in one direction and the gift of night in another.

Then there is the operation in Egypt, in Stonehenge and other areas around the world that dealt with trepanning or making a hole on top of the skull. It gives modern male archeologists and medical doctors a great deal of trouble. It is only because the left hemisphere of their brains has become so tightly entrenched in rationalism that what had been a universal practice during the time of mother centrality had to be totally suppressed, obliterated and destroyed. It goes back to meditation or any other means of moving into the trance state to gain the ecstasy, courage and knowledge that has been part of that magical experience.

Here's how it works. The Tantrists explained it with their chacra system. There have been considered to be seven chacras or spiral energy wheels in the human body. The chakras had been perceived to exist along the spinal column. There also had been perceived that a double spin of energy called the electro-magnetic shakti of the Kundalini serpent energy that lay dormant at the base of the spine could be awakened with different activities. For the mothers it was the high fast panting birthing breath during childbirth. For males it was castration, ritual, meditation, fasting, dancing, drumming, drugs, spirits, cactus, etc. It had been the job of the meditative male aspirant in order to gain the desired state of transformation that along the seven chacras they had to flush out the habit based fears that had been dammed up at the time of their helpless, panic stricken and conscious infancy.

The base chacra at the anus deals with the fear of death and starvation. Eat and be eaten is the motto of the first chacra. The images of famine locked in that base chacra have to be burned clean and released in order for the electromagnetic shakti of the Kundalini energy can be made to rise to the second level which is the sexual chacra at the level of the genitalia. At the second chacra dealing with procreation all aspects with sex and the fears associated with sexuality have to be burned clean, have to be neutralized. When that is accomplished the Kundalini rises to the next level, the third chacra and that is the solar plexus, the seat of power. All trapped fear driven images of hierarchy, domination, control and left hemispheric power have to be scrapped.

The chacras of survival, sexuality and power had been considered to be the lower three chacras with their dark aspect of the Kundalini energy flushing up negative images that had to be flushed out or burned clean. Then a movement occurs into the fourth chacra of the open heart which deals with all aspects of bonding, of motherly love, of the right hemisphere of the mother, of compassion, love for the infant, for the beloved, for the neighbor. With love placed tightly in the heart, judgment and rejection are jettisoned. After that a movement occurs into the fifth or throat chacra which is the chacra of creativity and communication containing the human voice which vibrates to the strings of the universe.

The next chacra is the chacra of the third eye. It is the chacra of inner vision. 'Many are called but few are chosen'. When the Kundalini rises to the sixth chacra with it comes an en*trance* at the center, into the *trance* state of transformation. All of these states are safe to meditate on alone. It is the movement into the seventh chacra of the opening at the top of the bony skull that has to be dealt with carefully. It is the chacra of the thousand petalled lotus called either Nirvikulpa Samadhi or Samadhi itself. In Hunduism Samadhi means death. You can return from the Nirvikulpa Samadhi like a hiBERnating bear(BARA) can return from its sleep. But you cannot make the return from the ultimate Samadhi.

There is also the apparent problem that when the risen neutral Kundalini energy moves up to the seventh chacra on top of the head it becomes arrested by the thick bony structure of the skull. It may give the aspiring adept a great deal of pain and even death. The movement from the sixth chacra of the third eye to the seventh chacra of the thousand petal lotus has to be done very slowly, methodically, under the guidance of a guru. The double serpentine coil of the heated Kundalini energy as it rises has to be slowly allowed to soften the bone on top of the skull to make its exuberant thousand petal lotus exit into the universe. If the movement is too rapid then much pain and dislocation can occur. When the movement is guided by a wise and knowledgeable guru, in time with much guidance the bony skull on top softens, creates a passage and allows the Kundalini energy to make its emergence up into the heavens. The aspiring adept now stands free of all of the infantile habits that the trapped images of existence has burdened them with. He becomes selfless, stateless, unencumbered by society's rules. With it often come the gifts of shamanism, of healing, prophecy and wisdom. Transformed males become child-like and have to relearn all new habits for survival. They pick up a begging bowl and go out to live at the mercy of their society, specifically in India.

They are often called 'soft in the head' for as their heated Kundalini energy rises it softens the bony structure of the skull. Flowing through them like through a tube or vessel, it emerges unimpeded out of the top of their head creating the thousand petal lotus scenario. They are no longer guided by the laws of their society becoming accepted as special and not too rational for their violent rational fear driven prattling left hemisphere has not only been stilled but transformed.

What happens when the energy moves up to the seventh chacra and the chacra is trapped by the bony material of the skull?

That is when trepanning comes in. Surgeons in Egypt, Stonehenge and many other areas of the ancient world knew how to make a hole on top of the head in the skull to allow the Kundalini energy to flow through and give the adept peace of mind and a journey into ecstatic transcendence.

The same area on top of the head dealing with exactly the same activity surfaces in ancient Judaism and is practiced to this day. Their Rabbis understood the movement of the Kundalini energy through the human body and its fear defusing power leading to self realization and possible enlightment. They knew that the magic of transformation and its inherent powers resided with the risen Kundalini out of the hole on top of the head that had to be not only cherished but protected. It also became a major symbol of their identity. They were aware that it was the Kundalini mother energy leading to a state of trance that defined them. That is why to this day that Jewish males wear a black, round cap, a *yarmulkah* on top of their heads to cover or enclose a 'spiritual' movement of the risen Kundalini up from the body of Mother Earth. That same cap covers the heads of popes but for them it is white. It pays allegiance to the ancient perception that the energy of life coming up from the body of Mother Earth made an exit out of the top of the skull. In PHASE TWO it had been redefined as dealing with their allegiance to a Father God *away* and *above* the body of Mother Earth. Like circumcision replaced castration, it is a symbolic left over from the time of female centrality and the acceptance of the right hemisphere of the human brain associated with mother source and an ancient balance that had been worshipped. This was before in PHASE ONE moving into PHASE TWO when the ancient practices had still been associated with the body of Mother Earth and not the 'hidden' Father God in the far reaches of the left hemispheric rational male brain.

The ancient practice of activating the Kundalini energy covered many bases but the most universal movement into trance had been through meditation. It is the focusing of the mind in meditation, with the birthing breath, ritual, drugs etc that the state of trance became a sought after state of being. The three overlapping dyads of RULE SIXTEEN in trance (TARANASA) as (TARA) (RANA) (NASA) hides in their linguistic coils their original source and meaning. (NASA) deals with the Latin nascence (NASA-) or giving birth. (RANA) deals with the wound on the mother's body that allows for the birth to take place. In Polish RANA means wound. (TARA) defines the terrain, (TARA-), the tor (TARA), the tar (TARA), the wound on the surFACE of Mother Earth from which the serpentine Kundalini energy as Her blessed lea line is born to assist mothers in birthing.

In PHASE THREE the *focusing* (FAKA-) became associated with orgasmic release of pressure. Pleasure became redefined and associated with males and *fucking* (FAKA-) leaving the 'spiritual' life of mysticism behind. The relics of religion took over the fears associated with death and the unrelenting fucking on the planet drove the planet into famine and territorial destruction. Both focusing (FAKA-) and fucking (FAKA-) contain in them the same dyad (FAKA-). (FA) deals with the fingers of fire as the rays of the sun emerging out of the horizontal rim on the body of mother Earth at dawn. (KA) deals with that which is small. So both fucking and focusing deal with the activity of the small human fingers and masturbation. The big fingers dealt with the four or five flaming fingers as the rays of the sun.

MEDITATION

There are many ways to meditate but the simplest and most direct cover five levels.

Level One; *RELAX*; Sit comfortably on a chair with both bare soles on the ground, with the back straight up. You can do the same in a lotus position with the anus flat against the body of Mother Earth. The first level deals with relaxing the body completely. Beginning with the feet, talk to the body and tell it to relax piece by piece. Make sure to especially cover the shoulders, face and all the joints where tension is stored.

Level Two; *FOCUS* on the area between the two eyes on top of the nose. It is the third eye the area to which you want the flashing light of the Kundalini energy to rise. Staying fully relaxed keep the concentration at the center and when the mind drifts bring it gently back to the center.

Level Three; *BREATH*; Become aware of the breath moving in and moving out. Learn to use the diaphragm and the lower part of the body to control the breath as you stay relaxed and focused on the air moving in and out of your body. As you concentrate on the breath start to become aware of the heat of the Kundalini energy engulfing the bottom chacra and beginning to spin up your spine.

Level Four; *MANTRA*, Find a word or phrase that when repeated bores the restless left hemispheric prattling mind and quiets it down. It also establishes a resonance of stillness that fuses with the peaceful energy of the universe.

Level Five; *MALA*; To engage the restless fingers find a mala, rosary or any form of prayer beads that also engage in the focusing quality of concentration.

Relaxation, focus, breath, mantra and mala will work for you.

HETEROSEXUAL MALE - EUNUCH UNCLE

In PHASE ONE human females were defined primarily as potential mothers and dealt with the bearing, nurturing and the survival of children. That was not the case with their male offspring. Under the best conditions their male children faced a perilous future. Cultural conditions for human beings in PHASE ONE at the time of female centrality had been massively different. Reality was defined from a female point of view. Because male bodies did not produce babies, male children were either undefined or considered as objects that could be manhandled and transformed.

In PHASE THREE as male role in specific procreation had become known and males defined their reality from their needs and their points of view, their perceptions of reality made a complete turn-around and the exploited and manhandled objects universally became women, a condition that exists to this day having its evolutionary source out of the brutal Northern Congo River male chimpanzees.

In PHASE ONE at the time of female centrality male children at birth were assigned into different roles. One dealt with the protection of the family which fell to the castrated first born sons, the eunuch uncles. The other dealt with the peripheral heterosexual males with fighting over turf in concert with all other male animals and with often violent mating.

The clan of humanoid mothers needed protection from the savage conditions of the savannah. Evolving as a branch from the brutal North Congo River male chimpanzees they and their children were systematically raped and kidnapped. They had no one to protect them. Specific paternity was unknown. The changing sexual cues in the females left them at the mercy of any rogue male and more to the point, the band of brothers who had been pushed out at puberty because of their violence and rampant sexuality.

There was no pair bonding, no sense of paternity. Marriage was a distant possibly which surfaced with male role in specific paternity becoming known in PHASES TWO and THREE with the be-gats of the Hebrew Bible.

Why male bodies did not produce babies was a mystery to them. Baby boys were born with bodies that were almost the same as the bodies of baby girls. Except on the bottom of their trunks they had a set of organs which made no sense to the perplexed mothers. Very early on, mothers thought that the *test*es were in*test*ines that had become dislodged and hung outside of their boy's bodies.

Along with watching their small pets becoming violent at puberty there began the process of assumption making. They thought that if the testes were removed and a cleft was created on the little boy's body that mimicked the cleft on the little girl's body, then maybe the little boy would be able to bear children. They knew that it was the coagulated blood inside of the mother that made the baby, so if the lower part of the trunk on the body of a little boy was cut and was made to bleed that might also make him into a mother. They not only created a wound on his lower trunk but because the testes were in the way, they excised them and castrated their sons to make them more like their daughters and capable of becoming mothers.

What resulted with the process of castration was not only did his body did not produce babies but an unanticipated result entered the scene. He became docile, emerging with a cultural plus that created the possibility of survival. With no testosterone finding its way out of his testes and rushing through his veins at puberty, as a newly created peaceful citizen he could remain in the family set up and assume the role of protector. Not only that but physically still in a male body he was usually bigger and stronger. As a son, brother and nephew he could protect the family. There existed another plus for a castrated first born son who often also became a shaman (she man) or (IS HAMANA) a human (HAMANA) being which had been defined as the mothers HUM and a linguistic movement into HUManity. His left hemispheric brain joined across the corpus callosum and fusing with the right hemisphere of the mothers at the center became balanced. The lib of castration became the lib of liberation from his violent self.

The castration of first born male babies in PHASE ONE became a universal practice to protect the human family. Linguistic tracks exist around the whole ancient world in the names of castrated individuals, sacred and safe places as the result of the dispersal of the eunuch protected family. They became the avuncular, eunuch (HANAKA) uncles (HANAKALA) to their mothers subsequent children that contain two overlapping dyads (HANA) and (NAKA) out of RULE SIXTEEN. (HANA) is one of the original names of the sun (IS HANA) and deals with the male aspect. (NAKA) surfaces as the name for the metaphoric snake (IS NAKA) of the Kundalini energy as the female aspect. Together they represent the eunuch (HANAKA) (HANA-NAKA) as representing the sun (IS HANA) guided by the ubiquitous Kundalini snake (IS NAKA) making his journey through the body of Mother Earth at night to which the human eunuch (HANAKA) standing on the side of his mother became associated as the subsequent psycho-pomp or solar guide and protector.

Using the twenty five RULES OF ORIGINAL SOUND DISCOVERY (ROSD) it will become apparent that castration of the first born son was an ancient universal practice that lasted for thousands of years and surfaces all over the world as humanity's ancient ancestors dispersed after many of the great cataclysms that periodically befell the beleaguered continent of Africa.

When the male essence became eliminated through castration in the creation of a eunuch (HANAKA) the two hemispheres of the human brain became even, the over evolved violent left hemisphere of the human brain became balanced and the light in the third eye could find its way home. The name of eunuch (HANAKA) like a leit motif in a symphony surfaces all around the ancient world, if often apparently linguistically disguised. It surfaces as concepts, in the name of boys, in places and in relationships.

In Amharic sank (IS HANAKA) means even, the eunuch (HANAKA) with the balanced brain. In Chinese Yang E (HA(YA)NAGA) means to castrate. The original Yang of Yin Yang was the castrated solar disc that traversed through the portals of night guided by the sun. Aya (HAYA) is light in Persian and dawn in Assyrian. For the Bemba tribe in Africa–sanika (IS HANAKA) as light reiterates the same concept. For the Hebrews the holiday of light is Channukah (HANAKA). Anki (HANAKA) had been an Egyptian air god. Anak (HANAKA) Krakatoa as the son of the Indonesian volcano, Krakatoa, establishes the son Anak (HANAKA) as the castrated eunuch (HANAKA). The Egyptian Ankh (HANAKA) covers many bases but the most obvious is that it is based on first born son castration. Isis his sister put him together without his penis. The frozen male body of Asti found in the Alps had also been castrated. Echoes of echoes. For the Basque a boy's name is called Inaki (HANAKA). There is a city called Ankara (HANAKAra) in Turkey. On the other side of the world the Inca (HANAKA) surface with their own hidden linguistic links to the eunuch (HANAKA) priesthood. In Mexico Tihuanako (-HANAKA) had been their major deity, then there is Pumapunku (-paNA-KA) in the Andes. In the jungles of the Amazon River a tributary surfaces with the name Shingu (IS HANAGA), The (K) and (G) are interchangeable. Inga (HANAGA) Stone in Brazil, Inga (HANAGA) Mongolian God. Ionic (HANAKA) brings us forward into Greece. The scribes of old must have been eunuchs (HANAKA) for the primary tool for their linguistic expression had been ink (HANAKA).

Then a movement into the realm of mystery and into the protective uncle (HANAKALA) becoming a spiritual protector, guide and god. Other names surface to extend the linguistic cover of watchers and protectors. In Finnish enkeli (HANAKAla) is the name for an angel (HANAGAla). The (K) and (G) are also interchangeable. In Finnish henki (HANAKA) is the name for ghost or spirit. Henki (HANAKA) is also a Mongolian mountain Range. There surfaces the realm of special powers, of the creation of gods and special human beings, privy to the trance state, the shamans of old, not extraterrestrials but humans with extended powers in their extended skulls. In the Sumerian epic of Gilgamesh his friend is Enkidu (HANAKAda) or the (DA) gift of the eunuch (HANAKA). He is short, hairy, friendly and eats berries, SOUNDS like the not so ancient Neanderthal. The Annanaki (HANANAKA) surface as the Gods of Sumeria. With the Greek (NANA) as a double negation of night at the center dealing with the moon we are moving into PHASE TWO and the short worship of the nightly male gods. Anki (HANAKA) surfaces as the Sumerian brotherhood of the snake (IS NAKA). A company of Buddhist monks is called a sangha (IS HANAGA). Castration in Amheric is sanga (IS HANAGA). On the other side of the world for the Maya sian khan (IS HANAKAhana-) is where the sun is born with (KAHANA) covering another concept. How about the North American tribe of Seneca (IS HANAKA)? Then there is the country of Senegal (IS HANAGAla) and Anglia (HANAGAla), present day England. The Sinclair (IS HANAKALA) family of Scotland having links with the Templars and the castrated uncles (HANAKAla) bears rediscovering. Then there is the name for a Polish sled as sanki (IS HANAKA). In English sled (IS LADA) deals with the lady (LADA) as the leader (LADA-) who led (LADA) the ancient migrators. Were the great and massive stones of Stonehenge slid (IS LADA) along on sleds (IS LADA) during the winter? But last and not least is the Biblical heavenly spirit, the Enoch (HANAKA) who like the birds also defied gravity and sailed away into the Tibetan 'intermediate state' of heaven. Shanghai (IS HANAGA) and Shangrila (IS HANAGA-), the K and G are interchangeable. The Naga people of Harrapa = serpent (IS HARAPA) dealing with the Kundalini energy of the snake and serpent.

In South America, along the Amazon River Basin hidden in the deep impenetrable jungle there lives a massive boa constructor with the name Anaconda (HANAKA-) who is saddled with virgin birth and is self perpetuating. Just to name a few, more will follow.

Since it was the female family unit who joined the other creatures in waking up the sun at dawn, the castrated first born sons became their mothers closest not only protectors but assistants in the singing of aves at dawn to awaken the sleeping sun and wailing at twilight at the death of the solar orb.

When the hint of the rosy light of dawn spread across the Eastern sky, the birds stirred even before dawn, bursting into a cacophony of rapturous song to awaken the slumbering sun from its nocturnal sleep. As the golden glow in the East spread out into the belly of air above them, apes howled, and screeched their welcome. Even human beings joined in the exuberant chorus of gratitude, singing and dancing, clapping their hands, thumping their heels that Mother Earth at dawn, heavy with the burdens of night, in one of Her great labors out of Her pregnant belly at the horizon ready to have Her most helpful offspring, heaved the coagulated and solidified sun up into the heavens. In PHASE TWO the emerging eunuchs became the solitary priests who officiated over the rising and in time the setting sun.

In PHASE TWO the heterosexual band of brothers including other humanoids, circling the periphery of the female clan and mating with the females established their power, territoriality and dominance above ground. The castrated eunuch brotherhood claimed the caves and mountain tops dealing with the dual passage of the sun and its passage *above* Mother Earth's belly of air, Her creative surFACE and through Her womb of transformation within Her bowels *under* Her surFACE.

The rest of the maturing *not castrated* male brothers, as testosterone filled their veins, violence became their major activity and beards sprouted on their chins. As the birds returned to their nesting grounds, and the herbivore migrations began their march in March to greener pastures, they were shoved out at puberty to create the roving gangs, the 'band of brothers' that circled the periphery of the female family unit. That was only part of the story, for there existed other bands of humanoid brothers who were more violent and unstoppably sexual who took advantage of the peaceful herds of females and who raped the more peaceful ranks of the humanoid and human creatures.

Due to the growth of fear in the human creature based on the panic stricken awareness of their helplessness at birth and the shift from the nose to the eye and the accumulated bank of images to which fear was becoming trapped, human beings becoming more and more competitive losing their ability to organize themselves into peaceful, roving family units. All that they could do was to watch how other creatures organized themselves to survive.

Their apparently closest relatives were the primates, among them the chimpanzees, who came in two distinct packages and share ninety-eight percent of their genes with human beings. One was the violent, male dominated Jane Goodall chimps of Gambia North of the Congo River Basin with the destructive father chimps brutalizing the mothers and forming alliances, scheming, stalking and killing solitary males from other groups, deflowering them and ripping out their thorax. The other chimpanzee group South of the Congo River Basin was the peaceful matriarchal, sharing, sexual Bonobo who were more cooperative and mother centered.

It seems that the violent left hemispheric male dominated patriarchal Gambia chimps moved evolutionarily down the line into the early Cro Magnons polishing off all other competition moving into the contemporary *man*kind ranks. The relatively placid sexually active matriarchal Bonobo moved evolutionarily through the much maligned and misunderstood right hemispheric peaceful Neanderthal, the Saan, Hadza and Sumeria and then into *hum*anitys underground mother centered current human present.

HIERARCHY

When there is more than one sibling most creatures will develop a pecking order, or a *hierarchy*. To mate, all males have to become the top dog and get rid of their rival. There have been cases when one twin will kill its sibling in the womb. Birds will shove the smaller chicks vying for food out of the nest as will hyena cubs. Among human beings sibling rivalry is the first sin in the Hebrew Bible as Cain kills Abel. There are actually only three genetically based sins; jealousy, exploitation and vengeance.

The role of *hierarchy* and its importance in the ancient world has to be dealt with since it was a major factor in the past and still remains as class or caste systems in the sub strata of contemporary society.

There have been three levels of *hierarchy* that have their roots in animal behavior and that express themselves through mothers, through heterosexual males and through what evolved to be the eunuch priesthood to whom and because they too had a permanently empty belly male homosexuals became attached. The males and the eunuch priesthood share similar antecedents. The female roots are different.

THE CURSE OF THE ALPHA MALE,
'You Owe Me'

A multi track system evolved propelling its way into the future and established systems of hierarchy that are with us to this day. One dealt above ground, upon the surface, with the heterosexual often violent males, second born sons, who in predatory gangs with the seeds of territoriality and unrelenting sexual 'go' alive in their genes, led by the control and power driven *alpha males* circled the periphery of the female herd, stalking, chasing and killing other males to establish mating primacy while raping and kidnapping the women and their children. Male hierarchy is genetically based on power, control and sexuality. To that end male body size, physical strength, size of penis and male group cohesion plays a major role.

Human creatures evolved to play different roles. The human female evolved to create small replicas of herself and to bring that replica to maturity. The human heterosexual male evolved to impregnate her with sperm that brought with it the possibility of change. The avuncular eunuch uncles evolved to protect her and to assure the survival of the family unit with the bonus of shamanism to share.

The gradual shift from a girl to a woman happens very quietly and almost imperceptibly. When menstrual blood spots her buttox she is ready to make babies. She doesn't have to do much else but just to sit and wait. That is not the case with young boys. Young boys go through a much more perilous passage even beyond what their cultures and castration might dictate.

Young boys face a tripple whammy. First in order to mate the heterosexual male has to conquer the reigning *alpha male*. The butting of male heads in the animal world including sperm whales, attest to that fact. Once they depose the *alpha male* they have to mark their territory. Without a territory they cannot mate. Territory supplies a food supply that is very important to the females. Sexuality and violence exist together in the hypothalamus of the male brain. Once they conquer the *alpha male* and establish mating rights over his territory they have to beguile the female of the specie. This may prove to be the most onerous task for he has to overcome the fear of his mother, the first giant in his life, in order to subjugate and mount the object of his lust.

MALE LINE UP

What happens to the not so *alpha males*? They scheme in the bushes trying to overthrow the boss. Forming secret alliances they look for an opening of weakness to depose him off the top of the male hierarchy. The *male line up* is ironically like a pyramid. There emerges one *alpha male* at the top. His job is to *win,* to become top dog at all costs to lie, cheat, kill and destroy. In the process of scheming he focuses his brain into the singular left hemisphere leaving his gentler mother based right hemisphere behind. Then under him there are two or more vice-males who do his bidding. Vice has its own meaning. Under them there are more as armies are formed to keep the power and control and so on endlessly down the expanding both vertical and lateral lines.

The group of vice and *alpha males* at the top get all the goodies; power, control and females. They begrudgingly for favors, (bribes or tips) mete out some of the remains to the expanding pyramid below them. Each level has a lower level to look down on. A need is established in the male pyramid to have someone to look down on to make sure no one is gaining on them. On the same power or control level there is established a need to compete, to shove the next to you out of the proverbial nest and to claw your way as far up to the top as you can.

Each level has its own rules, has its own markings, flags, insignias, hats, uniforms, tattoos, names, codes, languages, religions, slogans, food, arm bands, greetings, initiations, handshakes, and limitations except for the *alpha male*. He makes his own rules. So what exists in the male line-up is the ultimate desire to get to the top, to *win*. Male primary function is the competition to *win* at all costs. It is rabid power driven competition to primal genetic control that drives males to ascend to the top. Nothing stands in their way, not social constructs, not the need for community, not the need to protect their families. Patriotism may be invoked, so may religion. Tradition, language and territory may be dragged in. But the fundamental reason for male violence has come through the evolutionary primal thrust to win at all costs to become the singular top dog with power and sexuality. The killer gene in *alpha males* is a moot point and exists without question.

For heterosexual males to get the 'job done' becomes a secondary importance. Women's primary thrust is to cooperate with each other in order to get the job done, the job is bringing a baby to maturity. That is one of the major differences between the sexes.

Males in the line-up look to depose the line above them and are tormented by the fact that the line below them may be gaining on them. To that end they form alliances and the most salient of their alliances may be based on 'you owe me'. That is the male mantra. Deals are concocted, most often secret deals to depose the existing *alpha male* and create new power bases with nepotistic family and friends who owe each other the expanding universe.

Mothers cannot say to a new born helpless infant 'you owe me'. It would not make any sense. They need the cooperation of other mothers to help them to raise an infant. Contemporary human tragedy is marriage and the two parent family unit where the often young mother is isolated and has no help from other women in a similar condition.

What also surfaces out of male behavior and the male line up residing in the single focused right handed, left hemispheric male brain is a double contradiction. One is the consolidation of power under one *alpha male* head. To that end all the members of the pyramidal line-up claw their way to get to the summit, the Alps or *alp*ha at the top.

The other contradiction is the segmentation into smaller and smaller units to give each male member under the *alpha male* his own line up, his own turf, or his own power base, his own silo. Rank which is related to 'rut' and 'must' enters the male hierarchal scene. The segmentation creates pockets of power that in selfishly protecting their own turf, male power brokers often ignore and destroy the whole assemblage. They create *silos of protected turf*. The same process exists in corporations, clubs and all other male organizations. In protecting their own turf they do not share information and create pockets of isolated often unrelated knowledge. The systems cease to work for the whole assemblage. The stultifying chains of bureaucracy deal with the fact that each level of the male hierarchy has to be dealt with. There can be no jumping over the head above you without dire consequences. The whole chain of command often grinds to a halt.

Back to the consolidation under one *alpha male*. Human activity cannot be dispersed, therefore in mankind's condition following the pyramidal set up whole regions and activities have to have one male leader. There ultimately has to be one world government. All religions have to fuse under one God. All media have to succumb to one master. All agricultural production has to be dictated from one corporate source based on a single industrial crop. All languages have to be fused into one. To that end endless wars are instituted and where women, children and the helpless have become the major victims.

Mankinds *alpha male* behavior cannot honestly be dealt with as an expression of an ancient evolutionary animal based thrust for power and control but has to be hypocritically hidden under the folds of good and noble rationalizations; ie patriotism, sanctity of religion, establishment of democracy, expansion of civil rights, delivery from oppression, call to duty and honor, brotherhood, etc. etc, etc.

Alpha male behavior is from the top down and in PHASE THREE it is universally expressed through brutal dictatorships and through either communistic or capitalistic corporate power, both are antithetical to democracy. They deal with the male left hemispheric modality which doesn't allow for the right mother hemisphere with its compass of compassion to show its head. Filling the pages of HIS STORY as warriors, warlords, chiefs, emperors, generals, dictators, pharaohs, tsars, caesars, kings, kaisers, feuhrers, presidents, prime ministers, CEOs, popes and other secular upper class dictatorial rulers suppress women and do massive environmental injustice to the patient body of Mother Earth.

The not so *alpha males* and there are many men of good will in whom the right hemisphere is still active and who are aware of the injustice, who snuck in the bushes and mated with the more than willing females, evolving into the foot soldiers, workers, slaves, serfs, peons, peasants and indentured servants. As members of the lower classes they often but not at all times became the personal property of the upper class *alpha male* rulers.

The actual physical activity of human males works in concert with the activity of the penis. *Direction* is the 'gift of' (DA) the *erection*. That's the beginning. To erect is to establish, to build something, be it a penis, a building, a musical masterpiece, or a theory in physics. The reigning theory, or a current masterpiece, or an erect penis has to be destroyed for a new masterpiece to emerge. An erect penis goes through what has often been called a 'petit mort' or a small death as it is deflated ie ejaculates in a woman's body. It dies to its former grand empowered state. *Therefore human males have to destroy what they have created in order for a new creation to take SHAPE.* Their penis shows them the way. They have to rape, murder, declare war, bomb, torture, kill in order to be able to start again, ie have another empowering erection. Massive destruction of people, buildings and the environment has to take place based on the activity of the penis.

In PHASE THREE words have evolved that declare war on a flaccid penis even when Mother Earth reels under the weight of human fecundity. Up is better than down. WHY? Because an erect penis often points up to the sky not down to the body of Mother Earth. Hard is better than soft also WHY? Because a hard penis declares that it is ready for action. A flaccid penis hides its shame under tunics, except for the New Guinea natives who sheath their penis in a long bamboo pole. The longer the better. No shame there.

There is also the *concept of opposites* based on competition. The opposites deal with ends of possibility as black and white perceptions of reality. It has to be either large or small, black or white, loud or soft, good or bad, friend or foe. It cannot be gray. The linguistic process in PHASE THREE is based on the exclusive *either or and not with the inclusive and.*

If your perception is linear of the left male hemisphere and not holistic circular of the right mother hemisphere then there must be a beginning and an end. In PHASE THREE with the risen God or gods *away* and *above* the body of Mother Earth, be they the moon, the sun or the stars there has to be a beginning and an end. That is what defines a line. A circle does not. A circle goes round and round recreating the same repetitive pattern but as a spiral on a different level. That may be why there are so many 'mysterious' circles and mounds on the body of Mother Earth that harken back to mother centrality. With male interpretation of reality in PHASE THREE and the linear orientation locked in the left hemispheric male mind *all* monotheistic patriarchies contain a beginning and an end.

Moses in cahoots with God created the ten commandments that begat the Biblical Genesis on one linear end. The battle of Armageddon is waiting on the other end of the line. Muslims began their story with Mohammed and their Apocalypse only echoes the same linear story. Not to be left out Christianity came up with a beginner in Christ on one end of the line and Armageddon and the rapture on the other. Male monotheistic patriarchy has to have a beginning and an end. That is the way that the male linear left hemisphere in the human brain works. There are many, mostly men and a few brain washed women who are chafing at the bit for the end times scenario to begin.

At the time of female centrality in PHASE ONE there was no perception of linear beginnings and no ends. It was a time of *endless becoming*. The Egyptian Goddess Sais said, I am all that was, that is and that is yet to come'. In PHASE THREE as all aspects dealing with motherhood as source had to be obliterated, the Hebrews ascribed that saying to their patriarchal monotheistic God in (Revelation 1:8).

As beginnings and ends began to filter through ancient reality, the beginning out of the surFACE and body of Mother Earth and of individual mothers had to be obliterated. Clitorectomies entered the scene to obliterate the power inherent in the birthing breath of the mothers as did black robes and burkas on women to hide their bulging bellies. Male violence and sexuality embraced the ancient male source in PHASE THREE as the penis became the sacred organ of creation.

Linguistically it will become apparent that many names have evolved trying to define the activities of the penis even after male role in specific paternity has become known. There are echoes of the old days out of PHASE ONE when its role was not so clear.

The Greek males in PHASE TWO as their knowledge of their role in paternity was hanging by a thin thread, called the penis an *orchis*. If that doesn't SOUND like *orchid* I'll back track. An orchid is an air plant. It is not rooted to the body of Mother Earth, or to the tree that exists as its host. That is what the Greeks thought that the male penis was, an air plant, not rooted to the female body but an air plant with a life of its own as a citizen of the air. They also must have believed that the penis was beautiful as most orchid plants have a tendency to be overwhelmingly stunning.

There is only one hope for the human race and breaths should not be held. Men of good will and all the mothers of the world have to somehow devise scientific ways, no longer castration, to thicken the corpus callosum that stretches between the two hemispheres of the human brain and begin to pour the right hemispheric hormones of compassion and cooperation onto the left hemispheric right handed male brain that has become stuck in ruthless competition, violence, fantasy, greed, lying, exploitation, destruction and an unfolding universal madness.

The wars that have evolved between the power bases of heterosexual males, and castrated first born sons have expanded to include the body of Mother Earth in PHASE TWO as Her son the sun declared war on Her and the linguistic battle bears witness to the fact that as long as Mother Earth remained in PHASE ONE the central and most powerful creator, She reigned victorious. In PHASE TWO and THREE the power bases shifted and heterosexual males took their emerging deity, their daily shining sun up into the heavens *away* and *above* from the physical body of Mother Earth and the eunuch priesthood took their sinking sun into the underground caves to emerge as the monotheistic patriarchial religious systems in PHASES TWO and THREE.

There emerged an entrenched battle between the two male power bases that exists to this day. The heterosexual males above ground became the kings, dictators, CEOs and rulers. The castrated brothers along with shamans and male homosexuals became the power bases of religion as the popes, priests, rabbis, mullahs, and deacons. Women have been pushed out of this power construct altogether. They don't even exist on the periphery as their sexuality has been compromised through laws and ritual and their compass of wisdom and compassion flagged as weak and unimportant.

FEMALE SEXUALITY

There is little confusion in animals concerning their availability to mate. The cues are very specific and direct. Male carnivores, like lions are always on 'go'. To bring the female into heat, they kill off the milking cubs of the former reigning king establishing their own mating rights. Male elephants come into a very testy stage called a 'must', verb and noun. They too start trumpeting around, fighting off other males, looking for a receptive female. Most herbivore males come into 'rut' in the spring and fall at the time when the females flow with estral ruddy droplets of blood. It is also the time when males lock horns and establish primacy for territorial mating rights. The butting of male heads and the butting of female buttocks becomes a repetitive categorical imperative. The males circle the estral females, their noses on the level of the rumps, licking the air with their tongues and also with their tongues licking the hind quarters of their receptive quarry to determine their sexual availability.

Like the electron circles the nucleon, like the Earth circles the sun, like the sun circles the galaxy, the electro-magnetic push pull of procreation on all levels as a circular spin rooted to the center is constant and unrelenting. The seasonal or unstructured random pavan, populates the body of Mother Earth with Her multi faceted aspects of creation.

THE NOSE KNOWS

The mating dance among humans has not been so relatively simple. Originally it was the animal snout that alerted the males to the availability of females to mating. The females seasonally passed blood and as the scent sent upon the wind, the nostrils of the males quivered as they lined up to mate. That simple solution had been left behind with the herbivores. They still responded to the seasonal solar clock.

Human males faced a future dilemma as changes in female receptivity caused a great deal of subsequent confusion. As they became bi-pedal their noses on the level of the female rump had been left far behind with the quadrupeds. They still remained like the carnivores ready to 'go' but the sexual cues from the females were shifting. There is no apparent linguistic information how the human female began to menstruate in tandem with the twenty-eight day cycles of the moon.

The process must have evolved out of our humanoid ancestral past that has left no record in the scarce fossils that have surfaced to further confound contemporary humanity. A rare clue surfaces out of the two words dealing with passage of blood out of the bodies of female creatures. One is *estral*. The other is *menstrual*. The estral passage of blood out of herbivores as estrus is seasonal, based on the solar clock occurring in spring time and in the fall, around the Spring and Fall Equinox.

The humanoid female left the seasonal, solar based clock behind. She began to pass blood based on the more closely spaced lunar clock. It must have been an evolutionary adaptation to assure the survival of the specie.

The word menstrual is the word estral with the phonemes of 'mens' (MANASA) preceding it. Mene (MANA) is one of the names for the moon (MANA). The syllable (SA) on the end of (MANASA), deals with blood. The second dyad (NASA) deals not only with the nose (NASA), the primary sense organ in most animals for smelling the female in heat, but with nascence (NASANASA) or the repetitive activity of being brought forth into existence.

The dyad (MANA) deals with the mother (MA) and the concept of 'holding'. The phoneme (NA) deals with the concepts of 'emergence on the surface' or 'the negation of a former state'. That is what the moon (MANA) had been perceived to do, like a nocturnal celestial hand, mano (MANA), is hand in Spanish), it held and released the tides on the body of Mother Earth and the blood in human females. So the lunar word 'menstrual' associated with human females, is the expanded solar word for 'estral', which had been associated with herbivores and deals with the cyclical lunar passage of blood out of female bodies.

THE EYES HAVE IT

The signals from the female shifted the male sexual perception from the acuity of his nose to the acuity of his eyes. The male still looked for the red specks of bloody receptivity that alerted him that she was ready for mating. Except that the cues were shifting. The bloody spots on her buttocks only meant that the human female was menstruating, not necessarily expressing the categorical imperative of her loins. He, like the carnivorous male lion was not dependent on either the solar or the lunar seasonal clock to mate. He was always set on 'go'. She was not. Just because a female passed blood it didn't mean that she would present her hindquarters to receive the present that he offered. Her cycles of receptivity were based on the more closely spaced phases of the moon. He had stepped out of that celestial continuum. Even though he had to watch her buttocks for flecks of red blood, those flecks no longer alerted him of her availability to mate.

Shifting from the nose of smelling to the eyes of seeing did not solve the problem. It only exacerbated it. The violent activity of rape entered the human scene. In the animal kingdom females may present their hindquarters as an act of submission, but if the female is not sexually receptive most males will not mount her. It became a different story in humanoid and human beings. Females found alone were often either raped or kidnapped. For the protection of the family equally violent and abusive customs evolved to protect the women and their children. First-born sons were castrated to become the protective uncles to their sister's children. Second born sons were either pushed out at puberty, or maimed to become the subsequent smiths and shepherds of the still migrating mother based clusters of humanity.

Human females are the most fecund between their periods, when they ovulate. This began to present a problem. Cohabitation around both the solar and the lunar clock had to take place for the vulnerable specie to thrive and to endure. The human female had to be offered an incentive to mate even when she was not receptive, when she was not at the peak of her fecundity. To that end Mother Nature gave her a double whammy in the form of pleasure and bonding.

SECTION ONE

EVOLUTION OF PLEASURE IN WOMEN

There are two major evolutionary factors that fed into the evolution of pleasure in women. One deals with bi-pedal locomotion and the freeing of the front paws that in the primates were developing into sensitive fingers and hands. The moving, grasping hands fell at the area of the human genitalia. There were no pockets into which they could be stored when not used. Hanging in space they looked for any pleasurable activity. The linguistic record flourishes with information that they found it in masturbation.

The other factor deals with the last stages of labor in birthing mothers. After her water broke she had to squat, she had to breathe hard, she had to pant to push the large headed baby out of her body. If you pant long and hard enough, you activate the electro-magnetic shakti of the Kundalini Bastrika Breath that finds its home at the secret sacral bone of the trunk, creating the second wind that often carries you into a trance, and the trance activates the ecstasy of orgasmic satisfaction that accompanied the birthing experience of the ancient mothers.

THE CLITORIS

Here's how it worked. The clitoris stuck out between the folds of the vulvic lips, in the SHAPE of a tongue or a beak. In Polish the clitoris is affectionally called a 'dziobek' (JABAKA) and means 'little beak'. The beak (BAKA) is an object that actually jabs (JABA) in English, from the avian declination. It is the primary organ of sexual pleasure in a woman. The clitoris as an organ of pleasure evolved on a tandem track that had its ancient roots out of humanity's bi-pedal locomotion and the overwhelming growth of fear.

As the human creature became erect, the narrow hips of the human mother did not keep up with the growing head of the fetus. Many died in the throes of labor. Stories of orphans swell the pages of human history. To house the growing bank of image driven facts, the fetus had to be born more and more helpless, the head had to become smaller and smaller and to fold on itself in order to slide through the mothers birthing canal. As a helpless, but conscious newly born infant, the birthing process for a baby had its own often dire consequences. It began to create its reality based on its perceived total helplessness. Born into a body that like a jail didn't work and through a filter of panic driven helplessness it developed a total dependence on the mother.

For the birthing mother a series of activities assisted her in the job of expelling the large headed fetus out of her body. One was the fast, high panting Kundalini Bastrika Breath that activated the centers of pleasure, obliterating the pain, moving into a trance state and bonding with the baby.

The other was the use of the hands in masturbating the fetus out of her body. The internal spasms like the peristalsis of digestion in the colon pushed the feces out of the body, so in the birth canal the orgasmic spasms of birthing of the vagina also pushed the fetus out of the uterine canal. Ancient mothers and accompanying midwives understood the role of the spasmic orgasms that assisted early mothers in their efforts to bring forth a baby. When the head of the fetus pushed against the stretched open clitoris from the inside, creating not only agonizing pain but great pleasure with the closely spaced contractions which not only helped to push the large headed baby out of her body but to erase all the accompanying pain and to bring the laboring mother into multi orgasmic satisfaction. *That is why women are capable of having multiple orgasms.* It was an evolutionary assist during their extended labors to bring forth babies that expanded for some, not many, into orgasmic pleasure during coital sex with their male partners.

The head of the penis from the outside, caressing the clitoris during coital sex, became like the head of the baby caressing the clitoris from the inside during the act of delivery. That may very well be the reason that the penis is called 'a head'. It may be that it has a mind of its own, but the more ancient links seem to exist with the birthing mothers. It brought some of the birthing mothers to orgasmic pleasure on both levels, with the baby and with the male partner.

As the trance state enveloped them, mothers orgasmed, experienced great pleasure, satisfaction and the possibility of bonding with the male partner as they had bonded with the baby. Ancient links of pair bonding based on shared pleasure began to evolve as an evolutionary plus.

Out of masturbation after the freeing of the hands, the growth of pleasure in women and the relief of pressure in men, the assistance during the last stages of labor, the role of the hands in bringing forth a baby, moved out of the possibly original need to use the free hands to scratch an itch. The moist pubic area on the human body must have been host to many creatures, such as the contemporary crab, that gave our ancient ancestors another reason to scratch that unrelenting itch. The human crotch (KARAJA) has linguistic links with the need to scratch (IS KARAJA), and establishes the primacy of the hands not only in masturbation and in birthing but also in scratching.

Many years down the line in PHASE THREE in Egypt, the highest and most secretive God Amun or Ammon (HAMANA), the underground sun, daily masturbated all of 'existence' into being. His creative priesthood must have gotten the idea that masturbation produced a baby from somewhere. Were they dealing only with the observable physical activity of the use of the hands in masturbating a baby out of a mother's body? The first dyad in Amun (HAMANA) as hama in Greek, means 'together with'. Mano (MANA) in Spanish means 'hand'. It seems that the highest and most secretive Egyptian nocturnal solar God created all of 'existence', out of the activity of being 'together with his hand', or masturbating. Neat. Handmaidens of God on all levels take on new meaning. The Biblical Hebrews outlawed masturbation altogether, for it fell afoul of the idea that all of existence came out of the mind of God. If masturbation either by the ancient mothers, or the Egyptian deities produced a baby, then where do you put the mind of God as the ultimate creator? Men who masturbated would become blind. That was bad enough.

Women were dealt a harsher fate. Genesis 4:16 "I will greatly multiply thy sorrow and thy conception." *In sorrow* shalt thou bring forth children and thy desire shall be to thy husband and he shall rule over thee." The admonition by the Hebrew God Jehovah covered a lot of bases. It implied that there was a time when birthing for mothers was not so devastating and painful an experience. Something else preceded the admonition. Something that had made the birth process not only bearable but possibly pleasure filled. The admonition established a six thousand year madness that solidified into dogma, not only in Judaism, but Christianity and then in Islam. Catholic nuns have had to shower in their habits so that they did not see or touch their bodies. Muslim women wear burkhas to cover their faces, obliterating their identities. They also wear heavy black cape like tunics to cover their bodies in order to obliterate the obvious, that babies use their bodies as a vehicle of passage, that they are the apparent parent.

In PHASE THREE as male centrality overran the planet the penis not only became sacred but became defined as the only source of the female orgasm. In reality only about thirteen percent of women 'come' during intercourse. The rest eighty seven per cent have to become great actresses to keep their male sexual partners happy. The penis evolved to deposit the sperm as far up the vaginal canal as it could go. It was an evolutionary assist that some women if fucked long enough would reach the orgasmic state. Many never do.

ORGASM-ORGA(NI)SM

In the construction of language there exists an ancient linguistic clue that included the experience of pleasure during the birthing process. Farfetched as it may sound, in spite of the speculative evidence to the contrary, the orgasm obviously created a new orga(NI)sm. The two are related. Not too many contemporary women can honestly say that, even though some may have secretly experienced something akin to the experience.

What you have in the center of the word 'organism', is the phoneme (ni (NA) of the new baby and the concept of (NA) representing 'negation of a former state' or the' emergence on the surface'.

The baby emerging out of a female orgasm has its roots out of female centrality in PHASE ONE before specific male role in procreation had become known. When language was becoming codified specific male role in procreation was unknown and the sex act was not associated with the creation of a baby. The Egyptian God Amun (HAMANA) seems to represent the ignorance dealing with birth. If a mother masturbated to bring forth a baby then he too would masturbate to create 'all of existence'. Was it through his semen (IS HAMANA), or through the actual process of digital masturbation? If it was the former then we are still dealing with female centrality in PHASE ONE. If it was the latter then we are dealing with male role in procreation having become established and enforced through a celestial deity in PHASE THREE.

Obviously the categorical imperatives of creation still left much to be desired. Not enough babies were being produced to keep the specie from becoming extinct. Both mothers and babies died in the often grueling, last stages of labor. Not all human females evolved with the masturbatory orgasm at their fingertips. Clutches of female relatives were becoming systematically disbanded through inter tribal marriage. Another evolutionary wrinkle entered the already overburdened collage. Out of the confusing shift to lunar passage of blood in the female and her fecundity between her periods and the male shift from his nose to his eyes, there must still have been a paucity of humanoid and then human off spring.

PASSION

There emerged something even more ancient that had been lurking in the evolutionary bushes. It had not as yet been used as a means to create more electro-magnetic fusion and the physical product of that fusion. The next evolutionary assist to draw the sexes together was *passion and the act of falling in love*. The Karuna of subsequent Tantric mother love, extending to the sexual partner entered the picture. It began its journey with the pleasure associated with the masturbation that accompanied the orgasms of the birthing mother. Moving out of the realms of automatic electro-magnetic polar attraction, it obscured not only discretion, but judgment and reason, making the object of *passion* irresistible, like the new born infant had been made irresistible to the mother. It took the impassioned victim into an infantile state that existed at the breast. There has been much nuzzling, kissing, cooing, gooing, necking, locking in on the face and even baby talk. Sensuality, the pleasure locked in the skin and awakened by the fingers, the massage as the message from the mother, exploded on the scene to be shared by all. That may be one of the reasons human beings lost most of their body hair and why women are less hairy than men. They need an extra boost of sensory pleasure to remain locked in the coital embrace.

It was and is a time of such pure joy, such pure comforting bliss and such *passion* that only the state associated with the breast of the mother could assure the swelling of the waning ranks of the human species. Pundits have called it madness. Some have denied its existence. They even call it sentimental romanticism. It is only because they have not yet experienced it themselves. Some never fall victim to it. Not all have been traveling on the same evolutionary track. It is a process still unfolding. The tragedy associated with the evolution of *passion* is that it is fickle. Once the fusion is made there is no great need to perpetuate it. Marriage based on *passion* contains a mass of pitfalls. You have to deal with the real person.Sooner or later *passion* dissolves and leaves the victim ready for the next encounter. Like snowflakes in the sun *passion* often dissolves without a trace.

RAPE

Like a pruned plant, threatened with its survival goes into the production of flowers and subsequent fruit, so the human male, having to fight other more aggressive alpha males, and then to mount the first giant of his life, a female extension of his mother, became overwhelmed by the massive and staggering input of his senses. Not only was his nose still vaguely active, but his eyes gave him no rest. With fear associated images he galloped into the morass of single focused coital penetration, most often leaving the product of that penetration behind. The medium became the message. The sexual act became the end result, not a bridge to that result. The baby became lost in the frenzy to copulate. The creatures on the planet and the planet itself have been pushed to the edge of extinction by the mass of fear driven, evolutionarily and psychologically pruned human males. The rite of passage of circumcision, although having more ancient links with female centrality and first born son castration, the activity associated with the pruning of the penis on the physical level, echoing the internal fears, has not helped the matter much.

The next step contains in it interesting implications. It is not the drama played out between males and females that has taken millions of years to unfold. It is a drama being played out by human males and the universe. Women have been left out of the next step altogether. For it is a game of creation longed for by males, without using the female body, or the female essence. On one level it is the push into space *away* and *above* the body of Mother Earth, to establish life in outer space, without the dependence on the mother essence on any level. The other deals with the creation of actual life without using the female form as the cubicle of creation. It is the game of cloning, of robots, of extra-uterine procreation. It is the game of slave and monster creation. With it comes the devaluation of the mother essence, of caring, compassion, co-operation, of bonding at the breast, of passion within the heart, and of the possibility of playful, joyful human intimacy. It is the end to human joy.

The negation of the mother as the obvious birth giver, as the apparent parent, has been going on for at least six thousand years. There was a time in PHASE ONE when the personal mother and the great body of Mother Earth were at the center of creation. There was a time when female experience defined what was real. It was at that time when language began to take form and bears witness to that ancient experience. Life came out of individual female bodies. They had no problem with that observation. Life and death was a given, was a cycle of constant repetitive returns.

There was no one as yet at that ancient time to argue with the perception that the volcanic crater (KARATARA) on the body of Mother Earth was the original creator (KARATARA). The third dyad (TARA), deals with the terrain, terra firma, the surFACE on the flat round surFACE of Mother Earth, the tip, top or edge (TA) out of which She gave birth to the sun (RA). The second dyad (RATA), deals with the ratio (RATA), the circular sweep of the suns constant return. The first dyad (KARA) deals with creation (KARA-) itself, with smaller aspects (KA) of the sun (RA). It is the cavity, the cubicle, the cave, the caldera, the crater out of which She not only created Her greatest off- spring, the sun, but She created Herself as Herself through the lavic blood that poured across Her surFACE creating the crust of land upon which Her creations, Her creatures could have their being.

The WARP of the fabric in the SHAPE of SOUND contains many aspects of ancient reality that can be documented by the SOUNDS that were becoming codified. They include the *right hemisphere* of the human brain which had been associated with the ancient mothers working in tandem with the linear male left hemisphere of the human brain. They were relatively balanced creating the birthing breath of the mother and the castrated first born son leading to the mystical state of trance and a stepping into another level of transformative experience that houses within its magical coils not only the SHAPE of the mythical snake but ecstasy, wisdom, courage, healing and prophecy.

It all began in Africa with the clusters of mothers and their children *following the migrating herds* across the great verdant savannahs. Within the familial circle they had been accompanied by the eunuchs, the castrated first born sons and the band of brothers on the periphery of violent heterosexual males.

They relied on their perceptions and what they saw around them. Their Mother Earth was a *flat round surFACE and body* that ended in all directions around them at Her often distant horizontal rim. Working with Her helper the sun both had been considered to have been a single creative force.

The original time keeper had been the moon who not only ruled the nocturnal sky, circled the body of Mother Earth every twenty eight days but did that circulation thirteen times a year. The moon had been considered not only as *a ruler, a measurer of time* but a ruler over the monthly menstrual cycles of women. When a young girl began her period she joined the ranks of other mothers, the queens of the clan, the ruler at the time when the SHAPE and SOUND of human communication was becoming codified.

It was a time of mother centrality in PHASE ONE when female fecundity had been of paramount importance. The birth of a baby had been the greatest gift. Male role in specific procreation had been unknown. At birth a little girl had been defined by the triangular *SHAPE of her pubis*. Since male role in specific procreation had been unknown a male baby was defined as one more,(I) by the *SHAPE of his penis*.

SECTION TWO

OF PHASE ONE
SHAPE *of* SOUND

The WOOF of my linguistic fabric

PHASE ONE

DEALS WITH THE BEGINNING OF THE STORY OF
LANGUAGE AND HOW TO REDISCOVER THE CONSONANT

SOUNDS and SHAPES

FROM WHICH THEY EMERGDE USING

THE RULES of ORIGINAL SOUND DISCOVERY

(ROSD)

LEIT MOTIF IN MUSIC

When listening to a symphony, you can either hear the whole tapestry of SOUND interwoven, superimposed, suspended upon the vibrating air, or you can pick out a single instrument and follow it as it weaves its way through the caverns created by other textural and harmonic fusions. When you listen to a single instrument and the *leit motif* that it carries, as the SOUND washes over you, you become aware of the underlying repetitive pattern inherent in that *leit motif*. As it is repeated either by other instruments, or by the whole orchestral assemblage you recognize it like an old familiar friend, and jump to it, grateful for a hook on which to hang your experience of beauty, understanding and rapture.

There are times when the *leit motif*, or melody moves along the pathways of SOUND almost unrecognizable but the ear the ever present consort of auditory vibration tunes in and brings subtle complexities of meaning to consciously recognizable patterns.

So it happens with the single SOUNDS and the phonemic clusters that comprise the words that human creatures use to communicate with the world over. At first hearing, the SOUNDS seem to represent a cacophony of unrelated babble. Once you find the identifiable consonants and universal SOUNDS, once you discern the underlying *leit motif* in the syllables or words, you can take them back to their most ancient and original sources which expand with the fulfillment of meaning.

Within the syllables and words of the world there exist familiar old friends that chart the beginning of human communication. Once those ancient consonant SOUNDS become isolated, like the *leit motif* can be isolated in a symphony, the meaning that they carry, even when buried in the echoing caverns of other SOUNDS, become very clear. They emerge with a constancy that is comforting to the ear, bringing with it the keys to subsequent ecstatic response and appreciation.

SECTION TWO OF PHASE ONE

TABLE *of* CONTENTS

Leit motif in music	118
The capital letters of the Western Alphabet (WOOF)	121
Synopsis of the FIVE STAGES	122
HABA	125
HADA	138
HALA	146
HAMA	147
HANA of Emergence	152
HARA of the Belly	155
HASA	156
HAYA of Light	157
HAWWA (HAWA) or HEVEH (HAVA)	158
The Role of PROCESS expanded, sun (IS HANA)	159
TWENTY-FIVE RULES OF ORIGINAL SOUND DISCOVERY (ROSD)	168
RULE ONE: Monogenesis	168
RULE TWO: STAGES, Five Stages expanded	172
RULE THREE: Consonants	174
RULE FOUR: Work back from original sounds	181
Birds (BARAda);	194
A tribute to the birds	203
RULE FIVE: Names of natural phenomena	209
RULE SIX: Phonological Correspondence	218
RULE SEVEN: ANLAUT or first letter in a word	219
RULE EIGHT: Anastrophe, Palindrome, Reflection, Inversion	221
RULE NINE: Place the A(ah) SOUND behind every consonant	245

RULE TEN: H (huh) SOUND before vowels	247
RULE ELEVEN: EMPHATIC letter S	250
RULE TWELVE: A (ah) SOUND in any and all of the languages	260
RULE THIRTEEN: Double dyads, same consonant SOUND	283
RULE FOURTEEN: Repetition of Dyads	292
RULE FIFTEEN: Repetition of Words	318
RULE SIXTEEN: Overlapping of DYADS and TRYADS	324
RULE SEVENTEEN: Homonyms or puns within the language	326
RULE EIGHTEEN: Homophones	334
RULE NINETEEN: METAPLASM	363
RULE TWENTY: BUZZ words, Derogatory descriptions	368
RULE TWENTY ONE: Turn to Goddesses	374
RULE TWENTY-TWO: Metaphoric Creatures	379
RULE TWENTY-THREE: Symbols	391
RULE TWENTY-FIVE: Vowels	416

SECTION TWO

THE CAPITAL LETTERS OF THE WESTERN ALPHABET

The WOOF of my linguistic fabric

The claim made by some linguists that the meanings carried by the capital letters of the Western Alphabet subsequently emerging as both female and male as gender specific out of Middle Eastern societies may not be valid. More to the point, the SHAPES of the capital letters of the Western Alphabet and the SOUNDS associated with them came out of more ancient social prehistoric clusters based on female centrality originally out of the continent of Africa.

The specific original alternate meanings locked in those ancient mother based symbols that are known contemporarily as the capital letters of the Western Alphabet have mostly been lost, on one hand due to natural disasters; to cataclysmic upheavals, shattering earthquakes, devastating floods, droughts, famines, even an ice age that resulted in disastrous human dislocations and on the other hand due to the dawning of the knowledge of male role in specific paternity and the subsequent shift from female to male centrality. A shift occurred from the left handed primacy of the mother to the right handed primacy of the father, from the holistic approach of the right hemispheric mother to the single focused linear over evolution of the left hemisphere of the emerging father, from cooperation to competition, from the worship of the physical body of Mother Earth, to the worship of a mythical Father God in the sky *away* and *above* the body of Mother Earth. This shift resulted in the conscious redefinition and obliteration of the female essence as the father devised his own rules and his own fantasy as contemporary history (HIS STORY). The only links that remain to that ancient time of obliterated female centrality in PHASE ONE are the SOUNDS that have become codified in the capital letters of the Western Alphabet. In PHASE ONE there existed a shared specific progression in the way that the SOUNDS created as human communication became associated with the SHAPES that evolved to define them.

Synopsis of the FIVE STAGES

Synopsis of the *FIVE STAGES* of linguistic tonal evolution dealing with the SHAPE and SOUND of the capital letters of the Western Alphabet which will become apparent using The twenty-five RULES OF ORIGINAL SOUND DISCOVERY (ROSD)

STAGE ONE; INDIVIDUAL MOTHERS FACE;
> Keeping in mind that in PHASE ONE the SHAPES of the capital letters of the Western Alphabet initially as SOUNDS emerged as the SHAPE of the organs out of the INDIVIDUAL MOTHERS FACE, then in;

STAGE TWO; FACE or surFACE of MOTHER EARTH;
> They expanded to embrace the metaphorically flat round maternal surFACE that was the FACE of MOTHER EARTH then in;

STAGE THREE; INDIVIDUAL MOTHERS BODY;
> Expanded further to include the organs, processes, qualities and functions on the INDIVIDUAL MOTHERS BODY, then in;

STAGE FOUR; METAPHORIC BODY of MOTHER EARTH;
> Further expanded to metaphorically include the organs, processes, qualities and functions on the all encompassing BODY of MOTHER EARTH.

STAGE FIVE; CREATURES;
> At some period along the way in PHASE ONE the SOUNDS and SHAPES associated with the processes, qualities and functions of creatures such as insects, birds, bees, snakes, dogs, elephants, lions, bats, the octopus also entered the picture.

Like the individual human mothers as surrogates and daughters of Mother Earth in the creation of smaller replicas of themselves shared the same organs and pushed food out of their mouths, out of their round flat faces in *stage one*, so Mother Earth in *stage two* also fed Her creations after She too pushed them and their source out of the many holes, or mouths of creation out of Her top, tip or flat round surFACE.

Since She too had been perceived to have a round flat surFACE then She also have had to have a mouth, a break or a wound at the horizon line out of which She regurgitated or gave birth to the sun, moon, stars, clouds, even birds. If they had noses then She too as their great Mother must have had a nose somewhere. She also had to have had eyes, a jaw, cheeks, chin and a moving tongue, mostly a mouth.

Her mouth must have existed on the edge of that circular sweep around Her surFACE that ended at the horizon line, like individual mothers had in the circular sweep of the skull that contained hair on one side and separated by the ears, a round relatively flat hair free face on the other.

The individual mothers chewed morsels behind that lower hole on their faces and when the food was finely milled and lubricated they regurgitated the morsels to their eager young. Therefore Mother Earth must also have had a break in that flat horizontal rim on the edge, a break, a mouth in Her horizontal surFACE out of which the sun, moon, clouds, stars, even birds and insects were regurgitated back up to Her surFACE.

They posited that Mother Earth swallowed the heavenly bodies into Her waiting maw in the West, depending where they were on their migratory trek into either that looming line of mountains that looked like a great mouth of repetitive top lips at the edge, or She swallowed them into that watery wall of water. They have to had passed through Her fiery internal womb of transformation below Her crusty mantle, under Her very skin, using Her mysterious rivers of water and blood as a liquid tunnel for their great journey, She regurgitated them back up to Her surFACE on the other side. In the process of regurgitation she not only fed but maintained all the existing life upon Her magnificent generous surFACE.

Since in *stage one* the individual mother had a tongue that lay on the bottom of her mouth and pushed edible morsels up to the surface, then in *stage two* somewhere at Her circular edge within Her mountainous mouths Mother Earth must also have had a tongue that pushed the heavenly bodies and the birds up to Her surFACE.

To the job of holding on to and maintaining life in the *first stage* of mutual sharing of facial organs, between the individual mother's face and the surFACE of Mother Earth, an expansion occurred which began to include the naming of other organs on the individual mother's body and the body of Mother Earth in *stages two and four*.

What had been individual organs on the mothers face not only supported and maintained life, but fed into the creation of the SHAPES and SOUNDS that became the capital letters of the Western Alphabet, expanding to include other organs, processes, qualities and functions.

In *stage three* the individual mothers face and mouth as the source of much wondrous activity expanded to include the rest of her being. Her body including many of her organs, expanded to include the processes, qualities and functions that also emerged as the crucible that created and maintained life; the mammaries, tits, the mons veneris, hands that held, legs that moved, fingers that caressed, the mind that collected images and memories.

In *stage four* on the body of Mother Earth, Her round flat surFACE also expanded to embrace the processes, qualities and functions that She shared with Her surrogates; the mammaries became snow capped mountains, the tits became tetons, the mons veneris became the cleft between two mountainous mounds, the hands (manos in Spanish) that helped, became the bloody aspect of the sun, Mother Earth's greatest helper. The mind became associated with Mother Earth's other helper, the moon, the menstrual time keeper and ruler of the nocturnal sky.

Then in *stage five* other creatures especially birds, even insects played their metaphoric roles in adding to the codification of human communication at the time of female centrality in PHASE ONE.

MOTHER EARTH and the SUN at one (atone) with each other

At the most ancient time of SOUND codification in PHASE ONE Mother Earth had been considered to be *at one* with the sun. The sun sailed through the belly of air *above* Her surFACE in the primal uni-verse classification creating the linguistically diverse syllable for the belly of air as the unvoiced, expelled HA (ha) SOUND.

Using RULE TWELVE of the RULES OF ORIGINAL SOUND DISCOVERY (ROSD) to that unvoiced H (ha) SOUND, had been added the melody carrying voiced A (ah) vowel, becoming (HA). Accompanying the (HA) SOUND emerging SHAPES of the subsequent capital consonants of the Western Alphabet took their turns in defining the SHAPES that defined the WARP of ancient reality. The two syllables dealing with the body of Mother Earth as (AH) and the belly of air above Her surFACE as (HA) became the (AH-HA) dealing with the activity of the breath defining the (AH) as the beginning of life and the end as (HA).

There is also the perception that the A(ah) SOUND is not only a vowel but a consonant. There may have been a time that the A (ah) SOUND as a consonant led some of the words.

With the addition of mixed consonant SOUNDS to the belly of air above Her surFACE, out of RULE FOURTEEN, there surfaces a plethora of words and concepts. One of the first will deal with the birth of a baby and the establishment of the repetitive activity or habit (HABATA) through a filter of panic stricken helplessness.

SECTION TWO

HABA

For the Egyptians AB (HABA) originally in PHASE ONE defined the heart soul, one of the seven souls given to a baby at birth. In PHASE TWO AB emerged to define the father and water as his seminal fluid.

One of the most ancient dyads of the sun out of PHASE ONE as (HABA) deals with the sun and Mother Earth being *at one* with each other. The (HA) deals with the belly of air above Her surFACE. The (BA) deals with the suns repetitive 'two in one' activity of rising and setting giving birth to the process of habit (HABA-). The letter H (huh) comes directly out of the body of Mother Earth with the letter A (ah) blasting open on top to let the fire drenched air of the exploding volcano create the breath above Her surFACE and the letter (H).

The SHAPE of the letter B comes directly out of the two full bulbous lips as seen in profile on the individual mothers face ergo the 'two in one' scenario creating the one mouth. RULE NINE; Habit with the addition of the A (ah) SOUND after every consonant becomes (HABATA).

HABA, of habit (HABATA) is one of the ancient names of the sun dealing with an activity. What is a habit (HABATA)? A habit is an act that when repeated enough times becomes an automatic response and is no longer based on conscious choice. After it entrenches itself as an automatic response, it then establishes its own set of insistent demands that cannot be easily dislodged.

For human beings original habits (HABATA) are the neuronal pathways in the brain that are laid as tracks or canals of subsequent behavior. Upon being born, with the first breath, the human infant begins to lay down the tracks of what will become its subsequent habitual (HABA-) life defining patterns.

The newly born infant is also flooded with the immediate numbing realization that the body in which it is encased does not work. With the dawning awareness of its helplessness panic sets in. The only way to defuse the panic is to get the eyes that are lovingly staring down at it, to keep staring.

The newly born helpless infant becomes an attention getting machine. If those eyes look at it when it smiles, it will keep smiling. If they look at it when it cries, it will keep whining. If it cries and there is no apparent response, it may give up and come to the sad conclusion that no matter what it does it won't get what it wants or needs. A feeling of helplessness begins to lay down its tracks.

Those neuronal pathways laid down as deeply grooved behavior habits filtered through a human beings panic stricken infancy follow it for the rest of its life, often stultifying the creatures every move. They become in adult life the alien, often erratic behavior patterns of depression that sabotage (IS HABATA-) its every effort.

If they become etched into the psyche through an extra added dose of image based trauma, they can become the root of panic geometrically multiplied, emerging as obsessions (HABA-).

In animals those habitual patterns of behavior are called 'instinct', an immensely unfortunate and evil left hemispheric name which implies that animals do not rationally choose aspects of their behavior and are not privy to feelings and reason.

The concept of human habit (HABATA) was shared by the symbiotic relationship on the one hand between Mother Earth and Her surrogates, the creative mothers on Her body and on the other hand with Her major off spring, the solar disc travelling through Her belly of air above Her surFACE. They surmised that if among human beings there existed an activity that had them locked into habitual patterns, so that same activity must have occurred upon the generous flat surFACE and body of their majestic all encompassing Mother Earth.

Among Mother Earth's many original repetitive habits (HABATA-) was the major one of the sun being regurgitated into light and life out of Her mouth at Her horizontal Eastern rim every morning and swallowed back into Her waiting maw, the watery wall of death on the Western rim every night.

The linguistic construct of (HABA) deals with the double movement of the repetitive, predictable, habitual (HABA-) passage of the sun in and out of the body of Mother Earth. The phoneme (HA) deals with the belly of air above the body of Mother Earth through which the sun rose at dawn and set at twilight. The letter (B) is the symbol for the two full lips on the mothers face seen in profile in stage one emerging into the concept of 'two in one'. It takes the top lip and the lower lip working in tandem to make the single context of the mouth, ergo 'two in one'. The unvoiced (T) at the end of habit (HABATA) deals with where the activity took place at the tip, top of the tongue in stage one and then subsequently on the surFACE of Mother Earth in stage two at Her horizontal rim.

It was the activity of the ancient sun at the time of female centrality in PHASE ONE moving in and out of the body of Mother Earth through the name of Haba that defined the concept of repetitive habit. If Her major solar off-spring sank into a body of water in the West, the reflection in the water as it disappeared out of sight, was of great turbulence. The sinking sun in the West looked like it was shattered into bits as it trembled upon the gory waves of its descent. The death of the sinking sun into the bloody waters in the Western sky created a variety of perceptions. One was that Mother Earth's flat circular surFACE swallowed the sun into Her great mouth on the edge in the West for it to pass through Her underground internal intestines, in order to be transformed and reborn at dawn in the Eastern sky. Mother Earth was perceived to have eaten the sun. There was no doubt about it, as the sun disappeared off Her flat surFACE at Her side, its round shattered solar disc slipping down reflected in the standing waters looked like She ate it. The number eight (8) surfaces here.

In Egyptian Abtu (HABATA) the fish of Isis as Mother Earth swallowed the penis of Osiris every night into Her Western watery Abyss (HABA-). It was the job of Isis his sister after she recounted the magic word to put him together. Another myth recounts the story that he as the setting sun was chewed up into many pieces before he was swallowed by the body of Mother Earth and his sister Isis put him together without his penis. The Egyptian story out of PHASE TWO recounts ancient links to the castrated first born son, as Mother Earth's swallowed sun.

For the early Egyptians one of the seven souls given to a child at birth was called the Khaibit (KABATA or HABATA) 'the shadow'. A habit (HABATA), like 'a shadow' followed the creature all of its life based on decisions made out of a missing frame of reference at birth and a panic stricken realization that it was helpless and locked in a body that didn't work.

The most ancient linguistic perception of the sun as a constant returning reality establishing the concept of reincarnation, for the Hebrews Haba meant 'after life'. Olam (HALAMA) Haba dealt with 'the world to come'. The Olam (HALAMA) deals with the solar (IS HALA-) disc belonging to the (MA) of Mother Earth. There is an intimation here that in PHASE ONE the ancient Hebrews believed in an 'after life' connected with the passage of the sun, with reincarnation and the systems of worship belonging to the all encompassing body of Mother Earth.

In Swahili to worship is abudu (HABADA). The Amharic name for the snake, the symbolic electro-magnetic Kundalini energy, the guide of the sun on its way to transformation had been Abad (HABADA). In Abada (HABADA) the Arabic word for 'eternity', the letter (H) at the beginning, using RULE TEN had been dropped off. It deals with the ultimate passage of time, of the sun rising and setting and in PHASE TWO with a shift into male centrality. The sun, as the emerging male symbol of 'source', *away* and *above* the body of Mother Earth, in PHASE TWO measuring the unrelenting passage of time defined the habitual (HABATA-) passage in and out of Her body as the moon had done in PHASE ONE.

In the Arabic word for 'eternity' as Abada (HABADA) the 'gift of' (DA) as a verb, the activity of the hands, replaces the noun, 'place' of the 'tip', top (TA), of (HABATA), on the body of Mother Earth, where this activity took place. Nouns as things and places may have been the first to be named, verbs as activity followed suit. With male realization of their role in specific paternity in PHASES TWO and THREE the movement became *away* and *above* the body of Mother Earth as 'source', into the male 'source', as watery reflection, sun, sky, stars, heaven, penis and ultimately the left hemispheric mind of a hidden Father God in the ethers.

The habitual, dual (BA) movement of the sun above and below the plane of Mother Earth creating the passage of time, is expressed with Abada (HABADA) the Arabic word for 'eternity'. Since it is already based on the (AH) vowel SOUND, then it represents one of the most ancient, original words, not having been contaminated by the subsequent 'SHAPE shifting' vowels. The concept of reincarnation seems to have been deleted as the habitual passage of time encoded in the Arab Abada dealing with 'eternity' and not with the cycles of constant returning.

As a symbol, the SHAPE of 'eternity' lying on its side, one circle next to each other is the same as the SHAPE of number eight standing straight up with one circle on top of another. Another factor emerging here is that 'eternity' lying on its side looking like the number eight and the SHAPE of the activity of the eye as a reflective system is SHAPED like a closed double loop. In Spanish ojo (HAJA or HAHA) is the eye and ocho (HACHA or HAJA) is the number eight. They are almost linguistically indistinguishable. The activity of the eye of seeing and the SHAPE of the sun making its daily descent into the Western wall of water became related in Abada (HABADA) the Arabic word for 'eternity'. You could see (IS HA) only when the sun rose and spread its light in the Eastern sky at dawn. On the individual level you could only see when there was light from the sun and if there was light of life in the eyes of a living creature.

Ancient mothers of wisdom the sagas, knew the ways how to neutralize the stultifying habits that sabotaged (IS HABATA-) a lifetime through the experience and mapping of the electro-magnetic shakti of the Kundalini energy.

Under the temple of a Greek Goddess there was not only a spring, but a cave, a pit called the abaton (HABATANA). A virgin oracle sat upon a three legged stool above the opening in the body of Mother Earth and in a Kundalini induced trance shared her wisdom with the questing adept.

A human being caught in the net of habitual destructive repetitive panic based behavior, could spend time in that pit like cave under the temple, face their greatest fears, become transformed, incubated, cooked clean and like the sun become *'born again'* to a new life free of panic. The pits of transformation, the abatons were usually located over Lea or Kundalini electro magnetic prana lines that suspended the searching adept into states of ecstatic bliss. This process had been automatic with the birthing breath of the birthing mother. It became shared with others through contact with the Kundalini energy, castration and multifaceted ritual.

For the ancient Hebrews, the process of trans-formative renewal was given a time, the Shabat (IS HABATA), or Sabbath (IS HABATA), every seven days on Saturday, when the stultifying fear driven habits (HABATA) of a lifetime could be faced, and through prayer and devotional d'avening (DA) 'gift of HAVANA) dealt with and defused. The seven days of transformation for the Hebrews establishes ancient links with the seven dual chacras, the Ida and Pingali of the Tantrists. Both deal with the reclamation of their even (HAVANA) distribution of process using the number seven (IS EVEN or HAVANA) with the Kundalini electro magnetic prana energy as a main factor in that transformation.

As the knowledge of male role in specific procreation and the primacy of the linear left hemisphere of the brain gained ground in PHASE TWO all aspects of women's ancient knowledge were becoming if not stolen, obliterated. The magical healing powers of the Greek abaton (HABATANA) literally went underground.

In PHASES TWO and THREE as the redefinitions proliferated, for the Hebrews the magical abaton (HABATANA) of the Greeks out of PHASE ONE became redefined as the dreaded Abaddon (HABADANA), the 'Spirit of the Pit'. What had been the 'place' (TA), the top on the body of Mother Earth, where transformation could take place, became an activity, the 'gift of' (DA), the dreaded underground Abaddon (HABADANA). The (T) and (D) are interchangeable.

It would seem that the Arabic Abada (HABADA) as 'eternity' became something more prosaic in the Hebrew Abaddon (HABADA-) dealing with 'the spirit of the pit'. We are in PHASE THREE entering the realm of left hemispheric male 'religious' fantasy.

It is the hands that give and take. The sun was considered to be the helping hands of Mother Earth. When the primacy of the solar disc as the 'two in one' activity (BA) emerges over the primacy of Mother Earth and Her air (HA), there surfaces male centrality. What had been the abaton (HABATANA), a place of healing and transformation within the body of Mother Earth in PHASE ONE, as the redefinitions proliferated She became replaced by a Father God *away* and *above* Her surFACE. The dreaded Hebrew abaddon (HABAdana) moved into the bleak future and in PHASE THREE faced a perilous future creating the subsequent fires of the Christian hell.

For the Greeks Hebe (HABA), was the 'virgin' form of Hera (HARA) the Mother of the Gods. She dealt with the process, the dual movement of beginnings of the sun emerging out of the belly (HARA) of air (HARA) above the surFACE in and out of the body of Mother Earth. Her mother Hera (HARA) was the Goddess that personified not only the great belly of air (HARA) above the body of Mother Earth, the actual place where many of the ancient male Gods especially the sun (RA), of the sky, thunder, space and subsequently the left hemisphere of the brain, had become gestated.

Hebe (HABA) as the Virgin Goddess was the dual process of the sun rising into the belly of air (HARA), beginning a new day and setting into the womb of transformation, beginning a new night. The process of 'beginnings' defined her as a 'virgin'. There seemed to be no other apparent input into the process of creation. Male role in specific paternity in PHASE ONE was unknown. Without Hebe (HABA), the Gods would die. They would no longer be immortal. Passing through the belly of air above the body of Mother Earth they would not have the cycles of solar based time through which they could establish their reign. 'Hail Mary Mother of God' has ancient antecedents.

In Anatolia Hebat (HABATA) was the 'cupbearer of the Gods', 'dispenser of immortality'. As the 'dispenser of immortality' she had links with the sun because it rose and set every day without pause creating the endless cycles that became one of the metaphors for reincarnation, immortality and habit (HABATA). In Spanish the word for sol (IS HALA) as the sun, has the same linguistic root as the word for soul (IS HALA).

As the sun rose out of the darkness and death of night to its light every morning, so the human soul would rise to a new life of light after its passage through the darkness of death. The letter (L) at the end of sol (IS HALA) deals with the *angular* SHAPE of the emergence of the sun out of the horizontal surFACE or side of Mother Earth at dawn. It has had its origins out of PHASE ONE and out of the SHAPE of the tongue (lengua in Latin) in stage one, the angle that lay on the floor of the oral cavity. So it must have been that for the sun to emerge at dawn and help Mother Earth to maintain Her creations it had to be pushed up or regurgitated up to the surFACE by Her ever ready internal tongue in stage one and later on by Her hands in stage three.

For the Maya on the other side of the world, who dealt with three cycles expressing their understanding of time, their primary solar clock was called the hab (HABA). Using the same phonemic dyad of the sun rising and setting (BA) into the belly of air (HA), it establishes the possibility that after one of the great planetary cataclysms and subsequent human dispersal off the continent of Africa the Mayan culture had its origins across the great oceanic divide on the other side of Mother Earth.

The Anatolian Hebat (HABATA), the Goddess of Immortality not only has links with the Arabic Abada (HABADA) and is a variant of the Biblical Eve (HAVA), whose reign began in the EVEning, with the passage of the sun through the trans-formative entrails of night. The letters (B) and (V) are interchangeable made in the same area of the mouth. In the tropics near the equator, there was an EVEN distribution of day and night that happened when the sun rose in the morning and set in the EVEning. EVE, the harbinger of the menstrual moon, was also known as Hvoh (HAVA) in Persia and Heveh (HAVA) or Hawwa (HAWA) in Mesopotamia.

The Mesopotamian Eve as Hawwa (HAWA) deals with water (WA) at the Western wall, into which the sun sank and was swallowed by Mother Earth in the EVEning, to begin its journey of trans-formative rebirth. The EVEning time became sacred because it was considered the time that the sun passing through the entrails of night within the body of Mother Earth used to coagulate, reassemble itself, become transformed and to rise pale and wan to a new day in the Eastern sky creating the even balance of day and night at the equator.

In PHASE THREE as the sun came to represent male primacy on the planet, the moon was shunted to a second place and the Biblical EVE (HAVA) as the daughter of EVEning was also given her demotion.

In Spanish haber (HABAra) means 'to have' (HAVA) establishing links with the Biblical Eve (HAVA) of EVEning. What she had was the birth of night in the EVEning, out of Her vulvic (VA) aperture, the volcanic (VA) vent (VA) on the body of Mother Earth that flushed up the moon, sailing through the belly of air (HA), at night. In PHASE ONE it was the moon that counted the passage of time. It was the moon as the *ruler*, the master and measurer not only of time but of the ruby red russet drops of estRUs that coincided with the human mothers period at the end creating her as the *ruler* of her clan.

The passage of time counted (KANATA-) by the cycles of the moon, became associated not only with menstruation but with the female cunt (KANATA) out of whose vulvic aperture the lunar celestial clock became the 'dispenser of immortality'. In cunt (KANATA) the phoneme (KA) dealt with Mother Earth and all individual mothers who created smaller reflections of themselves. (NA) deals with 'emergence on the surface' or 'change from a former state'. (TA) at the tip, top or edge, tells its own story. (KA) deals with some aspect of smallness. So the cunt (KANATA) is the place on the tip, top or edge of the trunk (TA), out of which there occurs an 'emergence on the surface' (NA) creating a small reflection of the mother (KA). In Polish kont (KANATA) is an angle and the angle on a female body is the triangular vulva.

The Iberian (HABArana) Peninsula, in time surfaced within the Spanish language. As major cataclysms rocked the African continent over its multi thousand year history, many of its inhabitants scattered over the planet. One of the closest immigrations occurred North from the Sahara Desert across the Mediterranean Sea that could easily be crossed by boat. It can be ascribed to the Iberian (HABArana) Peninsula that the Habanera (HABAnara), a very lively Spanish dance had its origins on that peninsula.

Another Spanish dyad for word surfaces here and that is habla (HABALA) as speech. It is so perfect a linguistic example that it almost boggles the mind. On the level of the human being, the (HA) deals with the breath. (BA) deals with the two lips moving in concert to create the one mouth that creates the SOUND emerging into speech. And (LA) deals with the angle that lies in the cavity of the mouth as the tongue (lengua in Latin), that not only tells lies, but obfuscates meaning. The breath (HA) using the mouth (BA) as a vehicle of passage uses the tongue (LA) to create cogent speech, ergo the Spanish word habla (HABALA).

Since Mother Earth shared all of the processes, qualities and functions with Her surrogates, the individual mothers of the specie, She too went through the same, if a bit tortured process. The (HA) of (HABALA) as speech was the belly of air above Her majestic surFACE. As in the human case, the (BA) were the two lips approximating to create the SOUND. It became the activity, the dual journey of the sun moving in and out of the two mouths at either side of the horizontal rim on the surFACE of Mother Earth. One mouth regurgitated the sun in the East at dawn, the other mouth swallowed the sun in the wall of the Western waters.

Since the movement of the sun had to have holes on the Eastern horizontal rim and the Western side in order to move in and out of Her great surFACE, they assumed that it was originally in stage two Her two mouths. It moved in stage four to become Her two vulvic lips, Her anus or a wound at the edge. In Polish the word RANA means both 'wound' and 'dawn'. How could that be? At the time that this particular concept emerged in PHASE THREE and male centrality, the passage of the sun out of the body of Mother Earth at dawn was perceived to have been through a cut, a wound in Her side, Her horizontal rim. At other times it was through the other orifices. In the Polish word rana as both 'wound' and 'dawn', the phoneme Ra deals with the sun. The letter (NA) deals with either with 'emergence on the surface', or 'change from a former state'. This may have been the time in PHASE THREE dealing with clitorectomies when women had to be cut open to give birth.

What was it that the Egyptian obelisk (HABALAsaka) in concert with the Spanish habla (HABALA) had to say? Was it like a sacred tree joining the surFACE of Mother Earth and Her greatest helper the sun above Her? Or was it in PHASES TWO and THREE like a penis (PANASA) that also acted as the link that brought the two different aspects together?

In the word Spanish a *leit motif* seems to surface for Spanish (IS PANASA) contains within it the word for penis (PANASA). The –ISH at the end of SpanISH dealt with 'one who is like'. Was it a time when the heterosexual males were finding their own primacy in PHASE TWO as they dispersed over the world? The penis (PANASA) deals with the passage (PA) into birth (NASA). NASENCE (NASANASA) the Latin word for repetitive birth. It could also go in the direction of PAN (PANA) as the name for man in Polish and his blood (SA) as semen that added to the creation of life.

After the shift into male centrality in PHASE THREE the name of the wandering tribe of Semites became known as Hebrews (HABArawa) with their origins out of Hebe (HABA) the Virgin Goddess of Immortality. Hebe surfaces down the line and into the future as one of the derogatory names for Hebrews.

The concept of virginity deals with a dual process. It originally dealt with Mother Earth without any help recreating Herself, out of Herself, by Herself as land during a volcanic eruption *and* either regurgitating or giving birth to the reconstituted solar disc every morning.

It was universally believed that the flowing menstrual blood once it stopped flowing on the outside, coagulated inside of the individual mother to create the baby. The same process was metaphorically shared with the body of Mother Earth. The volcanic crater (KARATARA) was the original creator (KARATARA). It was the crater out of which lava poured across Her surFACE coagulating into land that made it possible for all of her terrestrial creations to have their being.

In the words crater (KARATARA) as creator (KARATARA) you have three overlapping dyads (KARA-RATA-TARA). The (KARA) deals with Mother Earth as the creator of smaller (KA), aspects out of Herself, such as lava, soil, rubble, rocks, dust, smoke, at one with the helping hands of the sun (RA). The (RATA) deals with the return (RATARANA) of magma back up from the fiery bowels within the body of Mother Earth. And (TARA) deals with the terrain, the tor (TARA), the tar (TARA) that boiled up and blasted its way to the heavens during a volcanic eruption creating land upon Her surFACE. The word magma (MAGAMA) tells it all. (MA) the Mother, be-getting (GA), the Mother (MA), virgin birth, parthogenesis in action.

The (WA) at the end of Hebrew (HABARAWA) although silent, deals with water (WA) and the wailing at the Western Wall where the male sun (RA) as 'helper' was sWALLowed by the great body of Mother Earth as it set into the great waters in the West, ushering in evening, the time not only of darkness but of solar death.

The word for war (WARA) deals with the battle between the body of Mother Earth as water (WA), swallowing the sun (RA), every night and the sun fighting for its life on the way to its nightly doom (DAMA) gift of (DA) the mother (MA). With the addition of (DA) at the end of war to get word (WARADA), it becomes apparent that it deals with the 'gift of' (DA) war (WARA). So it was the use of language that defined one of the differences that begat war. This seems to be the time when the singular focused left hemisphere of the male brain gained supremacy over the repetitive quality of the circular mother based brain as males began to question female centrality with their God Ra taking up the cudgels against the primacy of Mother Earth.

The metaphoric activity on the body of Mother Earth in PHASE TWO must have been in some way related to the battles that must have been raging between the female and male human creatures on Her body.

The Wailing Wall in Jerusalem, although redefined, is still a place of grief and prayer for the Jews. The (RA) in Hebrew (HABARAWA) surfaces with a clue that the ancient desert wanderers spent a great deal of time in Egypt to have incorporated the sun God Ra into their name as the 'doer' and 'helper' of Mother Earth.

The name for Arab (HARABA) bears a striking resemblance to the name

Hebrew (HABARA-), except that the two last syllables are transposed. The Arab name deals with 'place', the belly of air (HARA) above the body of Mother Earth through which the sun made its dual (BA) passage. The Hebrew (HABARA-) name, deals with the Virgin Goddess Hebe (HABA) as process, representing the dual (BA) habitual 'activity' of the sun and of 'beginnings' into day and into night. It also deals with Bardo (BARA-) the Tibetan 'intermediate state'.

A similar construct surfaces in the Yoruba name for the 'master of the sky' as Obtala (HABATALA). The (O) at the beginning of the name implies, that is associating it with the SHAPE of the solar disc and maleness. As 'master of the sky' he was no longer the sun, as the son and helping hands of Mother Earth. In PHASES TWO and THREE he became her husband, passing above Her body, no longer working with Her as one familial unit, but *apart* and *above* Her, as Her lord and master. He not only became Her lord and master, but his Earthly representative became Oba (HABA) 'the divine king'. In Polish oba (HABA) deals with the concept of 'both'. His brain had become even, had become balanced through castration, both sides working in concert through ritual for him to become a male leader out of PHASE TWO.

As the celestial deities reorganized their relationships, they reflected the reorganization that was occurring among human beings on the body of Mother Earth and how mothers were losing their ancient power to the emerging fathers. Reality at the time of female centrality was defined from a female point of view. As male role in specific procreation was becoming apparent, in PHASES TWO and THREE the name for the emerging FATHER, was the one who made HER FAT/FATHER. It establishes the emerging fact that not only the fat belly of the mother but he too could be seen as the *apparent* parent.

At the time of very ancient female centrality in PHASE ONE, as babies emerged out of the bodies of the mother, specific paternity was unknown. Male children were unidentified. They did not understand male role in specific procreation. Boys (BAYA) were perceived to have the 'two in one' linguistic concept (BA) locked in them. They had a female body like his mother and male genitalia like the other male members of his group. The (AYA) in boy (BAYA), deals with what he would eventually become, the protector of the family, the castrated eunuch shaman uncle, presiding over the rites of the rising and setting sun. Aya means light in Persian and dawn in Assyrian.

The name for brother (BARATARA) comes out of that same ancient 'two in one' perception. Along the way, the I of 'one more', of the individual self, became attached to growing boys. As they matured and most left the clan, wandering in groups along the periphery like elephant males, they were redefined again with the vowel (O) that began to represent maleness surfacing with the zero (IS HARA) of the empty belly (HARA), in time attaching it in PHASE THREE to the SHAPE of the circular disc of the sun (O) and its growing primacy as male source *away* from and *above* the body of Mother Earth.

The name for brother (BARATARA) on one level establishes its links with the dual essence perceived in the boy. But if you separate the 'BR' from the 'OTHER', you realize the ancient perception that the boy and the brother were not like the mother. They were not the M, of the M OTHER, they were the 'OTHER'. They were also the alien, the ANOTHER, the 'A NOT HER'. They became defined by the zero (IS HARA) of the permanently empty belly (HARA).

In Japanese and Hebrew the name for belly is HARA. The Japanese belly surfaces in HARA-KIRI as the suicidal disembowelment due to loss of face. For the Hebrews there is a double source for HARA. It not only means 'pregnant belly' on a mother's body but also 'sacred mountain', the Eastern bump on the body of Mother Earth, where the sun was born every morning. Mt. Ararat (HARARATA) the place of the landing of Noahs ark and Har (HARA) Magido the prophesized Armageddon, the linear end of the left hemispheric mind, the ultimate battle of the Apocalypse.

The word for belly as HARA also defines the word for zero (IS HARA). The HARA as the zero (IS HARA) comes to define the permanently empty belly that human males carried within them before their role in specific paternity beginning in PHASE TWO became known.

When the shift was occurring from female centrality in PHASE ONE to male centrality, in PHASES TWO and THREE males redefined themselves as the sole source of creation. The empty belly of HARA, as zero (IS HARA) moved before the 'one' of individuality. Male source emerged out of the space *before* the zero (IS HARA). Out of where? The emptiness, the abyss, the fallen side of Mother Earth, the hidden source out of the emerging power of the left hemisphere of the brain, out of the mind. The vowel SOUND of (O) still defines maleness at the ends of nouns in the Romance and Slavic languages.

The phoneme (BA) dealing with the dual passage of the sun in and out the various apertures on the body of Mother Earth became *reflected* to emerge as Ab, (BA/AB) and ab (HABA) or abba (HABA), became the name of the 'father' in Middle Eastern societies. The AB (HABA) originally had been associated with the heart-soul given to a baby at birth in Egypt. As male role in specific paternity became realized in PHASE TWO he was given the reflected under water name of AB (HABA) or ABBA (HABA) his heart-soul name. Ab (HABA) is also the name for water and had been associated not only with watery reflection but with seminal fluid. In PHASE THREE the father emerged as the sole creator of the baby assuming its most definitive name.

The linguistic reflection of deities and names followed a pattern that was created at the time of ancient female centrality and the singular worship of the body of Mother Earth. Mother Earth had been considered to be a dual presence. She was land and She was water. The land above the surFACE (IS HARAfasa) was reflected in the still standing waters below Her surFACE. The land above dealt with life. The reflection in the still waters was considered to be the land of death below Her surFACE. The first born son, the brother to his sisters, the uncle and protector to the mothers subsequent children, became part of the eunuch priesthood officiating over the rites of the setting sun and the reflection of life in the standing waters of death. The reflected surFACE of water and the underground caves above and within the body of Mother Earth became the domain of the transformed balanced, liberated males, the eunuch uncles, the avuncular ancient co-heads of the human family. The reflected standing dark waters became their domain.

As heterosexual males began to understand their role in specific paternity in PHASE TWO, they took over many of the rites of the ancient eunuch priesthood. The search for the 'father', as the male 'source of creation' began. It not only incorporated, scrapped, but obliterated much of this ancient historical and linguistic mother based knowledge, and redefined women as either mothers, whores or slaves and with clitorectomies destroying the ecstasy and power inherent in their birthing breath.

Having links with the death of the sun, in its repetitive habitual aspect, is the name for texts written for the dead and their 'beginning' into a new life, in obituary (HABATA-).

The Virgin Goddess HEBE (HABA), representing the process of the journey of the sun rising and setting, ushering the beginning of both day and night, hidden in her former ancient name would have been amazed at the permutations that her name as 'process' evolved into. She would have been amazed that her virginal name of Hebe (HABA) became associated with habit (HABATA), the unrelenting passage of time having its links with the habitual rising and setting of the sun and the moon.

In the word obituary (HABATARA) the ultimate habit (HABATA), rears its redundant head. For obituary is the literal acknowledgement of the habit of death. The (RA) at the end of obituary (HABATARA) deals with the sun as the doer, the helping hands of Mother Earth that as time, let no one pass through.

HADA

The solar FALL off the side (IS HADA) of Mother Earth to hide (HADA) under Her Western rim. HADA deals with the (DA) 'gift of 'the belly of air (HA). The actual dyad hada surfaces in Hebrew meaning 'to sretch out'. Since it contains within its linguistic folds the 'gift of '(DA) air (HA) with both phonemes based on the A (ah) SOUND then it must be assumed that it is very ancient. It also becomes apparent that the 'stretching out' is out of the body of Mother Earth in stage four and the stretching out is done by the rays of the sun as fingers and hands, stretching out at dawn, like newly awakened human beings often do, to the joy of its new light and stretching out in despair as the body of Mother Earth swallowed them into Her Western horizontal mouth.

A similar concept surfaces in Phoenician with yod (H(AYA)DA) as the hand. The (AYA) in the center deals with light in Persian and dawn in Assyrian also defining the solar light sinking into the side (IS HADA) of Mother Earth as Her helping hand. In Lithuanian to put into or to insert is IDETI (HADAta). As the side (IS HADA) it harkens back in stage four to the body of Mother Earth.

Had (HADA) deals with past tense in English, part of the verb to have dealing with past containment. So both the Hebrew HADA and the Phoenician YOD (HA(YA)DA) deal with the rays of the sun as the fingers of Her helping hand stretching out of Her Western side (IS HADA) as they descended into Her body at twilight.

For all intents and purposes the sun hid (HADA) into the body of Mother Earth for the night. How did in PHASE THREE the concept of a *hidden* male Father God in the sky *away* and *above* the body of Mother Earth come into being? Linguistically it has to go back to the sun that disappeared off the Western rim into the body of Mother Earth at twilight. It hid (HADA) from sight under the hide (HADA) or skin of Mother Earth into Her horizontal Western side (IS HADA). In Lithuanian oda (HADA) means skin, or hide (HADA). The SHAPE of that disappearance or hiding became encoded in the angular SHAPE of the fall off the edge of the flat round surFACE of Mother Earth at Her horizontal rim, becoming encoded in the SHAPE of the number seven, siedem (IS HADAma) in Polish. In Amharic admas (HADAmasa) is the Western horizon where this activity took place. Both the number seven in Polish as siedem (IS HADAma) and the horizon as admas (HADAmasa) in Amharic deal with the mouth on the Western side (IS HADA) of the surFACE of Mother Earth in stage two where the sun was daily swallowed.

On the individual mothers body the *hidden* (HADAna) internal spaces were the skull with the eyes and ears that held back the avalanche of information from the outside. The senses are not there to open creatures up to information. The senses are there to keep the content of the universe from swamping human beings. Autism may be the overwhelming swamping through the left hemisphere of the brain in which linear information is stored.

There was also the hidden (HADAna) cavity of the mouth that held the tongue out of which SOUND emerged along with masticated morsels. In Hebrew the mouth is hodes (HADAsa) linking it to the side (IS HADA) on the surFACE of Mother Earth Her mouth into which she ate the sun, hid (HADA) it from sight. The other hidden area was the vulvic aperture and abdomen where the hidden magic of creation took place. Behind the vulvic aperture was the anus that held the digested contents of ingestion. The activities of SOUND out of the skull, baby out of the abdomen, feces out of the anus were all hidden from sight, were all apparently mysterious internal, magical processes originally associated with the individual mother which then metaphorically expanded to embrace the surFACE and body of Mother Earth.

What had been hidden (HADAna) inside also were the teeth, odo (HADA) in Greek. The tongue may have done the milling, but it was the teeth at the tip of the gums that did the tearing apart of downed prey. The teeth hidden in the mouth separated the morsels into manageable pieces. It was initially the mothers mouth that did the separation of death from life whether it was of living creatures or plants, fruit or tubers.

Also in PHASE ONE that separation had been associated with the carnivores and their hunting habits. The mothers whether alone like the cheetah and leopard, or in prides like the hyena and lioness, did all of the hunting and caring for the young. To s*mother* the downed prey establishes the mother as the caretaker and killer. The word to s*mother* hides (HADAsa) in its linguistic folds the carnivore *mother*.

Then there is the next perception that needs a bit of linguistic twisting. To our ancient codifiers of SOUND and language the next step was a bit creative. They metaphorically expanded their perception of separation as that which came out of the flat round surFACE of Mother Earth to that which emerged out of Her body. They put Her round flat surFACE and body together as a single unit. The round flat face emerged with a mouth on either side (IS HADA) out of which in the East the sun was regurgitated and another mouth, the mouth on the Western side (IS HADA) that swallowed and killed the rays of the sun as they sank out of sight ushering in the darkness of night. There emerged the two sides (IS HADA) of Her round flat surFACE as the source of the the two mouths, the regurgitation of the sun in the East and of the swallowing of the sun in the West.

When the sun was regurgitated at dawn it brought with it life and light giving birth in the Eastern sky to the angular SHAPE of the letter (L) of enlightenment and living. The sun emerged up as the angle of ascent into the light of its own creation. As rays of splintered fingers of the solar hand stretched across the body of Mother Earth they caressed Her and Her creations to awaken into their own lives. The letter (L) dealing with the LA of the LAdy of the LAnd dealt with the future. To 'stretch out' as branches, or the rays of the sun attaches itself to the original hada in Hebrew. Both are the gifts of air, as is hed (HADA) the 'echo' in Hebrew.

After the sun passed through Her belly of air above Her surFACE it descended into the Western abyss encoded in the angle of its descent and the SHAPE of the number seven. The number seven, siedem (IS HADAma) in Polish became universally mythologically established as the number of separation and death. It had its links with the ancient migrations but originally in PHASE ONE it dealt with the angular SHAPE of the fall off the horizontal edge, the death of the sun at twilight.

So the occurence of the two mouths of Mother Earth on either side of Her surFACE established the time of beginnings of separation and of death. In time it became Her volcanic vulva, Her anus and even Her armpits that came into play as the killers of the sun. The most perplexing dealt with the sun as it appeared out of a wound in the Eastern sky and disappeared to its doom in the Western horizontal cravasse. The sun said goodbye to its light in Basque as adio (HADAYA) and adios (HADAyasa) in Spanish. The (AYA) in both the adio (HADAYA) and adios (HADAYAsa) deal with the Persian word for light and in this case, its loss.

As the birth of the sun gave us the angular SHAPE of the LA of the lady ushering life and light, so the angular SHAPE of the number seven gave us the death of the sun at twilight. Mother Earth shed (IS HADA) the rays of the sun at twillight. There had been much pain odyne (HADAna) in Greek and blood odol (HADAla) in Basque, as She shod (IS HADA), hid (HADA) or swallowed the rays of the sun and their blessed light. She not only seduced (IS HADAsa) the sun at night but hunted it down, adan (HADAna) in Amharic.

Individual mothers of the specie did not give birth out of their sides. Some lying on their sides during labor may have looked that way but it was apparent to them that the hole on the end, the tail end of a creature and the hole on the bottom of the trunk on a human mother was where the small replica of the mother made its appearance. That vulvic hole on the bottom of the trunk became associated with the volcanic hole on the body of Mother Earth. Both flowed with red menstrual or lavic blood, the SASA of another declination.

When periodically in concert with the moon, the blood emerged on the surface, on the potential mothers flanks it announced that a death had occurred in the hidden womb inside of her body. The blood did not coagulate to create a reflection of the mother within her hidden recesses. It flowed freely on the outside. The menstruating female would not become the apparent parent.

Mother Earth replicated Herself as land and the individual mother created another but smaller version of herself. The mysterious process of replication was not an activity that occurred on the surface. It was not apparent. It was *hidden* deep inside of both the individual mother and the all encompassing body of Mother Earth.

The 'menses' in Swahili are hedhi (HADA). In Hebrew idda (HADA) defines 'the monthly period'. Both have ancient links with the side (IS HADA) on the body of Mother Earth where the lavic menses of creation made their ascending descent. The concept of hidden (HADAna) out of the side (IS HADA) gained momentum. The side (IS HADA) as the ravenous mouth remained in the linguistic record as hodes (HADAsa) in Hebrew.

To further confuse these ancient mother based perceptions when in PHASE THREE the ancient Hebrew defined the *hidden*, they came up with the male mind of God as the *hidden* creator up in the heavens *away* and *above* the body of Mother Earth. The *hidden* contents of the mouth or the *hidden* baby in the womb were left behind. The hidden became secreted in the left hemisphere of the male side of the human brain. It was really the human brain that created everything. But that it was not what it came to be redefined in its misinterpretation. The idea (HADA) went much further. God was *not* originally *hidden* in the human brain. God as a giver of laws dealing with human behavior was *hidden* in the far recesses of the cosmos. Michaelangelo understood the hidden process. In his painting of the Sistine Chapel ceiling with the finger of God on the right side of the ceiling extended toward *man* as the creative source and the SHAPE of the left hemisphere of the human brain in which language, violence and primal sexuality had been stored.

What Michaelangelo had been saying in his painting and not too obviously because of the Inquisition, was that God as the *hidden* is a creation of the left hemispheric human male mind.

The whole original female centered PHASE ONE story dealing with the birth and especially the death of the sun had been left behind along with the processes inherent in the female body and the body of Mother Earth. Linguistically they surface like a leit motif in a symphony but the constancy of the ear has to be tweaked to hear the refrain.

When you say that you had (HADA) something, it usually means that you ate it. And so the linguistic pancake. In Sanskrit ada (HADA) deals with eating. In Greek edein (HADA-) also means to eat, as edere (HADA-) does in Latin. In Hebrew sader (IS HADAra) means dinner. Had it dealt with the individual mother then eating would *not* have been the gift of air (HA). It would have been that which had been eaten, the individual object of ingestion. So all the above processes dealing with eating in which the dyad side (IS HADA) is contained deal with the side (IS HADA) of mouth-body combine of Mother Earth in PHASE ONE. In Hebrew hodes (HADASA) means mouth including Hadassah (HADAsa) a women's organization.

But there is also Hades (HADASA), the bloody (SA) side (IS HADA) as the mouth on the Western horizontal rim on the body of Mother Earth, It dealt with the separation of the sun from life into death and the subsequent in PHASE THREE Christian hell. Hell (HALA) has links with the Greek eelyos (HALAsa) dealing with the sun and its death at twilight creating the shades (IS HADAsa) of night. Hades (HADASA) was the Lord of Death consort of Hecate (HAKATA), (HAKA-KATA) the all embracing Mother Earth as the hacker (HAKA-) and cutter (KATA-) of the sun at twilight.

Shadow (IS HADAwa) comes out of that linguistic configuration. For a shadow is that which is cast upon the water (WA), the reflection that is like the real thing but is really an image of the real thing. The real thing was apparent but the reflection contained within it is the hidden reality of that which was above. Water is hydro (HADAra) in Greek.

A much more expansive interpretation of water as the killer of the sun surfaces mythologically in the Greek Hydra (HADAra). Her name gives us a clue, but who she actually had been goes much deeper. Defined as a serpent like sea dragon with snake like gifts, when one head was cut off two appeared in its place. She had a poisonous breath and left bloody tracks when killed. There are two ancient myths that surface in the creature called the Hydra (HADAra). One deals with the journey of the Kundalini snake as the guide of the sun once the sun had been perceived to have been lost in the underground watery maze. The serpent could be a snake, a dragon, a sea monster any one who fit the bill of guiding the sun back up to the light. The snake was not only considered to be a guide of the lost under ground sun but the metaphoric SHAPE carrier of the electro-magnetic Kundalini energy that sourced by the sun rising up through the crusty mantle of Mother Earth and entering the soles of human beings bringing them the gifts of ecstasy and knowledge.

There is also in that first configuration the concept of killing one head and two others grew back. The expanding universe makes its appearance here. There must have been a perception that went back to the molecular level of procreation. The original concept of birth dealt with the splitting of the mother molecule in half begetting two daughters. The daughters begat four more and geometrically down the line to accommodate this endless separation the universe or cosmos had to expand.

In the word cosmos (KASAMASA)) there glimmers an answer. The (SA) at the end is the blood of the mother (MA). (SAMA) in Polish means She alone. And (KASA) deals with the coos (KASA) where the mothers (MA) blood (SA), alone (SAMA), out of Her hidden coos (KASA), created all that was. Mother Earth recreating Herself as Hebe (HABA) the virgin, Herself out of Herself, virgin birth, parthogenesis in action had a snake in South America who performed the same function. The anaconda (HANAKANADA) can reproduce living young without male input.

But that is not the end of the story with Hydra (HADARA) she also had a poisonous breath and left bloody tracks wherever She went. SOUNDS like a volcano emerging like a nose out of the water spewing poisonous gas and a stream of lava out of Mother Earth's fiery depths. The Hydra (HADAra) may have come out of the water but She embraces within Her two aspects the watery expanse and the round ground of being of Mother Earth. We are dealing with PHASES TWO and THREE when male centrality gained momentum and all that Mother Earth created and represented had to be maligned as evil and summarily destroyed.

'Gift of air' as the Basque hodei (HADA or HADAYA) defines an actual gift of air. Falling off the Western side (IS HADA) into the abyss below created the concept that the sun had been heir to 'the gift of' air. An extended gift of air had also been considered as an idea (HADA) or (HADAYA). An idea (HADA) in Greek deals with looking. Idein (HADANA) deals with seeing. An ideal (HADALA) dealt with the picture in the mind.

Before the names of objects separated them from their ground of being there was no separation of the left hemisphere of the mind from the right hemisphere, they were balanced. The bifurcation of the two hemispheres started to occur when the objects perceived and named began to establish their own stories based on the why (Y) of their shared bifurcated periphery.

How is it that when human beings read actual words they create images in the mind and make their home in the brain? The ancients understood the power of words to create an alternate reality. Myths abound of secret words that had to be spoken to get at the gift inside. To spell had been understood to create a spell. It was to those images created by the words in the mind, the eyes of seeing, that left hemispheric fear had come to be linked. It was to those images trapped with fear that acted as a voice over giving the human creature no rest that they turned to means of stilling that fear and a rising into the realm of fearlessness which the birthing breath of the mother established creating an endless search and growing ritual for men. They travelled the world over looking for the right words to open the Sesame (IS haSAMA) that most often remained locked.

Associated with the ancient migrations were the two hundred thousand year old movers across the planet in a semi-annual procession following the herbivore herds. The Hadza (HADASA) people, the Olduvai Rift Valley Gorge hunter gatherers trudged across the planet semi-annually following the herbivore procession to the promised land of the verdant savannah. To move is cedere (IS HADAra) in Latin. It was moving to the side (IS HADA), to the area out of which the sun descended into the abyss of night. In Greek hodos (HADASA) deals with 'way' or 'journey'. In Polish chodzi (HADA-) means 'to walk'. In Persian a 'guide' for the journey is hadi (HADA). For the Hebrews Chadassah (HADASA) is a women's organization. It was the ladies (LADA-) who led (LADA) and were the leaders (LADA-) of the ancient migrations. They all deal with a movement toward the edge, to the then perceived side (IS HADA) of Mother Earth where the rain was falling.

The Western side (IS HADA) of Mother Earth where the death of the sun became encoded because it dealt with the male aspect of darkness, becoming a repository of many deities dealing with its demise. In PHASE ONE the life above the surFACE dealt with the mother. The reflected shadow (IS HADAwa) across a quietly standing stretch of water became associated with maleness, especially the eunuch priesthood.

In Amharic Adan (HADAna) the hunter surfaces as Mother Earth hunting and eating the sun (IS HANA) every night. It is out of Her Western side (IS HADA) where She swallowed the sun every night that this activity occured.

In Greek to eat is edein (HADAna). The pain that the sun must have experienced when it was masticated into little splintering bloody bits in Greek is odyne (HADAna).

The Phoenician and Cannonite God became Adon (HADAna), the one who at twilight nestled into the side (IS HADA) of Mother Earth. He surfaces as Adonai (HADAnaya) in Hebrew, also expressing the same concept as the sun disappearing off the side (IS HADA) of Mother Earth with the addition of (AYA) the Persian light becoming a celestial deity during PHASE TWO when the sun became a Hebrew transient god. The other Hebrew solar deities came up with names such as Samson, Samuel and Simon.

The Greeks took it a step further and came up with a beautiful male god hero Adonis (HADAnasa). He was no longer singularly a god becoming a transformed human but had been able to have children as the (NASA) at the end of his name indicates. Also for the Hebrews their Almighty God had been called a Shaday (IS HADAYA) or Shaddai (IS HADAYA) containing in his side (IS HADA) the AYA of the Persian light of the sun. The Hebrew God SOUNDS like a shadow (IS HADA) or a reflection. In Sanskrit their sun god had been Aditya (HADATAYA) also containing the (AYA) of the Persian sun light in his name. The Hebrew priesthood must not have thought that it was so painful for their name for splendor was hod (HADA) or the sight of the setting sun into the side (IS HADA) of Mother Earth. It was the wall of water into which the sun had been swallowed every night killed to its light that in PHASE THREE became the Hebrew wailing wall.

Cydippe (IS HADApa) statue sufaces in a Romanesque Cathedral with one leg and one foot missing leaning on a pastoral staff. SOUNDS like the crippled eunuch shepherd who became the herder of sheep during the last stages of mother centrality having links with the rites of the setting sun. Lib means not only to castrate but includes the activity of maiming.

For the Egyptians their God of the setting sun had been called Set (IS HATA), the (T) and (D) are interchangeable. The setting sun set into the tip, the edge, or the side (IS HADA) on the body of Mother Earth before the side of Mother Earth became a male domain in PHASE THREE dealing with the loss of the sun and a plunge into darkness. Hudi Gamma (HADA gama) was a Hindu Mother Goddess with transvestite castrated priests worshipping Artemis and Cybele. The Persian name for the Hebrews had been Yehudi (hayaHADA).

For the Sumerians Side Ninti (IS HADA nanata) was a Birth Goddess who enabled women to make babies out of their bones, their ribs and out of their sides (IS HADA) like Mother Earth did. Here we have intimations that the Biblical Adam having Eve out of his rib may have lifted the process from the Sumerians. It may be why so many native civilizations collect the bones of the deceased in order for them to make a clean journey into reincarnation.

The name for side (IS HADA) as an end or termination of the sun surfaces in Latin as the name for death itself in mother murder as matri-cide (-SADA (IS HADA), father murder as patri-cide (-SADA, IS HADA), insect murder as pesti-cide (-SADA (IS HADA), murder of self as sui-cide (-SADA (IS HADA). The linguistic leit motif of the linguistic symphony surfaces only if you give it a chance. Not to be left out is sidereal (IS HADArala) of the stars *away* and *above* the body of Mother Earth.

HALA OF ASCENT

HALA deals with the angular vertical SHAPE of the suns emergence out of the horizontal Eastern mouth on the flat round surFACE of Mother Earth that became encoded in the letter L originally associated with the tongue emerging at an angle out of the individual mothers mouth and neck in PHASE ONE. The tongue is Lengua in Latin.

In Ur (HARA) of the Chaldees 'the supreme God' in PHASE TWO was called EL (HALA) and has his origins in the belly of air through which the sun made its passage. In Greek, the 'sun' as eelyos (HALASA), containing in it not only the vertical angular SHAPE of the emergence or regurgitation of the sun out of the Eastern mouth on the surFACE of Mother Earth encoded in the letter L, but with (SA) of the coagulated lavic blood that it was perceived to have been constructed.

Using the RULE EIGHT OF REFLECTION for the Greek sun eelyos (HALASA), without the (SA) of the blood at the end, the construct emerges as (HALA/LAHA). The sun above the plane as eelyos (HALAsa) becomes reflected as the 'hidden' sun within the body of Mother Earth at night as (LAHA). For the Hawaiians LAHAR (LAHA-) means Mother Earth the container of the nocturnal sun. In South Africa the KALAHARI (kaLAHAra) Desert surfaces with a similar construct.

In the African language of Wolof the word for 'hidden' is loh (LAHA). It was also perceived that the sun emerged upon Mother Earth's surFACE, not only at a right angle, vertically out of Her flat circular horizontal surFACE but it came out of a cavity, a containment, a hole (HALA), the 'hidden' break of the circle at the horizon line.

The Polish word for 'wound' and 'dawn' in PHASE TWO, surfaces here as rana. The (NA) in rana deals with 'emergence on the surface' or the negation of a former state', of the sun (RA). The hole (HALA) or break at the edge also gave birth to the letter (C=kh) of creation the letter (G=jee) of generation and (G=gh) of be-getting with the circle ending at the horizon line broken, made into a hole, to let the sun through to be born to the light and life of a new day.

The sun born out of the broken circle at the horizon line when it emerged out of its watery depths became the 'whole' of creation, with the silent (W) of water leading it. As above so below, the reflected reality in the silent standing waters of the Okavango River Delta became encoded as the total or 'whole' cycle of life and death, the Yin Yang of the Chinese expanding also in PHASE TWO into the male-female construct.

The solar disc as HALA the SHAPE of emergence also surfaces, but not so obviously in the Spanish name for the sun as sol (IS HALA). It shares its journey of trans-formative rebirth through the entrails of Mother Earth with the human soul (IS HALA). Since the solar disc had been perceived to be immortal because it always returned at dawn, so the human soul (IS HALA) had been perceived to go on the same journey. That ancient perception in PHASE ONE substantiated the universal belief in reincarnation.

Then there is Alaska (HALASAKA). It establishes its links with an ancient perception of source. The tryad (HALASA) at the beginning establishes the sun, the Greek eelyos (HALASA). The (KA) at the end comes up with that which is small. The (LASA) deals with the SHAPE of the movement of the small solar disc up and out (LA) of the lavic body (SA) of Mother Earth. So Alaska hides in its linguistic coils not only the name of the small sun but how it emerged out of a volcanic eruption. The land of the midnight or small sun comes into focus. What were the Greeks doing in prehistory in Alaska to give it that ancient linguistic name?

HAMA OF BLOOD

HAMA, Ema (HAMA), or heoma (HAMA) in Greek is the name for 'blood'. The phoneme (HA) is the breath in the belly of air above the body of Mother Earth. (MA) deals with the universal mother in all of the languages of the world except the Japanese where she is called HA-HA associated with the birthing breath. When the sun died to its light, when it was swallowed into the great Western wall of water on the body of Mother Earth, it left a crimson footprint of its violent demise upon the bloody shimmering waters. It then was perceived that Her blood hid below Her crusty mantle going through the process of menstruation, coagulation and maintenance before it emerged pale and wan back upon Her surFACE. Mother Earth not only chewed the bloody solar disc into small edible pieces but shared the process with Her surrogates, the individual mothers of the specie.

It began out of the process of food ingestion in the individual mother as she chewed the morsels and regurgitated the masticated milled mash for her waiting brood. The ema (HAMA) of the Greek blood deals originally with the felled prey that as bloody mash was shared by the mothers with their hungry offspring.

As the SOUND of language was coming into its own in PHASE ONE it fell to the mother to teach her offspring how to survive, how to eat that which was safe. The most ancient original SOUND may have been the SOUND of humming (HAMA-), indicating which morsels were edible.

The hum (HAMA) of the individual mother also includes the giving of *assent*, of the teaching of her children that the food she was chewing in her mouth was m-m good, or edible *as sent*. She not only chewed tubers and berries, but also the felled bloody prey of birds and small animals that she often regurgitated to her waiting brood. MA expands into the concept of 'holding' and 'maintaining' extending to the body of Mother Earth.

HAMA is the dual symbiotic activity of the Mother Earth's belly of air (HA) above Her surFACE 'holding' (MA) the sun and the sun as the blood of life 'maintaining' the body of Mother Earth. When Mother Earth ate (8) the sun at the Western horizon, it dissolved into a bloody gore filled river that coursed underground through Her veins to become three creative processes; menstruation, as lavic blood that poured out during a volcanic eruption to create land, coagulation into the integral disc of the sun to be reborn at dawn, maintenance to keep Her alive and powerful. When Mother Earth ate the sun, she put Her lips together at the horizon and hummed (HAMA-) her acceptance that the sun was good, that it was worthy of being eaten, of being transformed through Her internal womb of re-creation.

The activity of humming (HAMA-) as acceptance, was shared by the individual mothers when they approximated their lips and hummed (HAMA-) to their children that the food they were *tasting* as they *tested* it, was edible. HAMA deals with the sanguine quality of the sun, as that which was not only 'bloody' but 'hopeful'.

Mother Earth said yes to the eternal habit of becoming. She hummed (HAMA-) Her acceptance to the goodness of the bloody sun, that it was ready not only to be eaten, but that it was worthy to pass through Her body to be transformed, ie coagulated into the integral disc of the sun on one hand

and as the outpouring of Her lavic menstrual blood into the creation of land upon Her surFACE on the other.

Keeping in mind that ema (HAMA) in Greek deals with 'blood', in its aspect as the bloody sun struggling for its life in the Western waters becoming the familial 'maintainer' and 'helper' to the body of Mother Earth the following Goddesses and other creative aspects enter into the mix.

Ama (HAMA) had been the Great Goddess of Mesopotamia and the East. Amma (HAMA) for the Dogon tribe of Africa as a male deity takes us to PHASE TWO. He created Earth and married her. The clitoris of the Earth as a nest of termites rose against the divine phallus, Amma (HAMA) had to cut it out to be born. Interpretation. Obviously Amma (HAMA) was the male sun in its bloody aspect cutting through the rim or edge on the body of Mother Earth, the circle ending at the horizon line. It not only gave birth to the broken letter (C=kh) of creation, and (G=jee) of generation and (G=gh) of be-getting, but the explanation and justification of a much more ancient practice of clitorectomies on human females. One of the Dogon twin children was a smith, a culture hero. He has links with the castrated, maimed and limping eunuch son out of PHASE TWO. The common name of Smith (IS MATA) surfaces in England.

Amata (HAMAta) (HAMA/MATA) The 'beloved' vestal virgin, bride of God in Rome out of PHASE TWO. The eternal virgin was Mother Earth creating Herself out of Herself without any external input in PHASE ONE. (HAMA) deals with her bloody aspect and MATA is the mouth (MATA) of the mother(MATAra).

Amaterasu (HAMAtarasa), the Japanese 'Heaven Illuminating Lady' out of PHASE ONE, who as the Goddess of the Sun, was at one with the body of Mother (MATA-) Earths terrain (TARA-). The (SA) at the end of her name, along with (HAMA) at the beginning, deals with the sun as a 'bloody' helper in the creation of light above Her surFACE. Following a universal trend of obliteration of the mother In PHASE THREE in the fourteenth century she became redefined as a male God.

Ambrosia (HAMAbarasa) supernatural red wine of Mother Hera, as the blood (HAMA or SA) of life. Spirits were used to awaken the BARA, the transformed conscious 'intermediate state' of the Tibetans. Mother Hera of the Greek triad was no longer Hebe a virgin. She had become a mother with the flow of lavic blood out of her belly (HARA).

In Persia a priest (eunuchized male), named Zarathustra, (IS HARA-) offered the sacrificial libation of the heoma (HAMA) plant as the ambrosia

(HAMAbarasa) drink to bring about a 'renewal' of the universe, bound up with the sun as blood, and with the cycle of the year. Since reincarnation and the soul going through the same journey of reincarnation as the sun (sol in Spanish) had been debunked by the Sumerian prince Gilgamesh, in PHASE TWO new systems of human belief and reorganization had to be established.

In Persia In PHASE TWO it became a battle between good and evil, light and darkness, heaven and hell, the left male hemisphere and the right mother hemisphere. In other words it became a battle between the body of Mother Earth and the emerging male sky gods representing the sun *above* and *away* from the body of Mother Earth. Light above Her surFACE became the 'good'. The sun sinking out of sight within the body of Mother Earth in darkness on its way to become transformed and reborn at dawn, became the 'evil'. Heaven as the domain of the emerging sky Gods, specifically the sun, becomes the 'good'. Hell (HALA) as the place where the sun set in the West, into the great hole (HALA) on the body of Mother Earth, to cook its way through Her burning interior became the 'evil', on its way to eternal damnation. The 'gift of' (DA), 'evil', became reclassified as the devil (d-evil).

In India, ambrosia (HAMAbarasa) as the elixir of immortality is made from the plant called soma (IS HAMA). For the Egyptians it was the SA or the 'wise blood of the mothers'.

The rush to rediscover the roots of immortality takes many different turns, but it seems to go back to the creative aspect of blood, Greek ema (HAMA), heoma (HAMA), Egyptian SA as the 'mothers wise blood', is the thread that runs through the universe to create a continuum, an immortality on the physical level of the specie, if not the 'spiritual' personality of the individual. That journey takes on a different route.

What becomes confusing is the fact that the sun in one of its permutations was believed to have been a bloody disc that was swallowed in the West by the body of Mother Earth at twilight. That is what the religions of the Middle East picked up on and turned it into the madness that exists to this day in the judgmental, joyless religions established by Abraham (habaraHAMA). He not only was a Hebrew (HABARA) but contains in his name the (HAMA) of Mother Earth's blood, the bloody sun as the elixir of immortality.

In Egypt the priestesses as 'singing mothers' were called shemat (IS HAMATA), (HAMA/MATA). The first dyad as (HAMA) either deals with the fact that the 'singing mothers' hummed (HAMA-), or the fact that they worshipped the Mother Earth-sun unit in its bloody Greek ema (HAMA) aspect. The second dyad as (MATA) deals with the mouth (MATA) of the

Section Two

mother (MATARA) in PHASE ONE before Her son RA at the end of the (MATA) dyad, became 'the doer', Her 'helper' out of the end of PHASE ONE and the beginning of PHASE TWO.

The Egyptian priests who officiated over the rites of the sun God Ra were called SHEM (IS HAMA). It may have been that Shem (IS HAMA) or Sem (IS HAMA), as the sons of Noah (NAHA) who had his own problems with the sun not returning, became the Semites (IS HAMATA), which goes back to the 'singing mothers' shemat (IS HAMATA) out of PHASE ONE. Semites (IS HAMATA) have more than ancient linguistic links with the Hamites (HAMATA). Both groups emerged out of worship of the ancient bloody Mother Earth-Sun, at one configuration.

The subsequent solar heroes of the Bible in PHASES TWO and THREE, surface with the ancient name for the bloody sun in them. Samson (IS HAMAsana), who as the sun God Shams-On (IS HAMAsa hana) or Shamash (IS HAMAsa) lost his power with the shorning of his hair, saara (IS HARA) is hair (HARA) in Hebrew.

Hair to the human head was like the rays of the sun were to the body of Mother Earth, Her celestial hair (HARA) that rose like branches through Her belly of air (HARA) at dawn. A bald pate was the sign of the castrated eunuch, but there was hope for Samson, for his hair grew back and he destroyed not only Delilah the Goddess with the gift of the yonic door, but the temple of her matriarchal reign. She was a metaphoric symbol for the body of Mother Earth who made him weak, ie dimmed his light, shaved his hair (the rays of the sun), as he descended into Her body for the night ie she seduced (IS HADASA-) him, CHADASSAH (HADASA) again.

There is also Samuel (IS HAMALA) who embodies in his name the small (IS MALA) sun (HAMA), the sun dead to its light, the 'dread lord', the 'leveler', 'judge' of the dead. Simon (IS HAMANA) establishes his links with the hated Egyptians and their highest God Amun (HAMANA), 'the hidden one' who masturbated existence into being every night. Maybe that is why the ancient Hebrew's were so adverse to masturbation. Blindness was a high price to pay for self gratification.

In the 'new world', the Aztecs did them all one better. To keep the bloody corridors within the body of Mother Earth lubricated with internal rivers of blood for the nocturnal journey of the sun, they sacrificed living victims on the altars of their dread that the sun would not return and that the soul would not be reborn.

With the enduring growth of violence against women and their children in PHASE TWO many women isolated themselves into tightly knit kinship groups to protect themselves against male rape and the kidnapping of their children into slavery. They were called the Amazons (HAMASANA), a name that they shared with the Biblical solar hero Samson (IS HAMASANA). Therefore in PHASE ONE their power base was the body of Mother Earth and Her relationship to the exuberant birth and the bloody death of the sun. She and the sun were considered to be one unit at this most ancient time. Mother Earth was the original virgin, for She gave birth not only to the sun by Herself, but to the land upon Her surFACE. She created Herself, by Herself, out of Herself. Male role in specific procreation was unknown. The Amazons were the ancient daughters of Mother Earth and were dangerous remnants of the old order as male dominance and their male Gods in PHASE TWO co-opted the scene. The Amazons as the creative power of women having its links with the creative powers inherent in the body of Mother Earth had to be not only obliterated, but their very existence had to be denied.

The African Berbers, who still retain some of the ancient mother centered customs, have the uncle as the head of the family. Paternity is known but not worshipped. The Berber women choose their husbands and divorce them at will. The ancient name of the Berbers is Amazigh (HAMASAGA) having links with the Amazons (HAMASANA), the amazing free women who covered much of the ancient North Africa, Middle East and Southern Asia.

HANA OF EMERGENCE

HANA, the sun (IS HANA) is a process that as (NA) 'negates a former state' or 'emerges upon the surface' and deals with change. When the sun rises in the East it negates (NA) the darkness of night (NA-). When it sets in the West it negates (NA) the light of day. The (HA) in (HANA) deals with the belly of air (HA) above the body of Mother Earth into which the sun rises. The process of reflection surfaces here also. It is clearly illustrated in the name of the Biblical 'grandmother' Hannah, (HANA/NAHA) who as the dual activity of the sun (IS HANA) reflects itself above (HANA) and below (NAHA) on the body of Mother Earth.

In PHASE ONE above Her body, the sun (IS HANA) had been considered to be Her helper, a relative, an aunt (HANATA) or even a grandmother, the Hannah of the Bible, also Hana as the grandmother in Old Iranian.

Below the plane (NAHA) deals with death and non-being and with nihilism (NAHALA-). In Latin nihil (NAHALA) means 'nothing'. In Polish nachalna (NAHALANA) is the word for 'pushy'. That is the state of the impatient

Section Two

dead carrying the seeds of life, waiting to re-emerge upon the surFACE, their impatience guiding them to push up through the mantle of darkness into the light, to be reborn to a new life. For the Bugotu, vunuha (vaNAHA) 'is the sacred place where men wait while sacrifices are being offered'. Out of the Bible in PHASE THREE, ark builder Noah (NAHA) also has had to deal with the demons of darkness represented by falling rain obscuring the sun and the subsequent swell of water that became the Biblical flood.

The many names of Goddesses; Ana (HANA), Anna (HANA), Ananta (HANATANA) Ananke (HANANAKA), Anath (HANATA), all deal with some aspect of the sun (IS HANA) as that which 'negates a former state' and 'emerges upon the surface' (NA).

Ana, Anna, (HANA), 'Lady of Heaven' in the Middle East and around the Mediterranean. The sun as the 'Lady' that illuminated the sky, was considered not only to 'emerge out' of the body of Mother Earth, out of the mountains at Her side in PHASE ONE, but to be at one with Her.

Ananta (HANATANA) The Hindu Serpent Goddess whose coils enfolded the sun (IS HANA) every night. The third dyad (TANA) comes from the ten (TANA) fingers that 'held'. In Latin tenere (TANARA) means, 'to hold'. The serpent or snake (IS NAKA), the rising Kundalini energy of Mother Earth had been considered to be the guide of the sunken (IS HANAKA-) sun (IS HANA) on its way to rebirth in the East, not only guided, but as the Serpent Goddess Ananta (HANANATA), embraced the sleeping solar disc at night. Ananta deals with the electro-magnetic Kundalini energy as the sleeping snake waiting to awake and to guide the sun to unwind to the light of a new day.

Ananke (HANANAKA), The Greek Goddess as 'necessity', another name for 'fate'. She was considered to be married to Chronos, father time and as such contained in herself the double aspect of 'time' and 'fate'. Because the third dyad in her name as (NAKA) is the name for the snake (IS NAKA), she is also associated with the passage of the sun (IS HANA) within the body of Mother Earth at night as the (NANA) double negation dyad of the moon establishes. Guided by the Kundalini energy as the metaphoric snake both the sun (IS HANA) and the moon (NANA) create the cycles that marked not only time, but the inevitability of 'fate' as a cycle of inevitable 'necessity'.

For the Egyptians the ankh (HANAKA) was the SHAPE of 'life', the round disc of the sun (IS HANA), emerging vertically out of the body of Mother Earth, pushed up to the surFACE with the help of the ubiquitous metaphoric Kundalini snake (IS NAKA), who like a tongue, shoved the ancient sun out of the body of Mother Earth and showed it way back up to Her surFACE. This perception had been shared at different times by not only the snake but the tongue, hands and fingers on the body of Mother Earth.

Eunuch (HANAKA (HANA-NAKA)) had been a castrated member of the ancient priesthood, the transformed male shaman uncle (HANAKALA), the psycho-pomp who officiated over the rites of the setting sun and as the guide of the sun (IS HANA) transforming its way through the body of Mother Earth, sharing his duties with the ubiquitous Kundalini snake (IS NAKA).

Uncle (HANAKALA), was the castrated first born son, the eunuch (HANAKA), uncle (HANAKALA) who shared in the protection of his mother's and sister's children. He was also the priest who stood at his mother's side officiating over the rites of the dead, and of the rising and setting sun (IS HANA). Channukah (HANAKA) Jewish 'festival of lights' having its roots in the sun (IS HANA) above the plane and the sun below the plane guided by the Kundalini snake (IS NAKA) to be born to its new light. It has links with the Egyptian ankh (HANAKA) the PHASE ONE eunuch (HANAKA) the uncle (HANAKALA) and the Sinclair (IS HANAkala) family in England (HANAgala). The (K) and (G) are interchangeable.

Sanguis (IS HANAGA-) as 'blood' in Latin, reiterates the perception that the sun (IS HANA) with the help of the ever ready KUNDALINI snake (IS NAKA, NAGA), the letters (K) and (G) are again interchangeable, floated through the entrails within the body of Mother Earth on a sea of blood to be reborn in the East. Sanguis (IS HANAGASA), establishes its links with the sun (IS HANA) and (SA) of sanguine out of SA the Egyptian 'wise blood of the mother'.

Sanguine (IS HANAGANA) in English means not only 'bloody' but also 'hopeful'. It seems that the return of the sun to shine in the sky may have been open to question for so many of the ancient rites deal with assisting the sun on its bloody passage so that it would be born again in the Eastern sky. Like the sun, 'hope 'sprang eternal out of the human heart. These perceptions may have had their origins out of an extended period of time when the sun was absent from the sky, when it rained endlessly flooding the soggy body of Mother Earth, or when a volcanic eruption obscured the light of the sun creating a cold dark and desolate wintry landscape. The Biblical Noah dealt with the former problem. The Aztecs really went overboard with this concern. As also hopeful it dealt with the menstruation inherent in the young girl that she would be ready to bear children.

Saint (IS HANATA) in PHASE THREE is a being having the enlightened god like characteristics associated with the sun (IS HANA) after having gone through the trans-formative process of having his 'sins' (IS HANA) castrated or burned clean by divine intervention in the abaton, ie originally passing through the trans-formative solar sourced oven within the body of Mother Earth, to become the terminus in the fires of the Christian hell in PHASE THREE.

Anath (HANATA) in the Middle East had been considered the twin of the Goddess Mari the 'Lady of Birth and Death'. She was called the 'Lady of Heaven' by the Egyptians, establishing her links with the sun (IS HANA). She was also fertilized by the sacrificial blood of men, not by their semen, since blood had been considered as the only source of life. This was in PHASE ONE before specific paternity became known. Her reputation survives as the killer of gods ie the spatial solar creations away and above the body of Mother Earth, representations of male search for their role in specific 'paternity' and 'source'.

On the other side of the world in darkened caves decorated by the Maya, part of male sacrifice had been the piercing of the penis in order for it to spurt with blood. It has links with the African custom of male mutilation of the penis in the creation of the universe and the flowing of blood, for the role of semen had not yet come into being.

HARA OF THE BELLY

Both the Egyptian houris (HARASA) and the Quechua huari (HARA) share ancient origins. The dyad hara in Hebrew defines the belly and deals with pregnancy harah (HARA), or that which can only take place within the female belly (HARA) or the approximation of a belly on the body of Mother Earth, the mountain or har (HARA) In Hebrew. The two words define the fact that the mountain har (HARA), on the body of Mother Earth, was pregnant, harah (HARA). It gave birth to Her son, the sun (RA) into Her belly of air (HARA) above Her surFACE. On the other side of the world, for the Japanese hara also means belly. HARA KIRI in Japanese deals with disembowelment, or the act of suicide based on preserving honor by slicing the belly in half.

It was perceived that in the dyad HARA, had been the belly, or the pregnant mountain. The sun (RA) rose out of the mountains at dawn, into the belly of air (HA), above the surFACE of Mother Earth. It was the ancient belly of life above Her surFACE through which the sun of daylight sailed that had been reflected by the womb of re-creation as the passage through the sun of night and death below Her surFACE. That was the area where the ancient houri (HARA) presided, in both the old and the 'new' worlds.

In PHASES TWO and THREE the priestess of 'great supernatural powers', who officiated over the rites of the dead, helped them in their passage of rebirth, healed the living, helped babies to be born as midwives and taught men how to pleasure their partners, became redefined as whores (HARA-). The ancient women believed that they needed no intercessors, no priests or rabbis to commune with their great Mother. Their states of trance created an entrance into the center, into where the fires of creation boiled and brought forth their fiery truth. All mothers and their children were the great Mother, only in individual, segmented, perambulatory forms. There was no separation. The separations and a great yearning for a reconnection came later. The yearning did not come to reconnect with the mind of the Father God in the sky. Human beings were never part of that rarified essence. The yearning to reconnect deals with the ancient grief that somehow, somewhere, a separation had occurred between humanity and the awesome body of Mother Earth and that the tools have been lost for humanity to find its way back.

Was the lament of Christ on the cross 'Eli Eli why hast thou forsaken me?' a belated realization that transformation and rebirth didn't come through the mind of God, but through the awesome body of Mother Earth? Was His emergence out of a cave an afterthought or a link to a very ancient mother based past? Leonardo Da Vinci emerged as a genius after he spent two years in a cave.

HASA OF BLOOD

HASA deals with the sun above the surFACE on the skin of Mother Earth. It deals with the rising of the sun in the East (HASAta) and the setting of the sun in the West. The Greeks called Hespera (HASApara) the nymph of evening who lived in the gardens of the West. In the East (HASAta) Homer called Eos (HASA) as being 'rosy fingered dawn'. The Vedas called Usha (HASA) as dawn, mother of the rays of the sun, eternally young, who brought enlightment. She was the daughter of Brahma, with whom he committed incest. Brahma as the male God coupled with the sun. In Polish the dyadic construct of usta (HASAta) deal with 'lips', and the 'lips' that are dealt with are the horizontal 'lips' on the body of Mother Earth out of whom the sun was born or regurgitated in the East (HASAta) at dawn.

The concept of dawn and beginnings are dealt with from another direction. The sun rising in the Eastern sky began not only the day but also the year for Easter (HASAtara) fell at the time of the Spring Equinox when the estral (HASAtarala) flow of blood from the buttox of the herbivore mothers announced that the time for the migration had begun. It was the time of parting and the time of beginnings. Hosannas (HASAnasa) were sung on two levels, the greeting to the birth of the sun ushering a new day and the expression of joy that the migration to the promised land of the greener savannahs had begun.

HAYA OF LIGHT

The dyad HAYA deals with the SHAPE of light itself. In Persian aya (HAYA), means 'light'. In Assyrian aya (HAYA), means 'dawn'. The letter A (ah) deals with the Alpha of beginnings, either as the triangular SHAPE of the volcanic cone that begat land, or the triangular SHAPE of the mountains that begat the sun at dawn. It was the light of the sun that actually awakened the body of Mother Earth from the slumbers of the dark night into the glow of a rosy dawn, as the birds sang their welcome and human beings sang their hallelujahs (halalAYA).

The letter Y flanked by the two letter A's on either side (AYA) stretches across the boundaries of Mother Earth and Her female surrogates in the creation of life. The letter (Y) is the SHAPE of the female pubis. The sun may have emerged out of the twin peaks, the mountains on either side, straddled by the two letter A's, those two helping hands that masturbated the sun out of Her pubis, but life as the light of the sun emerged out of the body of Mother Earth. With the first opening of the baby's eyes (HAYA), at the time of birthing, light as life came into being through the laboring bodies of individual mothers.

For the Yoruba tribe in Africa, Iyaloda (HAYALADA) (HAYA YALA LADA) a mother priestess as the midwife contains in her name not only the AYA (HAYA) of 'light' and 'dawn', but also the name of 'lady' (LADA) as her third dyad. Her second dyad as (YALA) not only surfaces with the color of dawn as yellow (YALA) but links it to the SHAPE of the female pubis. It also establishes the fact that there was a lot of Yelling (YALA-) by everybody when the sun awoke from its nocturnal slumber.

In Wolof their name for God in PHASE TWO is Yalla (HAYALA), including the (LA) of the Lady of the Land, as the SHAPE of the pubis on the female body, keeping yellow as the color of the sun. Dropping the (Y) of the female pubis, can the name of Allah in PHASE THREE be far behind?

For the Birhors of India, also out of PHASE TWO, their 'headman' named NAYA stands on his left leg with the right leg resting on his knee, like a stork (sounds like the crippled smith).

In Spanish the name for 'today' dealing with the rising of the sun at dawn is hoy (HAYA). In Polish hojna (HAYANA) means 'lavish', 'munificent', the 'best' and 'highest', the one who gives without waiting for gratitude or reimbursement. SOUNDS like the Polish hojna (HA(YA)NA) is dealing with the sun (IS HANA).

HAWWA (HAWA) or HEVEH (HAVA)

Mesopotamian name for Eve (HAVA). The name of Eve deals not only with evening, the beginning of night and the even distribution of day and night at the equator, but with the time of day at twilight when the sun set in the West. The second dyad in (HAWA) as the letter (W) deals with the setting of the sun in the evening in the Western wall of reflective water. To make that observation they must have been on the Eastern side of either a river, or a great lake.

It was the showers (IS HAWA-) in the distance, the fall of water from the sky, that showed (IS HAWA-) them how (HAWA) to proceed to the greener pastures. There was exuberant joy when the sun rose to help Mother Earth in Her great labors of creation and maintenance. There was also overwhelming sadness when the sun set in the West, at the end of its journey being chewed into little pieces and swallowed by the great horizontal Western mouth of Mother Earth. The helping hands of light pulled the sun down. It disappeared into the great maw off the horizontal plane, or descended into the peaks of the looming mountains, or sank into the great reflective rivers on the opposite shore. Weeping, wailing and the holding of wakes at the waters of the Western wall accompanied the death of the sun, beseeching it to awake at dawn and bless them with its wondrous light.

Whatever the avenue of its disappearance, along with the darkness, a great panic filled sadness settled upon many of the creatures on the body of Mother Earth. The perils of the dark night and of nocturnal predators who could smell out, not only the newly born calves, but also the terrified clusters of migrating humanity as they climbed up trees, clung to craggy ledges and huddled in darkened caves.

Section Two

The Role of PROCESS expanded

THE SUN (IS HANA)

One of the most ancient names of the sun (IS HANA) had been based on the dyadic structure of the word based on the (HA) SOUND defining the SHAPE of the belly of air above that supported the activity of life and through which the sun (IS HANA) sailed every day. In PHASE ONE it dealt with a tri-parted reality. One dealt with the sun in the air *above* the surFACE of Mother Earth. The second dealt with the sun *upon* the body of Mother Earth. The third dealt with the sun *below* Her planetary plane.

The (NA) SOUND in the sun (IS HANA) deals with the process of the suns emergence on the surFACE of Mother Earth. The (NA) SOUND stands for either 'emergence on the surFACE' or 'a change from a former state'. Some words will use more rules than others but the word sun covers many of the bases and has had its origins out of the side view of the nose (NASA) on the mother's face in stage one and the dual process of breathing in and out and the smelling of and the rejection of food. It also came out of an ancient time when in PHASE ONE Mother Earth and the sun had been considered as one familial unit.

As the Twenty Five RULES OF ORIGINAL SOUND DISCOVERY (ROSD) become familiar, it will become apparent that in English the word for sun (IS HANA), the word for hand (HANAda), the word for SOUND (IS HANAda), the word for song (IS HANAga) and even sanity (IS HANAta), come from PHASE ONE and emerge from the same ancient mother-sun based linguistic roots. The many names for the sun extend their linguistic solar fingers defining a host of ancient and contemporary processes. Using a multitude of rules to rediscover their ancient meanings, the further dissection of the word for the sun follows.

SUN (IS HANA).

RULE ELEVEN; The SOUND of the letter S (ss) is an EMPHATIC dealing with 'it is', remove it from the beginning words. SUN becomes (IS UN).

RULE TEN; Place the letter H (huh) before a word that begins with a vowel, (IS UN) becomes (IS HUN). Many of the words beginning with a vowel often dropped the unvoiced (H) SOUND.

RULE NINE; Place the A (ah) SOUND behind every consonant. (IS HUN) becomes (IS HANA). The A (ah) SOUND became the first codified both vowel and consonant SOUND. It established the concept of the Alpha of beginnings with the (AH) SOUND associated with the intake of the baby's first breath.

Cobbled together the word for the sun emerges as (IS HANA). HANA as the sun (IS HANA) defines the sun in its passage *above* the body of Mother Earth through Her belly of air. The phoneme (HA) deals with the belly of air, the breath above the body of Mother Earth. The phoneme (NA) deals with two concepts that had their inception in the activity associated with the nose on the mother's face. One is 'the negation of a former state'. The other is 'emergence on the surface'. So the sun as it spreads its brilliance upon the surFACE of Mother Earth in the Eastern sky at dawn negates the state of perilous darkness of night. When it sinks (HANAka) out of sight into the watery horizontal rim in the Western sky it negates the blessings of daylight.

RULE EIGHT; ANASTROPHE, PALENDROME, REFLECTION. If the SUN (IS HANA) deals with the passage of the sun through the belly of air during the day, then its *reflection* in the still waters of Okobango River inland delta deals with the passage of the sun after it sinks out of sight in the Western waters, swallowed back into the body of Mother Earth for the night. Mother Earth ate the sun drawn by the number eight (8).

Not only are the subterranean tunnels within the body of Mother Earth wet, dark, convoluted and cold, but darkness envelops the nocturnal sun below the plane. Nothing is left of its light above the surFACE as its r*eflective* self guided by the ever present sagacious Kundalini snake slithering its way through Her hidden intestinal canals makes its way back up to the light to help the sun to emerge pale and wan, regurgitated and triumphant, a winner in the light of the Eastern sky.

The linguistic evolution of the word for the sun (IS HANA) as the solar disc above the plane during the day follows the same process of *reflection*. The dyad HANA as the sun (IS HANA) above the plane, becomes NAHA, (HANA/NAHA), the reflected sun below the plane.

RULE NINE, placing the A (ah) SOUND behind the consonants the Latin word nihil (NAHALA) stands for 'nothing', or the *reflected* (NAHA) of the sun (IS HANA) (HANA/NAHA) becoming nothing, negating its power over the darkness of night.

The (LA) phoneme at the end of nihil (NAHALA), deals with the angular SHAPE of the sun in one of its other linguistic manifestations as the Spanish sol (IS HALA) or the SHAPE of the angular emergence of the sun at dawn out of Her horizontal rim in the Eastern sky.

Section Two

The (LA) of (HALA) in (NAHALA) has its roots in the angular SHAPE of the tongue in stage one pushing food out of the mother's mouth. It expands to include the mouth of Mother Earth in stage three also using Her hidden tongue to push the sun out of Her mouth at Her Eastern horizontal rim. (HALA) is one of the names of the risen sun in PHASE ONE. When it rises in the Eastern sky, the SHAPE of the vertical angle of the risen sun becomes encoded in the letter L for light and life. When it descends into its watery grave in the Western horizontal rim it becomes encoded in the SHAPE of its fall off the flat circular side (IS HADA) of Mother Earth and into the SHAPE of the subsequent number seven (7) (IS EVEN) associated with life and death or (HAVANA) the passage into transformation.

RULE FOURTEEN; Repetition of DYADS, deals with two different consonants based on the same A (ah) SOUND as (HA) and (NA). The actual name Hana surfaces as the name of the Old Iranian clan matriarch out of PHASE ONE at one with the sun. If the clan mother in ancient Iran ruled as the wise old matriarch then the same qualities were shared as the wisdom of Mother Earth who was the *ul*timate ruler. Mother Earth and the sun at the time of humanity's most ancient heritage (HER IT AGE) were considered not only to be one uni-versal unit, but a very close knit female (FAMALA) based family (FAMALA), mirroring the human family on Her surFACE. At different times, other relatives stepped in to play the role, the aunt (HANATA) as a helper was also considered. To Mother Earth, the sun (IS HANA) as the old Iranian matriarch Hana had been considered to be out of PHASE ONE a wise old female and comforting grandmother.

As the helping hand (HANADA) to Mother Earth, the sun in many of its aspects and definitions surfaces with the actual word for hand (HANADA) in English as (DA), the *'gift of'* the sun (IS HANA). On Egyptian stelas the solar disc is shown as the rays of the sun pointing down and ending in right hands that helped Mother Earth.

RULE TWENTY ONE; GODDESSES; Anatolia contains the tryad of the Grandmother Goddess Hannahanna (HANAHANA) (HANA-NAHA-HANA) also carries the helping hand of the sun (IS HANA) in her name. Her name deals with three aspects of the sun (IS HANA) as a continuous process, above the plane as (HANA) of shining (IS HANA-) in daylight. Below the plane she survives as the nihil (NAHA-) of Latin nothingness, night and darkness, to emerge back up above the plane as the shining (IS HANA-) sun (HANA). In Her name she completes the triangular cycle associated with the journey of the sun; uni-verse, *above* the surFACE of Mother Earth, *upon* the surFACE of Mother Earth and *below* the surFACE of Mother Earth.

RULE FIFTEEN; Repetition of WORDS; Hannahanna becomes the Hannah of the Bible, also as the wise old Earthly grandmother and originally out of humanity's prehistoric heritage as the celestial helping hands of Mother Earth carrying light up to Her surFACE during the day and dragging it back down into nothingness for the night. The name Hannah (HANA/NAHA) reflects itself and covers both bases; *above* as the shining sun (IS HANA) and *below* as the dark sun of nothingness, the Latin nihil (NAHA-).

RULE SIX; PHONOLOGICAL CORRESPONDENCE; The letters H (huh), K(kh), and G(gh) because they are made in the same area in the oral cavity are often interchangeable. In the words nihil (NAHA-) in Latin for 'nothingness', the snake (IS NAKA) and Nagas (NAGASA) the ancient serpent Kundalini blessed people of India, all deal with the nether aspect of the sun at night under the plane of Mother Earth. Through the nothingness of the dark night the ever present metaphorical Kundalini energy symbolized by the snake and serpent slithering through the convoluted internal intestines guided the sun back up to the light. Not only do they share a similar activity and place but the letters H, (NAHA) of the Latin nihil (NAHALA) of nothingness, the letter (K) of (NAKA) of the snake (IS NAKA) and the serpent people of India as the (G(gh) in Nagas (NAGASA) also reflect their origins out of the same area of the oral cavity of the mouth.

RULE NINETEEN; METAPLASM, transposition of letters. In Polish the word for 'munificent' and 'lavish' is choiny (HAYANA) containing within the ancient construct of (HAYANA) the Aya of light in Persian and dawn in Assyrian. The Ya of the Yaay (YAYA) in the African language of Wolof defines the *'mother'* or *'old woman'*. In this case the light of the sun is not only the *'old woman'* but the *'mother'* which means that the body of Mother Earth and the sun in PHASE ONE were considered to be the uni-verse, at one, or one complete unit. In Polish jaja (YAYA) is the name for eggs, another creative mother based source.

There emerges a progression in the following perceptions. It is not Mother Earth's mouth in stage one that does the swallowing of the sun in the West and regurgitating it in the East but there is a movement in stage three into the rest of Her magnificent supportive body.

As the sun rose in the East, its fingers as rays of light stretched up into the heavens and like stilettos pierced the pall of darkness with the promise of dawn across the newly lit sky. The sun (IS HANA) was dependable, like the two hands (HANAda) of the individual mother were dependable, always working in concert. No matter what happened, the sun rose out of the body of Mother Earth every morning out of the mysterious cleft between Her gestating mountains in the East. At twilight it sank back into Her even more mysterious watery waiting maw in the West. It created a succession of ands (HANAda) of cyclical solar repetitions.

At the beginning of each day, one hand (HANAda) carried light up to Her surFACE to resume its job of maintaining life. At twilight the other hand pulled the light back down, to begin its trans-formative journey of rebirth through Her body, to rise, or be 'born again' in the East. *Above* the plane and *below*, rising and setting working in tandem, the sun like the hands of the mother the universal maintainer were predictably dependable.

The concept of sanity (IS HANA-) came from the habitual predictability of the rising and the setting of the sun. It could always be depended on. The word sane (IS HANA) also has ancient links with the sun (IS HANA). It was not like the 'shape shifting' moon that disappeared periodically. It was not like the clouds, that almost always came seasonally, but sometimes delayed to end the drought sourced famine in the parched savannah. It was not like the stars that turned like a great wheel in the night sky changing their patterns to the searching eye.

The sun was always there at dawn, consistently a flat, often pale and wan circular disc, filled with the promise of light, ready to travel across the belly of air and do its job. When its job was over, it silently, without any fanfare, set back into the body of Mother Earth. It was truly a dependable helper.

Everything came to life when the sun rose at dawn. When a hint of rosy light spread across the Eastern sky, the birds stirred even before dawn, bursting into a cacophony of rapturous song (IS HANAga) to awaken the slumbering sun from its nocturnal sleep. As the golden glow in the Eastern sky spread out into the belly of air above them, apes howled and screeched their welcome. The SOUND (IS HANADA) as the 'gift of (DA) the sun (IS HANA), spread to all the corners of their ancient light drenched savannah.

Even human beings joined with aves (HAVA-) in the exuberant chorus of gratitude, singing (IS HANA-) and dancing, clapping their hands, thumping their heels, that Mother Earth at dawn, *heavy* (HAVA) with the 'hidden' solar disc, in one of Her great labors, out of Her pregnant mountainous belly at the horizon line, ready to *have* (HAVA) Her most helpful solar offspring, *heaved* (HAVA-) the sun up into the *heavens* (HAVANA).

RULE TWENTY TWO; METAPHORIC CREATURES, Some of the concepts of 'hidden' had their source out of the mothers body and the bee hive

(HAVA), where the activity of the queen bee, of 'being', continued her singular unrelenting egg laying in the secret hidden recesses of the bee hive. The queen bee was one of the major metaphoric symbols for Mother Earth who also singularly created life out of the secret 'hidden' internal recesses within Her body. On one level on Her surFACE She created plants and burrowing creatures, on another level on Her tip at Her horizontal rim She gave birth to the sun, moon, stars, clouds and even birds.

In Polish the word for a bee hive is *ul* (HALA) and on one hand morphs into the English word for *ul*timate, (HALA-) and on the other hand has links with the Spanish word for the sun, sol (IS HALA), and the English word for hole (HALA). For it is out of the hole (HALA) or wound on the horizontal Eastern rim of the body of Mother Earth that the sun, the Spanish sol (IS HALA) was perceived to have been born every morning at dawn.

Also in Polish the word for 'hidden' is chova (HAVA). In PHASE THREE the redefined 'hidden' Hebrew God Yahveh (YHVH) (YAHAVA) or Jehovah (JHVH) (JAHAVA) through the second dyad (HAVA) in his name, establishes his links with the ancient mother based 'hidden' sun waiting to be born out of the metaphoric *'hidden'* bee hive (UL) as the body of Mother Earth in PHASE ONE.

The (YA) of Yahveh (YAHAVA) is a throw back to the PHASE ONE mother centered past when the letter (Y) as the SHAPE of the pubis out of stage two defined the place out of which creation issued forth from the female body. The pubic SHAPE was shared by the body of Mother Earth as one of the SHAPES of the openings of solar creation, the pubic cleft between two mountains out of which the sun emerged every morning.

RULE SEVEN; ANLAUT, The first SOUND or letter in a word often establishes its meaning.

The above names for God in Hebrew as Yahveh and in Wolof the name of God as Yalla, emerging out of the SHAPE of the pubis (Y) on the female body and the SHAPE of the cleft between two mountains on the body of Mother Earth, establish their links with the birth of the ancient sun out of mother centrality in PHASE ONE. In Persian Aya means *'light'*. In Assyrian Aya means *'dawn'*.

If the name of Yahveh came out of a more ancient past in PHASE ONE, then the name of Jehovah looked to the future. For the (JA) in Jehovah (JAHAVA) establishes its SOUND with generation (JA) and its links to the newly emerging representative of the sun, the Christian Son (IS HANA) of God who as Jesus (JASASA) also appropriated the name of the supreme

Greek male deity Zeus (SASA) in His name. The East represented by Jehovah of the Hebrews and the West represented by Zeus of the Greeks met on more than one level in the name of Jesus.

RULE TEN; Place the letter (H) before words beginning with a vowel. In PHASE THREE the Middle Easterners dropped the (Y) SHAPE of the female pubis at the beginning of the name for the Wolof deity Yalla, and it became ALLA (HALA) and can go in a variety of directions, one emerges as Allah (HALA) of the Muslims. As (HALA) it has links with the sun, eelyos (HALA-) in Greek.

RULE EIGHT; ANASTROPHE, PALENDROME, REFLECTION It can also go in the direction of REFLECTION for LA is REFLECTED by AL, (AL/LA) and establishes ancient links with the Mid Eastern sun AL (HALA)) and the body of Mother Earth (LA) as the one creative uni-versal REFLECTIVE unit out of PHASE ONE moving into PHASE TWO.

Sometimes, depending where the human travelers following the herds were on their migratory trek, the sun rose out of the flat plane on the body of Mother Earth at the horizon, out of Her very side or mouth on the Eastern horizontal rim. At other times the sun rose out of the mountains that were considered to be great gestating bellies that held the solar disc before it was born, the hara of the Hebrews. Then there were times, when the sun seemed to rise out of the depths of the waters, reflecting its glory as it separated itself from its watery self, ascending into the great belly of air above Mother Earth's surFACE. At all times, as the sun rose, it was greeted with a noisy welcome that held much reverence, love and joy. The sun was considered Mother Earths greatest offspring, her major helping hand. As it daily rose out of its watery womb it had been perceived to win (WANA) its battle for survival. The (NA) deals with 'emergence on the surface' and (WA) deals with the waters out of which it made its appearance.

The perception that the sun was Mother Earth's 'helping hand' also surfaces in Polish using a different set of phonemes. In Polish the name for 'hand' is reka (RAKA). The phoneme (RA) out of PHASE ONE deals with the Egyptian sun God, Ra. The phoneme (KA) deals with the body of Mother Earth in Her job as ultimate creator of smaller aspects of Herself, out of the X of the female buttox halved vertically and by the SOUND specifically associated with egg laying birds. The phonemes (RA) and (KA) together, establish the fact that the sun (RA) and the body of Mother Earth (KA) like actual hands worked in tandem. At the time that this dyad came into being at the very end of PHASE ONE they were still considered to be at one or one unit of creation.

How the Egyptian sun god Ra linguistically surfaces way up in Poland defining a process out of PHASE ONE of mother centrality, is anyone's guess.

Paintings of the sun as the helping hands of Mother Earth emerge with pristine clarity on the walls of Egyptian temples after Akhenaten or Amenophis IV in PHASE THREE, shifted from the worship of many deities into the worship of a single solar deity, the Aten (HA(TA)NA), as the solar disc with his solar rays as extended hands pointing downward. At the end of the solar rays were open right hands ready to help Mother Earth in the job of maintaining life upon Her body. The fact that the depicted hands are right hands deals with the fact that it exists in PHASE THREE and the perception that it was the right hands of the father, not the left hands of the mother that were being presented as the sole solar maintainer and helper. The body of Mother Earth as singular source in PHASE ONE had already been left behind.

The Hebrew priesthood that as slaves trapped in Egypt, took this concept one step further and created the monotheistic 'hidden ' God, the underground God, the reflected God, the metaphoric hidden bee hive (HAVA) as the helping hands of Jehovah (-HAVA) after He morphed out of His solar past but still setting into the body of Mother Earth and as his name indicates was *'hidden'* from sight. In PHASE THREE Christianity brought the solar disc back up to the light as the son (IS HANA), the risen sun (IS HANA) Jesus of the same *'hidden'*, formless left hemispheric God.

The sun also helped to bring the clouds billowing back out of the body of Mother Earth, out of Her side at the horizon line. The drenching showers out of Her belly of air coincided with the estral flow out of the bellies of herbivore mothers (as above so below). The rains created the marshes. Marshes exploded with insects. Insects alerted the birds to make their semi annual pilgrimage. The coming of the rains and the passage of birds stirred the blood of the migrating herbivores into movement to the wet and marshy 'greener pastures', followed by the rag tag human mother based family.

The sun and the moon, after they passed across the belly of air above Her surFACE descended into the mysterious swallowing maw in the West. They emerged on the other side in the East out of the subterranean recesses within Her body. It was as if the sun and the moon were not only helping hands to the body of Mother Earth, but were also like the air that went in and out of Her body and the bodies of living creatures.

If in English the sun (IS HANA) was the helping hand (HANADA), gift of (DA), the sun (IS HANA) during the day, then in Spanish the moon (MANA) was also a helping hand but at night. Manos (MANA-) are hands in Spanish.

It was also perceived that when the sun rose to the light of day, it said yes to life, like the hum (HAMA) of the individual human mother said yes to life, as she indicated that the food that she was chewing was not only edible, but safe and ready for ingestion. Both the sun and the mothers hum SOUND used the air as a vehicle of passage.

The hum (HAMA) of the individual human mother indicating that the food was edible became associated with the metaphoric mouth of Mother Earth swallowing the heavenly bodies, especially the sun, eating them in the West, indicating that they were good, that they were ready to become transformed, ready for them to pass through Her internal oven (HAVANA) to emerge into the dawn of a new life.

One of the processes that the sun went through after it disappeared bloody and tattered into the body of Mother Earth was to become Her maintaining blood, ema (HAMA) in Greek.

At different times in their predictable semi annual passage, the sun always sank, died to its light, was swallowed back down into an open mouth, or maw in the Western horizontal rim. The fact that it was swallowed by a *mouth* (MATA) on the edge of the surFACE of Mother Earth in PHASE ONE by a break in the circle around them that ended at the horizon line, almost never varied.

The perceptions of the birth of the sun out of the body of the great maternal womb were more imaginative. As it rose out of Her horizontal side in the Eastern sky at dawn, sometimes the sun not only emerged out of Her mouth (was regurgitated), but it also emerged out of Her horizontal vulva. At times, metaphorically Her anus and even Her armpits came into play.

The most ominous hole out of which the sun emerged out of the body of Mother Earth was when it had been considered to be a wound at Her circular horizontal siderial rim. The horizontal circle had to be cut open by the stiletto like rays of the sun as cutting fingers, (F), for it to emerge out of Her body at dawn. The SHAPE of the cut on the horizontal circle gave birth to the letter (C-kh) of *'creation'*, the letter (G-jee) of *'generation'* and (G-gh) of *'be-getting'*, bear witness to that circular break around them at the horizon line, the round ground of being out of which life and light carried by the sun emerged out of a wound, to dwell vertically as life and light upon Her surFACE. In Polish RANA deals with both wound and dawn. Not to be left out rain (RANA) comes out of the same linguistic dyad.

TWENTY-FIVE RULES OF ORIGINAL SOUND DISCOVERY (ROSD)

RULE ONE;
Monogenesis The Single Source of Language

Most of the existing languages of the world evolved out of the remnants of humanity that survived the last series of cataclysms and climate changes in and around Equatorial Africa. As SOUNDS they even go further back to the African continent into the time of female centrality out of PHASE ONE. As climactic conditions shifted and the migrations of the herbivore herds adjusted to the changing patterns of the falling monsoon rains, the expanding use of human language occurred out of the Olduvai Gorge with the Hadza people, the Saan Bushmen of the Kalahari, the Berbers of the the Sahel, and the Ethiopian Highlands, bordering the ancient expansive and still verdant Sahara Desert, then North into the regions above the desiccating Sahara and North Africa, above to the Iberian peninsula, East into the sub continent of Asia, then North East into the Tundra and the great echoic stretches of Asia, eventually West to Europe and across the expanse of the great sea to (what has been described as the 'new world) of native Americans and the Maya of Central America.

With the loss of rainfall in what is now the Sahara Desert, the migratory patterns of the herbivore herds would have shifted South to the Sahel followed by the migrating clans of humanity. They do have their linguistic origins out of the perpetually even distribution of the seasons, one wet the other one dry and out of the even distribution of day and night, the latter process occurs only at or near the equator.

As there are no actual lines of demarcation delineating countries on the globe, so there are no real lines delineating ancient languages and or, existing contemporary tongues no matter how apparently diverse they seem to be. The categorization of languages is for the sake of study and is as arbitrary as are the boundary lines that separate countries on the global map. The categorization of languages emerged out of PHASE TWO as left hemisphriric linear mles began to create their own systems to which they created new and specifically male understood languages.

Depending on the changing patterns of climate which dictated the ancient migratory marches of herbivores and humans, language emerged out of mother based experience in PHASE ONE and out of shifting areas in equatorial Africa spreading in time with migrating humanity in ever expanding circles to all of the corners of the ancient world. Their linguistic and mythical journey can be tracked through mother centrality, the universal worship of the Kundalini snake electro-magnetic energy, addiction to the numbers three, seven and thirteen to the persistent and expanding role of the much misunderstood and ignored universal eunuch priesthood.

As humanitys ancient ancestors populated the far reaches of the planet, they carried with them the phonemes that created the original SOUNDS. The only potsherds that remain from those very distant times are the SOUNDS that are still carried upon the wind. Like leit motifs are often hidden in a symphony, they lie hidden in *all* of the contemporary languages of the world.

The ancient dispersal covered a period of many thousands of years. It predates known and often guessed at ancient cataclysms and climactic changes that sent humanitys ancestors searching for food and new places to inhabit. They may have traveled by foot, by caravan or dugout canoe, even in reed boats. With an approaching tsunami or a shattering volcanic earthquake, they may have had to leave behind all that they held dear, but they carried with them their babies, their identifiable tattoos, their experiences, their belief systems and their mother sourced songs that those experiences and those belief systems gave voice to.

Like the code of the molecular DNA existed at the beginning of creation and continues to exist in contemporary life forms, so the SOUNDS that existed at the beginning of human communication still maintain their ancient integrity, if only the RULES to decipher them could become known. The waves of recognizable SOUND carried by humanity, the woof as the leit motif of the fabric, splaying out from the center in all directions, some echoing in both of the hemispheres of the new world', some surfacing in the far reaches of the South Pacific, some poking their way through the contemporary SOUNDS still made by the Maori of New Zealand, while others lying hidden in isolated pockets of the world, not as yet explored by 'civilization', will in time and with patience give up their ancient and single sourced mother based linguistic secrets out of PHASE ONE.

To believe that language popped up spontaneously around the world is simplistic nonsense. Language spread its specific mother based origins into a wide global net from a single mother based African source. To say that language popped up here and there in distant locations that had no links to each other based on evolutionary impulses that have no common source is like saying that dogs in all of their diversity have no common ancestor. It's like saying that Chihuahuas and the St. Bernard didn't both evolve out of the wolf and like spontaneous combustion burst fully blown upon the canine scene.

There may have been a time that it was believed that the great diversity among dogs came from different species. But if you trace them back through their genes, you realize that *all* dogs have their primal beginnings out of the wolf. The magical thing is that the wolf is still with us and the diversity that emerged out of that specific canine creature can be studied. So it is with language. The cacophony of original SOUND used by human beings to communicate can be traced to a single mother based source out of Africa.

The original mother sourced SOUNDS that began language, surface in *all* of the contemporary languages of the world. After they are recognized they can be followed like a leit motif can be followed in a symphony, or read like the molecules in a DNA sequence.

The contemporary SOUNDS may SOUND very different to the modern ear, but the Chihuahua doesn't look very much like its ancestral grandparent the wolf, neither does the St. Bernard. Even more fantastic is the reality that the Chihuahua and the St. Bernard, who don't look at all alike have a common ancestor.

Like the convoluted journey through the history of canine evolution can be traced back to the wolf, so the cacophonic cluster of contemporary language can be traced and its shining skeletal frame exposed as having its original source out of specific areas in Africa dealing with the face of the individual mother and the metaphoric surFACE of Mother Earth.

The most ancient origins of language primarily as SOUNDS wedded to the SHAPES that come out of PHASE ONE of humanity's mother centered heritage (HER IT AGE). Magically and mysteriously they surface as the still recognizable SHAPES of the contemporary capital letters of the Western Alphabet, having their ancient original, physical dawning out of the clusters of mother based families who following the herbivore herds for an extra supply of milk guided humanity across the varied terrains of ancient Africa.

Examples of MONOGENESIS and the lack of linguistic borders using the example of the Eye. In Polish in its most ancient linguistic word out of the individual mothers face the eye is OKO. The two O SHAPES on either side of the letter K establish the eyes as two visual orbs that flank the letter K at

Section Two

the center. The letter K has originally been the letter X halved vertically, the place above the nose and between the two eyes where the criss-crossing of the body and brain occur. It is also the area of the third eye where the focus into the realm of the electro-magnetic shakti of the Kundalini trance has its brilliant explosion.

The eye on the human face had been perceived to reflect reality. That same activity had been expanded to metaphorically include the surFACE of Mother Earth. Her great *seas* were there to *see* that which was reflected above Her. In the central expanses of Africa there exists an internal river delta called the OKAvango that floods periodically creating a verdant savannah and marsh for the foraging creatures and migrating humanity.

The consonants stay constant. The vowels do their SHAPE shifting dance. The *oka* in *Oka*vango as the inernal sea establishes it's links with the Polish *oko* as the eye that *sees* on the surFACE of Mother Earth. On the other side of the world in Florida there is an expansive relatively placid inland sea called lake OKEechobee, another placid body of water, another inland *sea* that *sees* the sky. In Namibia Lake Ochikoba may have been its linguistic pre genitor. In Polish ochy also means eyes. Then a bit further up in Georgia you have the OKEefenokee Swamp another *oko* on the surFACE of Mother Earth that sees and reflects the sky. In British Columbia even further up, the OKInagen River flushes with its reflective glory. Further West in the grand open Pacific Ocean the Island of OKInawa shifts gears a bit. It is an island with the name that begins as a eye *oko* in Polish. Broken down linguistically the (WA) at the end deals with water. The (NA) deals with either' a change from a former state', or an 'emergence on the surface'. The *Oki* establishes the eye. So *Oki*nawa is the island that emerges (NA) out of the watery (WA) sea that like an eye *(OKI)* reflects the sky.

There are probably more, but the similar word surfaces around the world specifically in Poland as the ancient OKO. It has its origin even further back as OXO and even further back using RULES of ORIGINAL SOUND DISCOVERY (ROSD) with both Oko (HAKA) and Oxo (HAKASA) establishing the reflective process of water as a *hacking* (HAKA-) agent. Originally the hacking (HAKA-) quality had been associated with the hook (HAKA), the lower jaw on the human face in stage one and the carnivore animal snout that did the hacking. It expanded to include the hacking quality on the body of Mother Earth and Her aqua (HAKA) the Latin water as the hacker (HAKA-) of reality in twain.

RULE TWO;
Stages

There are FIVE STAGES delineating the SHAPE and SOUND of the capital letters of the Western Alphabet out of the individual mothers face including the metaphoric surFACE of Mother Earth. In their own individual way they are their own pictographs. Eventually obvious, but apparently hidden meanings are locked in them.

Stage One; Individual Mother's Face;
The most ancient recognizable SOUNDS that became the consonant capital letters of the Western Alphabet out of PHASE ONE had initially been wedded to the SHAPES of the organs that created them out of the INDIVIDUAL MOTHERS FACE.

Stage Two; Surface of Mother Earth;
Since individual mothers were considered to be surrogates in the creation of matter upon the SURFACE of MOTHER EARTH they metaphorically expanded to include the implied organs on the apparently flat round surFACE of Mother Earth.

Stage Three; Individual Mothers Body;
Then as organs, process, quality, function and concepts they began to emerge to include the SHAPES of the various pertinent parts on the INDIVIDUAL MOTHERS BODY.

Stage Four; The Body of Mother Earth;
Following a preset pattern of perception dealing with the various pertinent parts on the INDIVIDUAL MOTHERS BODY a further expansion occurred to metaphorically include the all embracing BODY of MOTHER EARTH.

Stage Five; Other Creatures;
The SHAPES and SOUNDS of other creatures; bees, snakes, elephants, bats and octopus (KRAKEN) lions especially birds were added to the linguistic mix.

Many of the letters and writing itself out of PHASE ONE and mother centrality faced to the left as if written by the left handed mothers and persist to this day in Hebrew, Early Brahmin, Etruscan, Phoenician, Early Greek, Tyrrhemian, Faliscan, Lydian, Early Latin, Siberian, Celtic. In PHASE THREE as male role in specific paternity was becoming known, with the over evolution of the linear single focused left hemisphere of the human brain,

Section Two

many of the letters and writing itself shifted to the right as if written by the right hand of the fathers.

As there have been THREE PHASES that defined the shift from female to male centrality, so there also have been FIVE STAGES within PHASE ONE that moved singularly from the SHAPE of the organs on the individual mother's face that emerged as the capital letters of the Western Alphabet, to the SHAPE of those same organs as they have been perceived to exist upon the metaphoric surFACE of Mother Earth. The same facial organs that the individual mother possessed were believed to have existed in that big round flat maternal surFACE under their feet that ended in a circular sweep around them at the horizon line.

Like the individual mothers who pushed food out of their mouths, out of their round flat faces, Mother Earth also fed Her creations after She too pushed them and their source of maintenance out of Her top, tip or surFACE.

The individual mother chewed morsels behind that lower hole of her mouth and when they were finely lubricated she regurgitated them to her eager young. Therefore Mother Earth must also have had a break in that rim on the edge, a break in Her horizontal flat round surFACE out of which the sun, moon, clouds, stars, even birds were regurgitated back up to Her surFACE. They posited that She swallowed the heavenly bodies into Her waiting maw (MAWA) in the West onto that looming line of mountains that looked like a great mouth (MATA) of repetitive top lips at the edge and then when they had passed through Her womb of transformation under Her crusty mantle, under below very skin, She regurgitated them back up to Her surFACE on the other side.

If on the individual mother's face the top lip of her mouth (MATA) was in the SHAPE of the letter M, then it's reflection as the bottom lip was SHAPED like the letter W. On the body of Mother Earth the bottom lip as the letter W reflecting not only the the M of the mountains but Her mat (MATA) of matter(MATA-), became associated with and defined by quietly standing pools of water (WATA-) that when splashed over them made them wet (WATA).

If on the face of the mother the angular nose rising out of her face acted as a vehicle of passage for the air that went in and out, then the noses on the body of Mother Earth must have been the volcaNOES that blasted air up to the surFACE and the islands that rose out of Her watery depths staining the belly of air above them with purple plumes of unfurling smoke.

The most ancient origins of language primarily as SOUNDS wedded to the SHAPES that come out of PHASE ONE of humanity's mother centered heritage (HER IT AGE), magically and mysteriously surfacing as the still recognizable SHAPES of the contemporary capital letters of the Western Alphabet, having their ancient original, physical dawning out of the clusters of mother based families who following the herbivore herds for an extra supply of milk guided humanity across the varied terrains of ancient Africa and then the world.

RULE THREE,
Consonants

Consonants are constant their SHAPE and SOUND carry the meaning. Con deals 'with' and sonant deals with the SOUND that is carried. The SHAPE shifting vowels carry the melody. Ancient humans and chimpanzees had trouble making the consonant SOUNDS. Earliest human SOUND of the Saan of the Kalahari was open mouth singing without the use of CONSONANTS. In the North Eastern part of Turkey there still exists a village in which the women communicate with bird SOUND. Some ancient mothers also hummed which in time gave them their name by another group of humanoids as the HUMming creature that came to be defined as HUMan. The present of making CONSONANT SOUNDS had been given to the Neanderthal with their hyoid bone ready to give more specific meaning to the SOUNDS that they sent forth out of their mouths. The Neanderthal had trouble making the vowel SOUNDS. The lack of vowel SOUNDS also surfaces in Hebrew. Yahveh began His life as YHVH. Curious?

Both the Hadza (HADASA) of the Olduvai Gorge and the Saan of the Kalahari Desert, genetically proven to be the two oldest tribes in Africa used clicks in their communication. Clicks are also used as communication among the dolphins. The earliest occupants of the African continent were not only great mimics but must also have been expansive oceanic travelers to incorporate the clicking SOUNDS of the dolphins into their languages.

The Letter M;
The letter M may have been the original SOUND of HUMming (HAMA-) as the individual mother taught her children what was safe to eat. The only SOUND that can be made when the two lips are approximated and food is being savored, milled and masticated in the MOUTH (MATA) is the M-M-M SOUND of acceptance. The SHAPE of the letter M is the SHAPE of the top lip of the mouth on the mother's face in stage one and came to define her as

the *M* of the *mother* and not the *other*.

On the body of Mother Earth the letter M of mouth (MATA) dealt with the mat (MATA) of matter(MATA-) sharing its SHAPE of the mountains around Her round flat surFACE in stage two, the many mouths (MATA-) that regurgitated the sun at dawn and swallowed it in the West at twilight. Why many repetitive mouths that had been the mountains on the body of Mother Earth? Because the suns emergence and exit on the horizontal rim varied from one side to the other with the passing of the seasons during the course of the year.

The Letter N;
Nose (NASA) Not only was the food given *assent as sent* but there was also the nasal SOUND of rejection that had been associated with the nose (NASA). The SHAPE of rejection and the letter N deal with the protruding proboscis of the nose on the human face as seen in profile. Like an island stuck out of water on the round flat aquatic surFACE of Mother Earth, so the nose stuck out of the round flat human face. The only SOUND that can be made when the tongue is pushing food out of the mouth in the process of rejection is the nasal SOUND of negation. The letter N associated with the nose emerged to define the process of 'negation of a former state' and 'emergence on the surface' also dealing with the breath moving in and out. The nose (NASA) as the Latin nascence (NASA-) defining birth joins the ranks of beginnings.

The Letter L;
The tongue (TANAGA) is the angle (L) that lies on the floor of the oral cavity of the mouth and tells lies giving us the original SHAPE of the letter L out stage one. The darting snake like object evolved to savor, mill or push food out of the mouth as the tongue (TANAGA). (TANA) deals with the process of holding tenere (TANA-) in Latin with the ten (TANA) fingers. (NAGA) is one of the names of the snake (IS NAKA). The (K) and (G) are interchangeable. It gives meaning to the SOUNDS that drift by as language becoming Lengua (laNAGA) in Latin. In PHASE THREE with the definitions of male body parts having their dawning the penis became the lingum (LANAGA-). The (NAGA) of the snake like tongue (taNAGA) surfaces also in English. Forked snake like tongue telling lies harken back to their PHASE ONE origins.

To name things is to separate them from their existing reality. With the naming of things into words the tongue helped to create an alternate state of being that found its home in the *linear* left hemisphere of the human brain.

The evolution of humanity and a movement away from the continent of Africa created some full sensuous mouths to become thinner, no longer defined by the two full bulbous lips encoded in the letter B of ancient Africa. The L of the angle of the two thin lips of Asia and Europe creating the one mouth entered the scene.

In PHASE ONE on the metaphoric body of Mother Earth the tongue as the risen angle in the Eastern sky shoved the sun out of the round flat surFACE of Mother Earth for it to be regurgitated by the *LA*dy of the *LA*nd into Life and Light out of Her Eastern orifice. It gave birth not only to the letter L of the angled individual mother's tongue defining Mother Earth by the *LA* SHAPE and SOUND but also gave birth to the round SHAPE of the letters G (jee) of Generation and G (gh) of be-Getting. Both circles as the letter G on the flat round face of the individual mother and the flat round surFACE on the circular horizontal rim of Mother Earth have the tongue sticking out of the circle of creation encased in the SHAPE of the letter C of creativity which is the top part of the laterally halved letter S of isness. In PHASE THREE as male role in procreation had become established the angle defining the SHAPE of the letter L became the LINGUM or the Asiatic penis and the angle dealt with penal erection.

The Letter B;
The African mother's bulbous sensuous mouth cannot be left far behind. The original letter B dealt with the two full lips as seen in profile on the individual mother's face in stage one making up her mouth extending to embrace the babble (BABA-) of the baby (BABA), the Tower of Babel (BABA-), the ancient Babylonians (BABA-) and the Hebrew Bible (BABA-). Also in Hebrerw one of the names for the father is baba. The Polish baba as the old wise woman cannot be far behind and not to be left out the transformed human male in Hinduism with the Mother Earth Kundalini energy of prana alive in him is also called a Baba. The letter B establishes the concept of 'two in one' or both dealing originally with the two lips in stage one. On the body of Mother Earth it defines the bio (BAYA) of life as the creation of life out of the many regurgitating lips, mouths or mounds on Her surFACE. The letter B in bio (BAYA) deals with the 'two in one' habitual passage of the journey of the sun in and out of the body of Mother Earth, the aya of light and dawn out of Persian and Assyrian. The letter L of the tongue (Lengua in Latin) at the end of babble (babaLA), Tower of Babel (babaLA), Babylonians (babaLA-), Bible (babaLA-) establishes the two lips in the making of SOUND belonging to the *LA*dy of the *LA*nd.

The Letter J;

Then there is the lower mandible on th individual mothers face, the movable lower jaw that goes up and down SHAPED like a hook (HAKA) that hacks (HAKA) morsels into manageable pieces. It is encoded in the SHAPE of the letter J reflecting the hook (HAKA) like SHAPE of the lower jaw. It is also associated with the making of SOUND, for it hacks SOUND into manageable, recognizable segments that became words.'In the beginning was the word' may have its origins here for it deals with the Hebrew Bible and the name of the Jews (JAWA) as the original users in PHASE THREE of divine pronouncements, or segmented SOUNDS. The name Jew (JAWA) has it's origins not only with the jaw (JAWA) in the making of manageable segmented SOUND but with the lower mandible dealing with the reflective pools of standing water as aqua (HAKA) that hacked reality in two creating the upside down reality of male *source* in PHASE TWO out of the body of Mother Earth. The four upside down female statues out of Nineveh, Saint Peter being hanged upside down and Mussolini sharing the same fate harken back to the darkened caves where bats hanging upside down created their darkened nocturnal homes becoming in PHASE THREE aspects of darkness and evil.

The SOUND of CH;

May not come out of a single CONSONANT but it does emerge out of the dual activity of the CHeek and CHin when CHewing or CHeering is done inside the cavity of the mouth. The circular letter C with the opening on its side establishes the round flat circle of the individual mother's face with her mouth open. The letter H deals with the air (HA) that the open mouth of the mother uses to make the air SOUND. Put the C and the H together you get the SOUND of the CH out of the oral cavity behind the CHeek and CHin. When used in CHirping it has much to do with birds and their young begging for food. As the concept of beginnings it is related to Change, Children and CHoice. The CHI energy emerging up from the surFACE of Mother Earth is the Kundalini electro-magnetic energy rising and creating the eventual possibility of life. It may have been the SOUND that created the name for China as the birds flew to their nesting sites North and South away from their African homes.

The Letter P;

The letter P deals with the SHAPE of the top lip and the SOUND of Plosive Passage of SOUND carrying air up to the surface out of the individual face of the mother in stage one and the exPlosive volcanic surFACE of Mother Earth in stage two.

The Letter T;
Tip (TAPA), top (TAPA) deals with Tips, that which is either on the Top or edge. The Teeth are at the Tips of the gums. The Tip of the Tongue lies behind the Teeth. The Throat sits on the Top of the Trunk. The Trunk with the Tits sits on Top of the legs. On the bodies of elephants the Tusks are at the Tip of the head. The Trunk is at the Tip of the body. On the body of Mother Earth the Tips are at Her horizontal edge. Out of Her Tip, her horizontal round flat sidereal surFACE there emerge the sun, stars, moon, clouds even birds. Out of Her Top all other THINGS have their being, Tar, Tor, Terra firma, Trees and the concept of three.

The Letter V;
Although not seen on the outside of the mother's face there exists the letter V on the inside of the mother's throat. It is the SHAPE of the Vocal chords that create SOUND. It is also the SHAPE of Vision that splays out of the visual cavity. On the surFACE of Mother Earth the letter V as SOUND is associated with the Vibrant Volcanic eruption that creates land on Her surFACE. The letter V also gives birth to the Vulva and Vagina, the places of creation on the individual mother's body, where a di*VISION* occurs when she becomes the ap*parent parent*.

The Letter W;
Is the SHAPE of the bottom lip on the face of the individual mother. It is the reflection of the SHAPE of the top lip that became encoded in the letter M. One reflects the other creating the 'two in one' of the mouth. It is the letter that when puckered up defines the woo of wonder, wailing and woe. On the body of Mother Earth the reflected letter M of the looming horizontal mountains is the Wall of Water encoded in the letter W. It is also the Western Wall of Water into which Mother Earth declared War on the sun, chewed him into little bloody pieces and sWALLowed him. The letter W in its most expansive consideration defines not only Water but War and has ancient links with the death of the sun and in PHASE THREE the Israeli Wailing Wall.

The Letter X;
The letter X Is not apparent on the surface of the individual mothers face. It exists at the metaphoric third eye between the two actual eyes above the nose. It is the area where a criss-crossing occurs. The left side of the body is controlled by the right hemisphere of the brain. The right side of the body is controlled by the left hemisphere of the brain. It is the area of transformation that is associated with the left handed mother's Kundalini birthing breath

and with right handed ritual for men. As a letter and number the letter X also deals with the SHAPE of the buttox as seen from the back and the ten (X) months of lunar gestation associated with human birthing when the abdomen is disTENded.

The letter X means ten in Latin and the concept of holding, tenere in Latin surfaces here with the ten fingers. *The Runic hooked X deals with male role in specific procreation having been established in PHASES TWO and THREE.* For the hooked X contains the erect penis that has been added to the X of the ten months of lunar gestation of the mother's pregnancy. It harkens back to the abib (HABABA), the penis like erect corn on the stalk of the Hebrews harvest. Also in Hebrew AB and Baba are the names for the father.

The letter A

The letter A can be considered either as a CONSONANT or a VOWEL. The triangular SHAPE of the letter A (ah) comes out of the three sided volcanic cone on the surFACE of Mother Earth. As SOUND it is the intake of the first breath of a baby as it is slithered forth into life. The letter H as HA is the SHAPE of Mother Earth exHAling and blasting open the A(ah) SHAPED volcanic cone on top to create the escape of air up through Her surFACE encoded in the letter H. The AH-HA of the breath inhaling and exhaling are like two sides of a coin. Leading both the Western Alphabet and the Finnish Akkoset it deals with the alpha of beginnings

The Letter F;

The SOUND of the letter F deals with fillibratiion. The SHAPE of the letter F does not come out of any organ on the individual mother's face. It comes out of the body of the individual mother, her four or five fingers extending to the surFACE of Mother Earth as the SHAPE of the fingers of the helping hand of the sun, that like exuberant four or five fingers of fire stretch out across the firmament of dawn as Mother Earth awakens to the sun. The five fingers of the mother deal with work and the maintenance of the infant. The four fingers without the opposable thumb deal with male not as the maintainer of the infant. In the Western sky the reluctant fingers as rays of light stretching in all directions are drawn back down into Mother Earths body making their transformative journey home.

The Letter K;

The SHAPE of an open bird's beak as seen in profile making the cooing SOUND of bird song. It has no apparent links with the SHAPES out of the individual mother's face, or the surFACE of Mother Earth except in North

Eastern Turkey. As a halved vertically CONSONANT it tells a different, if appealing story dealing with the letter X (KASA) of the coos (KASA). The letter K exists out of the letter X halved vertically (K) of ultimate creation out of the buttox of the female making smaller (KA) aspects out of her blood (SA).

The Letter Q;

Can be mystifying for it deals with Questing and searching for answers to the original peripheral, undefined male state and the castration and leg mutilation of male offspring. As the limping slaves they Quested for answers for their sorry condition establishing the round circle of the sun (O) and the zero of the permanently empty belly (0) *away* and *above* the body of Mother Earth as their source and subsequent gods. The smiths and shepherds limped along on one leg, so the round circle of the sun (0) metaphorically gained the one limping leg becoming their symbol of Questing and limping on one leg across the sky. Metaphorically they established their source expressing their links to the round circle of the sun trailing along on one leg also limping across the sky. It became their solar symbol defining their Quest giving rise to the letter Q, the solar circle (0) with a mutilated trailing leg of questing.

The Letter R;

SOUND deals with the raging, roaring, rampaging volcanic eruption. The SHAPE of the letter R deals with the triangle of the volcanic cone of Mother Earth on the bottom (A) and the circle of the male sun (O) on top. Halved vertically it creates the letter R. The male circle of the sun on top and the triangle of the mother on the bottom establishes the letter R as coming out of PHASE TWO when male supremacy was becoming paramount and *above* the body of Mother Earth.

The letter S deals with 'isness'.

It is the breath of life out of the sissing calderas on the body of Mother Earth. It is also SA the lavic blood out of Her body and the SA out of the blood of the individual mothers body creating the SASA dyad at the end of female names; miSS, laSS, goddeSS. It is also the SHAPE of Mother Earths life as movement encoded in spirals and hurricanes. The letter S also gave birth to one of the perceptions dealing with the letters C (see) above halved vertically as in see of the sea and the lower C (KH) as in cadaver, container, corpse.

The Letter Z;

The voiced aspect associated with the letter S. As the letter A (ah) beginning the Alphabet as Alpha had been associated with motherhood and the beginning of life, so the letter ZED evolved as the last letter of the Alphabet associated with the Father not only as source as in Zeus but also as the end. The linear aspects housed in the left hemisphere of the human brain deal with beginnings (A) and ends (Z), the Alpha and Omega of another declination.

The letter Y deals with a double reality;
The original letter Y is the SHAPE of the female pubis on the individual mother's body. On the body of Mother Earth it is the SHAPE between two mountains out of which the sun had been regurgitated at dawn. With the castration of first born sons and the maiming of the subsequent sons for shepherding and working at the forge as smiths, the questing males began to ask why (Y) of their peripheral state. Along with the over evolution of the left hemisphere of the human brain due to linear speech and writing and the asking of WHY of their peripheral state, the letter Y of the bifurcated brain came into being. In PHASE THREE with monotheistic patriarchal religions the left hemisphere of the father's parted from the right hemisphere of the mothers creating the bifurcated brain encoded in the letter Y (WHY), ushering a time of violence, chaos, rampant sexuality, irresponsible procreation and war.

RULE FOUR;
Work Back

Work back from the original codified ancient SOUNDS locked in both contemporary and obsolete languages. Deal in the way they have been pronounced' not in the way that they may have been written.
   Bardo (BARAda) Tibetan 'INTERMEDIATE STATE
   State of trance, suspended animation after death before rebirth.
   The BARA dyad with (da) the gift of (BARAda) splays out in many linguistic directions;
   There are a variety of linguistic clues out of PHASE ONE that deal specifically with the movement of the electro-magnetic Kundalini energy that activate the transformative state of trance. Some clues hide in (HANAKA) and (KAHANA), others surface in (HAVANA). The (SASA) dyad also hides in its linguistic coils many of the secrets of transformation. One of the most universal and inclusive examples exist in the dyad BARA.
   The BARA dyad defines what the Kundalini experience includes on a variety of what evolved as mostly subsequently mystical 'spiritual' levels; what is it for, why is it, who is the recipient, where does it come from, how it is

manifested, where it has been experienced, how it has changed over time.

The linguistic beginning of BARA deals with the letter B that defines the 'two in one' SHAPE of the bulbous mouth as seen in profile on the face of the individual mother. Dealing with both the top and bottom of the mouth working in concert, it encloses the contents within, be they food, moisture or SOUND. It extends to include the 'two in one' scenario of the two sides of the human brain hooked together across the corpus collosum working in concert as one *balanced* entity.

The same process is shared by the surFACE and body of Mother Earth. She too has a metaphoric mouth on either side of Her flat round horizontal surFACE that held the promise of life and maintenance from within Her body. With Her bulbous mountainous mouths She swallowed the heavenly bodies, especially the sun on one side and regurgitated them on the other. The process is encoded in the letter B and the 'two in one' scenario of the sun rising out of Her Eastern mouth and setting in Her Western mouth creating the Bio of life.

The letter R deals with Mother Earth and specifically with Her greatest helping hands, the sun. The SHAPE of the letter R defining the sun comes out of the volcanic triangle of the mother on the bottom, with the male circle of the sun on top halved vertically. As RA in PHASE THREE the sun becomes a male deity for the Egyptians. In PHASE ONE the sun began its life as the helping hands at one with Mother Earth. The SOUND encoded in the letter R comes out of the bottom half, out of the volcanic eruption as the roaring, rampaging, raping solar blood that had been chewed and swallowed by the maw of Mother Earth at Her horizontal Western rim. With the addition of the original A (ah) SOUND the BR becomes BARA.

What does the BARA dyad proclaim? It proclaims a state of such majestic transformative being that words fall short to define it. It also exposes a state of trance dealing with leadership, ecstasy, courage and power that has been universally suppressed and as often as not obliterated. Why? *Because it originally dealt with mother centrality and power.* That magical power had been originally experienced by the birthing (BARA-) breath (BARA-) of the mothers and subsequently universally experienced by humans spanning a multitude of conditions and to have been originally sourced by the body of Mother Earth. The dyad BARA defines not only one of the states of transformation and trance but also the 'INTERMEDIATE STATE' of an alternate state of suspended animation.

The necessity for the ecstatic trance of transformation that became part of humanity's experience came out of the birthing breath of the mother, the castration of the first born son and the use of ritual for many others. With it came the over-evolution of the left hemisphere of the human brain in which the image locked together with fear had become stored. With the numbing realization of a baby that it is locked in a body that doesn't work came the growth of panic at its helpless state. The image came to be meshed with fear. With the over-evolution of the linear left hemisphere as source came unending prattle, anguish, depression, misery, doubt, shame, tension, restlessness, stress, anger all the negative emotions that came to saddle the human creature.

As talent became a gift of attention for the under appreciated human being, so Mother Earth also threw up the Kundalini experience to ease the torment inherent in the human creature which included the birthing pains of the human mother. Mother Earth knew that within Her magnificent body the fires of the solar wind made life upon Her surFACE possible. The solar wind barreling toward Her body had been responsible for the creation of the *lea* lines beneath and across Her surFACE. It was along the *lea* lines on Her surFACE that She shared a multitude of creative powers with Her creatures.

The ancient migrators following the tracks that Mother Earth had laid down for them often felt a pulse of pleasure, of well being and a feeling of being stoned. Some coincided with animal pathways that had been used by the herbivore herds for thousands of years as they migrated back and forth across the African savannah. Caves that they passed along their semi-annual trek also filled them with ecstatic reconnection inherent in the womb of creation. They also knew that at certain times of the year those feelings of pleasure intensified as they did with different practices of ritual and drugs. Times of day, of the month, of the year also awakened their pleasure. Places on the magnificent body of Mother Earth rocked them back and forth as they moved into states of trance filling them with the gifts of healing, prophecy and well being.

The most profound experience had been experienced by Individual mothers in the last stages of labor as their fast, hard panting breath (BARA-) awakened the latent electro-magnetic Kundalini energy that lay dormant at the bottom of their trunk, at the sacred sacral bone which then shot up their spine in a double serpentine energy coil. The movement of the Kundalini within the mother during the time of birthing (BARA-) not only filled her with ecstasy but made her a fearless protector of her baby.

Because males did not experience the birthing breath of fearlessness, ecstasy and power that had been given to all mothers they called it a mystery which in time became defined as mystical mysticism.

When not giving birth, to still their overactive prattling left hemisphere the ancients of both sexes pursued the activation of the energy through a variety of means. They believed in balance and evenness. To that end everything that they pursued had to have the concept of evenness activated in them. Peace and well being had been prized. Violence and chaos within the clan in PHASE ONE at the time of female centrality had apparently not been tolerated.

They lived at or near the equator where there was an even distribution of day and night. There was also an even distribution of the ancient year at the time of the solstices and equinoxes. Their migrations following the herbivore herds created a back and forth even circle across the savannahs of Africa based on the coming monsoons and drought. To keep the universe on an even keel their brains (BARA-) also had to be balanced. Violence and war upset the balance. Means had to be found to create and maintain that peaceful balanced state.

The birthing (BARA-) breath (BARA-) of the individual mothers created the first journey into that sequestered state of trance. They also knew that the state of trance created a *fusion* at the center if they concentrated deeply and strongly enough to push the large headed baby out of their bodies. So did *focusing* intently of any kind; fasting, dancing, chanting, drumming, rocking back and forth, repeating favorite words, twisting beads through the fingers, use of specific plants, sex, and at the feet of gurus. For many Christians hair shirts, flagellation and pain became their rational focus into transcendence.

As the Kundalini energy rose up through their bodies it burned (BARA-) out their infantile habits, freed them of their fears, blessed them with ecstasy, the gifts of prophecy and healing, making it possible for them to survive with joy and peace. This was all at the time of female centrality in PHASE ONE. The Goddess Maat of wisdom and justice of the Egyptians weighed the human soul at death against a feather. If the soul was heavier than the feather it did not pass. Sadness and anger made the soul heavy. The ancient Egyptians had been admonished to be joyful or they would not pass into immortality.

The gift of trance (TARANASA) had been inherent out of the body of Mother Earth. The three *overlapping* dyads (TARA) (RANA) (NASA) reveal their unique story. (NASA) deals with the Latin nascence NASANASA) meaning birth. (RANA) establishes the wound or break on the body of Mother Earth out of which the birth occurred. In Polish rana means not only wound but dawn relating to the birth of the sun out of the body of Mother Earth.

(TARA) is the tor (TARA), the tar (TARA) that emerged out of the volcanic body of Mother Earth and created land, or the terrain (TARARANA) up on Her surFACE.

The state of trance is the Kundalini energy that emerged out of the wound (RANA) or vent on the turbulent (TARA-) body of Mother Earth giving birth (NASA) to a new balanced and even (HAVANA) state of being. As the sun had been 'born (BARA-) again' to a new dawn, so the human being had been 'born (BARA-) again' to a new life.

Out of the birthing breath of the mother in the last stages of labor she moved out of the 'INTERMEDIATE STATE' of being pregnant I'bur (haBARA) of the Hebrews (haBARA) into motherhood. Her birthing (BARA-) breath (BARA-) as air not only had been established as an 'INTERMEDIATE STATE' between death and rebirth but carried her into the ecstatic trance associated with the rising of the electro-magnetic Kundalini energy through her body.

The imbalance within human families occurred when young boys turned pubescent, when their veins bulged with testosterone and violence became their way of being. The only way that they could share their special gift of balance that had been given to mothers at the time of the birthing (BARA-) breath (BARA-) was the act of castration and the creation of eunuch uncles that had been practiced on their first born sons to protect the human family. Non castrated males circling the periphery were on their own as the band of brothers that became the subsequent bandits surviving as heroes of ancient myth jumping on their steeds trying to find the power inherent in the Kundalini experience.

The BARA dyad came into its own with the ecstatic experience of being stoned, of rocking back and forth, of being goose-pimpled with the shower of truth and with a tossing around in an uncontrolled spasm and vibration (vaBARAta-). With it came a torrent of possibilities. The state of *trance* not only created an *entrance* at the *center* but moved into the unchartered field of unlimited possibility. In the state of trance there are no rules to limit any possible thought. *It exists as if the dream state had become conscious.* All exists in the NOW and is the present of the present. The future can be prophesized. The past can be known. The present can be healed.

There are those who have been known to be born with or to possess those powers, mothers acquired it with the birthing breath. There have been transformed males like Christ, Mohammed, Moses, Buddha. Some have been animal whisperers like Rasputin, dog whisperers like Cesar Milan, sleeping healers and prophets like Edgar Casey and last but not least Nostradamus. There have been many, many women along the way with those powers who have been called witches, succubus and burned at the various stakes.

The trance state nullifies the state of one sided, unbalanced rational left hemispheric conscious reality. You enter another level of multifaceted being and become suspended in an experience of otherness. While awake you enter the state of the elusive conscious dream.

Actual WORDS played a role in defining the qualities of the Kundalini transformative awake while dreaming state. In Aramaic the magical Abracadabra (haBARAcadaBARA) reveals its meaning as, 'I create as I speak'. Ancient mothers understood that words painted pictures in the mind creating another reality and were therefore eminently powerful as spells that spelled out the possibility of control. For the Basque who have been very closely related to the ancient source of the Western Alphabet out of PHASE ONE berba (BARAba) (BARA/RABA) defined the word. SOUNDS like verb (VARABA), the B and V are interchangeable made in the same area of the mouth. Coming (BARA) and going (RABA) reflecting itself, the emerging 'word' had been considered to be sacred.

To spell not only meant to break (BARA-) down a linguistic construct but to cast a spell, a SOUND that could cause a change in the vibrational (vaBARAta-) construct of the universe. The casting of a spell through the use of words had been considered to be a magical occurrence.

In Polish dobra (daBARA) is the '(DA) the 'gift of' good and the good is the trance state (BARA). This was still in PHASE ONE before the fear driven left hemispheric rational mind of the right handed males swamped the right hemisphere of the left handed mothers.

In Swahili BARA defines contentment and BARA BARA meaning exactly right is contentment repeated. Both dyads deal with the trance state as highly desired. For the Ethiopians, a benevolent helpful spirit is adbar (hadaBARA) and has links with one of the names for the setting sun falling off the side (IS HADA). In Swahili a blessing is BARAka. The (KA) on the end establishes smallness and the fact that there is a larger gift than the actual blessing. 'Many are called but few are chosen' and that is the mysterious gift of transformation.

The Tibetans went for the categorical imperative and called the state between death and reincarnation the Bardo (BARADA) which actually means an 'INTERMEDIATE STATE'. It is the (DA) 'gift of' the BAR (BARA) dealing with the intuited state between death and reincarnation. It is similar to the

Christian Limbo. There is an implication here that human beings didn't actually totally die and a break (BARAka) or bar (BARA) existed between the two states. Living creatures, especially human beings separated from the body, became transformed and waited for the next state of being.

Another word that bears witness to the process dealing with the 'INTERMEDIATE STATE' of suspended animation on a practical, physical level is the state of temporary sleep that a hibernating (haBARA-) bear (BARA) experiences during the winter months.

The transformed males, among who were the castrated first born sons often becoming shamans dealing with healing and prophecy carried in their names their state of being. In the Ashanti tribe in Africa the actual BARA dyad is a name for a sorcerer or magician who had experienced the rising fire of the Kundalini shakti energy.

In Basque BURU (BARA) was the name given to a leader (LADA-), one at the end of the line on top with the balanced brain (BARA-). In PHASE ONE the original leader (LADA-) of the ancient migrations had been the lady (LADA). In PHASE TWO the one who also became a leader (LADA-) had been the transformed male, the castrated first born son who stood at the side of his mother with the Mother Earth Kundalini energy alive in him. In Basque, the crowning with the Kundalini energy had been called Bures Kundu (BARAsa KANADA) containing in the word BURES (BARAsa) the 'INTERMEDIATE STATE' of trance, the (SA) of the individual mother's blood and Kundu (KANADA) of the magical Kundalini (KANADA-) energy up from the body of Mother Earth.

In Lithuanian Burtinan sas (BARAtanasasa), the sorcerer and magician as the transformed male covers even more bases. He not only includes the (BARA) dyad of the ecstatic Kundalini vibration (vaBARAta-) but the (SASA) of the individual mother's menstrual blood (SA) and the lavic blood of Mother Earth (SA). At the center there sits (TANA) dealing with the ten (TANA) fingers that did the holding. The Latin tenere flushes up a perception from the past to hold with the ten fingers.

The trance of transformation in Hindu is Digam BARA. Also for the Hindus Brahma (BARAhama) one of the triple Gods hides in his name that he was a transformed male deity. The dyad (HAMA) deals with the blood of Mother Earth ema (HAMA), or heoma (HAMA) in Greek. In Hebrew their patriarch was Abraham (haBARAhama) linguistically very close to Brahma (BARAhama) of the Hindus. AB is one of the names of the father in the Middle East. BARAbbas was the son (BARA) of Abbas. Depending on the time the definition occurred he may have been the transformed, castrated or circumcised first born son of Abbas. Why was he spared when Christ was crucified? Because in PHASE THREE he was the son of the father (AB). Christ straddled the fence being the son of the Virgin Mother Mary. Harking back to the time of the villified mother centrality in PHASE THREE that fact may have been His downfall.

Other than having accompanied the birthing (BARA-) breath (BARA-) of the mothers there existed two specific times of the year when the Kundalini energy had been high and the state of transformation had been practiced when young boys were castrated and crippled. One happened at the time of the Spring Equinox with the arrival of the birds (BARADA) and the other had been at the time of the Autumnal Equinox with the departure of the birds (BARADA) when the balance of the global clock had been extended to the traditions of early mothers in PHASE ONE. It was also a dual time of birthing (BARA-) of breeding (BARADA-) of the resting herbivores and of a break (BARA-) in the migratory circle of returning back to their welcoming rain drenched verdant savannahs.

The 'INTERMEDIATE STATE' leading to transformation came to define closely the castrated first born (BARA-) sons, who were no longer male and not really female existing in that 'INTERMEDIATE STATE' of suspended sexual animation. The brother (BARAdara) or (BR-OTHER) was the other with the (BARA) dyad of transformation defining him.

The (BARA) name surfaces in other languages. Brat (BARAta) is a fresh spoiled kid in English. Brat (BARAta) is brother (BARAdara) in Polish. Brat (BARA-) is the not only the castrated but crippled Amharic smith. Burdingile (BARAnagala) surfaces as the name of the smith in Basque. It also contains the (NAGA) or snake (IS NAKA) of rising, twisting shakti of the Kundalini energy. The (G) and (K) are interchangeable.

Castration or eunuchanization of first born sons had been linked to homosexuality because both carried in them an empty belly and neither male could become the apparent parent. It may have been that in PHASE TWO when the ancient migrations came to rest in farming, agriculture and husbandry the first born sons were joined by the second and subsequent sons who were not only castrated but crippled to keep them enslaved and incapable of running away. The word lib of castration and liberation from their violent selves enters the scene.

With the arrival of the birds (BARADA) at the time of the Spring Equinox first born (BARA-) sons at puberty (paBARA-) went through the process of castration when violence bearing hormones beset their bodies and their beards (BARA-) began to show on their chins, broda (BARAda) in Polish. Barbers (BARABARA) not only shaved their chins but performed the act of castration on their bodies. As a relic of the past, the twisting white (milk) and red (blood) of the barber (BARABARA) pole announces that small surgery could have been performed in situ.

There exists to this day a tribe of people called the Berbers (BARABARA) who embody many of the concepts related to the ancient mothers. More recently the name Barbarosa (BARABARA-) attached to a Roman emperor surfaced and barba (BARABA) in Italian means red Beard (BARADA). Scientists have discovered that the Neanderthal may have had red hair. The Biblical David also had red hair as did Mother Mary. Many ancient societies contain fear drenched mythologies of very violent red haired people. Some have called them Vikings. It may have been that they were ancient Berbers (BARABARA). Hitler honing in on ancient mythologies named his attack on Russia the Barbarosa (BARABARAsa) campaign. Ironically he must not have known that their ancient perhaps non blond Aryans had Neanderthal roots.

The act of castration created the shaman who became the smart, the bright (BARA-) light in his brain (BARA-), having gone through the process of liberation. Lib means castration. Libra (LABara) had been the Goddess holding the scales of balance. Castration created a balance in his young brain (BARA-) negating his violence. In Japan Subaru (IS haBARA) means to unite. The act of castration created a uniting of the two hemispheres of the brain (BARA-) across the bridge (BARAja), the corpus callosum in the brain (BARA-) a liberation (laBARAta-) from his violent self and a movement into subsequent transformation.

There existed in PHASE ONE a double bladed ax called the labrys (LABARAsa) of both (LAB) and (BARA) used by the priestesses of ancient Amazons that linguistically bear witness to the rites of castration (LIB), crippling (LIB) and transformation (BARA). The double bladed ax must have been used as a tool by the crippled smiths and shepherds for LABrys has links with LABor. As ancient traders traversing around the ancient world their economic process dealt with bartering (BARA-) their goods. Where does bribery (BARABARA) fit in here, for it must.

The often reluctant first born son went through the process of brevis (BARA-) or the abbreviation (haBARA-) of his genitalia. His castration lifted the burden (BARA-) of violence from his arms, brazos (BARA-) in Spanish. When the Spanish brazos (BARA-) were brought (BARAta-) together like the two sides of the brain (BARA-) were brought together they created a heart felt embrace (hamaBARAsa). With those freed arms the LIBerated adept became a masterful painter. In Polish obras (haBARAsa) is a painting and establishes linguistic links with the Saan of the Kalahari Desert who were great painters and very possibly painted for a time after the last glaciations in the caves of Spain and France.

There were many ancient times when the state of transformation had been so desired and many castrated young men became instant celebrities (is halaBARAta) upon having their genitalia removed. This occurred under the reign of Apollo the Greek sun god, Helios (HALAsa) representing the sun eelyos (HALAsa). The discarded male genitalia had been buried under an altar (HALA-) on top of the mountain close to their solar deity.

As the great helper and protector of the mother's children the hapless young man also assisted her in the rites dealing with life and death. Here we regain our links with the "INTERMEDIATE STATE". To bury (BARA) dealt with one of his responsibilities. Burial (BARA-) at the time these concepts reigned in Tibet had been perceived to be an 'INTERMEDIATE STATE" between death and reincarnation. In Basque buru (BARA) dealt not only with the chief who officiated over the rites of the dead but with that which was final.

At the grave site he was also the great singer or bard (BARAda) who like the birds (BARAda) lifted his voice up into the heavens. In PHASE THREE the ascension dealt with the Egyptian pharaohs who held the world in balance as they flew to heaven in their wooden barques (BARAka). The ascension to heaven in Hebrew and Christianity dealt with winged angels, crippled saints and Christ. The contemporary singers with heavenly female angelic voices didn't die a silent death. They surfaced in Catholic churches as the castrati, or castrated holden (HALA-) tenors bearing (BARA-) their high plaintive soprano voices up into the heavens.

The castrated males were called the dry ones, brut (BARA-) in French extending to brute (BARA-) in English possibly associated with the much maligned Neanderthal.

In Polish the name of the bachelor's button as chaber (haBARA), emerges as the non married transformed bachelor or dry male. In Herbew (haBARA) Bris (BARAsa) deals with circumcision as does berit (BARA-). Both create the 'INTERMEDIATE STATE ' of being in between the care free state of boyhood and the responsible state of manhood. In PHASE THREE the act of castration had been replaced by the symbolic act of circumcision. A moyl, the traveling Hebrew circumsizer sucked on the tiny bloody penis helping it to heal, or perhaps establishing its bloody fertility. Only blood had originally been considered to be the single creative source of life. That is why animals had been koshered (KASArada) to drain them of their magic creative blood. It brought them back to the coos (KASA) of the mothers blood (SA).

A bridge (BARAja) had been considered as a transformative area existing between the two eyes at the bridge (BARAja) of the nose, the 'INTERMEDIATE STATE' creating transformation. In PHASE THREE it expanded to become a practical place of passage between two rivers. Other places of passage occurred at the brim (BARAma), the edge, the border (BARAdara).

In Polish the brama (BARAma) as the *gate* or place of passage exists as an opening into another level. It SOUNDS like it linguistically extends to the Hindu God Brahma (BARAhama) and the Hebrew Abraham (aBARAhama). Not only transformed male gods but actual places on the surFACE of Mother Earth had been considered to be portals or gates of passage into transformation.

For the ancient Hittites Beren (BARAna) Kuyu (KAYA) were caves of passage in Turkey. (KAYA) deals with the small (KA) light (AYA) is light in Persian. Baran (BARAna) in Polish is a male sheep or ram. In PHASE TWO and THREE totemic male animals replaced totemic female animals. Gabrinas (gaBARAnasa) Island existed off the coast of France. The Iberian (haBARAna) peninsula must have been the same place of passage. Both places have been the homes of sheep herding or rams, baran (BARANA) in Polish.

Ubar (haBARA) had been an ancient quarter a city buried (BARA-) under the sands of the desert, a convergent place of trade, a route of passage in the Sahara Desert. The same could be said of an oasis (haSASA), an intermediate place of transformation where water could be found. Water as a conductor of electricity like gold held many different values. One had been the movement of the Kundalini energy through it. Christian baptism and the Hebrew mikvah enter here.

For the Hebrews I'bur (HABARA) meant pregnancy. Pregnancy had been considered as an 'INTERMEDIATE STATE' between barreness (BARA-) and birth (BARA-). The state of pregnancy as I'bur (HABARA) gave its name to the Hebrews (HABARA).

Britain (BARAtana) the holder of the Brat (BARAta) at Star Brae (BARA) contains hundreds of English Earth mounds. Places of passage, the 'INTERMEDIATE STATE' between life and death had been burial (BARAla) grounds or caves in Salisbury (is halaBARA) and Avebury (havaBARA).

Gibraltar (GaBARAtalara) had been named as the place of passage, a gate between two continents. On the other side of the great oceanic devide is the Barbados (BARAbadasa) Island across the briny (BARAna) sea off the coast of North America. Like Alaska (HALASAKA) seems to have links with the Greek sun eelyos (HALASA), there surfaces Siberia (IS haBARA) as an 'INTERMEDIATE STATE' dealing with another linguistic mystery.

The most notable people of the Sahara were the Berbers (BARABARA) who as the Tuareg had been related to the ancient mothers. The uncle had been the head of the family and women were free to choose and to leave their husbands. The (BARABARA) linguistic construct also surfaces in Swahili as that which is exactly right. The Berbers (BARABARA) must have been ancient people who had been considered to be exactly right in their experience of a balance within an alternate reality. The (BARABARA) dyad as the original SOUND of bribery (BARABARAS) and barber (BARABARA) echo with strange linguistic links.

Then there were deities or gods who circle around the edges and bear examining. There was a god of the Hittites named Kumbari (kamaBARA) who became pregnant by eating his own penis. SOUNDS like the Hebrew moyl. By ingesting his own penis Kumbari (kamaBARA) must have spilled a lot of blood. It was blood that had been perceived to be the source of creation. This opens up a host of possibilities. In the Middle East one of the names for water is AB. It has also been the name of the father. Had the male semen been considered as water and the fructifying liquid that brought forth life? Was this at the time in PHASE TWO when male role in specific paternity was becoming known that also surfaces in the Runic hooked X? The number X (KASA) is the Roman ten and establishes its links with the ten months of lunar gestation and the place of that gestation the mothers coos (KASA). The Runic hook within the number ten is the erect penis as part of the ten lunar month gestation processs. We are in PHASE TWO with male role in specific paternity becoming known.

Then there is the case of oral sex. Had women been satisfied through cunnilingus and that activity had been mistakenly thought of as bringing forth a baby? Ingesting your penis might create the same outcome. Does the Hebrew moyl sucking the penis reek with other possibilities that the penis would bear (BARA) children alone like the Egyptian god Amon? It is not unlike young girls in the United States in the early Twentieth Century thought that kissing would make them pregnant. Universal sexual ignorance and madness knows no bounds.

Section Two

In Alexandria Abraxas (haBARAkasa) a god with two snake feet had been worshipped. The electro-magnetic Kundalini energy entering the human body at the bottom of the feet like a double snake emanation then coiling up the spine or coos (KASA) created the experience of transformation. The two snake feet on the god Abraxas (haBARAkasa) not only establish the state of transformation with his (BARA) dyad but the X (KASA) shows us an area where the energy emanated from, the coos (KASA) or the sacred sacral area on the female body. The double spin of the Kundalini energy as symbolized by the snake entering through the bottom of the feet and coiling up the spine surfaces for the Hindus as the Ida and Pingali, the solar and lunar channels that emanate from the body of Mother Earth bringing with them transformation. The Greeks went for the medical Caduceus with the two entwining serpent spinning up the spine with bird (BARA-) wings on top of the stem.

For the Greeks in PHASE THREE the three headed dog Cerberus (IS haraBARAsa) with his three serpent tails guarded the gates of hell. The number three is the numeric symbol of the Mother. The Greeks already in PHASE TWO and THREE defiled the patient body of Mother Earth as the demon (DAMA-) out of the mother as the dame (DAMA). The place of damnation (DAMA-) was hell, the fires that burned (BARA-) within the belly (HARA) of Mother Earth. Hell in this case was also a place of transformation and harkens back to the day when the sun had been considered to be guided by the snake and to move through the entrails of Mother Earth re-coagulating and rising as a solid solar disc at dawn. The three canine heads deal with the bitch, the kur, the brilliant courageous transformed individual mother and her three sided vulvic patch. The three serpent tails deal with the three sided volcanic cone on the body of Mother Earth that blasted the Kundalini energy up to Her surFACE illuminating the night sky with the fires that became the Christian hell (HALA). It has its links with the solar(IS HALA-) disc that went below Her surFACE to be cooked clean in Her internal oven (HAVANA) before it rose clean, coagulated and bright, 'born again' on Her surFACE.

On the body of Mother Earth the air that passed across Her surFACE had also been considered an 'INTERMEDIATE STATE' between Her body and the path of the heavenly bodies above Her. In that barrage (BARAja) of air the birds (BARAda) had their being. They, because they used the sacred breath (BARAta) of air as a vehicle of passage had been considered sacred.

BIRDS (BARADA);

The dyad (BARA) with either the (T) or (D) at the end because both are made in the same area of the mouth, emerges with a host of possibilities. Because the coming and departure of birds (BARAda) semi-annually played such a major role in establishing the passage of time as a celestial clock as they clacked their way across the belly of air, it is to the birds (BARADA-) that we will turn in our linguistic journey. It is also to the birds (BARA-) that we turn to *when* the process of castaration occurred.

In Latin 'aves' (HAVAsa) are birds (BARADA-) or ancestral spirits. In PHASE THREE they became the feathery angels (HANAGAla) of male centered monotheistic patriarchal religions the castrated eunuchs (HANAKA) no longer bound to the body of Mother Earth but creatures of the Tibetan 'intermediate state'of air. The letters (K) and (G) are interchangeable.

Mother Earth as the 'bio' of life embraced the 'two in one' concept. The sun rising and setting daily establishing the word for habit (HABA-) also joins the ancient 'two in one' picture. The specific mother with a baby in her watery womb, in her ab*dome*n also reflected the 'two in one' process. The (RA) of (BARADA) or (BARATA) deals with the solar disc. Both (T) and (D) establish either the 'gift of '(D), or the place on the tip, top (T) on the body of Mother Earth where the activity occurred.

Not to be left out, the birds (BARADA-) fall into that same category. Their two pointed open beaks gave birth to one of the the SHAPES of the letter K as seen from the side defining the process of 'two in one' expanding into the fecundity of egg laying birds and one of the concepts for smallness. The oral internal CAvities in bird (BARAda) heads out of which so much onomatopoeic SOUND emerged gave birth (BARAta) to the same SOUNDING letter C (kh), the bottom part of the letter (S) halved laterally.

Obviously birds (BARADA-) had two wings (B) that gave them power over the gravity of Mother Earth as they soared into that 'INTERMEDIATE STATE', Her belly of air. Their most important activity dealt with their coming and going in the Spring and Fall Equinoxes at the time of the ancient migrations. Out of the cold Northern reaches they rose in great soaring drifts clacking their way South to the warm climates of welcoming Africa. They did the same with the Southern wind that blew them to their tropical wintry nests. Their coming and going semi-annually established a time of ritual and change. Birds (BARAda) as creatures living in the'INTERMEDIATE STATE' of *air* (breath) must have been immensely important to the ancient people named the Berbers (BARABARA) who share major linguistic links with their transformative experience.

It was a group of mother based wanderers who survived an ancient cataclysmic disaster that sent many of their neighbors to inhabit diverse areas of their beloved Mother Earth. Many of the Berbers (BARABARA) stayed put at the Sahara desert and the Sahel as their North African savannahs turned to sand and they clung to a migratory life, trading from place to place alighting at their distant oasis. Because they were at home with the birthing (BARA-) breath (BARA-) of creation as they awakened their state of trance during the last stages of labor, they became defined by the repetitive BARABARA name. It is the same repetitive ancient construct that exists in the Latin name for birth as nascence (NASANASA).

Some Berber (BARABARA) tribes, like the matrilineal Tuareg stayed as the 'free people' not absorbing the customs and laws of other male centered emerging desert groups. As the 'free people' the freedom was not only for males but dealt with women far into PHASE THREE who flourished with sexual freedom to choose their husbands and to leave them at will.

In the seventh century a Berber (BARABARA) queen, Al Kahina (-KAHANA) emerged with all of the characteristics of the great women out of PHASE ONE, she was considered to have been a great leader, a mother, a mystic with great charisma who led her people against the invading Arabs. Since the tide of history was against her, she was defeated and her story ended as the story of great women leaders ended all over the world.

There was an ancient tribe of Jewish priests called the kochanin (KAHANA-) in Lemba that carry a linguistic clue to the Al Kahina (KAHANA) of the Tuareg, Berbers.

One of the names of the Berbers (BARABABA-) was Imazighan, or individually Amazigh, the 'free people'. Did their sexual freedom and capacity to rule of the ancient mothers set them apart? Were they the ancient much maligned Amazons? Was the birthing breath part of their experience that gave them fearlessness in the protection of their babies and with it a power to lead, heal and prophesize? They leave a hidden linguistic legacy that has remained not only constant but reveal a pattern of their dispersal.

We begin with the Berber (BARABARA) migrating matriarchal clusters who lived their lives moving back and forth, 'two in one' (B), across the ancient verdant pre-glacial and flood drenched Sahara Desert. To the East existed the Great Rift of the Olduvai Gorge and the Highlands of Ethiopia out of which Mother Earth regurgitated the sun at dawn. To the West was the Atlantic Ocean and the maritime stretches on the West coast of Africa into which the sun was swallowed at twilight into the body of Mother Earth, died to its light, the setting places of Morocco, Mauretania, and the home of the rampaging Moors.

Its ironic that the linguistic construct for Berber (BARABARA) in its most ancient descriptive form is based on the A(ah) vowel SOUND defining the mother centered 'free' people is also the root dyad (BARA) for the much defiled barbarians (BARABARA-).

When male centrality over ran the planet in PHASE TWO with the dawning knowledge of male input in specific paternity, were the ancient mothers who demanded their antediluvian sexual freedom considered barbarians (BARABARA-)? Was the Biblical Lilith part of that ancient group? She wanted to retain her sexual position on top with Adam which had become verboten. He took a more suppliant mate in Eve. Lilith's loss of grace and in PHASE TWO her redefinition as a hag, a witch, the succuba and cause of male nocturnal emissions, a killer of children, pales to what wise, independent women were to endure in the subsequent years.

The Barbarian (BARABARA-) women were not only considered by the emerging male power bases in PHASE THREE as sexually 'free' but as close to their search for pleasure as a definition of savagery of their ancient redefinitions allowed. *The constant male enemy as the sexual freedom for women entered the ancient scene.* The Garden of Eden (HADANA) from which Lilith extricated herself, comes from the same root as hedonism (HADANA-) or the experience of pleasure. Was that the barbaric (BARABARA-) 'freedom' defining the Tuareg, cum Berber (BARABARA) mothers that had to be erased from the male based and redefined planetary historical and linguistic scene with the introduction of clitorectomies beginning in PHASE TWO?

In PHASE ONE a male child had been considered to be of two genders. He was born with an apparently female body like his mother, but he had an extra set of genitals like the other male members of his group. Boy (BAYA) in English is the name for a male child. Beginning with the anlaut of the letter (B) it echoes the 'two in one' concept. In Persian aya (HAYA) means light. In Assyrian aya (HAYA) means dawn.

As the first born (BARA-) son, the oldest brother (BARA-), potential first uncle he had to be castrated to become the protector to his mothers and sister's children. He entered the 'INTERMEDIATE STATE', no longer a male and not fully a female. It was a rite of passage that occurred at puberty (paBARATA). One set of first born (BARAna) boys was castrated as their reproductive organs were cast to the wind, or buried (BARA-) in a cavern. The

Section Two

other young males, younger brothers (BARADA-) at puberty (-BARATA) coming into their sexual violence were stricken from the familial clan to either circle the periphery, like male lions and male elephants, or to find new mates far from home. Many ancient civilizations put them to work on enormous monuments and buildings to keep them from doing harm.

In PHASE TWO linguistic and mythological clues surface that smiths as the ancient brats (BARATA-) in Amharic, were also eunuchized and crippled second born sons who worked at the forge of the sun, creating the simple tools of survival in PHASE TWO and subsequently the metal weapons of war in PHASE THREE. All the limping smiths leaning on their staffs, and shepherds leaning on their crooks symbolized by the storks balancing on one leg who brought babies, and the letter Q of questing, dealt with their peripheral and maimed state represented by the crippling of young boys.

The castrated firstborn son as the avuncular head of the family and spiritual force with his mutilated brothers helped to sustain the growing centers of what became civilizations in PHASES TWO and THREE in North Africa, the Middle East, Europe, Southern Asia, the British Isles and Scandinavia. In PHASE THREE with the emergence of monotheistic patriarchal religions the shepherds crozier or crook became a symbol of power for the Egyptian pharaohs and the Christian Church fathers.

Hybrid (haBARADA) contains in its linguistic construct links to the brother (BARADA-). Assisting in the rites of the rising and setting sun he was associated with the solar disc in all of its phases. The word hybrid (haBARADA) establishes its links with an ancient tribe of people, the Hebrews (haBARA-) who after one of the great cataclysms at the Sahara or the Sahel, scattered North West to the peninsula of Iberia (HABARA), and even much farther north to Siberia (IS HABARA). There is a link here with the larger brained and much maligned Neanderthal.

There were more than one humanoid and human species inhabiting the planet before the last ice age. Were the larger brained Neanderthal part of the hybridization (HABARA-) that exists in the Hebrew (HABARA-) name? Because they were considered to be smarter due to their larger brains (BARANA) were the Hebrews (HABARA-) considered arrogant and filled with hubris (HABARA)? In PHASE THREE their special intellectual status was blamed on the worship of a single male father deity *away* and *above* the body of Mother Earth. It may simply have been that they were intellectual hybrids (HABARA-). Is that the reason that the Hebrew Bible admonishes its followers not to wear clothing made of two fabrics creating a hybrid

(HABARAda) on their bodies and an ancient forgotten memory of a different linguistic source linking them to the vilified centrality of the ancient mothers?

Had there been sexual contact between the two divergent groups, birth (BARATA) may have been a problem. To abort (HABARA-) the trans specie fetus may have entered the picture. The brother (BARATA) as the Polish brat (BARATA) was also considered to be a hybrid (haBARADA-) with the female body and male genitalia, as were castrated first born sons and male homosexuals. The (T) and (D) made in the same area of the mouth are interchangeable. The brother (BARATA) surfaces in the name for a cunt containment, the brothel (BARATAla) or bordello (BARADAla). Both contain the LA as the LAdy of the LAnd or a female centered harem. It was the eunuch servants, the first born brothers (BARADA-) that kept the women enslaved in a harem in PHASES TWO and THREE to service the peripheral brothers who had been rejected at puberty to become the reigning sheiks and Chinese despots and to assure their specific progeny. They not only kept the women enslaved but were the servants, the bakers of bread (BARADA) and the cooks of bubbling broth (BARATA)???

For the secretive Kogi Indians of Columbia in South America who descend from their jungle hills to appear occasionally at the cities to warn the towns people that by exploiting the planet they are destroying the body of Mother Earth. Their first born son is called a MA, like the mother. He has been probably castrated to assume her name and her powers. The second born son, the brother (BARATA-) is considered to be the accursed trouble maker and is shunned from the village, which has echoes of a past out of Africa.

In PHASE ONE the second born heterosexual sons were pushed out at puberty (paBARATA). In PHASE TWO both the eunuchs and the heterosexual sons were maimed and crippled to work at the forge and care for the flocks of goats and sheep and the maintenance of the expanding and changing familial unit. They formed alliances with other similarly rejected second born (BARA-) and subsequently born sons, in time forming the roving male gangs of related siblings, the 'band of brothers' that became the bandits and still surface in military campaigns. They became the marauding armies of emerging territorial kingdoms that exist to this day.

Baradar (BARADARA) Persian stands for brother (BARADARA). In Sanskrit Bhratr (BARATARA) means 'support' as the older brother (BARATARA) was not only the eunuchized avuncular uncle but the 'support'

Section Two

of his mothers and sisters families. In PHASE TWO as control shifted from the mother to the father the support system became the establishment of a farming economy based on ownership of land and of violence filled territoriality.

The Hindu epic poem Mahabharata (-BHARATA) as either 'support' or brother (BARADA), the (T) and (D) are interchangeable, deals with a big (MAHA) battle of Krishna and the five brothers (BARADA-).

In Egypt the Primal Goddess Mother Isis searched for the scattered remains of her brother (BARAdara) Osiris, after reciting the magic WORD, she found and reassembled his diverse parts with everything but his penis. SOUNDS like something out of the PHASE ONE past when the peaceful existence of the social unit was more important than the left hemispheric male violence that was to sweep the world in PHASES TWO and THREE.

The semiannual coming and going of birds (BARADA-) in the spring and fall ushered in the rite of shaving the beards (BARADA-) of the castrated young boys by the barber (BARABARA). As the castrated eunuchs they entered the priesthood and stood with their mothers and uncles at the rites of the rising and setting sun. The emerging priesthood hailed with aves the birth (BARATA) of the sun in the Eastern sky at dawn becoming the bards (BARAD-) of old wailing at the watery Western grave at the loss of the sun at twilight.

In Polish the word for beard (BARADA) is also broda (BARADA), or the 'gift of' (DA) the emergence of 'two in one' (B) the male child with his reproductive testosterone glands excised, emerging from the ordeal with the female essence singularly alive in him. With the removal of his male organs he became not only the peaceful protector of his mother's children but also due to the ritual practice of castration he entered the 'INTERMEDIATE STATE' becoming the shaman, healer and prophet.

There emerged the perception that the castrated young boy became smarter, he became brighter (BARATA-), his brain (BARA-) had become more balanced due to the surgery. Since they somehow understood that the brain (BARA-) existed behind the brow (BARA-) in the skull, they also ascribed that the large brain (BARA-) behind the brow (BARA-) was covered by a brown (BARA-) African skin.

The SHAPE of the letter B comes out of the SHAPE of the two lips on the human face as seen from the side. Since the lips are apparently bulbous as the SHAPE of the letter B proclaims, then we are dealing with a brown (BARA-) race of people who originally may have migrated North to the Sahara to become the ancient mother centered Berbers (BARABARA-), cum Tuareg.

For the emerging Christians in PHASE THREE the supporting 'good man' became Barnabas (BARANA-) who was not only a Levite and filled with 'the holy spirit' but was called the 'encourager'. It SOUNDS like the Sanskrit brother as the support system.

The eunuchs were considered to be bald and hairless. They exercised so much power and celebrity (IS halaBARATA) as the brothers (BARATA) of the sun (HALA), that young boys craved to become part of their social construct. They shaved their heads and succumbed to castration. The subsequent habit of shaving the beard (BARADA) may have its roots out of the power base that the eunuch priesthood possessed. The celibacy of priests in the Roman Catholic Church may have its origins here. It may be an ironic coincidence that in the twenty-first century a plethora of men shave their heads and proudly display their shiny bald pates.

The Egyptian Sphinx has a lion's body with ostensibly a male pharaonic head. The male head is clean shaven. He has no goatee plastered on his chin as do later Egyptian pharaohs. The massive statue is much older than has been postulated. It comes out of a time in PHASE TWO when the brother (BARADA) based eunuch priesthood were considered to be the beardless (BARADA-), bald and hairless rulers. They were supplanting their mothers at the throne. As the heterosexual male ostracized base, the peripheral band of brothers was gaining momentum in PHASES TWO and THREE. To retain their thrones of power the eunuch priesthood plastered goatees on their bald chins.

Then came one of the many disastrous cataclysms on the beleaguered continent of Africa that periodically displaced the ancient migrators. They scattered in all directions as the global recurrence of the eunuch (HANAKA) name proclaims. Some went across the Mediterranean Sea up to Spain, then further North to the BasQUE country that bears in its name the QUE of QUEsting of their peripheral state. Then on to France where the brut (BARATA) defined not only wine but the castrated man as the 'dry one'. Passing the rest of Europe especially the Alps, we have to pause over Asti the frozen ancient mummified man who had been found murdered there. It has been proclaimed that he was five thousand years old. It is not often mentioned by the male scientists that he had been castrated.

Further up North, the Sami people of Scandinavia share DNA links with the Berbers (BARABARA-) that go back nine thousand years. On their way North the migrating Berbers BARABARA-) must have passed through Poland. It explains why so many words in Polish seem to have links with the

Barbary (BARABARA) Pirates and why the name of Barbara (BARABARA) is so common.

If one group went North to become the feared and dreaded Vikings then another turned West through Brittany (BARATA-) and then to Britain (BARATA-). Here 'the dry one' became the brute BARATA), or the uncivilized barbaric (BARABARA-) pagan Druid who built Stonehenge next to the river of passage, the river Avon (HAVANA) reached by a wide avenue (HAVANA) creating a bridge (BARADA) an 'INTERMEDIATE STATE' between this world and the next. As males searching for their source *away* and *above* the body of Mother Earth the next stop was not only across the great divide of the Atlantic Ocean but HAVANA, the stop over to the seven (IS HAVANA) sisters, the Pleiades from whence in PHASE TWO they believed to have been descended. They called them Shet (IS HATA) Ahad (HAHADA) of the birthing (BARA-) breath (BARA-) of the mothers.

At their ceremonies at Stonehenge they ate masses of boar (BARA) meat, not because pigs were expendable but because they knew that pigs were not only smart but sacred and ingesting their flesh would assist them as a bridge (BARADA) of passage on their journey into immortality.

The shift to the left hemisphere of the human brain (BARA-) left behind and obliterated the knowledge of the role that animals played in human passage across the bridge (BARA-) of death.

The brute (BARATA) may have been the Neanderthal male with his larger brain (BARANA), the bright (BARATA) one with red hair and stocky build who surfaces as Enkidu (HANAKADA) in the epic of Gilgamesh and later on as Lug in Europe. Both may have been considered the brutes (BARATA-) who became the bards (BARADA-), the traveling singers of romantic ballads, perhaps even the Romany or Gypsies from the ancient Harrapan culture in the Indus valley, subsequently the castrati tenors of contemporary Catholicism.

How does all of this surface in a country with a name like Britain (BARATANA), or the holder (TANA) with the ten (TANA) fingers of the brat (BARATA) the exiled younger brother (BARATARA)? In British a different dilemma surfaces as Brit-ish or one one who is like (-ish) a brother (BARATA) or a brat (BARATA), or an ancient exiled, castrated and often maimed smith. Smith is a common English name. Broken down linguistically smith (IS MATA) is one who either belonged to or was like the mother (MATA-) having links with PHASE ONE and mother centrality out of Africa.

Before the maternal name of a female became mother (MATARA) it was (MATA) out of PHASE ONE. One of the sources of (MATA) is not only the mouth (MATA) of the mother sMOTHERing carnivore prey and masticating food but also the nocturnal moth (MATA) associated with the moon whose job was pulling tides across the body of Mother Earth and counting (KANATA-) time with the monthly passage of blood out of the female cunt (KANATA). Since mathematics (MATA-) also begin with (MATA) then counting (KANATA-) with the cunt (KANATA) with the thirteen month lunar moon had also been the counter (KANATA-) with both belonging to the ancient mothers.

During the day the beautiful butterfly fluttering through space was associated with the sun. The butterfly in Spanish on the Iberian (haBARANA) peninsula is mariposa and mariposa in Spanish is a derogatory name for a male homosexual.

A secret cult of devotees surfaces at this ancient time with the name of the mother (MATARA) out of PHASE ONE but with traditions and symbolism out of PHASE TWO and the bloody sacrifice of the bull, the male cow. The cult of Mithras (MATARA-) expressed the ancient perception that only the blood of the mother coagulating inside her body made the baby. Since they sacrificed a bull and the bull was becoming a male deity especially in Crete for the Minoans, we are in PHASES TWO and THREE when male animals replaced the female animals as totemic symbols with their sacrificial blood pouring over the despairing males. Bull fighting as mucho macho male activity in Spain is a throwback to that ancient practice.

The ancient stories as experiences of the migrating mothers out of PHASE ONE became denigrated to the position of an unknown and unreal reality and the reign of mysterious myths (MATA) the time of the ancient mothers as in PHASES TWO and THREE due to the shift from the left handed mothers to the right handed fathers with the advent of writing itself, reality became linear and became redefined and rationalized out of male experience dealing with the answers to the why of male periphery.

It is to the Barbaric (BARABAR-) cum Tuareg Amazons working in concert with the ancient Neanderthal that we may owe our Western Alphabet and to English itself for the SOUNDS that emerged from the SHAPE of those letters that had their origins out of the individual mothers face and metaphorically out of the surFACE of Mother Earth.

The Romans with their love for organization and violence spreading their left hemispheric powers across the ancient world went after the Barbarians surrounding them. There is a perception that the Barbarians were all 'pagan' tribes. The word Barbarian was not an adjective defining the uncivilized hordes surrounding the 'civilized' Romans. The word Barbarian was an actual name of an actual people, the Berbers out of the desiccating Sahara who migrated not only to Northern Europe but to the British Isles and then to Ireland. Off the coast of Scotland the Heberdies (haBARADAsa) Islands also show links with the Barbarians as does the Sinclair (IS HANAKALA-) name that defines the ancient mother based head of the family, the castrated uncle (HANAKALA).

Recently a magnificent grave had been discovered in Ireland of a rich, well appointed woman with her carriage and personal belongings to assist her in her journey to the next world. The Barbarians of Ireland cum the Druids (DARADA) believed in reincarnation as did the Egyptians and the Neanderthal. A woman may have been their leader. It is a similar grave of a powerful woman that has been discovered in Southern Russia. The discovery has sent scientific male archeologists into a tail spin. They also discovered that the system of governance of the Druids (DARADA) was from the bottom up and democratic and not from the top down of authoritarian fascism. Democracy (DAMA-) is a system of ruling out of the mother's shared experience out of PHASE ONE.

Because the Druids left no writing and orally transmitted their traditions and history, their brains didn't begin to tilt to the left hemisphere of linear thought, unbridled sexuality and violence. They may have been the 'free people' of the Tuareg cum Berber.

It was in PHASE THREE that 'THE WORD' written by the right hand of the fathers ascended to the throne subsequently with the emerging power base of the left hemispheric dictators. This same process happened the world over as the violent male centered band of brothers with the gene of power and war alive in them conquered the clusters of peaceful female centered families called the Barbarians. Another factor surfaces in Ireland. They were known for their metal work, for working at the forge, for being smiths and having settled a disappearing island off their coast called Hybrasil (haBARAsala). The word Brasil (BARAsala) surfaces here and the dispersed migrators may also have settled the far reaches of South America, as they did the islands of Barbados (BARA-) and Bermuda (BARA-).

A TRIBUTE TO THE BIRDS.

In PHASE THREE along the villification of the snake, of women and the exploitation of the body of Mother Earth, the moniker of 'bird brain' became associated with our avian relatives. Along with so much redefinition, it is also a lie. An off hand remark that 'it is for the birds' deals with the same perception. Birds are far from being slow on the uptake. They have learned how to levitate and with their soaring flight negate the laws of gravity. Specifically and at the right moment with great wisdom they leave their oncoming cold and wintry nests and head for warmer climates in Africa. Somehow, navigating by an internal magnetic compass (Lea lines) they always found their way in both directions, migrating away from the creeping cold of their wintry reaches and after their job had been done with the drought stricken savannahs behind them, wheeling in great departing circles away from their African nests. As descendents of the dinosaurs they, along with sharks and crocodiles have the most ancient history. Everything that has evolved to create aspects of survival, birds have in one way or another internalized. We, so high on our totem pole contain the sum total of all that the birds have learned along the way.

They are master builders and weavers as many of their nests proclaim. They are also creative architects. Not to be outdone some species have an esthetic sense and are distinctive designers. Others create music that is so specific and varied that a word evolved to describe it as onomatopoeia, or bird SOUND. Many birds such as the Sand Cranes and Canada Geese are so devoted that they mate for life. Others are less dedicated. Many share in the care of their young. Some mothers feign a broken wing to deter predators. Others lay their eggs in the nests of other birds and save themselves the burden of raising their young. Some like company. Others prefer being alone. The variety of bird qualities is endless. To think that birds don't think or feel is ignorance on the highest level.

In Egypt there is an Ibis headed bird God named Thoth (TATA) who is the God of wisdom. Where does wisdom reside? In the brain, where there is the possibility for thought (TATA). The Egyptians understood the magic inherent in birds. They buried the mummified Ibis in sanctified graves. WHY? Because birds flew up to heaven. They were masters of that 'INTERMEDIATE STATE'. What did they know that we have forgotten? Then you have the feathered serpent of the Maya and Aztec on the other side of the world, the Kundalini energy *away* and *above* the body of Mother Earth taking flight into the heavens (HAVANA).

The BARA dyad may harken back to very ancient times but it shares its constancy with the codified SOUND of the consonants in the native languages, not in the way that the words may have been written. The consonants are relatively constant. Like the 'shape shifting' moon, the vowels that carry the

SOUNDS are often fickle. As the carriers of extended SOUND the vowels are often heir to improvisation, although some, at times, like the A (Ah) SOUND may respond to the rules of constancy. Like the unvoiced letter (H) has been dropped off from words beginning with a vowel, so the letters (K) and (W) at the beginning of words are often unvoiced.

KNOW= NOW (NAWA)

It goes back to the nose. It is the nose that KNOWS even though the letter (K) defining smallness is silent belonging to the small individual mother not the large Mother Earth. The (NA) deals with 'emergence on the surface' or 'a change from a former state'. The (WA) deals with water or the emergence out of a reflected watery reality. As an aspirating and smelling organ on the mothers face the nose comes with a unique evolutionary story. All the senses criss cross in the body. The left side of the body is controlled by the right hemisphere of the brain. The right side of the body is controlled by the left hemisphere of the brain. They criss-cross at the area of the bridge of the nose. But the nostrils of the nose do not criss-cross they go straight up on a dual track into the olfactory bulb of the brain. The nose may be the oldest sensory organ. The universe may be governed by the sense of smell. A mother smells and hears her baby. The chick can smell and hear its mother. A male in rut smells the estral female in heat. In both sexes pheromones floating on the air activate sexual attraction.

The nose (NASA) creates the activity of beginnings. In Latin nascence (NASANASA) means repetitive birth. Birthing establishes the activity of beginnings. Beginnings occur in the NOW moment. The sense of smell also occurs in the NOW moment. Like sNOW itself it passes quickly. Therefore to KNOW is to be in the NOW. *The NOW moment is not an idea in the mind. It is an experience in the body. The body never lies.* The NOW moment of experience is the present of the present. Ideas float around like vowels. It is difficult to pin them down and they change. But the body is always true to itself. When it is excited it flushes itself with goose pimples. When it is hungry it eats. When it is thirsty it drinks. When cold grips it, it covers itself with clothing and seeks shelter. When it has to go, it goes. When an alien host attacks it, it raises its temperature and burns it out of its system. The body should be listened to. The body always tells the truth.

Because it exists in the NOW, the experience in the body is a series of NEW occurences, or KNEW occurences. For the moment that an experience happens it is already old hat, it has already passed, it is already past tense. Somebody, somewhere KNEW what they were putting together in our linguistic story and like a leit motif in a symphony it gave us all the clues to find the singular ancient theme out of PHASE ONE.

The silent consonant (K) at the beginning of Knose, Knew, Know may give us pause but since the SHAPE of the letter (K) is a birds beak in profile and since also the letter (K) deals with birds, smallness and beginnings then we are dealing with the smaller creations out of the body of Mother Earth.

The letter K may also have its origins out of the letter X of the buttox halved vertically facing in opposite directions. The SOUND of (K) as (KH) (KAHA) also defines the cough (KAHA) of death and that may be the reason that dealing with live experience in the NOW (NAWA) for it acts as a silent reminder at the beginning of active words. But existing there even silently, it never lets us off the hook. It is reminding us that even with the present of the present, or the experience in the NOW, we are forever facing the watery (WA) entombment and that we are a small (K) guest on this planet.

PHANTOM=FANTOM (FANATAMA);
The (PH) of PHANTOM and the (F) of FANTOM dealing with the pronunciation or SOUND are made in the same area of the mouth. They as a consonant are made by the air being exploded through the top lip.

The SHAPE of (FA) and the SHAPE of (PA) come out of the two sets of frontal appendages. One set of frontal appendages as the (FA) in stage ine the five fingers on the human body and the other set of frontal appendages as (PA) the pads of paws (PAWA) on the lower part of the body of a carnivore creature. The (FA) of fingers on the human body may have morphed into the (PA) as the paws of power on the lower front feet of a carnivore.

The original PHANTOM may have been a stalking carnivore leopard, cheetah or lioness silently, on carefully padded paws (PA) slinking its way through the myriad obfuscating dapples of the forest or through the deceptively tinted tawny grass of the savannah, difficult to see and dangerous.

The SHAPE of both the paws (PA) extended and the palm of open fingers (FA) are like the fan (FANA) in FANtom (FANATAMA). In Polish (NA) means upon and (TA) in English deals with the top or tip, the tail end, as the paws and fingers are on the tip, top or ends of the extended appendages. The (MA) at the end of PHANTOM deals with the mother and among the carnivores it is the mother who does the singular job of hunting for her cubs. The carnivore mother sMOTHERS her prey as she grabs it with her paws and brings it down. It is in her paws (PAWA-) that her power (PAWA-) resides. The (WA) in paws deals with water as the passage (PA) of reflective watery (WA) death. It shares its aspect as prey with the sun being smothered by the watery body of Mother Earth in the Western horizon. It is what the prey faces when it is brought down by the hungry predator.

In PHASES TWO and THREE as fear and the panic stricken image led to fantasy, the carnivore mother stalking her prey through the bushes became the anthromorphized ghostly PHANTOM killer, the ghostly presence in the jungle or tall grass. Early human beings in PHASE ONE leaving the jungle and the savannah behind had to contend dealing only with the violent weapon carrying busy and dangerous fingers (FA) of their human neighbors.

PHALLUS (PALASA) and FALLUS (FALASA);

The PHALLUS is one of the names for the penis. Its definition emerged out of a time in PHASE ONE when the role of the penis as a specific co-parent was still unknown. Out of a similar linguistic basket both words surface in Polish in their own unique ways. PHALLUS (PALASA) In Polish deals linguistically with a finger palec (PALASA). It goes even further back in English into pole (PALA). A Polish finger was SHAPED like the English pole (PALA). The (PA) deals with passage. The (LA) deals with the *angle of emergence* dealing with the Eastern sun out of the body of Mother Earth. It goes even further back for (PALASA) is also the linguistic construct of not only place (PALASA) but palace (PALASA). Were ancient palaces made of poles? Maybe. But that is not the direction this is going.

We have to pick up the Phallus (FALASA) and realize that we are dealing with the name of a movement. In Polish fala, in (FALAsa) an ancient word based on the (ah) SOUND means a 'wave' on the watery surFACE of Mother Earth. The (FA) in fala deals with movement, with the fingers (FA) of water that as waves create movement, they stretch out across the beach, grab the unwary, and entomb the water logged. What does a wave do? Like a finger it goes up and down. What is the major activity of the penis if you don't know that it also made babies? In PHASE ONE male role in specific procreation was unknown. The phallus was only seen as the organ on the male body that like a wave went up and down.

Expanding its extra curricular activities as the Polish finger as palec (PALASA) it evolved linguistically as the extra finger that pleasured their partners. Masturbation must have been one of the most ancient sources of birthing, pleasure and stress relief. Where did all of this activity take place (PALASA) in the palace (PALASA). Palace must have been very important for the generic name of place (PALASA) comes out of the same linguistic construct as palace (PALASA). It was in those ancient pleasure (PALASARA) palaces (PALASA) that the holy women, the houris taught males how to pleasure their partners. Great loss.

With the addition of the (RA) at the end of pleasure (PALASARA) we are entering another territory. For RA as the sun had been considered the doer, the helping hands of Mother Earth. If the (LA) of pleasure (paLAsara) dealt with LAdies, then the RA of pressure (paRAsara) dealt with men and stRess relief.

In PHASE THREE in the Middle East Ra represented 'that which existed forever' and had its roots in the Egyptian sun God Ra. On the other side of the world still in PHASE ONE for the Maya 'that which existed forever was LA' and harkens back to the Lady of the Land, the pLAnet and Mother Earth. A similar linguistic construct surfaces in the words play and pray. Play (PALAYA) as a joyful activity dealt with the mother as the Lady of the Land in PHASE ONE. Pray (PARAYA) as in pariah (PARAYA) entered the scene in PHASES TWO and THREE as the solar deity (RA) needing veneration co-opted the scene into male centrality.

Again in Polish another word raises its unruly head and that is palic (PALAJA) or (PALACHA) dealing with fire. Here we are again entering the territory of Mother Earth. Was it the finger of fire that snaked its way up through Her volcanic vent orgasming Her into a shattering eruption that created the land upon Her surFACE out of Her crater (KARATARA) the original creator (KARATARA)? There was no doubt that fingers played a major role in sexual pleasure.

Whole=hole (HALA);
Along with Hana and all the other dyads, in Spanish sol (IS HALA), is one of the earliest names for the sun. The sun rising at an angle (LA) out of the surFACE, or body of Mother Earth in the Eastern belly of air (HA) has been one of Her helping hands. The hole (HALA) at the Eastern rim had to be rendered by the stiletto like rays of the sun, the fingers at the edge, or the angle of the tongue that regurgitated the sun up to the surFACE allowing for the light to shine through. With the silent (W) as the anlaut it establishes its links with water and the nascent emergence of the sun out of its mysterious watery depths on the Eastern shore (IS HARA), the watery belly of Mother Earth. Mother Earth as the hole of creation on Her round ground of being becomes the whole of creation with the addition of (W) of Her watery womb.

Write=rite (RATA);
To write is to document the ritual (RATA-), to write it with the right hand of the father in PHASE THREE. (RATA) also deals with the ratio (RATA) of

a circle. A ratio is a fixed portion. It is not open to the majestic flow of the universe. To rationalize (RATA-) is to explain, to find an answer to the WHY. It is like a boomerang that always returns (RATA-) to the sender establishing the rut and must of another declination.

Wrong=rong (RANAGA)(RANA/NAGA);
The (RANA) in Polish stands for both 'wound ' and 'dawn' on the surFACE or body of Mother Earth. RA deals with the sun. (NA) deals with 'emergence on the surface'. It was perceived that the snake (IS NAKA, NAGA), the (K) and (G) are interchangeable, as it guided the sun on its journey through the dark intestines of the night, like the stiletto fingers it also assisted in creating a wound at the edge, the horizontal rim out of which the sun was born at dawn. Because it deals with what is not right but what is wrong, and what has been left, then we are dealing with male centrality in PHASE THREE.

RULE FIVE:
Names of Natural Phenomena, Especially out of Africa

Olduvai (HALADAVAYA) Gorge contains in its hidden linguistic folds a host of possibilities that throws a light on its origins out of PHASE ONE. (HALA-LADA-DAVA-VAYA) the four overlapping dyads reveal their own story. Reading from right to left as it was done originally by the left handed mothers of the Hebrew, Early Brahmin, Etruscan, Phoenician, Faliscan, Lydian, and Siberian, there had been others. Aya is light in Persian and dawn in Assyrian. If you stood on the West side of the great divide, the Olduvai chasm that snaked its way North-South of Eastern Africa, the light of the sun as aya in Persain and aya at dawn in Assyrian rose out of the other side out of that cleft, that great valley (VA) that gave birth to it, creating the first dyad of (VAYA).

There were times as they migrated back and forth across the great continent of Africa that the sun rose, or was regurgitated out of the mountains but in this case it was vomited (VA) out of the great and gorgeous gorge, the Eastern mouth on the surFACE of Mother Earth. The (VAYA) at the end is the SHAPE of the movement of light out of that volcanic cleft, mouth, or any via (VAYA). (DAVA) establishes the 'gift of' (DA), of (VA) or the gift out of the volcanic vulvic vent on the body of Mother Earth out of which She birthed the sun every morning. (DAVAYA) takes it a step further for it deals with the whole concept of the (DA) 'gift of' the via (VA) of the light (AYA).

The source of that light at dawn came out of two processes, one was Mother

Earth herself as the lady (LADA) of the Land giving birth to the sun at dawn. The other were the actual rays of the sun as Her great stretching stiletto like fingers that broke the rim at the horizon and helped the sun to rise at dawn to awaken Her sleeping children. The helping (HALA-) hands, morphs into the Spanish sol (IS HALA) and the Greek sun as eelyos (HALA-).

The Olduvai Gorge linguistically is the place on the Eastern side on the continent of Africa out of which the sun had been perceived to rise every morning out of a deep vulvic volcanic cleft on Her body spreading Her gift of dawn and light upon Her sleeping creatures. It also throws light upon the contemporary repeated dogma in PHASE THREE that the ancient 'pagan' people were so ignorant that they believed that if you walked too close to the edge of the world you would fall off, as you might on the edge of the Grand Canyon. In PHASE ONE teetering on the edge of the Olduvai Gorge may have given birth to that ancient rather obvious observation.

The Masai Mara is a tribe in East Central Africa. It must be ancient for it is based on the originally codified A(ah) vowel SOUND. It also deals clearly with two major ancient components. One is the MA of the mother as MARA RIVER also in East Central Africa, the home of the Masai Mara tribe. The other is Ra the Egyptian solar deity, the helping hands of Mother Earth. The MARA dyad surfaces all over the world for it gave birth to many of the MARine (MARA-) concepts and environments.

The name of MARA may have evolved out of the latter part of PHASE TWO when Mother Earth (MA) and the sun (RA) seemed to work together in the linguistic construct of MARA. They may have reflected the relative peaceful reality that existed on the planet between women and men as they migrated together and raised their children as a cooperative group. It wasn't to last, for in PHASE TWO the shift out of female centrality was beginning to take place. Males were beginning to realize their role in specific procreation and began their search for their fathers and their own Gods *away* and *above* the body of Mother Earth, ergo the begats of the Hebrew Bible.

The climactic conditions also shifted as did the migratory patterns of the herbivore herds. There are linguistic clues to the fact that the migrations following the falling monsoon rains in the distance covered many areas in Africa. The savannahs emerged in different areas that were sought out by the pregnant *mares* and by the following clumps of humanity. With the mare (MARA) as a female creature with her womb of water in her belly we are still in female centrality and in PHASE ONE. There emerged a time when the climate shifted to such a degree that people migrated North to the Sahel and

Section Two

then even further North to the then verdant Sahara.

The Sahara also went through its own desertification every twenty thousand years, due to a polar shift, most recently ten thousand years ago but before it did its marine (MARA-) environment slid over to the West coast of Africa where the sun was swallowed every night, killed to its light, resisting and fighting all the way, giving names to the tribes and places, the Moors (MARA-), of Mauritania, (MARA-) and Morocco (MARA-). The Maori (MARA) of New Zealand who left Africa fifty thousand years before may have been part of that African marine (MARA-) configuration.

Then in PHASE TWO a shift again occurred in the relationship between mothers and their male children. Emerging male knowledge in their role in specific paternity extended to embrace the metaphoric relationship between Mother Earth and the sun. Since mothers and Mother Earth dealt with life *above* the reflected surFACE of water, then initially searching for their specific father, males took over the domain of the underworld, the reflected reality of death *below* in the still waters.

The words in the language deal with that reflection. The MARA dyad of Mother Earth becomes reflected to become the male RAMA (MARA/RAMA) as do most of the other deities (MAYA/YAMA) etc. The MA was *above* the surFACE of Mother Earth. The RA was the male deity who dealt with the sun that had set into the Western waters dying to its light being swallowed by Her great maw. Every night She killed him, ate him, as he struggled not to set into Her open maw, stripping him of his light. Resenting his role as the constant victim he as the sun rose into the sky and separated himself from the creative source of Mother Earth. With his role in specific paternity becoming known he emerged in PHASE THREE as far away as possible above in Mars (MARA-) becoming Her war lord and master.

What was occurring on the mundane plane was the primal war between mothers and the emerging fathers that began to be reflected on the body of Mother Earth between Her and the emerging sons of the sun. The power struggle on the Earthly plane was echoed on the universal battleground as the male God of War became MARS (MARASA).

In MARA the (MA) as water as the marine (MARA-) environment was also associated by the (WA) SOUND associated with *water*. For along with Mars as the male God of War *away* and *above* the body of Mother Earth there surfaces war itself as Mother Earth (MA) as the watery (WA) grave in the West swallowing the sun (RA) every night became the cannibalistic villain that had to be destroyed. The marine (MARA-) environment and the watery

(WA) terminus of the sun in the Western horizon became the words that evolved into Mars the God of War and war itself.

The (MA) of the mountainous mouths as the top lip on the individual mothers face and the top lip on the surFACE of Mother Earth came together with the reflection of the (M) of the top lip into the (W) of the bottom lip extending to the waters, the bottom lip on the surFACE of Mother Earth. Both the top lip (MA) and the bottom lip (WA) created the mouth, the watery maw (MAWA) that ate the sun every night.

In PHASE THREE there began the male journey into the destruction of the female source of creation, be it the individual mother, or the more extensive body of Mother Earth. As males established their dominance over the individual mother as the creator of life out of her body, she had to be shackled, restrained, clitorectimized. Her power rested not singularly out of the fact that she enjoyed sex. Her power emerged out of the birthing breath in the last stages of labor that activated the powerful Kundalini energy of trance. It eems ironic that the Statue of Liberty in the New York harbor has shackles or chains around her feet.

The bi-pedal upright birthing mother had to squat, pant hard and fast (HAHA) to get the large headed human fetus out of her body. The high fast panting breath acting like a bellows awakened the fiery solar sourced electro-magnetic Kundalini energy of shakti lying at the base of her spine. As it coiled upwards through her body like a double snake, it burned out most of the traces of fear that she carried as a young girl. The ecstatic trance state that the Kundalini energy awakened in the panting mother defused any source of panic and made the mother, any mother, a fearless defender of her baby.

Fearlessness is the major part of the 'spiritual' journey and is the leading aspect of 'self realization'. As the head of the fetus worked its way down out of her body, her uterus began to spasm, began to orgasm to help her in the process of birthing. The head of the fetus as it moved down through the vaginal canal brushed up against the clitoris and caused it also to spasm or orgasm. The peristalsis of the uterine orgasm assisted by the pressure by the head of the baby gave the mother not only pain but ecstatic pleasure and on that wave of bountiful joy she bonded with the product of her great labors. It may well be that the male penis called 'the head' gave pleasure to the mother from the outside as the baby's head gave the mother pleasure from the inside.

There was another gift to the birthing mother with the birthing breath. As she moved into the Kundalini trance, she by becoming fearless opened areas of experience that not only dealt with fearlessness but with a movement away from the close ended rationalizations of the left hemispheric brain into the open ended flow of the universe. Fearlessness brings with it the fusion of the two hemispheres of the brain. That fusion as the 'intermediate state' is the doorway or bridge to transformation, balance, wisdom, prophecy, healing, leadership and all the aspects that have been called mysticism. It is also the bridge to the state of trance and the mystery of where that state of trance resides. Taking a clue from the Australian Aborigines as they 'walk about' in their 'dream time', *it may be that the state of trance is the dream state brought to the level of consciousness.*

Males were not privy to that ecstatic experience. They yearned for the powers of the mothers. Tales of young men seeking for many trials of discovery echo that ancient search. Mothers were very powerful. They realized that it was the activity of the clitoris in its orgasmic state that made the mother powerful. It was the clitoris of the mother that became the enemy. It was the clitoris of the mother that had to be removed. War was declared on the mother's body, especially the clitoris. The clitoris was not only removed but the wound of mutilation was sewed up and only a small hole was created for urine and menstrual blood to pass through. "Ye shall bear your children in pain" to repeat the phrase by the Hebrew God Jehovah. Was there a time when women did not bear their children in pain? It would seem so. In PHASE THREE as the practice of clitorectomies or the removal of the whole organismic vulvic ovular circle became the practice of Northern Africa, the Middle East and Southern Asia, to give birth women had to be hacked apart. The wound scenario entered the picture. It exists to this day in the same areas of the world as unclitorectomized girls cannot find husbands and Arab boys masturbate to pictures of mutilated women.

In PHASE THREE Mother Earth had to suffer the same fate. Her singular source of creation had to be denied as the heavenly solar deities, the stars and then the heavenly Father took over the singular male sources of creation. Not only Mars rose up into the heavens but war was declared on the body of Mother Earth. She became abused, defiled, polluted, destroyed, gouged, desecrated, exploited and Her many creations suffering the same fate slowly became extinct.

SAHARA (IS HAHARA) (HAHA-HARA);

The Sahara on the body of Mother Earth as one of the places of early humanity contains in its linguistic folds the (HAHA) of the individual mothers birthing breath. For haha is the name for the mother in Japanese. In all of the rest of the world the SOUND of M defines the mother. So much for disparate areas of the world coming up with the same SOUND. The M SOUND defining the mother is monogenesis in action. The (HARA) dyad in Sahara (IS HARA) deals with the belly of air (HARA) that in Hebrew means both the pregnant belly and holy mountain. (HARA) also means belly in Japanese. The watery shore (IS HARA) is also the source of the birth of the sun or another belly of source on the watery body of Mother Earth.

So the Sahara (IS HAHARA) Desert is the result of the birthing breath (HAHA) that Mother Earth who gave birth out of Her belly of air (HARA), as She was birthing one of Her major creations, the desiccating sun. The (HAHA) dyad defines the mother in Japanese. In the process of birthing the sun with her schorching rays the ancient African verdant savannah shrunk into the desiccated Sahara (IS HAHARA) Desert that exists to this day.

Another name pops up as a solar deity in Ahura (HAHARA) Mazda the Persian sun god. He rose above his twin brother Ahriman (HAHARAMANA) whom he deposed and threw out of heaven to reign underground. The 'two in one' aspect surfaces here with the solar twins. It tells the story of the sun in its twin aspect as passing through the belly of air above the surFACE of Mother Earth and the other twin moving through the underground intestines within Her body. The sun above the plane was not only filled with light and was considered good but the sun below the plane was dark and was considered to be evil. Much has been made of this observation.

The Sahel (IS HAHALA);

It sits across the equator where the days and nights are of equal duration and where the concept of evenness and balance may have had its origins. It contains within it a variety of possibilities. The (HAHA) as the birthing breath of the Mother defining the name of the mother in Japanese. This time it deals with Mother Earth linked to two possibilities. One is the (LA) of Mother Earth as the pLAnet. The other is (HALA) of the Spanish sol (IS HALA). It would seem that the Sahel (IS HAHAla) was an earlier place of origins out of PHASE ONE with not only the birthing breath of Mother Earth (HAHA) but at the time in the uni-verse when the body of Mother Earth and the solar (IS HALAra) diisc had been considered to be one unit. That had been the most ancient perception of reality.

There is another clue in the Hebrew Caballah as the Zohar (IS HAHARA). The Caballah linguistically has links with the creature of passage, the horse, or mare, caballo in Spanish. It also has links with the same linguistic source as the Sahara (IS HAHARA). Since it contains the (RA) of the Egyptian solar deity in its name then it would seem to emerge out of PHASE THREE when the diasphoric Jews wandered around the Sahara (IS HAHAra) desert and described their source out of that desiccated but sacred place out of that ancient dichotomy.

It also reveals the battle for power in PHASE THREE between the eunuch priesthood and the emerging heterosexual band of brothers who became the subsequent ruling bandits. The eunuch priesthood bemoaning their mutilated state became relegated underground whom Ahriman represented. The sun above the plane as Ahura Mazda emerged as the deity of the emerging fathers. Ahura (HAHARA) Mazda was originally the Mother on both levels with her birthing breath (HAHA) that survived as the definition for the mother in Japanese. The (HARA) is Her (HARA) belly of air (HARA) into which the sun rose every morning. The twin solar brothers surface all around the mythological world representing the two aspects of the sun; above and below, light and darkness, good and evil, and subsequently in PHASE THREE heaven and hell. The Biblical Enoch follows the same trajectory as Ahriman, as do all the angels thrown out of heaven to dwell in the darkness underneath the mantle of Mother Earth. Fallen angels, ones who had been thrown out of heaven had been heterosexual males in whom the Kundalini had awakened and they could mate with Earthly women.

A curious SHAPE emerges representing a letter in Hebrew as heh (HAHA). It is SHAPED like a three sided box with no bottom. It is similar in SHAPE to the Russian letter P. It too surfaces with the dyad (HAHA). It looks like a birthing stool. Not to be outdone in Chinese the same SHAPE surfaces defining Pi or a dragon. Pi also defines the one moving foot and is also part of the definition of a circle. The circle in many of its forms etched into the ground goes back into prehistory and PHASE ONE.

The SHAPE of the birthing stool is often contained within a circle. On the body of Mother Earth the same birthing stool SHAPE is echoed in the menhir or dolmen. They contain two upright massive stones with a lateral lentil on tip, like a box with no bottom.

If the individual mother squatting on a stool during birthing with the high fast panting breath could activate the Kundalini energy to get the large headed fetus out of her body as she was overwhelmed with goose pimples and ecstasy, then the same experience must have been perceived to be shared with the body of Mother Earth.

They knew that if they crossed specific areas on the body of Mother Earth, they could feel the ecstatic Kundalini energy rising from Her as they responded by becoming stoned and by rocking back and forth. They called those tracks of pleasure lea lines for they lay upon the Lady of the Land.

Those ancient beings out of female centrality in PHASE ONE before they lost their ancient knowledge that the body of Mother Earth was a ball floating in space, mapped the body of their overwhelming maternal context with a grid that when they stepped on it, they could always depend on it to make them feel the flow of ecstatic pleasure.

That same grid as the seven Tantric chacras, charted along the human spine established how this solar sourced electro-magnetic Kundalini energy of shakti moved through the human body. The Greeks counted twelve systems that had to be faced to become transformed and self-realized as in the twelve labors of Hercules. The Tibetans and the Hopi Indians count five. If it was the birthing breath of the individual mother (HAHA) that sent her into paroxysms of ecstasy, then metaphorically Mother Earth must also have been moved into ecstatic states as She shared that same birthing experience (HAHA) giving birth to the Sahara (IS HAHAra) and Zohar (IS HAHAra).

Since the experience dealt with moving into a trance state then they felt that it was a movement from one area to another, a passage through a door, through a defined opening. On Mother Earth's body that opening human beings in PHASE ONE constructed in the SHAPE of the menhir or dolman under which the ecstatic breath (HAHA) of the birthing mother could be experienced. In Hebrew the SHAPE of a dolman or menhir is a box with no bottom, standing on two legs and has been called the heh (HAHA) or the birthing breath of the mother. As they passed or sat under those menhirs and dolmen they could enter that 'intermediate state' of the Tibetans and be moved into another level of experience.

The lateral lentil on those massive stones in Stonehenge and other areas of the world, are not there to keep the massive stones from toppling. They were placed there to concentrate the energy of trance that created not only a yoking at the center but an entrance, a portal into a state of ecstatic transformation. It was that state of transformation that originally in PHASE ONE only mothers experienced with the birthing breath. It brought with it a variety of gifts; power, healing, prophecy, leadership, and fearlessness making the mother, any mother, a fierce protector of her baby.

During the trials of 'spiritual' discovery the first thing that has to be jettisoned is fear, whether it is called ego, or negativity, or a closed heart. 'Self-Realization' is the first step dealing with clearing out the fear. The stables flushed by the two Herculean rivers, (two twining Kundalini snakes) in the Greek Labors of Hercules deal with that chacral manure removal of fear laden habitual debris.

Males not able to experience the birthing breath of the mothers went in a variety of ways to touch the hem of that ecstatic outpouring. It seemed to surface automatically in the castrated first born son of the mothers who became the eunuchs and uncles to protect their families. In PHASE TWO many young heterosexual heroes jumped on their steeds and cleared out their chacras by doing battle with a dragon, monster, one eyed giant, any looming object (Mother Earth), which only meant that they were dealing with their fears and looking how to experience the ecstatic birthing breath of the mothers.

The Biblical story of Adam deals with the snake, the Kundalini energy as the coiling serpent up the human spine who dispensed great wisdom and knowledge. Eve already knowledgeable about its ecstatic power of the birthing breath wanted to share it with him. He had *not* gone through all the clearing out of his lower chacras that are necessary for it to take hold and since we are in the Bible and PHASE THREE of male centrality we are *not* dealing with castration. He had to stay a heterosexual male, so both are driven out of the Garden of Eden, (HADANA) the place where pleasure had its hedonistic (HADANA-) home.

The birthing breath of the mothers as the source of creation competed with the hidden mind of God in the ethers, so she has to be stripped of her power and pleasure. The celestial God Jehovah admonished her that she would bear her children in pain, no longer will the ecstatic birthing breath be part of her experience. Adam not to be left out completely, had his penis circumcised, for it to spurt with blood, for blood had still been considered as the only source of life. Circumcision had become a symbolic act replacing ancient castration.

RULE SIX;
Phonological Correspondence

Over time some consonants may have become interchangeable, especially if they are made in the same area of the mouth. Simplify them to expose their original meaning.

H in Spanish as young, joven (HAVANA).
H (huh) in English anlaut for h in hand, Hebrew harah (HARA) pregnancy
H in Polish chova (HAVA) hidden, Hebrew JeHOVAH hidden God
H in Hebrew in Chanukkah (HANAKA) holiday of light
K (kh) in English charisma (KARASAMA)
K (kh) Kali Hindu Goddess, kont (KANATA) Polish corner, cunt
C (kh) English cave (KAVA), corpse (KARAPASA), coos (KASA)
X (ks) is (KASA), ax (HAKASA), exit (HAKASATA)
Q (kue) (KA or KAYA), que (KA) why in Spanish, quest (KASATA)
G (gh) as in ghost (GASATA), silent (H)
G (gh) in English get (GATA), Polish gura (GARA) mountain
G (jee) as in genius (JANASA), gee (JA), giant (JAYANATA), gyno (JANA)
J (jee) as in Jenie, as judge (JAJA), hedge (HAJA), range (RANAJA)
DZ (jee) in Polish as dziadzia (JAJA) old man
S (SA), sage (SAJA or (IS HAJA)), stone (IS TANA)
C (see (SA), cent (IS HANATA), century (IS HANATARA)
SH (IS HA), She (IS HA), shine (IS HANA),
Z(zee)=(SA) zero (IS HARA), zebra (IS HABARA), zenith (IS HANATA)
T(tee)(TA), Tetons (TATANA) mountains, tea (TA) drink
TH (tuh)(TA) thing (TANAGA), mouth (MATA), beth (BATA) Hebrew house
D (dee) (DA), body (BADA), demon (DAMANA), deal (DALA)
Dh (duh) (DA), dug (DAGA), dust (DASATA), devide (DAVADA)
B (bee)(BA), be (BA), beast (BASATA), being (BANAGA),
B (buh) (BA), bust (BASATA), must (MASATA),
P (pee)(PA), appeal (HAPALA), peer (PARA), pass (PASA)
Ph (puh or fuh) (PA or FA), push (PASA), food (FADA), phallus (FALASA)
F (fuh) (FA), fur (FARA), foot (FATA), finger (FANAGARA)

V (vuh)(VA), vent (VANATA), volcano (VALAKANA), vulva (VALAVA), valley (VALAYA), valve (VALAVA), woda (VADA) water Polish, dawno (DAVANA) way back Polish,

W(wah)(WA) water (WATARA), wind (WANADA), war (WARA) double u)(WA), Hawwa Mesopotamian Eve,

Y (yuh)(YA), you (HAYA), yes (HAYASA),

Y (WHY) woo,

Y jutro (YATARA) Polish tomorrow, jest (HAYASATA) Polish is.

RULE SEVEN;
Deal with the ANLAUT, or the first letter in a word.

When the ANLAUT is a consonant, it usually establishes the meaning of the word that follows it.

The M ANLAUT; The most ubiquitous name that covers the body of Mother Earth is the name of the individual mother. Almost all of the names for the mother across the Globe begin with the ANLAUT of M, except in Japanese where it is associated with the HA-HA of the birthing breath. The SHAPE of the letter M deals with the mouth (MA-) of the mother (MA-), her top lip teaching her offspring what is safe to eat and what is to be avoided and discarded. She does this as she MAsticates the food in her mouth humming (haMA-) its edibility as she savors it. Her children mimic (MAMA-) her and learn the lessons of gustatory survival.

The concept of having a mouth and eating, expanded to include the metaphoric (MA-) surFACE and body of Mother Earth. If the individual mother had a slit on her round skull with hair on one side and a series of holes on the other, then their all inclusive MAternal global context also had to sport the same fanciful if metaphoric configuration.

On the flat round surFACE of Mother Earth there were obviously many (MA-) holes, many (MA-) slits that not only breathed with life but supported a multitude (MA-) of promises. The major (MA-) ones were not as apparent as the massive (MA-) chasm of the Olduvai Gorge. They existed as perceived notions on the two sides of the flat surFACE of their great Mother.

Because Mother Earth was much (MA-) larger than their individual mothers, she must (MA-) have had many (MA-) more (MA-) holes, but they settled for the many mouths SHAPED like the mountains (MA-) on either side of Her flat round surFACE from which the sun emerged at dawn and sank back into Her at twilight. She, like their individual mothers must (MA-) have eaten the sun at twilight and then vomited (-MA-) or regurgitated it back up to the surFACE at dawn. The same (-MA) process expanded to include the other heavenly bodies and even the birds.

The two great facial holes on either side of Her flat round horizontal surFACE were perceived at different times as different apertures. The most (MA-) ancient in stage two dealt with the two mouths of their great Mother, doing the job of swallowing in the West and regurgitating in the East. Then there came a time when it extended as both entrances and exits on the sides of the body of Mother Earth. The perception shifted when it came (-MA) to be believed that it was a series of wounds at Her horizontal sides that created the swallowing and regurgitation of the heavenly bodies. In Polish that concept emerges at the 'rana' dyad defining both wound and dawn. Ra deals with the emergence (NA) of the sun at dawn creating the wound at Her side.

The concept of wound as a source of creation out of Mother Earths side, surfaces in the Hebrew Bible as the birth of Eve out of the side of Adam. They, in PHASE THREE took the ancient Sumerian story of creation and restated it as male based. That same perception also hides behind its linguistic shutters the advent of clitorectimies, the wounds created on the mothers body for the baby to make (MA-) its entrance. When a baby made its enTRANCE in PHASE ONE accompanied by the trance filled breath of the birthing mother, it burst forth on the unfurled wings of a trance state.

An endless litany of words emerged to define the creative mother in all of her individual and Her majestic (MA-) glory. She was considered to be the magnificent (MA-) master (MA-) who created more (MA-) of everything and many (MA-) others. It was on Her mat (MA-) of matter(MA-) upon Her surFACE that Mother Earth made (MA-) all that was.

In PHASE THREE the MASTER with the MA of the Mother (MA-) with the change of the definitive vowel from (A) to the (I) of one more, emerged into the MISTER. There also occurred a shift in the power structure as the master of the mother not only became the mister but became the pastor of the father. Ma Story as the mystery associated with the birthing breath of the mother became Pa Story of the Pastor. And the *mist of the mister* as reinvented fantasy of the fathers emerged to hang like an impenetrable blanket over the real World.

Section Two

RULE EIGHT.
Anastrophe, Palindrome, Reflection, Inversion

Reading backwards and forward.

'Able was I ere I saw Elba' —Napoleon Bonaparte

It is the INVERSION, or the REFLECTION of syllables within a word, or words themselves that dealt with an eminently important ancient understanding of balance. The original perception of REFLECTION out of PHASE ONE and stage one dealt with the two lips on the human face. The top lip, the SHAPE encoded in the letter M as the mouth of the humming mother, was perceived to have been REFLECTED by the SHAPE of the bottom lip that became encoded into the SHAPE of the letter W. The two parts one above and one below were separated and joined by the line of the mouth. The same balance had been perceived to exist within the human brain. The two hemispheres had been considered to REFLECT each other, to be balanced when compassion of the right hemisphere of the left handed mothers was balanced by the linear logic of the left hemisphere of the right handed fathers.

On the surFACE of Mother Earth in one of its permutations in stage two, the letter W dealt with the REFLECTIVE quality of water, whose quiet often glassy surface mirrored in its mysterious depths the reality above. The concept comes into sharper focus on the surFACE of Mother Earth not only as the REFLECTED surface of water (W) below, but also the SHAPE of the mountains (M) above. As She lay on Her side, the line of separation and joining was the mouth at the horizon, into which the sun was swallowed every night, Mother Earth ate it. The mountains above were REFLECTED in the mysterious depths of the standing waters below. The waters, REFLECTING a mysterious containment in their depths, became the domain of death.

The number seven (IS EVEN) before it became (IS HAVANA) enters the picture at this point. As our ancient migratory trekkers looked in the distance at pools of quietly standing waters of the Okabongo River Delta they saw a complete REFLECTION as a dual reality in the waters before them.

'Look' they must have cried at the REFLECTED aquatic apparition before them, 'IS EVEN'. The REFLECTION of their world above in the waters below was an 'even' (HAVANA), if often temporary, magical replica of their world. The word even (HAVANA) also surfaces at the time of the ancient migrations when the thirteen month lunar year was broken up into two equal halves, one coming and one going, with the seventh (IS HAVANA) month of September as the pivotal fulcrum of separation and change.

In Persian the concept of balance goes right to the source. For in Persian the word for even as hattah, HAT/TAH reflects itself. The (HAT) REFLECTS the (TAH) creating a balance, an evenness within the word itself.

It may very well deal with the belly of air (HA) at the top (TA) and its REFLECTION at the top (TA), or surFACE where the air (HA) is. The concept of evenness taking it even further back into PHASE ONE deals with the original perception of the even activity of the breath (HA) going in, as inHAlation and out, as exHAlation.

Writing shifted direction in the ancient world. In PHASE ONE it flowed right to left as if written by the left handed mothers of the Brahmins, Etruscans and Hebrews and many others. Then in PHASE TWO with the evolving primacy of singularly linear thought facilitated by writing itself, resulting in the lop sided development of the left hemisphere of the human brain, it shifted direction from left to right, to be written by the right hand of the fathers. The direction in many of the capital letters of the Western Alphabet follow a similar pattern.

There also existed a concept of balance. The dual reality above and below at, or around the equatorial Sahel, was associated with the passage of the sun above and below the body of Mother Earth. It created a balance, an even distribution of day and night in the EVENing. The equal distribution of day and night also echoed the perception that during the day when the sun shone there was life above Her surFACE. When the sun went down and the darkness of night spread its often icy fingers of death on a variety of levels; the sun died to its light, it was swallowed into the Western wall of water.

One of the most ancient definitions out of prehistoric China of the Yin-Yang in PHASE ONE follows the same perception. The Yin (YANA) was the sun above the plane, above the body of Mother Earth. The Yang (YANAGA) was the sun lost to its light under the plane, under the skin of Mother Earth following the snake (IS NAKA) through the dark and convoluted corridors of night. The (G) and (K) are interchangeable.

In PHASE TWO male role in specific procreation was becoming known and the 'source' out of the body of Mother Earth was being shared, with male role in paternity becoming known in PHASE TWO Yin-Yang was redefined establishing the female as the Yin and the male as the Yang forever spinning through space.

Since the transformative journey of the sun under the plane of Mother

Earth was as real to them as the reality above in the belly of air, then there was an equal value placed on the mysterious realms under the plane of Mother Earth, be it within Her entrails under the ground around them, or in the REFLECTIVE surFACE of the mysterious waters.

All of the words that emerged out of that ancient time REFLECTED what they perceived. If their reality was a process that REFLECTED itself, then the words that emerged defining those perceptions followed the same rules. They became the dyads of overlapping phonemes that could be read, not above and below, up and down associated to the journey of the sun, except perhaps in Chinese, but forwards and backwards, and even sideways like the rays of the sun at dawn that flowed laterally across Mother Earths surFACE caressing Her body as they gently spread their fingers of light across Her eagerly waiting skin.

Level (LAVALA) (LAVA/VALA);

The shared phoneme is (VA) and it shares its REFLECTIVE concept of evenness and balance with the Persian hattah using a different set of phonemes. To be 'on the level' is to be real, is to be telling the truth, to be balanced. Nothing could be closer to what is basically real and true than the first dyad (LAVA), the magmic lavic menstrual blood as source out of the body of Mother Earth that coagulated into land. Land is the ultimate reality and the definition of truth itself. The (VA) at the center of level (LAVALA) deals with the volcanic vent below the surFACE of Mother Earth. When the lava makes its emergence on the surFACE pushed up and out by the ever ready angle of the tongue (LA) it creates gorges, crevasses, and valleys (VALA-). So linguistically (LAVA) emerging above the surFACE of Mother Earth REFLECTS the (VALA) below Her surFACE. It became the word for natural law (LAVA). In Polish the (V) SOUND is written with a (W).

Magma (MAGAMA) (MAGA/GAMA);

The shared phoneme is (GA). The Mother (MA), begetting (GA), the Mother (MA). Mother Earth creating or REFLECTING Herself out of Herself, by Herself out of Her magmic, or lavic menstrual blood, in the process creating Her offspring, the solid coagulated spread of soil as land above Her surFACE. Soil (IS HALA) was perceived to have its beginning out of the bloody coagulate of the sun, (sol (IS HALA) in Spanish), that erupted as lavic menstrual blood out of the flaming crater creating land or soil upon Her surFACE. The word solid (IS HALADA) deals with 'the gift of' (DA) the sun, sol (IS HALA) in Spanish. Once the liquid solar sourced magma flowed down the flanks of the volcano as lava, it coagulated, and hardened into soil (IS HALA). So soil (IS HALA) had its source out of the sun, sol (IS HALA) in Spanish. Strangely haunting perceptions of reality.

Ganga (GANAGA), (GANA/NAGA);

The Ganges River in India. The same reflective reality was perceived to exist in water. The shared phoneme is (NA) which is either 'emergence on the surface' or 'a change from a former state'. The river Ganga emerged on the surFACE (NA) begetting (GA) torrents of water from below to above not unlike the journey of the sun. (GANA) deals with the Greek gyno (GANA) defining the female. The REFLECTED (NAGA) deals with the ever present guide of the sun the ubiquitous snake (IS NAKA, NAGA). The letters (K) and (G) are interchangeable. In India the sacred River Ganga (GANAGA) was Mother Earth recreating Herself as water.

In PHASE TWO after a bit of fancy foot work by the woman hating priests of Manu, the Ganges River sprang out of the left foot of the male blue skinned God Vishnu. The linguistic links remain to the mother centered view of creation out of PHASE ONE. The left side of the body has always been associated with the female. The letter V in Vishnu has linguistic links with volcano, vulva, vagina, all vents of creation as vias of passage out of the body of Mother Earth and the individual mother. In the English word magma, Mother Earth replicates, recreates, REFLECTS Herself as land. In the Indian word Ganga, Mother Earth continues with the same activity as water. Both have their ancient linguistic source out of the body of Mother Earth in PHASE ONE.

Cusco (KASAKA)(KASA/SAKA);

Capital of the Inca (HANAKA) empire. The eunuch (HANAKA) uncle (HANAKALA) surfaces here as a displaced immigrant after one of the major prehistoric cataclysmic eruptions on the continent of Africa. The SOUND of the shared phoneme is (SA) of either the mothers blood; SAngre in Spanish and SAng in French, or the inHERent spinning spiral (SA) SHAPE of 'source' and bloody lavic effulgence out of the body of Mother Earth.

The first phoneme as (KASA) deals with one of the areas of creative 'source', the female coos (KASA), the place of creation of smaller (KA) aspects out of the blood (SA) in the mothers body. In Spanish the word for house, a place of containment is also casa (KASA).

After one of the great African cataclysms as the bands of our ancient ancestors spread out to distant shores they brought with them the SOUNDS that they carried as communication. The concept of evenness and balance was crucial to their understanding of their reality. They named many of the cities that they settled around the globe after those concepts of balance. The city of Cusco (KASAKA) on the continent of South America contains in it the name for the concept of REFLECTED balance carried by the ancient mothers and their castrated first born eunuch sons. It was believed that castration and a loss of testosterone created a balance in their brains.

Tibet (TABATA) (TABA/BATA);

The shared phoneme is (BA) and (BA) stands for 'two in one' or 'both' (BATA). There may have been a perception that Tibet (TABATA), in the far reaches of the Himalayas, was a place where a balance, a REFLECTION also occurred, where a company of Buddhist monks was called a sangha (IS HANAGA), having linguistic links with the eunuch (HANAKA) priesthood and where a lea line of the emergent solar wind passed under the surFACE of Mother Earth and fused both (BATA) of the two hemispheres of the human brain together creating the balance necessary for the trance of transformation and a journey into the far reaches of the Akashik record or the cosmos. It echoes the perception of the Bardo the 'intermediate state' that the soul endured before it was reincarnated. Shangri LA (IS HANAGArala) linguistically surfaces as one of the places named for the ancient eunuch (HANAKA) priesthood. The (K) and (G) are interchangeable.

Laurel (LARALA) (LARA/RALA);

The shared phoneme is the (RA) of the sun. Within the dyad (LARA) there exist clues as to its source out of the ancient mothers. Lar (LARA) is the left side of a ship. The ancient mothers were associated with left handedness and the left side of the body. There must have been a great deal of traveling across the great oceanic divide by human mothers to name the left side of a ship after her. A ship has been called a she, also named for a woman, the one who as a leader did the traveling.

The laurel (LARALA) as a balance emerges out of PHASE TWO when the sun (RA) and Mother Earth (MA), as the LAdy of the LAnd were one unit of creation in the maintenance of what was real (RALA). It was a time of peace and balance between males and females on the planet in PHASE TWO that had been REFLECTED by the body of Mother Earth before the concepts of war and the emergence of the God of War Mars in PHASE THREE came into being. A branch from the laurel tree signified a token of peace harking back to PHASE ONE.

Madam (MADAMA) (MADA/DAMA);

The shared phoneme is (DA) and (DA) is 'the gift of' the individual mother (MA) and Mother Earth (MA) bringing forth the 'gift of' (DA) life. Dama is 'lady' in Polish and also defines 'lady' in the Romance languages. As a dyad based on the A(ah) SOUND dama has very ancient roots. It also shares its mother based roots with the head, the dome (DAMA) as the area where thought is housed. It is shared by the linguistically balanced vulva (VALAVA) as the valve (VALAVA) of another declination.

Since it morphs into dama, we are dealing in PHASE ONE with the mother being defined as the thinker. She is also the source of another apparent physical creation. For out of her abDOMEn she also creates life. In PHASE THREE as all aspects dealing with the superiority of the mother as the ultimate creatress were being shoved underground the the gift of (DA) the mother (MA) became a male God, the dominus (DAMA-), the dominant (DAMA-) doer.

Dam (DAMA) is one of the names for a herbivore mare. When it switches to a human mother it begins to define a process of dealing with the coagulated blood that had been perceived to create a solid baby. Male role in specific procreation in PHASE ONE was as yet unknown.

The bottom of the belly created a dam (DAMA) that stopped the menstrual blood from flowing out. It created a blocking up so that the menstrual blood once it stopped flowing on the outside could do its job of coagulation on the inside. It is out of her abDOMEn that the mothers created life. It also shares its roots with the head, the dome (DAMA) as the area where thought is housed. Since it morphs into dama, we are dealing with the mother as the thinker. As the thinking mother she becomes the teacher, the creator of subsequent culture, the role model, the story teller showing by example how her children were to survive.

In Polish the actual home that the mother creates is called the dom (DAMA) and deals with domesticity (DAMA-) in English. In PHASE THREE for the Russians the house where their politicians hopefully do their thinking is called a duma (DAMA). In Polish the verb duma (DAMA) deals with very heavy thinking. Following all those names dama establishes the 'gift of' (DA) the mother (MA) on a variety of levels. Where the word dumb (DAMABA) comes from is a tricky question. It seems to emerge in PHASE THREE as the 'gift of' (DA) the Russian duma. Closer to home democracy (DAMA-) has its links with the compassion of the right hemisphere of the mothers.

As the REFLECTIVE (MADA) of (DAMA) it deals with what the mother (MA) gives (DA) coming and going. In 'spiritual' thinking a dam (DAMA) is an obstruction, a DAMming up of the free flowing Kundalini energy up the spine. When the ascending Kundalini energy is trapped by fear in the three lower chacras, negative results occur. To be DAMned in PHASE THREE came to be accursed by God. In PHASE ONE it meant that not only the blood was DAMmed up to create a baby but trapped or DAMmed up energy had to be released by the birthing breath of the mother.

For the Hindus the energy spiraling up the spine is called shakti. For the Catholics it is the Holy Ghost. Since we are dealing with the word dam (DAMA) then it is the Kundalini energy flowing out of the body of Mother Earth the ultimate mother as the dama, that has to be set free.

Test (TASATA) (TASA/SATA);

The shared phoneme is (SA) as the blood of the individual mother and the ever creative spiral source and lavic outpouring out of the body of Mother Earth. The (TA) at either end deals with where the activity occurred at the tip top on their bodies. The original test (TASATA) for humanity was whether a helpless vulnerable human child could survive to maturity. Life on the open savannah, on the surFACE of Mother Earth, on Her tip, top on Her expansive terrain was full of peril. Small replicas of the mother, be she herbivore or human were part of the carnivore diet.

In PHASE TWO as specific male role in paternity was becoming realized and the redefinitions proliferated, the test (TASATA) became associated with pubescent young men. His major rite of passage was to test his mettle against other males in order to be able to mate. (The butting of heads among male animals scenario). He could kill a lion or another tribesman. He could allow himself to be mutilated and tortured. He could be isolated in the bushes for an extended period of time. He could have his penis bloodied. It was a passage from childhood into manhood which was based on the development of courage, the conquering of fear and the denial of pain. He had to pass a series of tests (TASATA).

In PHASE TWO there emerged the realization that the male played a role in the creation of a baby. He may not have had the belly that distended with life but he had an extra set of organs that were necessary in the creation of life in a mother's belly. The only other organs that he had that were different from his sisters and could do the job of baby co-creation were the two orbs on his lower trunk and the movable finger that hung above them.

Since it was only the young man who had to past a TEST to mate, girls became ready when with the cycles of the moon they began to menstruate, then for the male child the singular organs on his body that dictated the activity of TESTING became known as the testes (TASATA).

In PHASE ONE males were undefined. Their role was mysterious. Specific paternity was unknown. They were not the apparent parent. Because they were considered as the surrogates of Mother Earth little girls were defined by the letter A(ah) related to the triangular SHAPE of their pubis and the triangular volcanic cone on the body of Mother Earth. Little boys were considered to be one more and defined by the I of the individual self related to the finger like SHAPE of the penis. The concept of one more in PHASE THREE surfaces in Latin at the ends of words such as alumni. The one more concept surfaces in names all around the ancient world.

Since the belly of the mister housed no babies there evolved a mystery of what his role could be. The word mYstery houses the pubic Y of the mother. As in PHASES TWO and THREE he began to define himself, he threw a blanket of obfuscation across the terrain of truth out of the ancient mothers. The mist of the mister entered the scene. As mastery had been the domain of the ancient mothers another wrinkle entered the scene and was becoming replaced by pastory. The limping shepherd became the maimed pastor so that he would not run away, herding his flock of sheep, leaning on his crook, spreading his WORD far and wide as pronouncements borne on the wings of fantasy and adult fairy tales spread the mist of the mister across the land. In PHASE THREE the crook of the limping pastor tending his flock became the staff of the subsequent bishops and popes of the ruling religious hierarchies. The eunuch uncle was not the father (FAT HER) he did not make (HER FAT), the REFLECTION tells its own story. The concept of the father making her fat come out of PHASE TWO when specific male role in procreation was becoming known.

It was a different story in PHASE ONE. The mothers thought that the TESTS associated with male TESTICLES were inTESTines that had fallen out of their bodies. They tried to shove them back in. That didn't work. So they removed them completely, creating horrific practices that led to the eunuchization of their first born sons. It resulted in placid young men who could protect the family as uncles on one hand and shamanic healers and prophets on the other.

In the sexual drive there is no room for choice as the names for male animals in rut among the herbivores or must in male elephants establish. At the time of rut or must most male animals become very TESTY. In PHASE THREE TESTosterone came to define human male virility. As competition continued to spread its wings across the land, the TESTS that males subject themselves to deal with total power, control and the thrust to win at any cost. The seat of power is not necessarily the size of the TESTICULAR construct in competing males, but money. TESTing involves gambling and when gambling defines universal economic systems then HUManity *AND* MANkind are in a lot of trouble.

Vulva (VALAVA) (VALA/LAVA);

The shared phoneme is (LA) having links with the Lady of the Land the great Leader of the ancient migrations on the continent of Africa. The letter (L) in stage one came out of the angle of the tongue (lengua in Latin) in PHASE ONE. When it establishes its links with the body of Mother Earth it becomes the angular SHAPE of the suns emergence up and out of Her horizontal rim in the Eastern sky. When the perception surfaced that it was the tongue that pushed the sun out of the body of Mother Earth we are dealing with the process of regurgitation. Mother Earth vomited (V) the sun up to Her surFACe to help feed Her children.

The angle extending to the female body also dealt with the SHAPE of the pubis, the (V) angle on the bottom of her trunk. In Polish an angle or corner is called a kont (KANATA) establishing its links with the cunt (KANATA) which is another name for the vulva.

The vulva (VALAVA) also REFLECTS itself as (VALA/LAVA) as the place of creation out of the body of Mother Earth, Her volcanic (VALA-) vent that gives birth to land. As magma the lavic (LAVA-) flow surfaces and spreads like a cape across the skin of Mother Earth creating the land (LA) out of Her volcanic (VALA-) cone.

The vulva (VALAVA) REFLECTING itself also defines the valve (VALAVA) for a valve is an angle of a turn around. The blood coagulated in a mother's body and after ten lunar months of gestation and a disTENded abDOMEn, a miniature REFLECTION of the mother makes its appearance on the surface. Then a turn-around occurred again as the blood restored its flow. It was in the mother's body that the turn around into life occurred.

The vulva (VALAVA) also establishes the relationship between the volcano (VA) on the body of Mother Earth and the vulva (VA) on the individual mother's body as the double place of creation. It echoes the same concept of many other symbolic and linguistic creations, the SS at the ends of female names, and the two overlapping triangles in the Star of David.

It becomes apparent that the concept of level (LAVALA) houses within its folds the same set of phonemic structures as does the vulva (VALAVA). The level (LAVALA) reflected the concept of balance and truth as in PHASE ONE in the ancient mother defined world the bearing of children out of the vulva (VALAVA) took primary priority.

A similar process of INVERSION or REFLECTION followed the naming of Goddesses and Gods. Goddesses in PHASE ONE existed mostly in daylight above the surFACE on the body of Mother Earth dealing with personifications of specific aspects of Mother Earth as the grantor of wishes. Then as the triad of creation She also took over the underground realms within Her body dealing with the passage of the sun and with death as creatress, maintainer and absorber.

The emerging male Gods in PHASE TWO took over the realm of Mother Earth in Her tri-parted aspect as absorber under the REFLECTIVE surFACE on Her body and with darkness. In PHASES TWO and THREE separation myths recall the story, creating their own male 'source' vaulting over the domain of Mother Earth and sailing directly into the heavens *away and above* Her body.

The naming of Goddesses and Gods followed two separate tracks. As the letter B follows the letter A, so in PHASE ONE many of the original names of Goddesses in Africa began with the letter A. The A(ah) SOUND could be considered either a vowel but in some cases it remained as a consonant at the beginning of some very special words. Many of the subsequent emerging male names of Gods in PHASE TWO began with the letter B. The progression from A to B deals with sequence.

The naming of Gods in PHASE TWO expanding into PHASE THREE also dealt with the INVERSION or REFLECTION of mother based symbols and words. As water on the body of Mother Earth REFLECTED the reality above, so female names became REFLECTED by male names in the reality below.

Mothers dealt with the rites of passage, of bringing life into being and with the rites of ushering life out. The passage of the sun dealt with the constant return, the birth and death of the sun that became associated with the tandem journey of birth and death of the human soul.

The mothers dealt with the passage of the soul and the sun on its transformative journey through the body of Mother Earth. In time, as priests, the castrated male sons created power bases of their own. They took over the rites of the dead. Their dominion was specifically underground in the REFLECTIVE darkness of water.

Above ground, as specific male role in procreation was becoming known in PHASE TWO, males as roaming gangs, as the rejected bands of brothers, continued to fight over mating rights and over the territories that were becoming settled.

It was out of the underground male, eunuchized, and in time homosexual priesthood that the INVERSION of the established mother based words came into being. The emerging priesthood presided over the underground domain dealing with death that was REFLECTED in the standing waters having links with the sun. Words as the names of emerging Gods associated with the male priesthood began to emerge REFLECTING that mirrored reality. In PHASE TWO names of the ancient Goddesses became REFLECTED into the names of emerging Gods.

Mama; MAMA/AMAM;

MAMA as the title of the Egyptian Great Mother Goddess of the 'nourishing breasts' of the ancient world above ground, in PHASE ONE became REFLECTED in PHASE TWO as the Egyptian underworld male God, AMAM the 'eater of souls'. The balance of above and below was maintained. What AMAM represented was Mother Earth swallowing the sun as the Spanish sol (IS HALA) into Her Western mouth every night. In Hebrew AMAM means, 'to be higher', 'to surpass'. The MAMA dyad in PHASE ONE dealt with the ancient Mother on all levels. In a convoluted way as the redefinitions began to proliferate in PHASE TWO, the REFLECTED MAMA dyad in Hebrew as AMAM went up into the sky, becoming 'higher' and 'surpassing' the physical reality of Mother Earth that existed below. They as the solar deities had won the war. She could no longer eat them in Her Western waters. They sailed up into the heavens to establish their own bases of power.

In Egyptian AMAM became reflected in the other direction as the underground 'eater of souls'. Both lost their links with their original Mother based source above ground. The Hebrews rose into the sky *away* and *above* the body of Mother Earth. The Egyptians stayed with the body of Mother Earth but established their REFLECTIVE base underground.

AMAM (HAMAMA) contains in it the dyad (HAMA) and hama stands for blood, ema (HAMA) in Greek. AMAM as the 'eater of souls' may very well be one of those ancient puns. For in Spanish sol stands for the sun that was swallowed by the maw on the body of Mother Earth in the West as it set into the scarlet bloody waters of its final descent. Its REFLECTION into the waters of its entombment created the number eight. The mountainous mouths at the horizontal rim of Mother Earth ate the sun. As the redefinitions proliferated obscuring their origins out of female centrality confusion filled the ranks of the emerging words.(The mist of the mister syndrome).

Maya, MAYA/YAMA;

MAYA was the holder (MA), of the light of dawn (AYA). The AYA dyad emerged as 'light' in Persian and 'dawn' in Assyrian. Both deal with the sun above the surFACE of the body of Mother Earth. MAYA REFLECTED became YAMA, the Japanese 'Lord of Death' and deals with the subterranean journey of the sun under Her surFACE. For the Hebrews the day of atonement (AT ONE-) is known as YOM KIPPUR (YAMA KAPARA). YOM (YAMA) in Hebrew deals with day. Day (DAYA) in English (DA) is 'the gift of' (AYA), light in Persian and dawn in Assyrian. In Ugarit Yamm (YAMA) was the 'prince of the sea', into which the sun sank and died to its light. For the Bemba tribe in Africa the maternal uncle, the castrated oldest brother was called Yama. As the 'lord of death' or 'the prince of the sea' he helped his mother and sisters to officiate over the rites of the setting sun as it was daily swallowed into the Western wall of watery death. In Polish jama (YAMA) stands for 'gorge' or 'crevice' and performed the same function on land. On the continent of Africa the gorge or crevice was the long deep canyon of the Olduvai Gorge out of which the sun was perceived to have been born if they stood on its Western rim. If you stood on the Eastern rim it was the deep cavern, the place on the other side where the sun sank to its death.

The Y shape between the A (ah) of the tips of the holding hands on either side of AYA, is the SHAPE of the female pubis (Y) on the body of Mother Earth, the crevice on the edge, the Olduvai Gorge, the Great Rift on the continent of Africa, out of which the trudging migrants traversing back and forth, were constantly overwhelmed by the blessing of light of the rising sun at dawn and of the curse of the darkness of the setting sun at twilight.

For the Buddhists MAYA was the mother of Buddha, the holder (MA) of the light (AYA), for the Buddha was considered to be the enlightened savior, who preached denunciation and nothingness, stilling the voice-over, fear driven left emisphere, bringing forth peace and serenity.

In the New World, the MAYA people, one of the early re-settlers off the continent of Africa, left when the passage of time had still been reckoned as a cyclical continuum, a helixical twisting through space, not as the subsequent straight line of Western right handed left hemispheric brain perception. Their name MAYA means, 'holders' (M) of the 'light' (AYA) on three levels; lunar, solar and cosmic. They may have spread their dominion as far North as the peninsula of Florida. The MAYAKA River deals with the MAYA as the small (KA) in the Northern reaches of Florida. The city of MIAMI not only deals with the one more as the male child but MIAMI (MAYAMA) REFLECTS itself as belonging to the ancient PHASE ONE balanced Mother. It was on the Eastern coast of Florida that the sun rose at dawn giving birth to the name MIAMI (MAYAMA). AYA is light in Persian and dawn in Assyrian with the Mother (MA) above and below creating the ancient linguistic balance. In Polish the left hand associated with the ancient mothers is smaja (IS MAYA) and in the nineteenth century in Poland it had been considered to be the hand of the devil and had been vilified.

Mara; MARA/RAMA;

In Africa the MARA River in the Masai Mara is one of the areas of the ancient migrations in the Serengeti Plain and the linguistic source of many of the subsequent watery marine (MARA-) constructs.

Another area of migration may have been the Sahara savannah (IS HAVANA) thousands of years before it became a desert. The following MARA based names may have emerged out of the perception that the sun sank or was swallowed by the body of Mother Earth off the West Coast of Africa. The Moors (MARA) of Mauritania (MARAtana) and Morocco (MARAka) also figure in this ancient marine (MARAna) based configuration, further afield the Maori (MARA) of New Zealand left Africa fifty thousand years before. Note the I of one more at the end of Maori.

The MARA construct out of PHASE ONE deals with Mother Earth as water and surfaces as mer (MARA) the 'sea' in French, mare (MARA), the 'sea' in Latin, mar (MARA) the 'sea' in Spanish, Morze (MARA-) as the 'sea' in Polish. It also moves into the word mirror (MARARA), the reflective surface of water. In Russian the word mir (MARA) means 'peace' and that was what the REFLECTED reality of life was seen to be, the peaceful state of death.

For the Northern peoples from Europe to India, MARA was the Goddess as the 'old crone', the bringer of death. In Polish, the word for 'death' is smierc (IS MARAja). In French, mort (MARAta) means 'dead', 'defunct', 'gone'. In Spanish it is muerte (MARA-). In Polish to die is umarl (haMARAla). It deals with the resistant sun (RA), setting into the body of Mother Earth (MA) for the night, dying to its light, pulling its REFLECTION into the darkness of the waters below. The second dyad (RATA) deals with the ratio (RATA), the habitual cycle of returns back and forth, above and below the plane, the valve of another declination. The god of war Mars having vaulted *above* and *over* the body of Mother Earth and sailing into the heavens in PHASES TWO and THREE defined the war that had been occurring between Mother Earth and the resistant sun as she ate it at night

One of the the ancient names for the sun, as (HAMA) the bloody coagulate out of PHASE ONE surfaces in umarl (HAMArala) the Polish word 'to die'. For the sun died to its bloody fingers of light as it splattered across the Western sky descending into the horizontal side of Mother Earth. Also in the Polish word umarl (haMARAla) 'to die' there exists the second dyad of (MARA) which reiterates the death of the sun (RA) in the embracing waters on the body of Mother Earth (MA).

The MARA dyad deals with the ancient perceived war between Mother Earth (MA) as water, swallowing the sun (RA) into Her great Maw (MAWA) or watery (WA) stomach at twilight. It emerges (haMARAja) out of PHASES TWO and THREE when the battles for gender supremacy between women and men began to be fought on a massive scale as men began to learn their role in specific procreation.

To murder (MARAdara) someone, is to send them on their journey across and into the cradling arms of passage across the waters. Ironically murder in its most ancient form is the 'gift of' (DA) the sun (RA). It means that you went on the same journey of trans-formative rebirth as the sun. You died to the light in your eyes, as the sun died to the rays of light that were snuffed out when it set into the waters in the West, into that great waiting maw (MAWA) that swallowed it at the end of each day. In Polish a similar SOUNDING, but more ancient word for murder (MARAdara) is morda (MARAda) that also deals with murder and slaughter. The Polish word mord (MARAda) expands into morda (MARAda) and is associated with a vulgar description of a snout, or the hacking jaws of a carnivore mother, the ultimate murdering smotherer and has its links with the individual carnivore mothers mouth.

In Latin 'death to weeds' was attributed to the lowly 'hoe', or marra (MARA), the 'shim' (IS HAMA) of another declination. For the Semites Mara or Marah was associated with the 'passive weight and darkness of the deep sea-womb' often translated as 'the bitter', as the briny, salty water of the coastal marine (MARANA) seas.

For the Buddhists MARA was a tempting demon of darkness, i.e. death.

As a male, MARA emerges linguistically intact in PHASE TWO, but his origins go back to PHASE ONE to mother centrality and the dark REFLECTIVE surFACE of the ancient standing seas (mer, mar, mare, marine) the holders (MA) of the setting dying sun (RA) within the body of Mother Earth.

Some of the ancient migrants who left their homes in Africa and settled far from their ancestral lands, were the moors (MARA), further afield, the 'dream time' Australian Aborigines, and the Maori (MARA) of New Zealand.

The Moors (MARA) were Berbers who traversed the desolate stretches of the Sahara Desert and emerged out of Mauritania (MARAtana) and out of Morocco (MARAka) the North West coast of Africa. Morocco (MARAka) in North West Africa bordered the Atlantic Ocean on one side and the Mediterranean Sea on the other. It was on the Western shore that the sun set into the great sea, was swallowed by the maw (MAWA) on the edge of the body of Mother Earth off the Western coast of Africa. The maw (MAWA) is the place at the edge, the tip on the body of Mother Earth where the sun was held (MA) beneath large expanses of water (WA), before She either regurgitated it to sail above Her surFACE in the East at dawn, or swallowed it for it to swim (IS WAMA/MAWA) as best it could at twilight guided by the ubiquitous snake, below Her surFACE in the West. When She sWAllowed the sun, it no longer WAllowed beneath Her WAtery WAll of death at tWILLigt. She ate it as the SHAPE of the number eight illustrates. It died (DAYADA) to the light of its day (DAYA).

The Polish 'hand' as reka (RAKA) in Morocco (MARAKA) the second dyad surfaces here also as the helper of the passage of the sun (RA) into the murky (MARAka) marsh (MARAsa) below.

On the 0ther side of the world in Melanesia Marawa 'a powerful spirit' brought death to mankind. Not only is his name based on three syllables associated with the A (ah) SOUND of the ancient mothers, but the (WA) at the end establishes his links with water, the area on the edge of the body of Mother Earth into which the sun died to its light every night. The process of Mother Earth swallowing the sun at twilight has a very wide global linguistic distribution.

Mauritania (MARATANAYA) offers some hope for it deals with TANA as the third dyad and that is the ten (TANA) fingers of 'holding' that held the rays of light at dawn. AYA as 'light' in Persian and 'dawn' in Assyrian surface here also. Because (MARA-) leads the linguistic perception defining death we are establishing the fact that we are dealing with linguistic concepts out of the body of Mother Earth as the watery grave of the sun.

There are two words that cry out for some exploration. One deals with marriage (MARA-) as marital (MARATALA). The other deals with war and mortal (MARA-) combat as martial (MARATALA). The answers would seem to be obvious where the connection exists. We are in PHASE TWO for both words deal with the battle for power and the definition of source between the mothers and the emerging fathers.

In marital (MARA-) we are dealing with the institution of marriage (MARA-) as the eternal battleground that became echoed as martial (MARA-) upon the body of Mother Earth as she fought to kill the light of the sun every night and establish Her dominance at night even in death.

But the reality changes as time moves from PHASE ONE into the subsequent PHASES of TWO and THREE. On one level the (MA) of Mother Earth as the 'holder' of the sun (RA), at one with him, be he her son, lover or husband, moved into a celestial marriage (MARA-), the very short period of time when male and female cohabited and were at peace with each other. The Zoa tribe of the South American Amazonian Basin must have gotten out of Africa at that ancient time of peaceful sexual coexistence. The mother of the clan has four husbands, cohabitating with all of them and while not establishing specific paternity they all mutually take care of the children.

Then in PHASE TWO as males were becoming aware of their specific role in procreation back in Africa, the fact that the (MA) of Mother Earth swallowed the sun every night, killed it to the life of its light, was a bit of a problem to them. They became associated with the sun as a male deity. As procreative males, the band of brothers began to create their own Gods *away* and *above* the body of Mother Earth. They associated themselves originally with the solar disc as their symbolic representation. They were the gangs of brothers that had been pushed out of the clan at puberty making the sun their own using the SHAPE of the circle of the sun to replace the SHAPE of the zero of the permanently empty belly.

Mother Earth swallowing the sun every night, killing it to its light, led to open warfare, (the Samson story of the Bible), the martial (MARA-) confrontation that led to marital (MARA-) discord.

In PHASE TWO the battle between Mother Earth as physical 'source' associated with the females as mothers and the celestial bodies associated with the 'rational' males as fathers as 'source', went into full swing. The battle between the two belief systems is exemplified through the raging competition between the Goddesses and Gods of the Greek and Roman Pantheon. In PHASE THREE the Gods and then the single male Father God won, but in PHASE TWO they were still in marital (MARA-) and martial (MARA-) confrontation.

It is no wonder that Mars (MARASA) became the God of War. What his name and symbolism exemplify is the raging battle for supremacy between the ancient Mother Earth, the (MA) of marine (MARA-) creation and the emerging solar (RA) Father God in the sky, losing his light and power within Her body every night. She had to be destroyed along with Her daughters and beginning in PHASE TWO, She was. In PHASE THREE as the Mother, a participant in the story of creation She was obliterated altogether.

RAMA (MARA/RAMA) OF REFLECTION;

Mother Earth (MA) holding and giving birth to Her son, the sun, as helper (RA) out of Her standing waters became the REFLECTED reality of RAMA, the male sun (RA), emerging lord and master in PHASE TWO, holding the body of Mother Earth (MA) in place UNDER him. (Shades of Lilith in the Adam Biblical story in Genesis). The solar disc above the volcanic cone shifted in his role from the male son as helper in PHASE ONE and TWO, to the male sun as master in PHASES TWO and THREE.

In Polish rama emerged as the name for 'frame' (FARAMA). The lord and master who had been the helping hands, became the frame, the holder encircling with his arms (HARAMA) and fingers (FA) not only the body of the individual female but as the square gained momentum with the four points on the compass, encircling Mother Earths horizontal rim (RAMA). With that perception the number four became a symbolic male number.

The circular sweep that ended at the horizon line, the rim (RAMA) as the body of Mother Earth and the circle of the sun as one unit out of PHASE ONE, with the cross at the center, created by the passage of the sun East and West and the passage of the birds North and South, became replaced by the square that became a male symbol. The triad was the ancient symbol of the mothers. As one (I) more of an undefined male child added to the number three became number four emerging as a square and dealt with maleness. The circle contained by the square became the frame (FARAMA) the Polish rama, the male arms (HARAMA) that in PHASE TWO and THREE enclosed the body of Mother Earth as they enclosed the body of the individual female. When the symbolic square is in a circle we are in PHASE ONE and female centrality. When the symbolic circle is in the square we are in PHASE THREE and male centrality.

On the mundane level the same activity created the harem (HARAMA) that held the pregnant bellies (HARA) of the mothers in the frame of male arms (HARAMA). The holding of the female in place when she was not sexually receptive and raping her evolved into the large arms and strong upper torso on the male body.

For the Egyptians the God Amun who masturbated all of existence into being every night, in PHASE THREE shared his name with a native sheep also called amun, whose male offspring was a ram (RAMA). The Egyptians opted for the rampaging ram (RAMA). The Hebrews stayed with their goats, although Egyptian male and female pharaohs in PHASE TWO wore goatees plastered on to their chins establishing their links with the indispensable nanny goats who provided milk for the migrating mothers out of PHASE ONE. At one time as the eunuch priesthood gained ascendancy over the circling males at the periphery, the Egyptian pharaohs as the original hairless eunuchs plastered goatees on their chins.

All the members of the Zoa tribe of the Amazon River Basin wear a tube pierced through their bottom lip that hangs down their chins. It looks very much like a symbolic goatee. Since they do not have goats in the rain forests of the Amazon then they must have gotten their ancient tradition out of Africa.

The Hebrews, harking back to PHASE ONE and mother centrality worshipping goats for their life sustaining milk supply and meat on the hoof, grew full beards but shaved the sides of their heads and grew the pais, long forelocks, like goat ears, to pay homage to the milk providing and life sustaining nanny goat.

Also in PHASE TWO moving into PHASE THREE, the RAMA dyad became attached to many of the deities associated with male Gods as 'source'; RAMA KRISHNA in India, RAMSES in Egypt, BRAHMA in India, ABRA(HA)M in Semitic North Africa, RAMBAM the Hebrew articles of teaching, RAMPANAORA of Madagascar, REMUS and ROMULUS as founders of ROME, ROME and the Vatican in Italy, moving into kingly castes as the ROMANOVS of Russia. In Europe a country bore the name of RAMA as Romania (RAMANAYA). For the Hindus the epic poem of RAMAYANA in PHASES TWO and THREE set the stage for male centrality. For the Muslims the feast of RAMADAN carried on the tradition, establishing its links not only with the REFLECTED sun but with the actual process of REFLECTION.

As male role in specific procreation was becoming known and the heterosexual gangs above the plane and the eunuch priests below the plane began their battles for power, there occurred a melding of power bases with the mothers sandwiched between them and then in PHASE THREE squeezed out of the picture altogether. The rampaging (RAMA-) male gangs above the plane fighting for territory and mating, becoming the rulers, emperors and kings appropriated the Gods of the underground priesthood, along with their reflected names.

The totemic animal became the rampaging Ram (RAMA) of procreation and physical immortality above the plane, replacing the mothers snake as the shower of the way for the sun to emerge from its underground maze, blessing humanity with a belief in reincarnation. The Babylonian Epic of Gilgamesh in PHASE TWO put a nail into the coffin of that ancient belief and threw the Middle East into religious turmoil that reverberates with faith based chaos to this day.

HANA/NAHA;

The great 'grandmother' Hannah (HANA/NAHA) of the Bible, follows a similar construct. It also deals with an 'even', reflective linguistic construction, but this time it deals with cycles, with the emergence of the sun (IS HANA) above the surFACE on the body of Mother Earth and its folding back under Her surFACE (NAHA). At that very ancient time in PHASE ONE the sun was considered not only as a helpful relative to the body of Mother Earth but at one with Her, echoing the familial construct of Her daughters but specifically the grandmothers.

The second dyad of Hannah (HANA/NAHA) as (NAHA) deals with the reflection of the sun (IS HANA) in the waters at the Western wall of death. In English the word that emerged dealing with the nullification of life, is nihilism (NAHA-). (NAHA) as the reflection of (HANA) deals with the reflection of life into death. (NA) deals with the 'negation of a former state'. (HA) deals with the belly of air out of which and into which existence makes its circular return. In Latin-NIHIL (NAHAla) is 'nothing', or the 'negation' (NA) of the sun, eelyos (HALAsa) in Greek.

For the ancient Hebrews NAHASH (NAHA-) was the 'serpent God', the one who guided the sun and the soul after they died on their underground trans-formative journeys of rebirth through the dark and bloody (SA), intestinal corridors of nothingness within the body of Mother Earth.

For the Aztecs Nahual (NAHALA) (NAHA/HALA) 'protective animal spirit of the nether world' performed a similar function. It may have been the ubiquitous snake (IS NAKA) out of Africa. The (H) and (K) are interchangeable. The second dyad (HALA) deals with the sun, sol (IS HALA) in Spanish.

Nehellenia (NAHALANA) as a Norse Goddess represents the nether moon, the moon of the dark night (NAHA-) when both the sun and the moon are absent from the sky. In Latin Luna (LANA) is the Goddess of the moon. The moon sailed across the dark night sky as the sunken sun passed beneath the watery depths to fuse with the rivers of blood that carried it to the surFACE of new land, or of a new dawn.

For the Upper Nile Egyptians Nekhbet (NAKABATA or NAHABATA) is the vulture Goddess, of death and rebirth. The snake (IS NAKA) surfaces here also. What also surfaces in the name of the vulture Goddess Nekhbet (naHABATA) is the English word habit (HABATA). For both life and death as the continuum of existence were considered to have been habits of never ending return, 'the two in one' phenomenon encoded in the letter (B) that was associated with one of the names of the sun (HABA) out of PHASE ONE.

The turn around of the vulvic valve surfaces here also. Hannah (HANA/NAHA) as the Biblical 'great' grandmother, her name reflecting itself out of PHASE ONE, was also one of the names of the sun (IS HANA), the grandmother as the helper to her granddaughter, the body of Mother Earth, moving above Her body as the sun (IS HANA) and below Her body as (NAHA) of either nothingness or the metaphoric Kundalini energy as the snake. In the following words the (HA) of (NAHA) and the (KA) of (NAKA) are interchangeable. For it was the ubiquitoius Kundalini snake (IS NAKA), that guided the sun through the subterranean entrails within the dark and convoluted body of Mother Earth on its way to trans-formative rebirth.

The Jewish 'holiday of light', CHANUKKAH (HANAKA) contains within it the same construct as the Egyptian ankh (HANAKA). Both deal with some aspect of the sun (IS HANA) and the metaphoric Kundalini snake (IS NAKA) and 'spirituality'. Linguistically the first dyad deals with the sun (IS HANA) above the plane. The second dyad (NAKA) deals with the snake (IS NAKA) under the plane guiding the sun through the intestinal body of Mother Earth to its rebirth at dawn. It contains the same construct as the REFLECTED dyad (NAHA) of 'nothingness'. The letters (K) and (H) are interchangeable. So the Jewish Chanukkah (HANAKA) and the Egyptian ankh (HANAKA) deal with the dual activity of the sun, rising (HANA) and setting (NAHA, NAKA), to which the journey of the human soul had hopefully become attached.

Like it or not, they harken back to mother centrality out of PHASE ONE and both for the Egyptians and for the Hebrews, the concepts within Chanukkah (HANAKA) and ankh (HANAKA) originally dealt with reincarnation and reincarnation dealt with the rebirth of the sun at dawn, to which the journey of the soul had become attached.

The rites of passage of both the sun and the soul as they made their descent into the underworld was officiated over by the eunuch (HANAKA) priesthood. The priests as the castrated first born sons of the mothers worked in the subterranean darkness assisting the sun, and the soul to be 'born again', the sun to the light of a new day, the soul to the life of a new body.

The castrated firstborn son was the eunuch (HANAKA) and the uncle (HANAKALA) to his sister's children. The eunuch (HANAKA) as uncle (HANAKALA) also officiated over the rites of the setting sun at the side of the mother in many of Her aspects as LA, the lady (LADA) of the land (LANADA). So 'Chanukkah', 'ankh', 'eunuch' and 'uncle' have ancient links with the dual aspects of the sun setting in the West and rising in the East, assisted by the subterranean priesthood. In the Bible, out of PHASE TWO, the convoluted story of Enoch (HANAKA), the eunuch (HANAKA) bears reexamination for in PHASE THREE, it deals with aspects of heaven, hell and angels (HANAGALA) laying the groundwork for them to burst into full bloom in Christianity. The fallen angels had been considered males who were not eunochs and not even homosexuals, they were males who were either born with the balanced Kundalini energy alive in them or through ritual gained the blessings associated with that singular experience. They could mate and have children with Earthly women creating their own bases of power.

Akka, (ACCA), (AK/KA) (HAKA);

The 'water drawer' Goddess of AKKAD, the midwife, Greeks called her ACCA (HAKA). As the 'water drawer' she drew reality on her surface. In Central America on the other side of the Atlantic divide she was called not only ACAT (HAKATA) but Akna (HAKANA) establishing her links with the surface of water as the REFLECTIVE eye of Mother Earth, the oko (HAKA) in Polish and okno (HAKANA) as window. She not only REFLECTS herself in her name, as AC/CA (HAKA) the Water Goddess but was also the personification of a process on the body of Mother Earth as the hacker (HAKA-) of existence into two distinct and equal pieces.

For the Greeks she was also Hecate (HAKATA) the trinitarian Goddess who not only midwifed the sun God every morning but ruled heaven, Earth and the underworld, as an ongoing process defining life, death and reincarnation. In her name there exists not only the (HAKATA) of the hacker (HAKA-) in the first dyad, but the (KATA) of both the cat (KATA) as the cutter (KATA-) in the second. The lioness, the great hunter as a cat (KATA) became a living metaphor for cutting (KATA-) or hacking (HAKA-) of death from life. Hecate (HAKATA) was associated with the moon, the time that the nocturnal cats (KATA) began their nightly prowl.

The hacking quality was associated out of PHASE ONE and stage one, the hook (KAKA) or the SHAPE of the jaw on the bottom of the skull that did the hacking, the separation of death from life most notably noticed in the carnivorous mother cats (KATA) as they s*mother*ed their prey.

On the body of Mother Earth the hacking of reality into two parts, into life and death, dealt with the REFLECTIVE quality of water that also hacked reality into what was above and what was REFLECTED below. The Latin word aqua (HAKA) as 'water' bears witness to the hacking or REFLECTIVE perception that had been associated with water. ACCA (HAKA) as a water drawer and Aqua (HAKA) as water in Latin share very ancient linguistic roots. The ancient Goddess as ACCA in PHASE ONE became demoted to the Latin aqua as plain water in PHASE THREE as all aspects of Mother Earth and Her Goddesses became obliterated.

The Sphinx with the body of a lioness and the head of a woman, may very well be an ancient metaphoric symbol of Mother Earth and the hacking quality represented by the lioness as a majestic hunter separating death from life resulting in the accompanying belief in reincarnation.

The 'water drawer' in the name of ACCA does not necessarily mean that with a swinging bucket she drew water from a well. That has been the universal interpretation of 'water drawer'. Originally out of PHASE ONE it meant that ACCA (HAKA) as a 'water drawer' created a picture, made a drawing of the REFLECTED reality in the standing waters. As a midwife she assisted in the birthing of the sun, for at this ancient time in PHASE ONE the sun must have risen out of the waters on the Eastern rim of the Olduvai Gorge.

Assa (AS/SA);

The name for 'gum Arabic' ASSA as the sticky 'gum', is what held it all together. When chewed by the teeth and gums, the solid piece of 'gum' became a sticky mass. It evolved out of the perception that the activity of baby production emerged not only out of the coagulated, sticky internal blood, but out of the cleft on the female buttox, her very 'ass', which as the sacrum (IS HAKA-) had been considered to be a sacred (IS HAKA-) mysterious place, the place where she was hacked (HAKA-) apart.

The stickiness of the flowing blood went through a mysterious hybridizing process that coagulated into a solid baby. Cloven hooved animals, as ruminant quadruped mares, sharing their milk supply with the migrant mothers in PHASE ONE, were sacred to them. Their cloven hooves divided lengthwise, reflected not only the cloven SHAPE of the buttox, but also metaphorically the process of blood coagulation, of it sticking together inside of their bodies, to make a baby behind the cleft. In PHASE TWO as all traces of creation out of female bodies were becoming obliterated, the madness continued as even cloven hooved animals suffered the same vilified state.

For the Hebrews the back end of a quadruped herbivore was not only associated with the mothers place of creation, her ass, but was not considered clean enough to be eaten. Only the front part of a herbivore was considered clean enough and kosher (KASARA) enough to be eaten. The back part was considered unclean. The 'curse' comes to mind.

On the body of Mother Earth a clove (KALAVA) is a rocky cleft, a gap, or a ravine. The second dyad as (LAVA) bears witness to the fact that the rocky cleft, gap or ravine had been caused by the lavic (LAVA-) outpouring out of the body of Mother Earth. It had been caused by a discharge of Her menstrual blood out of the deep recesses within Her, and out of Her surrogates in the creation of life out of their individual bodies, out of that vertical wound on the bottom of their cloven buttox.

The cloven hooved ass also called a donkey, bred with a horse, created a non-reproductive hybrid, a mule. Within the word donkey (DANAKA) a clue surfaces why patriarchal 'saviors' like Jesus in PHASE THREE, rode into Jerusalem on an ass's colt. The implication is that an ass's colt was a hybrid, a transformed non-reproductive male (MALA), mule (MALA). In Polish mala means the 'small she'.

The second dyad in an ass or donkey (half of a mule) is (NAKA) and it is the ubiquitous metaphoric Kundalini snake (IS NAKA), the guide of the underground sun that surfaces here also, if not too obviously. As the snake guided the sun to be reborn in the East to reign over the terrain of Mother Earth, so in PHASE THREE the mule carried the modern 'savior' Jesus, i.e. son of God, the human male into the city of his new reign ABOVE ground. It was not only the snake (IS NAKA) in PHASE ONE that guided the sun and the soul on its journey of rebirth. As the eunuch priesthood, the hybrid males, psychopomps, Hermes, considered neither as men or women, but as male hybrids, what became the androgyny in male form (neither an ass or a horse, but a mule) existing in the 'intermediate state', came to dominate the process and activity of transformation, taking over the rites of transformative rebirth from the birthing breath of their mothers.

Replacing the snake (IS NAKA) in PHASE TWO, as priests, psychopomps, showers of the way, they became the sole guides for the sun and the soul to gain at first their reincarnation in PHASE TWO, then one step better, emerging out of the darkness into the white light of the sun and their immortality in PHASE THREE.

Laden down with all the products of human reproduction, and questioning if there was enough room up in heaven Christianity evolved a single male Christ to be the savior, to become reincarnate, to take on the sins of the world, as the lowly goats had done for the Jews, except that Christianity was more ambitious. Not only would the sins be carted away, but eternal life would be promised for the supplicant, the believer, the generous faithful.

On the body of Mother Earth one of the major evacuations out of Her fulminating calderas along with lava was the ASH that fell upon Her surFACE and with the sticky lavic blood pouring across Her skin, coagulated into land. Cinders that became the epic of Cinderella, the goose girl tell their own story, how Mother Earth in Her most awesome aspect as creatress in PHASE TWO and THREE became the stepdaughter, the outcast, the peripheral female waiting for the prince to save her. The castrated son disappeared in the mists of time but through her lost slipper she would be rediscovered by the prince and resettled upon her rightful throne. Convoluted redefined story of the maimed and limping smith and shepherd becoming associated with the young bride including the the flow of the Kundalini energy up her right foot. It could only be experienced through bonding with the prince.

Two closely related English words throw light on the shift that occurred from female to male centrality, as victor (VAKATARA) and victim (VAKATAMA). The victor at the end of the third dyad has the male (RA) of PHASE THREE in it. The victim, also at the end of the third dyad that emerged in PHASES TWO and THREE has the phoneme of the mother (MA) in it.

Clove (KALAVA) (KALA/LAVA);

The clove as the rocky cleft on the body of Mother Earth surfaces not only in cloven hoofed herbivores but also echoes the SHAPE of the buttocks on the female body and surfaces in the aromatic spice that is SHAPED like the ancient Egyptian ankh (HANAKA). The ankh is trying to remind us of the fact that the possibility of trans-formative rebirth can come only through the body of the mother, be she the personal mother, or the body of Mother Earth.

When the 'doer' as RA enters the picture, the clove becomes cloveR. Clover is the three lobed plant, representing the triad of the ancient mother. In PHASE TWO and THREE as male centrality took center stage, the three lobed clover echoing the triad of the ancient mother was pushed aside by the SHAM of shamrock, the four lobes of good luck representing the left hemispheric emerging perception of male centrality and essence.

RULE NINE;
Place the A(ah) SOUND behind every consonant.

The A(ah) SOUND was the first vowel SOUND to have become codified. Its original SOUND came from the first breath of a new born baby, the A(ah) as the Alpha of beginning. Its original SHAPE came from the triangular volcanic cone on the body of Mother Earth that created land and the possibility of the beginning of life upon Her surFACE. With the codification of the A(ah) SOUND the journey into syllables began. The A(ah) SOUND is not only a vowel, but is also defined as a consonant and may be governed by its own very specific rules. For sentient creatures it had been linked with the inHAlation and exHAlation of the breath (AH-HA), of air going in and of air coming out supporting the activity of life.

For the human mother it is the specific SOUND of the panting breath during the last stages of labor (HA-HA) that not only creates the electromagnetic Kundalini energy of shakti but has been associated with the cosmic orgasm of the birthing breath of the mothers. HA-HA is also the name for the 'mother' in Japanese.

On the body of Mother Earth the SHAPE of the letter A(ah) comes out of the mountains, of the ten fingertips of the hands touching at the edge, creating the tent like SHAPE of the volcanic cone, one of the sources of the breath of life, and as land, the support system for existence upon Her body.

During a volcanic eruption the letter A, closed on top, the SHAPE of the fingertips touching creating the triangular tent like cone of creation, became blasted open for the HA-HA of Mother Earth's panting breath, giving birth to land, to Herself out of Herself and to the SHAPE of the letter H.

The places of Sahara (IS HAHARA) and the Sahel (IS HAHALA) may have been named after the activity associated with the breath of birthing (HAHA) of the tropical scorching sun out of the body of Mother Earth.

For the Hebrews the vowels, especially the A (ah) SOUND had been left out altogether and only consonants had a place in their historic linguistic beginnings. Some scientists have discovered that the much maligned and under appreciated Neanderthal although it had the hyoid bone could not make the vowel SOUNDS. They could only make consonants. In Sanskrit every consonant had to have the A (ah) SOUND of life creation and maintenance associated with it. The following A (ah) based dyads start the journey into human codification of speech and the many changes that occurred on that journey.

PARA;

The dyad para as steam or mist in Polish in stage two deals with the surFACE of Mother Earth at dawn in one of Her aspects as the rising, undulating mist hugging the receptive hills accompanied by the rising sun, Her breath exHAling into the sky, passing upwards out of the valleys on its way to the open heavens. The other steam as para also in Polish deals with the air spiraling (IS PARA-) out of Her calderic fissures and vents creating the belly of air above Her surFACE. (PA) deals with passage. RA deals with the morning light of the sun as the source of the steam gently winding itself around the body of Mother Earth caressing Her as it brushed across Her tender skin. In Sanskrit the word priya (PARAYA) becomes the beloved. The beloved had been considerd to be the light (AYA) carrying mist that passed (PA) or wound its way across the body of Mother Earth at dawn.

The original PARA dyad emerged as pour (PARA), pyre (PARA), por (PARA), pro (PARA), per- (PARA), pure (PARA), peer (PARA), pare (PARA), pair (PARA), -per (-PARA), pore(PARA).

-TO GODS EAR

In Hebrew the word hed (HADA) means 'echo'. (DA) is 'gift of' air, or the breath (HA) out of the body of Mother Earth. So an 'echo' as hed (HADA), in Hebrew, what would be considered across language boundaries and time, is (DA) 'the gift of' air (HA).

The word 'echo' (HAKA) in English contains its own very similar antecedent. Like the hook (HAKA) of the lower jaw hacks (HACK-) food into two or more pieces, so the echo (HAKA) also hacks (HAKA) the air carrying SOUND into two or more pieces. In one direction it is created by the SOUND creating source; as bellowing thunder, a crashing rock slide or rapturous singing. In another direction it reverberates back repeated, to be heard by the ears.

A similar leit motif surfaces in Wolof, in the word addu (HADADA) that means 'to answer'. Both the Hebrew hed (HADA) as 'echo' and the Wolof word addu (HADADA) as 'to answer', embracing the two (D)s deals with (DA) as the double 'gift of', (HA) air. A similar phonemic construct surfaces in Polish but with a slightly different twist. The word odda (HADADA) in Polish means 'to give back'. In English to 'add' (HADADA) deals also with a sort of 'giving back', or accumulation. Is it not what the Hebrew 'echo' and the Wolof 'answer' and the English 'add' and Polish odda do? They 'give back' the 'echoing" SOUND. They create an 'answer' that is a 'give back' to a question. How they give back is through the gift of air as a vehicle of passage. An idea (HADA) is also the 'gift of' (DA) the air (HA). It also becomes apparent that the consonants stay constant, but the vowels create their own melodic 'shape shifting' dance.

RULE TEN;
Place the letter (H) before words beginning with a vowel.

Along the way many words that now begin with a vowel once had the SOUND of (H) before them. For the sake of simplicity the letter (H) became not only unvoiced but often dropped off altogether.

In Greek heureka-eureka (HARAKA) means found.
What does the finding?
The hand reka (RAKA) in Polish.
In Latin harena-arena (HARANA) means sand,
in Latin haruspex-aruspex (HARASAPAKASA) soothsayer,
Egyptian Hapi-Apis (HAPASA) the bull,
Semitic Hadad-Adad (HADADA) Storm God,
Hebrew Har Magido-Armageddon (HARAMAGADA-).

In Israel another mountain surfaces as Ararat (HARARATA) assuming that before the anlaut of the letter A (ah) the letter (H) had been dropped off. Then there is the mountain named Hermon (HARAMANA) where Christ along with Enoch had experienced their celestial transformations. These two mountains have the (hara) dyad in common. The hara dyad surfaces in Hebrew as either pregnant belly, or holy mountain. In Japan hara also shares its links with the belly in hara kiri or disembowelment. Both haras deal with the evacuation out of the belly, be it the individual mother or the belly of Mother Earth.

The hara dyad as the (HA) out of the belly of Mother Earth and (RA) as Her begotten sun establish links with individual mothers, for harah in Hebrew means pregnancy. The word harah as the Hebrew word for pregnancy reflects itself with (HARA/RAHA). The shared phoneme is (RA) of the sun. It is not unlike the concept of the valve at the vulva, or an echo, the place of a movement back and forth, menstrual blood flowing out, coagulating inside and a baby returning back up to the surface.

On the body of Mother Earth it is the sun (RA) that journeys in and out, back and forth out of the body of Mother Earth. Ruah (RAHA) is the air (HARA) reflected as (HARA/RAHA) or breath originally of Mother Earth through which the sun passes daily out of PHASE ONE. In PHASE THREE in Hebrew it emerges as the breath of God. The Kundalini energy rising up from Mother Earth the universal maternal deity becomes totally obliterated.

The electro-magnetic Kundalini energy emerging out of the body of Mother Earth in PHASE ONE becomes the male Father God as the Holy Spirit orchestrating reality out of the sky *away* and *above* the body of Mother Earth. Another Goddess as Rhea (RAHA) deals with a reflection of hara, (RAHA/HARA) the belly of air (HARA) above the body of Mother Earth. She as the Greek Mother of Gods is defined by the flow, the flow deals when the menstrual and estral blood that begins flowing with the flowering of a young girl into womanhood. As the Mother of Gods Ruah (RAHA) is Mother Earth for without Her as their platform there would be no place for the Gods to have their being. 'Holy Mary (MARA) Mother of God' takes on new meaning.

The belly as holy mountain in Hebrew establishes its links with mountains or mounds on the body of Mother Earth out of which the sun was perceived to have been born at dawn. That is why the mountains were holy. To create their hallelujahs at dawn our ancient kin folk had to position themselves West of the rising sun to become aware that the sun rose out of the Eastern sky out of either Her round mountainous belly, between the two peaks that created the SHAPE of the pubis or a spread of quietly standing reflective water. It dealt with Mother Earth giving birth to one of Her greatest creations, the sun. The other was the effulgence of menstrual lava creating land upon Her surFACE.

Har (HARA) Magido as Armageddon (HARA-) not only deals with the plain upon which the world would end during the Apocalypse, but with the mountainous belly Hara that borders it in the East giving birth to the sun.

Mount Hermon (HARAMANA) (HARA-RAMA-MANA) holds on to its anlaut, the (H) at the beginning of the tryad. (HARA) deals with the belly of air (HARA) that gave birth to the sun. The (RAMA) dyad establishes that we are already in PHASE THREE and the Mother as (MA) follows the (RA) as the male sun God. The (MANA) dyad deals with the moon (MANA) as the nocturnal helping hands of Mother Earth manos (MANA-) as hands in Spanish. The name of Mount Hermon may have come out of the time in PHASE TWO when male deities were still subterranean cave dwellers fighting for their emergence out of the 'dark night of the soul' to dwell separate from the body of Mother Earth *above* Her surFACE.

The hara dyad covers a multitude of bases. It is the air (HARA) that hovers over the surFACE of Mother Earth. 'To be' as are (HARA) joins the activity of breathing with being. Hairs (HARA) on the human head are likened to the rays of the sun to the surFACE of Mother Earth. In Hebrew saara (IS HARA) is hair. Samson the Biblical solar hero losing his hair symbolizes the loss of his solar rays and his power. In destroying Delilah he destroys the matriarchy. (HA) deals with the belly of air (HARA) above the surFACE of Mother Earth. Within the individual in stage one it deals with inHAlation and exHAlation with breathing and with being alive.

Ra on the other hand covers many more bases. In Egypt it is the most important deity as the sun God. In Sanskrit it deals with fire, with royalty and with exaltation. In Sanskrit we are in PHASE THREE for the shift *away* and *above* the body of Mother Earth has already occurred. RAA out of Hebrew as bad takes us to PHASES TWO and THREE when the body of Mother Earth (A) and the sun (A) were considered as one unit and not very favorable, being blamed for the desertification of the Northern savannah into the Sahara Desert.

For the Semites RA of the solar god away from the body of Mother Earth was 'that which existed forever' as opposed to the Mayans who believed that it was 'LA of Mother Earth as the pLAnet that existed forever'.

Using another vowel RU, RUS deals with the RUSset color of blood. It surfaces in the word estRUS and the passage of blood on the flanks of the female herbivores along with the arrival of birds announcing the semiannual time of the ancient migrations. To RUle came out of that dyadic construct. For it was the moon that measured or RUled the night sky with its monthly passage which coincided with the menstruation of human females. In PHASE ONE it was the moon who was not only the RULER of time but also established the capacity of women to RUle when they flowered with the flow of their estRUS, RUSset, Ruby Red blood.

In Linear B the phoneme RU is SHAPED like the pubis or trident.

As our ancient ancestors scattered to the far corners of the world after one of the cataclysmic African disasters, one of the places was North to the regions that became Southern RUSsia where graves with majestic women queens have been uncovered. Along the way the RUS of Russia fused with the Vikings, who may have given that land its name. The color red of blood remains in the RUSsian lexicon to this day emerging as the red flag of communism, but that may be another story.

RULE ELEVEN; EMPHATIC,
Take the hissing SOUND of S (ss) off words beginning with the letter S

The letter S is an EMPHATIC and at the beginning of words stands for 'it is', 'isness', 'blood' and the concept of 'existence'. It begins to establish the noun verb combination that subsequently emerged into the sentence. At the end of words, in English, the letter S deals with plurality, or 'isness' extended. Also at the end of English words the (-ish) SOUND establishes a concept of similarity, of one thing being like anotheras brack-ish. As (-ist) it moves into defining 'one who is' as in art-ist.

The concept of repetition at the end of some English words dealing with specific aspects of women such as miSS, laSS, princeSS, hosteSS, or even GoddeSS, the first (S) deals with the blood of the individual mother as the creative source of individual life; SA in Egypt is the wise blood of the mother. Sang (IS HANAGA) blood in French, Sanguis (IS HANAGASA) is blood in Latin. Sangre (IS HANAGARA) blood in Spanish,

The second (S) deals not only with the spiral, conical, triangular SHAPE of hurricanes, dust devils, and whirlpools on the body of Mother Earth but with Her lavic menstrual blood, Her magnificent and majestic expressions of source underlying Her creation of the physical universe having its origins out of the sun (IS HANA) and the solar guide as the metaphoric Kundalini snake (IS NAKA) worshipped by the eunuch (HANAKA) priesthood. The (G) and (K) are interchangeable.

Show (IS HOW), (HAWA);

Out of the ancient migrations on the continent of Africa in PHASE ONE it deals with showing (IS HAWA-) the way to the falling water (WA) or rain out of the sky and how (HAWA) to proceed toward the 'promised land ' of the falling showers (IS HAWARA-) and the verdant wet savannah teeming with bugs, birds, flowers and greener pastures. (HA) deals with the belly of air above the body of Mother Earth. (WA) deals with Her whole (W) dual aspect as not only Her round ground of being, but also as falling WAter in the distance, one who shows (IS HAWA), or is the shower (IS HAWA-) of the way. Water (WATARA) (WATA/TARA) the terrain (TARA-) on the body of Mother Earth (WA) establishes the fact that the terrain was not only rained upon from the belly of air above but became blessedly wet (WATA).

In the Sahara Desert a wadi (WADA) is the gift of (DA) the water (WATA-). The (T) and (D) are interchangeable. In Amharic watate (WATATA) defines rain. Not only the body of Mother Earth becomes wet (WATA) when showers drench Her surFACE but also human beings succumb to the same aquatic embrace when they sweat (IS WATA).

Slick (IS LICK), or (LAKA);

To lick (LAKA) is to make the object slippery (LAPA-). To like (LAKA) it as a small lake (LAKA) of spittle is formed to accomplish the task. It is the two lips (LAPA) and the tongue, lengua (LA(na)GA) in Latin, that makes the object slippery (IS LAPA-). (LA) deals with the mothers face in stage one when the two thin lips seen in profile in PHASE TWO are accompanied by the angle of the tongue. (PA) deals with passage or movement across. Mothers lick (LAKA) their young to free them of dangerous smells, to create bonding and because they like (LAKA) to do it. Babies lick (LAKA) the mother's breasts, teats or udders in order to stimulate the flow of milk, in the process spasming her uterus, assisting it in its healing.

The phoneme (KA) in the lake (LAKA) of spittle deals with the creation of smaller aspects out of female bodies. Coinciding with the ancient migrations, the time of birthing occurred on all levels when the noisy waves of calling, clacking (KALAKA-) birds returned to their nesting sites on the lake (LAKA) drenched savannahs either at the Mara River, the Okovongo Delta or the preglacial verdant Sahara. Herbivore mares gave birth to their foals activating their lactating (LAKA-) udders bursting with lakes (LAKA-) of milk. The definition of lactating (lakaTATA-) creates its own symphonic leit motif for it contains in its linguistic folds not only the wet lake (LAKA) but the double (TATA) of titties (TATA).

At the time that the birds semi-annually either arrived or departed an activity dealing with young pubescent boys also took place. The clacking (KALAKA-) of the birds establishes its links with kaleka (KALAKA) which means cripple in Polish. It was a time at the dual equinoxes when rites of castration and crippling of pubescent boys took place.

Sword (IS WORD or (WARADA);

A verbal (WARAba) order, the word (WARADA) has been used as a weapon of conversion, if necessary by force, through the use of the sword (IS WARADA). The two overlapping dyads are (WARA) and (RADA). WARA deals with war (WARA) as the symbol of death. (RADA) in Polish means advice as 'gift of' (DA) the sun (RA).As a verb (WARABA) the word war deals with an activity dealing with violent confrontation.

The two phonemes of (WA) and (RA) deal with the battle between female and male power bases expressed through the metaphoric ancient battle between the watery (WA) body of Mother Earth and the heavenly bodies, especially the sun (RA).

Mother Earth as the waiting maw of water (WATARA) swallowed every aspect that rose out of Her, especially the emerging male metaphoric 'source' as the sun every night. She killed it to the life of its light as She ate the rays of the sun at twilight. She was perceived at to be at war (WARA) with it. As the sun disappeared back into Her body in the bloody Western horizontal rim She always won (WANA). But in the East as the suns rays lit up the morning sky, the sun rose into the heavens at dawn and also won (WANA) if temporarily, reflecting the never ending battle between the female Mother Earth and Her male consort the sun. (WA) deals with water and (NA) deals with either 'change from a former state' or 'emergence on the surface'.

The Samson story and his shorn hair deal with the symbolic rays of the sun being shorn by Delilah as a Biblical metaphor for the patient body of Mother Earth ready to swallow the rays of the sun, Her hair, morphing into the mythological locks (LAKA) of Samson.

(RADA) the second dyad, is the 'gift of' (DA), the sun (RA). In Polish, rada means 'advice'. 'Advice' is given through the use of the word (waRADA). If the word (WARADA) doesn't work, then the sword (IS WARADA) is used. It seems that language itself was considered to be so important that it was used as a weapon. The secret word of emerging male centrality in PHASES TWO and THREE had to be used to open a lot of Sesames (SASAMASA) or (HASAMASA) the doors to transformed males internalizing both the energy of Mother Earth and Her lavic blood (SA) and the essential blood of the individual mother (SA) as the fallen angels (HANAGALA) of the Bible.

In PHASE THREE as part of male history (HIS STORY) the WORD established the Biblical beginning of existence itself, for nothing was perceived to have come before it. 'In the beginning was the word'. That may have been only partially true. As a redefinition of ancient reality 'the word' did come out of the beginning of male centrality and the shift into the right hand of the Father with the secret codes of writing. The spoken SOUNDS of language did not come out of PHASE THREE and the anthropomorphic mind of God. It originated out of PHASE ONE and the hard working, birthing, nurturing, teaching, maintaining individual mothers face.

The left hemisphere of the human brain has been discovered to house the linear activity of language. The left hemisphere also contains the endlessly repetitive fear drenched aspect of contained imgery that is associated with sexuality and violence.

A word (WARADA) through its anlaut as the letter W, having connections with water, expands the understanding of closely related perceptions. A word, the name of a thing, is not a referent. It is a reflection of the thing. It is not the thing itself. Water, aqua (HAKA) in Latin, on the body of Mother Earth performed the same function. It reflected a reality above the surFACE, not the surFACE itself. It was an image that like the eye, oko (HAKA) in Polish, hacked (HAKA-) reality into two pieces. On the body of a creature through the use of the eye one reality existed inside and the other reality existed as the reflected image on the outside.

On the body of Mother Earth one reality existed above the plane. The other reality was reflected in the waters below the plane upon Her body. As a name or word it reflected the thing, but was not the referent or the thing itself.

Work (WARAKA) enters this picture, for work (WARAKA) is the small (KA) result of war (WARA) perpetrated on early humanity. Work was done by the conquered slaves who toiled for their conquering owners creating the reWARD and often the aWARD of brutal war (WARA). No nobility of labor here. It could also go in the direction of (RAKA) as the individual hand in Polish declaring WAR on the sun pulling the sun down into a watery (WA-) grave in the West killing its rays of light (RA).

In PHASE ONE at the time of female centrality the world (WARALADA) (WARA-RALA-LADA) was the real (RALA) home of the lady (LADA) where the warring (WARA-) battle between the sexes symbolized by Mother Earth eating the sun in the West was fought. With the removal of the (LA) phoneme of the mothers tongue (lengua in Latin) creating specific words, out of the mouth of Mother Earth, the world (WARA(LA)DA) not only lost the (DA) as the 'gift of' the tongue as the SOUND making organ but also the (LA) defining the the lady (LADA) of the Land. She lost the battle as unrelenting war (WARA) between the mothers and emerging fathers with their knowledge of specific paternity upon the planetary plane in PHASE TWO entered the ancient scene.

Clues often hold on tightly to their ancient source and meaning. In the Polish word for war is wojna (VAYANA). The (V) and (W) are interchangeable. There exists the (AYA) dyad that establishes its links with light in Persian. Also in Polish the (W) SOUND is pronounced as a (V). So wojna (VAYANA) as war in Polish reiterates the same concept that the waters (WA,VA) on the body of Mother Earth created the celestial war by swallowing the light (AYA) of the sun.

There had been another war that existed on the Afrian savannah. It dealt with a swarm (IS WARAma) of locusts that declared war on every blade of grass and flowering tree. As they broke free into the warmth WARAmata) of the ascending sun, their swarm (IS WARAma) declared war (WARA) on the helpless plants of Mother Earth.

The sword (IS WARADA) held by the rock at Avalon removed by King Arthur echoes with some very ancient perceptions. The end of the tale as the Lady of the Lake takes the sword (IS WARA-) with her sinking into the engulfing waters symbolizing the death of female centrality. With it resulted the loss of the right hemisphere of the brain and the even balance that it once created. With the creation of human language adding to the loss taking with it ancient gifts that can only be surmised.

Slight (IS LIGHT or (LATA) not heavy;

The vertical emergence (LA) illustrates the SHAPE of the rising illuminating sun into the belly of air out of the body of Mother Earth, out of Her edge, tip, top (TA), floating with the lightness of a feather through the glistening sky at dawn. The sun and birds in the 'intermediate state' sharing their celestial ascent as emissaries out of heaven morph into subsequent angels in PHASE THREE out of an ancient redefined history. No extra terrestrials here.

Smola (IS MOLA or (MALA);

It linggistically bridges three languages, In Polish it is 'tar', in Greek it is the 'magical energy of the Earth', the fires within that force bubbling tar up to Her surFACE. Smoldering (IS MALA-) in English comes to mind. Also in Polish the word mala means 'the small she'. It expands to include a process inherent in the workings of Mother Earth. As She gave birth to Herself, as she spasmed, orgasmed and created land upon Her surFACE through a bloody menstrual magmic volcanic eruption, the land that She created was Her child, Her off-spring, as such it was a small (IS MALA) replica of Her. (LA) deals with the angle of emergence of either the sun or lava out of the flat, circular surFACE of Mother Earth. (MA) deals with the great Mother Earth as the 'holder' and 'maintainer' of life out of Her lavicly created land and life, having its origins out of the light of the sun.

Saara (IS HARA);

In Hebrew is the word for 'hair' (HARA). The rays of the sun (RA), emerging out of the edge of the surFACE, the face or skin of Mother Earth at dawn, into the belly of air (HARA), were considered to be like hair (HARA) emerging out of a creature's skin or hide. The ancient Hebrew hair must have considered to have been wavy, for in Maori, the name of the undulating 'intestines' that are housed in the belly is maHARA. Hair was also considered to be immortal like gold and honey for on a mothers head it never stopped growing.

The Biblical story of Samson, the solar hero, deals with him as the symbol of hair shorning (IS HARA-) establishing the perception that hair had power, for we are dealing here with stage two, with hair that was to the human skull as the rays of the sun were to the head of Mother Earth. It was Mother Earth every night at twilight who ate the rays of the sun, declared war on him, shorned the solar disc, made him bald, took away his power, made his skull shine like the bald pates of the eunuchs. The blind Samson was shorn not only of his hair but of his other great power, the power of sight that can only be used when the rays of light shine across the plain and the dark pall of night is lifted. Visual acuity is also the primary source of male sexuality.

In Hebrew hara emerges to mean two other things. One hara means pregnant belly. The other Har (HARA) is holy mountain. The Hebrew mountain was perceived to be holy because the sun was believed to rise out of it at dawn. Har Magido is the plain around the mountainous belly Har (HARA) that gave rise to the prophecy of Armageddon. Here we see an example of rule ten where the letter H at the beginning of the word Armageddon has been dropped off.

Samson establishes his own story reflecting the use of rule eleven. For Samson (IS HAMASANA) contains in his name both dyads reflecting the most ancient names for the sun. (HAMA) deals with the sun in its bloody aspect setting into the grisly waters of the Western sea and the sun (IS HANA) in the SHAPE of its emergence (NA) and descent (NA) in and out of the belly of air above the body of Mother Earth. In Greek ema (HAMA) is the name for blood linking it to its bloody passage.

Far afield in Japan the belly is also called hara, and Hara Kiri means disembowelment, dealing with the restitution of honor for disgraced military leaders. The Japanese word Kiri (KARA) establishes its own links with Polish. In Polish kara means punishment. Can the single source of language much further back out of Africa be denied?

Smote (IS MOTE or (MATA);

The mouth (MATA) of the mother (MATARA) establishes the killer. In Spanish matar (MATARA) means to kill. Smother (IS MATARA) expands on the perception of killing associated with the mother (MATARA). What is dealt with here is the carnivore feline hunter, the lioness, the pride mother as the supreme and ultimate killer who clamped her jaws or mouth (MATA) around the neck of her pray as she brought it down and smothered (IS MATARA-) it.

The Sphinx with the body of a lioness and the face of a woman may be the personification of the mother lioness as Mother Earth, the ultimate killer. Everything that She gave birth to, She not only killed but reabsorbed back into Her body.

Skin (IS KANA);

Tha skin (IS KANA) is that which establishes the kin (KANA) of kinship, kindness (KANA-) and the child, 'kinder' in German. (KA)deals with the 'creation of smaller replicas of the mother'. (NA) deals with 'emergence upon the surface', or 'change from another state'. The (-ER, -OR, -AR) on the ends of the words wat-er, moth-er, mat-ar, deal with the sun (RA) as the male helping hands, the doer, the helper to the body of Mother Earth. (KANA) is also the volcanic cone (KANA) of ultimate creation, the birth of land on the body of Mother Earth.

Sand (IS HANADA);

Sand is (DA) the 'gift of' the sun (IS HANA). When the equatorial sun burned the land clean there was nothing left but sand. Sand (IS HANADA) has the same linguistic antecedents as hand (HANADA). Both come from the intense activity of the sun (IS HANA), one out of the uni-verse and having been AT ONE as the helping hand (HANAda) of Mother Earth, the other as total destroyer of life, leaving only desiccated burning sand having ancient links with the Sahara and Kalahari Deserts of Africa. A dessert is that wich came after.

Cinder (IS HANADARA);

Cinder contains in its linguistic coils the 'gift of' (DA), the sun (IS HANA), from another direction, from the burning effulgence that covers the land after a volcanic eruption. It deals with the perception that the sun passed through the internal fires within the body of Mother Earth after it set into Her body in the Western sky. Because its reflection in the waters below was a splattered gory red it was believed that one aspect of the sun was the blood that coursed through the body of Mother Earth. As Her menstrual blood it flowed down Her flanks during a volcanic eruption accompanied by other emanations that also seemed to be associated with the bloody fires of the sun such as cinders and ash.

Strategy (IS TARATAGA);
Strategy deals with territorial ambitions and the accumulation of land as a power base. Without the EMPHATIC (S) at the beginning of the word STRATEGY, there emerges TRATEGY and with the last two syllables (-TEGY/-GEDY) transposed into TRAGEDY and the beginning of scheming, plotting and violent confrontation of the Northern Congo male chimps, into the Homo Erectus and then singular left hemispheric MANkind.

Shin (IS HANA);
Shin is one of the areas where the magical wind of the sun (IS HANA) carrying the much misunderstood Kundalini energy enters and leaves the human body. Achilles lost his power when the arrow of his enemy punctured his shin (IS HANA) or heel (HALA) both deal with the ecstatic energy of the electro-magnetic solar (IS HALA-) Kundalini, the original God energy emergent upon the surFACE of Mother Earth.

SOUND (IS HANADA);
SOUND is associated with the (DA) 'gift of' the sun (IS HANA) as the creatures on the body of Mother Earth who rose before dawn to greet the light of life and warmth in the Eastern sky with their hoots and hollers grateful that the pall of the dark night had been lifted. Human beings with their aves and hallelujahs thumping their hollow logs and drums with their thumbs also joined in the chorus. It must have happened daily for thousands of years for SOUND (IS HANADA) to have been associated with the sun (IS HANA) having risen in the Eastern sky.

The SOUND and SHAPE of the letter (S) as an emphatic or verb at the beginning of words establishes the 'isness' or being of the following verbal construct. It goes into other multifaceted definitions. Not only does the letter (S) deal with 'isness' but with plurality at the ends of words, also establishing one 'who is' as (-ist), and one who 'is like' as (-ish). At the ends of words the double (SS) tells its own if hidden story. It is not an accident that in PHASE ONE important names of women often end with a double (SS), such as miSS, laSS, GoddeSS, mistreSS, hosteSS, sorcereSS, waitreSS, and actreSS.

What the double (SS) at the ends of female names in PHASE ONE tells us is that the one defined by the (SS) at the end of the name has become an individual mother and in the process of becoming a mother has flowered not only with a baby but with the Kundalini breath of ecstatic birthing. She has internalized the two aspects of motherhood; the *blood* energy of the individual specific mother as the one (SA) and the triangular spiral cone SHAPE of Mother Earths electro-magnetic *lavic* menstrual energy as the other (SA).

With the Kundalini birthing breath she becomes fearless in the protection of her off spring. Mothers will kill to defend their young. Fearlessness is the primary quality of the 'spiritual' path and becomes sought after as self-realization. It is fearlessness that allows the adept to journey up toward the light without dragging the habits created through the filter of a helpless panic stricken infancy.

With the experience of the Kundalini and the birthing breath there also occurred the movement into trance, into shamanism, into the mystery of mysticism, of prophecy, healing and leadership. The perfect example that still historically surfaces has been the leader and mystic mother Al Kahina of the Tuareg Berbers.

The human tragedy and the shift from female to male centrality originally dealt with males not knowing their specific role in the procreative process and their inability to share in the experience of the birthing breath. The birthing breath of the mother as high fast panting in the last stages of labor acting like a bellows awakened the dormant Kundalini energy sleeping at the base of the spine. It masturbated the clitoris into orgasming during the birthing process as the head of the baby pushed against the clitoral beak from the inside also during sexual activity experienced pleasure with the head of the penis masturbating the clitoris from the outside. It was the clitoris of the mother that was the seat of her power. In PHASE THREE it was the clitoris that had to be removed as clitorectomies slashed through the lives of the birthing mothers.

The first born son was castrated to protect the human family from marauding males who had been pushed out of the familial unit at puberty and who circled the periphery of the human herd. There were also foreign humanoid marauders who decimated the familial unit. The process of castration made the young boy into a docile eunuch with his testosterone hormones compromised. He joined his mother in the rites of the rising and setting sun. He also developed the same qualities that the birthing mother

Section Two

possessed becoming not only the brave protective avuncular uncle but the shaman, healer and a prophet. Creating a base of his own power he became as powerful as the ancient mothers in PHASE ONE.

The peripheral human males circling the female herd yearned to experience the birthing breath of the mothers and the apparent power that it endowed upon them. To that end *it is only the males of history that go on quests for all the symbols dealing with the male search for the power inherent in the birthing breath of the mothers.* They have given that search different names, searching for the golden fleece, the holy grail, the killing of many dragons, leviathons, snakes, pythons, dispatching one eyed monsters. The Iliad and the Odyssey among many others are stories of males on their journey to defuse their fears and to join the mothers in their ranks as powerful rulers. Their stories of conquest and bravery surface in most of the mythologies of the world. The twelve labors of Hercules define the same journey.

If not jumping on their steeds to do battle with their panics they moved into meditation, drugs, spirits, alcohol, fasting, dancing, chanting, humming, davening, placing themselves at the feet of a shaman or guru, during specific times of the day, of the year, at specific places on the planet to become transformed and to touch the hem of ecstasy and power.

The electro-magnetic shakti energy of Kndalini is neutral. It can be expressed as good or evil based on where it becomes trapped in the human being along the chacral wheels. The Tantrists in their chacra system explain the role of evolution in the expression of the Kundalini energy. The use of systems of fear defusion created a set of transformed males.

It is in those transformed males that a new set of letters begin to surface. They are not as obvious as the double (SS) at the end of female names as mothers. To become transformed they had to create another category, not only of angels and birds that rose into the sky like the sun but they had to become more than human. They had to become defined as gods.

The list of transformed males who exhibit the internalization of the mothers blood energy (SA) and the spiral energy of Mother Earth (SA) to create the (SASA) dyad blessing them with special powers surfaces most clearly with the Lithuanian Burtinin Sas (-SASA) who is defined as a sorcerer and a magician. It expands into the Greek Zeus (SASA), Sysyphus (SASA), Perseus (-SASA), Jesus (-SASA), Moses (-SASA), Ramses (-SASA), Theseus (-SASA), Aziz (haSASA) Syrian Lord of the underworld, Azazel (haSASA-la) Hebrew sacrificial goat of atonement, Gods eunuch rival. The Sisterian (SASA-) monks, the 'ancient ones' as the Pueblo Anasazi (-SASA) of the

American South West Indians who had no writing and depended on the oral tradition of story telling establishing their source out of PHASE TWO of transformed males. The symbol of the goosepimply moment of truth as the goose in Lithuanian is zasis (-SASA). The magical place of survival in the desert is an oasis (-SASA). Also in Greek Physis (-SASA) was defined as the Goddess of growth and nature, ie Mother Earth. Not to be left behind Kyesis (KAYASASA) is pregnancy in Greek covering many bases. It not only includes the blood of the individual mother (SA) and the light (AYA) emerging out of the body of Mother Earth but Mother Earth (SA) as the creatress of smaller aspects (KA) out of Herself.

One of the greatest tragedies that has occurred on the planet after the abuse and vilification of women and the destruction of Mother Earth in PHASE THREE, is that Adolph Hitler understood the use of the Kundalini energy, but in him it did not rise above the solar plexus, the chacra of total control and power. He was the personification of the violence ridden left hemisphere of the human brain gone amuck using the (SS) dyad to represent the Aryan base of racial supremacy. His gifts of oratory swayed masses of people into a state of universal trance. As an aspect of fascism he ironically expressed the left hemispheric linear rational brain of the then conquered Germanic civilization; rule from the top down, uniformity, creativity, writing, music, poetry, invention on one hand, violence, brutality, war, destruction, carnage, corruption, rivalry and competition on the other, leaving behind the love, bonding, cooperation, kindness and compassion in the balanced brains of the mothers. The Kinder on all levels was left behind. Any dictator who sways masses of people by his oratory has the Kundalini energy alive in him and is trapped at the solar plexus the power chacra.

RULE TWELVE;
Find SINGLE syllables followed by the A (ah) SOUND in any and all of the languages of the modern and ancient world.

All original codified syllables by the ancient mothers in PHASE ONE were based on the A (ah) SOUND. When they surface in contemporary language they reveal their most ancient and primitive source. Discover the links that they may have in common. The letter A(ah) is considered to be both a vowel and a consonant. When it follows a consonant it is considered to be a vowel. As an anlaut, or at the beginning of a word it is often dealt with as a consonant. When the A (ah) is inhaled it is an unvoiced anlaut. When the (HA) SOUND is exhaled it is a voiced vowel.

The Neanderthal could not have made the vowel SOUND. The early Homo Sapiens could only make the vowel SOUNDS. As they met they put the two together when the vowels of the Homo Sapiens became added to the consonants of the Neanderthal to begin their journey into the future as did the cohabitation of the early Homo Sapiens and the Neanderthal must have done. The Hebrews kept the vowels out of their alphabet altogether holding on to the ancient tradition of the mothers out of PHASE ONE as the YHVH of Yahveh establishes. In India they went into another direction and embraced the A(ah) SOUND of the breath as part of both life and death (AH-HA) associating the SHAPE of A(ah) with the triangular SHAPE of Mother Earths volcanic cone, the SHAPE of land and life creation and female centered.

A Hindu sage Samketa Paddhai declared 'AH is the first of all letters and HA is the last'. In PHASE THREE in India the A(ah) SOUND by the female hating Manu priests became associated with males as female centrality and its source out of the organs on the mothers face shared by the surFACE and body of Mother Earth became redefined and suppressed.

BA-Egyptian, 'winged soul, survival of dead',

The phoneme BA establishes the concept of 'two in one' out of PHASE ONE and stage one based on the two bulbous lips in profile on the mothers face working in tandem to create the mouth. It expanded to embrace many other concepts that were based on the 'two in one' construct. Birds have two wings that use the air as a vehicle of passage and the two sides of a beak that sang, also used the same air to float their SOUND. Birds were considered to be the guides of the soul sailing upward into heaven and immortality in PHASES TWO and THREE. Life and death were two sides of the same coin.

As creatures of flight that sang their way through life having ancient links with the eunuch (HANAKA) uncles (HANAKALA) who in PHASE THREE morphed into winged angels (HANAGALA) and gods. The dyad of the sun (IS HANA) reflects their solar (HALA-) ascent.

Words had been considered to be sacred because like the birds and the sun they used the vehicle of air for their passage. They existed in that sacred 'intermediate state' of the Tibetans. It was the belly of air above the surFACE of Mother Earth that supported the magical activity of life and the accompanying magical soaring of SOUND.

BA-Chinese 'eight';

BA is the reflected circular orb of the sun rising in the Eastern sky and setting in the Western horizontal rim at twilight creating the 'two in one' scenario. When it sank out of sight into the bloody waters of the Western sky it was perceived that Mother Earth ate it. The SHAPE of the letter eight (8) of the round disc of the sun reflected in the waters below comes out of that perception. Ba is also the name of an ancient long forgotten tribe of people in China.

BA in Bemba 'be';

BA reiterates the 'two in one' concept. To 'be' deals with either the individual mother creating a Baby out of her Blood, or the Body of Mother Earth creating the Bio of life aBove Her surFACE. It contains the bee of being symbolic concept.

BA Swahili 'father';

(The father followed the mother as in the Western Alphabet the letter B followed the letter A). In PHASE ONE before male role in specific procreation became apparent, a male was considered to be of two possible genders; one that he was born with a body like the mother, the other was that he had extra genital parts like the other male members of the clan. The English name for Boy comes out of that ancient perception. It may also define the two orbs or Balls that hung from his genital area and in PHASE TWO came to define the emerging father and the growing knowledge of male role in specific paternity. The concept of father as the one who made HER FAT/FAT HER came into being. Ba is the reflection of AB (AB/BA) which is also the name for father and water in the Middle East. The water may have dealt with either the reflective surface of water which had become the domain of male source or the name and reality of seminal liquid that begat the baby out of PHASE TWO and male awareness of their role in specific fatherhood.

DA 'gift of';

The SHAPE of the letter (D) comes from a variety of areas; on the body of a mother it is the closed fist in stage three that when opened shares in the bounty of giving. On the bodies of creatures it is the dome (DAMA) of the skull in stage one that housed thought and shared accumulated knowledge. On the body of the mother in stage three it is the SHAPE of the distended abDOMEn. In Hebrew Dam (DAMA) means blood out of which the baby had been created. In Swahili blood is damu (DAMA). In Persian a dam (DAMA) is a snare, or a collection point. In PHASE ONE it was perceived that the menstrual blood that had stopped flowing on the outside was dammed (DAMA-) up inside at a collection point in the belly to coagulate and to create a baby. The coagulated bloody liver became that collection point. The delivery from the liver scenario defines the process of birthing. With the understanding of the 'spiritual' movement of the Kundalini energy up the spine, to become DAMNed, was to have had the Kundalini energy DAMMed up and not moving freely along the Chakral spins bringing joy and well being to the creature.

DA in Sanskrit 'she who gives', 'she who bestows';

It could also go in a variety of directions. It is the mothers hand that when opened gives and bestows edible morsels to her children. It is her accumulated knowledge out of her dome (DAMA) like skull that she shares with her offspring leading to their survival. It is also the mother's abDOMEn that gives birth and bestows life out of her creative body. Dama is the name for a special lady in Spanish and Polish. It is (DA) 'the gift of' the Mother (MA). In Amharic dam (DAMA) deals with blood as the special gift of the mother same as the Hebrew dam (DAMA). The red surFACE of Mother Earth, Her russet clay in Africa gave birth to the name adam (haDAMA) that in PHASE THREE surfaces as the name of the Biblical first man. It was the body of Mother Earth that gave every thing that Her children needed.

DA in English 'to divide' (DAVADA);

The birth of the baby divides from the mother creating the 'gift of' (DA) of vida (VADA), or life out of her vulvic (VA) aperture. Vida (VADA) is life in Spanish. David (DAVADA) as the Biblical hero carries in his name the overlapping dyads and the process of reflection and inversion. As division (DAVA-) the process of seeing or vision divides the reality equally, outside from the image on the inside as memory. Linguistically it deals with balance,

DA in Bugotu 'future';

The (DA) 'gift of' life in the creation of a baby out of the mothers abdomen creates the future.

DA in Russian as 'yes';

It nods its head to the concept of giving and the 'gift of life'.

DA in Spanish 'he, she, it gives;

Out of PHASE THREE it embraces all concepts of giving.

DA in Polish as 'give' also on unrestricted levels;

Give (GAVA) deals with the (GA) of begetting and (VA) deals with either the vulva, vagina (VA) construct on the individual mothers body, or the volcano (VA) on the body of Mother Earth. During a volcanic eruption Mother Earth gives forth Her bloody magmic discharge creating land upon Her surFACE bestowing all with the promise of a planetary nest. It could also go in the direction of the gift (GA-) out of the waters (WA). (V) and (W) are interchangeable in Polish. The five fingers of doing enter here. It is also the V created by the open palm of the thumb on one side and the four fingers on the other.

FA-Swahili= 'to die';

In Swahili the war between the swallowing bloody waters as the body of Mother Earth and the rays of light as the Fighting Fingers of Fire of the Flaming sun descending in the Western Firmament disappearing into the relentless triumphant body of Mother Earth. Every night the sun died to its rays of light as She ate it. The two lateral bars on top of the stem of the letter (F) deal symbolically with the solar fingers as the rays of the sun pulling the sun down into the darkness of night.

FA in Chinese= 'issue, to give out,';

The Five Fingers of Fire drew the sun back into the body of Mother Earth they also pushed the sun out of Her Eastern rim as the Fingers of Fire, the helping hands of the sun spread across Her waiting surFACE and caressed Her into giving birth, to issue out Her gift of light and life.

FA in English 'face, or to shine';

FA establishes its links with the sun as the shining object in the sky above the surFACE of Mother Earth. The concept of the shining human face is a mythological perception born out of a mother's bonding love for her baby and the babys reaction of love to her face.

GA (gha) in Sanskrit is Singing (IS HANAGA);

It also deals with Giving and Moving. When the sun moved out of the body of Mother Earth at dawn it gave Her creatures the gift of life and light. To awaken the sun and her guide the snake (IS NAKA) from their nocturnal sleep, they gathered at the foot of the birthing mountains and Sang (IS HANAGA) their rapturous welcome. The (G) and (K) are interchangeable. To sing (IS HANAGA) also deals with the ubiquitous eunuch (HANAKA) who were the bards, the ancient singers. The (K) and (G) are interchangeable.

JA (YA)-Finnish 'and' (HANADA);

The creation of another one deals with addition and the concept of one

(HANA) more. Since we are dealing with one (HANA) more, then we are in female centrality out of Mother Earth and the systematic repetitive journey of the sun (IS HANA) creating the one more concept of its rebirth at dawn. The and (HANADA) concept also deals with the sun as the helping hand (HANADA) of Mother Earth the 'two in one' of the sun rising and setting working relentlessly and habitually in tandem.

JA (YA) Polish= 'I am';

JA deals with individuality (hanaDAVADA-), or the one who is divided (DAVADA-) from the mother, be she the individual mother or the body of Mother Earth. When one is divided (DAVADA) from the mother, one moves into 'the gift of' (DA) vida (VADA) or life in Spanish. In vida (VADA), (DA) is 'the gift of' and (VA) is the familiar vulva vagina (VA) construct on the individual mothers body and the volcanic vent (VA) on the body of Mother Earth.

JA (YA) Swahili, Arabic, Finnish= 'to come', (KAMA);

It may deal either with the migratory march arriving on the promised land of the verdant savannah, or with having an orgasm. As the herbivore mares arrived in the verdant savannahs they dropped their foals. The (KAMA) of coming deals with (KA) making smaller creations out of (MA) the mothers bodies. Or it may have been part of the birthing process of a human mother as the high fast panting breath orgasmed the baby out of her body, by coming up to the surface accompanied by the ecstasy of the orgasming birthing breath. In either case it deals with joyful arriving on the scene and with ecstatic birth.

JA (YA) German, Swedish, Danish, Finnish= 'yes';

It says yes to life as; I am, of coming, and of life creation, all the above. Yahweh (YAHAVAHA) or Jehovah (JAHAVAHA) enters the picture as in PHASE THREE He rises into the ethers and becomes the yes sayer not only to life but becoming the male source of all creation.

JAA in Swahili means to get full and it deals with eating; It says yes to food (FADA), the 'gift of' (DA) of the fingers (FA). On the other hand JAA as being full also deals with the negation (NA) of being full, as NJAA establishing being hungry and famine as the semi annual monsoon rains refused to fall on the parched savannah or failed to come at all. It is in Swahili that the SHAPE of the letter (J) as the SHAPE of the lower mandible of the jaw on the mothers face the organ that does the cutting and eating surfaces very clearly and gives veracity to the concepts of 'and' 'one more', 'yes' to the process of eating.

HA-Anglo Saxon= 'how' (HAWA);

After the MA of the mother as the top lip of her mouth creating the humming SOUND that the food was edible in PHASE ONE, the next codified SOUND may very well have been the HA of the birthing breath. For it was the human mother who asked HOW to do the things that she needed to do to keep her offspring alive. In PHASE THREE males asked the WHY of their peripheral state. In PHASE ONE at the time of female centrality it was the mother who defined reality. The answers to the HOW of survival were one of her greatest tools.

With the (W) at the end of HOW we are either dealing with the bottom lip on the face of the mother or the bottom lip on the watery surFACE of Mother Earth. With the watery surFACE of Mother Earth during the time of the most ancient migrations across Africa it was the sHOWers in the distance that sHOWEed her the way to the verdant savannahs and by following the herbivore herds HOW to get to the promised land of plenty. The HA of the Anglo Saxon HOW (HAWA) as a single dyad retains its (H) SOUND before the vowel and is very ancient. The water surrounded island of Hawaii (HAWA-) may not have been that isolated. Or it may have dealt with the one more at the end of Hawaii of the undefined PHASE ONE boy child.

At the Gobekli Tepe ruins in Turkey that go back eleven thousand years there are perfectly chiseled enormous blocks of standing H SHAPED monoliths. What did they mean to our ancient Mediterranean ancestors? Did they have anything to do with the language and the importance of the breath, or was it the SHAPE of the opening on top blasted apart by a volcanic eruption that was a metaphoric symbol of their importance.

HA in Portuguese, Spanish, Italian= 'it is';

The specific naming of things came with the emergence of language out of female centrality in PHASE ONE. To name something is to separate it from its background, to make it stand alone, to make it more important. It also creates its state of independent being and alerts the young what thing, plant or animal is safe for ingestion. Children shove everything into their mouths. They have to be taught what is safe. Naming an object gives them the knowledge of survival.

HA in Hebrew= 'tabernacle';

Upon becoming aware of their role in specific paternity in PHASE THREE the Hebrews in the creation of their father God sailed into the sky *away* and *above* the body of Mother Earth. Their first sacred place of worship was the sun which sailed through the realms of the sky, through the belly of air above the body of Mother Earth. The vault of the sky housing the sun and other celestial bodies including the stars became the Hebrew (haBARA) temple of worship, their TaBERnacle. In PHASE THREE it became the place of the hidden, invisible mind of God also floating in the ethers. In the word for TaBERncle you have the dyad of BER (BARA) of the 'intermediate state' of trance of the Tibetans which included soaring birds (BARADA) who flew in the 'intermediate state' of air and the castrated brothers (BARADA-) who existed in the 'intermediate state' neither male and not female.

The word temple gives it all away. It is the temple of the forehed that gives birth to thought. It is thought that created the male God who rose to be worshipped in the temple.

HA in Persian=light (LAYATA);

The light of the Persians shares its linguistic meaning with the (AYA) also of light and dawn in Assyrian. The HA of light in Persian deals with the vault of air (HAra) above the body of Mother Earth into which the sun had to stretch its way to the surFACE to be reborn at dawn. The aya (HAYA) dyad deals with the specific pubic SHAPE of creation (Y) between two mountain peaks on the body of Mother Earth out of which the sun was born or regurgitated in the Eastern sky.

HA in Bugotu of the Solomon Islands 'to breathe out';

In the process of breathing, in one direction the air as the breath is taken in (AH), in another direction the air or the breath is expelled (HA) or let out. The AH-HA of inHAlation and exHAlation is linked together like the two sides of a coin. On the body of Mother Earth the activity of the volcanic cone echoes with the same process The blast of the volcanic eruption breathes the air up to the surFACE.

A) on the body of Mother Earth are closed on top She becomes the triangular cone of potential creation expressed through the SHAPE of the letter A(ah). In the process of exploding or erupting during a volcanic eruption She blasts air up to Her surFACE, not only creating the air above Her surFACE as Her majestic exHAlation but the open on top letter H of the exHAled breath.

HA in Egyptian, Aruba (HARABA)='large house';

In Spanish house is casa(KASA) and casa establishes a case for the coos (KASA) of the individual mother as the house of creation. Since it is a large house then the Egyptian house of creation may very well be Mother Earth and the belly of air (HARA) above Her out of PHASE ONE. As (HA) it may also deal more directly with the belly of expelled air through which the sun sailed every day, made its daily home both above the surFACE of Mother Earth and at twilight went to sleep beneath in the underground intestinal tunnels within Her body (BA-). There was no larger house than the one provided by the tri-parted body of Mother Earth above, upon and below for Her (HARA) solar offspring.

HA-HA Japanese= 'mother';

All the other languages on the planet define the mother by the humming SOUND made by her top lip in the process of alerting her young what was safe to eat, codified in the letter M. The Japanese are the only ones that deal with the repetitive birthing breath of the individual mother in the last stages of labor. She had to pant hard and fast (HA-HA) to get the large headed fetus out of her body defining her as the Japanese mother.

Mother Earth also panting expelling Her tropical birthing breath gave birth to the Equatorial Sahel (IS HAHAla) and the Northern Sahara (IS HAHAra) the desiccated scorched desert. In Old Basque zahara (IS HAHARA) as 'old' may have links with the passing of the verdant Sahara into desert history. For the Hebrews ze'ah (IS HAHA) defines sweat. It must have been obvious to the ancient Hebrews that the high fast panting breath of the mother giving birth covered her with a patina of sweat (IS WATA), or water (WATA-). In Sanskrit the birthing breath of the mother in PHASE ONE created the reverence for life that surfaces as ahinsa (HAHAnasa). The (HAHA) as the birthing breath, the (HANA) as the sun (IS HANA) and (NASA) deal with the birth of the sun created the reverence for life. One of the Hawaiian Islands is Oahu (HAHA). Not only the how (HAWA) of the maintaining mothers surface here but also her birthing breath (HAHA) like emerging noses smoked their way up to the surface of the Pacific waters. Not to be left out the state of Ohio (HAHA) shares that ancient linguistic destiny with a giant sculpture of a terrestrial serpent on Her sacred ground . As an area of passage the Seven Starry Sisters in the heavens as the Pleiades on the body of Mother Earth in PHASES TWO and THREE surface in the search for male centrality *away* and *above* Her body are also called Shet (IS HATA) Ahad (HAHAda).

KA-Egyptian 'twin soul of a dead person';

The concept of twinning surfaces in many mythologies the world over. It usually deals with the two aspects of the sun rising in the Eastern sky as one twin the other twin setting in the Western sky. Same concept as the two hands working in tandem. In PHASE THREE they are often called brothers. The rising sun in the Eastern sky dealt with life and the living person. The setting sun in the Western sky dealt with death (of the sun) and the dead person. As the KA in Egyptian it establishes the possibility that the twin associated with the KA was the smaller of the two. The twin dealing with the living rising sun was the bigger of the two.

It may also extend to the coming and leaving of birds as the SHAPE of the letter K of a birds open beak illustrates. When the birds arrived with the coming monsoon rains like the rising sun life flourished on all levels. When the birds left, with the desiccating savannah behind them, their leaving left the sky empty of their rapturous presence. It was as if the sun had set over the silent scorching surFACE of Mother Earth. Set (IS HATA) is also the name of the Egyptian sun God SETting in the Western waters.

Another source of the letter K deals with the the letter X of the buttox in stage three as seen from the back halved vertically as did the halving of the mothers body while giving bith or egg laying. One aspect of the letter K deals with smallness.

KA Hindu 'twin of Buddha'(BADADA);

The Buddha had been the 'enlightened one' having links with the sun of daylight. The twin of Buddha was the setting sun of night and its dark passage within the body of Mother Earth. In his name the Buddha (BADADA) carries the concept of duality 'the two in one' of the letter (B). And the (DADA) as the double gift of coming and going. It reflects the same perception as the Egyptian solar twins rising and setting. It also is smaller than the sun of daylight and the sad silence left by the birds. In Polish budzi (BADA, BAJA) means to be awakened. If not in the writing but in the SOUND, the Polish budzi (BAJA) reflects the fact that the Buddha is the 'awakened one', like the sun at dawn. with the sun of dawn shining upon him, he became enlightened.

To that scenario could be added the flowering bud (BADA). A bud (BADA) is the 'gift of'(DA) duality (BA). When its petals are closed it exists in the state of potential, like a tulip. When its petals open wide due to the shining and warmth of the sun establishing itself not only as the result of enlightment but that it is ready for much heavy duty business with the flowering of creation. A TULIP bud (BADA) opens the TWO LIPS, the two emerging petals of creation that awaken the possibility that we are talking about the two vulvic lips of the pubis.

KA-Hebrew= 'like (LAKA), the';

Something is 'like', the something is defined by the individual 'the' dealing with an aspect of reflection. When something is reflected we are dealing with a body of still standing water that as a lake (LAKA) reflects the reality above, is 'like' the reality above. If the reality above dealt with life then the reality below dealt with death of the sun under the mysterious reflection in the dark waters. It is those dark convoluted rivers of passage that had to be crossed to get to the promised land. Who wandered through those underground grottoes? Along with Gilgamesh, the sun and the moon.

KA-Middle East='place of burial';

The place of burial, the ancient cemetery was on the West side of the river, or a body of water. The syllable KA dealt with the smaller creations like the sun out of the body of Mother Earth. Where the KA of the Egyptians as the twin soul of a dead person, and the KA of the Buddhists as his twin the dark sun, and the KA of he Hebrews as to be 'like' and the KA in the Middle East as the place of burial was the place where the sun died to its rays of light. It became smaller. The KA in all of these words deals with the sun setting, dying to its light and the birds descending semi-annually into the Northern darkness of the horizontal rim giving the KA its SHAPE as the open beak of arriving and departing like the sun.

KA-Slav= 'soul';;

The Slavic soul (IS HALA) also deals with the journey of the sun. In Spanish the sun is sol (IS HALA). It was believed that the human soul (IS HALA) took the same journey within the body of Mother Earth as the sun, sol (IS HALA) in Spanish, to be reborn to a new day at dawn, The soul when a human being died would be reborn to a new body. In PHASE ONE all the ancient cultures emerging out of Africa believed in reincarnation. In the Epic of Gilgamesh the Sumerian prince took the same journey as the sun through the body of Mother Earth at night and debunked that ancient belief. The Hindu culture escaping the heresy inherent in the pronouncements of Gilgamesh held on to the promise of reincarnation.

KA-Chinese= 'song';

What else but bird song as cano (KANA) in Latin with the SHAPE of their open beaks arriving to usher in the day of birthing and singing. (KA) in one of its manifestations is the open beak of a bird as seen in profile. (NA) deals with either 'change from a former state' or 'emergence on the surface'.

KA-Bemba= 'diminutive';

Primarily it deals with Mother Earth creating all aspects smaller than Herself (KAKA) out of Her majestic volcanic buttox .It also deals with birds laying their endless eggs making innumerable smaller aspects of creation while coming and going. With their open beaks (K) they sang their way through the heavens.

-KA= Polish 'diminutive female';

Sharing with the Bemba diminutive, or what is small but more specifically with the female; dziewczyna =girl, dziewczyn*KA* =little girl, kobieta=woman, kobiet*KA* little woman, pani= woman, panien*KA* = little girl. In Basque girl is nesKA (NASAKA) Nasa deals with birth and that is what a girl does, she gives birth. Basque contains ancient linguistic links with PHASE ONE and mother centrality. The big female is Mother Earth.

Hidden in the name for Alaska (HALASAKA) we have an aspect of smallness dealing with the sun. The first three dyads as (HALASA-) deal with the sun eelyos (HALASA) in Greek and the Greek sun God as Helios (HALASA). Alaska then becomes the land of the small (KA) sun eelyos (HALASA) in Greek. Is that not an apt description of the far North as the land of the midnight sun? Who gave them that name, the ancient Greeks? What were they doing in Alaska when language was becoming codified in ancient PHASE ONE?

KAA= Swahili 'sit, stay, charcoal';

Here we are dealing with Mother Earth and the result of a volcanic explosion and the making of kaka, that awful offal. It is the lava that as potential dirt pours down Her flanks that is admonished to sit and stay and to make land, Her smaller creation upon which that as dirt creatures could have their being. And it is the charcoal that is created during that blast that darkens the sky and showers Her body with charcoal and cinders also smaller aspects than She is as their overwhelming maternal matrix.

The double AA deals with lavic terrain in Hawaiian as creation of the ground of being out of the body of Mother Earth and also AA the name of a river in Latvia as Her other major aquatic creation. For the Finnish it establishes the name of their alphabet as the AAKKoset covering both bases; Mother Earth and Her triangular cone of creation as AA (HAHA) of the birthing breath as (HAHA) and the open beaks of the semiannual arrival of birds as (KAKA).

LA- English='echoic sound';

The letter L originally out of stage one in PHASE ONE dealt with the angle of the tongue lying on the floor of the oral cavity. In Latin lengua (LANAGA) stands not only for the tongue (TANAGA) in creating meaning goes up and down but surfaces in English as that which is created by the tongue, ie language (LANAGA-). In PHASE THREE with the expansion of names for young boys that which also moved up and down but this time on a male body had been the lingum (LANAGA-) or Hindu penis. In PHASE ONE the capacity of the trance state out of the birthing mothers and ritualized shamans, were based on solid truth. Males began to create their reality out of the answers to the WHY of their peripheral state. There are no real answers to the WHY. They have to be made up.

THE ANSWER TO WHY IS ALWAYS A LIE.

In PHASE THREE because the (NAGA) dyad as the SHAPE of the snake (IS NAKA, NAGA) surfaces in both the tongue (taNAGA) and language (laNAGAga) we have to assume that we are dealing with a creature with a lying forked tongue like a snake (IS NAKA) . The (KA) and (GA) are interchangeable. In the Middle East women fillibrated the air with their tongues at the arrival of triumphant warriors. The fillibrating of the air with their tongues may have been a promise of more than just lallating their welcome.

LA Swahili= 'to eat';

Not only the mouth of the mother was used in the eating of food. To masticate it and make it slippery enough to slide down the gullet, the tongue,(lengua) in Latin, the angle lying on the floor of the oral cavity had to be used to do the job of milling (MALA-) it into small (IS MALA-) pieces and lubricating it in the oral cavity.

LA- Sanskrit= 'Earth';

Mother Earth had been considered as the maternal context, the LAdy as the LAnd that defined the pLAnet giving birth to everything, even the heavenly bodies out of Her round, fLAt circLAr horizontal rim. It was the angle of emergence of the sun, moon, birds, clouds even the stars that used the SHAPE of the angle of the tongue as a metaphor for their emergence up to the surFACE. It was also one of the beliefs in PHASE ONE that Mother Earth pushed the heavenly bodies and birds out of their nocturnal sleep up to Her surFACE with Her tongue, She regurgitated them. That may have been one of the reasons that Light and Life became defined by the angular SHAPE of the tongue (Lengua in Latin) encoded in the letter (L) as the SHAPE of the sun became evicted up to the surFACE in the Eastern sky at dawn.

For the Middle Easterners in PHASE THREE it was the male sun RA *away* and *above* the body of Mother Earth 'that existed forever'. For the Maya across the great watery divide 'that which existed forever' was the LA of Mother Earth as the great Mother who gave birth to the sun who was at one with Her in the creation of light, life and land upon Her surFACE.

LA of Maya= 'eternal truth, that which existed forever';

For the Maya the LA of the Mother was not only 'that which existed forever' like Mother Earth their pLAnetary nest but was also 'the eternal truth' as nature.

LA of Aztec= 'Mother Goddess of the sun God Quetzalcoatl';

She as Mother Earth gave birth to the sun God, be She in the Middle East in PHASE TWO as Ra, or on the continent of what became in linguistic PHASE ONE the Americas as LA. 'Holy Mary Mother of God' for the Christians falls into that same category.

LA Spanish= 'she';

A baby boy had been called a he (HA). A baby girl with the addition of the (S) before her name establishes her as the one who out of her blood (SA) creates a baby. The S plus HE becomes a SHE. It is the same construct as man and WOman. Man is a male person without the watery WOmb of a WOman. The same surfaces in male and FEmale. It was the FEmale with her two hands and five FIngers that did the work of tenderly tending to her inFant with her hands and FIngers. In China mounds on the body of Mother Earth, the LAdy of the LAnd are called a SHE. The same concept surfaces in Ireland.

MA- 'mother in all languages' except Japanese;

The SHAPE of the letter M comes out of the top lip of the mother. It is the SHAPE that defines the activity of HUMming and assenting to the fact that the food is edible as sent. The only SOUND that you can make when you are savoring the food to make sure that it is safe, is the SOUND of HUMming. The HUMming SOUND defined not only HUManity but the creature that HUMmed who had HUMor and joy, came out of HUMus, out of the body of Mother Earth and was HUMble of her beginnings.

MA in Basque= 'kiss';

It was obviously the mouth (MATA) of the mother (MATARA), her two lips working in tandem that created and held the blissful kiss.

MA in Finnish= 'country soil';

Here we are dealing with the mountainous mouths and mounds on the body of Mother Earth, the tarry terrain on Her surFACE, as the ultimate Mother.

MA in Burmese= 'young woman';

It would be she who would become a MA at her quintessence when she flowed with her menarche (MANARAJA) or her first menstrual flowering, in time becoming the monarch (MANARAJA). It echoes the same concept as the RU of RUler dealing with her RUddy blood and the moon (MANA) as the RUler of time in concert with her menstrual flow. Meter (MATARA) as the mother (MATARA) establishes the same ancient mother as the counter in line with the phases of the moon. When she had her first period menarche (MANARAJA) the young woman became not only the potential mother but the subsequent monarch (MANARAJA) and ruler. Matematics (MATA-MATA-) repeated as a reality came out of the perceptions of the mother (MATA-).

MA in Sanskrit='tongue';

It is the tongue of the mother, the angle that lies on the floor of the oral cavity of the mouth that masticates (MA-) the morsels, milling them around, making them smaller.

MA in Persian='we, what';

It is the individual mother (MA-) that creates the we (WA) out of her hidden wet (WATA) watery (WATA-) womb. It is Mother Earth (MA) that creates all that is, the what (WATA) above Her belly of air with the coming of the wet (WATA) rain of survival and below under Her watery (WATA-) surFACE. In PHASE ONE human beings had been at one with the essence of Mother Earths Kundalini energy using watter as a conductor.

MA in Hebrew= 'what';

The Hebrew what (WATA) also has links with water (WATA-). The mystery associated with death resided under the still waters that reflected the reality above. The endless human inquiry and fear has been based on the question of WHAT existed after death in the murky waters below Mother Earth's surFACE.

MA in Indo-European='Goddess of indulgence, source, all seeing, immortality';

Mother Earth in PHASE ONE had been considered to be the Goddess of indulgence, or the one who gloried in the joy of human sexuality and did not judge or restrain female sexual behavior. It was out of Her all incompassing body as source that everything emerged, the celestial bodies and birds out of Her horizontal rim, the plants and burrowing creatures out of Her soil and large herbivores and carnivores that crouched and scurried across the savannah. She was the source of everything. In Egyptian She was represented by the all seeing owl, the MA'A who rotated her head in every direction which was associated with human mothers. You couldn't be single focused, left hemispheric and linear to keep the infant from doing damage to itself. You had to have eyes in the back of your head. The MA'A as the Egyptian owl fit the symbolic metaphor as its head spun around in every direction. It is the MA of the mother that created the (A) of another daughter that the Egyptian owl signifies. The owl as a great hunter also regurgitates food for her chicks.

MAA-Bugotu= 'fearless';

When a mother (MA) went through the birthing breath and the state of ecstatic trance that the high fast panting activated, upon awakening the Kundalini energy she became the fearless protector of her baby. She also awakened in herself the capacity to rule, heal and prophesize. The fearless state has been the state that emerges as self realization in the 'spiritual' journey. It has also been the state sought by all the male heroes who went after the quest to search for the state of ecstatic fearless liberation. The two (AA) s in MAA represent the triangular volcanic SHAPE of Mother Earth (A) and the reflected triangular pubic SHAPE (A) on the individual mothers body. Both create the perceived SHAPE of source and creation that led to evenness, balance, courage and liberation. It also surfaces as the earliest SHAPE of the Star of David.

NA-Persian= 'no, neither';

If the hum of acceptance of masticating food defines the top lip, the (M) of the mother, then the SHAPE of the letter (N) of the nose in profile surfaces with the (N) SOUND of negation as the food is pushed out of the mouth. The only SOUND that you can make when the food is evicted, or regurgitated is the nasal (N) SOUND of negation associated with the nose. The (N) SOUND is either 'emergence on the surface' or 'change from a former state'. It is saying to the food, no and neither. In no case are you edible.

NA in Polish= 'upon';

When something is evicted or pushed out of the mouth it has to land somewhere. In Polish it lands upon a reluctant surface.

NA in Swahili='and, by, with';

When something emerges upon the surface it becomes an individual object dealing with an activity of repetition. To eat in Swahili is a process where you are not only 'by' but 'with' your food and by repeating the process of eating creating an endless succession of 'ands'. The possibility of holding the food up to the mouth deals with the activity of the hands (HANADA) who create the endless flow of ands (HANADA).

NA in German='not';

The food as sent is 'not' edible. It is not ready for ingestion. It engages in the concept of negation and the nasal SOUND associated with the nose.

NA in Chinese='which, what';

The shoving of food out of the mouth separates 'what' is edible and that 'which' is not edible accompanied by the nasal SOUND of negation. The naming of things created a separation into which or what they were perceived to be.

PA-English='place of definite position, serial order';

The SOUND of P (puh) air being ploded out of the top lip deals with the SHAPE of the top lip as the major creator of the unvoiced B (buh). The letter (P) usually deals with an aspect of passage, or movement through.

PA in Persian='foot, leg';

As a movement through, or passage, it is the paw or foot of a carnivore that slinks through the underbrush after its prey. In Latin pied (PADA) defines a foot. In Polish pada deals directly with that which falls down, which is what a feet do, they fall down to the ground, one after another or serially. In both words (DA) is 'the gift of' and (PA) deals with passage. Spider (isPADAra) is an insect that falls directly on its prey.

PA in Wolof='father'; One who follows the body of the mother and falls on her during coitus.

RA-Egyptian= 'solar deity';

The letter R is made up of the circular male sun on top and the volcanic triangle of the Mother on the bottom halved vertically. It comes out of PHASE TWO when the two sexes worked in tandem but the male sun was on top and the mothers triangle was on the bottom which means that we are moving into PHASE THREE and male centrality.

It was the electro magnetic solar wind piercing the poles on the body of Mother Earth, burning its way through Her center and emerging upon Her surFACE as the RAging, RAmpaging RAping volcanic eruption that gave the SOUND to the letter R and the Egyptian Ra as the Sun God.

RA in Semitic= 'that which existed forever',

For the Middle Easterner males upon becoming aware of their specific role in paternity as they moved *away* and *above* the body of Mother Earth in order to create the father and to establish their own Gods, the sun became one of their major deities. The fact that they existed in the scorched, sun drenched Sahara may have added to that perception. For the Maya in the lush tropical jungles of Central America it was the LA as the LAdy of the LAnd 'that existed forever'.

RA in Sanskrit='royal, exulted, high';

It was the solar disc as it soared high across the sky becoming worshipped and exulted for its rays of blessed light in PHASE THREE became the sole ruler on high, the sole royal celestial God. Mother Earth as the ruler, with Her russet ruby red blood associated with the menstrual tugging of the moon was demoted and left behind.

RA in Swedish, Danish='original state';

It was the sun that had been considered as the source, as the creator of the original state, not the body and surFACE of Mother Earth. We are in PHASE TWO of budding male centrality and the male Gods of the sky *away* and *above* the body of Mother Earth with the solar God RA as their major deity.

RAA-Hebrew='bad', RA'A, 'evil', RHA='the red one', When the Jews were enslaved by the Egyptians in PHASE TWO, they must have rejected all aspects of Egyptian religion and RA their major solar deity. The double (AA) in RAA takes us back into Mother Earth (A) and the human mother (A) out of whom issued the Alpha of creation. The Hebrews must have rejected both the RAA as bad and RA'A as evil because it had been associated with the ancient mothers as in PHASE THREE their knowledge of specific male input in procreation and male centrality was gaining momentum resulting in the begats of the Bible. The emergence of the (A) as the surrogate daughter of Mother Earth became redefined as evil, the work of the subsequent devil, the 'gift of' (DA) of evil. The double AA in RAA takes us back to the definition of Mother Earths terrain as defined by the double AA of repeated volcanic eruptions.

The red one (RHA) takes us to the setting sun in the Western sky as Mother Earth ate and swallowed the mauled solar disc leaving a trail of blood on the reflective surFACE of the engulfing waters. On land much of the soil in many parts of Africa is also made of red clay as Mother Earth devoured all that she created. The RHA (RAHA) as the red one may have links with the red haired Neanderthal who also had been considered evil. The Biblical hero David had also been red haired as had Mary Magdeline. Here we are dealing also with the concept of androgyny, the Mother Earth-sun combination both creating survival in one majestic body. The solar disc of the male on top and the triangle of the mother on the bottom gave us the SHAPE encoded not only in the letter R but in the keyhole, the place of passage reflecting the androgyny that occurred in the balanced brain. The eunuch first born son became the priest associated with that passage though the keyhole created by the balance of the external and internal hemispheric aspects.

SA-Swahili= 'seven';

At the time of the ancient migratins in PHASE ONE, seven (IS EVEN) became established as the even (HAVANA) number of September and separation. If you counted the beginning of the migrations in March then six months later the herbivore herds dropped their foals, came into estral heat and in the seventh month began their journey back. It was a time of separation from their verdant savannah (IS HAVANA) and a trek back to their mountain homes in September. In Latin sept means both seven and separation. It also established the concept of reflection as the seven (IS EVEN) apparition of what was real and what was duplicated on the surFACE of the waters. Seven also surfaces as a number, as the solar angle of descent in the Western rim, falling to its doom (DAMA) into the underground transformative chambers within the body of Mother Earth.

-SA= Basque ='feminine form suffix';

The SA establishes the blood of the mother; SAng in French, SAngre in Spanish and SAnguis in Latin. It establishes her intelligence as SAge and SAgacity. It also deals with plurality at the end of female nouns. Sais (SASA), pais (PASA) land surFACE, coos (KASA), casa (KASA) Spanish house.

SA in Wolof='your';

It deals with possessiveness, with the pointer finger pointing away dealing with motherhood and what belonged to her out of her blood. There was no SA of the father as 'your' so we are still in female centrality and PHASE ONE when specific paternity was unknown.

SA in Egyptian='goose';

Wise blood of the mother. In Lithuanian zasis (IS HASASA) is the name for the goose. The goose had been considered as the carrier of truth due to the fact that it had goosepimply puckers all over her skin. When a moment of truth hits you, the truth showers you with a flush of goose pimples. The (SASA) on the end of the Lithuanian zasis (IS HASASA) establishes the goose as reflecting both truths out of the individual mother (SA) and the body of Mother Earth, the other (SA).

The goose (GASA) also hisses like the gas (GASA) that hissed its way up to the surFACE through Mother Earths vents creating the air above Her surFACE that supported the multifaceted activity of life. Cinderella had also been called the goose girl with her relationship with both the volcano and with transformation.

SA in Sanskrit='wind, snake, air, bird, Vishnu, Siva';

As the wind SA dealt with air and movement and the Tibetan 'intermediate state'. Before male role in specific procreation had become known in PHASE ONE many women exposed their buttocks to the wind to become pregnant. The wind felt as the movement that they wanted to recreate in their bellies. The Trobriander women of the South Pacific according to Malinowski still carried that belief into PHASE THREE. Male role in specific paternity took a long time to take root.

The wind, air, snake and bird cover a similar base. It was through the belly of air that the sun made its daily journey guided by the ever vigilant snake. As an area of passage, the air above the body of Mother Earth was also the arena for birds. It had been considered as the 'intermediate state' and worshipped as SAcred. Vishnu and Siva out of Hinduism have their own antecedents. When the Kundalini enegy awakens in the human body, the nail on the big left toe often turns black. The big left toe nail on the body of Vishnu not only gave birth to the river Ganges but also to the big black toe nail. For some reason he was also colored blue. It may have been because he had been associated with the color of the great expansive blue seas. The Maya painted their children blue before they sacrificed them into the surrounding holy cenotes. Can Mayan origins out of both Africa and Asia and their religious systems be doubted?

SA in French='his, hers, its';

Possessive pronouns based on all three definitive categories of human beings defined by their blood SAng in French.

SAA in Swahili='hour, time';

In PHASE ONE, time was based on the thirteen month lunar calendar. It was the passage of the menstrual blood of the mother (SA) that counted time in tandem with the phases of the moon. The moon as a ruler measured time. A ruler was also the female who ruled when she came into her menarche (MANARAJA) becoming the monarch (MANARAJA). The Raj

(RAJA) was an ancient name of the ruler originally out of the first blossoming of a young girl. In PHASE THREE when all the redefinitions became linguistic reality Raj (RAJA) became the name of a male monarch. The double (AA) in SAA includes the body of Mother Earth as one who also flowered with Her lavic blood and created the land upon Her surFACE. One A(ah) dealt with the individual mother. The other A(ah) dealt with the body of Mother Earth. The (AA) construct surfaces in Finnish as the name of their AAkkoset or alphabet. The Finnish (FANASA-) people SOUND too much like the Phoenicians (FANASA-) to be discarded lightly. They had been considered magnificent sailors and when their Mediterranean home may have been flooded they could have migrated further up North into Finland. Their language like Lithuanian and Basque has very ancient preHIStoric often mother centered roots.

SA'A-Arabic='hour, movement';

The passage of lunar time in PHASE ONE establishes not only the hours of the night but movement itself out of the blood of the mother (SA). SA with the apostrophie SA'A sends the message that one A(ah) emerged from another A (ah). Since the first syllable is a SA then we are dealing with the mothers blood creating another one like herself. Also if daughters were surrogates of Mother Earth then the SA'A may deal with Mother Earth (A) creating another one like Herself, another daughter as the second (A).

SA in Hebrew-SHA'AH (IS HAHA) ='hour';

Somehow the HA'AH deals with the birthing breath of the mother but backwards with the exHAlation coming first and the inHAlation (AH) following it as AH-HA. As HAHA it may have links with the huh (HAHA) that defines the number seven of reflective evenness and separation.

ZA-Hebrew='moved';

The movement with the voiced ZA could only deal with the coagulated blood (SA) in the mothers belly with the growing fetus starting to kick.

ZA Polish='after';

Deals with what comes after the high panting breath and the bloody (SA) baby appears upon the surface. As the letter A(ah) came first establishing the Western Alphabet so the letter Z(zed) came not only after but last, Alpha and Omega, A to Z, female to male, beginning to end.

ZAA Swahili= 'To bear offspring', deals with a similar concept out of the mothers blood (SA) coagulating around the liver (LAVARA), as the fetus is panted and pushed up to the surface. She delivers (daLAVA-) it from inside

Section Two

to outside. On the body of Mother Earth it is the lava that flows out of Her livid (LAVADA) volcanic crater that creates one of Her major creations, land upon Her surFACE.

TA-English= 'the, thee, thou';

Deals with separation into distinct categories at the tip, top using the tip of the pointer finger to distinguish differences, to point things out and to give them names.

TA in Polish= to, tamto (this, that);

Same concept flourishes in Polish as things are pointed out linguistically by the tip of the pointer finger. They also exist upon the surFACE, at the tip, top or edge on the body of Mother Earth.

TA in Chinese= 'he, she, it';

Same individual things defining human beings, targeted by the tip of the pointer finger.

VA-Spanish= 'he, she, it goes';

Dealing with movement; voy, vas, va, vamos, vais, van. It may have links with the volcanic (VA) body of Mother Earth covering all bases, when She was considered to be female-male, the ultimate balanced right hemispheric androgyny.

VA in Sanskrit= 'to blow','water';

Also deals with movement, the swirling wind as a creative blowing source, and the trembling WAVES upon the waters that never seem to remain still.

VAA-Bugotu='to open' (of mouth?);

Looking at the letter (V) sideways it emerges looking like the open beak of a bird and may have links with the voice (VA) or SOUND that emanates from it. It may also morph into Mother Earth (A) creating another (A) as Her daughter out of Her volcanic (VA) vent.

YA-Swahili= 'of';

In PHASE ONE the (YA) dealt with the mothers pubis as the SHAPE of creation. It was also the SHAPE of the sun rising from between two mountain peaks at dawn. Creation emerged or was out of the body of the female and her pubic SHAPE. In PHASE THREE as source was redefined not only out of the heavens but out of the bifurcated left hemispheric male mind questing for answers to the WHY of their periphery, the YA of Yahveh emerged triumphant.

YA in Sanskrit='air';

As male deities emerged denying the body of Mother Earth as source, the only area that was not taken by the all encompassing Mother, was the belly of air above Her. It was through the air above the body of Mother Earth that most of the celestial deities representing the emerging male source had their being. It also has links with the concept of an idea. For an idea floats upon the air like a bird or like an opinion. Pinion defines a wing that also floats upon the air. An idea is a figment of the imagination. Imagination plays a role in the growth of the bifurcated brain (Y) as it splits away from the HOW of the mothers in PHASE ONE to the WHY of the fathers in PHASES TWO and THREE.

THE ANSWER TO WHY IS ALWAYS A LIE.

YA in Chinese= 'swallow bird', 'flying';

The birds on their wing take to the air as a vehicle of passage, clacking their way back and forth across the sky semi-annually making that enormous migration that was like an ancient clock. The oPINION as a birds wing raises its head here also. It may have been that the SHAPE of a swallow bird high up in the sky reflected the SHAPE of the letter (Y).

WA -Chinese='dig';

On the mothers face the (WA) was the bottom lip reflecting the (M) of the top lip. Since the bottom of the individual mothers face did not ostensibly do the digging, then we are dealing with two possibilities, one is the busy, grunting sow, the endlesss digger and tiller of the soil and the other is the (WA) of Mother Earth as torrents of rushing water (WA) dug (DAGA) their way across Her surFACE.

It was the torrent of water out of the celestial body of Mother Earth as rain that created the bounty of survival. On the individual mothers body it was the mammary gland, the dug (DAGA) that also flowed with milk, the emerging liquid of survival. (DA) is 'the gift of' and (GA) is the activity of beGEtting.

WA in Swahili='to be';

When the water sack broke in the womb of the pregnant mother and the amniotic fluid poured out of her body, she created the future and the possibility of being. The fetus floating in the mothers womb upon being pushed up to the surface established the concept of to be. On the body of Mother Earth, to be emerged as the concept of 'two in one' and bio. One WAs the ground of being or soil. The other WAs the great waters that often surrounded them.

WA in Bemba= 'fall';

Water fell from the sky as rain. It created the weather, or WET HER. It made HER WET. Same linguistic concept as the FAT HER, the one who made HER FAT, or pregnant. The fall of water from the sky as the coming monsoons was a blessed event and the beginning of the ancient migrations to the verdant grassy savannahs of the promised land.

WAA-Wolof='person';

Here we are dealing with the definitin of a female person out of PHASE ONE. The one (A) defines the individual mother. The second (A) defines the body of Mother Earth. Together they establish the concept of source out of female persons while also defining them. On the body of Mother Earth in Hawaiian AA deals with lavic terrain. Across the world in Latvia AA deals with a river and water. It is out of the individual mothers watery womb that a person came into being.

WA'A- Arabic='awake';

To have been born was to have awaken into the life on top of the surFACE of Mother Earth. It is also the emergence out of the WAtery womb of the individual mother. Before one was born it was believed that one was asleep, on the other side of reality under the reflective surFACE of the dark and mysterious waters. Since in PHASE ONE reincarnation was a universal belief, they who waited to be reborn were asleep in the Bardo the 'intermediate state' of the Tibetans or the subserquent Christian Limbo. At birth the sun awakened to a new day and a creature awakened to a new life.

RULE THIRTEEN; REPETITION,
Find DYADS, or linguistic constructs of the same syllable repeated, based on the A (ah) SOUND;

MAMA- Egyptian='nourishing breasts';

Mama Is 'ancient universal name for the mother of the nourishing breasts' The SHAPE of the letter M of the top lip established the mouth of the mother as the hummer in stage one indicating that the food was edible. It expanded to include other organs, processes, qualities and functions as the nourishing aspects of sustenance out of the mother's body her breasts or mammaries (MAMA-). Since originally it was the mouth of the mother that established her as the source of regurgitated food for the baby in stage one, then the MA of the 'nourishing breasts' or mammaries (MAMA-) as a source of food is a subsequent addition in stage three.

BABA-Polish ='old lady';

The 'two in one' aspect of balance codified by the letter (B) deals with the Polish Baba having both qualities in her out of PHASE ONE. As she became the revered and enlightened clan matriarch she had been considered to be at one with an aspect of the mothers Blood (BA) and another aspect of Mother Earth through Her lavic blood creating the Bio (BA) of life. Same linguistic structure as the repeated (SS) of the bloody duo, the (AA),the Alpha of beginnings, even the (KK) of smallness.

BABA as Hindu sage;

After the male adept went through his ritualistic transformation in PHASES TWO and THREE he became as enlightened and as wise as the Polish Baba.

BABA- Hebrews BABA= the father;

The one that came after or followed the A(ah) of the mother.

DADAD=(DADADA) Persian 'to give';

The gift of (DA) is thrice given, out of the mothers DOME as thought, out of her abDOMEn as a baby and out of her blood (DAM) in Hebrew and Amharic. SoDOMy and freeDOM enters the picture here.

DADA became the deified son of an incestuous union in West Africa.

HAHA=Japanese 'mother',

Almost all of the other languages of the world establishes the M or MA of the mother as the sharer and teacher about the edibility of food. It is only in Japanese that the birthing breath (HAHA) of the mother surfaces establishing the awakening of the Kundalini experience during the birthing process. How it survived in Japan would be an interesting study. Were the Japanese mothers not clitorectomized? Did they escape that brutal destiny?

JAJA (YAYA) in Polish is 'eggs';

It is the mother hen, the bird that lays the eggs out of her pubic (Y) area.

YAAY (YAYA) in Wolof is 'mother' or 'older woman';

It is the mother hen that lays the endless Polish eggs jaja (YAYA) out of her pubic (YA) area.

KAKA-Bugotu ='older sibling';

There had been a celebration or ritual at the time that the birds either flew off or returned to their nests. The 'older sibling' was the castrated first born brother, who had been castrated in concert with the SOUNDS made by the cacophony (KAKA-) of the birds at the time of the spring and autumnal equinox.

KAKA in Swedish = 'cake';

A cake (KAKA) is that which was cooked (KAKA-) in an oven. When a mother bird sat on her eggs and kept them warm, she had been perceived to have cooked them to maturity. The same was perceived to be with the disappearence of birds into the body of Mother Earth at Her Northern rim and in the Southern reaches of Africa. As they passed under the mantle of Mother Earth through Her internal oven they too must have been cooked (KAKA-) to maturity.

KAKA in English = 'feces', (FASASA);

When food went through the specific creature it was thought that it was due to some sort of transformative cooking (KAKA-) inside the belly for it to emerge steaming out of the body. The same process was believed to have been shared by the body of Mother Earth. The sun, moon, stars and even birds were swallowed on one side, disappeared underground into Her oven and became transformed to rise triumphant on the other side. They were like the feces emerging out of individual creatures body as they rose in the Eastern sky upon Her surFACE.

(SASA) at the end of feces (FASASA) endows the feces with very admirable qualities out of the blood (SA) of the individual mother and the energy of lavic existence (SA) out of the body of Mother Earth. Feces were the product of ingestion and the end result of the support system of life itself. The KAKA dyad relates them to the birds especially the mother hens (HANA) who not only warmed their eggs into maturity but like feces emerged out of the horizontal rim, the anus (HANASA) on the body of Mother Earth. As eggs and small aspects of creation Ka defined them as being small to remain linguistically as one of the sources of the dyad for smallness

When the birds returned to their nests they brought with them not only their rapturous song but blankets of feces, or KAKA that covered the ground under their nests creating the fertilizer that encouraged the growth of flowering plants and a bevy of insects that fed their young. On the body of Mother Earth it was the sun (IS HANA) that had been considered to be both the solar egg and the hen (HANA) when it was originally at one (ATONE), a single unit with the surFACE and body of Mother Earth.

LALA- Swahili = 'lie down';

It is the angle of the tongue in stage one lying on the floor of the oral cavity that makes the LALA SOUND of lallation LALA-) and lullabying (LALA-). It also assists in the lubricating and liquefying of food. On the body of Mother Earth in stage four it is the angle of the rising rays of the sun at dawn piercing the gloom of night to lie across and as it passes caressing the surFACE of Mother Earth.

Female animals and probably human mothers licked their babies. They believed that the spreading rays of the sun caressed with their solar fingers and licked with their tongues the surFACE of Mother Earth as they warmed Her body into life at dawn.

LA'I LA'I Hawaiian 'first woman;

La'I La'I Is associated with Mother Earth, the LAdy of the LAnd creating the LA of Herself extending to Her daughters. The (I) of one more becoming associated with the earliest definition of a male child. It may very well be in PHASE TWO when both females and males criss crossed the oreaens in trade and discovery.It is not unlike the Runic X of ten month lunar gestation accompanied with the penal dash of mutual cohabitation.

NANA moon In Dahomey, Greek, Uruk, Sumerian, Phrygian Queen,

Nana Buluku, moon, sun, first man, first woman.

NANA is a double negation.

Pushing food out of the mouth because it is not edible establishes the nasal SOUND of no, of negation and the SHAPE of the nose in stage one as it is seen in profile. The Nana of double negation covers many bases.

When daylight fades, the onrush of darkness negates the light of day. The negation of the light of day is defined by the (N) of Night. It is no longer defined by the (L) of Light. It is the moon that sails across the dark negated lightless night sky. That is the first (NA) of Nana as the name for the moon. The second (NA) deals with the moon after it sets back into the body of Mother Earth during the daylight hours and it makes its underground journey within the dark convoluted bowels of Mother Earth. When the dyad Nana surfaces in Dahomey, Sumerian, Uruk, Greek, and Phrygian what we are dealing with is the male eunuch priesthood in PHASE TWO that at that specific time worshipped the moon *away* and *above* the body of Mother Earth.

Ninsun (NANAsana) was an Akkadian Goddess

Who in PHASE ONE knew all knowledge, had the Kundalini experience of the birthing breath and found the dynasty of Ur. It may have been in

PHASE TWO when the sun had not as yet become the separate major male celestial deity.

The clue exists in the name of the 'witch doctor' in Bemba as nanga (NANAGA). The picture comes into clearer focus with the word nangu (NANAGA) as 'neither', 'nor', also in Bemba. What it establishes is that the 'witch doctor' as nanga (NANAGA) was a *shaman* and was nangu NANAGA) 'neither', 'nor', a man or a woman. He no longer had the genitalia of a man and didn't really fit the category of a woman. He was the castrated eunuch, the in between person, the BARA- as the 'intermediate state' of the Tibetan declination.

The (GA) deals with be GEtting and (NANA) deals with the moon. The (NAGA) of the snake (IS NAKA, NAGA) becomes the begetter or guide of the moon back up to the surFACE. It also creates the relationship with the eunuch (HANAKA) priesthood who worshipped the snake as not only the Kundalini energy guiding the sun through the portals of the dark night, but also the moon through the light of day below the surFACE of Mother Earth. The (K) and (G) are interchangeable.

Nun (NANA)

In PHASE THREE the Roman Catholic nun (NANA) was blessed with a similar moniker. She too represented a double negation staying a virgin, not having sex and having a permanently empty belly establishing her persistent linguistic links with the nangu (NANAGA) as the 'neither', nor' concept of the castrated male of the Bemba tribe in Africa.

In Lemba also in Africa there existed a tribe of Hebrew priests named the kochanin (kahaNANA) who must have been associated with the moon, as the (NANA) at the end of their name implies. They were probably castrated first born sons. Kochanin (KAHANA-) moves into the direction of hidden 'mysticism'.

Once heterosexual males took over the rites of the sun and made the solar disc their deity, in PHASE THREE the castrated eunuch priesthood who were already dealing with the rites of the setting sun and darkness, took over the total worship of the twice darkened moon (NANA).

In Chinese ning (NANAGA) means 'peace'. It is the same original linguistic construct in Bemba as the eunuch nangu (NANAGA), and the witch doctor nanga (NANAGA) who dealt with the passage of the moon through the night sky. All three deal with the castrated first born son as the peaceful eunuch who became the transformed shaman or witch doctor.

Other clues surface for in Chechua the name for milk is nunu (NANA) having links with the cow that jumped over the moon in nursery rhymes and the white color of the lunar disc. Except further back in time in PHASE ONE it was the nanny (NANA) goat who provided the milk for the migrating mothers. The job was shared by the nanny (NANA) or wet nurse, the original sister or nun (NANA) who also provided care and an alternate supply of milk for the infant. In PHASE THREE for the Hebrews the poor nanny goat became the bearer of sins and had been shoved out of the tribal circle to forage in the desert. But the Hebrew priests didn't completely forget her as they shaved their heads but left the peis or what looks like goat ears on the sides of their heads.

There were name places around those ancient desert establishments that surface with the (NANA) dyad such as Ninevah (NANAvaha) and Lebanon (LabaNANA). Ninevah hides within its linguistic folds the name that surfaces with numbing intensity as it REFLECTS itself, Nineveh (NANAVAHA/HAVANANA) or HAVANA.

The Ananaki (HANANAKA) (HANA-NANA-NAKA) out of Sumeria had been considered to be half brothers. Same construct as the two aspects of celestial twins rising and setting, this time dealing with both the sun (IS HANA) and the moon (NANA). The snake (IS NAKA) giving SHAPE to the Kundalini energy slips in here also. With their bird wings and heads they had been considered creatures of the air associated with a celestial deity. Their father was Anu (HANA) and the names of the brothers were Enki (HANAKA) and Enlil (HANALALA). The Anu (HANA) father is the sun (IS HANA) and his two sons are the different aspects of the sun rising and setting. Enlil (HANALALA) is the risen sun as the (LALA) at the end of his name proclaims. It is the angular SHAPE of the suns emergence out of the Eastern rim creating the letter (L) that surfaces here. The other sun or brother Enki (HANAKA) is the sun (HANA) under the plane of Mother Earth guided by the ubiquitous snake (IS NAKA) same as the most ancient Yang (hayaNAGA) of the Chinese.

What we are dealing with here is both the female based Enlil (HANALALA) and the male based castrated eunuch ((HANAKA) Enki (HANAKA). Their source comes out of PHASE TWO when both genders had been represented as celestial Gods. It also becomes apparent that we are dealing with the eunuch (HANAKA) priesthood that officiated over the rites of the rising and setting sun. At dawn they joyfully welcomed the sun Enlil (HANALALA) with lallating (LALA-) tongues. At twillight wailing at the Western wall they watched the rays of the sun (IS HANA) grow smaller (KA). In the solar brother Enki

(HANAKA) as they descended into the body of Mother Earth losing their light they were castrated of their power becoming eunuchs (HANAKA).

Anu (HANA) as their solar father has links with the anus (HANASA) and we are dealing with a transitional state. The sun is not regurgitated out of the gestating mountainous mouths or bellies of Mother Earth. It is not evicted out of Her volcanic vents. Since we are dealing with eunuch sensibility and anal sex, then birthing begins to appear out of the anus. Mother Earth as their all encompassing matriarch had been blessed with that singular event. Benin (BANANA) as a tropical African country Benin may have been blessed with the birth of bananas (BANANA). Or it may have been that they worshipped the dual (BA) aspects of their lunar (NANA) deities.

The Creatress Queen Nana Buluku (BALAKA) not only deals with the moon (NANA) but also with the sun. For the sun had been perceived to also create a double negation. As it rose into the light of a new day it negated the darkness of night. When it set back into the body of Mother Earth it negated the rays of light that passed across and caressed Her surFACE.

The Buluku (BALAKA) deals with the small (KA), angle (LA), of duality or 'two in one' (BA). It does define the 'two in one' passage of the sun back and forth rising and setting, above and below, as does the moon. So NANA as a double negation is able to cover many bases.

PAPA-Phrygian = 'mother';

Papa deals with the passage of mlk out of the lactating mammeries as paps (PAPA-).

PAPA in Hawaiian='creatress of milk out of her paps' (PAPA-);

It surfaces on the other side of the body of Mother Earth as the lactating (LAKATATA-) individual mother. The small (KA) and angles (LA) on the upper part of her body are reiterated by her titties (TATA-). It has links with LA'I LA'I the first woman in Hawaiian and the the more expansive body of Mother Earth, the pLAnet as the LAdy of the LAnd.

PAPA in Bugotu='to carry pick-a-back';

In Bugotu the PAPAya tree is blessed with a double perception exposed in its SHAPE. On one level it could be the body of the mother with the titties high up on her trunk, her paps (PAPA) in PHASE ONE bringing nourishment to her subjects or it it could have been the penis like trunk with the fruit like balls high up on it in PHASE THREE symbolizing the Papa of the father. The upper body of the mother or the penile trunk of the father carry the cluster of fruiting titties or balls high up on the trunk or 'pick a back'.

PAPA in English father;

It may have links in PHASE THREE with the unvoiced SOUND of the voiced Hebrew Baba as the father. Baba as the Hebrew father emerged as the god Baal in many of his forms and followed the mother Goddesses; Artemis, Aurora, Athena, as the letter B of two in one followed the letter A of the volcanic cone establishing the concept of beginnings.

PAPA Roman Catholic 'pope';

The Roman Catholic Pope became not only the spiritual Papa also in PHASE THREE but the physical father shaman on the body of Mother Earth reflecting the celestial father reigning supreme in the ethers. Due to the establishment of marriage he reigned supreme in the family unit.

SASA of blood source,

SASA the tail end of certain female names and transformed males; One (SA) deals with the individual mothers blood. In Egyptian Sa is the wise blood of the mother, SA is intelligence in Hebrew. SAng is blood in French, SAngre blood in Spanish, SAnguis blood in Latin. The other (SA) deals with spiral SHAPE of 'source' as the internal spin of isness that as lavic blood gave birth to the external activity of life on the body of Mother Earth.

In the human being the two winding streams of electro magnetic Kundalini energy of shakti fuse and separate as they spin their way up the spine. It is associated with the Kundalini energy having been awakened and spun up the spine activated by the birthing breath of the mother. The two awakened streams define the birthing mother as fearless, wise, capable of leadership, healing, caring and free from illusion. In Greek gnosis (ganaSASA) means knowledge. In Lithuanian nosis (naSASA) deals with the nose or snout. The NOSE KNOWS enters the scene here. In Bemba naosa (NASA) is the name for a rudder. Is not that what a nose does and is like a rudder, it points you in the right direction? It is the red or ruddy flow of blood that becomes the reason for the pointer, the direction of the erection. As zasis (IS haSASA) the Lithuanian goose with the shower of truth covering its body with permanent goose pimples.

The (SASA) dyad of the two energies working in tandem define the following; miss (maSASA), princess (paranaSASA), Goddess (gadaSASA), priestess (parasataSASA), hostess (hataSASA) and hallowed places such as Knossos (KanaSASA) of Minoan Crete, Mount Parnassus (ParanaSASA), linking it with the princess (PARANASASA). The prana (PARANA) in mount Parnassus (PARANA-) and the princess (PARANA-) in Hinduism define the prana or shakti, as the female Kundalini Mother Earth energy that activated all three male Gods. Physis (faSASA) as Mother Nature in Greek and the oasis (haSASA) is Mother Earths blood as water that nourishes Her creatures. The Lithuanian cloud debesis (dabaSASA) whose emergence out of the rim on the body of Mother Earth at the beginning of the monsoons announced a time of plenty.

As males understood the role of the birthing breath and the power inherent in the experience, after they clitorectomized most of the women in PHASE THREE and excised their seat of power, they too pursued it through a variety if means; ritual, meditation, fasting, drugs, dancing, drumming, chanting, trials of fear defusion, places on the planet, places in time, individuals in whom the energy had risen, castration. When they reached a level of transformation they gained the (SASA) dyad at the end of their names; Jesus (JaSASA), Zeus (SASA or IS haSASA), MO'asses (MaSASA) Persian founder, Moses (MaSASA) Hebrew leader, Sisyphus (SASA-), Ramses (RamaSASA), Perseus (ParaSASA). Theseus (TaSASA).

In PHASE THREE the Hebrew Garden of Eden defining the beginning of humanity has been called Genesis (JanaSASA) containing both the individual mother's blood (SA) and the lavic (SA) of Mother Earth. The GENE-) of Genesis (JANA-) gives it away as having its ancient links with the mother. For gyna (JANA) not only defines the woman in Greek as in gynecology but as the Jenie (JANA) that emerges out of the rubbed bottle. The bottle with its long neck has long been considered as the symbolic SHAPE of the long necked vagina with the uterine ball at the end. Rubbing it deals with masturbation that releases the baby during birthing and the orgasm during the pursuit of pleasure and tension relief. The fall of man in the Garden of Eden has much more ancient links leading to a repressed if not a disturbing past.

TATA -'my father' in Bemba

TaTa is the unvoiced DADA as the gift of the father. Male input into paternity in PHASE THREE had been considered to be *external* made by the tip (TA-) of the penis and testicles. Female input of the mother was *internal* created by the vulva, vagina, ovary construct. In PHASE THREE the TATA dyad of the father took over most of the mother's role as source on many levels including the role of her titties (TATA-).

RULE FOURTEEN;
Repetition of Dyads

Create DYADS, or linguistic constructs of different A(ah) based syllables repeated.

BARA-Ashanti in West Africa is a sorcerer, magician who inhabits the 'state of trance'. A state of trance dealt with being suspended between this apparent reality and another not so apparent one. It was an enTRANCE at the center. The center was the pulsating light in the third eye that had become opened as a result of the Kundalini experience. An enTRANCE at the center for mothers dealt with the result of the high, fast panting of the birthing breath that as the massive concentrated focus led to mysticism. For males it dealt with multileveled ritual. For both it resulted in an ecstatic transformation which led to a variety of gifts; leadership, wisdom, healing, prophecy and for some, at different times into a glimpse of immortality.

The Ashanti BARA dyad as the sorcerer carrying in him a 'state of trance' originally dealt with the two hemispheres of the human brain being yoked together across the corpus collosum, balanced and working in concert. When the state of trance occurred it was as if a bar (BARA) had been erected between this reality and the reality experienced during the trance state when it put to rest the relentless voice over left hemispheric rational, prattling ego centered God besotted brain.

rance (TARANASA) as an overlapping tryad contains within its linguistic folds the (TARA) which is the terrain of Mother Earth and an emergence out of that terrain (NASA) or nascence (NASANASA) as birth in Latin. The (RANA) has grave overtones for it deals with 'wound and dawn ' in Polish. It was out of the wound of dawn (RANA) out of the body of Mother Earth (TARA) that the birth (NASA) of a trance could be experienced. SOUNDS like the experience of the Kundalini energy rising up from the body of Mother Earth along Her lea lines. It could be assisted on its journey with elexirs such as alcoholic spirits, mead or beer (BARA), a mysterious ecstasy producing plant ambrosia (hamaBARAsaya) and Amenita Muscaria the fly killing hallucinogenic mushroom. Ambrosia was thought to have been brought to humanity by doves ie birds (BARADA). In India it was called amrita, a kind or honey or nectar manufactured by bees. Both are creatures of the air as are the enraptured shaman or the birthing mother as they vibrate (vaBARAta-) in paroxysms of ecstasy.

The state of trance as a suspension between this reality and the next was also believed to be shared by the process inherent in the journey of the sun above and below the body of Mother Earth. The SOUND and SHAPE encoded in the letter (B) as the 'two in one' concept dealt with the sun (RA) rising and setting, moving above and below the body of Mother Earth. When the sun was above in daylight, it barred (BARA-) the darkness of night. When it was below at night it barred (BARA-) the light of daylight. The round flat surFACE of Mother Earth was like a bar (BARA) 'in between' night and day.

The Tibetan Bardo (BARA-) deals with the 'intermediate state' or that which is 'in between', after death and before reincarnation . The DO in Bardo deals with 'the gift of' the intermediate state. In English a bar (BARA) divides two areas, one on each side, it bars (BARA) the way. A bar could be a lateral pole barring the way, or it could be a series of vertical poles creating a jail, barring egress. It exists as a division between two sides. In the word break (BARAKA) it also deals with two sides with the crack or break in the middle. The (KA) at the end of break (BARAKA) establishes the fact that it is a small break, as in a trance and not a massive break between day and night that occurs on the body of Mother Earth.

The 'intermediate state' of the Tibetan Bardo (BARA-) defined not only a 'state of trance', the BARA of the Ashanti sorcerer but expanded to define other similar conditions. To hibernate (haBARAnata) was to exist in a state of suspended animation, of being 'in between' this reality and the next. What creature became associated with hibernation? Of course the bear (BARA). Would not beer (BARA) be considered as a state of suspended animation of that 'in between' state wandering around in the realm of spirits?

It was piles of ingested boar (BARA) bones that had been found at Stonehenge. Pigs especially sows were considered to be not only very intelligent but sacred. In Polish swienty (IS WANATA) as holy has very close linguistic links with the English swine (IS WANA), or again in Polish as swinia (IS WANA). To win (WANA) takes us back to the sun as it daily won (WANA) its battle emerging (NA) triumphant out of the watery WA) emtombment from within the body of Mother Earth. The sow (IS HAWA) as a wise mother surfaces as sowa (IS HAVA) also in Polish. (the (V) and (W) are interchangeable. For sowa (IS HAVA) is a wise old owl. She like the individual mother spun her head around and could see in all directions. It is a condition that individual mothers have to have in order the keep their eyes on their growing toddlers. In Egyptian MAA is a wise old owl. SAVAnt (IS HAVA-) as one who is very smart surfaces in English. She also sHOWed her children what foods were edible, and how (HAWA) to survive. Not only were pigs wise but they were also sacred. Once the redefinitions began to proliferate, in PHASES TWO and THREE it may be why the Hebrews forbade the eating of pork.

Above the body of Mother Earth what creatures floated 'in between' the body of Mother Earth and the sun? You don't have to travel far a field to discover that the birds (BARAda), or 'the gift of' (DA) of (BARA-) used the 'in between state' of air as a vehicle of passage. It may be the reason why birds in PHASE THREE became symbols not only of flight but of transformation becoming the templates for the 'watchers' the eunuch (HANAKA, uncles (HANAKALA) and subsequently in PHASE THREE angels (HANAGALA). The (K) and (G) are interchangeable.

The Tibetan Bardo (BARADA) occupies the same state. The 'gift of' (DA) the bar (BARA). It defines the area of suspended animation, the 'in between state' that the soul experiences after death waiting to be sent forward into another level of existence, or being sent back to reincarnate into another body to do it over again, similar to the Roman Catholic limbo.

For some the 'in between state' became a bridge (BARAja) of passage across the great divide. The bridge extends to embrace the bride (BARADA) who had also been considered as a bridge of passage between a carefree girlhood and responsible motherhood. For the Hebrews the male rite of passage is called a bar (BARA) mitzvah. The passage for girls is called a bas (BASA) mitzvah. The RA in BAR mitzvah deals with the male sun in PHASE THREE. The bas (BASA) mitzvah deal with the (SA) of the blood of the emergent woman. The 'spiritual' bridge in stage one dealt with the bridge of the nose where the meeting at the center created the balance inHERent in the trance.

In so many cultures after her time in female centrality in PHASE ONE, the young girl belonged to the joyful clan of her mothers family. In PHASES TWO nd THREE after she became a bride and married, she lost her name and identity becoming a slave to her husbands family. The bridge of passage had been an overwhelming burden (BARADAna) for the young bride. To embrace (hama BARAsa) is to use the two arms, brazos (BARAsa) in Spanish that bridge the gap of the 'in between state' that exists when the arms are not conjoined.

It had been considered in PHASE ONE that motherhood defined a woman. To be denigrated as barren (BARAna) was an 'in between state' that couldn't define the woman as a carefree girl and not yet as a mother. For boys in Hebrew that 'in between' state in PHASE TWO had been defined as a bris

(BARA-), for a bris as circumcision covered two bases. It was the 'in between' state between the ancient practice of castration and leaving the penis in it's natural state and as a ritual of passage between a relatively carefree boyhood and a movement into the mature male clan.

Then there are the Straights of Gibraltar (jaBARAlatara), not as a bridge of passage but a movement through, an 'in between' connection between two entities, the Atlantic Ocean on one side and the Mediterranean Sea on the other. The Scottish Islands of the Hebrides (haBARADASA) surface with birdies (BARADASA) right in their center. What story does the ancient city of Barcelona (BARA-) in Spain have to tell us, or Bristol (BARA-), or even Berlin (BARA-)?

It may seem ironic but a bar (BARA) in PHASE THREE in a restaurant also creates an 'in between state' separating the drinkers from the tenders. Just a thought.

Another 'in between state' had been defined by the Tantrist as Nirvi Kalpa Samadhi. At the end of an intensive ritual often a state is reached where the adept floats upon a cushion of air oblivious of their surrounding reality. It is a state from which a return is possible. The word Samadhi (IS HAMADA) in Sanskrit means death, Nirvi Kalpa Samadhi means the small death where all the systems of the body slow down and are often imperceptible. When that state is reached the adept moves into a state of trance, an entrance at the center leading to transformation and the place that reverBERates with a thousand questions. Where do they go when they enter that trance state? It would seem that much value could be gotten if that state could be made conscious.

BAYA Swahili 'bad';

The concept of dualty, inherent in the letter (B) as 'two in one' associated with the the AYA of light in Persian and dawn in Assyrian surfacing as being 'bad' can only deal with drought and a time of famine when the semiannual monsoon rains failed to arrive on the scorched African savannah. In must have been a time when the light of the sun (AYA) appeared relentlessly every morning at dawn (AYA) and gave the parched creatures below no relief from their desiccating surroundings.

BAYA Hindi 'left';

BAYA can deal in PHASE ONE with either the 'left' handed path of the mothers, or in PHASE THREE as male centrality gained momentum that the mothers had been 'left' behind. As the left handed path of the mothers the ancient calendrical svastica spun to the left, as did the journey of the devoted

Muslims, seven times around the sacred Islamic shrine, the Kaaba. It seems ironic that the migratory march began left-right, left-right leading (LADA-) with the left foot of the ancient lady (LADA) leaders (LADA-).

BAAYA Hebrew 'problem';

A different set of perceptions surfaces in the Hebrew BAAYA as a 'problem'. It exists in the double (AA) construct. For (AA) dealt with a variety of female sources; In Hawaii AA deals with the terrestrial terrain. In Latvia AA deals with a body of water. It also deals with the triangular source of creation as the SHAPE of the volcanic cone on the body of Mother Earth (A) and the vulvic triangular patch (A) on the individual mother's body originally as a mother symbol which in PHASE THREE became redefined as the Star of David. In PHASE TWO male role in specific paternity was becoming known and males began to create their own Gods *away* and *above* the body of Mother Earth. All traces dealing with the female body and the body of Mother Earth as source, became a 'problem' and as they moved into the hidden heavens had to be done away with.

The AYA in baAYA deals with the duality associated with light and dawn. Was it a time when the sun refused to rise in the Eastern sky and bless them with its light due to an extensive time of a great rain?

CARA(KARA) Spanish, Portuguese face (FASA);

The surFACE of Mother Earth had been the big flat round face (FASA) in the very beginning in PHASE ONE when the body of Mother Earth and the sun had been considered as one unit. The solar disc had also been considered as a round flat face (FASA) floating above in Her belly of air as a baby floated in the pregnant mothers sac. In time it became an unblinking eye, two helping hands working in concert, Her son, Her partner, Her husband, a solar deity apart from Her body, all the above and more. The face of the moon had been more apparent and the Man in the Moon became an iconic figure. The sun went through more symbolic permutations. But in PHASE ONE the solar (RA) face as KARA had been considered to be at one if a smaller (KA) companion of Mother Earth.

Mother Earths face (FASA) takes us back to the bloody (SA) fingers of fire (FA) that yanked the sun down into the gory blood filled bath as Mother Earth swallowed it in Her Western horizontal rim forcing it, guided by the snake, to swim through the underground entrails under Her surFACE. The letter C (kh) of the face as Cara deals with the round skull with hair on one side and a large opening for the mouth on the other. On the flat round surFACE of Mother Earth it was the open mouth at Her horizontal rim that regurgetated the sun at dawn and swallowed it at twilight.

CASA (KASA) Spanish house, English coos (KASA);

Since the Spanish casa (KASA) contains in it the (SA) of the mothers blood then we are dealing with the coos (KASA) of the mother as the other container, the cunt as the counter of lunar time. Both the coos (KASA) and the Spanish house as casa (KASA) are small (KA) containers of creation out of the individual mothers blood (SA).

DANA-Celtic Horse Goddess of Irish, Danish and Russians;

'Great Mother Goddess and her sacred serpents', The distended letter (D) began its life as 'the gift of'. The letter (N) leaving behind its source out of the nasal SOUND of the regurgitated food and of knowing, but establishing its concept as' change from a former state' or 'emergence on the surface' reveals the Goddesses major activity as a giver, as one who pushes things up to the surFACE out of the body of Mother Earth. Goddesses were personifications of Mother Earth with all of Her processes, qualities and functions. Her sacred serpents were the Kundalini lea lines upon Her body. One such serpent still exists as a mound of a twisting snake in Ohio.

Horses had very close links with women in PHASE ONE. They were considered to be creatures of passage. In Polish kon (KANA) has the same linguistic construct as the volcanoc cone (KANA) of creation, the volcano on the body of Mother Earth. In Polish koniec (KANA- NASA)) means the end. The NASA means birth into another reality or reincarnation. The horse was considered to have carried the body across the distant horizon, across the great divide of death. The Horse Goddess Dana gave her name to the Danes, based on the A(ah) SOUND it is very ancient. She with her sacred serpents expressed the Kundalini energy rising up from the body of Mother Earth as her power base.

DANA Persian 'learned';

To be learned was to have had the gift of (DA) knowledge 'emerge up to the surface', and a 'change from a former state' (NA) of ignorance. It is a gift that accompanies the rising of the Kundalini energy.

DANA Polish 'that which is given';

The (DA) establishes the 'gift of' and (NA) in Polish deals with upon. So the Polish dana deals with an expression of service, or placing something upon another thing.

DASA Old Iranian, Persian 'ten'.

(DA) 'the gift of' blood as (SA) deals with the 'ten' months of lunar gestation when the Egyptian 'wise blood of the mother' (SA) knew what to do inside of the mothers body as it coagulated into the making of a fetus. The concept came out of PHASE ONE when male role in specific paternity was unknown and the individual mother coagulated the blood (SA) in her body to create the fetus. She created the infant herself. The perception expanded to embrace the body of Mother Earth defining Her as also making everything by Herself, *The Eternal Virgin*.

DASA Sanskrit 'gift of blood';

Very directly (DA) is 'gift of' and (SA) is blood.

DAVA Persian 'medicine, drug';

Something that like a gift (DA) came from below either out of the vagina on the individual mothers body or out of the water on the body of Mother Earth. The (V) and (W) are interchangeable. Or it was the transformed mother after her birthing breath who became the healer of her children. She knew which plants and soils had medicinal properties with which to heal her children, like the elephant matriarchs and chimpanzee mothers.

DAWA Swahili 'medicine';

Probably came from the same linguistic roots having its links with water (WA). Perhaps water contained properties that have been lost to us. It may explain in PHASE THREE why so many religions use water as a sacrament. It has been described as a symbolic washing away of sins. There may have been more practical and more profound uses of water. Water is a conductor of electricity. The Kundalini electro-magnetic energy passes across water. Water as a conductor of electricity may have been considered part and parcel of the Kundalini experience associated with the broken water sac at the time of birthing and the birthing breath of the mother. It may be why so many legends deal with the passage over water after death, since birth and death had been associated with the process of reincarnation.

DAWA 'Ethiopian river' is 'the gift of' (DA) of water (WA);

The English word dew (DAWA) has links with the Ethiopian water DAWA. The word dawn (DAWAna) surfaces here also. Dawn was 'the gift of'(DA) of the 'emergence' (NA) of the sun out of its watery (WA) grave out of the body of Mother Earth at dawn (DAWANA) as Her body was sprinkled with dew (DAWA). The sun had won (WANA) its endless war (WARA) against the darkness of night.

FADA, Persian sacrifice;

Sadly a 'sacrifice' was the 'gift of' (DA) of the fingers (FA). It could have been a human or an animal sacrifice but the fingers (FA) of the hand had to do the job of killing and blood letting. On the body of Mother Earth it was the fingers of fire (FA) in the Western sky that as the rays of the sun pulled the sun down into the gory waters within Her body. As the maw of the mountainous mouths of Mother Earth ate the sun, it was a 'sacrifice' to Her, so that She could defecate it, push out Her feces (FASA-) on the other side so that it would rise again at dawn and create Her enlightened with light surFACE (-FASA). The Sumerian Annanaki and their solar God Anu (HANA) of the anus (HANASA) bear witness here.

Many subsequent civilizations leaving behind the original perceptions made in PHASE ONE out of female centrality continued with the 'sacrifice' of humans and animals to create the bloody corridors for the sun to navigate through guided by the ubiquitous shakti serpent. The Minoans, Aztec and Maya filled that bloody category. Others in the Middle East used water as a vehicle of passage for the rebirth of the sun. In PHASE TWO that led to war (WARA) as the solar disc (RA) began its battle against its demise in the Western wall of watery (WA) death. (WA) plus (RA) equals war (WARA). It may have been a perception that the world (WARALADA) was a place that was in a constant state of war. That could have emerged out of any of the PHASES. Eat and be eaten has always been the global motto defining life and the base chacra of the Tantrists.

FALA-Polish = 'wave';

A wave goes up and down. On the human hand the fingers (FA) are like angles (LA) that not only go up and down but in many directions. Actually the major activity of the five fingers is to flap up and down and with the opposable thumb to hold things creating the (V) SHAPE. A wave could also mean a greeting or a goodbye, the Hawaiian aloha (HALAHA). Across linguistic corridors in Greek a phallus (FALASA) is also like a wave, the Polish FALA, it too goes up and down when filled with blood (SA). As a greeting, the *erection* of the phallus points in a specific *direction*. The direction it points to is the gift of (DA) the erection. How that was dealt with in the ancient past is open to conjecture. First born sons were castrated so that was not their problem. In PHASE ONE heterosexual males were permitted only to mate, circling the periphery of the female groups, they resorted to a variety of activities, with the changing of female sexual cues, their major ones dealt with kidnapping, rampaging, rapacity and rape.

FANA Sufi ecstatic union with the divine;

The Sufi were also known as the Whirling Dervishes who twirled, danced and viBRAted themselves into trance. The (NA) deals with 'emergence on the surface' and (FA) deals with the flaming (FA) fingers (FA) of fire (FA) within the body of Mother Earth that as the solar wind cum the Kundalini energy rose up through Her surFACE. It entered the soles of human feet blasting its way up the spine, transforming the seeking adept with the ecstatic birthing breath of the mother.

In PHASE ONE the Kundalini energy had been considered as female, the energy rising up from the body of Mother Earth. In PHASES TWO and THREE it was reinterpreted as falling down from the sky entering the top of the head and plunging downward. It became reinterpreted as being divine or father sourced down from the sky no longer sourced up from the body of Mother Earth. In PHASE THREE the Kundalini energy has been redefined in the Judeo-Christian tradition as God. For the Muslims it is Allah, for the Cabbalists as the Shekhinah, for the Hindus as the Shakti and for the Roman Catholics as the Holy Ghost.

FANA; Arabic 'annihilation and non being';

When the state of trance was activated, the ego or where the fear has been trapped is annihilated and a new being enters the fray. What the Kundalini burns out with the double fingers of fire flaming (FA) up the spine are the habits created in the panic stricken infancy when the new born baby realizes that it is helpless, that it is locked in a body that does not work. It creates all of its subsequent habits through a filter of panic stricken fear. The risen Kundalini with the psyche burned clean, the new being has to relearn all their activities without the burden of fear in the process becoming self-realized. The Kundalini fires (FA) burn clean their infantile habit driven old self and emerge (NA) born again to a new life.

PHANA (FANA) Greek 'to seek';

In PHASE ONE women were privy to the birthing breath. It made them powerful and fearless. It was the clitoris engaged during the birth of a baby that was the major source of their ecstasy. As the head of the baby pushed against the beak of the clitoris it spasmed and orgasmed the baby up to the surface. The multiple orgasmic birth based on the panting breath in the last stages of labor spun the laboring mother into a trance state. The trance state transformed her from a carefree girl into a fearless mother. Males were not privy to that birthing experience. It was through ritual that they could touch the hem of that awesome ecstasy. The Sufi did with twirling and dancing. Others used multiple means. For the 'seeking' males it was a journey of discovery. In PHASE ONE it was native to all women who became mothers. In PHASE TWO as clitorectomies entered the scene with the removal of the clitoris and the whole vulvic structure, the Kundalini experience became mysterious, in time mystical. It was no longer something natural that was shared by all mothers. It became a mystical phantom (FANA-) much desired and little understood. Because it became a phantom (FANA-) it gained all kinds of mysterious intepretations as connected with the devil, satan, voodoo worship, witchcraft anything that could not be explained by the left hemispheric rational male mind. That ignorance exists to this day as women born with the gift of ecstatic mysticism have been called dangerous witches and in the past have suffered horrific fates.

FARA; Persian, 'up, above, upon';

The RA gives it away as dealing with the sun (RA) high up in the heavens. (FA) deals with the splayed rays of the sun at dawn like fingers (FA) of fire (FARA) piercing the pall of night to rise triumphant in the Eastern firmament (FARA-) . With the addition of 'upon' we are dealing with the rays of the sun spreading upon and across, caressing the surFACE of Mother Earth, as they cross Her patiently waiting body at dawn aglow with new found pleasure.

FARA Swedish 'danger, fear';

A feral (FARA-) animal is a wild 'dangerous' creature no longer able to be domesticated. It strikes fear (FARA) in the human heart. There were good reasons to keep as far (FARA) away from such a creature as distance allowed. It could also go in the direction of fire (FARA) that would have been considered to be dangerous and fearful (FARA-).

FAVA=English 'bean';

A bean (BANA) deals with 'emergence on the surface' (NA) of duality (BA). It takes a more basic turn as the FAVA bean, for it deals with the fingers (FA) and the vulva (VA). As the seed of life, the bean is SHAPED like a fetus, it too is the seed of life gestating under the surface. Dealing with the (FA) of the four or five fingers, it may deal with masturbation during the birthing labors to help get the large headed baby out of the bi-pedal mother's narrow pelvis and out of her vagina (VA). This was before the birthing breath kicked in. A seed (IS HADA, or SADA) is 'the gift of' (DA) of the blood (SA), of the creature and sap (SAPA) is the blood (SA) of the plant (PA).

FATA-Latin = 'fate';

As fate (FATA) the fingers (FA) could go in many directions. They could help the fetus (FATASA) to emerge on the surface through masturbation. Human fate (FATA) as the future (FATAra) is based on the survival of the new born. On the body of Mother Earth the fingers of fire (FA-), as the sharp rays of the sun acting like stilletoes, pierce the fabric (FA-) of dawn helping the sun, Mother Earth's major off spring, to make its emergence on Her sur-FACE, on Her tip (TA-), top (TA-). Feet (FATA) as movement in any direction also define fate (FATA).

HARA-Hebrew='holy mountain, pregnant belly,' Japanese= 'belly';

It becomes apparent that the Hebrew and Japanese hara deal with the same aspect of the belly, gut or stomach. But the belly covers a multitude of bases. In Hebrew harah (HARAHA) means pregnancy. It also reflects itself (HARA/RAHA) dealing with pregnancy as a reflective process of the mother creating another one like herself. As the belly (BALALA) it deals with the SHAPE of emergence (LA) of duality or 'two in one' (BA) out of individual mothers bodies and out of the body of Mother Earth. On the mothers body it is the ball (BALALA) that she carries in her belly (BALALA) as she goes on with her labors. In Lithuanian defining the gut, or intestines it becomes zarna (IS HARAna) linking it with the Hebrew and Japanese belly as hara. For the the Maori (maHARA) also defines the intestines, or that which lives in the belly (HARA).

In Basque it jumps to 'being born', the process of evacuating the fetus out of the body as sortu (IS HARAta). The (RATA) dyad in (IS HARATA) of the Basque 'being born', defines the journey of the fetus as a return (RATA-) back up to the surface. We are also dealing with the concept of source (IS HARAsa) having links with the belly (HARA) of air (HARA) above the body of Mother Earth through which the sun (RA) made its daily reappearance.

The Lithuanian sun as aurinko (HARANAKA) (HARA) (RANA) (NAKA) not only reiterates the same concept but adds to it the sun's return (RATA) and (RANA) the ever present Polish 'wound of dawn' scenario out of which the sun was born with the help of the snake (IS NAKA). In Tibetan shar (IS HARA) deals with the Eastern mountainous belly out of which the sun made it's entrance. In Hebrew hara also means holy mountain. WHY? Because the sun had been perceived to have been born out of the mountains, out of the pregnant bellies on the Eastern edge of the African continent. That is why har (HARA) defines the Hebrew mountain as Ararat (HARARATA) and Har Magido the current PHASE THREE Armageddon and Mount Hermon

(HARAmana) the place of Enochs and Christ's transformation.

On a more personal level the rays of the sun emerging out of the body of Mother Earth at dawn were considered to be not only Her flaming fingers but Her hair (HARA). In Hebrew hair is saara (IS HARA) with the double (AA) construct through its center establishing hair as having magical properties. When it started growing on a girl baby's head it never stopped growing until the woman died. Males lost their hair when they were eunuchized or became bald naturally. The magical power that had been perceived to exist in women's hair had to be denied, had to be covered. Women entering Roman Catholic churches until very recently had to cover their heads and women in Muslim countries could face a beheading if their burkas slipped and exposed their power source, their hair. Chassidic wives still have to shave their heads when they marry wearing wigs for the rest of their lives. Roman Catholic nuns also have their hair shorn (IS HARA-) covering it with a habit. HABIT? The madness continues.

Like the sun, honey and gold, hair had been considered to be immortal, it never stopped growing. The Hebrew Sara (IS HARA) as a princess goes back to PHASE ONE when princesses were extensions of the body of Mother Earth, surrogates (IS HARA-), her daughters in the creation of replicas of themselves. The Mother of the Gods in Greece was Hera (HARA) heralded (HER-) as the queen of heaven. It was through the realms of air (HARA), *away* and *above* the body of Mother Earth that the celestial male Gods had to pass to create their growing male *source* in PHASES TWO and THREE. She also gave birth to her (HARA), the female on one hand and the hero (HARA) with the (O) at the end, the transformed male on the other.

The story of Samson, the solar hero with his locks of hair shorn (IS HARANA) by Delilah tells a different story. It is not of seduction. It deals with the patriarchy killing the matriarchy. When Samson's hair grows back, ie when the sun with its rays of sun are reborn at dawn, he regains his power and topples the shrine (IS HARANA) of Delilah's matriarchial reign.

Then there is the concept of zero (IS HARA) that establishes its links with the hara of the Hebrew and Japanese belly. For zero (IS HARA) defines the empty male belly. Males and eunuchs were considered to have permanently empty bellies. With the dawning of male knowledge of their role in sprcific paternity it surfaces as a definition of their source out of zero (IS HARA) before the one, in PHASE THREE.

The female belly made one more, defining the female baby with the A(ah) of the mother and the male baby as the one (I) of the undefined individual self. Since it was the female belly that created the one more, then as males began their search for source, they gaining in primacy, defined their role as *PRECEEDING* the one (I) of the self. The origins of male centrality then emerged as an idea out of the zero (IS HARA) of the empty male belly. It could go in any direction. The female body became redefined as a furrow into which the male planted his seed. She was only a container not a participant. In PHASE THREE it went into the Big Bang of the male orgasm spasming into being all of creation. The cosmos (KASAMASA) has its ancient linguistic roots out of the coos (KASA) of the mother (MA) and Her blood (SA). The (SAMA) in the middle deals with she alone in Polish, the ancient Mother Earth as the eternal virgin. The zero (IS HARA) became glorified as establishing its importance in mathematics (MATA-) but its original meaning had been redefined. The mist of the mister has one of its origins here.

As a concept, the dyad hara has some other unique properties. For in Spanish ser (IS HARA) means 'to be'. That could deal with the belly of air (HARA) that supports the life of the sun both working in concert with the body of Mother Earth creating the possibility of being.

On the other hand in Polish ser (IS HARA) is the word for cheese. The word ser (IS HARA) as cheese in Polish deals with a process. The process involves what the ancients believed was the transformation that the moon as flowing milk went through when it set back into the body of Mother Earth. It curdled to become the round ball of cheese floating trough nocturnal space. It became not only the holder of nourishment but also of light. With the dawning of light, whether during the day or night, there was a perception that a beginning had occurred, the moon had risen, it was born, it came into being. Enter the Spanish ser (IS HARA) defining the concept of 'to be'.

Or it may have been much more prosaic. The ancient migrations had no way to store an alternate supply of milk for the nursing mothers. The curdled cheese could be carried over wide distances and may have dealt with the possibility of survival or being.

HANA-Old Iranian='clan matriarch grandmother';

As the aunt (HANATA) came out of the linguistic construction of the ant (HANATA) mound and the bee defined the be of being, Hana defined the sun (IS HANA) working in concert with the body of Mother Earth in PHASE ONE as the hen (HANA) who laid the golden egg of the sun (IS HANA). She was the old Iranian clan matriarch to whom all turned for her great accumulated knowledge, as they did to the matriarch in the elephant herd. In Basque zahar (IS haHARA) means old. It could deal with the hara dyad as the old mountainous belly out of which the sun emerged every morning. Or it could mean that it was the Sahara (IS HAHARA) Desert on the body of Mother Earth in Northern Africa that was older than human memory. Old (HALADA) hides within its linguistic coils not only the dyad for the solar (IS HALAra) disc but also the lady (LADA) who was at one with the sun. Both were (DA) 'gifts of' very ancient times.

KARA-Sanskrit is ray of light;

KARA deals with the creation (KARA-) of smaller aspects out of the female buttox symbolized as the letter (X) halved vertically dealing with (KA) the creative aspect of that halving. The KA deals with the creation of smaller objects either out of the female body or the larger body of Mother Earth. The ray of light is the creation out of the body of Mother Earth, Her finger of fire piercing the horizontal rim that lights up the Eastern sky at dawn. The letter X as ks (KASA) SHAPED like the buttox seen from the back is the maker of smaller aspects (KA) not only out of the female coos (KASA) but also out of her blood (SA).

Kara also deals with a different aspect of creation (KARA-) having the SHAPE of a birds open beak (K) leading the flock. It has to deal with birds and their return at the time when the body of Mother Earth erupted with the semiannual monsoons and the bodies of mares dropped their foals. It was a time of creation (KARA-) of making small things (KA) with the help of the sun (RA) on all levels. Birds (BARADA-) had been considered as the 'in between' soarers that used the currents of air sharing their aerial assault that had also been done by the rays of light. They, like SOUND itself also used the air as a vehicle of passage, the 'in between state' of the Tibetan Bardo. Since the air as the living breath had been considered to be sacred then not only the rays of light but the birds became tarred by the brush of divinity. Rays of light could have been considered as the small (KA) suns (RA).

KARA Polish='punishment';

The departure of birds (KA) had been seen as a punishment when they left their noisy presence with the skies empty of their song. With their departure, the rains (RA-) died and also stopped falling. It was current with the two equinoxes, the one in the spring and the other in the fall dictated by the journey of the sun (RA). As pnishment the Polish kara may have links with the Old Norse Valkyrie (valKARA) as the Goddess of Death who chose the warring soldiers who would die and who would live. She had been depicted as a swan maiden and further back as a raven, the bird of death

Val Kyrie (valaKARA) = 'swan queen';

Deals with birds (KA) and their movement across the sky giving birth to so many concepts such as angels, the in between state of flying, and all the fantasies that the emerging left hemispheric brain gave birth to in PHASE THREE. The name of the swan is hansa (HANASA) establishing their links with the sun (IS HANA) as also the fellow traveler through the realms of air. Closer to home the swan (IS WANA), like the sun at dawn (daWANA) won (WANA) its battle against the dread of the coming cold in the Northern sky.

-KABA-Bemba='hot';

It became hot in the African savannah when the birds (BA) with their open beaks (K) singing their way across the heavens returned to their summer nesting sites in order to lay their endless small (KA) eggs. The big egg was the sun. Or it may have its links with the KAABA on the peninsula of Arabia that has had its source out of a flaming 'hot' meteorite.

KAMA-Vedic='erotic desire';

In PHASE ONE at the time of the Spring Equinox there occurred an estral orgy when the herbivore mares came into estrus at the time concurrent with what evolved in PHASE THREE as the Christian Easter. It was the start of the ancient migration that began to march in March toward the falling rains in the promised land of the verdant savannahs. During the Autumnal Equinox in September after the mares dropped their foals, there was much butting of horns and the butting of buttocks as the journey back to their beloved mountains began. The kama of coming (KAMA-) dealing with an orgasm may have some of its revelations here.

KAMA-MARA-Buddhist='erotic desire';

With the MARA at the end of KAMA MARA we are not only dealing with the mares (MARA) that gloried in the mating dance with their butting partners but also with the passage of birds (KA) back and forth across the African sky. The 'erotic desire' embraces the body of Mother Earth seducing the sun back into Her waiting watery arms, the marine (MARA-) seas. As the sun descended slowly into the Western waters it was sheared of its rays of light. Mother Earth embraced the sun and in the process killed him. She killed the suns hair making him bald and powerless like a eunuch or Samson. It has links with the drone being mpaled by the queen bee. The birds enter the picture here as the small (KA) mothers (MA), who assisted Mother Earth in the creation of life on Her surFACE.

GAYA-Greek= 'Mother Earth';

As the Romans borrowed from the Greeks, so the Greeks borrowed from the Assyrians and Persians. In Greek Gaya is based on the most ancient A (ah) SOUND. Mother Earth is described as the begetter (GA) of AYA, as light in Persian and dawn in Assyrian. In PHASE ONE the body of Mother Earth did not twirl around the sun of subsequent scientific discovery. The flat surFACE of Mother Earth gave birth to the sun and all of the celestial migrants out of Her flat circular Eastern rim, out of Her magnificent all encompassing body. She created it all. Some times she regurgitated the sun out of Her mountainous mouths at the edge. There were other times when She gave birth in stage three out of Her gestating bellies. Even Her vulvic lips and arm pits came into play. As the redefinitions proliferated in PHASE THREE the arm pit stage resulted in the Biblical tale of Eve emerging from Adams side or rib. Close enough to arm pits.

Not to go too much further a field, in Hebrew there are the goyem (GAYAma) and what do they tell us linguistically? That goyem were and are non Jews. They belonged to the ancient pagan belief that Mother Earth, the Greek Gaya, was their ancient deity and the source of all creation.

The same can be said for homosexuals who are called GAY (GAYA), not because they are more joyful than the rest of humanity. They too have their links in mother centrality in PHASE ONE and a balance between their two hemispheres of the brain. Lesbians are totally devoted to the mother. Castrated or homosexual males have had in one way or another their testosterone compromised harking back to links with mother centrality.

LARA-Indo European 'Mother Goddess';

(LA) deals with the SHAPE of emergence of the sun (RA). So LARA is the SHAPE of emergence of the sun out of the body of Mother Earth, out of Her Eastern horizontal rim. Working in concert, the (LA) of Mother Earth and the (RA) of the sun both establish the most ancient duo of creation at the beginning of time in PHASE ONE creating the LA as the LAdy of the LAnd.

The letter (L) in stage one also deals with the SHAPE of the angle of the tongue lying on the floor of the oral cavity, Lengua in Latin. The sun needed help to be born at dawn. Singing, clapping with their hands, thumping on their drums accompanied by the avian symphony did not seem to be enough to awaken the sleeping sun. So Mother Earth as the LAdy of the LAnd complied by using Her internal tongue (LA) to push the sleeping sun up to the surFACE bringing with it Her food as the gift of not only warmth but Light and Life to all of Her creatures. The letters of G (gh) of begetting and G (jee) of generation having their source out of the circle C (kh) of creation have their linguistic tongues stiching out as they push their creations to the surFACE.

LARA Roman 'Goddess of the Hearth';

The sun not only complied by bringing life and light up to the surFACE on the LAdy of the LAnd. It also brought warmth and the fires that accompanied the scorching sun (RA). Mother Earth had also been considered as an enormous oven. They could see Her boiling cauldrons in the volcanic craters, as the fiery lava poured down Her flanks and deep in their caves as tubes of magma coursed down to the sea. Prometheus and Odin may have been punished for bringing fire to human beings but many thousands of years before in PHASE ONE mothers used fire to keep away beasts at night, to keep warm and in time to cook. The burning of the eternal flame as part of many ancient rituals comes from the mothers keeping it alive at the hearth. The loss of the flame may have been a great tragedy on the open carnivore laced savannah.

LAVA-English= 'volcanic effulgence';

The angle (LA) here deals with the volcanic (VA) cone, the two lips of the crater creating two angles that allowed the plume of fiery magma to spill over the volcanic rim and spread land across Mother Earths surFACE. She had to make two major creations; one was the coagulated sun that was born as a solid round disc at dawn. The other was the effulgence of LAVA that as coagulated land, like a gift of skin covered Her surFACE.

MARA-'African river';

Here the marine (MARA-) environment of water, surfaces in Kenya and Tanganyica dealing with Mother Earth. (RA) deals with Her major offspring the sun. It was perceived in the Eastern side of the great divide, the Rift Valley in Africa that the sun rose out of the body of Mother Earth in the Eastern side and was swallowed back into Her maw in the watery West. Mother Earth ate the sun at twilight. She swallowed it and killed it to its rays of light. That is why they reasoned sunsets were often blazing bloody red fiery flames of the setting sun splattered like crimson droplets across the ominously darkening Western sky, mirrored in the glistening gore filled waters below. The round solar disc of the setting sun in a liquefied state as the splattered blood in the Western sky slid out of sight and having to swim through the blood filled intestines had to become transformed, to solidify, to cook, to coagulate to be reborn as the inlegral solar child of Mother Earth at dawn. 'He is risen' they greatfully often shouted as the sun made its appearance.

As male role in specific paternity was becoming realized in PHASE TWO, they began to fight back, to kill and to pillage the clusters of women with greater intensity. That same fight extended to the body of Mother Earth. She killed the sun every night. She ate it. The SHAPE of the number eight is the reflected SHAPE of the sun sinking into the bloody gore filled Western waters. The dyad MARA surfaces as the beginning of the word for murder (MARA-), Mother Earth murdering the sun every night.

MARA Hindu='Death Goddess';

The Hindu 'Death Goddess' as MARA reiterates the same concept, Mother Earth (MA) murdered (MARA-) the sun (RA) as it slid out of sight back into Her body at twillight. In Polish the vulgar name for the snout of an animal is morda (MARAda). For it is the snout as morda (MARA-) that murders (MARA-) its prey. Here the story of Samson had its beginning. The hair on his head representing the rays of light on the body of Mother Earth become shorn by Delilah. She, acting like Mother Earth tries to murder him or render him powerless.

As the God of War, Mars (MARA-) the marauder (MARA-) becomes the male deity *away* and *above* the body of Mother Earth in PHASE THREE fighting his battle against Her up in the sky.

MARA Buddhism='fear of death';

It is the fear of death that is the killer, not death itself. As Franklin Delano Roosevelt entoned 'You have nothing to fear, but fear itself'. It comes out that same concept of Mother Earth swallowing the sun into Her Western waters killing it to its rays of light that extended to the fears of death inherent in most human beings.

MARA Slavs 'nightmare hag';

The concept of Mother Earth (MA) murdering (MARA-) the sun in Her Western waters spreads to invoke other concepts while staying true to the original intent. The 'hag' is the female body of Mother Earth in stage four. When the sun was murdered as it was swallowed in the Western marine (MARA-) stretches of water darkness descended on the vulnerable creatures of the savannahs. It became night, the negation of light. The stultifying fear of darkness fused in the night into the demonic dream state. As a demonic state of fear, human imagination played a massive role. A cloud in the sky was just that a cloud in the sky floating by with the promise of rain. That was to the good. But if there was a great deal of stress on the open savannah, or if some hallucinogenic drugs were taken, the cloud with its shape shifting phantoms could become demonic and frightening. In Polish a cloud is chmura (haMARA). In Greek the same linguistic construct surfaces as chimera (kaMARA, or (chaMARA) something completely unrealistic, a frightening monstreous hybrid which is what human imagination constructs, the SHAPE shifting clouds in the sky as unrealistic demons. Not too far a jump to angels with wings, humans with bird heads, animals with human bodies, the list becomes endless. For iMAGInation deals with MAGIc and magic deals with presto digitation. Now you see it. Now you don't. Isn't that what a cloud does? The demon is up there and in a thrice it is gone. In the Middle East in PHASE THREE they even had men who were called the Magi (the (I) as the male one more) for they dealt in PHASE THREE with the emerging deities of male fantasy and imagination.

MARA Semites= 'passive weight and darkness, briny and bitter';

The Semites opted for the open ocean where the marine (MARA-) waters were briny, salty and not potable. They also harkened back to the MARA dyad as dealing with the darkness of night. 'Passive weight' is not a joyful concept. To bring back some concept of the mother as the benevolent sea, for humanity yearning for mother love in the Middle Ages, Mother MARY (MARA) had to have been resurrected.

MALA-Polish ='small she';

It was the mother (MA) who using the angle of her tongue (LA), teeth, chin and cheeks chewed the food for the toothless baby, milled (MALA-) it in her mouth, made it into small (IS MALA) pieces before she regurgitated it and she smiled (IS MALA-) as her baby gobbled it up. In Polish mala is a small (IS MALA) she.

MANA-'universal lunar queen of heaven, maternal power';

Takes us back to the frightening powers of the night of which the SHAPE shifting moon (MANA) was the major deity. Because the moon (MANA) was associated with menstruation (MANA-) for most of human history out of PHASE ONE it belonged to the ancient mothers. (MA) deals with the mothers. (NA) deals with its emergence on the surface to begin its journey through the night sky.

As eunuchs began to experience their negative journey due to castration, the moon (MANA) as the Greek Nana became their double negation. The (NANA) at the end of many of their names establishes that double negation. The first (NA) had been perceived to be absent from the sky during the day. Travelling through the darkness of night defined the second (NA). In the South Pacific MANA has been a powerful spirit of creation. For the Hebrews MANNA (MANANA) was a nourishing food that fell from heaven. It surfaces with the Spanish word for tomorrow. Since time had been reckoned by the lunar calendar in PHASE ONE was the food that fell from the sky as Manna (MANANA) a promise of life and tomorrow? Or was it a convoluted symbolic manifestation of female menstrual blood that also created the future?

MAYA-Hindu= 'Virgin Goddess of the Moon';

She gave birth to the enlightened one, Buddha, MAYA was also the actual name of Buddha's mother as Mother Earth. Elephant tusks stabbed her on her side and she gave birth to the enlightened one, the one filled with light (AYA). It emerges out of early PHASE ONE when MAYA as the holder (MA) of light (AYA) is not impregnated by a penis but by an elephant tusk. Shades of Eve out of Adams rib. The concept of impregnation and male role in paternity in PHASE TWO was becoming known but as yet the object of that impregnation had not been established.

The elephant Ganesh is the Hindu God of beginnings. MAYA like GAYA and RAYA, glow with the AYA of light in Persian and AYA of dawn in Assyrian. The moon brought the beginning of light to the night sky. It, like Mother Earth in PHASE ONE had been considered to be female and also a virgin. There was no apparent input in the moons creation. She like menstruation just appeared and disappeared based on her own whim.

MAYA dealt with Mother Earth as the mother (MA) the holder of light (AYA). She gave birth to it or regurgitated it. The light issued forth from Her horizontal side at dawn, whether it was born to be as light out of the temperamental SHAPE shifting moon or from the helping hands of the sun.

On the other side of the body of Mother Earth, across the great divide of the open sea the same name of MAYA as a place and people surfaces in Central and South America. They too defined themselves as the holders of the light, or the enlightened ones. They proved it to the world by becoming great city builders, astronomers and mathematicians.

On the Central West coast of Florida there is a river called the MAYAKA. Could it be that the (KA) either establishes the migratory coming and going of birds that defines the small (KA). The MAYA who lived further South in

Central America in the country called Guatemala (GATAMALA)? A moment of hair standing on end. Was not the Buddha's other name in India Gautama (GATAMA-) Buddha? The (LA) on the end of Guatemala (gatamaLA) is like the (LA) on the end of the name of the eunuch (HANAKA) who became the uncle (hanakaLA) also surfacing in the African country of Senegal (IS HANAGAla) . The G and K are interchangeable. It deals with the same linguistic construct. The only explanation seems to be that the Indian Buddhist shamans or eunuchs traversed around the world and established bases as far as the 'New World' way before Columbus. There are other familiar mythological landmarks, the worship of the snake as the feathered serpent conjoining the serpent of the ancient mother with the birds as the 'in between' creatures of the air. There are no explanations how the Mayans disappeared. What exists are ruins of an advanced massive civilization that was often bloody and cruel. Along with the Myakka River in Florida there is the city of Miami (MAYAMA) hiding in it's linguistic folds the (MA) as the holder of the light (AYA) and the one more (I) of PHASE ONE definition of a boy. It also flushes up the YAMA as not only the killer, but as a reflective dyad MAYA/YAMA) as the place at the end of the world where one fell into the abysmal abyss.

There is a word that surfaces in Polish dealing with the left hand of the mothers and it is smaja (IS MAYA). To have been born left handed in Eastern Europe in PHASE THREE was to have been cursed and considered a child of the devil. *The left hand had been tied up in a sock and the child had to learn to use the right hand.* Since the females in PHASE ONE had been left handed they must have masturbated with the left hand. That is why masturbation by the Hebrews had been considered the work of the devil and deeply punished by the emerging male deity in PHASE TWO.

In the city of Tabasco in Mexico there have been discovered enormous stone carved heads. They are taller than most humans and their features are not Indian but Negroid (NAGARA-). And then there is the Niagara (NAGARA or NAYAGARA) falls and river further up on the North American continent. Along with Havana and Lake Okeechobee and even further North the Okeefenokee Swamp having links with the Okobongo Delta in Africa they are giving us clues that ancient African people travelled around the world way before Europeans made their descent there.

MAIA-GREEK= 'Virgin mother of the enlightened one, Hermes';

The same mythology continues for the Greeks with the changing of the vowel from (Y) to (I). The SHAPE of the letter (Y) comes out of PHASE ONE and the female pubis (Y) as the place of source. The Greek (I) deals with the male defined as 'one more'. Hermes (HARAmasa) as the *messenger* (MASA-) of the Gods hides in his name his links with the mother. The message that Hermes brought from the moon was that of menstruation. It was Her (HARA) belly that spilled forth the message (MASA-) of the menses. Delete the letter (N) from the word menses and you get meses (MASA-) or the second half of HerMES (-MASA) name.

MAIA Out of PHASE ONE is also the bringer of something specific to young girls dealing with the light of the moon since Hermes is also the 'enlightened one'. Buddha out of PHASE THREE went into self denial and denunciation of the physical body. Hermes on the other hand was much more practical. He dealt with procreation and fertility beginning with a young girls period. Linguistically in PHASE THREE the mess (MASASA) that surfaces out of the deleted menses (MA(NA)SASA) is similar to the curse (KA(RA)SA) that emerges out of the coos (KASA).

MAAT Egyptian 'mother of truth and justice';

For the Egyptians MAAT (MATA) weighed the human soul at death against a feather. If the soul was heavier than the feather then it had to do it all over again. What made the soul heavy? Sadness, anger, vengeance, depression all the negative emotions weighed the soul down. Egyptians were admonished to be joyful or else the Goddess MAAT would not let them pass through to be reincarnated. The double (AA) at the center of MAAT deals with her as being both the individual mother defined by the first A(ah) of her reflected vulvic triangular patch and by the all encompassing Mother the body of Mother Earth as the second A(ah) of the triangular volcanic cone.

MATTA-Gypsy='supreme mother';

As the 'supreme Mother' we are dealing with a double reality the body of Mother Earth, on whose mat (MATA) of matter (MATA-) all have their being and whose surrogates, Her daughters whose mouths (MATA) masticated or milled their food, who created mathematics (MATA) who codified ancient SOUNDS, who lallated them to sleep and could not have been considered anything but supreme.

MAGA-European= 'Grandmother Goddess';

Maga deals with the great ancient grandmother (MA) begetting (GA) all of reality out of Her prolific body into the third generation (GA).

NALA='a smith';

helper to the Hindu God Rama. Standing on his left leg, he was the crippled smithy working at the forge of the sun. Since he was working for the god

Rama then we are in male centrality in PHASE THREE. The one legged stork became a symbol for the one legged smith. The smith (IS MATA) may also have been a eunuch and a midwife helping with the birthing process. That may be why as the bringer of babies the stork standing on one leg became associated with him. It may also be that in the spring when the storks returned to their Northern nests there had been an explosion of births among the creatures of the newly lit spring.

NASA-Sanskrit= 'nose';

The nose (NASA) establishes its beginning with the first breath that a new born baby takes. It is with the first breath that the journey into life begins. In Latin nascence (NASANASA) deals with the process of birthing. The (NA) phoneme deals with 'emergence on the surface' or 'change from a former state'. Originally in stage one it dealt with pushing inedible food out of the mouth creating the nasal SOUND of negation. The 'emergence on the surface' originally dealt with the food being rejected. As the process of birthing it dealt with the baby being pushed to the surface and the babys first nasal breath. It then moved into the nose (NASA) as the organ of smelling, of recognition.

NAKA Wolof='how';

The NAKA dyad has usually been associated with the snake (IS NAKA). There may have been questions among the Wolof tribe HOW did the snake guide the solar elctro-magnetic energy of the Kundalini out of the darkness under the body of Mother Earth to be reborn at dawn. With the (W) at the end of the word HOW there is an aspect of the suns passage through Water. If it was a passage through water then we may be dealing with the ancient migrations in PHASE ONE when the sHOWers in the distance sHOWed them HOW to proceed to the greener pastures.

NAGAS-Vedic='Serpent people';

Serpent (IS HARAPA) out of the Indian Harrapan (HARAPA) culture of the ancient Nagas based n the worship of Mother Earth and Her Kundalini energy symbolized by the ubiquitous snake.

PADA-Sanskrit ='leg, foot';

Pada deals with the 'gift of' (DA) passage (PA). With (PA) as the leg, or foot there surfaces the possibility that the foot is a paw (PAWA) taking it back to the creatures that had paws and were human pets like cats and dogs. It also deals with the Latin leg as pied (PADA) and moves into the same gift of (DA) passage (PA).

PADA Polish = 'fall';

What the Polish pada deals with is the foot, leg or paw that falls to the ground during walking or running. It also deals with the spider (isPADAra) falling down upon its entombed prey.

PADD=Wolof 'to trip someone';

The pada (PADADA) dyad deals with some aspect of walking with the lower extremities or pieds (PADA-) feet in Latin. With the double (D) (DADA) it may be that when someone fell down, or had been tripped they did it with the gift of (DADA) or both legs.

PARA-Polish 'steam';

On the body of Mother Earth when the sun (RA) raised its head at dawn and passed (PA) across Her surFACE, water vapor transformed itself into mist or steam. The steam like fog or mist gently caressed the undulating hills and valleys. In Sanskrit priya (PARAYA) deals with 'the beloved'. The beloved as PARA the light of dawn (AYA) wound itself around the awakened body of Mother Earth like a vine winds itself around a tree. The concet of winding around each other with the beloved as in priya (PARAYA) when in PHASE THREE shared pleasures during the sex act as rape entered the scene, it became the pariah (PARAYA).

PARA Bugotu 'to burn, to scorch';

For the Bugotu Islanders of the South Pacific PARA is closer to the boiling steam that rose out of the volcanic vents on the body of Mother Earth out of Her steaming calderas, and blasting geysers. It dealt with the passing (PA) of the broiling sun (RA) within the craters (KARATARA) the original creaters (KARATARA) on the body of Mother Earth.

PALA Bugotu 'carry in the arms';

One of the linguistic sources for human arms is the fact that they had been considered to be like hanging poles (PALA-) attached to either side of the trunk. The (PA) deals with passage and the (LA) deals with the angle that the arms create when they rise up from the shoulders, or bend at the elbows. In Polish palce (PALA-) define individual fingers that are like little poles (PALA-). To 'carry in the arms' you not only have to use the large poles as the arms but the small poles as the fingers to hold and to carry.

PASA Latin 'gentle mother';

When a young girl passed (PA) her menstrual blood (SA) she was on her way to become a mother. With luck she was gentle and filled with peace (PASA) and love.

PATA Maori father;

PATA may have its links with petra (PA(TA)RA) as rock. It may be what defined a swollen erect hard penis. With the addition of the (RA) of the sun in PHASE THREE as the emerging male deity Petra (PATA-) in Jordan became a series of buildings and temples that are hewn out of solid rock. Also in PHASE THREE it moves to define Saint Peter (PATA-) the petrified rock as solidified tradition upon which Christianity had been established. He had been crucified upside down reflecting an ancient percepticin of reality based on the upside down reflection in the standing waters defining male source. They seemed to use the hanging upside down cave bat as a metaphor for the subsequent symbolism.

RAMA-Hindu= 'deity';

The RAMA dyad is a reflection of the MARA dyad out of PHASE ONE (MARA/RAMA) establishing Mother Earth as Her marine (MARA-) environment. In PHASE ONE it was the rim (RAMA) on the horizontal edge of Mother Earth that encircled Her flat round surFACE and body. At this point in time the horizontal rim (RAMA) had been perceived to be encircling water. As male centrality gained momentum in PHASE THREE the rim (RAMA) not only reflected the MARA dyad (MARA/RAMA) but became the male arms (haRAMA) that encircled the female body during coitus as the horizontal rim (RAMA)the source of the sun encircled the body of Mother Earth. The sun was emerging as male source *away* and *above* the body of Mother Earth. In Hinduism and in many other countries he became a male deity.

RAMA Polish='frame' (FARAMA);

In this case the frame (faRAMA) are the fingers (FA) of fire (FARA) that framed or encircled the horizontal rim (RAMA) on the body of Mother Earth at twilight as the male encircled the body of the female during coitus. It is the same concept in PHASE THREE as the harem (HARAMA) that encircled the female into sexual slavery.

RANA-Polish ='wound', 'dawn';

In Polish rano (RANA) means dawn and rana means wound. Here we have the wound of dawn scenario. The encircling horizontal rim on the body of Mother Earth had to be cut by the stilletto like fingers of the first rays of the sun (RA) at dawn (RANO) creating a wound (RANA) out of Her side. It echoed what had been happening to mothers as they gave birth out of the 'wounds' on their sides. In PHASES TWO and THREE birth could not have happened naturally out of the vulva for as clitorectomies entered the scene the clitoral circle had been removed and sewn up allowing only urine and menstrual blood to flow through. The birth had to occur out of the 'wound' created on the mother's side. When males began to understand their role in specific paternity in PHASES TWO and THREE they created the fantasies that males gave birth also out of their sides as in the Biblical Adam.

SARA-Biblical 'Maternal Queen Goddess';

Sara (IS HARA) was the belly of air (HARA) above the body of Mother Earth who gave birth to the sun. The belly of air (Hebrew and Japanese hara) was Her creation, as was the terrain under Her. She created it all, the air above, the land upon, the labyrinth below, the sun that joined and separated the two sides becoming the queen mother who ruled in PHASE ONE. As a Maternal Queen Goddess Sara (IS HARA) was one of the major personifications of Mother Earth at one with the sun.

SAARA-Hebrew='hair';

Saara (IS HARA) reiterates the concept of hair (HARA) being to the human head as the rays of the sun were to the head of Mother Earth. It was also the fact that hair on a woman's head never stopped growing. Hair like gold, honey and the sun was immortal. That was its secret value. Samson's tale of hair cutting on males and burkas hiding the hair on femalers take on different meanings.

SAGA-Norse='speaking woman, sage';

When a woman went through her 'change of life', the blood (SA) that had stopped flowing on the outside, reconstituted itself in her brain and turned into wisdom. She like the matriarch of the elephant herd became the wise woman who guided (GA) her family wherever it needed to go, to water holes, to the verdant savannah, to medicinal plants. It was her words of power in the naming of things that showed them the way. That is still the reason that mothers live longer than fathers.

TARA-Indo-European='Goddess of the Earth';

The Tara construct comes out of PHASE ONE when the Goddess of the Earth contained within Herself both Her tarry terrain (TA) and the sun (RA). The separation myths had not yet occurred. She created the tor (TARA) out of the smoldering tar (TARA) that flowed down Her flanks creating the fertile terraces (TARA-) that in PHASE THREE fed the growing sedentary populations. As Tara she had been the capital of Ireland and a Goddess.

YALLA-Wolof='God';

In Wolof the God as Yalla must have come out of PHASE ONE because his name begins witht the pubic (Y). When male Gods began to appear on the linguistic landscape the (Y) of the mother had to be obliterated and Yalla became Alla or Allah (HALAHA). The word Allah (HALA/LAHA) reflects itself as both aspects of the sun, above the plane as AL (HALA) and below the plane as LAH (LAHA) establishing the fact that as a God he was also a balanced transformed male. The (HALA) on top, above the body of Mother Earth is the Spanish sol (IS HALA) of the sun, the Greek eelyos (HALA-). The reflection underneath In Wolof is loh (LAHA) and it means hidden dealing with the nocturnal sun.

ZABA-Hurrite myth 'God of war';

ZABA (IS HABA) deals with duality (BA), the male brain bifurcated asking for answers to the why of their periphery. Having links with the sun fighting for its life at the end of each day not having faith in the fact that it would rise at dawn becoming a male deity of War, like Mars. The ZA as the voiced SA deals with blood and the crimson splattered waters in the Western watery wall of death that temporarily entombed the sun.

ZABA Polish='frog';

The fairy tales of the frog turning into a prince, becoming transformed after he had been kissed by a princess has some mysterious overtones. Was he the Hurrite God of War who left his violence behind when he kissed the princess, shared her Kundalini passion of ecstasy? Was it at the time when some heterosexual males acknowledged their humanity became less violent and took part in the female (FAMALA) family (FAMALA) circle?

RULE FIFTEEN;
Repetition of Words

HANNAHANNA= (HANA/NAHA/HANA) Anatolian 'Grandmother Goddess', 'Mother of the Virgin Mari', Christian, 'Mother of the Virgin Mary';

The 'Grandmother Goddess' covers many bases as the sun (IS HANA), above the plane reflected under the plane as (NAHA) and back above the plane as (HANA). It comes out of the most ancient time based on the A(ah) vowel SOUND and the fact that the sun had been considered at one (ATONE) with the body of Mother Earth acting as a single unit of creation and source.

It also becomes apparent that the name of HANNAHANNA comes out of a most ancient perception for it no longer depends on the letter (S) of the sun (IS HANA) to preceed it.

The (NAHA) dyad at the center surfaces as the subsequent Latin concept defining nihilism (NAHA-) as the 'nothingness' that the sun sank into off the Western horizontal rim. The fact that it rises again in the East sharing its bounty of light establishes the sun as being daily reincarnated.

As the Mother of the Virgin Mari (MARA) or Mary (MARA), it deals with the emergence of the sun out of its nocturnal watery grave. The Mara River out of Kenya may have given birth to that ancient perception. It expanded to define most of the marine (MARA-) environments around the world as the human family dispersed following the unrelenting catastrophes on the continent of Africa.

Since in PHASE ONE Mother Earth had been considered a virgin, Her partner in the creation of life on the surFACE, Her grandmother the sun (IS HANA), had also been considered as a virgin. The individual mothers as either Mari or Mary as an extension of the maritime (MARA-) body of Mother Earth in the creation of replicas out of their bodies had also been considered as virgins. When male role in specific procreation was unknown in PHASE ONE all mothers, on all levels had been considered to be virgins. Their coagulated blood created life without any help from the outside.

SAWA SAWA-Swahili 'just right';

To do something correctly is to do it with some thought. You can't wing it. In Polish sowa (SAVA) is the wise old owl. Why is it wise? Because like Mother Earth her head spins around and it can see in all directions. It doesn't miss a thing. The (V) and (W) are interchangeable. For the Egyptians the owl defined the MA'A of the mother. The individual mother was also a wise old bird. To raise her children she had to have eyes in the back of her head. The owl also regurgitates her food for her young.

LAK LAK, (LAQ LAQ)-Persian 'stork', standing on one leg;

The stork standing usually on the left leg with the right leg tucked under him became a symbolic bird for the crippled and mutilated either smith or shepherd. With the LAK (LAKA) dyad he migrated to the lakes (LAKA) teeming with fish and frogs to spend his summer in the tropical sun of Africa at the time when winter settled over the Northern reaches.

The repeated dyad of LAK LAK may deal with the SOUND that the storks made with their open beaks clacking (KALAKA-) their way across the heavens. In Polish kaleka (KALAKA) means a cripple.

If the LAQ LAQ ends with the letter (Q) then we are dealing with the activity of QUEsting that began occurring in PHASES TWO and THREE as castrated and mutilated males began their quest for answers to their often peripheral state. Standing on the left leg has links with the Biblical Jason searching for the Golden Fleece. He had to keep his left foot free of sandals and in constant touch with the body of Mother Earth. He understood that the Kundalini energy, the original God, came up from the body of Mother Earth and you had to be in dirtect contact to be open to the power inherent in the ecstatic flow. The same perception surfaces with the Hindu God Vishnu for the River Ganges emanated from his left foot. Water had been considered to be the conductor of the Kundalini electro magnetic energy.

The stork became a symbol not only for being made into a one legged cripple but that he brought babies. Had he also been the metaphoric eunuch uncle who may have assisted in the birthing of his sisters children? He did return to Africa at the time of the autumnal equinox, the settling of nests, the birthing of babies and a time of great both avian and herbivore fecundity.

CHIN CHIN-Chinese 'kiss';

Occurring where? around the area of the lower jaw, the chin. But there is more. In Chinese the 'CHI (CHA or JA) is the mystical breath that filled everything between Earth and heaven'. What else fills the 'in between' area between Earth and heaven? Birds with their chirping (CHA-), cheeping (CHA-) SOUNDS that act like a semiannual clock migrating in great waves clacking their way across the sky. What makes the clacking SOUND? The lower mandible or jaw and on a bird, the movable lower beak that in a non avian creature would be the chin (CH-). The upper part of a face is the cheek that houses the oral cavity inside and stays put. It does not move. The same construct and activity surfaces with the lower beaks of birds.

Another definition of CH'I (CHA or JA) in Chinese is the 'female soul'. So the country of China (CHI-) was named not only around the coming and going of birds but also around the energy of air as the birthing breath of the mother being 'the female soul'. Much has been lost along the way.

SHING SHING (IS HANAGA)- Chinese 'star';

For the Chinese the star was considered to be like another sun (IS HANA), guided into space by the ever vigilant snake (IS NAKA, NAGA). The letters (K) and (G) are interchangeable. The stars have links with the eunuch (HANAKA) priesthood who beginning in PHASE TWO migrated not only around planet Earth, but metaphorically moved into the celestial heavens *away* and *above* the body of Mother Earth searching for their specific father and source.

In English the word 'star' (IS TARA) had been considered to be out of another perception. It was considered not to be another sun (IS HANA) like the Chinese hypothesized, but another terra (TARA) firma, another Mother Earth. In Polish the word stara (IS TARA) means, the 'old lady' and could cover both bases, the ancient sun and the ancient Mother Earth.

SING SING (IS HANAGA) Chinese 'greeting';

It may very well be that it was the 'greeting' of the sun (IS HANA) at dawn guided into light by the ever present snake (IS NAKA, NAGA), the SOUNDS (IS HANADA) made when the birds chirped their welcome, the chimps screeched theirs and human beings burst into a welcoming song (IS HANAGA) their hearts filled with gratitude thanking their benevolent Mother Earth for bringing the sun up to the surFACE. The ancient eunuch (HANAKA) surfaces here also. He was not only the singer of songs but from another declination the BARD (BARAda) of old having links with the intermediate state of the Tibetans.

KOWORO KOWORO- (KAWARA) Japanese 'curdle, curdle' creation myth;

The creation of the moon out of the watery (WA) depths. For some reason it had been considered as a small (KA) war (WARA). We are in PHASE THREE for the small war that existed dealt with the moon curdling reality out of the watery depths. The large war would have dealt with the coagulation of the sun. The moon associated as the white milk curdled its way through the night sky. The fragmented scarlet sun associated with blood coagulated inside the body of Mother Earth to emerge on Her surFACE as either menstrual lavic blood creating land or the integral disc of the sun.

TEN TEN-South American 'mountain peaks'. In Wolof, tund (TANADA) means 'mountain' as the 'gift of' (DA) the TEN (TANA) fingers meeting at the tips creating a tent (TANATA) like structure of the hands creating the SHAPE of the mountains and the *holding* of the sun at dawn. In Latin TENERE means 'to hold'. The (DA) on the end of tund (TANADA) of the Wolof mountain, deals with the 'gift of' (DA) of the ten (TANA) fingers creating a tent (TANATA) like structure. Its SHAPE encoded in the letter A of beginnings, that when blasted open on top into the letter H gave birth not only to air but to the sun at dawn. Since it was the tips of the fingers that did the parting and birthing of the sun, we are dealing here with masturbation and the accompanying orgasms as a process of birthing of a solar baby out of the body of Mother Earth. The word tender (TANADARA) comes out of the perception that it was the ten fingers that tended tenderly. Tetons (TATANASA); The three overlapping dyads (TATA) (TANA) (NASA) in French as 'breasts', the holders (TANA) of life (NASA) as nourishment in their titties (TATA), expand to include the body of Mother Earth and embrace the snow capped mountains, the breasts on Her body as the holders of milk upon their glistening snowy summits.

Taking the (TANA) dyad even further back into history, still in PHASE THREE there emerges the short lived Egyptian sun God Aten (HATANA) depicted with the rays of the sun raining down with open hands upon the body of Mother Earth. His great creater Atenkhamen believed that the ten (TANA) fingers at the end of those hands held the light of the sun and the singular possibility of life on the body of Mother Earth. His perception had been soundly thrashed and his face had been universally obliterated on all his statues and stelas.

GAL GAL-Hebrew 'wheel'.;

The Milky Way is the Galaxy, the wheel of stars rotating slowly from East to West through the night sky around the pole star. It still deals with the body of Mother Earth as the begetter (GA) of the Milky Way out of the break at Her side (LA), but Her milk is sourced from out of space. We are in male territory and PHASE THREE, no longer out of Mother Earths body, no longer out of Her milky tetonic white mountainous summits.

The Gal Gal as the Hebrew wheel magically surfaces in the word for gold. For gold (GALADA) is the gift of the Gal Gal the starry wheel in the overwhelming golden curve of the night sky. It was perceived that the Kundalini energy not only emerged out of the body of Mother Earth but was originally sourced by the sun in PHASE ONE and as the emerging male God out of the stars in PHASES TWO and THREE. The repetition of GAL GAL (GALA) not only deals with something happy, a festivity as in gala but also with a repetition, a double twisting of the Kundalini snake energy coiling up from the body of Mother Earth. Gold is a conductor of the electro- magnetic energy of the Kundalini. The city of Galilee (GALALA) associated with the transformed Christ carries in her name her source out of the cosmic reign.

DAN DAN-Persian 'tooth';

'The gift of' (DA), of 'emergence on the surface' (NA). As many teeth emerging out of the gums apparently do.

DAN DAN-Egyptian Stone

A small Egyptian stone pyramid with two human creatures, a male and a female emerging from it. It may have been a symbolic perception that all life on planet Earth had its beginning out of the triangular pyramidal SHAPE of Mother Earth making it possible for human beings to evolve on Her surFACE and to exist.

N'GORO N'GORO- (NA GARA) 'East African mountain';

GORA (GARA) in Polish means 'mountain'. The 'holy mountain' as the 'pregnant belly', the har (HARA) in Hebrew, or the begettor (GA) of the sun (RA). The (HA) and (GA) are interchangeable. (NA) deals with 'emergence on the surFACE' of the sun in the Eastern sky out of the 'pregnant belly' of the 'holy mountain' on the body of Mother Earth.

Both Niagara (NAYAGARA) and negro (NAGARA) may have had their linguistic beginnings out of the N'GORO N'GORO (NAGARA) crater. Who made that observation? Was there more than one group of humans who inhabited the Earth at the time that these SOUNDS emerged? Who was it that found their way to the continent on the other side of the oceanic divide in the Americas planting familiar African sourced names there?

A similar observation comes out of the definition dealing with 'human', the creature that hummed. Who defined them as the hummers, associating them with humus, the body of Mother Earth, who had a sense of humor, laughed a lot, and evolved into what became aspects of HUManity, not necessarily of MANkind? Where were the larger brained Neanderthal when all of these SOUNDS were being codified?

In the 'new world', the name for the majestic fall of cascading water is called Niagara (NAYAGARA), the 'emergence' (NA), out of the mountain gora (GARA) in Polish. Or it could go in the direction as the first dyad (NAGA), the snake (IS NAKA, NAGA) guiding the sun traveling on its underground journey through water within the body of Mother Earth to make its guided descent up and out of Her mountainous surFACE as a tumultuously tumbling light filled Niagara river.

For the Japanese a similar sounding name to N'GORO N'GORO as the East African mountain surfaces in a myth as Onogoro an island that had been created by stirring the water with a spear. The spear has links with the penis in PHASE THREE as does the sword of another declination. The myth establishes its links with gora (GARA) as the Polish mountain. In PHASE ONE the creation myth of source deals with the serpent Kundalini energy as the spear stirring the water of Mother Earth creating a spiral whirlpool of source.

LA'I LA'I Hawaiian 'first woman'

She not only sang, lallating (LALA-) her way through life, defining not only girls as the A (ah) proclaims but also boys as the (I) of one more at the end of her name in PHASE TWO establishes. As the first woman she like the sun emerged out of the body of Mother Earth establishing the angle of ascent in the East as the (L) of life and the (L) of light defining the pLAnet as the LAdy of the Land. With both the (A) of the female and the (I) of the male she represented Mother Earth as the ancient at one self perpetuating androgyny.

RULE SIXTEEN;
Create the OVERLAPPING of DYADS (two double syllables) and TRYADS (three double syllables or phonemes).

Perhaps to conserve space, we may never know the reason, but it becomes apparent that when you apply the RULES OF ORIGINAL SOUND DISCOVERY (ROSD) and have two or more DYADS, you become aware that you are dealing with the process of OVERLAPPING. The central phoneme of the syllabic construct shares a double function. It comes at the end of the first DYAD and at the beginning of the second. It contains similar antecedents as the words that create a balance in their construction like; level, kayak, Cusco. In PHASE ONE at the beginning of language construction it may have been a way of creating original sentences.

FUTURE (FATARA) deals with (FATA) and (TARA). The OVERLAPPED phoneme is (TA). The first dyad is (FATA) and it deals with fate (FATA), in Latin. The second dyad of (TARA) is the terrain, the terra (TARA) firma, the surFACE on the body of Mother Earth. The shared phoneme of (TA), deals with the tip, top or edge on Her body. (FA) deals with the five fingers of fire that not only fight (FATA) their way through the pall of darkness at Her horizontal side but as rays of light break free across the surFACE of Mother Earth. So logistically the future (FATARA) is the passage of fate (FATA) across the tip, top, or side of the terrain (TARA) on the body of Mother Earth. The feet (FATA) also surface as carriers of fate (FATA).

MAHARA (MAHA/HARA) as the 'intestines' in Maori;

It contains the overlapping dyads of (MAHA) and (HARA). Macha (MAHA) in Polish deals with 'movement,' 'undulation', as in a 'wave'. (HARA) is the name for belly as pregnant belly or 'holy mountain' in Hebrew and 'belly' in Japanese. What they share in common is the phoneme (HA) or the belly of air (HARA) which the sun had to pass through to be reborn at twilight. (MAHA) also means 'great' so we are dealing here with the great (MAHA) body of Mother Earth through whose internal intestines the sun had to pass through on its way to rebirth. The Maori left Africa fifty thousand years before, carrying with them their SOUNDS of communication, so human language itself must be at least that old.

Since the metaphoric snake surfaces in most of the mythologies of the world and like the M SOUND for the mother is also universal, then it becomes apparent that human language is much older than what we have been led to believe. It also becomes apparent that it planted its linguistic roots in prehistory out of Africa. If that is so, then who were the people that carried the SOUNDS of language with them after one of the great cataclysms sent them far and wide to search for safer shores (IS HARA) on which to sing their songs and to survive.

The red haired Neanderthal humans have to be considered, they lived concurrently with Homo Sapiens for more than eight thousand years, from twenty seven to thirty-five thousand years ago. Their brains were larger than their ancestral cousins, especially in the back. Had they been related to the ancient Atlanteans ? Were they an overflow of a catastrophe that sent them around the ancient world? What did those larger brains contain? Were they the people who built those ancient megalithic structures that pop up all around the world? Did their ancient civilization suffer a catastrophic meteoric attack from out of space or a nuclear winter due to a massive volcanic eruption? Did they survive in those European caves as the ice age covered them with numbing glaciers and they painted those magnificent painting on those cave walls harkening back to a time when all those creatures roamed the savannahs of Africa? Was there more to that ancient story? Clues keep popping up.

Somehow scientists in PHASE THREE have discovered that the Neanderthal had red hair. Stories abound how ancient people feared red haired invaders. Some thought it may have been the Vikings. Perhaps not. Italian women dyed their hair red because they felt that it was beautiful. Red hair surfaces in Ireland, Scotland and among some contemporary Jews.The biblical David had been observed as having red hair as did Mary Magdeline.

A variety of other characteristics also surface concerning the Neanderthal. Their apparently elongated lateral skulls had been copied by Egyptian royalty as we can see on their friezes. Mothers all over the ancient world and even today in some parts of the native world, flatten the skulls of their new born babies in order to elongate them. You don't copy that which you consider to be inferior. You copy that which you consider to be superior, smarter, more beautiful and more desirable.

The Neanderthal may have been shorter and stockier than their contemporary Homo Sapiens and didn't run as fast. That may have been their downfall. But they buried their dead in the body of Mother Earth in a fetal position with henna and flower petals around them, arranging the dead bodies for a rebirth, for some sort of reincarnation. They were not only smarter, were great painters, had red hair, but also believed that the human soul went on the same journey of rebirth as the sun (sol in Spanish). More than thirty five thousand years ago they believed in reincarnation. DNA studies of European elongated skulls depict them as not having the Y male chromosome. Is that what led to their demise?

Not only that they had compassion for each other and took care of their wounded or accident prone family members as reset bones that had healed surface in the fossil record. Did the eunuch priesthood exist among them? Were they the ones who had been the beginnings of humanity, the creatures that hummed? Did they have ancient links with the Tuareg or Berbers? Was it to them that we owe our alphabet, they who had to protect themselves from the marauding Homo Sapien males ready to kill everything that moved. Did they descend from the peaceful matriarchial South Congo Bonobo, as the Homo Sapiens descended from the patriarchial violent North Congo male chimpanzee? In the Epic of Gilgamesh his friend Enkidu (HANAKAda) gift of (Da) the eunuch (HANAKA) is depicted as hairy, short and as a worker or slave. He lived at the same time as the Sumerian prince and may have been the much maligned Neanderthal. They were privy to the hyoid bone in the throat that made only vonsonant sounds.

RULE SEVENTEEN;
Find HOMONYMS, or puns within the language, any language.

In Polish RANA means both 'wound' rana and 'dawn' rano (RANA); As a process the phoneme (NA) deals with the journey of the sun as 'emergence upon the surface', or 'the negation of a former state'. Out of PHASE ONE (RA) deals with the sun as the male helping hands and companion to the body of Mother Earth. The dyad (RANA) deals with the break, or wound in the horizontal circular flat rim on the surFACE of Mother Earth, at Her edge out of which not only the sun (RA), but all of the heavenly bodies were either regurgitated or evicted up to Her tip, top including the rain (RANA) carrying clouds.

The English HOMONYMS of reign (RANA) and rain (RANA) expand the concept of Mother Earth being the reigning (RANA-) queen containing in them compelling echoes related to a more ancient past when the blessed rains (RANA-) drenched the verdant savannahs and brought power to the rulers.

For the Maori, of New Zealand who left Africa fifty thousand years before, daRANA is a 'rainmaker', based completely on the most ancient A(ah)) SOUNDS. The 'gift of' (DA), rain (RANA), out of the same 'wound', rana in Polish on the edge of the body of Mother Earth at the horizon line that gave birth to rano (RANA) the Polish sun at 'dawn'.

In the word 'reign' (RANA), you not only have 'wound', 'dawn', 'rain out of the sky', but the source of all that bounty, the body of Mother Earth, the reigning (RANA-) queen (KANA), out of whose volcanic cone (KANA) land, Her most intimate creation appeared on Her surFACE. In the word queen (KANA) or (KA(WA)NA), the (WA) surfaces in the middle of the word as 'water'. Her explosive volcanic cones, like air aspiring noses rising out of Her watery depths also created the terra firma or islands upon Her surFACE. An island is just that 'is land'.

RATA In English;

There exist a series of HOMONYMS or puns within the language that originated as the solar dyad of (RATA) based on the ratio (RATA), the passage of circular returns. One was the word right (RATA). Another was rite (RATA). The most recent one in PHASE THREE has been write (waRATA).

During the time of mother centrality in PHASE ONE, right (RATA) dealt with that which was opposite of the left. The ancient migrating journey, as the march in March began with the left foot of the mothers; left-right, left-right. When the shift occurred to male centrality in PHASES TWO and THREE right (RATA) shifted into becoming judgmental and defined that which had been correct as defined by the emerging male hierarchy.

As males began to undersand the role of the birthing breath of the mother's and the power that was inherent in that ecstatic Kundalini experience, they set out on quests of their own in order to experience it. Those quests dealing with the why of their peripheral state evolved into rites (RATA) of passage from a carefree adolescence into mature manhood. They had to become fearless in order to either beat their fathers or join their ranks in order to mate. Many different linguistic configurations surface of how the journey of young males evolved.

There were many ways that their entrenched fear could be jettisoned. One was by facing it in the isolated abaton. Another was by transforming it into something else. The young heroes faced it by going abroad to encounter real or imaginary trials. They may vary in their definition but they break down into three main categories.

One dealt with facing the fear of Mother Earth and Her awesome natural power. That power was often represented by some sort of one eyed giant, snake, serpent or dragon. The one eye (Cyclops) dealt with the sixth chacra of inner seeing and the third eye of transformation. It also dealt with overcoming hurricanes, tornadoes and whirlpools. The second trial usually dealt with facing and destroying the power of the father. In order to become the top dog the young male adept had to overthrow the existing Alpha male and set up his own domain, made apparent in the story of Oedipus. The third trial dealt with wooing and winning the hand of the desired female. That could have been a gentle wooing with flowers as among some birds, or it could have been like among the Koala bear and dolphin as violent rape. The many ancient legends that surface all around the world retrace the steps of heroes who journeyed far and wide smiting everything in sight in order to become worthy of becoming subsequent members of the ruling power driven left hemispheric male configuration awash in PHASE THREE.

Then there is the other category of ritual (RATA-) that is less muscular and deals with transformation. It has its links with the first born eunuchized sons who internalized the mother energy through the loss of their testosterone based testicles. To that group were joined the homosexual males who internalized the mother essence before birth due to its loss as the father aged.

To reach the ecstatic Kundalini birthing breath of the mother's instead of facing their fears through actual confrontation and fighting, young heroes found other means to activate the trance state of fearless change such as; drugs, alcohol (spirits), dancing, twirling, chanting, meditation, starvation, rocking back and forth, meditating at specific times of day, times of month, times of year, places on the planet, places at the feet of a self-realized guru.

Ancient human beings had been defined as being either right or left handed. That may have been the major social separation. It had been believed in PHASE ONE that the left side of the body was female and the right side of the body was male. As writing (RATA-) began to enter the scene, in PHASE TWO it was originally done by the left hand of the Mothers. That can be seen in Hebrew, Brahmin, Etruscan and by a few others by the fact that it moved across the page from right to left, as if written by the left hand.

As male centrality gained ground in PHASE THREE and the male left hemisphere of the brain gained momentum there occurred a shift in the direction of the writing from left to right, as if written by the right hand of the fathers. It was the focus inherent in writing itself that as a linear process added to the single focus of the left hemisphere of the human brain. The left hemisphere housing violence and single focused male sexuality began to take over the circular orientation of relationship, compassion and caring of the right hemisphere of the female brain. An imbalance began to occur. To correct that imbalance and to save their family unit the ancient mothers castrated their first born sons to act as protectors of their and their daughter's subsequent children.

There evolved a dual reality for males. One dealt with the adolescent males evicted at puberty to roam at the edges of the female configuration creating the ubiquitous band of brothers scenario relying on mating, violence, control and power. The other dealt with the castrated eunuch uncle with his trance of transformation and his evolution into the shaman, the healer, the prophet, the dog whisperer, the inner vision person with the circular eye of transformation blazing in his forehead.

So the right (RATA) side of the body as in the male, the right side of the hemispheric brain as in the female, the rite (RATA) of passage to create a fearless balance and writing (RATA-) itself petrifying experience into tradition, has led humanity in PHASE THREE into a delusionary state.

Then there is the concept of returns (RATARANA) dealing with overlapping tryads (RATA) (TARA) (RANA) that dealt with passage as a ratio (RATA), or a circular journey created by the boomerang SHAPE of going in one direction on the body or terrain (TARANA) of Mother Earth after it emerged out of the wound of dawn (RANA) in Polish and then coming back. The ancient migrations established that ancient pattern traveling back and forth on the continent of Africa as did the journey of the sun (RA) above and below the body of Mother Earth.

There is a Biblical admonition in PHASE THREE that the desirable place was to sit on was the right (RATA) hand of God. As Christ said, 'I am all right (RATA), in me there is no left'. It takes on new meaning when the origins of theses phrases become understood. To further the sexual dichotomy inherent in the two hemispheres of the brain, Hebrews declared that the seed of female children emanated from a father's left testicle, while that of his male children emanated from his right testicle.

NAHA in Hebrew; To be slain, to be beaten, to wail, lament and mourn, to be blotted out of sight, as a HOMONYM in Hebrew covers a variety of bases; Primarly it dealt with the loss of sunlight.

The inedible food is pushed out of the mouth accompanied by the nasal (N) SOUND of negation. Na in Sanskrit means 'not' as the light of day is negated (NA) to become night (NA). It was the sun (IS HANA) that shone (IS HANA) during the day and shared its blessed light. The sun (IS HANA) reflected below the surFACE of Mother Earth emerges with a variety of different possibilities. On the body of Mother Earth the sun during the day above the plane was there above them and completely apparent. But under the plane at night because it was not apparent it became defined by a host of imagined possibilities. The process of reflection enters here for the sun (IS HANA) reflected becomes (NAHA) (HANA/NAHA). In PHASE THREE as males took over the linguistic landscape they made *reflection* of many of the ancient words their own. (NA) deals with the sun at night (NA-) and (HA) deals with the belly under the surFACE of Mother Earth. When the sun (IS HANA) was swallowed by the body of Mother Earth it was slain to its light, it was beaten, war was declared against it. To be beaten is to be eaten by the two lips (B) that did the eating. NAHA in Hebrew also means to be 'slain or beaten'; It was the sun that was slain, *beaten* and *eaten* by the swallowing lips of Mother Earth in Her Western horizontal rim as She killed the rays of the sun at night. The underground sun under the surFACE of Mother Earth was a reflection of itself (HANA/NAHA). As the sun died to its light the assemblage at the Western wall of the dying sun wailed, lamented and mourned its passing. NAHA in Hebrew also means to 'wail, lament and mourn'; As the sun disappeared into the Western horizontal rim on the body of Mother Earth, it was blotted out of sight, its light was diminished. In Hebrew NAHA also means to be 'blotted out of sight'. The sun needed assistance, needed a guide through the dark intestines within the body of Mother Earth to reemerge at dawn. NAHA in Hebrew expands to mean 'to guide, to lead'. The snake had been assigned that ancient position of leadership. In Hebrew HAHAS is the snake (IS NAKA) the (K), (G) and (H) are interchangeable.

For the Hebrews still in touch with their linguistic source out of mother centrality the sun under the surFACE of Mother Earth shared many other concepts and activities. Further down the line in Latin in PHASE THREE the sun once it set, fell off Her Western horizontal side disappeared into the abyss, or nothingness. In Latin NAHA gave birth to nihilism (NAHA-)

meaning 'nothing'.

In PHASE ONE the Harappan (HARAPA-) people out of the Indus valley in India defined themselves as the Nagas (IS NAKA, NAGA) or the worshippers of the snake or serpent (IS HARAPA-) . Why had they worshipped the snake? Because like all the other mythologies of the ancient world they believed that the symbolic mythological snake, had two major universal ancient jobs. One was its intuited double twining like journey up the spinal column as the Kundalini energy associated with the ecstatic and powerful birthing breath of the mothers. The other more apparently practical dealt with the mythological snake guiding the sun through its internal nocturnal passage within the body of Mother Earth for to be born to a new day every morning.

The serpent (IS HARAPA-) gives it all away. For defined by the name of the serpent (IS HARAPA-) the ancient Harappan (HARAPA-) people also share their name with the Indian sherpa (IS HARAPA) and Europe (HARAPA). All three deal with the mythological snake passing (PA) through the belly (HARA) or solar plexus of the individual mother and the other through the solar belly (HARA) of Mother Earth. The double P in HaraPPa may document that double passage; (PA) through the mothers belly and (PA) of passage through the belly of Mother Earth as the double (PP) twisting coil of the Kundalini energy. It surfaces as the double twisting spin on the Caduceus wand of healing in Greece.

At Mohenjo Daro in the Indus valley where the Harappan culture flourished, archeologists found no military fortifications among the rediscovered ancient ruins. It was a peaceful society betraying its source out of female centrality going back to PHASE ONE. They had links with the contemporary Sherpa (IS HARAPA) and amazingly linguistically with Europe (HARAPA). That may have been one of the migratory journeys out of Africa that the ancient dispersers followed.

Not to wander too far afield but to stay in the same meaningful linguistic pattern, in Finnish nuha (NAHA) means cold, as not only the night was cold, but the underground reaches within the body of Mother Earth in Northern Europe were perceived to be cold. In Basque negu (NAGA) meant winter with a similar concept as the Finnish nuha (NAHA) dealing with cold, establishing linguistic links with the Harappan Nagas (NAGA-) the serpent people.

In Persian naka of the snake (IS NAKA) dealt with 'end or conclusion'. The setting of the sun ended its journey above the body of Mother Earth and surrendered its intestinal passage to the guiding mythological snake (IS NAKA). In all of these words the (K)(G) and (H) are interchangeable.

There are three sets of English HOMONYMS or puns that need to be explored for they come with similar double meanings.

One is *rock*, the other is *stone*. The third one deals with SOUND. The noun rock is a boulder. The verb rock means to sway back and forth, to rock. The noun stone also means a boulder. The verb and adjective to be stoned takes on a different meaning. It deals with the process of transformation. The SOUND is that which is heard. To be SOUND deals with being healthy. There in lies a magnificent tale.

What is a stone (IS TANA)? A tone (TANA) is a SOUND that holds a certain vibration (vaBARAna-). A tone (TANA) also deals with the process of holding. In Latin tenere (TANA-) means 'to hold'. It goes even further back with the ten (TANA) fingers on the individual mother's hands in stage three that did the holding. As the ten (TANA) fingers that touch and awaken pleasure on the skin, so the tone (TANA) as SOUND vibrates (vaBARAta-) and activates a flow of goosepimples with the same response to the whole body.

The SOUND as tone (TANA) with the first phoneme (TA) deals with things (TANA-) that occur on the edge, on the tip, like the teeth that are on the tip of the gums, the toes are on the tip of the feet, teats are on the tip of the chest, things, such as trees are on the tip or top the body of Mother Earth. Having its origin as the nose seen in profile (NA) deals with either 'emergence on the surface' or a 'change from a former state'. It originally dealt with breathing in and out, smelling offensive food and shoving it out with the tongue, while making the nasal SOUND of rejection. In Polish the same concept surfaces but with a different set of dyads. Its as if after many of the African dispersals the ancient wanderers lost some of their ancient memories as the linguistic break proclaims. The concept of holding linking it to the rock (RAKA) surfaces in Polish as the hand that holds, or reka (RAKA). Lost are the ten (TANA) individual fingers that hold the tone (TANA), but the concept of holding shifts to the whole hand surfacing with another set of dyads. So the Polish hand reka (RAKA) like the rock (RAKA) held something.

It is the thumb thumping on a log or drum that causes a tonal and vibrational (vaBARAta-) response in the human body. When the rhythm is constant and the thumping goes on for an extended period of time and dancing accompanies it, then the activated trance creates an entrance into the balanced center creating the yoking of the two hemispheres of the brain working in concert and the beginning of transformation. It is a power that has yet to be truly explored and understood.

The drum (DARAMA) creates the 'dream (DARAMA) time' that the

Australian Aborigines experience as they communicate telepathically over long distances. The drum and the dream also create a story, the drama (DARAMA) that unfolds as the trance state takes over. It is in that dream state that an opening occurs, that on the wings of ecstasy goosepimples erupt upon the skin. The sensuality locked in the goosepimpled derma (DARAMA) brings with it fearlessness, leadership, healing, prophecy and wish-fulfillment. It is the gift (DA) of the sun (RA) by the body of Mother Earth (MA). The skin separates us from and connects us to the universe.

There is ongoing research that Stonehenge and other round *stone* circles around the world created a powerful area of transformation and of becoming *stoned*, as drummers (DARAMA-) sat inside of those stones and drummed together sending an echo that viBRated (-BARA-) not only the surrounding stones but the human BRain (BARA-) into alpha wave states that created a movement into that 'intermediate state' of trance and transformation. That may be one of the reasons that massive stone constructions around the world were used as sacred places of ecstatic ritual. Original 'sirituality' may have its origins out of a sense of shared pleasure and healing.

HUMAN BEINGS ARE ADDICTED TO PLEASURE.

Why else would they have sent themselves into states of stoned ecstasy? They didn't align their structures with the solar solstices and full moons in order to know when to plant their corn. They planted their corn when the leaves on their oak trees were the size of a mouse's ear. They aligned those ancient monoliths because they knew that at certain times of the year, at certain times of the month and even at certain times of the day, the Kundalini energy moving up from the body of Mother Earth, specifically up the left foot, was the strongest. They knew that if they got together at those specific times and formed their drumming circles surrounded by massive stones they would reach the height of ecstasy and become not only stoned but healthy and SOUND. Many other repetitive movements helped them on their transformative journey.

Rocking (RAKA-) back and forth in ecstasy, Hebrew males at the Western Wall and the Muslim boys in their madrasa's mumble their secret words. It was the shared ecstatic vibration (vaBARAta-) in the rocks at Stonehenge that caused them to rock back and forth and to become stoned. It is ironic that caged primates in humanity's zoos rock back and forth an activity that has also been observed in autistic children.

The same process may deal with the noun SOUND (IS HANAGA) as a HOMONYM defining not only something that impinges vibrationally on the ear but creates an adjective a SOUND and healthy body. What did the drummers at Stonehenge know at the time of mother centrality in PHASE ONE that has been suppressed, destroyed and forgotten by the left hemispheric rational brain of the fathers?

RULE EIGHTEEN;
HOMOPHONES, puns across the linguistic 'divide'

To continue, a Finnish word for 'stone' is kivi (KAVA). In Polish the verb for rocking back and forth is kiwa (KAVA). The Hopi sacred ceremonial circle gouged out of the ground and encircled in stone in the deserts of North America is called a kiva (KAVA). All these words relatively intact go back to the ancient place of worship within the body of Mother Earth out of Her Earthen womb, Her cave (KAVA) of creation. All over the world early humans not only found shelter, but worshipped in caves. There are links of cave (KAVA) worship to the Tuareg of North Africa and the early Berbers. They also used brain bending drugs such as caffeinated coffee, kawa (KAVA) in Polish.

The (VA) in cave (KAVA) deals with the volcanic (VA) vulva (VA), that created the caves, the magmic tubes within the body of Mother Earth that acted as vias of passage for Her lavic flows. The (KA) deals with all of the smaller (KA) things that emerged out of Her creative body.

Mother Earth using Her Kundalini electro magnetic pulse had been considered the matriarch that created and sustained everything. Like other matriarchs, specifically the oldest and wisest elephant, She was the oldest member of both the human and celestial family. In Bugotu of the South Pacific kave (KAVA) is the name for 'grandmother.' Any 'old woman' is KAE KAVE (KAKAVA). The repeated letter of (KAKA-) establishes its links not only with the semiannual passage of birds North and South across the luminous sky and the clacking (KALAKA) noise that they made establishing one of the movements of the ancient celestial clock (KALAKA) but with the repetitive nature of creation (KAKA) itself.

When the ice age descended on those original ancient migratory trekkers and subsequent builders of megalithic cities, they hid in those caves and survived the great glacial onslaught. In time with their memories intact they built other caves into the ground and covered them with wooden planks. In the Hopi Indian tradition those caves are called kivas (KAVA-) or caves

(KAVA-) dug into the body of Mother Earth where Her Kundalini energy could be concentrated and experienced directly. It was in those kivas that they danced, rocked back and forth and moved into trance states of transformation fusing the two hemispheres of the brain in the process becoming transformed and balanced.

In PHASE ONE on the wings of ecstasy the coven (KAVA-) of the transformed mothers with the birthing breath alive in them and the transformed male shamans performed the ceremonies dealing with fear elimination, leadership, healing, prophecy and wish-fulfillment.

To reach the state of balance, the left hemisphere had to become stilled. It was in the left hemisphere of the human brain that fear had become trapped. It was from the process of image accumulation in a straight line that the extended fear driven creature had to find relief. The fear became trapped with the image. Every time that the image was activated the fear surfaced. Every time that the fear surfaced the image popped up. The trapped image gave birth to imagination and the life of fantasy based on the answers to the why of male periphery. In Finnish kuva (KAVA) stands for image and deals with the image as the source of fear accumulation and its dissolution in the traditions experienced in the cave (KAVA).

Many of these perceptions were believed to have their emergence out of the cave (KAVA). In the word coven (KAVANA) there exists the concept of 'emergence on the surface' or a 'change from a former state' locked in the syllable (NA). As all forms of women's experience were becoming obliterated in PHASE THREE, the coven became a witches brew and destined like the wise witches burned at the stake for the scrap pile of history. Also in PHASE THREE the coven (KAVANA) of the mother's power base moved to embrace the Hebrew covenant (KAVANAnata) with a celestial deity *away* and *above* the body of Mother Earth into a male father God in the sky. Two clues emerge here. One is the repetitive (NANA) dyad which has links with the moon as a double negation. The covenant (KAVANANATA) of the early Hebrews establishes its ancient links with the coven (KAVANA) of the transformed mothers that was obviously practiced by the light of the moon at night. The other is the HAVANA overlapping dyad that establishes its own ancient heritage. The (K) and (H) in this case are interchangeable. It was the Arc of the Covenant that Moses stored the tablets of behavior recited to him by God. The search for the lost Arc of the Covenant, like male role in specific paternity has ancient roots.

HAVANA

Within the word HAVANA we are dipping into unchartered waters in more than one way. It covers so many bases that the linguistic landscape has to be carefully transversed. There do not appear to be any apparent cities in Africa that are called Havana. The one Havana that becomes apparent exists on the Island of Cuba. How did it get there? Hidden in the linguistic folds of so many African words, like the DNA stayed in the molecule, that original SOUND also stayed around in English, where surface the most ancient linguistic concepts dealing with Havana.

One deals with the ancient migrations across the African savannah (IS HAVANA). Another deals with the number seven (IS HAVANA). Then there is the simple word even (HAVANA), to name only a few. There is a linkage to the preceding concepts in the Hebrew word to D'aven (daHAVANA) which means to *rock back and forth*, the kiva in Polish, as if in a trance.

The Hebrew males understood the role of the rocking back and forth ritual in obtaining the trance state associated with the mother's mystical birthing breath.

After many of the African cataclysms and the desiccating Sahara, the ancient wanderers dispersed in many directions finding water and a warmer climate. Some went North to the French city of Avignon (HAVANAna). Others strayed even further afield onto the British Isles founding the city of Avon (HAVANA) reached by a wide avenue (HAVANA) at the foot of Stonehenge that led to the waters of passage across a great oceanic divide. It was across those waters of passage across the Atlantic Ocean that they came across the Island of Cuba and the city of Havana. The city of Havana was their haven (HAVANA) on their way to their concept of heaven (HAVANA) in the Pleiades, of the seven (IS HAVANA) starry sisters. We are touching on male centrality here in PHASE THREE for the concept of source is *away* and *above* the body of Mother Earth way up in the celestial realms. The Island of Cuba (KABA) has links not only with the Muslim Kaaba (KABA), the cube (KABA) SHAPE but emerging out of the square becoming the boxes as the tefilah that the Hebrews wear on their arm and forehead when they pray.

Then there is the number seven (IS HAVANA) the perception of even (HAVANA) enters here. The number seven (IS EVEN) comes out of the observation that a still body of water reflected upon its surface the reality that existed above it. It may have been the inland Okavango River Delta in Botswana that created an enormous spread of quietly standing water across the parched savannah IS HAVANA). Or it could have been the pre-glacial lake and river spread beneath the verdant prehistoric Sahara Desert. Someone traversing back and forth following the migratory herds coming upon the still standing water at the end of their journey and its reflection must have observed. Look! IS EVEN, the reflection IS EVEN and lo and behold the SOUND associated with the number seven (IS EVEN) came into being.

The number seven (IS EVEN) out of one direction and seven (IS HAVANA) from another, never knew that with the passage of time it would become a sacred and mystical number. It came to embrace a variety of extraordinary concepts. The most important one was that originally it dealt with the cycles of separation and death of the sun.

The seven day week was not an ancient perception emerging out of PHASE THREE. It was the fourteen day lunar cycle of the moon waxing and waning belonging to the ancient mothers in PHASE ONE that was definable, establishing one of the most ancient balanced twenty-eight day monthly lunar cycles. There was no original embarkation point defining the seven day week except in Herew when a day of rest had been forced on the slave masters of Egypt. That also came with the growth of male centrality and the primacy of the male number four that was becoming their symbolic number. Four even separate weeks had to be established in the month, as four points had been established on the horizontal compass squaring the circle of Mother Earths surFACE.

Taking it back to PHASE ONE and mother centrality human beings were guided by the thirteen month lunar calendar. As they migrated back and forth following the herbivore herds across the flooded savannah (IS HAVANA) they began their march in March or early April at the time of the Spring Equinox after the bellowing frenzy of the butting of male heads and the butting of female buttocks took place. They followed the herds in one direction for six lunar months, at the end of the six months the mares gave birth to their calves, mated and in the seventh (IS HAVANA) month, the month of September, if you begin the year in March, as the grass dried up, they turned around following the herds and headed back to their beloved mountains. In Latin sept is not only associated with September but with seven and separation.

In PHASE THREE and male centrality when the use of the irregular twelve month solar calendar of the fathers replaced the regular balanced thirteen month lunar calendar of the mothers, the butting of human female buttocks at the time of the Spring Equinox resulted nine months later when a new (NAWA) arrival that emerged upon the scene and a baby was born to the migrating human mothers in November (NAVAmabara) announcing a new member (maMABARA) of the group. The (V) and (W) are interchangeable.

There evolved a dual process of separation. One dealt with the breaking of the migratory year into two equal halves spinning around the fulcrum of seven, the sept of September. The other separation dealt with another duality, the separation of the foals as they fell off the bodies of their mothers at the end of their sixth month gestation period and the separation of the human babies as they divided off the mothers bodies in PHASE THREE after nine solar months in November.

The major migratory separation occurred in the seventh (IS EVEN-) month of what became September. It reflected the concept of evenness (HAVANA-) in *time* as the reflective waters established the perception of evenness on the body of Mother Earth in *space*. This journey was established for thousands of years in PHASE ONE with the mothers, their female relatives including the castrated first born sons in the center and the violent males circling the periphery. Marriage was unknown as was the knowledge of male role in specific paternity.

The same concept of separation and possible death dealt with a moment in time and gave birth to the SHAPE of the number seven (IS EVEN). When the sun came to the end of its daily journey across Mother Earth's belly of air, it either was swallowed, or slid into that great maw on Her horizontal Western side. The sliding off the side of Mother Earth had been documented in the SHAPE of the angle encoded in the number seven.

The birth of the sun in the Eastern sky ascending as an angle out of Her nurturing body giving birth to LAght and LAfe. In the West another separation occurred creating the number seven as the sun descended at an angle and disappeared into Her great waiting suicidal (IS HADA-) maw, mouth, darkness, abyss, nothingness, you can take your pick.

That separation, that fall off the edge off the body of Mother Earth, that death of the rays of light as Mother Earth swallowed the endlessly resistant sun, gave birth to the *SHAPE* of the number seven (IS EVEN). It was believed that there existed an evenness in existence, half of it was in life above Her surFACE and an equal half was in death below Her surFACE.

Another series of concepts concerning the number seven (IS HAVANA) deal with the journey of the Kundalini energy as the trance of transformation and its journey to death and rebirth in the stars.

The last and perhaps the most important evenness (HAVANA-) and balance deals with the fusion of the separated hemispheres in the human brain. Due to male questing and the asking of WHY (Y) of their peripheral state, the male mind became bi-furcated. The linear, single focused left male hemisphere carrying power, control, sex, fear, the image of imagination, rage and violence, as it separated from the right hemisphere of mother bonding of love and compassion, became over evolved creating the destruction of the right hemisphere of the mother's, resulting in the abuse of women and their children and the destruction of Mother Earth. Seven (IS EVEN) in one of its permutations came to represent the process of brain fusion at the center, the even (HAVANA) balance where the transformation of trance could find its home.

More other less pertinent words surface carrying similar meanings. The eve of evening (HAVANA-) breaks the circular pattern reflected in day and night. At the equator, evening breaks day and night into two even (HAVANA) halves. Biblical Eve had been considered half of God's creation, even though she emerged out of Adam's rib. The oven (HAVANA) *under* the mantle of Mother Earth had been considered half of Her reality. The other was the ovum (HAVAMA), the solar egg as Her helper existed at one with Her *above* Her surFACE.

HAKA or (IS HAKA);

MA SIKA (IS HAKA) in Swahili is 'heavy rains'. (HAKA) deals with the belly of air (HA) above the surFACE of Mother Earth (MA) creating the cascade of monsoon rains that hack (HAKA) themselves free at the horizontal rim out of Her body and thunder their way across the belly of air above Her surFACE. Everything that Mother Earth created was perceived to be a small version of Her (KA), even the rain (RANA) that emerged out of Her horizontal rim to fall upon the parched skin of Her savannah.

SIKA (IS HAKA) in Polish;

Sika means 'she pees' and deals with the same process of aquatic (HAKA-) hacking (HAKA-) not from the body of Mother Earth but from Her surrogate daughter, the individual female, who also makes rain (RANA) as urine (haRANA) out of her (HARA), belly as hara and the Polish wound as rana.

SIKSA (IS HAKASA) in Jewish;

Is the name for a gentile girl and not so complimentarily means 'she who pees' and like Mother Earth she also separates or hacks (HAKA-) herself free from the water within her. The (KASA) in her name establishes her as the bearer of the coos (KASA) from whence it was perceived that the emanation of water occurs and establishes her as unmistakably female.

SHIK SHIKA (IS HAKA IS HAKA) in Hindu, teacher lady;

Is 'a teacher lady', a surrogate of Mother Earth the ultimate teacher, twice blessed, a true equal (HAKA-), sharing the same processes of hacking

(HAKA-) free not only of her urine which seems to define her, but also an equal with the body of Mother Earth in the dissemination of information, a true *PEER*. Animals use their pee to establish territorial rights. They teach their own and others that they own the area that is guarded by their pee. Pee (PA) also deals with passage (PASA-) of a stream out of the body. It extends to the word piss (PASA) the SOUND associated with the passage of urine.

SHAKTI (IS HAKATA) in Hindu, electro magnetic current

Is the female principle of essence that as 'prana' of the electro magnetic Kundalini energy courses through the body and burns, or hacks (HAKA-) through the accumulated debris of habit, to free the adept into a subsequent joy filled, fear free existence. SHAKTI (IS HAKATA) has links with the English word for electric 'shock' (IS HAKA). It also surfaces as prand (PARANADA), which in Polish means 'current' and is 'the gift of' (DA) (PARANA).

It is the electro magnetic explosion of the double coiled metaphoric snake SHAPED Kundalini energy up the spine that as 'shock' (IS HAKA) and 'current' bursts through the body and hacks (HAKA-) the birthing mother, or the searching adept free of all the negativity that had been accumulated through a habit dominated lifetime that became trapped with the realization that at birth the baby had been born helpless, in a body that didn't work.

It is also the female essence that accompanies all male deities, like in India the mother sourced vowel A (ah), originally in PHASE ONE accompanied all the consonants. In PHASE THREE the female hating Manu priests redefined the language and placed the A(ah) SOUND of majestic importance associated with the volcanic SHAPE on the body of Mother Earth, behind male names.

SHEKINAH (IS HAKANAHA);

In PHASE THREE Jewish scholars not finding the journey through the mind satisfying enough turned to the sensuous (-SASA) gifts of the ancient mothers. The acknowledgment of the female principle in the Godhead, the SHEKINAH (IS HAKA-KANA-NAHA) emerges (NA) in the Jewish Caballah and carries with it the fusion of the female side of the brain with the male side creating a balance, and a movement into joy filled 'mysticism'.

The (KANA) dyad gives its ancient prehistoric mother based roots away, for it is the cone (KANA) of creation on the skin (IS KANA) of Mother Earth through which the Kundalini (KANA-) solar wind bursts forth, that is the source of ecstasy and transformation for the birthing mother out of PHASE ONE and the searching adept in PHASE THREE.

The (HAKA) dyad that surfaces in all of the former names deals with the hacking apart of one aspect of 'being' from another. In Latin aqua (HAKA) defines water as the hacker of reality on its reflective surface. It extends to other words defining the liquid substance. MA SIKA (IS HAKA) Swahili heavy rains, SIKA (IS HAKA) one who pees in Polish, SIKSA (IS HAKA-) Jewish name for young Polish girl peer, SHIK, SHIKA (IS HAKA IS HAKA) Hindu teacher, SHAKTI (IS HAKA-) female aspect of Kundalini energy, SHEKINAH (IS HAKA-) Hebrew female Godhead, all deal with the hacking (HAKA-) quality of water on the reflective surFACE on the body of Mother Earth. One reality existed as that which was above in life and the reflected reality dealt with what was perceived to be reflected below in death. Aqua (HAKA) as the Latin name for water establishes the salient quality of water as a reflective hacking (HAKA-) surFACE on the body of Mother Earth. It goes even further back into the SHAPE of the lower mandible, the hook (HAKA) on the snout of the individual carnivore mother in stage thee who did the hunting and the hacking (HAKA-) apart of prey.

The Latin aqua (HAKA) as 'water', symbolizes life as a process of constant change, of constant physical, intellectual, and of spiritual migration, of recycled returns, of unanticipated separations, into the subsequent universal concept of trans-formative growth and if nothing else, acceptance. What is, like justice, just is. Change is an ever changing cycle of apparent constants. What emerged was a state of freedom from panic stricken infantile habits, freedom from fear, euphoric acceptance and what came to be called mysticism.

Mysticism was native to women who in the last stages of labor, with the help of the second wind, the bastrika breath of the Hindus, with the help of their fingers orgasmed, spasmed and masturbated the large headed fetuses out of their bodies. Also at their fingertips was the inner vision that came with the opening into the universal container of the breath and the journey into nothingness. It could be Jungs subconscious unconsciousness, or the Akashik (HAKASAKA) (HAKA) (IS HAKA) record, or as yet a little understood area of creative reality. It could also deal with the dream state brought up to the level of consciousness.

SIKITU (IS HAKAta) in Swahili means 'nothing';

A 'state of being' pursued by the Buddhists, the hacking (HAKA-) or cutting (KATA-) free of desire and worldly possessions and a movement into the nothingness of the void.

ZOHAR (IS HAHARA) In the Hebrew Caballah;

Contains in it ancient linguistic clues out of PHASE ONE. The first dyad as (HAHA) is the repetitive fast panting of the birthing breath of the mother in the last stages of labor, when she moves into a state of orgasmic bliss as she gives birth to her off spring. For the Japanese HA-HA is the name of the 'mother'. The second dyad of Zohar (IS HAHARA) as HARA in Hebrew, deals with either the 'holy mountain' on the body of Mother Earth, or prosaically, the 'pregnant belly' of the individual mother. For the Maori the bowels or intestines were called maHARA. ZOHAR (IS HAHARA) has the same linguistic structure as Sahara (IS HAHARA) and may deal not only with Mother Earths dessicating breath but with the place of its ancient linguistic origin.

In the last stages of His agony, Christ hanging on the cross, cried out "Eli (HALA) Eli (HALA), why has thou forsaken me?" Mark 15:34. Was it because He realized that ecstatic transformation came through the *BODY* of the mother up from the body of mother Earth, not down from the sky from the *MIND* of God the father?

The temple in PHASE ONE had been the forehead, the third eye where the focus of transformation took place across the corpus callosum yoking the two sides of the brain. In PHASE THREE the temple as a place of spiritual activity became an erected edifice, a building, a synagogue, a temple. Michael Angelos painting of the Sistine Chapel ceiling contains the SHAPE on the right side depicting the hand of God extended contained in the SHAPE of the left hemisphere of the human brain. Somehow he understood that God emerged out of the left hemispheric male mind, not the other way around.

Out of Ugarit the 'supreme God' was called El (HALA). Similarly the name of the Hebrew God as Eli (HALA) takes it back to PHASE ONE when one of the names for the female sun as the SHAPE of the suns emergence out of the body of Mother Earth encoded in the letter L was hala, cum the Greek sun as eelyos (HALAsa).Eli also flowers with the i at the end of Eli as 'one more' of the individual self associated with a male child. It means that in the New Testament in PHASE THREE we are dealing with the male I as the 'one more' and the MIND of the father as the hopeful source of transformation and not the BODY of the mother.

The HAKA dyad goes further back into pre history and the time of female centrality in PHASE ONE and stage one, when the hacking (HAKA-) dyad was associated with the SHAPE of the hook (HAKA) on the face of the mother, her jaw and the hacking (HAKA-) done by the hook (HAKA) separating death from life of her prey. What did the jaw do once it separated the kill from its life. It chewed it apart into smaller (KA) pieces.

The hook (HAKA) on the body of Mother Earth, her lower jaw had been the water, the Latin aqua (HAKA) that separated the reflected reality of death below from the physical reality of life above. As the reality below the waters in death still in PHASE TWO became the domain of the eunuch priesthood, in Egypt the hidden one, the Lord of Death became Seker (IS HAKARA), the one who hacked (HAKA-) death from life. Sakarra (IS HAKA-) became the seven step pyramid to house the remains of the pharaoh on his journey across the sacred (IS HAKA-) waters into immortality. Since all of this activity was believed to exist under the reflective waters and was not apparently visible above the surFACE of Mother Earth, it emerged not only as sacred (IS HAKA-) but also as secret (IS HAKA-).

A curious addendum to this ancient aquatic perception exists in Polish with the following three words. They are szczy (IS CHA) which is another word for peeing, Then we have the word szczyt (IS CHATA) which means way up high. What brings them together is deszcz (DA IS CHA), for deszcz means rain, or the gift (DA) of peeing as szczy (IS CHA). It becomes apparent that we are dealing with the body of Mother Earth, because no matter how tall the female individuals who did the peeing may have been, they did not create rain. Curious throwback to female centrality and the origins of these words out of the body of Mother Earth and Her surrogate peer.

The throwbacks raise their heads to be reexamined as does the God Uranus (HARANASA). Before he came into being for the Greeks in PHASE THREE there was his consort Urenia (HARANA), the 'Celestial One' out of PHASE ONE. The (HARA) dyad establishes her as having a belly of air (HARA) out of which the rain (RANA) was born, out of both her wound and dawn, as rana in Polish. In PHASE THREE with male role in specific procreation becoming known the redefinitions proliferated resulting in the suppression of Mother Earth as the original God and the source of all of reality. The rain in this case became his semen that fell down from the sky as rain and fructified the body of Mother Earth. Instead of being the creator and source She had been demoted to act as a container of the male sperm (IS PARAMA).

In PHASE THREE the male sheikh (IS HAKA) of Araby became the hacker (HAKA-), the one who hacked (HAKA-) the virginal body of the female apart with his phallus in order to plant his seed in her fertile soil and keep her as a virtual slave in his harem (HARAMA). (HARA) is the belly and (RAMA) is the frame (faRAMA) of containment. It was a time when clitorectomies descended upon the poor girls. Their whole clitoral structure was excised and only holes were left for peeing and menstruation. Hacking apart by the phallus to have sex comes with horrendous implications as does giving birth.

No wonder birth had been considered to emerge out of the mothers side in Hinduism and out of Adams rib in Hebruism.

The hacking (HAKA-) jaw, the hook (HAKA) on the bottom of the mothers skull in PHASE ONE shifted in PHASE TWO and THREE into its primary organ of hacking (HAKA-) which was delegated to the male penis. For the Egyptians Seker (IS HAKARA) was the hidden one, the Lord of Death, or the sun at night under the body of Mother Earth. He had to hack (HAKA) himself free at Her horizontal Eastern rim to emerge at dawn to the light of a new life. In Arabic the penis became zekker (IS HAKA-). For the Hebrews male virility emerged as zakar (IS HAKA-). Not to be left out, further North in Poland more benevolently siekiera (IS HAKA-) surfaces as the name for the hacking (HAKA-) ax (HAKA-), or adze (HADASA). Bizarre, but there it is.

KAPA deals with passage; (PA) in the process of making smaller things (KA). A series of similar SOUNDING dyads (KA) and (PA) chase each other across the pages of linguistic prehistory.

CAP (KAPA; in one of it's manifestations in English is the small (KA) covering of snow or lava on the volcanic summit on the body of Mother Earth. Since both snow and lava deal with either melting or movement then (PA) is an apt description of their PAssage.

CUP (KAPA) is the small (KA) container that holds a liquid. (PA) deals with 'passage'. That's what a liquid does, it passes through the cup (KAPA) on its way to the stomach and as lava passes (PA) out of the volcanic cup (KAPA) upwards to emerge on the surFACE of Mother Earth as Her volcanic menstrual lavic blood or snowy cap (KAPA). In PHASE ONE and stage three, closed fingers of the hand were the first cup (KAPA) makers. In Polish fingers are palce (PALASA) having their origin out of poles (PALASA). Both were used for digging either for tubers, grubs or water.

KUPI (KAPA) for the Maori in New Zealand is 'water';

They may have left Africa fifty thousand years before but they still remembered their original African SOUNDS. It was the cupped (KAPA-) hands that held the water.

KAPIE (KAPA) in Polish means 'to drip';

The concept for the PAssage of water emerges on the other side of the world dealing with the same two dyads, (KA) and (PA).

KIPIE (KAPA) in Polish means 'to boil over';

We are dealing here with the mixed metaphors of water and volcanic fire out of the body of Mother Earth.

KAPALA in Polish means She of the 'dripping water'.

KUPALA (KAPALA) in Slavonic is 'water Mother'.

KOPALA (KAPALA) in Polish means She dug, or She kicked. In She dug we are dealing with a raging river as a torrential flood digging its way down to the lakes. She kicked, deals with Mother Earth kicking debris out of Her volcanic cup (KAPA) high up into Her belly of air creating both the massive explosion and the subsequent cap (KAPA) the caldera, on top of Her summit.

SCAPULA (IS KAPALA);

Before tools came into being In PHASE ONE the scapula (IS KAPALA) may have been the original digging tool. Its skeletal SHAPE reminds one of a shovel.

K'PALA (KAPALA) in Hawaiian is a 'shovel', a digging tool.

KAPOLI (KAPALA) in Bemba is a 'wild pig'. What does a wild pig do? It digs.

KOPIE (KAPA) in Polish also means 'to kick' and to dig.

KOPJE (KAPA-) out of Africa are 'piles of boulders' that have been perceived to have been kicked out of the body of Mother Earth during a volcanic eruption. On one level it deals with Mother Earth in Her aspect as the dripping, boiling water of the roiling rivers, and aquatic vents digging their way down steep ravines into the patiently waiting lakes.

On another level it deals with the cap (KAPA) that was blown off the top of the volcanic cone during a shattering eruption. Mother Earth in the creation of land as lava 'dug' Her way across as she 'kicked' boulders up into the air using what in Hawaii became a digging tool, K'PALA (KAPALA) a 'shovel'.

KAPOLI (KAPALA) in Bemba is a 'wild pig'. What does a wild pig do? It roots up the ground, it digs.

PELLE (PALA) in French is a 'shovel'. The 'shovel' used as a tool was a 'pole' (PALA), a 'digging stick'. The (PA) as passage through, of (LA) the angle. So the 'digging stick' was shaped like a hockey stick with a curved angle on the end to do the digging. In PHASE ONE it could have been the jaw bone of a large animal, a sharply angled branch off a tree, a bent finger, or a scapula (IS KAPALA). It could also have been the angle of lavic emergence out of the cup (KAPA) of the volcano as it blasted its cap (KAPA) into space. Mother Pele (PALA) is a common name for the volcano in the Pacific, sharing its linguistic roots with the Polish finger palec (PALAsa) that did the digging.

PALEC (PALASA) in Polish is a finger, its ancient linguistic source out of the human body in stage three.

PHALLUS (FALASA, PALASA);

On the male body the extra finger that pleasured women, was considered to be the blood (SA) filled phallus (PALASA or FALASA). On the body of Mother Earth, the pole (PALA) was the finger, the Polish palec (PALASA) of fire that rose out of Her subterranean recessive cup of the volcano and vertically pushed the lava up to Her surFACE.

PALIC (PALACHA) in Polish also means 'to burn' and establishes its links with the fiery volcanic eruption on the body of Mother Earth.

In the following words there are SOUND alikes and the letters (P) and (B) are often interchangeable.

KABILA (KABALA) in Swahili is a 'tribe'.

KOBYLA (KABALA) In Polish is a mare. A 'mare' was and often still is the name for many foaling herbivore mothers, especially horses who create a small caballo (KABALA) (horse in Spanish). Because the Swahili KABILA (KABALA) as a 'tribe' has links with the Polish KOBYLA (KABALA) who is a 'mare', we are dealing with the 'tribe' out of PHASE ONE, out of female centrality and out of the bodies of mares and tribal mothers. Family (FAMALA) and female (FAMALA) come from the same linguistic source.

As a creature of passage across the divide between life and death, the female horse, the mare horse played a large role in PHASE ONE. In Spanish the horse surfaces as caballo (KABALA). The links with Caballah (KABALA) can only be surmised. It goes back to PHASE ONE when cats, dogs and horses had been considered creatures and guides of passage.

The ancient Hebrews were 'tribes' of wanderers, i.e. migrants across the deserts of the Sinai (IS HANAYA), the land of light (AYA) in Persian, of the rising sun (IS HANA) at dawn (AYA), in Assyrian. CABALLAH (KABALA) in Jewish establishes its links with the 'tribe', the 'mare', as the female horse the kobyla (KABALA) in Polish and the body of Mother Earth as the begetter of the sun, taking it a few steps further into the ecstasy that began its life out of the female body and emerged into Chassidic mysticism.

KIPA (KAPA);

The yarmulkah cap (KAPA) that the Orthodox Jews wear on their heads is called a kipa (KAPA) and has links with the electro magnetic emanations of the Kundalini energy out of the seventh chacra of the Tantrists and out of the top of the head. Like Mother Earth created an alternate reality when she blew Her top, blew Her cap (KAPA), so the Chassidic Jews cover their heads with a kipa (KAPA) in an ancient acknowledgment of the source of that experience that harkens back to an earlier time of female centrality in PHASE ONE and the ritual experience of the eruption of the ecstatic Kundalini energy up from the body of Mother Earth rising through the body to exit out of the top of their heads.

Closer to home, BOI (BAYA) in Polish is 'fear';

The bifurcated left side of the human brain of the fathers adrift from the right hemisphere of the mothers, establishes the concept of not only 'two in one' that the letter (B) establishes, but of separation. Fear associating itself with the image gave rise to imagination, fantasy and the definition of reality as answers to the why of their periphery in adult fairy tales of the father. The (I) at the end of boi (BAYA) as one more associates it with a male child.

BAYA in Swahili is 'bad';

In PHASE ONE not knowing how to define a male child with a permanently empty belly, he may have been considered as a bad problem, especially at puberty. It may also deal with the the body of Mother Earth and the unrelenting light of the sun (AYA) turning the verdant Sahara into a desert with Her dessicating 'bad' breath.

BAAYAH (BAYA) in Hebrew; problem is 'a problem'. The problem dealing with young pubescent boys seems to expand across linguistic lines. It also expands to the body of Mother Earth and the time when the Sahara Desert turned into a sandy wasteland creating a problem of survival for the migrating Hebrews.

BAAY (BAYA) in Wolof is the name of the 'father', or 'paternal uncle'(HANAKALA) the castrated eunuch (HANAKA). It seems that the 'problems' relating to the socialization of young human boys had been of recurring and ancient concern. If a society didn't adequately socialize its young men, they became marauding gangs and the society dissolved into chaos.

In PHASE ONE the ancient mothers used the violent process of castration, mutilation and deportation of their sons to control them. In PHASE TWO, young males went through rites of passage to overcome their infantile attachments and fears. For the Wolof turning young men into 'fathers' and castrated 'paternal uncles' solved the problem. In PHASES TWO and THREE 'war' became a tool for the social control of young male rebellion against the power held by the authority of the aging fathers and surfaces as the second trial in all of those subsequent fairy tales. The first trial was the confrontation with Nature and Mother Earth.

BOY (BAYA);

In PHASE ONE with the anlaut of (B) establishes the concept of 'two in one' related to the letter (B). He was considered to be both a male and a female. He was apparently born with a female body but had an extra set of gentalia which associated him with the other males in the clan. The (AYA(HAYA) dyad of light in Persian relates him to the sun for he was destined to become the castrated priestly son who in PHASE ONE officiated at the side of his mother over the rites of the rising and the setting sun. In subsequent PHASES when he became castrated he moved into the Tibetan 'intermediate state' (BARADO) of not still being a boy and not really becoming a girl.

SYN (IS HANA) in Polish is 'son' (IS HANA).

SYN (IS HANA) in Greek is 'with'

SIN (IS HANA) in Spanish is 'without'

SIN (IS HANA) in English is 'loss of grace'

All the above words deal with some aspect of the sun (IS HANA).

SUN (IS HANA);

As -syn (IS HANA) in Greek is 'with' the body of Mother Earth shining above Her surFACE.

Syn (IS HANA); As son (IS HANA) in Polish deals very early in PHASE ONE with Mother Earth as the Mother of Her son (IS HANA), of it rising out of Her horizontal side at dawn. The pubic (Y) at the center off sYn establishes him as being at one with Her.

Sin (IS HANA) in Spanish is 'without' its solar rays of light above the surFACE of Mother Earth passing through the 'dark night' of the soul (IS HALA) under Her surFACE. Sol (IS HALA) is the sun in Spanish. HALA is another dyad for the solar (IS HALA-) disc.

Sin (IS HANA) in PHASE THREE dealt with loss of grace when the male solar deity morphed into a celestial Father God in the sky *away* and *above* the body of Mother Earth. A SIN (IS HANA) having its ancient links with the benevolent, predictable sun (IS HANA) came to represent unacceptable behavior, 'loss of grace' and a sin (IS HANA). It originally meant that the body of Mother Earth was without Her light, as darkness enveloped Her surFACE.

SYNAGOGUE (IS HANAGAGA);

Triple dyads (HANA) (NAGA) (GAGA). The sun (IS HANA) and son (IS HANA), the snake (IS NAKA, NAGA) the eunuch priesthood and (GAGA) surface in the word synagogue. We are in PHASE TWO of male spiritual territory. The place of worship of the ancient prehistoric mothers move out of the cave or the great seas into the temple (the forehead, mind, third eye) of the historic fathers. They are still dealing with the snake (IS NAKA, NAGA) Kundalini electro magnetic energy rising up from the the body of Mother Earth but transformed into a villain in the Garden of Eden, not as the beloved guide of the sun but as the carrier of some ancient magical knowledge that only Eve had been privy to. The mystical birthing breath of the mothers symbolized by the snake, serpent, dragon, worm surfaces here and had to be destroyed with subsequent clitorectomies. The Levites worshipped the Leviathan, the water snake (IS NAKA, NAGA) the watery body of the ancient Mother Earth.

All that ancient belief of 'source' out of the body of Mother Earth had to be suppressed and obliterated as male search for the father resulted in the creation of a male diety *away* and *above* the body of Mother Earth. The (GAGA) on the end of synagogue (is hanaGAGA) deals with begetting and the begetting deals with speech, the gaggle (GAGAla) at the top of the mountain close to their new temporary male deity, the solar disc. It became the altar of the priests cum rabbis creating a disparate reality based on the hidden MIND of the Father rather than the apparent BODY of the Mother. In PHASE THREE the hidden Father God makes His appearance and pushes the sun (son) off his celestial throne. All this continues to happen all around the Middle East except in Egypt for a short period of time with the god Atun. To this day in Japan in Shinto (IS HANAta) is still worshipped as the sun (IS HANA) god.

CHEEK, CHIN, Chicks;

Beginning in PHASE ONE at the time of the ancient migrations the CHEEK and CHIN come into play primarily out of the heads of birds. The CH sound is associated with beginnings and the SOUNDS made by newly hatched CHicks, emerging out of the bodies of CHickens, and other birds CHeeping their way into the SOUNDS of life. Their coming and going, North and South, on the continent of Africa established the beginnings and ends of the ancient migrations.

The Polish word for peeing as szczy (IS CHA) out of the wound on the horizontal side of the body of Mother Earth announcing the time of Her celestial peeing with the coming of the monsoons and birds at the beginning of the ancient migrations.

CHEW (CHAWA or JAWA);

Human beings dealt with food masticated within the oral cavity, wallowed in the wet (WA-) saliva for it to become slippery enough to be swallowed down the gullet. It is within the lower jaw (JAWA) on the bottom of the face holding the letter (W) reflecting the SHAPE of the letter (M) above, that the activity of chewing (CHAWA) takes place. What contains the activity of chewing is also the CHEEK (CHAKA) pouch. The activity of chewing begins the life of nutritive survival. Without chewed food there would be famine and a problem with survival. Mothers of many species, especially birds often chew (CHAWA) and regurgitate food for their young. (CH) and J(G-gee) are often interchangeable. Hidden in the word reGURgitate we establish links with the mouth of Mother Earth. For Mother Earth gave birth to Her greatest helper when She gave birth to the sun out of Her mountainous mouth. In the word reGURgitate is the dyad GUR (GARA) and GORA (GARA) in Polish means mountain. As She vomited or regurgitated the sun out of Her mountainous mouth in the Eastern sky, the sun, Her CHild, became the bearer of food for all living creatures and Mother Earth's greatest gift to the rest of Her CHildren.

CHI In Chinese is the 'mystical breath;

It filled everything between the body of Mother Earth and heaven'. It echoes the same concept as the Tibetan 'Bardo' of the 'intermediate state' that also reflected the concept of separation between the body of Mother Earth and the heavens. The (B) in Bardo (BARA-) deals with the 'two in one' concept with the sun (RA) either halving the sky at the equator or of moving above and below Her majestic terrain.

CH'I in Chinese is the 'female soul';

It seems that everything that existed between the body of Mother Earth and the sky was considered to have the soul of a female. Without a doubt we are in female centrality and PHASE ONE. There is an ancient community in China at Lake Lugu where the uncle is the head of the family, no actual marriage exists and women not only live with their mothers but are free to choose with whom they sleep.

CHU (CHA) in Chinese is 'beginning' and 'young bird';

At the time that the migrating birds returned to their nests in the tropical savannahs, they not only announced the 'beginning' of the ancient herbivore migrations but laid their own mounds of eggs creating a multitude of 'young birds'.

KUCHA (KACHA) in Swahili is 'dawn';

Dawn is the beginning of a new day. It is the birds that awaken before the sun has risen, and share their onomatopoeic song with the rest of the sleeping world. They wake up the whole jungle and savannah to help the sun on its journey across the brilliantly lit sky.

Section Two

A (CHA) in Bemba is 'dawn';

The SOUND of CHeeping, CHirping, cooing and clacking with their open beaks must have made such a racket that at 'dawn' no one, including the sun, could have stayed asleep.

CHEN (CHANA) in Chinese is 'morning';

It is the (NA) of 'emergence on the surface' and a 'change from a former state' that surfaces with the birds and their rapturous song greeting the sun in the 'morning'.

CIEN (CHANA) in Polish is a 'shadow';

For the Egyptians the 'shadow' as Khaibit (HABATA) was one of the seven souls given to a child at birth, and like a habit (HABATA) created at the time of their panic stricken helpless infancy could never be jettisoned. The sun emerging at dawn, negating the darkness of night created the light of day. The darkness of night hid the shadows from sight.

CHIZI (CHASA) in Chinese is 'a new born child';

(out of the mothers blood (SA). It has lnks with the CH'I of the female soul that gives birth to 'a new born child'.

CZAS (CHASA) in Polish;

Is both monthly lunar time and bloody (SA) periodic menstruation that creates a new born child,

CHILD (CHALADA) in English;

is 'a new born baby' the 'gift of '(DA), of (CHI) out of the LA of the mother and a beginning into life.

CALA (CHALA) 'Earth' in Bemba;

Deals with the body of Mother Earth as the LA of the Lady of the Land defining the pLAnet where the beginning of all life occurs.

CIELO (CHALA) in Spanish is 'sky';

Is the belly of air nto which the sun rises at dawn to begin a new day and the moon rises at twilight to begin a new night. In both cases they create new beginnings in the body above them.

CIALO (CHALA) in Polish is a 'body';

That which on a female (LA), is the container for the beginning of a new life.

CELLO (CHALA) is in English a 'musical instrument';

SHAPED like a female body'. As a female SHAPE begins the journey into life so the musical viBRation of a cello begins its journey into SOUND.

CHELA (CHALA) in Sanskrit is a young 'student';

Often a child or a slave to the master, as female bodies and the body of Mother Earth were considered to be slaves (IS LAVA-) to the process of menstrual and lavic (LAVA-) blood production.

Dealing with 'little things', what comes to mind is the Mexican CHIHUAHUA (CHAHAHA).

To continue in a similar vein of HOMOPHONIC SOUND dealing with 'beginnings'. The following words deal with the sun rising at the beginning of day, the sun setting at the beginning of night, and more.

MASHARIKI (MASHARAKA) in Swahili is 'East';

Reka (RAKA) in Polish means 'hand' and in this case deals with the sun as the helping hand of Mother Earth pulling the sun out of Her belly (HARA) at dawn. (RA) is the sun. (KA) is Mother Earth the maker of smaller aspects.

MAISHA (MAYASHA) in Swahili is 'life';

With the AYA of light and dawn in it. Life began on the body of Mother Earth with the birth of light in the Eastern sky. The dyad of MAYA surfaces here, as it does in Buddhism and in Central America.

SHAMASH (IS HAMASHA) of the Aramean Pantheon is 'the sun';

With the first dyad (HAMA) it originated out of PHASE ONE and the perception dealing with the rising sun as the bloody (HAMA) coagulate out of the body of Mother Earth, emerging as the solar disc. It has links with the Swahili name for 'life' as MAISHA and the 'East', as MASHARIKI (mashaRAKA). Echoes of a distant memory surface here for the sun surfaces as the helping hand of Mother Earth. In Polish reka (RAKA), the third dyad in MASHARIKI (mashaRAKA) is the word for 'hand'. It is the helping hand of the sun that rises in the Eastern sky at dawn creating both light and life and helping Mother Earth.

SHAMROCK (IS HAMARAKA);

In Ireland is the three lobed plant a trefoil, that in PHASE THREE became a symbol for the Christian Trinity, hiding within its linguistic origins, its source out of PHASE ONE. It too surfaces with the bloody sun (HAMA) and the triadic SHAPE representing the dual aspect of motherhood (SASA) as the triangular pubis on the body of the individual human mother out of which her blood (SA) creates a baby and the other (SA) as the spiral SHAPE of the lavic form (SA) out of the triangular volcano on the body of Mother Earth. As the helping hand (RAKA) of Mother Earth, it symbolically also represents its triparted journey of the sun; above, upon and below Her majestic planetary body.

BAALSAMIN (BALA IS HAMANA);

In the Aramean Pantheon was the 'master of the skies'. Who else but the bloody sun as (HAMA). In PHASE ONE the BA of the baby followed the A (ah) of the mother. In PHASE TWO the BA of the father followed the A (ah) of the mother. In PHASE THREE the BA became reflected to become the AB (BA/AB) not only of water in Hebrew but also the father. As the redefinitions intensified male names became the reflection of female names and the Gods assumed the reflected names of the Goddesses as the reflective quality of water originally established the Mother above the plane and the emerging Father below the plane. AB became the reflected name not only of Hebrew but of Middle Eastern fathers.

SHAMBALA (IS HAMABALA);

In Hinduism is a linguistic reflection of BAALSHAMIN, the AB defining the father in the Middle East as 'master of the skies'. SHAMBALA dealt with the body of Mother Earth and BAAL SHAMIN was Her male reflection in the sky. In Tibetan SHAMBALA deals with Shangrila (IS HANAGARALA), the mountain (GORA) in Polish, of the sun (IS HANA).

SHAMBLE (IS HAMABALA) is an English word that tells its own convoluted story.

SHAME (IS HAMA);

In PHASE TWO emerges as the beginning of Biblically inspired guilt dealing primarily with female nudity her sexuality and the mystical ecstasy accompanying the birthing breath of spiritual transformation originally experienced only by her.

SHAMAN (IS HAMANA);

Was a medicine man, one who dealt with 'hidden' powers that had been associated with the birthing breath of the mothers and its accompanying movement into power, ecstasy and healing. The same linguistic construct surfaces in PHASE THREE in the name for the Egyptian God Ammon, Amun (HAMANA) 'hidden' in his great temple, masturbating existence into being every night. The ram and goose were associated with him. It moves into omen (HAMANA) and amen (HAMANA). The Egyptian Hieroglyphic sign associated with amen (HAMANA) is a 'pregnant belly'. It gives pause to the perception that the hands of the mothers masturbated the baby into being. That is why the Egyptian god Amun had to masturbate in the dead of night hidden from sight to create the universe. They also used an implement to break the hymen (HAMANA) on a potential mother to make sexuality more pleasureful and birthing easier. All the above concepts were 'together with' the 'hand', mano (MANA) in Spanish from a slightly different direction;

SHAMASH, CHEMOSH;

'Sun God of Sippar' rival of Yahveh. If CHEMOSH (CHAMASHA) was not only the sun God, but the risen sun at dawn, a rival of Yahveh, (YAVAHA) then we are dealing here with the battle between the primacy of Mother Earth and the primacy of the risen sun *away* and *above* the body of Mother Earth in PHASE TWO, represented by the castrated first born sons who not only flourished through the underground priesthood but asked the 'why' of their peripheral state in the process of 'creation'. In Polish CZEMU (CHAMA) is the dyad for 'why', or (Y). (MASHA) surfaces here as the sun establishing its links with the Swahili life and also the Swahili East.

The YA of Yahveh in Hebrew has links with the SHAPE of the female pubis (Y), as does the name for God in Wolof originally as Yalla, (HAYALA). Out of PHASE ONE it is one of the names for the sun as Mother Earth's helper; aya (HAYA) as 'light' in Persian and aya (HAYA) as 'dawn' in Assyrian.

In Wolof YAAY (YAYA) is the name for 'mother', or 'older woman', out of which in PHASE TWO and THREE arose ALLAH (HALA) having links with the ancient sun, Greek eelyos (HALA-), as a single unit with the body of Mother Earth. In Polish the name for eggs is jaja (YAYA). Who lays eggs if not the mother, be she a bird, or a snake, or Mother Earth, the hen (HANA) that laid the golden egg of the sun (IS HANA). The same name covers both the mother hen (HANA) and Her offspring the sun (IS HANA), for in PHASE ONE they had been considered to be at one unit.

The color of the sun at dawn as usually a pale yellow (YALAWA) establishes its links not only with its emergence out of water (WA), but with the process of 'beginning' itself out of (LAWA, LAVA), whose emergence upon the surFACE creating land, established the possibility of the 'beginning' of terrestrial life.

CZEMU (CHAMA) Polish why;

The grief stricken tribute to the setting sun surfacing in the Polish word CZEMU (CHAMA) 'why' (Y). The wailing of 'why' at the watery Western wall of death, where the sun sank out of sight, died to its light, was swallowed by the body of Mother Earth where the accompanying eunuchization and maiming of young boys in those ancient caves occurred.

CIEMNO (CHAMANA);

In Polish means 'darkness'. The hand mano (MANA) in Spanish, pulled down the mantle of darkness and snuffed out (CHA), the 'beginning' of the life of the sun, associated with the SOUNDS made by chirping birds coming at the time of foaling and egg laying out of Swahili, Bemba and Chinese.

In PHASE THREE attached to the HAMA of 'blood' out of female bodies and the sun, there evolved the concept of SHAME (IS HAMA) dealing with the nude physical body of the mother and the passage of blood out of her pubic hole that made babies. It fell afoul of the male 'idea' that all of existence emerged out of the 'mind of God'. The process of birthing not only became hidden but menstruation as 'the curse' that accompanied it, became shameful. In the Middle Eastern societies burkas not only hide the 'seductive' female face but the flowing mantle also hides the obvious pregnant belly of the mother as the apparent parent.

SHAM;

There evolved a subsequent hope, which was represented by the five pointed starry pentacle of the oppressed women. The tryad of the mothers in PHASE ONE existed as part of their journey of centrality and power. Then in PHASES TWO and THREE it became number four of male control. Women fighting for their place in the sun came up with the five fingers of the mother and the five pointed pentacle as their emerging symbol. In PHASE THREE the pentacle became redfined as the star of Satan, of the devil, of all things to be feared. It tried to say that what had occurred in PHASE ONE was a SHAM (IS HAMA), it was a lie. Male questing for answers to their periphery in the birthing process, their asking of 'why' czemu in Polish, created a world based on the 'fantasy of the father', 'the mist of the mister', 'the fallacy of the phallus'. The ancient heritage of the mothers (MATAra) became redefined as myth (MATA). Male heroic search for ecstasy and fearlessness resulted in the asking of WHY (Y) of their peripheral state.

THE ANSWER TO WHY IS ALWAYS A LIE.

SHIM (IS HAMA) is a hoe;

With the growth of the left hemisphere, the right handed side of the brain, and ascent into territoriality, agriculture and the settlement onto conquered lands, there emerged a name for SHIM (IS HAMA) as a hoe that which cut into the body of Mother Earth preparing it for planting, made it bleed (HAMA) out of the red soil of Africa.

In PHASE ONE the sun at the equator cut the belly of air in half at the time when the belly of air through which the sun passed had been considered to be at one with the body of Mother Earth, Her bloody companion and family member. In PHASE TWO, as male role in specific paternity was becoming known the 'hoe' cut the body of Mother Earth in twain preparing it for the planting of the male seed. There follows an inescapable conclusion that the cutting of the female body in twain preparing it for the planting of the male seed was a reflection of the process of genital mutilation of individual women.

SHIM (IS HAMA) a wedge;

It is used as a 'wedge', or a piece of wood in carpentry to prop up a side, to balance it, to make it come out even. The concept of a male mind sourcing all of reality as the mind of God, put a 'wedge' (SHIM) between the human creature and the natural law of cyclical processes inherent in the body of Mother Earth. It created an imbalance.

As a prop it had to be metaphorically wedged in place to balance the male need to be the source of all creation. Mother Earth became an object of vilification, tilled mercilessly for the male seed to thrive. She had to be conquered, abused, exploited, a fate shared by Her daughters.

It seems a far stretch that the words shim (IS HAMA), sham (IS HAMA) have some relationship to the sun in its ancient bloody HAMA aspect. It does surface in the English word to SHIMMER (IS HAMA-) that is defined as light flickering, glowing, gleaming, shining brightly. Does 'blood' shimmer? No. Does 'shame' shimmer? No. Does a 'lie' shimmer? No. Does a 'wedge' shimmer? No. But the sun glows, gleams, shines, shimmers, as it reflects on the surFACE of the waters below. Coming out of ancient mother centered PHASE ONE, as one of the names of the bloody sun ema (HAMA) in Greek, also means 'one' (HANA), the reflected bloody gore that the sun sank into the open maw on the body of Mother Earth as it descended into its watery grave in the Western sky.

Before that, in PHASE ONE, and stage one was the hum (HAMA) of the mothers telling their children that the food was edible, mm good as sent, the lips 'together' creating the humming sound. The same process in stage two extended to the body of Mother Earth as She swallowed, as She ate the sun in the Western horizon. She put Her two lips together, the mountains on top (M) and their reflected mounds in the waters (W) below and hacked it free from its life, saying you are delicious, you are edible, you are worthy of transformation, to be cooked within my internal oven, so that you can rise to the light of a new triumphant day in the East.

GRUB (GARABA) in English as 'larva', 'to dig' and 'food'.

GRUB (GARABA) in Polish means 'grave';

To 'dig', 'grave' and 'food', have some common aspects in them. You 'dig' a 'grave' and you also 'dig' for 'grub' as tubers with your fingers or angled sticks, also while searching for food.

GRUB (GARABA) as 'larva' takes us further back into metaphoric ancient history. The larval stage of an insect is the stage where trans-formation, or a metamorphosis takes place. The moth or butterfly lays eggs, the eggs pupate, go into a stage of metamorphosis and emerge as caterpillars. The caterpillars go into a state of change form a chrysalis to emerge as moths or butterflies. They change from a recognizable worm, grub or caterpillar into a flying insect no longer locked to the ground. Its dominion becomes the 'intermediate state' of air.

The process deals with the same perception that was believed to be inherent in the journey of the sun above and within the body of Mother Earth. The bloody disc of the setting sun went through its own journey of transformation and rebirth within the body of Mother Earth after it set into the gory Western waters.

The lavic out pouring out of a volcano as a turgid liquid menstrual blood transformed itself into solid land. The coursing solar blood within the body of Mother Earth, under Her surFACE, pushing its way through Her intestines, through Her womb of transformation, changed itself out of the lava (LAVA) into a process that had its links with the larva, (LA(RA)VA) of insects, especially moths and butterflies. Then it moved into a process and into an internal coagulation of blood that created the integral disc of the sun at dawn. The (RA) in the center of (LAVA) into (LA(RA)VA) gives us a salient clue that we are dealing with the metamorphosis of the sun (RA) within the body of Mother Earth.

The phonemic construct of grub (GARABA) contains within it two overlapping dyads, (GARA) and (RABA). (GARA) is the mountain, gura (GARA) in Polish, the begetter (GA) of the transformed sun (RA), at dawn. (RABA) deals with the dual activity (BA) of the sun (RA) rising and setting encoded in the letter (B), as the two lips on the mothers face seen in profile in stage one which defined the concept of 'two in one'. So the larval stage of the grub was likened to the larval stage of the sun. Before it emerged into a new life at dawn it had been buried within the mounds of gestating bellies in the body of Mother Earth, as all things were perceived to have been, before they reappeared upon and above Her surFACE.

The ancient word grub (GARABA) as 'grave' in Polish, echoes that ancient perception linking the 'grave' of a human being as a place of transformation. To be buried (BARA-) in the ground, thousands of years later and into PHASE THREE, although the original meaning had been lost, was likened to the metamorphoses and larval stage of an insect and to the intestinal transformative passage of the sun through the body of Mother Earth using the butterflies and moths as symbols of the process in stage five.

As the ancient perceptions became lost or obliterated all kinds of other metaphorical fantasies took their place. The word grub (GARABA) as an insect in English and grave in Polish and the grave (GARAVA) itself in English, share another linguistic link. The (B) and (V) at the end of the second dyad are interchangeable in both words. They are made in the same area of the mouth.

CHRYSALIS (KARASA-);

Is a hard gold colored sheath of a butterfly, the state into which the larva of most insects must pass, before becoming an imago (HAMAGA). An imago is a 'perfect' stage of an insect after it metamorphoses. The golden color of the chrysalis and the (HAMA) of the imago (HAMAGA), the 'perfect' end product, establish their links with the ancient bloody (HAMA-) transformed sun out of PHASE ONE.

The rites of transformation were officiated over by the eunuch, non-reproductive priesthood, located within the bowels of the Earth, within the caves and burial chambers where the 'hidden' processes of transformation took place. Since the average human being at that ancient time had no knowledge of what happened to the sun once it set into that flat round maternal surFACE in the horizontal West and then was reborn to a new life at dawn in the East, then the soul once it was swallowed back into the body of Mother Earth must have gone through a similar process. The sun popped out of the body of Mother Earth at dawn as a new baby popped out of an individual mothers body every ten lunar months. The priesthood had a field day establishing the ancient belief of reincarnation that relied on the process of habitual, unrelenting solar rebirth.

Clues surface further with the English soul (IS HALA) and sol (IS HALA) as the Spanish sun. Both have links with the Greek eelyos (HALASA) as the sun in its aspect as that which emerges at a right angle out of the surFACE of Mother Earth codified by the SHAPE of the letter L representing the very ancient tongue out of PHASE ONE and stage one pushing food out of the individual mothers face, ie regurgitating it.

CHRIST (KARASA-);
Was not that He was hung on the cross (KARASA). Actually He was hung on a furka, a rood, a sort of crutch. The name of Christ (KARASA-) came out of the fact that He was a transformed male. He had gone through the process of crystallization, purification and transformation. He had been a chrysalis (KARASAlasa), had his sins burned out when He spent His time isolated in His desert cocoon. A crystal (KARASAtala) having linguistic links with Christ has been called a stone of transformation. He had internalized the female side of His brain, grew a wide bridge (BARA-) between the two hemispheres in the process thickening His corpus collosum. He became a hybrid, no longer purely male, but more like an androgyny, having internalized the female side of his brain. In PHASE THREE He became redefined as not singularly human but in some way a celestial deity as son of God, as Mother Earth in PHASE ONE had originally been the only source, the only God. In some ancient way He had links with the eunuch priesthood who were also considered hybrids.

In ancient days not only eunuchs became the keepers of the flame, asserting that they kept the sun alive through its intestinal journey within the body of Mother Earth. They were joined by male homosexuals. Male homosexuality has been understood to be the internalization of the female essence before birth. Often with that process came not only a balance but gifts of leadership, of creativity, of the 'spirit', of healing and of prophecy. The domain what became the monotheistic patriarchal 'religions' of the contemporary world came out of that ancient convoluted subterranean mystique.

MARIPOSA (MARAPASA) is the name for 'butterfly' in Spanish on the Ibernian (HABARAnana) peninsula;

It is also a derogatory name for a male homosexual, one who has gone through the hybridization process of internal transformation. A similar perception uses a series of different SOUNDS.

COCOON (KAKANA) is a larval stage of an insect;
The phoneme (KA) deals with the mother creating smaller replicas of herself, be she an individual mother, or Mother Earth. The (KA) repeated as (KAKA) in COcoon (KAKANA) on one level moves into a double creation of a fetus and of feces. The (NA) at the end deals with 'emergence on the surface', or 'the negation of a former state'. But here we are dealing with a process that had been likened to cooking (KAKA-). The fires within the body of Mother Earth in Her oven (HAVANA) cooked (KAKA-) the perambulating sun so that its lavic, liquid state became a solid disc of the sun, that like an egg

popped out of a hen's body, it too popped out of Her birth canal at Her flat circular horizontal rim, sometimes Her anus (HANASA) at dawn.

(KAKA) dyad is associatied with birds and the cooing SOUNDS that they made with their beaks as they returned to their nesting sites. As they sat on their eggs they also seemed to cook (KAKA) their chicks into being. Not only the eggs emerged out of the bodies of female birds but a fetus and feces (KAKA) also emerged out of the bodies of the mother apparently as a result of the internal fires associated with cooking (KAKA-). Here we have the feces as coagulated manure, fetus as coagulated blood and feta the cheese as curdled milk.

All of existence as it spent some of its time gestating within the body of Mother Earth went through a trans-formative process of cooking (KAKA-). The same process extended to the bodies of individual mothers in whose bellies the blood coagulated (KAGA-) and created a firm, small replica of the mother, steaming as it emerged upon the surface. The sounds of (K) and (G) are interchangeable.

PUPA (PAPA);

As the trans-formative stage of an insect, pupa surfaces in Latin as the name for 'girl', the young human female creature through whose body a trans-formation occurred. In PHASE ONE before male role in specific procreation had been known, her blood coagulated to create a baby.

In Polish it is more explicit, for a pupa is the vulgar name for the 'vulva'. Also in Polish a pupka (PAPAKA) is a small pupa. (KA) in Polish stands for the female diminutive out of the letter X of the buttox halved vertically. The pupa (PAPA) is the double passage (PA), one 'of blood', announcing that the girl had been ready for motherhood, the other (PA) that she is 'the via' of passage (PA), for the actual baby, the valve of the vulva phenomenon.

PAPA in English father. The papa dyad in PHASE TWO in English became associated with the 'father'. The concept came out of something more concrete than the concept of 'passage'. It was 'passage' indeed, but it dealt with the redefined perception of the male penis passing through the female body. PAPA is also the unvoiced BABA of Middle Eastern fatherhood.

PAPAYA (PAPAYA) tree in Wolof. Looks like a trunk, a penis, with the papaya fruit like testicles hugging it, way up on top as it reaches for the light, AYA in Persian.

PAA or PAPPE (PAPA) is father in Wolof.

PAPA for the Bugotu of the South Pacific;

Means 'to carry pick-a-back' which is what a papaya tree seems to do, carry the testicle like fruit 'pick-a-back' on its penis like trunk.

The many quests that human males set off on, from the golden fleece (FALASA), the golden glow of the sun as the shining phallus (FALASA), to the holy grail (GARALA). Grail (GARALA) and girl (GARALA) have the same phonemic construct. The dyad (GARA) is mountain, gura (GARA) in Polish. LA deals with the angle of the emergence of the sun out of the body of Mother Earth at Her Eastern horizontal rim. The girl (GARALA) in question may have been the virginal body of Mother Earth in Her aspect as the sole giver of birth to all that emerged upon Her surFACE; of plants, of the heavenly bodies and of birds.

Or it may mean that in PHASE THREE the Holy Grail (GARALA) is the search for the bloody cup of the last supper of Christ. The bloody cup may have been the girl (GARALA) who as Mary Magdalene carried the holy seed of Christ into the future i.e. the mother's gifts of; love thy neighbor, turn the other cheek, inclusion, tolerance, cooperation, nurturing, etc. Leonardo would have been pleased.

As the butterfly, the diurnal flutterer became a symbol for the transformation of the sun as it passed through the body of Mother Earth after it set at night, so the MOTH of the MOTHER became the symbol for the nocturnal trans-formative activity of the moon as it passed out of sight through the body of Mother Earth. The moth of the mother dealing with the moon established the moon as the messenger that brought menstruation and the beginning of motherhood, the subsequent Hermes as the messenger of the moon of the Greeks construct.

WANG (WANAGA) Swahili Queen of the West;

Bringing up the linguistic rear are the dyads of (WANA) and (NAGA). WANG (WANAGA) in Swahili is the 'Queen of the West'. The sun guided by the ubiquitous snake (IS NAKA, NAGA) sinking into the waters (WA) of the Western sea surfaces in this construct as the eternal loser. It is Mother Earth the 'Queen of the West' who is the winner (WANA-) as She cannibalizes him and sends him to begin his transformative journey through Her body.

WANG (WANAGA) in Chinese is 'to die, to hide, to perish';

We are dealing with the sun guided by the metaphoric snake (IS NAKA, NAGA) who lost its light in the Western waters as it sank, 'died, hid, perished into Her side, the Western horizontal mouth of Mother Earth as She swallowed him.

WANG MU in Chinese is 'mother';

We are dealing with 'Mother' Earth who swallowed the sun at Her Western watery horizontal rim.

WANGO (WANAGA) Australian 'boomerang';

The boomerang had been considered as a metaphor for the sun. For the sun always went in one direction and like the boomerang always came back. It also expanded to define the concept of reincarnation.

SWING (IS WANAGA);

Deals with going in one direction and of coming back.

UWINGU (HAWANAGA) Swahili 'sky';

The (HA) at the beginning of uwingu (HAWANAGA) establishes its links with the 'sky', the belly or air above the body of Mother Earth. It reiterates the ancient concept in PHASE ONE that Mother Earth and Her belly of air through which the sun passed were the winners (WANA-), were at one with each other. This perception of atoneness came before the shift into male centrality when in PHASES TWO and THREE the battle between the body of Mother Earth killing the sun to its rays of light merged into a planetary war reflecting the battles that were emerging between females and males on Her surFACE reflecting the hemispheric battle for supremacy within their brains.

WING (WANAGA);

In English deals with a bird that uses the sky as a vehicle of passage. The word for sky in Swahili is uwingu (haWANAGA). The word swing (IS WANAGA) also deals with the birds on the wing (WANAGA) semiannually migrating in one direction in the spring and then always coming back to Africa in the fall.

DOWN (DAWANA);

The movement down is the 'gift of' (DA) of winning (WANA-) and the winner is the watery body of Mother Earth as She overpowers the sun, Her son and he slips through Her lips as She swallows him in the West.

DAWN (DAWANA);

It is at dawn (DAWANA) as also the 'gift of' (DA) winning (WANA-), that the winner in this case is the sun. For no matter what happens it rises again at dawn (DAWANA). It follows the same trajectory as all the movements back and forth, the wings (WANAGA) that carry the birds, the wango (WANAGA) of the Australian boomerang, the swing (IS WANAGA). All of these activities occur in the Swahili uwingu (haWANAGA) as the sky, the belly of air above the body of Mother Earth. As the sun gets ready to make its appearance in the Eastern sky, the first tentative rays of the sun barely reaching over the horizontal rim on the body of Mother Earth, were likened to the downy (DAWANA) feathers on the body of a newly born baby chick making its entrance into the world.

RULE NINETEEN;
Check out METAPLASM or the transposition, adding, subtracting of syllables and letters in words.

Exit-exi(s)t, (HAKASATA)-(HAKASA(SA)TA);
To exist is to make an exit, or be hacked (HAKA-) free out of the bloody (SA) coos (KASA) out of the individual mothers body, or of hacking free of the bloody Western sun out of the body of Mother Earth.

Oni-o(m)ni (HANA) (HAMANA);
Add the birthing Mother Earth (MA) the maker of many omni (HAMANA), to the one oni (HANA) sun (IS HANA). Omni (HAMANA) deals with many humans (HAMANA).

Lava-la(ra)va);
To become the metaphoric hidden larva (LARAVA) of transformation, the lavic (LAVA-) internal fires as the solar menstrual blood as magma of Mother Earth have had to be helped along by the nightly underground journey of the sun (RA) through Her intestinal maze.

Lady-lord (LADA), (LA(RA)DA);
In PHASES TWO and THREE add the male god RA of the sun to Mother Earth, the LA of the LAdy of the LAnd, (LA(RA)DA) for him to rise above Her and become Her lord and master. She who had been the leader (LADA-) of the ancient matriarchal migratory group in PHASE ONE had to relinquish her position in PHASE THREE to the emerging lord (LARADA) the 'gift of' (DA) of the lady (LADA) as his role in specific paternity was becoming known. Her primary left hand (LARA) had been left behind.

Orgasm-orga(NI)sm (HARAGASAMA)-HARAGA(NA)SAMA);
SAMA in Polish, the dyad at the end, means she alone and that is what masturbation establishes. Masturbation is the creation of the spasmic peristalsis in the belly (HARA) of new (NI,NA) life, out of the pubic angle, the

rug (RAGA) or angle in Polish.

The birthing breath of the mother that created the orgasm was also the metaphoric flying rug or carpet of transformation as the myth of Aladdin's ritual passage into ecstasy metaphorically suggests. A drug (DARAGA) used as a hallucinogen is also the 'gift of' (DA) the rug (RAGA). If you rubbed the bottle ie if you masturbated yourself you could give birth. A bottle with its long neck and ball at the end had been considered like a vagina with the womb inside the mothers body. The genie (JANA) has linguistic links with gyno (JANA) the Greek name for woman. The three wishes dealt with the triparted reality that the SHAPE of the volcanic cone on the body of Mother Earth and the SHAPE of the pubis on the body of the individual mother represented as males rode off on their quests of discovery.

Sham-sha(lo)m (IS HAMA) (IS HA(LA)MA);

The male sham (IS HAMA) or blood letting in PHASE ONE being like the daughter with a baby in her belly, arose out of shalom (IS HALAMA) an ancient Hebrew greeting of peace dealing with the sun, sol (IS HALA). With the LA as the Lady of the Land deleted from shalom (IS HA(LA)MA) it became a sham (IS HAMANA). Ironically sham (IS HAMANA) aspires to have human (HAMANA) in his linguistic name as the empty bellied male aspired to have a baby in his belly.

War-word-wor(l)d-sword(WARA), (IS WARADA), world WARA(LA) LADA); Take the LA of the lady out of world (WARA(LA)DA) and you are in the left hemispheric brain in PHASE THREE 'in the beginning was the WORD...', add the emphatic (S) as blood to the WORD it becomes a SWORD. Remove the (DA) as 'gift of' and (S) as blood off the SWORD and you get WAR. War (WARA) reflected the battle on the planetary plane between the mothers and the fathers. It metaphorically explained how the body of Mother Earth in Her aspect as water (WA) swallowed the sun (RA) every night. The sinking male sun rebelled and fought Her on the planetary level as emerging males with their growing knowledge of specific paternity in search of their own father Gods did the same on the plane below. The same battle became linguistically codified in Mars (MARASA) the word for the God of War. Mother Earth (MA) as the Western coffin of water swallowed the reluctant raging, rampaging sun (RA) but this time he rose *away* and *above* Her body and sailed up into space as the new emerging base of male power base in PHASE THREE having links with and represented by the hidden mind of God.

War (WARA) created wards (WARADA) of the state and slaves;

A ward (WARADA) is the 'gift of' (DA) war (WARA). A ward is also a reward (RAWARADA) for the battle that had been won with the subsequent enslavement of the enemy. They as slaves and new wards of the winners were destined to work (WARAKA) for the rest of their lives. Work (WARAKA) is a small (KA) war. Not only that, but the Polish word for hand that does the work sneaks in here. The Polish hand is reka (RAKA) the second dyad in work (WARAKA). No nobility of labor here. In Polish a lip is called WARga. It is the WARga or lip on the horizontal surFACE of Mother Earth that declares war on the sun and does the killing. Originally it dealt with the mouth of the carnivorous mother that did the sMOTHERING.

The heritage of female defined humanity worshipping Mother Earth out of PHASE ONE should have read:

'IN THE BEGINNING WAS THE WORLD' (WARADALA) delete the LAdy of the LAnd out of WORLD (WARA(LA)DA) and surprise of surprises, in PHASE THREE and male centrality you get

'IN THE BEGINNING WAS THE WORD'. The myth of Avalon (HAVA (LA) NA) emerges here.

Have-ha(l)ve, (HAVA-HA(LA)VA);

To have (HAVA) a baby you had to halve (HALAVA) the lady. The concept of clitorectomies must have entered the scene in PHASE TWO in order to create this dyadic configuration out of the body of Mother Earth.

Lava had been considered the menstrual solar blood out of the body of Mother Earth that gouged and halved (haLAVA-) Her terrain in the process of its passage down Her flanks. It also expands in PHASE THREE to the rays of the sun cutting the horizontal rim of Mother Earth with their stiletto fingers, for the sun to be born at dawn. In this case it reflects the process of clitorectomies that was occurring on hapless women in PHASE THREE.

Hebrew (HABARA), Arab (HARABA);

The (BARA and RABA) dyads are transposed and reflected. The (BARA) dyad out of Hebrew (haBARA) and the reflected Arab (haRABA) dyad out of Arab tell their own story. Hebrew(HABARA) is halved by the SOUND associated with the letter (B) and the semiannual coming of birds (BARA-) halving not only the migratory year but the belly of air above the surFACE of Mother Earth hiding in its folds the dyad for the 'intermediate state' of trance. As most of the ancient words dealing with processes may have been reflected, so the word Arab (HA(RA)BA) establishes the duality of the sun 'the two in one' concept its rising and setting giving us one of the linguistic roots of the sun as (HABA) morphing into the English word for habit (HABA-).

Kosher (KASARA) and curse (KARASA);

The second dyads become (SARA/RASA) having an ancient relationship they became transposed and reflected. Both words deal with blood letting (SA) that have had their origins out of the female coos (KASA). Kosher (KASARA) has direct linguistic links with the female coos (KASA). In the word curse (KA(RA)SA) there emerges the male sun god Ra halving the coos (KASA) of Mother Earth in twain establishing the concept of a curse (KARASA) in PHASE THREE that became associated with the menstrual blood letting of quintessent girls. The coos (KASA) deals with the mother, be she the individual mother or Mother Earth with her or Her menstrual blood (SA) creating smaller (KA) replicas out of their bodies.

In PHASE ONE because blood had been considered to be sacred and the only source of life, the practice expanded to the blood letting and collection of slaughtered animals. Their blood had not been considered less sacred as in PHASE THREE their bloodless bodies were offered to the emerging male gods and devoured by the emerging priesthood.

Victim (VAKATAMA) and victor (VAKATARA) share a similar fate;

The (VA) at the beginning of both words establish them as emerging out of the via of passage for life, or the female vulva (VALAVA), the valve (VALAVA) of constant return up to the surface. Emerging LAVIC surges attaches it to the body of Mother Earth and Her greatest creation the land upon Her surFACE. It is the end phonemes (-TAMA and -TARA), that defines both of them out of PHASE THREE.

The female essence that as the mother (MA) became the victim (vakata-MA). The male sun as (RA) the emerging father became the victor (vakata-RA). It echoes the same linguistic constructs as MARA of Mars and WARA as war, as the watery grave of the sun. With the (TARA) at the end of victor (VATARA) it becomes apparent that territoriality (TARA-) and battles over turf (TARA-) enter the scene in PHASE THREE and that the migrations in PHASE ONE have been left behind.

Not to stray too far afield.

Vagina (VAJANA) and virgin (VA(RA)JANA);

Hide some nuanced clues. The (VA) of vagina establish that we are in the territory of creation out of the individual mother and her via of passage into life, her vulvic angle or patch. In vagina (VAJANA) there surfaces the dyad of gyno (JANA) and (VAJA). For the mythic Jenie (JANA) the bottle had to be rubbed for the magical giant to emerge. The SHAPE of the bottle is likened to the vulva and vagina. The vulva as the neck and the bulb at the end had been depicted as the womb of creation. When the clitoris is rubbed or caressed not only all kinds of orgasmic ecstasy associated with the Kundalini energy can take place but a baby is spasmed up to the surface. As the Kundalini energy winds its way up her spine the mother becomes the fearless protector of her offspring. The three wishes deal with the Kundalini internal explosion as the granter of wish fulfillment.

The virgin (VA(RA)JANA) with the vagina (VAJANA) also female has the (RA) of the male sun through Her linguistic center. Here we are dealing with the body of Mother Earth as the (V) of the volcano AT ONE with the round bloody disc of the sun (RA) as part of Her in PHASE ONE, still part of each other, not apart and separate. This was before male role in specific paternity became known and the separation myths peppered the linguistic landscape. At that ancient time the sun was considered to be Her helping hands and She remaining with the help of the sun as Her son, the eternal virgin creating Herself, out of Herself, by Herself, as land upon Her surFACE, mitosis, parthogenesis in action. The English Queen Elizabeth One must have had an inkling of the process.

Para- prava (PARAVA) pravo (PARAVA), Pravda(PARA(VA)DA;

Para in Polish as fog or mist, even steam upon the surFACE of Mother Earth is a very ancient word based singularly on the A(ah) SOUND dealing with the PARAde (PA) of the water vapor (vaPARA) rising out of the fulminating jungles hugging Her creations on the way to the open heavens. In Hindu the word priya (PARAYA) means beloved, for the fog or rising mist, was perceived to be like the beloved to wind its way across the surFACE of Mother Earth, like a vine winds its way around a tree, caressing Her to awaken and to help them on their journey into light and life. (PA) deals with passage. (RAYA) deals with the rays (RAYA) of the sun as the fingers of light caressing Her to wake up. The (AYA) deals with light in Persian and dawn in Assyrian.

The symbolic SHAPE of the heart in PHASE ONE originally had been likened to a vine climbing and twisting its way around a tree like the fog (PARA) wound itself across the surFACE of Mother Earth.

The SHAPE of the heart in not necessarily two swans with long thin necks ogling each other. In the tropics, especially in Africa, where all of this had its beginning the SHAPE of the metaphoric heart emerged out of the SHAPE of the two heart SHAPED lobes of the entwining leafy vine that created the coital embrace on the trunk of the tree. In PHASE THREE as all concepts dealing with the processes upon the body of Mother Earth were being suppressed and redefined, the beloved priya (PARAYA) became the accursed pariah (PARAYA).

Prawa (PARAVA) right also in Polish;

Deals with the right hand as opposed to the left. The SOUNDS of (V) and (W) are interchangeable. Still dealing only with the concept of difference as the A(ah) at the end signifies, it morphs into prawo (PARAVA) also in Polish, which means the rule of law and we are in linguistic male territory in PHASE THREE as the O(oh) at the end signifies. The rule of law emerges out of the right hand of the fathers which dealt with power and fantasy, not with the left hand of the mothers which dealt with natural law out of lava. The (W) and (V) are interchangeable. It moves into defining reality altogether out of the left hemispheric male fantasy construct and establishes itself as the concept of truth as prawda (PARAVADA), 'the gift of'(DA) the right hand as prawa (PARAVA) and the rule of law as prawo (PARAVA). It follows in the Northern reaches of Europe a similar progression as the homonymic puns; right (hand), write (law) and rite (expression of tradition).

RULE TWENTY;
BUZZ words and or DEROGATORY descriptions

Words dealing with female body parts, processes and activities; cunt, coos, ass, bitch, whore, harlot, fuck, frigg, tuat, clyde, tart, butt, nookie, crack, kurva, curse, cherry, beaver, box, puta, pudenda, snatch etc. etc. etc.

Cunt (KANATA)

The emergence (NA) at the tip, top, edge (TA), of smaller (KA) replicas out of the individual mother. Indian Goddess KUNDA (KANADA) represents the same ancient activity using the body of Mother Earth and Her volcanic cone (KANA) of creation. The (T) and (D) are interchangeable.

The experience of the electro magnetic Kundalini (KANADA-) energy is the explosion of the solar wind entering the magnetic poles on the body of Mother Earth, pushing up through Her body then entering the soles of human feet to nestle dormant at the base of the spine. The cunt (KANATA) also counts (KANATA-) menstrual time in sync with the phases of the moon. It is the kont (KANATA) the corner or rug as the vulvic patch in Polish that gives rise to the actual flow of monthly menstrual blood. One of the ways of activating the Kundalini energy is through the birthing breath of the panting mother another is the use of hallucinogenic drugs. A drug (DARAGA) is the gift of (DA) the rug (RAGA). In Polish the rug is a kont (KANATA), or corner. The story of Aladdin comes into sharper focus as he flew on the magic carpet of ecstasy ie the Polish rug or kont (KANATA), the much maligned cunt (KANATA). Also Aladdin (haLADAna) contains in his name the dyad for lady (LADA).

Coos (KASA;

The X (KS) (KASA) marks the spot on the buttox of the young female as she passes red blood and announces that she is ready to be read into the role of motherhood. (KA) deals with the creation of smaller objects and (SA) deals with the creation of them out of the mothers blood, SA is the Egyptian wise blood of the mother, SAng is blood in French, SAngre is blood in Spanish, SAnguis is blood in Latin. It has links with the semiannual coming and going of birds at the time of foaling and the fecundity of egg laying coos of birds.

Ass (HASA);

The place out of which life emerges upon the surface as coagulated blood on a female body when she gives birth to and has (HASA) a baby. It emerges as ASH (HASA) on the volcanic body of Mother Earth that coalesces into land. The ASS on the body of the birthing mother was the place where the Kundalini energy lay coiled and rose on the wings of the birthing breath. The movement of ecstasy up the spine has its origins at the sacrum, the triangular bone as the sacred place at the ASS.

The ASS as an animal in most of the THREE PHASES became related to the concept of hybrid transformation and evolved as a pack animal and a means of travel for many a savior or transformed male. Riding upon the back of an ass, mule or donkey became a means of entering holy places for Jesus and Mohammed. The double SS at the end of ass relates it to the SA of the individual mother and the SA of the spiral configuration on the body of Mother Earth.

Bitch (BACHA);

The female canine (KANANA) is the mother who created the beginning (CH) of life (BIO), out of her body. The (KANA) in her ancient canine (KANANA) name deals with the volcanic cone (KANA) of creation on the body of Mother Earth. Both deal with the creation of smaller aspects (KA) out of their bodies. The letter (B) in BITCH reflecting the concept of 'two in one' may deal with the number of pups that early wolves, the provenance of all bitches gave birth to. They may have been primarily privy to twins which the whole pack then raised.

With all the redefinitions from female to male centrality in PHASE THREE the bitch was left behind. The male dog along with the male bull and the male ram became male totems gaining supremacy over the female bitch, the mother cow and the cowering lamb as they lost much of their ancient primacy. Christ tried to bring the peaceful lamb of the mothers back into the picture. It remains only as a symbol not necessarily as a way of being. As the queen bee became the metaphor for the creative capacity of Mother Earth, so the bitch may have been a metaphor for the devoted quality of canine parenting that emerges out of PHASE TWO. The bitch is also one of the guides of passage along with the cat and the horse.

Nookie (NAKA);

The hidden snake (IS NAKA) surfaces in the female body, in her mysterious cleft or nook (NAKA). The mix up between the female body and the body of Mother Earth surfaces here. The snake (IS NAKA) was considered to be the metaphoric guide of the sun through the subterranean and hidden intestines within the body of Mother Earth. With catastrophic eruptions plaguing the African continent as humanity dispersed their memories may have mixed up the processes inherent in the female body and the body of Mother Earth. The teeth on the body of Mother Earth where She bit the sun into many bloody pieces surfaces as jokes of frightened bridegrooms who have had to face the toothy vagina and the possible loss of their vulnerable penis. There is also the possibility that there was the perception that the snake was the coiled Kundalini energy hidden in the mothers body, that was blown into uncoiling up the spine at the time of the birthing breath. The nook (NAKA) hid the snake (IS NAKA) at the base of the spine.

Whore (HARA), houris (HARA);

Be She Mother Earth or the individual mother she carries the belly (HARA) of life containment. In Hebrew har (HARA) is 'holy mountain' out of which the sun was born at dawn in the Eastern sky. It is also the 'pregnant belly' of the individual mother. In PHASE THREE she was redefined as a wanton woman and vilified as evil. For the valuable service that she performs she should get a host of medals.

Harlot (HARALATA);

The tryad hides within its linguistic coils the continuing shift out of PHASE ONE and mother centrality into PHASES TWO and THREE when the carrier of life as the individual female and the body of Mother Earth became totally compromised. (HARA) deals with the belly of creation. (RALA) deals with what was considered to be real (RALA) and not theoretical speculation and (LATA) deals with 'years' in Polish. With the passage of time the ancient mother as the source of power was not only demoted but slipped totally from view.

Fuck (FAKA);

The five (FA), fingers (FA), of fire (FA), in the Eastern firmament (FA-) as the rays of the sun, creating smaller aspects (KA) out of the body of the Mother Earth. As the creations of Mother Earth, Her rays became the helping outstretched fingers of the sun. On the female body the five fingers of the hands brought women to orgasm. When male centrality gained ground in PHASE THREE the process of fucking became associated with sexual intercourse and rape. 'To fuck someone over' is not to share love (LAVA) out of lava caressing the flanks of Mother Earth on its way down to the sea, but to put something over on them and to take massive advantage of them. Not a complimentary activity. Fuck (FAKA) also deals with focus (FAKA-) as part of the sex act dealing with one of the activities associated with transformation.

Frigg (FARAGA);

A Goddess in Europe also deals with the five fingers of fire (FARA) of the rising sun out of the body of Mother Earth that in PHASE THREE raped Her. On the individual female body it dealt with the rug (RAGA) in Polish, the pubic angle on Her body as she was raped. Linguistically War and Mars on and off the body of Mother Earth reflect that same ancient battle. She has been kept alive by giving her name to Friday.

Clyde (KALADA);

The lady (LADA) as Mother Earth who made smaller aspects (KA) out of Her body, out of Her clods (KALADA-) of clay (KALA). The Biblical Adam was perceivd to have been made out of the ground or clay of Mother Earth. It also establishes its links with clouds (KALADA-), for the ground may be dry but when clouds (KALADA-) release rain upon the surFACE of Mother Earths She turns into clods (KALADA) of clay.

Tuat (TATA);

Tuat is an Egyptian name for the uterine cavity on the female body that includes the underworld on the body of MOTHER EARTH. For the Phoenician TAAUT (TATA) was the snake that wound itself around the horizontal rim on the body of Mother Earth waiting for the sun to set in order to guide it through Her intestines. (TA) deals with the tip, top or edge, coming and going, rising and setting, guiding the sun to find its way back up to the surFACE at dawn.

The double (TATA) deals with both the tip (TA) on the body of Mother Earth Her tetons (TATA-) and the top (TA) of the body of the individual mother and her nourishing titties (TATA).

TART (TARATA) Besides being a culinary confection, the tart emerges out of (TARA), the terrain (TARA-), the tar(TARA), tor (TARA) on the body of Mother Earth. The (RATA) deals with return (RATARANA), or the completion of a cycle that included the rising and the setting of the sun emerging out of the 'wound' of 'dawn' RANA in Polish. As such what we are dealing with here is the singular unit out of PHASE ONE when the body of Mother Earth and the sun were considered as one. Tart (TARATA) not only reflects itself (TARA/RATA) but defines a sharp and sour flavor associated with the female, it must come out of PHASE THREE.

As the Indo-European primal Goddess she was known as the Hebrew Terah (TARA), Etruscan Turan (TARANA), Latin Terra Mater, or Mother Tara. In PHASE THREE the word strumpet (IS TARAMAPATA) belongs here. It establishes its links with the revered body of Mother Earth to which the individual female was related as Her daughter (DATARA) or (DA) 'the gift of' (TARA).

Crack (KARAKA);

The helping hand (RAKA) in Polish, of creation (KARA-), maker of smaller objects (KA), with the help of the sun (RA) as in breaking apart, creating a rift on the body of Mother Earth out of which lava could emerge up to the surFACE and create land. On the female body the crack of creation was the break at the buttox, or ass out of which her creation, a solid baby emerged.

The word crack (KARAKA) is a reflection of itself (KARA/RAKA). The shared letter is the RA of the sun. It was perceived that the fires of the sun were snuffed out as they were swallowed in the bloody gore filled Western waters eventually creating the volcanic crack on the body of Mother Earth as they moved up to Her surFACE coagulating into land. The other crack was the break or wound at the horizontsl rim out of which the celestial bodies and birds were born, the rana of another declination. It gave birth to the letters C (kh) of creation and G(jee) of generation and (gh) of begetting.

Kurva (KARAVA);

Polish whore, prostitute, again the primal creatress (KARA-) out of her vulvic or volcanic (VA) crater (KARATARA). One of the worst names that could be thrown at a woman. It comes out of PHASE THREE as the (KARA) of creation (KARAtana) becomes the lowest form associated with a mother. In Polish kara means punishment. It has links with the word for coos (KASA) becoming the curse (KA(RA)SA).

Box (BAKASA);

The coos (KASA) out of X (KASA), marks the spot, where the baby emerges after the red spots stopped flowing on the outside and the coagulation of the blood creating a baby began on the inside. The mothers coos (KASA) emerge as the dual source of both the blood (SA) and the baby (BA).

In PHASES TWO and THREE the four sided square and then the box became a male symbol. As boxes, the tefilah praying Jews wore them on their arm and forehead. The Muslims did them one better with the box becoming the cube (KAABA), their holiest site in Mecca. The box (BAKASA) has links with the process of baking BAKA-) and baking dealt with transformation which was perceived to occur within the body of Mother Earth before the sun rose out of Her fiery internal furnace at dawn.

Buttox (BATAKASA);

Both (BATA) mounds (BA) of creation, metaphorically speaking, echoing the shape of 'infinity' that cradle the hidden coos (KASA) within.

Curse (KARASA);

Actually the caress (KARASA) of blood (SA) as the dactyl rays of the sun across the skin of Mother Earth with the promise of creation (KARA-) associated with the SOUND of coos (KASA) made by the birds. In PHASE ONE the coos (KASA) on the female body with the emegence of the knowledge of male role in specific paternity and the creation of their solar gods (RA) *away* and *above* the body of Mother Earth. In PHASE THREE became the woman's curse (KA(RA)SA or punishment. Because her body not only flowered with menstrual blood but matured with the fruit of her labors, she had to become hidden and defiled.

Cherry (CHARA);

The sun (RA) carrying with it the beginning (CHA) of life. In PHASE ONE it lead to being charmed (CHARAMA) by the individual mother (MA) in whom the solar elecctro magnetic Kundalini energy exploded with life. In PHASE THREE the holder (MA) of the cherry shifted gears as mothers were losing their centrality and their CHERRY morphed into being wary or chary (CHARA). Wary (WARA) has in it the linguistic echoes of WAR (WARA). The cherry as the symbol of the creative force of Mother Earth in PHASES TWO and THREE does battle with the emerging male solar deity or the sun (RA).

Gautama Buddha not only had a mother named Maya, the holder (MA) of the light (AYA) but was born under a cherry tree. The CHERRY as one of the symbols for the pink clitoris on the female body establishes a different, if juicy meaning. In the word charismatic (KARASAMA-) we have glimmers of what the Kundalini energy activated in the birthing mother. In Polish sama means she alone. Echoes of masturbation and the birthing breath.

Beaver (BAVARA);

Furry animal, or the vulvic patch, the vulva on the female body (VA) out of which with the helping hands of the sun (RA), the bio (BA) of life makes its appearance.

Snatch (IS NAJA) or (IS NACHA);

In PHASES TWO and THREE takes us to the loss of choice for the hapless woman and the activity of subsequent rape. You have to grab 'it' fast, or snatch 'it', before 'it' gets away.

RULE TWENTY ONE;
Turn to Goddesses

Goddesses emerged on the human scene at the time of female centrality in PHASE ONE, thousands of years before the appearance of male Gods. They originally were specific personifications of the processes, qualities and functions that were perceived to exist in and through the body of Mother Earth.

KUNDA;

The Goddess that covers a multitude of bases and in many ways is the most universal although often linguistically hidden is the Hindu Goddess Kunda (KANADA). She establishes her origins out of the triangled volcanic cone (KANA) on the body of Mother Earth creating land out of Her lavic outpouring as the ultimate and singular source of creation, the original God. For the Goddess Kunda is the 'gift of' (DA) the triangular cone (KANA) of creation. The phoneme (KA) deals with the creation of smaller things out of Her body. As the 'emergence on the surFACE' or 'a change from a former state' (NA) defines Mother Earth with her volcanic outpouring as the primary and ultimate cone (KANA) of creation.

In Hinduism the Goddess Kunda as the risen Kundalini energy goes through a systemic progression throwing light on many of the varied concepts that follow. KU is the body of Mother Earth. KUN is the individual mother the one who emerges (NA) out of the body of Mother Earth. KUNDA is the name of the Goddess as 'the gift of' (DA) Mother Earth. KUNDALI deals with the angle of movement up to the surFACE. LI is movement in Sanskrit. KUNDALINI is the emergence (NI) of the angle of movement (LI) out of the Goddess KUNDA representing the body of Mother Earth (KU) and the individual mother (KUN).

For the Bugotu of the South Pacific, Ku is 'what comes first' or Mother Earth. It was Mother Earth creating land, or Herself out of Herself that came first. Without the body of Mother Earth 'coming first' as land there would have been nothing that could have come after.

In Greek Ku as either 'decaying' and 'destroying' dealt with the other end of the process that defined the body of Mother Earth. Everything that emerged upon Her surFACE was reabsorbed back within Her body through the process of 'decay'(DK) and destruction' becoming at one with Her.

With the addition of (NA) at the end of ku to become kun (KANA) we move into the cone (KANA) of creation that as the lavic volcano created land up to the surFACE of Mother Earth. For the Greeks khun (KANA) also deals with 'Earth' as the magnificent Mother who created everything. Not only lava emerged upon the surFACE of Mother Earth. In Chinese Kun (KANA) deals with the 'movement of a plant up from the body of Mother Earth'. There was no doubt for the ancient mothers in PHASE ONE that everything that in one way or another emerged out of the surFACE or body of Mother Earth was Her creation. Luoma Kunta (LAMA KANATA) for the Finns was Mother Earth as the sole 'creatress'. In Sanskrit the 'burning, violent lavic fires creating land' were called kanda (KANADA), the 'gift of' (DA) the volcanic cone (KANA) of Mother Earth.

The Kundalini energy enters the human body usually through the bottom of the bare feet while standing and through the anus while sitting. In Finnish kunta (KANATA) is 'base' or 'heel'. Achilles's loss of power dealt with his heel having been pierced by an arrow.

For the Basque cuna (KANA) deals with the cunt (KANATA). In Latin it is the cunnus (KANA sa). The double negation (NANA) associates it with the Greek moon. The (sa) at the end deals with the mother's menstrual blood that the moon activates into flowering. Closely associated the cunt (KANATA) counts (KANATA-) time with the cycles of the moon.

For the Finns (-KUNTA) deals with 'people' or a 'nation'. Also for the Finns to 'bear', or to 'carry' dealing with pregnancy is Kantaa (KANATA).

In Lithuanian to 'embody' is kunyti (KANAta). In Sweden kuni (KANA) is 'ten' dealing with the ten months of lunar gestation that the mother bore and carried the product of her subsequent labors in her disTENded belly. Kunas (KANAsa) in Lithuanian means 'body'. The (SA) at the end deals with the mother creating the baby out of her blood, SA the 'wise blood' of the Egyptians, SAng as blood in French. SAngre as blood in Spanish.

In German a child is kinder (KANADAra), for whom to be kind (KANADA) had been invented and a subsequent playground as the KINDERgarden was created.

In Bemba makunda (maKANADA) means to 'squat down' when giving birth. It is the mother (MA) who does the squatting. The American Indian word for woman is squaw. The 'beloved' and 'desirable' in Sanskrit is kanta (KANATA). In Polish a kont (KANATA) is the corner or rug the triangular pubic angle on the bottom part of the female trunk. The flying carpet of Aladdin surfaces here. The SHAPE of the triangular female cunt embraces the triangular SHAPE of the Sanskrit 'spear' or 'lance' as Kunta (KANATA). In Latin cantus (KANATAsa) is also the 'corner' SHAPE, the pubis on the female body with the (SA) of the mother's blood. In Sanskrit the cunt (KANATA) expands to include the LAdy in kandala (KANADALA) and means 'of a woman'. The (T) and (D) are interchangeable.

To diverge a bit, but still dealing with the ancient mothers, hiskuntza (hasaKANATAsa) is the Basque word for 'language'. The cunt (KANATA) of the mother surfaces here as the carrier of the good news and the origins of language. In English to repeat something over and over sarcastically is to cant (KANATA). In Latin canto (KANATA) means 'to sing'. Singing usually meant repeating the same song over and over perhaps sarcastically which deals with hearsay and heresy, both words out of Her say.

Kunigas (KANAgasa) is a Lithuanian 'priest', the eunuch (HANAKA) with the ubiquitous snake (IS NAKA) in his name along with the mothers blood (SA) taking us back to PHASE ONE and mother centrality. As the winged serpent the Mayan Ku Kul Kan covers a variety of bases. The Ku deals with Mother Earth. Kul (KALA) is the pLAnet, the body of Mother Earth creating smaller (KA) aspects out of Her body. As the winged serpent it may have had its origins out of the SHAPE of the passage of a flaming feathery comet linking it to birds or the metaphoric snake. The Kan (KANA) harkens back to the volcanic cone (KANA) of creation.

In England Canterbury (KANATA-) Cathedral barely gives up its linguistic secrets and is not only associated with the mother's cunt (KANATA) but

Section Two

with the murdered French Cathars. The history of the city of Kent (KANATA) in England also bears investigating.

Then there is the Hindu God Skanda (IS KANADA) who surfaces in the Northern people of Skandinavia (IS KANADAva-) containing in its linguistic folds not only the Hindu God Skanda (IS KANADA) but the country of Canada (KANADA) way across the great divide of the Atlantic Ocean. Then there is the word scandal (IS KANADAla) which surfaces in PHASE THREE and is associated with female sexuality. In the United States the state of Kentucky (KANATAka) establishes linguistic links with the small (KA) cunt (KANATA) or the vulvic cone (KANA), the creative lavic force out of the body of Mother Earth. The phoneme of KA surfaces as part of the University of Kansas (KANAsasa). Who knew what originally existed there to give it that name?

In PHASE ONE a series of words deal with the evolution of pleasure out of female bodies. In Lithuanian 'to be satisfied' and 'content' is called paten cunti (PATANA KANATA). The cunti (KANATA) is self evident as the cunt (KANATA). The clue lies in the paten (PATANA) with the passage (PA) of the ten (TANA) fingers across the cunt (KANATA), dealing with masturbation.

With the shift into male centrality in PHASE THREE and the ensuing clitorectomies maiming female bodies, nukenteti (naKANATAta) in Lithuanian means 'to suffer'. Also in Lithuanian kan kinti (KANA KANATA) deals with 'torment' and 'martyr'. It was the mothers being denied their birthing breath and the rise of the ecstatic Kundalini energy of Mother Earth that the Lithuanian words bear witness to that resulted in almost universal clitorectomies in many parts of the world that exist as a practice to this day.

Back to the continent of Africa, the country of Kenya (KANAYA) deals with Mother Earth as the maker of smaller (KA) aspects out of Her cone (KANA) of creation and like the candle (KANADAla) is the holder of the light, as aya in Persian. Sitting on the Eastern shores on the continent of Africa the sun rose out of the waters on Kenya's Eastern shore and like a candle (KANADA-) lit up Her sky.

The Goddess KUNDA (KANADA) of the Kundalini experience dealt with the transforming energy of Mother Earth that created ecstasy in the mother's who brought life up to the surface, making them through the process associated with the birthing breath, fearless protectors of their offspring, leaders, prophets and healers. The mother mystic and powerful woman Al Kahina of the Tuareg Berbers has a place here. There exists a nudge in the direction that not only Columbus but American Indians may not have been the first settlers of the 'New world'. The Vikings closely related to the Scandinavians (IS KANADA-) were obvious contenders but there were also the Welsh, the Irish and others.

Something even more distant raises its scaly head. There is a large boa constrictor in South America, a snake of massive proportions called the anaconda (HANAKANADA)(HANA NAKA KANADA) containing in its name a series of curious and mystifying linguistic implications. The sun (IS HANA) and the snake (IS NAKA) establishing the ubiquitous eunuch (HANAKA) (HANA NAKA) whose name was much more common and had its origins back in Africa.

But it is with the tryad of (KANADA) that a larger question surfaces. For (KANADA) is the original name of the Hindu Goddesss Kunda (KANADA) who expresses (DA) the gift of the cone (KANA) the triangulat volcanic SHAPE as the creative source out of the body of Mother Earth creating (NA) all the smaller (KA) aspects out of Her body. It deals with Mother Earth creating Herself, by Herself as land, vigin birth, parthogenesis in action.

But why would this large boa constrictor, the anaconda (-KANADA) carry the name of (KANADA) relating it to the singular creative aspect of Mother Earth as the virgin creatress. The ancient mothers who named it understood the process inHERent in the body of Mother Earth as the singular source of creation. They attached it to the massive metaphoric snake, but WHY? Because they knew something about it that we have only recently rediscovered. Female anacondas can reproduce without male anacondas input. They are procreative virgins like Mother Earth. And like Mother Earth who creates everything by Herself, they produce baby snakes by themselves not unlike the DNA of the elongated skulls found in Peru, Asia and Egypt that lacked the Y chromosome.

What are the implications? The virgin birth associated with the surFACE and body of Mother Earth existed at the time of female centrality in PHASE ONE, way before male input in specific procreation had become known. There is another linguistic clue much further North in the country named Canada (KANADA). The Goddess Kunda (KANADA) of the Hindu pantheon and the mother carriers of her worship may have arrived at the shores of North America way before both the Europeans and the Indians. Tracing it back through Skandinavia (isKANADAvaya) and the Vikings before them into Skanda (IS KANADA) a Hindu deity, gives linguistic pause. Then we have the Maya construct related to the Buddha. His mother had been called Maya, the holder (MA) of the light (AYA) in the country of Guatamala

(GATAMA-). Was not Gautama (GATAMA) Buddha part of his name? Was there massive traffic across the great Pacific Ocean from Asia landing on the Western shores of South America that gave us the Inca (HANAKA) also associated linguistically with the eunuch (HANAKA) priesthood? Then there is the ananconda (HANAKAnada) in those same South American reaches.

RULE TWENTY-TWO;
Metaphoric Creatures

There had been a period in human history in PHASE ONE when human beings considered themselves as part of the condition of sentient life. There were no separations between human beings and other creatures. As humanity succumbed to its fear driven over evolved left hemispheric violent future, it lost its links with the instinctual certainty that guided the creatures around them. They turned to many of their fellow travelers and used them as METAPHORS for their own behavior. Honing in on the most salient characteristics of their Earthly companions they used them as examples for their social configurations and as explanations of how the all encompassing body of Mother Earth worked. The most primal creature METAPHORS harken back to the ancient migrations in PHASE ONE, then as settlements evolved, other creatures were added to the mix.

Elephant;
The old matriarch of the elephant herd was the first to respond to the vibrations of thunder in the distance and the coming of rain to the parched savannah. As the herd led by the wise old matriarch moved to the 'greener pastures' in the far distance, other herbivores; wildebeests (gnu), zebras, gazelles, buffalo created a long parade behind them as the parting curtain of sHOWers in the far distance sHOWed them HOW to find their way.

The elephANT herd was one of the first templates for the matriarchal organizational structure that early human beings used. It was based on closely related sisters who were AUNTS to the newly born infants. The wobbly young infants were tended with great affectionate care and tenderness. She was the one leader (LADA-), the grand old lady (LADA) who led (LADA) them back and forth across the vast reaches of Africa, even the verdant prehistoric Sahara and that was the majestic wise old matriarch.

The word ELEPHANT (HALAFANATA) contains in it not only the SHAPE of the ears that act like a fan (FANA) on the creatures body to cool it and to rid it of pesky flies, but as LAFA deal with the life (LAFA) that had been promised by the falling rains in the distant savannahs.

The ELEPH- (HALAFA-) has the same linguistic origin as ALEPH (HALAFA) or ALPHA (HALAFA) of beginnings. It was the ancient elephant matriarch that began the march to a new life in March to the promising rain soaked savannahs of the Okobango River Delta. Elephants can sense vibrations over long distances and crashes of thunder awakened them to move toward the falling rains.

In PHASE THREE leaving mother centrality behind and the matriarch elephant as the beginner of the ancient migrations, for the Hindus the Elephant God Ganesh (GANASA), surfaced as the 'God of Beginnings'. The elephant mother matriarch who began the ancient migrations in PHASE ONE with the shift into male centrality in PHASES TWO and THREE morphed into the elephant male son of beginnings. The mythological male baby sitting of the lap of the Goddess became the redefined king. It surfaced with Isis and Horus for the Egyptians and with Mother Mary and Jesus for the Christians. In Ganesh (GANASA) the second dyad (NASA) deals with beginnings for in Latin nascence (NASANASA) deals with birth. As poachers have been decimating the elephant herds in Africa and Asia there remain only linguistic echoes of why they were so revered.

For the ancient Hebrews in PHASE THREE the same construct surfaces in Genesis (JANASASA) as the 'beginning' of the Old Testament. (JANA) deals with gyno (JANA or GANA) the Greek 'woman' who creates the beginning into life. (NASA) also surfaces as the Latin word for birth as nascence (NASANASA), the repetitive quality of birth, same as Mother Earth being a slave (IS LAVA), to lava itself as Her great creative outpouring over which She had no choice.

The (SASA) on the end of Genesis (JANASASA) establishes the Old Testament as having the transforming ability out of the individual mothers blood (SA) and the hidden lavic spiral (SA) energy of Mother Earth. Without being open about it, there is a perception that both of these energies fused into the Kundalini energy that men in PHASE TWO and THREE through ritual and universal castration began to share with the birthing mothers.

Birds;

The coming and going of birds semiannually also announced that it was time to begin the ancient migrations. They clacked (KALAKA) their way across the heavens and like a clock (KALAKA) semiannually greeted the herbivores who arrived to have their foals in the fall in the Southern Hemisphere and to champ on the newly sprouting grass. The coming of the birds from the Southern reaches and from the Northern cold where the sun never seemed to shine, was timed to the semiannual monsoons.

The rain made the grass sprout, the sprouting grass gave birth to flowers, the flowers soon filled with insects and that is what attracted the birds who swooped down on the insects in an orgy of feeding. They greeted old friends, found mates, built their nests, laid their eggs, reared their young, and as the terrain dried up they returned to their old nesting grounds North to Europe and Asia and South to the Antarctic.

The (KALAKA) tryad also creates a balance in the migrational year dealing with the birds. The clacking (KALAKA) clock (KALAKA) associated with birds surfaces with the KA on either end of LA the Mother Earth at the time of the spring and fall equinoxes which establish the equal distribution of time in the ancient lunar year. There is also another source for the SOUND related to the letter (K) of smallness. It deals with the coos (KASA) that birds made as they sailed across the vast belly of air above the surFACE of Mother Earth.

Another more questionable and singularly perceived balance at that specific time existed in Polish for kaleka (KALAKA) means one who is crippled. Castration and maiming of young boys and slaves to create a hormonal hemispheric balance of peace occurred at those special Equatorial, equidistant times.

Stork (IS TARAKA);

Like the helping hands of the sun, the stork (TARA-RAKA) also helped Mother Earth. The second dyad in stork is (RAKA) and reka (RAKA) is hand in Polish. The first dyad is (TARA) the terrain (TARA-) on the body of Mother Earth. So the stork had been considered to be a helping hand of Mother Earth at the time when all sorts of infants had been born. As the bringer of children in European fairy tales the stork has an ancient history. He arrived in the African Southern Hemisphere at the time that calving occurred in the fall. Standing on one leg he brought to mind the maimed smithy and the one legged shepherd who as eunuchs not only tended the forge and the emerging domesticated flocks but as midwives very possibly assisted in the birthing of life out of their sister's bodies.

The one legged stork accompanied by the maimed smith and limping shepherd came up with a letter all their own.

The letter (O) as both the circular SHAPE of the (O) of the sun and the zero (IS HARA) of the permanently empty male belly, associated with maleness at the end of Spanish nouns (muchacho, hermano), went through its own transformation. The eunuchized uncles, the limping smiths and shepherds began asking WHY of their peripheral state. They began to question their often sad fate. In Polish the word czemu (CHAMA) means why. The ancient Sun God of Sippar named CHEMOSH (CHAMASA) in PHASE TWO bears witness to the journey into male questing and the emergence of male solar deities. The sun is a round circle in the sky away from and above the body of Mother Earth. An Indian tribe on the Western coast in California is called Chumash (CHAMASA). How were they related?

The stork balancing on one leg became associated, not only with the bringing of babies at the time of the great foaling in the fall in the Southern Hemisphere, but with the maimed smith and shepherd. The letter (O), the zero (IS HARA) of the permanently empty male belly, and the SHAPE of the emerging male solar disc guided by the ever present metaphoric snake as the single leg, shared that leg with the linguistic symbol, and emerged in PHASE TWO as the letter Q, of questing. It was perceived to limp across the sky pushed along by the one leg like the eunuchized and maimed brothers limped upon the Earth. The quests follow them into PHASES TWO and THREE as they search for the golden fleece (FALASA), of their lost phallus (FALASA). What is more golden than the sun?

Goose (GASA);

For the ancient, mostly left handed mothers the realization of what was true (TARA) was an experience in the body. It was not based on the theoretical speculation out of the right handed left hemispheric rational male mind. The body always tells the truth. When it is cold, it shivers. When passion floods it, or an AHA moment of truth bursts upon the scene, it covers itself with goose pimples. When it is hot, it perspires. When it is hungry, it forages for food. When it is thirsty, it searches for water. When danger confronts it, it either flees, fights, or freezes, becomes rooted to the spot and thinks small. When it is pressured to defecate or urinate, it doesn't ask permission, it goes. When it is invaded by pathogens, it raises its temperature and boils them out of the system. When it is wounded, it coagulates around the wound and heals it. The body has a mind of its own vaguely related to the brain.

The brain asks questions. The female left handed right hemisphere usually asks HOW. The right handed male left hemisphere deals with explanations and rationalizations and usually asks WHY.

THE ANSWER TO WHY IS ALWAYS A LIE.

Section Two

The HOW of the mothers needs answers to survive with her children; HOW to find shelter, HOW to find food, HOW to find healing plants, HOW to know when the distant showers (IS HAWA-) show (IS HAWA) her the way. Questions are asked. When the answers to her questions come, when the AH-HA moment of realization floods her inner being, her body responds with its own shower of puckers or goose pimples across her skin. What the rash of goose pimples on the skin announces is that an answer of truth had been given to the questions that had been asked.

They had to come up with a METAPHORIC creature that symbolized the process. What creature has a permanent covering of goose bumps on its skin? Of course, the goose. Pluck it and what do you see holding the absent feathers in place, wall to wall goose pimples.

So when an AHA moment occurs, when an answer floods the body with a shower of truth, the body responds with gooseflesh. Why Latin came up with the apt linguistic metaphor is anybody's guess. But in Latin the name for goose is ANSER. That's right. The goose flesh on a goose is a METAPHOR for the shower of truth, or goose pimples on the skin, an ANSWER to a question. The mind like the moon, is a fickle companion, but the body never lies. If a shower of goose pimples floods your skin you are being given an answer to a question that you may, or may not have been consciously asking.

Thank the lowly goose (GASA) for being a METAPHOR for the moment of truth as an experience in the body and not a speculation of the mind.

The goose (GASA) also hisses and so does Mother Earth near Her volcanic vents and fissures as gas (GASA), Her creation of air, blasts its way up to Her surFACE. The creation of land out of the volcanic crater the original creator, as lava hardened down Her flanks, was the source of the most ancient law (LAWA), and that ancient natural law was the basis of truth. (W and V are interchangeable). Not only lava poured down Her flanks as Mother Earth gave birth to Herself, by Herself. There was also ash and cinders.

The epic fairy tale of Cinderella out of the cinders on the body of Mother Earth, was also called the 'goose girl'. For the volcanic cone on the body of Mother Earth was like a goose bump on the body of a human being. Both dealt with a moment of truth. The many mounds around the body of Mother Earth that are often called a SHE, give rise to the perception that they also share the bumps on the skin of the METAPHORIC goose. They in some mysterious way or another deal with an expression of a long forgotten and hidden truth. We have yet to plummet their ancient secrets.

The lost slipper being found by a prince bringing Cinderella back to her power base reeks with possibilities. We are in PHASE THREE when tt was only through the young prince that Cinderella could find pleasure. Masturbation had been forbidden, clitorectomies littered the ground. Jason searching for the Golden Fleece, limping along with his BARE left foot touching the ground establishes ancient prehistoric links that since the ecstatic electro magnetic Kundalini energy had been perceived in Greece to rise like the metaphoric snake up through the left side of the body that had been associated with the individual mother and the body of Mother Earth creating the (SASA) dyad. The graceful goose covered many bases.

BEE of Being;

As Mother Earth in PHASE ONE was the single creative source of everything, the ancient mothers needed a creature METAPHOR to symbolize Her great effort. She gave birth to all that emerged upon Her surFACE; plants, trees, scurrying creatures, and out of Her horizontal flat round surFACE all the heavenly bodies; the sun, moon, clouds, stars, including the birds. What other maternal creature held that same power base? There was nothing above Her plane that fitted their need. Plants and trees stayed put but were dependent on place, soil and the fickle monsoons. Herbivore mothers created mostly one baby at a time and had trouble bringing it to maturity. Carnivores also had a difficult time feeding their hungry pups. Birds laid a lot of eggs and gave birth to the letter (K) as the coo SOUND of smallness but they didn't control their environment flying back and forth across the skies looking for warmer places to rear their young.

Mother Earth stayed put as everything emerged out of Her internal womb, out of the hidden area under Her surFACE. At least that's what it looked like to them. They had to look UNDER the skin of Mother Earth to find an apt METAPHOR for Her single creative outpouring.

Insects began to look like possible contenders. They emerged out of hidden wombs, or often out of great circular balls that copied the womb like bellies of all mothers. Beetles had their day with the Egyptian sun as they rolled balls of feces in which to lay their eggs. Somehow they didn't evolve as a universal METAPHOR for motherhood. Spiders also had their day as the spinners of fate but the female spider impaling the drone after mating didn't seem to fit the bill. Air conditioned termite mounds came up for consideration and may have been the most ancient SHAPES for all those sacred standing stones that pepper the global landscape. Then there was the ant who almost succeeded in becoming a METAPHORICAL symbol for motherhood but in some way or another was pushed sideways off the throne into becoming the

Section Two

sister of the mother, the aunt and not the mother herself.

Then there was the BEE. Hidden in her hive, sometimes hidden in a crusty cacoon hanging off a branch of a tree but more often underground creating layers of hexagonal tablets in which to lay her endless eggs. It was she the Queen BEE, who like Mother Earth not only created her total environment, but was the single egg laying mother. Everything that emerged out of her awesome productive body worked in tandem creating the space for her and her off spring to survive. There were workers, there were nannies, there were soldiers, there were farmers tending the fungal gardens. She like Mother Earth created it all. It all slid out of her monstrous unceasing labors. The Queen BEE not only emerged as the perfect METAPHOR for the creative body of Mother Earth but emerged defining the concept of singular reproduction as BEEING. TO BE was to have had links with the BEE.

The BEE out of PHASE ONE is one of the few insects along with the ant that crept into the English language and stayed there symbolizing an ancient condition related to the mother's that had been left behind and almost totally ignored. Making sweet honey didn't resurrect the BEE from its state. This all came to be in PHASE ONE and the time of female centrality when everything had been defined from a female point of view. As males began to understand their role in specific procreation they began to destroy any and all traditions that dealt with Mother Earth as the single source of creation. The linguistic METAPHOR of the Queen BEE must have been so deeply ingrained that like the snake it could not be totally jettisoned. If it couldn't be jettisoned, then like the snake it had to be redefined as evil.

Here the slight of hand, the presto digitator, the maker of linguistic magic enters the scene. The eunuch (HANAKA) uncles (HANAKALA), the angels (HANAGALA), the Sinclairs (IS HANAKALA) of Scotland had to hide their origins out of mother centrality, so did the Queen BEE. The Queen BEE construct had to be made evil, the work of their new found devil, satan, dragon, any and all monsters that hailed 'source' singularly out of the body of Mother Earth.

Leaving the body of Mother Earth behind, questing males sailed into the heavens attaching their hopes to their major circular deity, the sun. In PHASE THREE the mind of a hidden male father God took residence in the sky *away* and *above* the body of Mother Earth. Also further on in PHASE THREE the sun as the son again entered the picture. Because 'pagan' Europeans longed for the mother who had been left out of the trinity, the Roman Catholic Church resurrected Mother Mary. It does go round and round.

Enter the number 666, mark of all that has evolved as horrific, as the devil incarnate, the Anti-Christ, the second coming of all destruction, of the apocalypse, Armageddon, you name it.

WHY the number 666? Because the Queen BEE had been created as the major METAPHORIC maternal insect for the capacity of single creation out of the body of Mother Earth. HOW did that happen?

Take the SHAPE of the BEE hive. The inside circle housing the BEE hive is based on the *six* sided SHAPE of the hexagon echoing the SHAPE of the larval BEE cell. That is the first *six*. Then count the number of triangles that the hexagon pushes out of its center and you get another *six*. If you lay two large triangles one upon the other that in PHASE THREE became the Hebrew Star of David, the two triangles add up to the *third six* and presto 666. That's not all.

The hidden hive stays in the language but it is no longer associated with the Queen BEE. It becomes in PHASE THREE, as male centrality gains momentum and all that is associated with Mother Earth has to have been destroyed, became redefined as Jehovah (jaHAVA). Chova (HAVA) in Polish means 'hidden'. The hidden hive (HAVA) of the Queen BEE, the METAPHORIC insect defining Mother Earth as the single creative physical source of creation becomes the new PHASE THREE definition of the hidden celestial male deity Jehovah (jaHAVA) as the mind of God orchestrating all of reality beginning with the 'big bang' of the male orgasm.

Six (IS HAKASA) and sex (IS HAKASA) contain some mysterious links here. August was the sixth month of the ancient migration if you count from March as the beginning of the ancient year just before the herbivore mares dropped their foals and in the seventh month all began their journey back to their beloved mountains. It was a time of the most profound expression of motherhood during that ancient era. Both six (IS HAKASA) and sex (IS HAKASA) contain in them the concept of hacking (HAKA-) the coos (KASA) of the mother. In the month of August the sixth month if you count March as the first month after the mothers dropped their foals, mating ensued before the journey home could begin. The hacking of the coos with clitorectomies and during cohabitation must have been already occurring on the planet among poor young girls to be reflected as an activity on the body of Mother Earth as the rana of the wound on Her horizontal rim for the birth of the sun in Polish declares.

Deborah (DABARA) or perhaps with the letters transposed (BARADA) had been the Queen Bee of Israel out of PHASE ONE and mother centrality. She had been the 'gift of' (DA) the (BARA) or Goddess of the sacred air, that in Tibetan defined the 'intermediate state', the Bardo (BARADA) as a place of waiting for rebirth (BARAta) between death and reincarnation. Other aspects used the intermediate state as a vehicle of passage like the birds (BARADA) who flew through the sacred air and who were also defined as belonging to that unique 'intermediate state'. In PHASES TWO and THREE the birds became male symbols of deified source. The bar (BARA) dyad had been associated with the eunuchized brats (BARA-) or brothers (BARADA-) who were also considered to be in the 'intermediate state', no longer males and not yet females.

Other creatures have also entered the picture.

BUTTERFLY, MOTH. In PHASE ONE during the day there was the butterfly, the fluttering insect of transformation. For the night associated with menstruation, the moth of the mother became hallowed. The ewe as the female SHEep in PHASE ONE belonged to the mother. In PHASE THREE the male sheep as the ram (RAMA) entered and swamped the picture. The same thing happened with the cow (KAWA) associated with the cave (KAVA) of the mother as the ultimate milk giver became transformed into the raging bull and the ultimate symbol of manhood. The (V) and (W) are interchangeable. The nanny goat as the migratory milk giver became replaced by the unrelenting sex God Pan, the ram prancing around with his long tail, horns and goat hooves.

Snake;

The metaphoric SNAKE (IS NAKA) appears in most of the mythologies of the world and is decidedly out of PHASE ONE at the time of Mother centrality. There are a variety of levels that have to be dealt with concerning the ubiquitous snake. One deals with HOW that sinuous creature came to be universally mythologically either revered or hated. Another dealt with the Kundalini energy rising up from the surFACE of Mother Earth that the coiling snake came to represent. The last one dealt with HOW that serpentine energy rose through the human body and what that rising accomplished.

The African continent went through a tsunami of catstrophies during its long and turbulent existence. At a very ancient time before the many dispersals that recurred it pushed the humanoid and then human creature all over the ancient world. Since the story of the snake is so universal then it must have happened at the beginning of ancient prehistoric codified time.

When an asteroid plowed through the belly of air above the body of Mother Earth and left a plume of debris that darkened the light of the sun, they must have wondered what could have happened that the sun could not find its way back up to the surFACE of their great Mother. Or when a trembling earthquake blasted its way into the heavens and created a dark winter cloud of ashen obliteration they must have wondered HOW they could help the sun find its way back up to the surFACE of Mother Earth. They believed that the sun had lost its way under the crusty mantle, within the subterranean intestines of the body of Mother Earth.

Since Mother Earth had been generous to them and provided for their needs they began to ponder how to help Her major offspring, the solar disc to find its way back up to the light. Because ancient brains at least two hundred thousand years ago were the same size as modern humanity we must assume that they tried to figure out the problem not unlike humans do today.

They were close to their animal cousins and used them as metaphors for their existence. The bee became the metaphor for Mother Earth with the queen bee expressing the same role of singular creation as Mother Earth defining the BE of Being. The ant with her mounds of creation based on another single mother with all the ants as aunts to each others children extended to define the female elephANT also based on the same aunt structure of cousins (kasa-).

So they wonderd which creature could assist the lost sun on its journey to be reborn in the Eastern sky and send its rays of blessed light to caress the surFACE of Mother Earth again. It had to be a creature that could travel within the intestines of Mother Earth after it had set into Her underground realms and guide it back up to the light.

They considered four legged creatures but their legs would obstruct their journey through the slippery intestinal walls of Mother Earth. Birds with their plumed feathery wings could only get sopping wet and further drag the lost sun down. Insects came up for considerstion but they were rejected as being too small to act as a guide of the majestic sun. Then someone must have had an AHA moment. How about the snake? Not only is it in constant contact with the surFACE and body of Mother Earth, slithering across Her skin, swimming through Her waters, but it would fit the intestines within the body of Mother Earth like a hand fits the glove. And so the most ancient perception of the value of the snake was born. Whether the sun sank into oblivion into the Western waters, or sandy deserts or looming mountains, even jungles, the snake knew its way around all of these places. It would guide the lost sun back up to the light. This whole scenario must have happened at the beginning of humanitys heritage for it to spread out and surface in most of the mythologies of the ancient world.

Then there is the expanding scenario of the snake as the SHAPE of the Kundalini energy not only guiding the sun back up to the light but as a electro magnetic current rising up from the surFACE and body of Mother Earth along Her Lea lines. The snake, the sun and Mother Earth became intertwined and at one with each other.

Human beings existing on the planet for at least two hundred thousand years went through a variety of perceptions dealing with reality and social constructs. What archeological digs have been telling us is that there were times when people believed that the body of planet Earth was like the sun and moon, a round globe floating through space. Upon that round ball they drew grid lines of the electro magnetic Kundalini energy which followed apparent Lea lines which they could experience as an ecstatic state of trance and a movement into a transformative state. That knowledge and what that knowledge bestowed upon our ancient ancestors along with others has been lost. With their prehistoric elongated skulls were times when they somehow knew how to manipulate matter and change massive rocks into closely fitted blocks of stone. Somehow they knew how to levitate enormous stones. The larger human brain of the eleongated skulls had a capacity of 25% more brain matter also surfacing in the larger Neanderthal cranium must have experienced conditions that we can only marvel at.

They surmised that this Lea line Kundalini enegy came in a double helexical spin which had its origins in the sun. As the solar wind barreled towards the body of the magnetized Earth it broke apart into two flows. One entered the poles becoming the Auroa Borealis in the Northern reaches and the Aurora Australis in the Southern hemisphere. As it entered the body of Mother Earth at the poles it then had to travel *through* Her fiery oven, Her flaming interior before it emerged cooked clean and vibrant upon Her surFACE. The other flow spread *across* Her surFACE and circled Her body like a frame of celestial solar arms. The double flow that entered the body of Mother Earth at the poles becoming cooked clean became the '*pagan*' mother source as the Kundalini energy up from Her interior. The solar flow that dropped directly from the sky became the ultimate male Father source and in PHASE THREE the subsequent redefinition of a celestial God.

The two solar flows one through the interior of Mother Earth and the other across Her surFACE became symbolized by the ever vigilant snake, serpent, dragon any one extended bare leg that slithered across Her ground, swam through Her waters and hung from Her trees.

Then there was the third perception that dealt with the Kundalini energy shooting up through the human body bringing with it massive 'mystical' change.

As it rose from the surFACE of Mother Earth it entered the human body through the soles of the feet, or the feet themselves while standing and through the anus while sitting. It had originally been experienced by the birthing mothers in the last stages of labor as they panted hard and fast to get the large headed fetus out of their bodies. The panting acted as a bellows fanning the Kundalini energy lying at the base of the spine to spin into action. As it rose in a double helexical ribbon, called the Ida Pingali of the Tantrists and the Cadesus (SASA) of the Greeks, it burned out the image laden fear that had been lying in wait to be released. Human males did not experience the birthing breath of the mothers which brought with it transformation. They called it a mystery, or a 'mystical' experience. They had to pursue it through other means such as ritual, drugs, meditation and other activities.

The panting mother became fearless as the result of the birthing breath as on a wave of ecstasy she bonded with the product of her labors. She also became not only fearless in the protection of her child but was endowed with the gifts of *lea*dership, healing and prophecy. Al Kahina of the Berbers comes to mind.

As far as I have been able to ascertain the chacras of the Tantrists are the only system that explains how the Kundalini energy up from the body of Mother Earth worked its magic through the human body.

They came up with the seven chacras. Each chacra was like an evolutionary system that dealt with the entrapment of fear.

- The base chacra at the anus, dealt with survival of eating and being eaten, the process of life on planet Earth.
- The second chacra at the sexual organs dealt with expression of sexual energy and the fears associated with its entrapment.
- The third chacra at the solar plexus dealt with power and hierarchy, and the establishment of violence and turf.
- The fourth chacra at the heart moves across the corpus callosum and fuses mother love with the infant.
- The fifth chacra at the throat, is the chacra of communication and creativity.
- The sixth chacra the third eye at the forehead, is the chacra of inner vision, total fear defusion and the beginning of self realization
- The seventh chacra is the chacra of transformation, the partial death from which you return (hiBERnation) and the total death from which

you don't. The partial death ushers in the process of enlightment.

The first three lower chacras deal with selfishness, violence and greed. The fourth chacra, the heart chacra of mothers love ushers in the promise of compassion, cooperation,tenderness and kindness.

It is to the SHAPE of the snake as the guide of the lost sun, the snake as the metaphoric double ribbon of the Kundalini energy rising along Lea lines up from the body of Mother Earth and the double helexical spin up the human spine that we owe our knowledge of the transformative proess. Each chacral process deals with concentratioin, with the fusion of the two hemispheres of the human brain at the center to create a balance from which fear had to be released.

The ancient mothers in PHASE ONE understood the process of fear defusion and the snake as its metaphoric symbol. When male centrality and the left hemisphere of the human brain overtook the global scene in PHASE THREE all things dealing with the mother energy had to be villified which included the state of transformation and the snake as its primary symbol.

Carrying the Kundalini energy of superior extensive knowledge the Kundalini snake tempted Eve and she shared it with Adam who wasn't ready to receive it and they both lost the Garden of Eden. The Leviathon, or water serpent had to be destroyed by the Hebrews. For the Greeks the Hydra with her snake hair fell into the same category.

RULE TWENTY-THREE;
Symbols

Check the names, SHAPES and metaphoric associations represented by ancient symbols and HOW they explained specific aspects dealing with the processes, qualities and functions of the individual mothers body in stage one and the surFACE and body of Mother Earth in stages two and four and their relationship to both of them.

YIN/YANG;

In PHASE ONE at the time of female centrality the original YIN (HAYANA), YANG (HAYANAGA) symbolic configuration dealt with the journey of the sun above the body of Mother Earth as YIN (HAYANA) during the day and through Her very intestines as YANG (HAYANAGA) at night.

The first linguistic clue surfaces in the first dyad as HAYA, for aya (HAYA) means both 'light' in Persian and 'dawn' in Assyrian. The ubiquitous metaphoric snake (IS NAKA, NAGA) in the second dyad enters the picture here as the Kundalini energy acting like the guide of the sun through the dark and wet subterranean intestines within the body of Mother Earth on its way to transformative rebirth. The (NA) at the end of both YIN (HAYANA) and YANG (HAYANAGA) deals with either' emergence on the surface', or 'change from one state to another'. Also in Chinese TAIYANG (TAYANAGA) deals with the snake (IS NAKA, NAGA) the light of the Persian sun aya (HAYA) below the surFACE of Mother Earth. The (TA) may find its origins out of the Assyrian aya as dawn and the PLACE in the Eastern sky, the horizontal tip (TA) from which the sun had been born.

The SHAPE of the letter (Y) on both the female body and the body of Mother Earth is the SHAPE of birthing, or the SHAPE of the pubis. On the individual female body the obvious emergence of life was through the triangular patch of the pubic hole. On the body of Mother Earth as the glow of light began to spread across the Eastern sky, the time that this observation was made it seemed to emerge from between two mountain peaks that stood at the rim, at the edge, at the horizon line, out of the tip of Her body. In Hebrew the mountain was known as har (HARA) or the 'belly', and the 'belly' dealt with the 'pregnant belly' the mountainous body of Mother Earth out of which the sun had been considered to be born. Also in Hebrew to be pregnant is harah.

Yang E (HA(YA)NAGA) in Chinese is castration and dealt with the underground sun symbolizing the castrated eunuch (HANAKA). The (KA) and (GA) are interchangeable.

The Chinese YIN (HAYANA) shares linguistic links with the Hindu YONI (HAYANA) that stands for the female pubis and vulva. In Lithuanian also as YONI she was the oven out of the lavic fires of creation spewing out of the body of Mother Earth. As IONE (HAYANA) she was the Semitic YONI (HAYANA). For the Etruscans she was UNI (HANA) or also YONI (HAYANA) the one (HANA) source of all creation.

As the YONI of all creation the dyad deals with the sun and the body of Mother Earth that had been considered to be at one with each other or one unit. All the above names deal with the SHAPE of the pubis on the body of Mother Earth (Y) and ther sun (IS HANA) and with light aya (HAYA), 'light' in Persian and 'dawn' in Assyrian. So all the above names are connected with the body of Mother Earth giving birth to the sun out of Her mountainous pubic belly.

Section Two

Taking it a step back and associating it with the female body out of stage three YANAKASHI (HAYANAKASA) was the name for a Bemba queen. The overlapping dyads deal with; the YONI (HAYANA) that linguistically contains the aya of 'light' and 'dawn' in it, the metaphoric snake (IS NAKA) as the guide of the sun, and the female pubis sometime called the kashi (KASA) but more commonly known as the coos (KASA). Both the individual female mother and the body of Mother Earth are covered in the name for a Bemba queen.

In Polish JASNA (HAYASANA) means 'light', as opposed to darkness, for the sun not only brought light and illuminated the body of Mother Earth but was as light as a feather in its flight across the sky. The word JA(SA)NA (HAYA(SA)NA) reflecting the process above it, halved by the (SA) of the solar energy, as the belly of air above the body of Mother Earth is halved by the journey of the sun across it. One not only reflects the other but bears witness to the process.

The YANG (HAYANAGA) of YIN/YANG originally in PHASE ONE dealt with the sun after it had set back into the body of Mother Earth, was swallowed by Her at the Western wall of death, to be guided in its transformative journey by the patiently waiting coiled upon itself snake (IS NAKA, NAGA). The journey of the ubiquitous snake guiding the sun was either through the dark mysterious rivers of water, or through the gory channels of blood. Both the dark water and the gory blood came out of the bloody horizontal rim of the setting sun in the Western sky and its bloody red splash of color at the end of its life. The sun and the snake working as a unit had been related to the internal intestines within the body of Mother Earth.

Some subsequent mythologies in PHASES TWO and THREE took up the water as the internal stream and washed a lot as the Hebrews did with the mikvah and the Muslims followed with absolutions at the entrance to a temple and the Christians with the rites of Baptism.

Others went for the blood as the via of passage for the snake guided sun and sacrificed human beings on the altars of their madness as the Aztec, Maya and others. Christianity blended the two with the rites of Baptism and the chalice of blood with Christ saying' drink of me for this is my blood', He was after all the metaphorical son (IS HANA) of the sun (IS HANA).

For the mythologies dealing with water as the source for the journey of the sun not to get lost within the body of Mother Earth dealt with the reincarnation of the individual soul. As the sun returned, or was born again to a new day, so the soul would be born again to a new life. In Spanish the name for the sun is sol (IS HALA) and has very distinctive links with the soul (IS HALA), out of the Greek eelyos (HALASA) that carries the blood (SA) of the sun in its name.

For the Aztec and Maya in Central America, the fear was not so much for the individual soul but for the fact that the sun might get lost within the maze within the body of Mother Earth and not make its appearance at dawn. They must have left Africa after a great cataclysm that had its roots in the sun not returning to the sky, either after great rains, or a cloud of ash after a volcanic blast. Their whole preoccupation was with the snake guiding the sun and with creating enough channels of blood underneath and within the body of Mother Earth so that the sun would not get stuck or lost in Her intestines. To that end human sacrifice filled the bill as shamanic priests killed everything in sight to create the rivers of blood that pulsed through the body of Mother Earth. To keep the blood pulsating to that end they also yanked out the beating hearts of their victims. The heart (HARA-) is also within the belly (HARA).

That whole process became established in PHASE ONE and the Chinese YIN/YANG representing the sun (YIN) above the body of Mother Earth during the day with a dot of the moon in it and the sun below (YANG) the body of Mother Earth with the snake guiding it through the perilous dark night, with the dot of the sun in it.

In PHASE TWO as male role in specific procreation was becoming known the YIN/YANG of creation became redefined as a female-male symbol with the dot of the female in the male side and the dot of the male in the female side. It echoes a similar cincept locked in the Runic hooked X. It too rpresents a female male symbol of ten months of lunar gestation in the letter X and the male penis entering the scene as the erect penis in the hooked letter X.

In PHASE THREE the SHAPE of the letter Y associated with the SHAPE of the female pubis emerged as the word WHY of male questing, based on the nature of not only their peripheral state but of the mutilation, maiming and castrating that had been visited upon them. As their role in procreation was becoming known in PHASE TWO another group of factors emerged in PHASE THREE and led to total male centrality.

Most creatures are composed of two sides. One side reflects the other. That duality also occurs in human beings and is reflected in the brain. The brain consists of two distinct sides that are connected by the corpus callosum, the via of passage, the bridge, the rainbow, the ladder that connects two disparate sets of human potential. The left hemisphere of the brain crisscrosses at the area of the upper nose and controls the right hand side of the body. The right hemisphere crisscrosses and controls the left handed side of the body. Since very ancient times the left side of the human body had been considered female and the right side of the body had been considered male.

Early writing usually moved from right to left. It has been postulated to have been written by the left hand. After the dextral shift into male centrality in PHASE TWO writing shifted and was perceived to have been written by the right hand. Dextral deals with (DA) the 'gift of' the extra hand and the extra hand originally was the right hand associated with maleness.

Along with the shift from the left handed tendency of the mother's to the right handed tendency of the father's, there also occurred the evolution of communication as partly a linear activity in human beings such as drumming, speaking, singing and most importantly writing itself. All of these activities are sequential in nature. One thing follows another in a straight line. In drumming, one tap on a drum or a hollow log follows another tap. In speaking, one SOUND follows another. In singing, except for a few Tibetan monks, only one SOUND can be made by the vocal cords at the same time. Writing whether right to left, left to right, or up and down, deals with sequence and a linear orientation. This linear focus fed into the left hemispheric male side of the brain and began to develop it beyond its role in physical survival into answering questions dealing with the WHY of their peripheral and much tormented state. The asking of WHY bifurcated the human brain. The two sides grew further apart, the SHAPE of the letter Y symbolism comes into play. There are no answers to WHY. The answers to WHY have to be made up out of fantasy, out of theoretical speculation, out of the careening turmoil within the brain itself. The images stored in the brain have to be rearranged and no longer attached to what is actually real. They have to create a dual reality that creates a place that men can call their own. It has to deal with speculation, the mist of the mister, the fallacy of the phallus for;

THE ANSWER TO WHY IS ALWAYS A LIE.

In PHASE THREE humanity is dealing with the burden of fantasy being pushed forward as truth. The fantasy of the father's is based on faith, on systems that suspend what is experienced in the body and forced to deal with what is offered by the mind. The fickle mind like the SHAPE shifting moon and SHAPE shifting vowels cannot be counted upon. Here the goosepimply goose might find an answer.

Efforts emerged to relink the two hemispheres of the brain before total annihalation of the specie occurs. To that end Mother Nature stepped in to help. She created the fusion of the male essence with the female essence before birth into what exists as homosexuality. Homosexuality is Mother Natures effort to somehow rebalance the human brain and take it out of the single focused, linear, exclusive, competitive, violent male orientation. When she created the Gays (Gaia) she was helped with what had already been occurring on the planet. There was a host of boys that were already stripped of their maleness through castration. An unanticipated tendency entered the scene for the castrated boys joined by the homosexual gays created the priesthood that officiated over the rites of the setting sun. What also became their domain is the area of mysticism that as trance created an altered state of consciousness. What the trance state revealed or professed to reveal was an answer to the age old questions dealing with humanity's greatest anguish that dealt with death, reincarnation and immortality.

In PHASE THREE the links with the body of Mother Earth-sun construct had been obliterated as new traditions were being established. But still the ancient SOUNDS rear their burkad heads and surface with the sad strains of mournful violins overwhelming us with the sun, its light, the snake, the triangular pubic SHAPE on the female body and the volcanic triangle on the body of Mother Earth, the questing male role in the scheme of things, and the madness locked in the left hemispheric right handed brain that has put the whole planet to flight.

In PHASE ONE the YIN-YANG dealt with the sun above the body of Mother Earth as YIN and the sun below the body of Mother Earth as YANG. With the shift into male inclusion in the procreative process in PHASE TWO it became the female and male forever spinning through space.

The Cross (KA(RA)SA);

Using RULE NUMBER NINETEEN out of; RULES OF ORIGINAL SOUND DISCOVERY (ROSD) dealing with METAPLASM or the removing or insertion of letters within a word began it's life as the time keeping Svastika.

The original perception of the CROSS, without the RA of the Egyptian male sun God at the center, (KA(RA)SA) in PHASE ONE dealt with the coos (KASA) or the house casa (KASA) of creation that was Mother Earth and the sun, out of the most ancient perception of source as the 'at one' construct. Casa (KASA) is house in Spanish. The (KA) dealt with Mother Earth creating smaller reflections out of Her body. The (SA) dealt with the sun in its creative aspect as coagulated lavic blood, the (SA) of SAngre as blood in Spanish.

With the addition of RA the Egyptian sun God through Her linguistic center, the ancient coos (KASA) became the cross (KA(RA)SA). A similar construct surfaces also in PHASE THREE with the coos (KASA) and the female period as the curse (KA(RA)SA).

With the inclusion of RA the Egyptian male sun God, it also becomes apparent that we are dealing with the relationship between Mother Earth and a specific solar movement across the sky. For the cross (KARASA) in PHASE ONE had also been considered a caress (KARASA). If we are dealing with the sky then what passed across (haKARASA) the sky or Her belly of air creating a cross (KARASA), was perceived to be a celestial caress (KARASA).

What was it that created such a sensuous passage across the sky caressing Mother Earths belly of air? During the day coasting East to West across (haKARASA) Her belly of air was the sun. At night the caress (KARASA) was left to the SHAPE shifting fickle moon. It was masturbation, or caressing of the clitoris that helped to deliver the human baby. Mother Earth giving birth to the heavenly bodies out of Her body must also have needed the masturbatory celestial caressing. The Egyptian god Amun who nightly masturbated all of existence into being in PHASE THREE must have gotten the idea that masturbation produced a baby from somewhere.

From North to South the caressing across the sky came from the rapturous semiannual flight of birds. The sun and moon East West in one direction and the birds North South in another created the celestial cross. In PHASE THREE as the number four became a male symbol the cross became a quadrant with the crisscrossing becoming two diagonal lines emerging into the squared horizontal rim. That male quadrant SHAPE above the body of Mother Earth in Her sky or belly of air was the original avian caressing cross (KARASA) that crisscrossed the sky.

The tender implications of the sensual passage of the sun, moon and birds paying homage and giving pleasure to Mother Earth dealt with what must have transpired on the plane below between females and males and must have had its origins out of PHASE TWO when there was a short period of peaceful coexistence between the sexes.

Another factor dealing with crisscrossed lines above the body of Mother Earth is the letter X (KS)(KASA). The letter X (KASA) deals directly with the coos (KASA). The age old saying that 'X marks the spot', is not something mysterious. It deals with the 'period at the end'. We are not dealing here with a sentence. We are dealing with the tail end on the female body, her buttox or coos (KASA). With the passage of blood, or 'the period at the end', it defines the specific house, casa (KASA) in Spanish, of creation out of the individual mother's body her coos (KASA).

To the SHAPE of the actual cross was added the SHAPE of the Swastika as the emergence of the sun in the East encoded in the anglular SHAPE of the letter L, the angle of the tongue pushing, or regurgitating the sun up to the surFACE.

The SHAPE of the suns descent off Mother Earth's body in the blood spattered Western sky was reflected by the SHAPE of the letter L of light and life in the East to become the number seven (7) on the Westrn side. The birds emerging semiannually out of the Northern and Southern reaches also created the angles of both ascent and descent.

Number seven is the 'SHAPE OF THE FALL' off the edge, the SHAPE associated with a multiplicity of terminations, primarily in PHASE ONE of the sun dying to its light. In Hebrew the same SHAPE of the angle of descent for the number seven only echoes the same ancient perception. It shares its origin with the ancient migrations in Africa that were based on the thirteen month lunar calendar. The year began in March or Aries when the march to 'greener pastures' in the distant drenched savannahs began. They trudged six months in one direction, rested, have birth and mated then in sept of September, the month of seven and separation in Latin, the journey back home began. So seven on endless mythological levels in PHASE THREE became a number associated with endings and with separation, in time with death.

It moves into the ancient use of the number seven in the seven step mastaba, the pyramid of entombment for the pharaoh, seventh heaven a place of repose after the last separation for both the Christians and Jews, seven chacras or energy centers of the Tantrists, the Pleiades the starry seven sisters or mothers, who judged the dead. Not to be left out the seven seals of the apocalypse. Seven is either a lucky number or an unlucky number depending where you alight upon the human mythical configuration. The list goes on.

When the metaphorical number seven surfaces we are dealing with two very ancient activities and concepts of separation and ending. One is based in the lunar based migratory trek and its semiannual separation to and fro from the 'promised land' of the verdant savannah. The other is based on the SHAPE of the sun's daily descent off the planet.

To that lateral configuration of the passage of the sun and moon East and West and the vertical passage of birds North and South that created the SHAPE of the cross across the belly of air. Placed one upon the other you not only get the caress of the cross but you get the SHAPE of the swastika, one of the most ancient symbols found from Iceland to Japan. In Sanskrit the svastika meant "so be it" or 'amen'. For the Japanese it was the ideogram for 'infinity'. In PHASE ONE the moon swastika pointed to the left and was associated with the Left Handed Path of the Goddess and women. In PHASE TWO the swastika turned to the right and the Right Handed Path was associated with a male God and subsequently Nazism. The (V) and (W) are interchangeable.

Because of its ancient role associated with God Thor and the Aryan ancestry, the Nazis adopted the swastika as their symbol. It once stood for something so simple and obvious as a celestial clock, with the passage of the sun, and moon, back and forth, and the birds up and down across the sky. It morphed into 'so be it', 'amen', 'infinity' and the Nazi symbol of brutality and power of the unimpeded right handed left hemispheric male brain in full swing.

The fact is that the SHAPE of the original swastika came out of the continent of Africa and illustrated the SHAPE of an ancient time keeper. The sun moving laterally across the sky delineated the passage of day and night, the twelve solar months and the changing of seasons once the movement away from the equator occurred in PHASE THREE. The passage of the moon at night established the thirteen month lunar calendar, and the cyclical phases of the moon. The vertical semiannual coming and going of the birds announced the time for the ancient migrations to begin their journey North and South across the African continent.

In PHASE ONE the primacy of Mother Earth emerged with the sign of the circle with the cross in it, or the horizon all around with the dual passage of sun, moon across and the birds up and down. In PHASE TWO as male role in procreation was becoming known and number four became a male symbol, the four sided square enclosed the circle that had been Mother Earth.

Square (IS KARA) and zakir (IS HAKARA) is penis in Arabic, the hacker (HAKA-) of the body of the female as he penetrated her, became reflected on the celestial level as the sun (RA) hacked the body of Mother Earth at the horizon, the (RANA) as wound and dawn scenario in Polish as he raped Her and set into Her in PHASE THREE. Kara means punishment in Polish.

In PHASE TWO the ancient three sided triangle of the mother as the SHAPE of the pubis on the female body and the three sided volcano on the body of Mother Earth was becoming replaced by the emerging four sided male square as the round huts and circles of the mothers became eplaced by the four sided boxed homes of the fathers.

It happened this way. Little girls when they were born were defined by the letter (A) and their capacity to make babies out of the SHAPE of the pubic triangle on their bodies and their association to the source of creation, the SHAPE of the triangular volcanic cone out of the body of Mother Earth. Little boys were puzzling to them. They had a body like the mother but they also had extra genitalia on the outside like other males around them. Their bodies did not make babies so they didn't know how to define them. They became defined by the SHAPE of the penis and one (I) more.

In PHASE TWO as male role in procreation was becoming known, male sexuality was perceived to be based on the eye (I) of seeing, the concept expanded into PHASE TWO when the one (I) became the I of the self. The concept of *individuality* out of the left hemisphere of the human brain began to replace the cooperative configurations of the ancient mothers. The mother as 'source' in PHASE ONE was becoming replaced by the father as 'source' in PHASE TWO.

Since little girls were represented by the (A) of the three sided triangle of both the SHAPE of the pubis and the volcanic cone, with the addition of one (I) more to the three aspects of the mother, the number four came into play. Three plus one becomes four. The four sided square (IS KARA) becomes a male symbol. It surfaces as the tefilah or boxes worn on the forehead and upper arm of Orthodox Jews. No longer is the four sided cross above the body of Mother Earth residing within the circle. The female circle now becomes contained within the male square. No longer is Mother Earth the larger context holding within Her the male offspring. The male squares like the male arms now encircle her and hold Her in their grasp.

An ancient symbolic configuration pops up in the SHAPE of a pyramid. The four sided square with the diagonals crisscrossing it becomes the context for the SHAPE of the pyramids as sources of fused power. The male square on the bottom of the pyramid has four female triangles above it. In PHASE TWO across the continent of Africa and in PHASE THREE for the Middle Easterners, the man as the square below had been allowed four wives, with the four triangles above him. Among the foraging and contemporarily settled Zoa tribe in the Amazon basin, a woman has four husbands and their legends recount that their ancestors had to flee their ancient homeland due to a great flood. They are a more ancient people out of PHASE ONE and Africa before the power shifted in PHASE TWO and the mother lost her power as the circle ended up within the square in PHASE THREE and the pyramid emerged as a symbol of male power.

The implications of sexual positions and the abdication of Lilith as not wanting to service Adam in the missionary position has very ancient roots.

It doesn't stop there. One upmanship comes into play as history HIS STORY barrels into the future with something more massive as the square is replaced by the multisided cube (KABA), the most holy shrine of the Muslims as the Kaaba (KABA).

In PHASE THREE the cross (KARASA) left behind the caress (KARASA) between the heavenly bodies, birds and Mother Earth to become a Christian symbol with Christ (KARASA-) crucified upon it. There is a misinterpretation here for Christ dealt with both the inherent power of the crystal (KARASA-) and the transforming activity associated with the butterfly chrysalis (KARASA-). The butterfly dealt with the transformative power of the sun during the day. The moth as the symbol of the menstruating mother dealt with the transformative power of the moon at night.

The separation myths surface here. To create their solar and then male Gods *away* and *above* the body of Mother Earth the separation had to be made complete. In PHASE THREE in Christianity an effort has been made to reconnect the solar deity with the body of Mother Earth through the transformative Christ (KARASA-) by fusing the body of Mother Earth with the sun (SON) above Her. The original meaning of the separation leading to male Gods *away* and *above* the body of Mother Earth became lost through suppression, obliteration, redefinition and destruction.

The emergence of the transformed Christ upon the planetary scene dealt with the values inHERent in the ancient mothers, in HER. It harkens back to the left handed path of the mothers to cooperate by turning the other cheek, forgiveness, kinship, helping the poor, healing, performing gifts of kindness, cooperation, compassion, and of loving thy neighbor. The Gospel of Mary Magdalene as Christ's major disciple recounts what has been left behind and obliterated.

What we sadly miss in our convoluted male dominated and redefined world is the unconditional love that human beings held for their magnificent and majestic body of Mother Earth.

Star of David;

Back to the triangles of the mother. In PHASE ONE in stage three, the individual females as the surrogates of Mother Earth in the creation of small replicas out of their bodies, both shared the perception defined by two triangular SHAPES, one as the triangular hairy SHAPE of the pubis on the trunk of the individual mother, and the other, the triangular SHAPE of the volcanic cone on the body of Mother Earth. Place one over the other and you get what in PHASE THREE emerged as the Hebrew STAR of DAVID.

Like the Chinese Yin/Yang, the two triangles did not originate as defining the female-male construct. That emerged in PHASE TWO and solidified in PHASE THREE. Hiding in the Biblical name of David (DAVADA) you get the double 'gift of' (DA) of the mother's (VA) of the hairy vulvic (VA) patch on the female body and of the volcano (VA) on the body of Mother Earth. The same concept surfaces here as the repeated (SS).

The name DAVID (DAVADA) not only reflects itself (DAVA)/(VADA) creating a balance, but contains within its linguistic coils vida (VADA) or the 'gift of ' (DA) 'life' in Spanish. In the Hebrew Bible in PHASE THREE it was David who slew the giant Goliath by a blow to his skull or third eye in the center of his forehead. The giant was the metaphotic Mother Earth. The blow dealt with the third eye in the forehead that can be activated on the way into a trance state and mysticism associated with the mother's birthing breath out of PHASE ONE. The same thing happened to the one eyed Cyclops.

The fact that David (DAVADA) with the balance apparent in his name, killed the Mother essence with a rock or stone takes us to the trance state of rocking and becoming stoned. What the story of David tries to tell us is that the balanced, transformed male with the birthing breath of the mother alive in him, having access to the Kundalini energy, no longer needed the mother energy and the state of becoming a eunuch to realize his transformation, so he killed the giant Goliath representing Her. The story of David illustrates the battle between heterosexual males using RITUAL to gain their transformed states, battling the Mother and her ancient power base. What these legends are trying to tell us is how the primacy of the individual mother and Mother Earth had become decimated. What it also establishes is the on going battle between the eunuch castrated priesthood and the emerging transformed heterosexual males. It is a battle that exists to this day.

One triangle superimposed on another triangle emerging as the six (IS HAKASA) pointed Hebrew STAR of DAVID also associates the six points with human sex (IS HAKASA) and expands to embrace human sexuality. For it was perceived that the male penis was like a weapon that hacked (HAKA-) the coos (KASA) of the female during the sex act. It may have dealt with deflowering a virgin, or with clitorectomies.

The ANKH (HANAKA);

In its SHAPE and ancient origin, the ankh (HANAKA) looks like the circular orb (O) of the sun on top being pushed up to the surFACE by a tongue like serpentine appendage out of the body of Mother Earth. It also looks like a clove, the aromatic herb. But it is with the Ankh (HANAKA) that we have to turn to to get the most salient clues. For the ANKH (HANAKA) hides in its linguistic folds the ancient name of the eunuch (HANAKA) priesthood. It dealt with the sun (IS HANA) on top and the guide of the sun, the snake (IS NAKA) on the bottom. It illustrates the same concept as the FIRST PHASE Chinese Yin Yang. It was the eunuch priesthood that dealt with the rites associated with the rising and the setting of the sun.

The SHAPE of the ANKH and its name bears witness to the fact that the eunuch priesthood reigned supreme in the Egyptian pantheon. The fact that Isis looked for her brother's body parts and reassembled him with every part but the penis takes us into PHASE ONE when the first born brother was castrated to act as the protector of his sister's children. There are many ancient names of all kinds of celestial deities that have in them the same eunuch (HANAKA) construct; the Ananake (HANANAKA), Channukah (HANAKA), Ankh (HANAKA), Anak (HANAKA) Krakatoa, Enki (HANAKA), Enkidu (HANAKADA) the friend of Sumerian Gilgamesh, Inca (HANAKA), the names of eunuchs ((HANAKA) at some ancient time out of PHASE ONE were not only universal but exhibited great power to have so many people, places and processes named after them.

Bindu (BANADA);

Is the Hindu circle with a dot in the center. That symbol covers a multifaceted story. In stage one out of the mother's face, it is the SHAPE of the eye with the pupil in the center, watching and learning how to survive becoming the universal pupil (PAPALA). When the pupil grows up and survives its infancy it joins the ranks of grown up people (PAPALA).

As it expands to include the body of Mother Earth, the Hindu BINDU is the human creature standing in the center of an enormous circle that ends at the horizontal rim equidistantly in all directions. The eye stretching to the edges of reality creates a round ground of being around them, with every creature creating its own airy womb. The circular SHAPE of the BINDU surfaces with a dot at the center. The dot is the period at the end and deals with mother cenrality out of PHASE ONE.

Then there is the concept of zero (IS HARA). When the circle of the mother's womb or belly had a dot in it, the dot represented her menstrual period. The period at the end scenario. It announced to the curious assemblage that her womb, her source of creation was empty, that there was no life in her belly, hara in Hebrew and Japanese, that there was a zero (IS HARA) planted within her belly.

When early humanity in PHASE ONE tried to define the role of men in the specific procreative process they were aware that males were creatures with a permanently empty belly. As the single source out of the mind of God gained momentum male creative reality had to emerge from somewhere. So it emerged BEFORE the zero (IS HARA) of the permanently empty belly. It emerged out of the space BEFORE the zero, like the 'hidden' God himself, it emerged out of the ethers, as an idea of the mind, as an opinion, as a reality BEFORE that which was physically real 'hidden' in the female womb.

The English word opinion establishes a clue. Here the birds come to our linguistic aid. For a pinion is a wing on a bird and keeps the bird afloat in the air, not unlike an idea (HADA). The Judeo-Christian name of God is Deus (DASA), which is plural as ideas (HADASA) since God in PHASE THREE had been perceived to create everything out of His mind. Hadassah (HADASA) as a Hebrew women's organization linguistically harkens back to its PHASE ONE roots. The (O) at the beginning of opinion established the word as being related not only to the round disc of the sun that also floats in the ethers, but with the concept of maleness as the zero of the permanently empty womb. Not to be left behind it also makes its appearance at the end of Spanish male names.

RULE TWENTY-FOUR; NUMBERS their ancient source. The spread of NUMBERS have their links with the ten fingers on the human hand and the ten claws on the paws of the carnivores. Number (NAMA MABA BARA) contains in its linguistic construct a series of intriguing possibilities.Perhaps numbers came before letters in the naming (NAMA-) of things. With the (BARA) dyad at the end we are dealing with the 'intermediate state' and a source of wonder and transformation. Had numbers been the first codified objects to have been given names (NAMA) and considerd sacred? In Hebrew numbers are associated with letters. The African country of Namidia (NAMADA) may have been the source of codified numbers (NAMABA-).

Teen (TANA);

As more numbers were added to the original ten (TANA) fingers they also become defined by the concept of 'holding', as thirteen (taraTANA), fourteen (faraTANA), fifteen (fafaTANA) etc. Not all the concepts emerge clearly but thirteen (taraTANA) deals with the thirteen lunar cycles that defined the ancient year of Mother Tara in PHASE ONE. It is one of the main reasons how the number thirteen became associated with the devil and with bad luck. In PHASE THREE as the male redefinitions proliferated, all concepts belonging to the body of Mother Earth along with Mother Earth Herself had to be suppressed and defiled.

Fourteen were the four (FARA) fingers of fire (RA) that burst through the fabric of dawn. Without the angle of the opposable thumb they could not deal with helping and holding of babies and became associated with males. The number fifteen includes the thumb, as the five fingers (FAFA) of fire (RA) that as rays of light clawed their way up to the surFACE. The number five in PHASE ONE dealt with the five fingers of holding, with the opposable thumb that did the holding associated with the mothers. The SHAPE of the letter V with the thumb opposing the four fingers surfaces in the Latin number five of the mother. The number four dealt with the four fingers of males who did not do the holding of new born children. It established four as their symbolic number.

The (TANA) dyad of ten (TANA) deals with (NA) as 'emergence on the surface' or 'a change from a former state'. The (TA) deals the tip or top on the body of Mother Earth. It moves to define the tent (TANATA) as the source of creation on the body of Mother Earth, the tent like triangular SHAPE of the volcanic cone and the inverted triangle of the hairy pubis. It moves to embrace the concept of tenderness (TANA-), the same as the caress of the crossing of the heavenly travelers across the sky and the kindness of the kin (KANA) out of the cone (KANA) of creation. In PHASE ONE the relationships between Mother Earth and all that caressed their way across Her surFACE was sensuous and beloved. That same condition must have existed among the individual mothers on Her plane.

The concept of one (HANA) out of PHASE ONE dealt with Mother Earth and the sun having been considered to be one single unit of creation. the 'emergence on the surface' (NA), into the air above her (HA). Along the way as the separation myths were being formed, in PHASE TWO the sun (IS HANA) became separate from the body of Mother Earth.

Many of the following words have their origins out of the passage of the sun. ON (HANA), the sun upON the body of Mother Earth. IN (HANA) the sun (IS HANA) withIN the body of Mother Earth. UN (HANA), the sun UNder the surFACE of Mother Earth. AN (HANA) the sun (IS HANA) ANother object ANgling through space. EN (HANA) deals with the journey of the sun (IS HANA) ENtering the space above the body of Mother Earth and on the other side ENding the light of day. EON (HANA) deals with the sun marking the passage of endless (HANADA-) time. On the human level because the process inherent within a boy had been undefined he became called as one (1) more. Added to the three of the mother he emerged with the male number four.

Two (TAWA);

The number two (TAWA) deals with reflection in the waters (WA) on the body of Mother Earth. One reality was perceived to exist above the surFACE of Mother Earth on her tip (TA), top (TA) and a second reality existed reflected in Her waters (WA). The concept has a relationship with the number seven (IS EVEN, or HAVANA) the same reflection 'as above so below'. There was also perceived to be an even (HAVANA) distribution of what was above in life (TA) and what was below in death (WA). It echoes the 'two in one' concept. Also on the human level the fetus floating in the watery womb of the mother created the concept of 'two in one' and gave birth to the letter (B) that became associated with both, babble, birth and the baby. The two in one on the human body covers a series of aspects; both, body, back, breasts, boobs, brow, brain, buzia (face) in Polish, brazos (arms) in Spanish. On the body of Mother Earth it desls with the bio of life.

Three (TARA);

Ancient Indo European primal most revered Mother Goddess Tara as Mother Earth, was worshipped from Ireland across the Middle East and India. The plane of land on the surFACE of Mother Earth that had been created by the triangular three (TARA) sided volcanic cone established the terrain (TARA-) out of the tar (TARA) that as lava spilled and coagulated across Her surFACE. From another declination it becomes the first (SA). The second (SA) is the blood of the individual mother that spilled monthly and when arrested like an internal dam in her body coagulated into the creation of a baby. Dam (DAMA) is the 'gift of' (DA) the mother (MA) in whom the blood had become dammed. In PHASE THREE with male role in specific paternity having become realized the internal dam within the mother became the damNed, or smothered in shame and accursed by the emerging male God.

The triad (TARA-) associated with the SHAPE of the triangular volcanic cone and the triangular SHAPE of the mother's hairy pubis emerged defining many of the processes, qualities and functions of the subsequent Goddesses covering many bases. One of the most ancient ones out of PHASE ONE reflected the family (FAMALA) unit based on the female (FAMALA) as mother.

The Goddess TRINITY surfaces all over the ancient world copying the construction of the human family unit resulting in the definition of early Goddesses as; the young girl, the mature birth giving mother and the wise old matriarch grandmother. The Virgin-Mother-Crone surfaces as Creatress, Preserver and Destroyer. It was the wise old Crone (KARANA), like the elephant matriarch, who was the *lea*der and wore the crown (KARA(WA)NA).

For the Greeks she was the Virgin Hebe, Mother Hera and the Crone as Hecate. In Ireland she was Ana, Babd and Macha. In India she was Parvati, Durga, and Uma. In Chaucer's time already in PHASE THREE she still remained female and was Luna in heaven, Diana on Earth and Proserpine in hell.

At the time of transition in PHASE TWO and a short lived balance and peaceful coexistence between the sexes there was a mixture of Goddesses and Gods that made up the TRINITY. The Babylonian trinity was Shamash the sun, Sin the moon, and Ishtar the star. In Greece the same construct was repeated as Helios the sun, Selene the moon, and Aphrodite the star. For the Arabian Christians there was God, Mary and Jesus replacing the Egyptian trinity of Osiris, Isis and Horus.

In PHASE THREE as males created their own Gods, the female aspect of the TRINITY was torally dismissed as male Gods co-opted the scene. In India Brahma, Vishnu and Shiva emerged as the Hindu TRINITY. Among the Germanic tribes the all male TRINITY included Woden, Thor and Saxnot. For the Christians in PHASE THREE the TRINITY became the Father, Son and the Holy Ghost. The Holy Ghost may have originated as the female Sophia, 'the wise one', cognate of Shakti and the Shekinah and the original Kundalini energy. As the male Christian hierarchy dismissed the female aspect in the Godhead, the Holy Ghost as the vilified mystical Mother Earth Kundalini energy of SHE dropped off the (S) of the mothers blood to become referred to as a 'he'.

The TREE (TARA) had been considered to be a creative force that had been perceived to unite the body of Mother Earth and the sky-sun construct. It was perceived to be made up of three (TARA) parts, the fan of branches shooting up into the air, the fan of roots creeping deep under the ground and the spindle SHAPED trunk that connected them. In Greek that spindle SHAPE is called atractos as both aspects above and below had been perceived to be attracted to each other. Again the relationship between the body of Mother Earth and all that passed across Her surFACE, in one way or another gave Her pleasure. Trees were worshipped all around the ancient world as carriers of the Mother Kundalini energy.

Four;

The four (FARA) fingers of fire (FARA) without the thumb that as the piercing rays of the sun spLIT the circular horizontal rim of Mother Earth to be born at dawn takes us ironically to stage four. The (RA) defines the sun and the (FA) deals with the SHAPE of the stiletto like rays of the sun that like the four fingers pierced through the circular horizontal rim of Mother Earth.

The number four (FARA) itself emerged out of a much more ancient concept of the mothers doing the work with their five fingers including the thumb.

Females of the specie, especially mothers were defined by the letter A(ah) associated with the SHAPE of the triangular volcanic cone related to the process of land creation. Since no babies issued forth from male bellies in PHASE ONE they were defined either by the O (oh) of the empty belly or by the concept of one more (I). The one more became the I, or one more of the individual self. At the end of the word alumni it still deals with more than one and plurality. Added to the triad of the females, three plus one became FOUR. FOUR emerged not only as a male number but also as a square (IS KARA). The emerging male perception of their uniqueness in PHASE TWO needing their own symbols, the female circle of Mother Earth around them ending at the horizontal rim became replaced by the square (IS KARA). The four sided square became the frame (FARAMA) of fire (FARA) at the horizontal rim (RAMA) in the Western sky where the sun had been swallowed or sank to its death.

The concept also established the FOUR cardinal points in the sky separate from and above the body of Mother Earth. The study of the skies and of the solstices and equinoxes as sources of power begins to emerge here as males turned to the skies to make them their own place of 'source' *away* and *above* the body of Mother Earth after their concept of source had been reflected in the standing seas.

For the Muslims the square did not seem to be enough. They created a four sided box, a cube (KABA) calling it the sacred Kaaba (KABA) and a place of pilgrimage in Mecca. To fulfill their spiritual duties they fulfill their haj by circling the Kaaba in an anti clockwise direction, or to the left that belonged to the ancient mothers. Worshipping the SHAPE of the square (IS KARA) cum cube or box, became a male preoccupation. To this day male Orthodox Jews wear sacred boxes, the tefilah on their foreheads and upper arms when they pray.

As the square (IS KARA) became the male symbol it linguistically began to echo the male genital organs that became associated with their new found source. For the Arabs the penis became zeker (IS HAKARA). The word for male virility in Hebrew became zakar (IS HAKARA). It had its origins out of the zero (IS HARA) of the permanently empty male belly sharing its linguistic links with the reflected Ethiopian Lord of the Underworld as Zar (IS HARA). In Polish Zar (IS HARA) defines the volcanic fires within the oven of Mother Earth. It seems like an unfortunate choice of words for the penis and virility, for it deals with the hacking (HAKA-) of the female body in twain during copulation. In Polish KARA stands for punishment. It must have been at the time when clitorectomies were performed on poor young girls and their clitoris was not only removed but their whole vulvic opening was sewn up. Only a little hole was left for menstruation and urination. The activity of hacking the struggling mother apart during cohabitation must have had horrendous consequences. When the same linguistic construct surfaces in Poland, closer to home it becomes more practical as siekiera (IS HAKARA), the name of the hacking ax (HAKASA).

As the male left hemispheric brain of the fathers split apart to gain supremacy over the right hemisphere of the mothers, John the Divine on the Island of Padmos reflected on the future that FOUR horsemen would create the end of the world, the Apocalypse. Its ironic that FOUR had been established as a male number.

Five;

If the male number four dealt with the four fingers of fire piercing through the fabric of dawn then five (FAVA) dealt with the whole hand and the FIVE fingers of the mother that comprise it. The opposable thumb comes into play here. Extended away from the four fingers, the angle created by the thumb creates the (V) SHAPE that surfaces in Latin as the number five (FAVA). (FA) deals with the fingers and (VA) deals with the angle created by the thumb. For it was the helping hand of Mother Earth giving birth to the sun (IS HANA) that was the 'gift of' (DA) the hand (HANADA). The sun helped Mother Earth in the maintenance of life above Her surFACE. It was Her FIVE fingered helping hand, the sun comprised of the four fingers and the thumb that did the holding, maintaining and helping of human babies. The four male fingers without the thumb could not do the job of making, holding and maintaining.

Six (IS HAKASA);

During the ancient migrations, it was in the sixth (IS HAKASA) lunar month that the herbivore mares dropped their foals. With the dropping of their foals they became privy to mating. Sex (IS HAKASA) entered the picture in August, for August was the sixth month if you counted March as the beginning of the ancient migratory lunar year. Six (IS HAKASA) and sex (IS HAKASA) bear a striking, if disturbing resemblance to each other. Both deal with hacking (HAKA-) apart of the coos (KASA). How was that possible since the foaling of mares is not necessarily that difficult. Some thing else must have happened to young girls on that ancient migratory journey across the continent of Africa in August. It was a time just before the turn around, the separation in the seventh month of September back to their home in the waiting savannah. In that ancient and much more practical time there was a specific instrument that deflowered young virgins to make sex more pleasurable and birthing easier. Not all mothers may have been privy to the birthing breath. Was August the time when that ancient deflowering ceremony took place? AU also means South. Was it a pointing South on the migratory trek that established the sexy sixth month of AUgust as the beginning of preparation for the journey back home? Six also deals not only with sex but with procreation. When the lower case letters of the Western Alphabet become known, it becomes apparent that they look like tadpoles, minnows or grubs. Check them out.

Seven;(IS HAVANA)

For it was in the seventh month of the ancient migratory lunar year beginning in March that the separation in September began. Seven (IS HAVANA) was the pivot, the turning point in the ancient thirteen month year. It created the even (HAVANA) distribution in time. As they trudged behind the herbivores back and forth across the African savannah (IS HAVANA) following the drenching monsoons they must have come across quietly standing pools of water. One area may have been the internal outpouring of the Okobongo River Delta in Botswana. Coming to a stop, the water created a wide quietly standing spread of water across the parched savannah (IS HAVANA). Not a ripple could be seen when the raging internal river came to rest. It was like an enormous mirror, an inland sea, or an aqueus eye that looked up and reflected the sky.

In that quietly standing blanket of water across the semi-annually soaked savannah (IS HAVANA) they must have observed that there was an even (HAVANA) reflection of their reality in the standing waters. They surmised that the reality above through which they passed dealt with life. The reflected reality across the surFACE of the waters on the body of Mother Earth dealt with death. Someone must have come up with the realization that the reflection created an even (HAVANA) balance 'as above so below'. Then there was a moment when another realization came into being with an AHA moment. Look someone may have observed, is even (IS HAVANA) and the number seven (IS HAVANA) was born. It established not only the concept of evenness but of the reflected reality in the waters below that dealt with death. Crossing crocodile infested waters to get to the 'promised land' and the bodies that were left behind in that watery crossing may have established the first perception that to get to the 'other side' in most religions you had to cross a perilous river.

Seven begins its journey into the future on many rails. As the sun descended into the blood splattered waters off the Western horizontal rim on the body of Mother Earth, as it was swallowed into Her great maw, the SHAPE of that precipitous right angle fall dealing with the death of the sun, became the SHAPE of the number seven (IS HAVANA) creating the even (HAVANA) distribution between day and night. The only place that it could happen was close to, or at the Equator.

With seven (IS HAVANA) emerging as a mystical number dealing with separation and death, the possibility of reincarnation became a reality. As the solar (IS HALA-) disc rose to a new day, so the human soul (IS HALA) could also rise to a new life. Sol (IS HALA) in Spanish is the name for the sun.

It was through the trance state that human beings could catch a glimpse into immortality. One of the ways of experiencing the trance state was through rocking back and forth. In Hebrew the word for rocking back and forth is d'aven (DAVANA) or the 'gift of' (D) aven (HAVANA). Then as cataclysmic eruptions crashed across the beleaguered continent of Africa scattering the clutches of early migrating humanity in all directions away from their savannah (IS HAVANA) home carrying their SOUNDS with them, some landed on the shores of France. The city of Avignon (HAVANA-na) in its name not only carries the African roots out of the savannah (IS HAVANA) and the even (HAVANA) distribution of day and night, but an inkling into the transformative trance state, the d'aven (d HAVANA) of the Hebrews. To become transformed meant that you had to be cooked clean in the oven (HAVANA) within the body of Mother Earth. You had to have the Kundalini energy burn through your entrapped fear. Crossing the channel into Britain, the Middle Eastern Amharic smiths as the brats founded the city of Avon (HAVANA) next to Stonehenge that could be reached by a wide avenue (HAVANA).

The Avon (HAVANA) River flowed to the Atlantic Ocean and that expansive ocean became the river of passage across the great watery divide into immortality. On their way across that great watery divide they found a haven (HAVANA) on the island of Cuba in Havana. This was all happening at the end of PHASE TWO into the beginning of PHASE THREE, for their search for immortality was *away* and *above* the body of Mother Earth. Their ultimate destination was the cluster of stars called the Pleiades, or the seven (IS HAVANA) sisters. It was there that they believed that they had descended from. It was at the home of the seven (IS HAVANA) sisters up in the heavens (HAVANA) that they would experience eternal life and their own immortality.

In subsequent British history King Arthur tried to resurrect the peaceful mythology of the ancient seekers with the city of Avalon (HAVA(LA)NA), including the LAdy of the LAnd, the Mother pLAnet as his peaceful 'source'. As the fear driven left hemispheric right handed human brain was driving hierarchal male beings into violent confrontation, he did not succeed.

But seven (IS HAVANA) remained in the language as the mystical number dealing with separation and death. In Hebrew to sit at the time of death is shivah (IS HAVA-) or the seven (IS HAVANA) days of mourning. Hebrews also cover the reflective surface of their mirrors after a passing so as not to see the reflection of their deceased. The Manorah contains seven candles. The number seven like the snake surfaces all around the the ancient world.

Eight;

The number EIGHT gives itself away as a pun. For it was the flat round surFACE of Mother Earth who ATE, (8) or swallowed the sun every night. As the solar disc descended into the blood splattered Western waters at twilight, it was believed that Mother Earth swallowed, or ATE the sun. The solar disc suspended above the horizontal rim on the body of Mother Earth created an even reflection. The SHAPE of that reflection, of the two orbs, one on top of the other, with the water between them, became the SHAPE of the number EIGHT. When it was turned on its side the SHAPE of the number EIGHT became the sign of infinity. Infinity then became a closed system turning round and round on itself, like the sun.

Mother Earth swallowing the sun, hunting (HANA-) it down every night represented what was happening on the plane below to the first born male offspring, led to the definitin of the world as the place of war as the sun (son) fought for his freedom.

As the sun was swallowed into the body of Mother Earth it coagulated within Her fiery oven (HAVANA), was cooked clean and after being guided by the metaphoric snake through Her underground intestines, it became transformed into the solid disc of the risen sun at dawn on one hand and the lavic outpouring of Mother Earth's menstrual blood coagulating into land on the other.

Nine (NANA);

The number nine (NANA) in one direction would take us into the double negation dealing with the definition of the moon, Nana in Greek. One negation (NA) dealt with the moon during the day hidden under the crusty mantle of Mother Earth finding its way through Her dark intestinal tunnels. The other negation (NA) dealt with the SHAPE shifting moon at night sailing though the night sky, negating the light of the sun, not really bringing too much light for the creatures below.

The moon as the consort of menstruation in young girls began their menarche (MANARAJA), a movement into possible motherhood and the ultimate monarchy (MANARAJA) of ruling. The moon bringing on the menarche created the process of beginning of the fetus, a time of the ten month lunar pregnancy out of their bodies.

As in PHASES TWO and THREE the transition into male definition of time began to depend on the irregular twelve month solar calendar of the fathers replacing the regular thirteen month lunar calendar of the mothers. It took ten lunar months for the fetus to become a baby. After the shift into male centrality it took NINE solar months for a baby to be born. The ancient migrations began their march in March after an orgy of mating with the oncoming of estrus (HASATARA) at Easter (HASATARA) time, the beginning of the ancient year. Human beings were part of that ancient carnival (KARANA-) when the flesh of the body was given its full sexual expression. In Latin carne (KARANA) means flesh. Flesh emerged as the KA out of the RANA or wound in Polish. Also in Polish KARA means punishment and NA deals with emergence on the surface. In PHASE THREE the physical flesh and pleasure of the woman had either been clitomerized or defined as a punishment.

For the herbivore mares the dropping of their foals fell in August the sixth month when their estral orgy of sex reached its fruition. For human mothers in PHASE THREE it took NINE solar months for them to give birth. If, as they did in PHASE ONE you start with the beginning of the year in March then the NINTH month is the month of November (NAVA-). November created a new member, November also defined Novo (NAVA) in Polish means new (NAWA). The (V) and (W) are interchangeable. In Spanish Nuevo (NAVA) means NINE. So something new and the number NINE also became interchangeable. The (W) in new and Nuevo deals with water. It was when the water sack broke in the pregnant mother that the journey into the navigation (NAVA-) of a new (NAWA) birth began.

TEN (TANA);

Ten deals with the process of holding. It is the ten (TANA) fingers of the human hand that do the holding. It is also the TEN lunar months of gestation that hold the fetus in the disTENded abdomen within a mother's body. In Latin tenere (TANA-) means 'to hold'. In Greek a 'worker who works with his hands' had been called a tekton (takaTANA) back to the ten (TANA) fingers that did the work. It expands to include the body of Mother Earth as the tectonic (takaTANA-) plates, Her ten (TANA) busy fingers ever ready to move the continents around.

The holding concept expands to include the ten (TANA) fingers of the hand that do the drumming during a transformative ceremony of dancing. The thumb may do the thumping but it is the whole hand with the ten (TANA) fingers that creates the rhythm and the tone (TANA). The tone (TANA) as it accelerates creates the state of trance that leads to transformation. It vibrates the stone (IS TANA) circles around the ancient thumpers into alpha wave states creating a vibrational state of becoming stoned leading to the opening of the portals into transformation.

The transformation occurs out of the body of Mother Earth as the Kundalini energy rising out of Her majestic body. During the birthing experience many ancient mothers experienced the birthing breath which carried them on the wings of ecstasy into becoming fearless mothers.

The NUMBER ten (TANA) as the Latin (X) also deals with the crisscrossing of the sky and the arrival of the birds North and South and the universal time of birthing. It is also the criss crossing at the third eye where the fusion of the two hemispheres of the brain across the corpus collosum due to the trance state create a balance, an evenness, a transformation. Not to be left out, the LETTER (X) (KS) (KASA) establishes the coos (KASA) of the individual mother creating smaller (KA) reflections of the mother out of her blood (SA). Her birthing breath became the trance state that evolved into the mysterious mysticism that all the ancient male heroes, jumping on their steeds quested to experience and some did. They became the Biblical fallen angels

Eleven (HALAVANA);

The number ELEVEN is just as mysterious. It may also deal with transformation. It hides in it's linguistic construct the word (HA(LA)VANA) or HAVANA with the LA of the Lady of the Land through its center, like the world (WARA(LA)DA) (WARADA) and Avalon (HAVA(LA)NA (HAVANA). The dyad (HALA) is the sun, as the Spanish sol (IS HALA). The second overlapping dyad is (LAVA) and that is the menstrual outpouring out of the body of Mother Earth that through the process of internal cooking within the oven (HAVANA) of Mother Earth coagulates, or is cooked into coagulated land. The third overlapping dyad is (VANA) and deals with the 'emergence on the surface' (NA) out of the (VA) the volcanic vent.

Could it have dealt with the time that the soul on its journey to heaven (HAVANA) on its way to immortality and a stop over in Havana after going through the oven (HAVANA) within the body of Mother Earth, Her lavic fires of the digesting sun to become purified and transformed. It seems to deal singularly out of the body of Mother Earth. But Mother Earth reflected metaphorically the processes that individual mothers went through on Her planetary plane. What could there be hidden in those cooking fires after the ten lunar months of gestation surfacing in the ELEVENTH (HALAVA-) month of separation in PHASE ONE that individual human mothers went through?

The (LAVA) dyad also deals with the capacity to leave (LAVA) as the magma leaves (LAVA-) the body of Mother Earth to coagulate on the outside and the fetus leaves (LAVA-) the mother's body after it had coagulated inside. The process of separation enters here.

Then there is the quality of bread as it rises with the addition of yeast. With the removal of the letter (E) at the beginning of ELEVEN it becomes leaven (LAVANA) that deals with the process of the bread rising like the belly rises on the pregnant mother. Like also the sun rises in the Eastern sky at the Levant (LAVANATA). In PHASE THREE the Hebrews obliterating everything that reminded them that a baby emerged out of the mother's body and not out of the mind of God removed the yeast from their plano convex bread creating unleavened matzohs so that they would not rise and not like the pregnant capricious female belly, would lay flat.

Twelve;

Deals with a time in male centrality in PHASE THREE when everything that belonged to the ancient mothers and the body of Mother Earth had to be redefined and suppressed. The round solar disc in the sky became a male deity *away* and *above* the body of Mother Earth. The solar disc had been redefoined to make TWELVE irregular rounds around the body of Mother Earth. It replaced the thirteen regular lunar circles that dealt with menstruation. That female lunar circling had to be replaced by the male solar definition of time. The thirteen lunar months in PHASE ONE which had been regular and balanced now began to reflect the lopsided number of days in the TWELVE solar monthly cycles in PHASE THREE. The ancient hemispheric balance of the mothers in many ways was becoming destroyed. In PHASE THREE the number TWELVE becomes immensely impressive as the number of followers that as apostles followed the transformed Jesus. The sun as the son emerges upon the mythological scene. The redefinitions go on.

The (W) at the center of TWELVE gives pause for it is dealing with water the reflected surFACE of death. The (TAWA) is two (TAWA) as the reflective reality in water establishes.

TWELVE may very well have meant the place where an ending occurred, the 'two in one', the even distribution of life and death at the waters edge. For the TWELFTH month has been the last month, the month of death OF THE YEAR in the male solar calendar. The year died at the end of the last TWELVE month period, before it began its journey again to establish it's 'two in one' (TAWA) habitual and immortal passage. This is where Janus of January comes in the arbitrary PHASE THREE looking both ways forward into the future and backward into the past.

RULE TWENTY-FIVE;
Vowels

The VOWELS are the carriers of SOUND. It is the consonants that carry the MEANING. Vowels occur in the SOUNDS made by many other animals. Primates hoot, screech, howl with their throats open without the consonants getting in the way creating much more specific meaning. Birds make more varied SOUNDS than any other creature, even human beings. They need all their cacophonic SOUNDS to wake up the sleeping sun at dawn.

It is not language that differentiates human speech from other animals. It is the use of consonants. The consonants stay relatively constant. It is the vowels that do their 'SHAPE shifting' dance and can't be pinned down. It is the vowels that established the most ancient relationship to singing. For it is the extended vowels that carry the melody.

The emerging Homo Sapiens with their links to the rampaging chimps of the Northern Congo region could not make consonant SOUNDS. The accompanying human creature, the Neanderthal could not make vowel SOUNDS. When they put the two together they came up with human language.

A(ah) is the SOUND of the first breath, the alpha SOUND that a baby takes as it makes its entrance into life. The A(ah) SOUND is not only made by the fully opened mouth but within the oral cavity it faces no obstruction.

Section Two

Its SHAPE as the letter A(ah) comes from the triangular volcanic cone that spews air up to the surFACE on the body of Mother Earth. It has links with the HA of the last breath as a person expires fillibrating the vocal cords on its last exit. The AH-HA construct of the first breath beginning life and the last breath expelling life works in tandem, like the two sides of a coin.

The A(ah) SOUND can be either a vowel or a consonant depending how it is used. It can also be a dipthong (AE) as in the English word mAke, sAne, fAte etc. In Hawaiian AE is an 'agreement' a 'yes' saying between Mother Earth (A) and the sun, that daily it will emerge (E) upon Her surFACE. Also in Hawaiian the emergence of the sun at dawn represented by the letter (A) establishes the concept out 'of' the suns emergence out 'of' the body of Mother Earth.

E(eh) comes in two packages;

One is the (E) as (eh). The other is (E) as (ee). One SOUND may have come from the SOUND of scrEEming and scrEEching due to an activity that is causing panic and a great deal of pain. The other not too far away and shorter, deals with (E) as (eh) dealing with the (eh) as in exit (eh) and exist (eh).

The SHAPE of the letter (EE) as part of scrEEming comes from the body of Mother Earth as the rays of the sun were perceived to puncture with their stiletto like fingers the horizontal rim on Her body. They perceived that She must have scrEEmed as She gave birth to the sun. The SHAPE of the letter (E) comes out of in this case the three fingers pointing to the right on the stem of the I, that do the piercing of the fabric of dawn. The scrEEming while giving birth must have come after the institutionalization of clitorectomies, the rana dyad as the wound (RANA) and dawn (RANA) in Polish. It is where at dawn Mother Earth scrEEmed Her way giving birth to the sun in the EEastern sky.

The EA became the letters symbolizing the Chinese EAst. The body of Mother Earth (A) in Chinese gave birth to Her sun defining his process with the SHAPE of the (E) of emergence (ee) upon her surFACE. For the Sumerians EA was the 'poem of creation'. The creation was the birth of the sun emerging (E) out of the body of Mother Earth (A). Same concept. Down the line for the Greeks in PHASE THREE EOS became dawn itself with the addition of the male circle, the O of the solar orb and emerging male deity. The SOUND of (EE) in Phoenician was HE before the letter (H) had been dropped off to become the bare (EE) of later linguistic evolutions.

I, the letter I is also the number one.

It can be (EE) or it also can be a diphthong in English as (AAHEE). It may deal with other concepts in other languages. In PHASE ONE it defined the body of a boy whose external testicles announced that he would never carry a baby in his belly. He was defined not by the A(ah) of his sister but by the one (I) more associated with his brothers. In Etruscan (I) is the number 'one'. In Polish the vowel (I) is pronounced as (EE) and deals with not only 'one more' but with 'and'. And is 'one (HANA) more' spreading its net to catch the sun, for 'and' (HANADA) is the 'gift of' (DA) the sun (IS HANA), the solar orb in the sky that created an endless cycle of days, or 'ands', in time becoming the male symbol of 'source'. In Wolof (I) is a plural as it is in Latin and in Polish.

O (oh) SOUND is made by the SHAPE of the open mouth;

As the SOUND of the letter A(ah) is the easiest to make and comes out of the throat with no obstruction, so the O (oh) SOUND in stage one emerges with a partial tightening of the muscles at the back of the throat. It also emerges with a partial tightening of the muscles of the mouth itself to create the round circle of the letter O (oh).

It too became associated with the males but further down the line in PHASE TWO as with their dawning knowledge of specific procreation they began to define the round solar orb (O) in the sky, echoing the zero (O) of the empty belly as their divinity of 'source'.

If Mother Earth and the sun at the beginning of PHASE ONE had been considered as a single unit, as the first 'one', then male 'source' had to come BEFORE the 'one' construct of Mother Earth and the sun. It had to come out of the zero (IS HARA), of the empty belly (hara in Hebrew and Japanese), the number of the emptiness that only the mind of the emerging sky God could fill. This came after the separation myths had their day and the body of Mother Earth and the sun had become rendered (RANA-) apart.

OO as (uu) takes us to the body of Mother Earth;

The SOUND may be made by both lips pursing up to create the constricted opening but it is specifically the bottom lip that is doing the (UU) as a result of the tightening. On the body of Mother Earth the bottom lip deals with the reflection of the letter (M) of the mountainous mouths at the horizontal edge. The letter that emerged as UNDER the top lip on the human face and as the letter (W) (double U), deals with water. The letter (W) bears witness to itself being made up of two under (U) scoops, that could have emerged out of either a (V) or a (U). In most subsequent words that evolved, the letters (V) and (W) are often interchangeable. The pursed up lips ooing into the sky wailed at the Western Wall of watery entombment as the rays of light of the setting sun slid within the body of Mother Earth plunging Her into darkness.

U;

As either the left behind (UU) or YOU created its own trajectory. It was in the female body behind her hairy pubis that a new YOU had been created floating in her watery belly. The SHAPE of the pubis emerges as the letter (Y) that defines not only the hairy pubis but the new YOU that emerged from it. In Polish U (uh) means 'within' as the baby was 'within' the mother's body. In Swahili (U) is 'you are'. In Persian (U) is he, she, it.

In Swahili an ancient almost forgotten process becomes defined by the (UA) meaning 'to kill'. What it tries to remind us is that there was an ancient time in PHASE ONE when the sun slipping 'within' the body of Mother Earth (A) under (U) Her surFACE was killed to its light.

SECTION THREE

THE SHAPE *of* SOUND

INDIVIDUAL LETTERS,
THE WOOF CONTINUES

LINGUISTIC BREAK

There exists a linguistic break, a great big hole in the fabric of what has come down to us as the SHAPES of the letters that fed into the creation of the capital letters of the Western Alphabet out of PHASE ONE and what has come down to us as the letters out of the Alphabets of Northern Africa and the Middle East out of PHASE THREE. It seems that a series of great cataclysms occurred. Perhaps it was the time of a great flood. Local myths mention it. In the rain forests of the Amazon basin in South America there is a Zoa tribe of people at peace with each other and their environment who claim that 'their ancient home was destroyed and recreated by a great flood'. For others it may have been a series of massive volcanic eruptions that brought an extended dark night which tore their landscape to shreds. Perhaps it was a time of an ancient ice age, perhaps all of the above.

Much had been lost along the way as they began to pick up the pieces. The letters that had been associated with the practical perceptions dealing with the HOW of survival, out of the face and body of the female as mother and the surFACE and body of Mother Earth in PHASE ONE, somehow became redefined as neutral body parts In PHASE TWO, then objects and then even further away from the physical universe into theoretical speculations and concepts based on the WHY of male periphery in PHASE THREE. They passed from being female based to gender neutrality and then into male centrality (actress became actor), in the process losing their ancient links with the female of the specie as their original source.

The specific face and body of the mother sharing her gifts of comfort and survival with her children had been left behind in many of the North African and Middle Eastern Alphabets that have come down to us. What remain as viable clues in the words of ALL of the languages of the world that exist as living potsherds are the SOUNDS that the phonemes still carry, the leit motif of our linguistic symphony, the DNA code waiting to be unraveled. For it is in the SOUNDS contained in the actual words that we can hear echoes of an ancient past that cannot be completely erased. The North African and Middle Eastern Alphabets that have come down to us and that have fed into the capital letters of the Western Alphabet are only approximations. It is the SOUNDS that expand into phonemic syllables and then into words that have to be dealt with to understand their origins and the source of their ancient meaning.

SECTION THREE
TABLE *of* CONTENTS

Linguistic Break	422
Consonants and the Neanderthal	425
Letter A	426
Letter H: AH-HA The Source of the letters	428
Letter M	439
Letter N	458
Letter L	471
Letter B	484
Letter P	499
Letter W	504
Letter V	512
Letter F	514
Letter D	517
Letter T	523
Letter S	527
Letter C	542
Letter K	547
Letter X	591
Letter Q	599
Letters CH	607
Letter G	609
Letter J	614
Letter I	617
Letter Y	622
Letter R	629
Summary	638
Conclusion	641
Changes	648

CONSONANTS AND THE NEANDERTHAL

The most ancient screeching SOUNDS to have become codified out of the northern Congo River violent male chimpanzees expanding to the more recent Cro Magnon and subsequently into the equally most violent Homo Sapiens as MANkind, were the vowel SOUNDS. Chimpanzees apparently do not make consonant SOUNDS. The consonants may have belonged singularly to the much maligned humanoid or even human Neanderthal. Their hyoid bone could not make vowel SOUNDS. Surprisingly, it is to the Neanderthal that we may have to turn for our consonants.

Since words as emergent consonant SOUNDS flowed out of the frontal area of the mothers head, out of the hole on the bottom part of her face, out of her mouth, lips, throat, jaw, including the nose, it is to those organs that our ancient ancestral mothers turned in PHASE ONE to create the SHAPES that magically emerged intact as the capital letters, cum consonants of the Western Alphabet, predating by thousands of years the often secretive obtuse alphabetic symbols that emerged out of the left hemispheric civilizations of North Africa the Middle East and Southern Asia. As males had been ejected from the mother clan at puberty they settled other areas. Clusters of male bsed territories gained the ground upon which they created their protected turf. What they also did was to create not only new bases which they protected with violence but they created new languages which only their cluster or city could understand. This led to male based universal babble as the Tower of Babble in the Bible proclaims. To this day male bases create their own language; such as doctors with medical terms and processes, corporations with mesmerizing names for their products. The best one deals with the police and their name for criminals as the 'alleged perpetrators'.

THE LETTER A (AH)

The letter A(ah) is an open mouth glottal stop, laryngial consonant.

It is defined as either a consonant or a vowel, depending on position and use. It may have been the first vowel SOUND to have been codified.

SOUND; InHAlation, the intake of the first breath of a baby through the open mouth.

SHAPE; Two SHAPES; First tent SHAPE of the *volcanic cone* (KANA) with the lateral line through the center. The other the tent SHAPE on its side with a vertical line through its center reminiscent of a bird's beak (K) and the *clitoris* (kleitor) in Greek.

MOTHER'S body; Tent SHAPE of the fingertips touching and the pubis reflected.

MOTHER EARTH; Tent SHAPE of *volcanic cone* (KANA) at rest, intake and exhalation of Her breath through calderic fissures and vents.

CONCEPT; Alpha of beginnings; SHAPE as land beginning out of volcanic cone on the body of Mother Earth and the clitoric beak on the body of an individual mother. SOUND of beginning of life, babys first breath. One of the major definitions is of the female essence out of the body of Mother Earth and the individual mother.

A (ah) AS ALPHA, THE LAND as WOMB, humanitys planetary nest.

All the many learned arguments notwithstanding, all the tomes agonizing whether or not there was a beginning and when it occurred, could be dispelled with a smidgeon of common sense. Forget about worrying about what came out of space and the big bang of the male orgasm. There could not have been any beginning of life without the planetary plane that has been the body of Mother Earth. For our ancient maternal ancestors not only the ground around them but also the wide stretches of standing water must have seemed to have come first. Without the land and water there could have been no life. All of life needs the solid and liquid body of Mother Earth upon which, within which, above which, through which it could have made its home to subsist and to survive. It needs the body of Mother Earth as its planetary nest.

Where did land come from? It is not a rhetorical question. For land obviously came from only one place. It burst up to the surFACE as lava through the planetary skin of the great Mother, belching smoke, dust, ashes, rocks with the volcanic eruptions that quaked and exploded upon Her spasming orgasmic surFACE, spreading lava and rubble kicked up from the deep inner recesses within Her body. As the effulgence spread across Her top engulfing Her like a cape, or as islands emerged like fulminating noses out of Her great oceans, they covered Her with a new skin, a new ground of being.

The wind and rain pummeled Her, creating chinks in that tough lavic hide. Waves of hot and cold air blasted across Her open surFACE creating fissures in which seeds snuggling against the wind could take refuge. Insects spread pollen. Birds descended upon the insects. Herbivores evolved. Predators adapted. Human beings survived.

It all began on the flat round surFACE of Mother Earth, with the cone (KANA) of creation, the triangular volcanic SHAPE that pushed itself up from the center, emerging out of Her skin (IS KANA), becoming the source of the cataclysmic eruptions that spread across Her surFACE and the source of all life that took root upon that great and awesome nurturing body.

The triangular SHAPE of that *volcanic cone* (KANA) on the body of Mother Earth, creating land upon Her surFACE, gave its SHAPE to the letter A(ah), the Alpha (HALAFA) of beginnings, who shared the process of 'source' with Her surrogates in the creation of life above their surfaces. They too had much smaller cones of creation upon their bodies, almost hidden, but always there, the places where life and the physical results of cohabitation emerged upon the surface, out of the beak SHAPE of the clitoris (kleitor in Greek), and out of the more internal areas of the vagina (V) and of vulva (V) and pubis (Y).

In the word Alpha (HALAFA) defining the letter A (ah), there exists another clue, for it relates not only the story of beginnings, but to half (HALAFA) of the story of life (LAFA), which came out of the hole (HALA), on either the individual female body, or the body of Mother Earth. The other half of the story, which was considered to be as important as life upon and *above* Her surFACE, was the transformative reflected journey through the dark realms of death *below* Her surFACE.

All babies had to go through the bellies of their mothers through the dark internal mysterious recesses under her maternal hide. As they navigated through those what had been perceived as internal intestines they became transformed, cooked solid, coagulated from the blood flowing within the mothers body, sending thanks to the liver, into a solid reflective object that emerged with appendages flailing.

The same thing had been perceived to happen to the creations of Mother Earth, especially the sun and the moon, once She swallowed them in the Western horizontal rim, they too became transformed in Her internal oven to emerge clean, shining and solid on Her surFACE.

An Indian sage Samketa Paddhai proclaimed that A (ah) is the first of all letters and HA is the last. It created the AH-HA of the breath.

The A(ah) SOUND established the intake of the first breath of a baby at the beginning of life. The HA, KHA, GHA phonemes of the last breath of the death rattle fillibrating the vocal cords on it's way out became a cluster of related SOUNDS which became associated with the end of life and with death. The AH-HA of the breath became the beginning AH and HA of the end.

Defining the major aspect underpinning the activity of life, words became sacred because as SOUNDS along with the birds (BARA-) both of the 'intermediate state' they too used the sacred airy breath as a vehicle of passage. The air supported the magic of words as it supported the magic of life. After the dextral shift into male centrality in PHASES TWO and THREE it became redefined as the Alpha of the mother establishing the beginning of the journey and the Omega of the Greeks, or the big OM, the OM of the father establishing the end of the journey and death. Life began with the A (ah) as the Alpha of the mother and ended with the O of the Omega of the father. The letters bear witness to their own prophecy.

THE SOURCE OF THE LETTERS
A(ah)

The most ancient triangular SHAPE of origins on the flat circular surFACE of Mother Earth, out of which air, lava and rubble blasted its way to Her surFACE, was the SHAPE of the *volcanic cone (KANA)*. It established the original perception as the Alpha of beginnings, for it created land, upon which life in all of its forms could take root and flourish. The paroxysm of birth as a volcanic eruption on the body of Mother Earth, as she created Herself out of Herself, by Herself, also shot up great blasts of air, which became defined as Her belly of air (HARA) above Her surFACE.

The concept of beginning surfaces in Swahili as Alfa Giri and defines the state before the sun made its appearance above Mother Earths surFACE creating the rosy glow of dawn emerging triumphant out of the Eastern mountainous bellies to the light of a new day. Alfa has links with the Greek Alpha and giri (GARA) deals with the Polish gora (GARA) or mountain.

At one point in time in PHASE ONE it was the volcanic eruption that was perceived to create the air above Her body. At others it was thought that the sun and the moon moving in and out of Her body were like the sustaining breath of life to Her. The A (ah) SHAPE of the *volcanic cone* (KANA) on the body of Mother Earth became associated with the process of breathing, of aspirating and of beginning.

The actual process of breathing and of the breath moving in and out on the body of Mother Earth needed more room than the closed cone at the top symbolized by the letter A (ah). In Her case the breathing was often violent and explosive. Out of the SHAPE of the letter A(ah) of the *volcanic cone* (KANA) closed at the top, there blasted a separation, the top parted and out of the triangular SHAPE of the letter A(ah) closed on top, a new SHAPE came into being emerging as the letter H (huh).

The SHAPE of the letter H (huh) emerged out of the violent volcanic explosion, when the volcanic crater no longer as the point at the top symbolized by the letter A (ah) opened up and made room for new land to be born carried on a blast of air. At one time in PHASE ONE the crater (KARATARA) had been considered as the sole creator (KARATARA).

The letter A(ah) represented a plethora of concepts dealing with their great Mother Earth as the beginner of life on Her magnificent surFACE. Before and after the shift into male centrality after the linguistic break in PHASE THREE some of the the Middle Eastern alphabets dealt with the triangular A (ah) SHAPE of the volcano and the SHAPE of the hairy vulvic patch on the individual mothers body. The triangular SHAPE on the individual mothers body symbolized by the letterA(ah) became associated with girls and the number three as the undefined boy became defined by the one (I) more and the beginning of the number four. The A(ah) SOUND remains on the end of girls names in the Slavic and Romantic languages. The I of one more surfaces in Italian in such names as Puccini, Verdi, Mussoini, Garibaldi. In Polish it also surfaces as Pulaski, Paderewski, Smolenski etc.There are many others as in Magi, Hopi and in Japanese the Samurai and Watanabi and things like sushi. Then there are places like Capri, Santorini. The young men rejected at puberty must have wandered all around the world as did their eunuch brothers.

The Alpha of beginnings as the letter A (ah) out of the SHAPE of the *volcanic cone* (KANA) of creation on the body of Mother Earth, surfaces as the symbol for the letter A (ah) in Lydian, Etruscan and Roman. Then the letter A (ah) as the SHAPE of beginnings on the body of Mother Earth, changes its direction, lies on it's side and peeks out from its ground of being on the body of the female, as the SHAPE of the *clitoral beak*, the place on her body out of which cohabitation and masturbation brought forth not only great pleasure and relief but a baby.

The *clitoral beak* lying on it's side establishes the SHAPE of the area of beginnings on the female body in Phoenician, Moabite, Old Indian and Greek. It echoes a lost perception that many ancient mothers must have lain on their sides to push their large headed babies past the *clitoric beak* out of their bodies.

In Linear B the letter A (ah) is HA retaining its anlaut of H which has often been dropped off words beginning with a vowel and has ancient roots not only with the AH-HA SOUND, but with the hard and fast panting breath in the last stages of labor (HA-HA) of the birthing mother.

It was the high, fast panting breath of the mother in the last stages of labor that activated the trance like state of the ecstatic Kundalini experience. For the Japanese HA-HA still remains as the definition of the Mother. The HA-HA SOUND was associated with the last stages of high, fast panting, as the birthing mother pushed the large headed fetus out of her body to begin its journey into independent life.

In Cypriotic the letter A(ah) is represented by another symbol that needs a bit of maneuvering to get at its original meaning. It too deals with the mother's body as the source of beginnings, but from a different direction. It hides in it's linguistic folds the *clitoris* (kleitor) in Greek.

In the Cypriotic Alphabet the letter A (ah) is symbolized by the SHAPE of the letter X,(KS) (KASA) halved vertically. It deals with an ancient name for the vulva as the creator of smaller aspects (KA) and is also associated with the SOUNDS made by birds, or their coos (KASA).

The letter X(KS) (KASA), originally came out of the bulbous SHAPE of the buttocks on the back end of females disappearing through the teeming savannah leaving its pungent scent of availability behind. The letter X(KS) (KASA) marked the spot, the area on the female body where red flecks of blood announced her receptivity and expanded to define the place where that receptivity occurred. The vertical line through the center of the letter X(KS) (KASA) emerging as the letter A(ah) on its side, halves the two buttocks in half in the process of birthing.

One of the ancient perceptions was that when a female menstruated, came into her menarche (one activity of beginnings), or when she gave birth becoming a monarch (another activity of beginnings) that her body was rendered, that a wound had cut her in half and she either bled (menstruated) or gave birth to a baby. To halve (HA(LA)VA) one entity is to have (HAVA) two entities. The mother and the baby separated, were halved to become two separate beings. The phoneme (VA) deals with the vulva (VALAVA) the valve (VALAVA) of unrelenting return. The phoneme (HA) as the HA-HA of the birthing breath deals with the breathing that accompanied the emergence of life upon the surface out of the vulva. The phoneme (LA) that halves (ha(LA)va) the buttocks creating life on the surface, occurs out of the mother, the LAdy of the LAnd. What contains and hides the spasming activity of the vulva, vagina construct that assists in birthing? The extruding beak of the *clitoris*.

In the overlapping dyad of halve (HALAVA) (HALA/LAVA) you get a bonus, for it contains the process out of the body of Mother Earth. It has within its structure the overlapping dyads of (HALA) and (LAVA). It was the LAVA that poured out of the calderic hole (HALA), which not only created land upon Her surFACE rendering the cone of creation, the body of Mother Earth in twain, creating the open top of the letter H of exHAlation. The (LA) at the center of the word halve (HA(LA)VA) as the LAdy of the LAnd, is one of the SHAPES of the angle of emergence of lava out of the calderic hole, to flow laterally across Her surFACE. The other SHAPE associated with the letter L is the emergence of the light (L) of the angle of the sun emerging out of the body of Mother Earth at dawn. In Spanish the sun is sol (IS HALA) emerging out of the hole (HALA) the break in the horizontal rim on the body of Mother Earth to highlight the beginning of a new day.

The letter A (ah) establishes its links with the letter K, also in Cypriotic. For the letter X(KS) (KASA), as the coos (KASA) vertically halved through its center, gives us two Ks coming and going, facing in opposite directions, (the concept of the valve of the vulva from another direction). The letter K relating to the SHAPE of the birds open beak may echo the pattern of the migrating birds semiannually coming and going North and South across the great open belly of air above the surFACE of Mother Earth.

The same process of vertical halving through the center occurs in the letter R. In PHASE TWO as male role in procreation was becoming realized it must have been at the end of that epoch for the round disc of the male sun was perceived to hOVER OVER the triangular *volcanic cone* on the body of Mother Earth. The male circular sun emerged abOVE the triangular cone on the surFACE of Mother Earth. The sun at this point in PHASE ONE had been considered as one of Mother Earth's creations, Her child as the golden egg of the sun, the OVUm that She as the Mother hen laid at dawn. It must have emerged out of the same perception that men straddled the female beneath them as they copulated with her. The triangular SHAPE of the volcanic cone of the Mother on the bottom with the round disc of the sun on top of Her became the template for the letter R.

Both the letter K and the letter R emerge out of the process of vertical halving which had to do with copulation and birthing, both established the process of beginnings. The letter K deals with the SOUNDS made by birds out of the SHAPE of their open beaks and with the letter X halved vertically of the buttocks creating the Ka of smallness and life. Also in Cypriotic it comes down to us as another SHAPE that stands for the letter A(ah) of beginnings. For the ancient migrations began at the two times of the year, which coincided when the migrating birds came and went North and South, vertically halving the great expanse of the African sky. As they obscured the light of the sun with their numbers, they clacked, cackled, cawed and cooed their way across, giving us the SOUNDS that emerged into the family of words which began with or contained in them, the K SOUND of beginning and of smallness.

What has come down to us out of the alphabets that emerged out of the Middle East after one of the great cataclysms of dispersal in PHASE THREE are symbols that come out of settled agrarian societies. They deal with a time when humanitys ancestors began to till land and to create extended settlements. They no longer migrated across the great savannahs of Africa. For the Egyptians, the Semites and the Phoenicians, the letter A (ah) as Alpha, Alef or Aleph, dealt with an ox, or a bull. Since they still dealt with the letter A (ah) as the Alpha of beginnings, keeping the concept, but shifting its origin, the male ox or male bull came first. How? He preceded the plow. It created the beginning of Agriculture and the creation of crops that led to the sustenance of life.

What had become lost in the redefinitions in PHASE THREE as the world reeled from the shift into male centrality, is the source of the letters out of the face of the individual mother and the surFACE and body of Mother Earth.

For the Maya, who seemed to have gotten away before the agrarian symbols began to emerge to confuse the linguistic landscape, the letter A (ah) represented by three diverse symbols dealing with the female body, and the dual aspect of the body of Mother Earth dealing with both life and death. The Mayan symbols do not deal with the passage of migrating birds, or of the heads of bulls or oxen. They go directly back to the original tri parted source. The round circle with a dot in it, the iota, the period, the Bindu of the Hindu as the first cause (KASA) deals with the belly of the female with the dot or period within it behind her coos (KASA) waiting to coagulate and to create a baby. It doesn't deal with the *clitoris* or the process of masturbation as the beginning of new life. The Maya already in PHASE THREE searched for their 'source' out of the heavenly bodies *away* and *above* the body of Mother Earth.

In PHASE ONE the circle with a dot in it was the human being standing in the center of a great circular sweep with the body of Mother Earth as far as the eye could see ending in a circle around them at the horizontal rim. Also in PHASE ONE in Hindi and Urdu it is the SHAPE encoded in the letter A(ah) accompanied all the consonants. To obliterate 'source' out of the body of Mother Earth in PHASE THREE, the letter A(ah) was left out of Hebrew, Persian and Roman. They became languages mostly of consonants as the YHVH of Hebrew proclaims. In PHASE THREE in India the woman hating priests of Manu went further and plastered the A(ah) SOUND at the end of male names.

When you have a simple linguistic circle, you generally have an empty belly, and all that it implied. When there is a dot, or a period within the circle, you are generally dealing with a menstruating woman. The letter A(ah) in Numidian is just a plain dot, another name for period. It was the bloody period patiently waiting in the female body to coagulate that was the source of the beginning of life. It seems that the Mayans after one of the many catastrophic dispersals may have had ancient prehistoric links with the Numidians of Africa.

The actual beginnings out of the body of Mother Earth establish themselves out of the next two Maya symbols. The triangular SHAPE encoded in the letter A(ah) represents the *volcanic cone* (KANA) of creation, where life began upon the land. The last Maya symbol for the letter A (ah) is diamond SHAPED and shows the triangular cone of creation above reflected as the trianhgular female pubis in the waters below. It creates the dual reality of beginnings. One beginning moves into life out of the triangular lavic cone of creation above the surFACE in the belly of air on the body of Mother Earth (SA). The inverted triangular hairy pubis moves into the beginning of life out of the body of the individual mothers blood (SA). The other meaning of the inverted cone deals with water and the reflection of the cone.

The Maya concept dealing with the letter A (ah) as representing the beginning into both life and death, is not too far away from the Greek concept of the Alpha (HALAFA) of beginnings. For Alpha (HALAFA), with the two overlapping dyads, dealt with half (HALAFA) of life (LAFA) out of the hole (HALA into which the solar (IS HALA-) disk disappeared at twilight. The other side of life was defined as death, the Omega of the Greeks, the big OM.

The Maya seemed to have created their own ancient symbols reflecting the same concepts but staying closer to the bodies of ancient Mothers with the source out of the letter A (ah).

In Greek delphos, (as the gift (D) of alpha) means the womb, the place of beginnings. The oracle of Delphi worked out of the Earth womb, beneath the temple of the Goddess, (the Goddess, as all Goddesses were, was in most cases the triple personification of the body of Mother Earth). It had been the sacred place of the Kundalini energy, the place of prophecy and healing in the ancient abaton, where the infantile panic stricken habits of a new and fully conscious baby were transformed and the questing adept emerged into a life with newly found freedom from fear. What the adept experienced in the abaton, in the cavity within the body of Mother Earth, the individual mother experienced with the ecstatic Kundalini birthing breath during her extended labors to push the large headed fetus out of her body.

The letter A (ah), followed by the letter B, led many of the alphabets that have come down to us that fed into many of the capital letters of the Western Alphabet. AAKKOSET, the name for the Finnish alphabet, is an exception. For both alphabets, the letter A(ah) as the SHAPE of the *volcanic cone* creating land and the beginning of life on the surFACE of Mother Earth came first. The individual mother of the second A(ah) joined Her. It means that in PHASE ONE they both originated out of the same ancient African place where mothers were held in such great esteem that the anlaut of A (ah), associated with the SHAPE of the triangular cone of creation out of the body of Mother Earth and lying on its side as the *clitoris* on the individual mother's body had become associated with them.

Hawaiian AA

It may be that the AA construct deals directly and singularly with the body of Mother Earth. In Hawaiian, AA stands for lavic terrain. In other words Mother Earth as lava (A), recreating Herself out of Herself as it plunges into the ocean creating land, the other (A). In PHASE ONE land had been perceived to create the only possibility of beginnings.

Swahili, KAA

KAA deals with charcoal and cool embers. (K) of KAA deals the creation of smaller aspects out of the body of Mother Earth associated with the passage of birds out of Her horizontal rim in the fall and in the spring. Charcoal and cool embers would fall into the category of beginnings, for cooling embers after a volcanic eruption fed into the creation of land.

SECTION THREE

In Finnish, to start or to begin, is ALKAA. Out of Amharic in Ethiopia, there is a word that joins the list and it is KAKKA. It too deals with what came first in the creation of land. KAKKA means 'coarsely ground'. During a volcanic eruption, not only lava, but rocks, ash, pebbles and gravel are ejected up to the surFACE and once they land, many are often 'coarsely ground'. KAKKA (KAKA) establishes links with the ancient perceptions that at the time that these dyads emerged in PHASE ONE, Mother Earth was perceived to have defecated (KAKA) Herself out of Herself up to Her surFACE, in small discernable, 'coarsely ground' pieces. It had been perceived that everything that emerged out of the body of Mother Earth was smaller (KA) than She was. Since it had been perceived that Mother Earth defecated Herself into the creation of land then defecation had not been considered to be an evil smelling sewage as it had become in PHASE THREE. The Egyptian beetle pushing a ball of manure into which she laid her eggs comes into full focus. She became a symbol for Mother Earth as the bee had become a symbol for another community of mothers. Defecated feces had been considered to be the stuff of life.

The SHAPE of the letter (K) as an open birds beak seen in profile associated with things smaller and as the *clitoris* (kleitor in Greek) also has links with the avian clouds of birds that came semiannually at the time of birthing and the beginning of the ancient migrations.

The letter A(ah) is defined as being a consonant and a vowel. That becomes a bit tricky. When is the apparently vowel A(ah) at the beginning of a word considered a consonant remaining in place and not becoming associated with the letter (H) as HA?

ABTU (HABATA) Egyptian;

Fish of Isis swallowed the penis of Osiris every night, fish not snake in this case as the guide of the sun. Mother Earth habitually (HABATA-) swallowing the male sun (son) in Her Western horizontal rim. Fish had often been associated with the female vulva. The Biblical Jason had been swallowed by a fish. Christ had been considered to be the fisherman of men.

ADITI (HADATA) Hindu Sun Goddess;

The 'limitless' Mother of the Gods. Mother Earth as the 'source' of all celestial divinities off Her Western hidden (HADA-) side (IS HADA).

AKKA(HAKA);

Eponymous Goddess of AKKAD, mid wife, water drawer, grandmother. As water drawer, midwife and grandmother she may have broken the placental sack to let the water flow out. On the surFACE of Mother Earth AK/KA became the reflection, the exact DRAWING or hacking on the surFACE of the waters of the reality above as in the Latin aqua (HAKA).

AMA, AMMA (HAMAMA);

Sumerian Great Fertility Goddess out of Her blood (ema (HAMA) in Greek, also reflected Herself as AM/MA, the MA creating another AM, or I AM that I AM.

ANDROMEDA (HANADARAMADA);

Ethiopia, Philistine Sea Queen, ruler of men, chained to a rock as a sacrifice to the sea monster. Shades of Prometheus. Mother Earth as the sea monster (Kundalini energy) to be destroyed in PHASE THREE as a physical reality of 'source' by being shoved up into the sky *away* and *above* Her body as a PHASE THREE constellation.

ANANKE (HANANAKA);

Greek Goddess of the moon (NANA) holding a spindle, the Greek atractos as the union with the sun (IS HANA) working in concert with both the moon (NANA) and the symbolic snake (IS NAKA). In PHASE TWO she had been the Goddess of force, inevitability, compulsion, necessity dealing with sexual congress and the names that defined her based on the menstrual cycles of the moon (NANA) and its result on women dealing with the universal law of procreation (NAKA) symolized by the Kundalini snake (IS NAKA).

ANU (HANA);

Irish Mother Goddess of the sun (IS HANA) or the anus (HANASA), ie the sacral, secret, home of the sacred Kundalini.

ANUKET (HA*NAKA*TA);

Egyptian Mother Goddess 'the clasper', the yonic (Y*ANAKA*) source of the Nile River out of the sun (IS HANA) symbolized by the metaphoric snake (IS NAKA), water pouring out of Her serpentine aquatic womb cut (KATA) free to tumble its way home.

ANUNAK (HANA*NAKA*);

Sumerian Gods of the moonlit (NANA) underworld, the eunuch (HA*NAKA*) priesthood as representatives of Mother Earth being at one (atone) with the hidden nocturnal sun (IS HANA).

ANAT (HANATA);

Phoenician, Ugaritic, Hebrew, Akkadian and Egyptian. Lybian triple Goddess of fertility, sexual love, hunting and war. 'I have come from myself'. Mother Earth as the 'source' of fertility, sexual love, hunter of the sun, declaring war on him and killing him every night. Also as the eternal virgin it is Mother Earth creating Herself out of Herself, by Herself as the source of her own fertility. In South America the boa constrictor as the ANAconda also generated her offspring without male input as does a humanoid creature with the elongated skull and a morning gecco in the South Pacific.

ANATH (HANATA);

Cannanites, Amorites, Syrians, Egyptians, twin of Mari, mistress of all the Gods, triple Goddess, Queen of birth and death, fertilized by blood of men not their semen, still out of the tail end of PHASE ONE. In PHASE THREE linguistically gave birth to ANATHema meaning anything consigned to damnation.

ANANTA (HANANATA);

Both the sun (IS HANA) linked with the moon (NANA), having risen upon the surFACE along the lea lines on the body of Mother Earth. Nato (NATA) in Polish means upon.

ANNA (HANANA);

Sumerian Lady of Heaven, hiding in her linguistic coils the sun (IS HANA) and Nana of the Greek moon working in concert.

APHRODITE (HAFARADATA);

Greek Goddess of love and beauty, trinity of (virgin, mother, crone), single creatress, governed natural world, half (HAFA-) of reality above her surface.

ARTEMIS (HARATAMASA);

Amazonian Moon Goddess, covered with bee cells her major metaphoric symbols. Mother Earth as huntress and maintainer, giving birth (HARA) in Hebrew to nurturing and killing all that she created.

ARINNA (HARANANA);

Hittite Great Goddess Mother of Her belly of air (HARA) of the moon (NANA) out of her horizontal wound (RANA).

ARACHNE (HARAKANA);

Greek spider as the spinner of fate. Human helplessness at birth trapped in a body that didn't work likened to a fly caught in a spider web.

ARTHA (HARATA);

Sanskrit, root Indo-European cognite of Mother Earth's belly (HARA) who supplied all the riches as they returned (RATA-) up to Her surFACE.

ARMATHR (HARAMATARA);

Iceland Mother of prosperity. Out of Her belly (HARA) with the male (RAMA) and Mother (MATARA) Earth working together to create wealth in PHASE TWO.

ARAMAITI (HARAMATA);

Iranian Earth Fire Goddess, mother (MATA-) of the people made of clay. Same as Adam. Devoted to peace.

ASHA (HASA);

Iranian 'truth', universal law, Vedic truth as fire (AGNI). Kundalini rising.

ASHESH (HASASA);

Egyptian Mother Earth as law giver, early form of Isis (HASASA). Lady of heaven, Queen of Gods, Law (LAVA) giving Mothers natural law.

ASHERAH (HASARA);

Semitic Great Goddess out of volcanic ashes.

ASHNAN (HASANANA);

Sumerian strength of all things dealing with the moon (NANA).

ASTARTE (HASATARATA);

Middle Eastern Great Goddess out of terra (TARA) of Mother Earth, the return (RATA-) of land up to the surface out of a volcanic eruption.

ASTRAEA (HASATARA);

Lybian Goddess of holy law, Libra. Lib of castration and mutilation.

ATALANTA (HATALANATA);

Amazonian Great huntress. The sun had been swallowed off the Western African coast in the maritime waters of the Atlantic Ocean as Mother Earth hunted and swallowed him at twilight.

ATERGATIS(HATARAGATASA);

Philistene fish Goddess, attar scent of vagina.

ATHENE (HATANA);

Greek virgin Goddess, ATI (HATA) mother, ANA Hurrian deity, also Goddess of fertility, sprung from head of Zeus in PHASE THREE fully armed and ready to do battle with the sinking sun.

SECTION THREE

THE LETTER M

The letter M is a bilabial voiced nasal consonant

THE HUM (HAMA) OF THE MOTHER in stage one

SOUND; Closed mouth humming, vibrating the roof of the oral cavity

SHAPE; The top lip on the mothers mouth (MATA)

MOTHERS BODY; mamaries, mons veneris, manos, mind

MOTHER EARTH; mountains, mounds, mar, maw

CONCEPT; holding, maintaining, masticating, making

Webster's New Unabridged Twentieth Century Dictionary contains the following observation. "There seems to be an ... abnormally frequent use of the letter M, or the SOUND that it represents... there seems to be a fondness for the letter M, from the Greek Mu". Not only is there a 'fondness' for the 'abnormally frequent use of the letter M' the world over, but a word slipped into both Greek and Latin defining the 'puzzling' phenomenon. The word is MYTAKISMOS and has surfaced in English as mytacism, or the extensive use of the letter M. Since Webster's New Unabridged Twentieth Century Dictionary has been compiled out of PHASE THREE, it would make sense that the SOUND and SHAPE of the letter M associated with the MOTHER on all levels would give the left hemispheric male compilers of the dictionary more than a moments quizzical pause.

The SOUND of the letter M and the phoneme MA are *hum*anity's oldest consonant . They define the processes, qualities and functions associated with the MOTHER, be she the individual *hum*an mother, or the more expansive metaphoric body of Mother Earth. The MA SOUND originated in Africa in PHASE ONE with the migrating mothers following the herbivore herds to greener pastures for an alternate milk supply. Over a multi thousand year heritage (HER IT AGE), in PHASE ONE before male history (HIS STORY) in PHASE TWO and THREE, the M SOUND associated with the MOTHER stayed constant as restless, perambulating *hum*anity circled the globe carrying with them their babies, their songs, their tattoos and the expanding use of meaningful clusters of recognizable SOUND.

Out of the most ancient PHASE ONE the letter M comes directly out of the SHAPE of the top lip of the mother's (MATA-) mouth (MATA) that closes over the oral cavity. It was originally associated with infant survival, with their mimicking (MAMA-) the mother, her teaching and with the maintenance of life. It deals with the SOUND of *humming* (HAMA-) M-M-M. The food is good. It is edible. As the mother put her two lips together, she *hummed* yes to the edibility of the food that she was savoring. As she was chewing the morsels, testing the food as she was tasting it, the only SOUND that she could make in her closed mouth (MATA), was the nasal SOUND of humming, alerting the children that permission was being granted, assent was given to the food that she was masticating. It was safe to be eaten as sent. Her offspring mimicking (MAMA-) her, learned what to eat, where and when to find it, how to pick, or catch it leading to their survival. When she rejected the food because it was distasteful or inedible, she shoved the food out of her mouth making the N SOUND of negation. It was the nasal SOUND that could be made when the mouth was otherwise engaged and the air had to be pushed out through the nose.

The nasal N SOUND expanded into the CONCEPT of 'negation of a former state', or 'emergence upon on the surface' originally associated with rejected or regurgitated food accompanied by the SOUND of air exiting through the nose. The MANA or the (MN) construct evolved into the ever widening cncept of 'holding' (MA) or 'rejecting' (NA).

In Hawaiian MANA is a 'chewed mass', food held in the mouth (MA), chewed by an adult for a child, and then regurgitated (NA).

The activity of *humming* associated with food testing was so pleasurable that it expanded into singing, defining the *humming* mother as the joy filled *hum*an creature, having a sense of *hum*or emerging out of the body of Mother Earth, Her *hum*us, *hum*ble of her origins, at one with her Maternal source.

Activating the pituitary gland sitting above the vibrating (vaBARAta-) palate the act of *humming* sent forth endorphins that in time evolved into the ecstasy carrying AUM (HAMA) or OM (HAMA), of Eastern religious practice. For the Greeks in PHASE THREE the big OM (HAMA) became OMEGA. Prophetically The A (ah) of Alpha the first letter of the Greek alphabet, began with the A(ah) of Mother Earths triangular volcanic cone. The O of OMEGA, the big OM, the last letter of the Greek alphabet ended with the father. The letter A(ah) surfaces on the ends of feminine nouns in Romance and Slavic languages. The letter (O) performs the same function on the ends of male nouns also in Romance and Slavic languages.

The phoneme MA defines the 'mother' in all of the languages of the world except in the Japanese. In Japanese the personal mother is HA-HA. Its not necessarily that she is so joyful at giving birth. It has more to do with the HA

Section Three

HA of the fast and high panting, the bastrika breath of Kundalini, that surfaces in the last stages of labor, awakens ecstasy and helps to push the large headed fetus out of the narrow hipped mother's body.

The dyad HAMA, not only dealt with the *hum* (HAMA) of the mother, but also with her blood. In Greek ema (HAMA) or heoma (HAMA) means 'blood'. It is associated with a variety of related processes. One deals with the blood coagulating, coming together with itself in the female body to create the baby. Male role in specific paternity was unknown in PHASE ONE when these SOUNDS were becoming codified and it was believed that the blood coagulated within the mothers belly all by itself to make a baby.

Another perception associated with (HAMA) deals with the liquefied bloody sun in the body of Mother Earth coagulating to create the solid integral solar disc, Her heavenly offspring to be born at dawn. It also dealt with the metaphoric lips on the body of Mother Earth perceived to be the horizontal divide where the top lip met the bottom lip at the edge of the extended circle around them. The top lip were the (M) of the mountains. The bottom lip were the (W) of the reflective surface of waters, the maw (MAWA) of another declination.

Out of Her body, as the ancient migrants traveled back and forth across the continent of Africa, the mountains emerged not only as swallowing mouths but also as gestating bellies giving birth to the sun. Mother Earth in Her aspect as the mountains, held the sun in Her mounds of creation. As it waited transformed, to push through the mantle of darkness and make its daily appearance upon Her surFACE. Out of Her aspect as water with large tracts of reflective swamps spreading out to the distant horizon, Mother Earth also gave birth to the heavenly bodies out of Her Eastern horizontal rim and swallowed them back into the other side in the Western waters. It was perceived that the mountains (MA) on top reflecting the waters (WA) below were the two parts that comprised Her lips, the broken circle of the mouth on Her surFACE. Those planetary lips of mountains on top and the waters on the bottom, closed around the setting sun as it splattered its bloody gore against the Western sky and became swallowed in the West. Mother Earth ate (8) it. As the two lips devoured the sun they *hummed* their acceptability that it was good as sent, that it was worthy of traveling through the subterranean entrails within the body of Mother Earth to be transformed and reborn at dawn. The bottom lip of the waters as a reflective surface absorbed the sun dimming it, as it sank out of sight. Sinking out of sight it seemed as if the sun and the waters merged, became 'together with', became at one with the aqueous body of Mother Earth. In Greek ema (HAMA) or heoma (HAMA) means 'blood'. The blood coagulating, to make a baby in the mother's body fused 'together with' itself. In Persian BAHAM (baHAMA) is 'together'. The phoneme (BA) deals with 'two in one', dealing with the activity of the blood coagulating in her body to make the baby and the 'two in one', of the baby being 'with' the mother. The other (BA) deals with the body of Mother Earth, killing the sun to its light in the West, putting Her two planetary lips together (BA) and chewing on the liquefied solar disc so that it became flowing blood, swallowing it for it to course through Her internal maze and become transformed into the solid integral disc of the sun to be reborn at dawn. The SHAPE of the sun setting in the watery Western horizon emerged as the letter eight (8) in English as Mother Earth ate it. In Chinese the SHAPE of the sun setting into the watery wastes in the West and rising out of the other side is encoded in the letter B that not only deals with 'two in one' but as the SHAPE of the bulbous lips seen from the side also stands for the number eight (8).

For the Hindus UMA (HAMA) is the 'Death Mother Goddess', the two lips on Mother Earth's mouth, the mountains on top, 'together with' reflected in the waters below, killed Her offspring, the sun. As it was being devoured in the West, in its bloody dismembered state it meandered through the underground entrails within Her body. That's why they needed all those subterranean metaphoric guides; snakes, cats, psychopomps, bulls, rams, to help it find its way back up to Her surFACE.

The body of Mother Earth may have swallowed her solar offspring every night, but she also without any ado, gave birth to it very quickly, in fact the next day. The body of the individual mother also gave birth, but she did not participate in the activity of swallowing her young.

In Swahili the M SOUND stands for 'plural'. In the process of birthing the mother creating one more of herself, creates 'plurality'. In Persian MA is 'we' and 'we' deals with more than one. In Burmese MA is a 'young woman'. In the Indo-European group of languages MA is 'intelligence'. In Sanskrit MA is the 'tongue', the expressor of 'intelligence' and the facilitator of deciding whether the food was edible, which takes common sense and good judgment. In ancient Europe, MA dealing with Mother Earth was the 'Goddess of Indulgence' and 'All Seeing Immortality'. For the Egyptians the owl as the letter M for MA'A represented by the 'all seeing' bird with the rotating head, who like the Great Mother Earth was not only the great ear who heard their inquiries but was also the great eye like the owl who saw in all directions. Like Mother Earth regurgitated the sun at dawn the owl regurgitated pellets

Section Three

of food. In Persian MA'A is 'with'. It could be that the M SHAPE of the top lip is 'with' the W shape of the bottom lip, creating the mouth. Or it could mean that the Persian MA'A is 'with' the baby in her belly. In Cypriotic, the symbol for MA is looks like buttocks holding a (U) in the mothers body. The baby (U) is 'with' the mother. In Linear B looks like the mating flight of the queen bee of be-ing, in the process of be-coming the lonely egg laying mother (like Mother Earth), with the male drone impaled under her.

The following dyads and triads illustrate the universal reach of the ancient M based SOUNDS associated with motherhood. The M SOUND as an anlaut establishes the MA of the individual *hum*an mother (MATARA) as the *hummer*. The T SOUND establishes the tip or edge of the mouth (MATA) partially encircling the bottom part of her face, creating the *humming* SOUND defined her as the *hum* maker. On the body of Mother Earth it deals with the mat of matter, Her tip, top, or mountainous edge. Creation out of Her TIP deals with Her edge at the circular horizon line out of whose broken circle She gave birth to the heavenly bodies and birds. Out of Her TOP, Her planetary skin She gave birth to plants, scurrying creatures, solidly planted trees, and perambulating *hum*an beings. The letter H deals with the breath AH-HA or HA-HA upon which the SOUND of *humming* became suspended.

On the body of Mother Earth it deals with the belly of air above Her surFACE through which all of life had its being. The Egyptian symbol for immortality as the ANKH, (HANAKA) related to the eunuch (HANAKA) is shaped like a clove (KALAVA). It may very well deal with the small (KA) round disc of the sun emerging as (LAVA) descending out of or into the top, tip of the body of Mother Earth. Since the sun was perceived to be immortal for it returned at dawn to a new day so the soul to gain immortality went through the same process. Like the sun, it had to descend into the body of Mother Earth, be buried (BARAda), become transformed and reborn to a new life. Many subsequent male based religious systems in PHASE THREE latched on to that mother based perception.

The following words all deal with names defining some linguistic aspect of the mother.

Swahili-MAMA
Welsh-MAM
Lithuanian-MAMA
Ancient Babylonian-MAMI
Sumerian-MATU
Sanskrit-MATA, MATRA

Russian-MATI
Polish-MA, MAMA, MATKA
Latin-MATER
Egyptian-MAT, MAHIR
Celtic-MATHIR
German-MUTTER
English-MOTHER
Greek-MITIR, METER
Chukchi-MITI
Spanish-MADRE
Russian-MADER
Swedish, Danish-MODER
Dutch-MOEDER
French-MERE
Norwegian-MOR
Australian-MARM
Portuguese-MAI
Assam-MAHARI
Vietnamese-ME
Chinese-MA, MAMA, MU

For the Maya MAMOM was the 'grandmother' who produced culture. As MAMOM she was also the 'grandmother' as pottery maker in Africa, Melanesia, Amazon, Peru and Egypt. The ancient pot was the symbol for the feminine uterus as the bowl, and the neck of the vessel as the vagina.

The vowels do their predictable 'shape shifting' pavan, but the M sound associated with the *humming* 'mother' stays constant. If it doesn't lead the pack, the M sound also surfaces within words defining the 'mother'.

The following words for 'mother' deal with some aspect of the activity of *humming* (HAMA-) or some aspect of the process dealing with her coagulating blood, ema or heoma (HAMA) in Greek. AM (HAMA) is 'mother' in Hebrew. Also in Hebrew AMAM means 'to be higher', 'to surpass'. In Arabic the 'mother' is UM, OM (HAMA). In Zulu it is UMAME (HAMAMA). Siberian Tungus myth OME (HAMA) is the 'matrix'. In Persian AMME (HAMA) is 'common people'. In Polish cHAM (HAMA) is also a 'common person'. In Latin and Greek AMMA (HAMA) was the 'spiritual mother'. For the Norse AMMA (HAMA) was the 'grandmother'. In Hebrew RAHAM (RAHAMA) means 'people', associated with the Egyptian male Sun God Ra out of PHASE TWO. In Greek AMA (HAMA) means 'together with'. In

Persian BAHAM (BAHAMA) means 'together'. The two lips approximated (BA), making the *humming* (HAMA-) SOUND by (MA). For the Assyrians UMMATI (HAMATA) were the 'high priestesses', 'mothers of creation'. The menstruating women who as mothers (MATA-) created life out of their blood, ema (HAMA) in Greek. In Hebrew shemat (IS HAMATA) were the 'singing mothers'. In Yiddish and Polish szmata (IS HAMATA), is a 'rag', worn as a badge of honor around her buttox. A 'rag' or a menstrual scarf has been and is used by women around the world during their periods. When a young girl reached her quintessence, or flowed with her red blood, she joined the 'mothers of creation', the ummati (HAMATA) in Assyria. It was a time of great singing and celebration, the shemat (IS HAMATA) of the Hebrews. Wearing a rag, szmata (IS HAMATA) in Yiddish and Polish, she joined the ranks of the 'high priestesses', who in PHASE ONE were the rulers and queens.

In Peru MAMA QUILLA (KALA) was the mother 'Moon Goddess'. She establishes her links with the Hindu Goddess KALI MA (KALA MA) in her aspect as creation and destruction associated with the passage of time (calendar KALA-) and the moon. Her daughter also a 'Moon Goddess' was MAMA OGILLO (HAGALA). The hag (HAGA) as a 'Holy Woman' and Hag (HAGA) was the cognate of Egyptian heq (HAKA) a predynastic matriarchial ruler who knew the ritual words of power, or hekau (HAKA). The second dyad (GALA) deals with 'mothers milk' and is associated with the ancient moon. For the Tartars MAMMA was Mother Earth. Turkish Mother Earth, MAMONT (MAMATANA) is the birther of Her major off spring the sun out of Her gestating, maintaining (MANATANA) mountains (MANATANA). The Sumero-Babylonian 'Goddess Mother,' of the primordial sea in PHASE ONE was TIAMAT (TAYAMATA), personification of the watery 'deep', Mother (MATA-) Earth in Her aspect as water, out of which all life and light (AYA) emerged. In Egyptian MA-NU (MANA) defines the 'abyss', or the wound on Her edge out of which Mother Earth gave birth to all of Her off spring. She held them within Her until they were ready and them She regurgitated, birthed or passed them up to Her surFACE. For the Maya 'dawn' as MANA, was the emergence of light out of the abyss of night, same for the Latin mane (MANA) as 'morning'. In the Maya 'dawn' as MANA, you are dealing with the holding (MA) and releasing (NA) of the light at dawn by the lips or hands at the horizon, the break in the circular sweep on the body of Mother Earth around them, that gave birth to the heavenly bodies and birds. As 'morning' in Latin MANE (MANA) deals with the SHAPE of the rays of the sun radiating out of the body of Mother Earth at dawn, like a mane (MANA) radiating out of a male lions head, one of the reasons why in PHASE THREE he came to represent royalty.

In PHASE TWO separation myths pepper the ancient landscape. The Sumero-Babylonian Marduk the son (sun) of Tiamat (TAYAMATA) divided his body that had been at one with the mother into the sky above and the Earth below. He performed the same function as Ra, the Egyptian sun God, separating the sun from the body of Mother Earth establishing the sun as the domain of the emerging male 'source'. By dividing the sea as TIAMAT in half, Marduk the son (SUN), established the diameter (dia(METER), the halving in twain of the unity of the circle that in PHASE ONE had been the watery body of Mother Earth and the sun. In Greek, the version of the halved Goddess Mother (MATARA) became Demeter (DAMATARA) to reign as the Goddess of Night, of the underworld and winter.

On the other side of the world the Maya 'grandmother' as MAMOM (MAMAMA). The Mayan MAMOM (MAMAMA) as 'grandmother' is MA of mother hood repeated into the third generation. She was not only associated with pot making but as the 'grandmother' she emerged out of PHASE ONE when the solar family of relatives were at one with the body of Mother Earth that included sisters, aunts, nieces, daughters and grandmothers.

On the body of the individual *hum*an mother the MAMA dyad expands to deal with her breasts, her mammaries (MAMA-) that flowed with life sustaining and maintaining (MANA-) milk (MALA-) and in PHASE THREE defined all lactating mammals (MAMA-). For the Tantrists MAMAKI (MAMAKA) was the Goddess of the 'fertilizing waters', the maker (MAKA-) of milk. Milk as liquid effulgence, the manure (MANA-) of the mother, made the baby grow and flourish.

The mouth (MATA) of the mother (MATA-) as the *hummer* and masticator, as the holder (M) and releaser (N) of food and SOUND, expands to include other activities of holding (MA) and releasing (NA). The most objective practical neutral example of holding (MA) and releasing (NA), surfaces in Chinese as MEN (MANA) and it defines a 'gate' or a 'door'. When a 'gate' or 'door' closes, it holds (MA) things shut, like the *humming* mouth of the mother closes around food that is being tasted. When it opens, it releases or pushes out the rejected contents making the nasal (NA) SOUND of rejection, establishing the concept of 'negation of a former state', or 'emergence on the surface'. The Chinese MEN (MANA) as a 'gate' or a 'door' could go into a more ancient esoteric direction out of PHASE ONE. For the 'gate or 'door' could be the mons (MANA-) veneris on the female body the 'gate' or 'door' into the holding (MA) and releasing (NA) of pleasure, blood and life itself.

Returning to the close proximity of the mouth of the mother, in Swahili meno (MANA) means 'teeth'. One 'tooth' in Swahili is jino. One tooth can't hold and release anything. It just hangs down from the top jaw or protrudes up from the lower jaw. The Swahili jino for one 'tooth' begs a question. Could the (J) deal with the SHAPE of the jaw and the (N) deal with 'emergence upon the surface', which is what a tooth does? It solitarily emerges out of the gums on the surface. It is only with many (MANA) teeth, meno (MANA) in Swahili working in concert, that you can create the activity of holding (MA) and releasing (NA). In Hawaiian MANA as a chewed mass of food that is masticated for a child by an adult comes close to the source. It is held (MA) in the mouth of the *humming* mother and when ready, regurgitated (NA) for the waiting young.

The sharing of edible food not only takes generosity but discretion, forethought and wisdom. For the Bemba MANO (MANA) is 'intelligence'. The mind (MANADA) within the skull is the 'gift of' (DA) holding (MA) and releasing (NA) of thought. In Sanskrit MENS (MANASA) is 'the mind', linking it to menses (MANASA) or the female 'period'. The female body holds (MA) and releases (NA) her monthly menses, or menstrual bloody (SA) flow. In Egyptian SA is the 'wise blood' of the mother. It knows all by itself when to flow, when to stop flowing and when to coagulate inside into the making of a baby. In Latin MUNUS (MANASA) means 'gift'. It is out of her mons (MANASA) veneris that the mother using her coagulated menses (MANASA) creates the 'gift' of new life. The first dyad (MANA) deals with the holding (MA), of the fetal blood and then after ten lunar months releasing (NA) of the baby. The second dyad (NASA) in Latin deals with nascence and nascence (NASA NASA) is the repetitive activity of birthing. The MANA related to the mons (MANASA) veneris may also deal with the functions of the hands (manus (MANASA) in Latin), massaging and masturbating the the large headed fetus to spasm and orgasm out of the mothers narrow hipped body.

The lunar month (MANATA) works in tandem with the female flow of menstrual blood. The moon (MANA) holds (MA) and releases (NA) the monthly flow of blood out of the female body. 'To think' in Lithuanian is MANYTI (MANATA) associating it with the female and her period at a specific time of the month (MANATA). A WOman is the mother, the 'holder' and 'maintainer' of the placental WAter sac that holds the fetus. A man (MANA) is a male creature who holds (MA) and releases (NA) the female during coitus, using his arms as a frame around her body. The same construct surfaces in Bugotu as mane (MANA) a 'male person', the one with a bush of hair eMANAting from around his face and head', like rays emanated from the surFACE of the sun. In Latin mane (MANA) is 'morning' dealing with the SHAPE of the suns rays as outstretched fingers of radiating hair. For the Maya MANA was 'dawn'. Both In Latin and in Maya the stiletto like fingers as the rays of light piercing the pall of darkness awakened the sleeping body of Mother Earth creating radiating piercing brilliance in the 'morning' at 'dawn'. In Spanish MANO (MANA) means 'hand'. For it was not only the fingers, or radiating hair that brought forth light, but it was the 'hands' that held (MA) and released (NA) the light onto Her waiting surFACE to create the 'morning' and 'dawn'.

The king of beasts, the lion with his radiating mane (MANA) the halo surrounding his massive head, likened him to the rays of the sun fingering their way into space at dawn. In PHASE THREE the lazy male carnivore sleeping eighteen hours a day became the king of beasts, replacing the female pride, primarily because the mane (MANA) around his head became associated with the SHAPE of the rays of the sun at dawn. When the sun became a separate male deity *away* and *above* the body of Mother Earth in PHASE TWO, the lion not only became the king of beasts, but because of his ray like solar mane (MANA) became a subsequent symbol of royalty. Since there are apparently no lions on the South Pacific Islands that contain the Bugotu tribe, then the related concept of a hairy halo around a male face and a corona like mane around a lion's head, must have their roots further back out of Africa. It may very well echo the fact that in societies where men want to maintain their dominance over women, they let their hair and beards grow, to become hirsute like the radiant splintering rays of the male sun fingering their way in all directions *away* and *above* their source of enlightment.

The hand (HANAda) is the 'gift of' (DA) the sun (IS HANA), the holder of light and warmth during the day in Her belly of air (HA-). On the body of Mother Earth the hand is the withholder of light and warmth beneath Her surFACE during the night (N). The holder (MA) and releaser (NA), dealing with the hands, surfaces in Spanish as mano (MANA), in Latin as manus (MANA-).

In Polish a derogatory term for the left hand of the ancient mothers, ending with the letter (A) of the female, is manka (MANAKA). In PHASE THREE among Polish Christians manka was derided as the hand of the devil. The second dyad in manka (MANAKA) is the snake (IS NAKA) representing the Kundalini energy establishing the left handed female as the daughter of Mother Earth in Her aspect as the serpentine guide of the sun and soul through Her body to be reborn to a new life, ie to be reincarnated. The ancient belief hidden in the dyad manka (MANAKA) dealt with 'paganism' out of PHASE ONE or the belief in the body of Mother Earth as the supreme and all encompassing creative 'source'.

In Hebrew MANA is a 'portion'. If you don't use the Swahili 'teeth' meno (MANA) to create 'portions', then you use the hands, the Spanish mano (MANA) to complete the process. Also in Hebrew MANA MANAH (MANAHA) means, 'to portion', 'to divide', same activity expanding to the Hebrew minha (MANAHA) as a 'gift'. A gift is that which is handed by the hands. The (NAHA) as the second dyad in minha (MANAHA) takes it back to the body of Mother Earth, to the Latin nihil (NAHALA) of 'nothingness', or the gift of the sun out of the subterranean void of darkness out of the body of Mother Earth. But the Hebrew MANA MANAH (MANAHA) comes from a much more ancient source in PHASE ONE. Mother Earth was believed to swallow the sun in the Western horizon. She killed it to its light. It disappeared into Her body. The creative and destructive power inherent in the sun being pulled down into Her, plunging the world into obliterating blackness. When Mother Earth ate the sun, she broke it into many pieces, she chewed it into many 'portions'. Before it could reemerge as the integral disc of the sun in the East, it had to reassemble itself out of the nothingness beneath Her planetary skin. It had to recoagulate itself in order to make its daily appearance. It had to transform and reflect itself out of the cold still underground of the Latin nihil (NAHA-) of 'nothingness', into the above ground triumph of movement, and the warmth of the blazing sun (IS HANA/NAHA). *As above (HANA) so below (NAHA).*

Closer to the mouth holding (MA) and rejecting (NA) is me'en (MANA), that in Hebrew means to 'refuse'. To 'refuse' as a verb, is to create refuse as a noun, and to reject what is given, either out of the activity of the mouth, or the activity of the hands. In Persian mane (MANA) means an 'obstacle'. It is with the hands that you bar the way, that you create an 'obstacle'. Or it could mean that you have come on a path facing a hairy male lion.

The Chinese share the AYA as 'light' with the Persians in their name for the 'full moon', that is MANYUE (MANAYA). The moon (MANA), was the hand (MANA), that held (MA) and carried the nocturnal (NA) 'light' (AYA), up and across the vault of the midnight sky. Periodically the moon also withdrew its light, plunging the nocturnal (NA) sky into impenetrable darkness. The light (AYA) of the 'full moon', its round perfect circle during the night, was like the light of the sun with its round perfect circle during the day. AYA in Persian means 'light'. The 'full moon' rising out of the body of Mother Earth was like the light of 'dawn' spreading into the dark corners of the night. In Assyrian AYA is 'dawn'. It could deal with the rising orb of the sun ushering a new day, or the rising full moon ushering a new night.

The mountains (MANATA-) and mounds (MANADA) on the body of Mother Earth were like gestating bellies that held the sun, moon, the heavenly bodies and even the birds before they were born, before they rose above Her surFACE to soar through Her belly of air.

The body of Mother Earth as mundo (MANADA) in Spanish is the ultimate 'gift of' (DA) holding (MA) and releasing (NA), of existence as it appeared above Her surFACE in life and as it disappeared below Her surFACE in death. The activity was so predictable and pedestrian that the English word mundane (MANADANA) evolved from that ancient perception.

In Hawaiian MANANA means 'to stretch out' with the arms and fingers extended, to loosen their grip, and radiate in all directions. On the body of Mother Earth the stiletto like rays of the sun like fingers and helping hands, or even strands of hair also 'stretch out', extend in all directions as they broke through the mantle of darkness. They were considered, not only to be reborn, but also to be regurgitated up to Her surFACE at dawn. In Hawaiian MANA is to chew food and regurgitate it for an infant by an adult. In Spanish MANANA means 'tomorrow' and 'tomorrow' is the gift of light carried by the repetitive emergence (NANA), of the hands of Mother Earth as the rays of the sun jostling awake the sleeping dawn.

As 'rays', 'branches', 'fingers' and 'hands' emanate from the center, so does 'SOUND'. The word manure (MANARA) has links with the sun (-ER). For the sun was not only regurgitated up to the surFACE at dawn, but at different times it was perceived that the birthing hole on the edge of the body of Mother Earth was an anus and what emerged from that anus was feces or manure (MANARA). In many of its aspects manure is like the helping hands that assist plants in their growth. Out of that perception Mother Earth swallowing all that She created especially the sun and defecating it up to Her surFACE after it passed through Her internal fiery furnace, was considered to be the ultimate manure maker.

MANA MANA in Hawaiian deals with the body of Mother Earth as it defines 'branches', 'extensions', 'sun with rays', 'fingers', 'appendages' of all kinds. All of these 'extensions' deal with holding (MA) and rejecting (NA). 'Branches' hold leaves and fruit and then let them go. The sun holds on to the 'rays of the sun' and lets them go when it absorbs them in the West. 'Fingers' at the ends of the hands are the supreme holders and releasers of all kinds of objects.

In Latin MANUal (MANA-) is that which is done by the hands, but shares the dyad MANU (MANA) with Maori men on the other side of the globe, for it defines their 'power' as residing in their hands. Other words surface dealing with the use of the hands. A 'MANUscript', is that which is written by the hand. To 'MANIpulate' is to presto digitate with the hands. A 'MANAcle' restrains the hands with handcuffs. 'MANUmission' sets the hands free. To 'MANAge' is to control with the hands. In Latin MANcus deals with being 'maimed' or 'crippled' through either inflicted or accidental injury. In Polish MANka or MANkut means 'left hand'. To 'MENd' is to fix with the hands. To 'deMANd' is the 'gift of' (DA) taking away with the hands. At the ends of words (-MONY) defines the act of holding and releasing; ceremony(-MA-NA) to the Goddess Ceres, harmony (-MANA) to the Goddess Hera, with the pregnant belly, matrimony (-MANA) to Matri or motherhood.)

On the ends of words, the suffix (-MENT) deals with 'the product or action of a verb', as in firmaMENT, docuMENT, vestMENT, fragMENT, atoneMENT, torMENT etc.

African Voodoo priests use man man (MANA MANA), their biggest drum to awaken the deep spirit of trance in the human psyche. It is the hands holding (MA) and releasing (NA) SOUND, thumping out repetitive rhythms with their thumbs and fingers that link man man to the activity of the hands. In Latin manus (MANASA) is 'hands'. A close relative to the 'hands' in Latin, is manes (MANASA), or 'the 'ancient spirits of the dead', that the African voodoo priests awaken by drumming with their hands.

For the Bugotu and many of the Islanders of the South Pacific MANA is 'magical power'. It could go in many directions. It could be Swahili teeth meno (MANA) the 'magical power' that creates milled and lubricated food for the survival of the off spring. It could be MANA the Hawaiian 'magical power', the process of chewing and regurgitating food for the waiting young. It could be the Sanskrit mind (mens (MANASA), that as the 'magical power' is so capable of working things out. It could be the Latin hands (manus (MANASA) that hold the 'magical power' MANUfacturing tools and weapons, holding a baby and foraging for food. It could be the moon (MANA) with its association to the monthly (MANATA) flow of blood (mens (MANASA) out of the mons (MANASA) veneris on the female body that is the 'magical power' that creates a baby. It could deal with men (MANA) holding the female with their arms as they share the 'magical power' of creation during coitus in PHASE TWO.

The whole picture becomes a bit fuzzy when the Biblical manna (MANA) 'falling from heaven', enters the linguistic scene. It probably had a double meaning; the female period (MENS) falling out of her body on one end. On the other end, the mysterious 'magical power' falling from the sky to activate the flow of blood in human females, governed by the cycles of the moon (MANA). The redefinitions and obfuscations in PHASE TWO lead to many confusions. What rose up from the physical body of Mother Earth in PHASE ONE, as the ecstasy carrying trans-formative Kundalini energy of the Tantrists, in PHASE TWO had to fall down from space, from the hidden mind of God in the sky, sun, moon and cosmos. What MANA does establish as 'magical power' in Bugotu, is that it deals with 'movement' and 'movement' deals with the whole cycle of existence of life above the plane (MA) and death below the plane (NA), that expands into the concept of holding (MA) and releasing (NA).

The mother (MATARA) was MATA in PHASE ONE before the -ER of the Egyptian male sun god Ra made his entrance as the doer and helper in PHASE TWO. She began her role as the ever present masticating, humming oral cavity in the mother's (MATA-) mouth (MATA) that maintained her hungry children.

On the flat maternal plane of Mother Earth the activity of creation occurred on two specific areas dealing with two different sets of off shoots. One dealt with Her circular sweep, the round ground around them ending at the horizon line, the solar plexus, the mouth at the edge, the rim at the tip (T) where the top lip in the SHAPE of the mountains parted to let the heavenly bodies and the birds to be born and to rise into Her belly of air. After Her solar passengers made their appointed rounds they were swallowed back into Her waiting arms, or into the horizontal hole in the Western rim.

The other was Her surFACE, Her crusty mantle (MANA-), Her skin, Her top (T) Her mat (MATA) of matter (MATARA) where plants, trees, burrowing animals, the fish that swam in Her sea and all the creatures that moved upon Her surFACE had their being. After they lived their lives, they fell down, died, decayed (DK) and were reabsorbed back into Her great body. Mother Earth was perceived to be the cyclical overwhelming, mysterious context of existence in both life and in death.

If the mouth (MATA) defined the individual mother (MATARA), then the mat (MATA) of material (MATARA), maternal (MATARA-) matter (MATARA) defined the body of Mother Earth. The mat (MATA) of matter

(MATARA), Her surface on top (T) and Her skin at the tip (T) were like a series of invisible, 'hidden' MOUTHS (MATA) that swallowed all that She created. If MATA deals with the mat of matter (MATARA) on the body of Mother Earth then the individual mother (MATARA), her surrogate in the creation of smaller aspects of herself shared the same organs, processes, qualities and functions. (TARA) the second dyad in matter (MATARA) deals with the terrain TARA-), the terra (TARA) firma, the mat of matter upon which all of this activity takes place. In English mote (MATA) is either a particle of dust or a hillock, a mound on the body of Mother Earth. Smote (IS MATA), the activity of killing provides fillers for the mounds on the body of Mother Earth.

For the Gypsies out of the Indus Valley the 'Supreme Mother Goddess' was MATTA (MATA). She may have been the maintainer and holder with Her hands in life, but She was also the releaser and rejecter in death. She was the great holder of warmth, movement and light. When She swallowed the sun, moon and all of the creatures that She created, She was considered also as a fearful dispenser of death and ultimate smiter (IS MATARA).

The following dyads deal with the destructive processes inherent in the body of Mother Earth. MATA as the dyad for the mother (MATA-) surfaces in Spanish as 'death'. In Latin MATA means 'to kill'. Mother Earth was the great killer and eater of life. She ate everything that She created. All that emerged upon Her surFACE was in one way or another swallowed back to make its trans-formative journey beneath Her skin, through the twisting, turning bloody rivers that carried the sun and soul underneath Her surFACE. When the sun set in the West, into standing stretches of water, the SHAPE of the sun sliding down into its reflective watery tomb was the number eight (8). Mother Earth ate the sun, swallowed it into Her great maw in the Western sky. In Arabic MAT (MATA) means 'to die'. In Arabic MOT (MATA) means 'death'. For the Canaanites MOT (MATA) was the 'God of Death and Sterility'. MAUT (MATA) in Hindi is 'death'. In Swahili MAUTI (MATA) means 'death'. Both in Hindi and Swahili they SOUND like the English mouth (MATA). Also in Swahili MAITI (MATA) means 'corpse'. The mouth (MATA) of Mother Earth ate, swallowed everything that She created, on Her mat (MATA) of matter (MATARA-).

For the African Pygmies MAAT (MATA) was the name for the 'womb' and the 'underworld' covering both bases. The mat (MATA) of matter (MATARA) dealt with light, warmth and motility (MATA-) above the plane. The place of transformation below Her surFACE dealt with darkness, cold dark stillness and the mysterious inevitable processes of transformation. She was known as MATU (MATA) in Sumeria and was 'cat headed'. Because cats could see in the dark, they were believed to be great companions for the departed soul and a guide on their journey to rebirth through the dark underground bloody rivers within the body of Mother Earth. As Mother (MATA-) she was the Egyptian MAT, or MAAT, in Sanskrit she was MATA or MATRA, In Russian she was MATI, In Latin she was MATER, in Polish she was MATKA, in Celtic she was MATHIR.

If the bee had been associated with the creative process of endless egg laying and bee-ing then two insects symbolized the process of transformation within the body of Mother Earth. For the nocturnal journey of the moon, she was represented by the nocturnal lepidopterous moth (MATA). For the djurnal journey of the sun, she was represented by the Polish motyl (MATALA), or butterfly. As (MATA) associated with the mother (MATA-) in PHASE ONE, she became symbolized by the nocturnal moth (MATA) in Her aspect as transformer of the milky moon on its way to become the ball of curdled cheese rolling through the night sky. As a metaphor (MATA-) for the moon, the moth (MATA) hunkered down in the dark, created a cacoon, slept, suspended its animation, awakened, emerged out of its chrysalis, spread its wings and like the 'shape shifting' moon took flight up into the night sky. The moth as an insect, became one of the most ancient symbols for the transformative process associated with the nocturnal journey of the moon on its way to rebirth.

But the nocturnal moth (MATA) also had an even darker more mysterious aspect. For the nocturnal moth was attracted to light, to flames and to its own destruction. When the moon rose into the night sky, passed through its trans-formative nocturnal journey, as the light of the sun rose in the Eastern sky the moth could not resist the fiery fingers of light and bathing in them, expired, like the moth expired to a flame. It emerged as the white eerie lunar disc floating in the daily sky.

The same process was inherent with the trans-formative journey of the sun as the Polish motyl (MATALA) or butterfly. As a caterpillar it wove a cacoon, hunkered down, then as a chrysalis emerged out of its self created mummy into a butterfly the Polish motyl (MATALA) and rose into the sunlit light filled sky, to flit through the flowers and recreate the process over and over again. Daylight dealt with movement, with life coming back into action at dawn. The fluttering animated butterfly stopping only to pick up pollen became a metaphoric symbol for motion (MATA-) and motility (MATALA-).

Section Three

For the Egyptians The Great Mother Goddess MAAT (MATA), before the human soul was ready to make its trans-formative journey through the body of Mother Earth had to have its soul the AB, weighed against a feather. If the heart-soul was heavier than the feather it flunked the test. What made the heart-soul heavy, was sadness, grief, anger, jealousy, calumny, lying and all the negative emotions. For the ancient Egyptians, Goddess MAAT admonished humans to be joyful, to live their lives in happiness and song. The Hebrew Shemat (IS HAMATA) of the 'singing mothers' (MATA-) surfaces here, as does the Garden of Eden (HADANA) of hedonism (HADANA-) and pleasure having its links with PHASE ONE, to become the wilted male based Paradise in PHASES TWO and THREE.

The Egyptian Mother Goddess MAAT (MATA) was also the 'All Seeing Eye' and the 'Spirit of Truth'. In Egyptian one of the symbols for the letter M, the owl with its 'all seeing eyes', and rotating head, was called the MA'A. As the measurer of the heart-soul MAAT, shared her capacity for measuring 'truth', with the Greek Goddess METER (MATARA) who also as a measurer, represented motherhood and had links with the moon. The moon measured the passage of time into thirteen lunar cycles. The lunar cycles coincided with the passage of menstrual blood out of female bodies. So the mother (MATARA) was the METER (MATARA), the measurer of time in tandem with the moon. Same construct as the RU of the RUby, RUsset blood of the RUler. The Ruler also has two meanings. One deals with 'measurement' of time in tandem with the cycles of the moon. The other deals with 'reigning'. Both were associated with the human female when she passed menstrual blood and became a potential mother and then queen. The beginning of her menarche (MANARAJA) created the new monarch (MANARAJA). The letter M as the ancient syllable of MA, mother on all levels, expands into the ever widening universal concept of, 'holding' measuring and 'maintaining.

Creatures of all kinds had been related to the passage into immortality. Ancient human mothers in PHASE ONE did not worship animals with human heads or humans with animal heads. The sheman, witch, or sachem after going into a trance declared which animal had been revealed to act as a guide into the hereafter and immortality of the particular clan or tribe. The American Indians represented their guides in Totem (TATA-) Poles. The Egyptians into humans with animal or bird heads like Thoth (TATA) and animals with human heads like the Sphinx.

When my sister Janina had been in the hospital Hospice sanctuary a few days before her death she looked around the crowded with relatives hospital room and pointing to the corner of the cramped hospital room," Look" she pointed to the corner, "I didn't know that they allowed cats into the hospital". We all looked in the direction that she had been pointing. The corner to which she had been pointing to was empty. We tried to reason with her. "Jasiu there is no cat in the corner." "Yes there is I can see it," and she pointed again to the empty corner. A few days before she died we again surrounded her bed. This time she asked us not to crowd her for the cat was sitting much closer to her on the corner of the bed.

Her almost to last words exposed the ancient mystery why the ancient Egyptians mummified and bred thousands of cats and buried them with the deceased. The cats had been the Egyptian Totemic guides into immortality. Thousands of years later they appeaered to my sister as she lay dying in that hospital room. Were they always there waiting for her to pass on so that they could perform their function? With the shift into the left 'rational' male oriented hemisphere of the brain what else had humanity been deprived of? We can only wonder.

Truth Will Out

The word truth (TARATA) as TARA/RATA, tells its own story. It deals with the double process of existence of life above and death below moving through the body of Mother Earth. The shared central phoneme as RA of the sun, defines both (TARA) and (RATA). Tara is not only the ancient primal Earth Goddess known from India to Ireland, but the linguistic root for all of the words dealing with the terra (TARA) firma, the tar (TARA) that created the terrain (TARANA), the terraces (TARASA) that grew crops, known as the Hebrew Terah (TARA), and the Etruscan Turan (TARANA). There was an Athenian orgiastic festival named after her as TARAMATA or Mother Tara. The (TA) deals with the specific place, at the tip, or edge at the horizontal rim where the sun (RA) emerged at Her surFACE. (RATA) deals with the ratio (RATA) or the circular cycle of passage that the sun (RA) made in its daily return (RATARANA) upon Her surFACE, or terrain (TARANA) out of Her tip at the horizon line. It is out of the 'wound' of 'dawn' at the edge or tip that the sun made its daily appearance on Her surFACE. In Polish rana, the third dyad in return (RATARANA) and the second dyad in terrain (TARANA) deals with both 'wound' and 'dawn'.

What the word truth (TARATA) deals with is the constant predictable return of plants back up to the surFACE of Mother Earth. It is after all Her association with the constant return of plants on Her surFACE that the Planet got one of Her names. The E in PlanEt deals with emergence or exit from one state to another. A seed (IS HADA) carries in it 'the gift of' (DA) life (SA) and no matter what happens, how long the drought may last, when the rains (RANA) come it will always awaken and force its face up into the light. Seedlings always manage to emerge upon the surFACE of Mother Earth.

Perambulating human beings didn't emerge directly up from the body of Mother Earth, so the next best thing was to name the place that was in almost constant contact with Her body, and that was the sole of the foot. In Latin the sole of the foot is planta. The sole of the foot may not be planted within the Earth, but it deals with the next best thing, constant contact.

Clues surface out of Spanish. In Spanish 'truth' is verdad (VARADADA). It has ancient links to the word for 'green' that is verde (VARADA). In fact it even goes into verne (VARANA) as 'summer' at the time of the vernal equinox when verdant green plants sprout vertically up from the body of Mother Earth.

At the base of all of these verses is the Spanish verb 'to see' as ver. Ver (VARA) is the emergence of the sun (RA) as the spreader of light making it possible 'to see' out of the ocular cavity, the via (VA) of passage for sight. On the body of Mother Earth it deals with the valley, vent, or volcano any V shaped opening that allows the light to shine forth making possible the activity of seeing (C-ing). It also deals with the break in the circlular oral cavity, the RANA dyad at the horizon line on the body of Mother Earth when at dawn She regurgitated Her celestial siblings up to the light.

From another direction vertere as 'turning' in Latin, is changing from one state to another. Putting the three ancient observations together TRUTH (TARATA) is a metaphor for the return of green plants back up to Mother Earth's surFACE. Green (VERDE) plants no matter how deeply they seemed to have been planted as seed potential they were always perceived to return (VERT) back up to Her surFACE.

So it was also perceived that TRUTH (VERDAD) no matter how deeply imbedded in the psyche, no matter how deeply overlaid by lies would always surface, would always break free, would always find its way back up to the light, would always out. That which is true (TARA) cannot be held back.

As a vertically growing plant, a tree (TARA) became an ancient metaphorical symbol for the process. The world over and in ancient Europe trees had been worshipped. What the word truth embodies is the fact that the knowledge of natural law is the basis of truth. Man made laws or divine pronouncements are at best theoretical speculations and don't necessarily deal with truth and justice. Justice is that which JUST IS, or the acknowledgement of natural law. The emergence of science shows us the way to understand truth and justice as observable, provable aspects of nature (NATARA), or that which emerges upon (NA), the terrain (TARA-), of the magnificent all encompassing body of Mother Earth.

After the linguistic break It becomes apparent that much of the SHAPE of the mother's mouth as the source of humming and teaching out of PHASE ONE has been left behind, except in Greek where the neutral mouth holds on as MU. Mother Earth still surfaces as 'water'. The ancient memory tries to make a comeback. In Phoenician, Semitic and Egyptian various SHAPES of waves appear on the redefined scene. For the Etruscans the letter M as an enclosure, the concept of 'holding' surfaces. Enclosure takes us to PHASE TWO or THREE implying staying in one place and not necessarily migrating. In Linear B, MA looks as if she were the queen bee in her mating flight over the impaled drone.

Cypriotic MA still holds on to the ancient concept of the mother's buttox as the source of life for it looks like the female buttocks with the U of a new life held above or within it. The Old Indian symbol of M holds curious implications, for it looks like the symbol for the place of a turn around. All of life was perceived to use the female body and the body of Mother Earth as a place of constant returns back up to the surface. The word vulva (VALAVA) and valve (VALAVA) deal with similar implications.

THE LETTER N
THE LETTER N IS A VOICED ALVEOLAR NASAL CONSONANT

THE NOSE KNOWS. It belongs to stage one on the mothers face.

SOUND; smell, nasal rejection of food, negation, exhalation of air,

SHAPE; the NOSE seen in profile on the mother's face,

MOTHER'S body; nipples, neck (NAKA), noga (NAGA) Polish leg

MOTHER EARTH; night, moon, volcaNOES, islands out of water

CONCEPT; 'negation of a former state', 'emergence on the surface', birth, beginning and end, movement in and out, knowledge

There are two major activities that deal with the letter N as defined by the NOSE in profile on the mother's face out of PHASE ONE. The primary one deals with feeding the eager offspring and teaching it what is NOT acceptable to eat which evolves into all kinds of extended concepts dealing with the process of *negation*, how to survive and with kNOWledge itself. The other deals with breathing in and out, with the beginning into life and with its ending in death. A whole plethora of linguistic possibilities emerge out of those two major nasal (NASA-) activities associated with the nose (NASA).

As the humming M SOUND made by the mother associated with masticating the morsels in her mouth encoded in the letter M defines what is safe and acceptable to eat, so the nasal N SOUND encoded in the letter N deals with food being pushed out of the mouth dealing with the concept of *negation* and what is not acceptable to eat.

All of the senses in the body of a creature, except perhaps of the jelly fish, crisscross at the bridge of the nose. The left hemisphere of the brain controls the right hand side of the body. The right hemisphere of the brain controls the left side of the body. The only sensory input that does not crisscross deals with the nose. The two nostrils of the nose go straight up on a parallel track into the olfactory bulb of the brain. The nose and the brain are intimately connected. As a result the sense of smell may be the oldest sensory opening that evolved within sentient creatures. The spiral spin of the cosmos, its electro magnetic attraction and repulsion may very well be based on the sense of smell associated with the cosmic nose (NASA).

In Greek nous (NASA) is the name for 'thought' or 'the mind' sourced by the brain obviously associated with the activity of the nose (NASA). It expands into the concept of 'knowledge' as gnosis (gaNASAsa). Both contain the nose (NASA) within their linguistic construct. 'To be known' in Latin is nasci (NASA). Also in Latin it is the nostril (NASAtarala) with its two tracks barreling into the olfactory bulb of the brain that emerges as being associated with 'knowledge'. For the nostril in Latin is naris (NA(RA)SA) and 'to be known' is narus (NA(RA)SA). We are in PHASE THREE for the sun (RA) as the male sun enters the picture with the nose as the male source of 'thought' and 'knowledge'.

There exists an ancient perception out of PHASE ONE that the nose cut the face in half and fused the two sides together. In Swahili 'half' is nusu (NASA) dealing with the position of the nose (NASA) on the mother's face. For the Cree Indians on the other side of the world the same concept surfaces but from a different direction. In Cree it is niso (NASA) associated with the 'number two' that defines the nose (NASA). It is the two sides of the nose as the nostrils (NASA-) on the central facial axis that create the single entity of the nose (NASA). In Persian the concept of 'two in one' surfaces with the word bini (BANA) defining the nose. The letter B (BA) establishes the 'two in one' concept originally dealing with the two lips on the mother's face as seen in profile creating the mouth expanding to define the 'two in one' concept associated with the two nostrils creating the single entity of the nose. The letter N (NA) establishes the concept of *negation* as an 'emergence on the surface' associated with the SHAPE of the nose as seen in profile on the mother's face.

There is a progression dealing with *negation*. *Negation* is a saying of no, of rejection, of separation from nature, from the ground of all inclusive being. The first separation that occurred for ancient human beings in PHASE ONE was the most primal and it dealt with the naming of things. Once you gave an object a name it became separate from its background. It *negated* its attachment to the whole. It became an independent entity. It could be recognized as either safe or dangerous. In the word name (NAMA) you have the (NA) of *negation* or separation from the (MA) or the natural body of Mother Earth.

The SOUND of M and NO may have come before any other SOUNDS that the mother shared with her offspring. The naming of things began with the cautionary SOUND of NO. Good smells and delicious objects that are good to eat do not need to be named. Their value is self evident as the nose follows the scent to their source. Since babies and toddlers stick everything into their mouths, it is the dangerous things that have to be guarded against by the ever vigilant mother. *It has been reported by a little boy who told his teacher that his name was NO, because that is what his mother always called him.* The anecdote is self evident. The nose (NASA) became the source of that primary NO saying as in PHASE ONE with the nasal SOUND of *negation* it pushed dangerous food out of the mouth.

That quality exists not only in the human mother's repertoire but in all maternal creatures who teach their offspring how to survive. It may not be universal in the sharing of SOUND in other creatures but their young mimic the mother and learn what is safe to eat by watching. In Hebrew n'um (NAMA) means either 'speech' or the 'naming of things'. N'um (NAMA) looks suspiciously close to the English word for name (NAMA). In Polish the word znam (IS NAMA) means 'I know' dealing with recognition of the object and a movement into knowledge. In Hebrew naba defines 'to speak', 'to sing', to 'bubble forth'. The (na) deals with 'emergence on the surface' or a 'negation of a former state' the (ba) establishes its links with the two lips as seen in profile encoded in the letter B and the concept of 'two in one'. When a bubble emerges out of a baby's mouth it is usually accompanied by the babble of SOUND.

Section Three

In Swahili to 'be full' and not have an empty stomach is jaa. When you *negate* the fullness of the stomach and the stomach becomes empty you get Njaa or 'hunger' and 'famine'. In Greek Nete (NATA) the Goddess of the Underworld dealt with night (NATA) and the negation of light above Mother Earth's surFACE. For the Egyptians Neter (NATARA) or nuter (NATARA) defined 'the womb of rebirth' and the priests wore artificial breasts. What you are dealing with here is a priesthood of eunuchs and transvestites in whom the process of birthing had been denied or *negated* through castration. They were not only neutered (NATARA-) but they had NO uterus. To neuter (NATARA) was to create 'not her', not the mother. As the castrated eunuch priesthood they reigned over the nether (NATARA) regions under the body of Mother Earth out of which She created Herself out of Herself with the solar blood that ran through Her veins without any external input, the eternal virgin. In PHASE THREE the MA of the mother with the letter N at the end becomes MAN, or from another direction, MA negated.

In Swahili a 'word' is neno (NANA) and to 'speak' is nena (NANA). Both deal with a double *negation* which will become apparent with the activity inherent in the Greek (NANA) for moon.

The next separation deals with the activity of recognizing edible food. That becomes an activity of the nose dealing not only with smelling but with the rejection or *negation* of what is inedible. The repertoire of food recognition expands into knowledge. That knowledge of what is safe expands not only into food but with specific primal scent that leads to the bonding between mother and baby, (the safest embrace in all the animal and human kingdom), with sexual estral receptivity, of when it is safe to mount the receptive female, with the marking of territory or what area is safe to protect from intruders, of catching the scent of prey, of following a scent to its source as magnificently expressed by the salmon. One of the tragedies for human beings is when they became bi-pedal they lost their sense of acute smell and shifted to the acuity of the eyes.

In Finnish to 'devour' is suuhunsa (IS hahaNASA) containing it its name both the nose (NASA) and the repetitive dyad of (HAHA) which has inks with the sun (IS HANA) 'devouring' everything in sight as it scorched the Sahara (IS HAHAra).

The major activity dealing with *negation* for all creatures, sooner or later was with death itself. Death *negated* the activity of life. The nose as a major sensory organ comes into play with that separation as dealing with the process of breathing. As long as the air was perceived to be pumped in and out primarily through the nose, the creature was defined as being alive. When the breath suspended its unrelenting passage and stopped, the creature became still and died. It separated itself from the living. It *negated* the process of life. With the baby's first breath as the air entered its lungs until the moment of its departure it was the nose that did its major job of airy maintenance. For the Wolof of Africa the 'nose' and 'life' are linguistically synonymous.

What happened to sentient creatures, especially human mothers had been perceived to be shared by the body of Mother Earth. She didn't go through the process of birth, neither did She die. She gave birth to everything out of Her surFACE and Her all encompassing body. What She did go through were the changes that Her creations visited upon Her. The major one was the shift from light into the darkness of night at the end of each day created by the unrelenting passage of the sun. At dawn the sun was born and with its light ushered in a new day (DAYA). Day is the gift of (DA) the Persian light as (AYA). At the end of its passage across the belly of air above Her surFACE it was swallowed back into Her patiently waiting maw. The light of a new day was *negated* by the onset of night. The N of night negated the L of light. The same process was shared by the 'shape shifting' moon. The darkness of the perilous night was *negated* by the blessed flourishing of day light.

If the air that creatures breathed in and out sustained them then the same process worked for Mother Earth. It was perceived that the sun and moon were at one with the air that Mother Earth breathed as they passed in and out of Her pulsating body. In PHASE ONE they all; the body of Mother Earth, the vault of air above Her, and Her celestial offspring had been considered as one interconnected unit.

The SHAPE of the letter N came out of the human nose (NASA) as seen in profile emerging from the relatively flat human face. The SOUND associated with the letter N came out of the process of *negation*, of the nasal SOUND of rejection in PHASE ONE as the food was being pushed out of the mouth with the tongue.

The (SA) in nose (NASA) spans a multitude of linguistic possibilities. The two major ones deal with the process of 'being' and of 'survival'. On the level of the individual mother it deals with her ever creative blood. The Sa as the 'wise blood' of the mother for the Egyptians knowing how to coagulate into the creation of a small replica of herself, the SAng in French, SAngre in Spanish, SAnguis in Latin. On the body of Mother Earth it dealt with movement itself. For it deals with the spin of the spiral as the inHERent process underlying creation itself. It is on the currents of air that the spiral spin of dust devils, tornadoes, hurricanes and whirlwinds can be perceived that bring forth massive change and the possibility of the creation of new physical form. The (NA) of change and the (SA) of lavic blood coursing through the body and the spiral crashing above and through the body of Mother Earth create the dyad representing the processes locked in the ubiquitous nose (NASA).

THE NOSE KNOWS

What is it that the nose knows? Before we expand into all of the possibilities, a small but valuable digression. To KNOW is to be in the NOW. In Swahili NA stands for 'NOW' and the 'present'. That which 'emerges on the surface' whether out of the individual mother's body or the body of Mother Earth occurs as an experience in the NOW. KNOWledge is the present of the present represented in the body. It is not an idea in the mind. The body never lies. The mind is a fickle companion. The most intimate basic sensory input into the brain is carried by the sense of smell. *Images created by the eyes and if not dammed up by trauma, float by.* SOUNDS received by the ears recede into the distance. The tender skin if not directly caressed loses its ability to share pleasure. You can live without seeing, hearing or feeling but you can't live without eating. It is the sense of smell that leads to testing the morsels as they are tasted. It all begins with the nose (NASA).

The activity of the nose establishes its reign of knowledge at the time of birthing. As the fetus begins its journey down the birth canal it ruptures some of the blood vessels in its mothers body. That is what it smells first, the smell of the mother's blood, the (SA) associated with the nose (naSA). As it takes its first breath, the ecstasy of the universe rising on the undercurrent of air fills its lungs with the promise of life. As the mother with her birthing breath rose on the wings of her Kundalini experience, so the baby also rose on the wings of the first breath. It associated its first breath with the ecstatic bloody smell of the mother and as often as not blasted its heart open as the air expanded its lungs and bonded with her for life.

The bloody apparition that emerged out of her body also gave the mother a nose full of her and the baby's bloody smell. That too assisted in the process of bonding.

The birth experience for the baby with the intake of the first breath through the nose (NASA) established the earliest perception of beginnings. In Hebrew nasab (NASAba) means 'to breathe'. The (BA) at the end establishes the breath as coming out of the two nostrils, defined by the (BA) as the 'two in one' concept. In Basque arnasa (haraNASA) deals with 'the breath' emerging not only out of the nose (NASA) but out of the 'belly' hara in Hebrew and Japanese. In Hindi the 'breath' is sans (is haNASA) and emerges out of the belly of air above the body of Mother Earth, the domain of the sun (IS HANA) Her nose (NASA) in the vault of the sky smelling and ferreting out the place of its terminus (taramaNASA) at the end of its daily journey. In Greek 'the breath' is pnos (paNASA) or the passage (PA) of the air through the nose (NASA).

The first breath of the baby also began the concepts of beginnings. In Latin nascence (NASANASA) is the repetitive activity of birthing as the beginning of life out of the dual activity of the nose (NASA). In Swahili anza (haNASA) means 'to begin'. It deals with the beginning on the body of Mother Earth and the beginning of day with the birth of the sun (IS HANA). Somehow it doesn't leave the nose (NASA) behind because at birth the sun (IS HANA) also had to take its first breath. In Finnish ensin (haNASAna) also deals with the body of Mother Earth and the concept of beginnings harking back to the nose (NASA) as the beginning of life through the first breath and the birth of the sun (IS HANA) as the first gift of light. For the Egyptians Nissa (NASA) in Ethiopia was the place where their God Osiris was born. Not to be left behind in Greek neos (NASA) means 'new' and what is 'new' usually comes first. In Hebrew Nisan (NASAna) is the name for the Spring Equinox, the first month, the beginning of the sacred Hebrew year. It was the time of the estral orgy at Easter when the males butted horns and butted the buttocks of the females once they smelled their bloody receptivity. The nose (NASA) in Nisan (NASAna) comes into play to define the time of the beginning of the ancient migrations. Also in Hebrew 'to bloom' and 'to put forth flowers', the beginning of the possibility of a harvest is naas (NASA) hiding in its linguistic dyad the primacy of the nose (NASA). Or was it perceived that the flower smelled the rays of the sun and burst into bloom as a token of gratitude.

As a concept of beginning the individual mother and the body of Mother Earth share a few possibilities. In Greek ganos (gaNASA) means the 'birth of the sun' or 'lightness'. In Turkish gunes (gaNASA) deals with 'the beginning of a new day', or 'the birth of the sun'. It was out of the body of Mother Earth that the sun rose at dawn to bless the hailing creatures with its gift of light. In Latin -gynus (jaNASA) is 'of the female' defined by the nose (NASA) of smelling, negating and breathing. It SOUNDS like genius (jaNASA). In Latin and Greek Genesis (jaNASAsa) deals with beginnings, as it does in the Hebrew Bible. For the Hindus the elephant God Ganesh (gaNASA) is the God of beginnings. To do something original and astonishing for the first time defines a genius (jaNASA). All of these concepts have their origins out of the nose (NASA) on the individual mother's face expanding to the concept of beginnings out of the body of Mother Earth.

For the mother the beginnings came earlier in association with the moon. For the moon in the night sky, the sky dealing with the *negation* of sun light, curdling internally within the body of Mother Earth, was like the mother's blood coagulating within her working secretly inside Her body creating a small replica of Her. The moon had been perceived to activate the menstrual blood in the young girl as she reached her quintessence. With the passage of her blood she became a woman and a potential mother. In PHASE ONE with the beginning of her menarche she joined the line of the subsequent monarchs. For the Basque a girl is neska (NASAka), or the small (KA) one who could be smelled by the male nose (NASA). Except due to the many changes in female sexual receptivity for thousands of years the blood on her flanks did not always announce her readiness to mate. It led to much confusion and the expansion subsequent universal rape.

The concept of beginnings associated with the nose (NASA) continues. Once a young girl began to menstruate she was open to being mounted. As male animals smelled the hind quarters of the females, be they carnivore or herbivore, they became aware, or gained knowledge whether the female was sexually receptive. It was the blood (SA) and the smell associated with that blood on the female buttocks that alerted the males to her receptivity. In Sanskrit for human beings nasa yoni dealt with 'a man's condition who could not copulate until he smelled a female yoni' or vulva. Yoni has ancient links with the Chinese Yin.

The word for vulva in Latin is cunnus (kaNASA). The active nose (NASA) again. Also in Sanskrit nas (NASA) is 'copulation' itself. Nus (NASA) in Wolof means 'to sniff'. In Latin nasci (NASA) means 'to be known, smelled or mounted'. The creature who unceasingly sniffs the ground is a canis (kaNASA) or the Latin dog. Having links with the female vulva cunnus (KANASA) also in Latin, the dog canis (KANASA) may very well have been a bitch. As the canine carnivore noses sniffing the ground never left the scent until they found their prey, so the sun and moon also followed a specific trajectory toward their ultimate goal apparently sniffing their way back into the body of Mother Earth. In Finnish nusskia (NASAkaya) means 'to sniff'. Since it contains not only the nose (NASA) that does the sniffing but the (AYA) of light in Persian and dawn in Assyrian we are dealing with the sniffing of the sun on its way to its nightly doom. For the Lithuanians the snout or nose is nosis (NASAsa). For the Maori 'male procreative power' was known as tanes (taNASA). His 'procreative power' is not only based on the activity of the nose (NASA) but on the ten (TANA) fingers at the end of his arms that held the female during coitus.

The subsequent evolution of beginnings deals with pregnancy. For pregnancy in a mother's body ushers in the possibility of subsequent creation. Creation is the stuff of beginnings. In Lithuanian nescia (NASA) defines 'pregnancy' as being the result of the nose (NASA) of smelling. Also in Lithuanian 'to carry, bear, bring forth' is nesti NASAta). It has linguistic links with the English word for nest (NASAta) the home of the house of creation. In Amharic sannasa (IS haNASA) as 'pregnancy' has links with the body of Mother Earth pregnant with the sun (IS HANA). In Tierra del Fuego the 'first people' were called onas (haNASA) having links with the sun (IS HANA). In Latin 'seeds' are called lens (laNASA), the (LA) deals with the angle of emergence that the seeds make out of the surFACE of Mother Earth at night by the light of the moon, Luna (LANA) in Latin. In Polish 'seeds', the carriers of the beginning of the life force are called nasienie (NASAna). Also in Polish 'to carry' is niesie (NASA) having links not only with the nose (NASA) but with the Latin 'birth' as nascence (NASANASA). Once a baby was born it established a family and belonging to a specific clan based on the activity of the nose (NASA) and its sense of smell. It established the posessive 'we' nos (NASA) in Latin. In Sanskrit 'our' became nas (NASA) and in Spanish 'our' became nous (NASA). In Polish 'our' emerges as nasze (NASA). Also in Latin 'our' emerges as noster (NASAtara) establishing its links not only with the nose (NASA) but also with the terrain (TARA-) on the body of Mother Earth as the all embracing familial context. It was the nose (NASA) that established the recognition between family members.

The moon was not only associated with the onset of menstruation, and its passage in tandem with female menstrual cycles, but with the subsequent onset of milk out of the mother's breasts. In Finnish nisa (NASA) is a 'teat', the nose like angle that protrudes from her trunk, like a mountain, the majestic teton protrudes from the surFACE of Mother Earth clad with a blanket of snowy white milk at the summit, like a volcanic island breathing air up to the surFACE pushing its nose (NASA) out of the sea as nesos (NASAsa) in Greek.

A baby is born with a pleasurable sucking instinct and the smell of the milk may guide it to the mother's emerging breast or teat. Because the moon had been considered as bringing forth milk out of the mother's teats after she gave birth it became defined as a nanny (NANA), or milk bringer. Stories abound that the moon had been like a ball of cheese floating through the night sky.

The moon surfaces as nana, a double negation. In Greek and Uruk nana is the name for the moon. When the sun set into the body of Mother Earth, the darkness of night *negated* the brightness of daylight as the doom of the *negated* light spread it's icy fingers upon the savage savannah creating the first *negation* as nighttime (NA). The second *negation* (NA) came during the daylight hours when the moon made its nocturnal trajectory through the underground vault of air nudging the sleeping body of Mother Earth to awaken to the newly risen rays of the sun caressing Her surFACE. Sailing above Her surFACE the moon created night, the first (NA). Navigating below Her surFACE the moon allowed for daylight, the second (NA). (NA) plus (NA) becomes nana the Uruk and Grecian moon. For the Wolof neen (NANA) means 'zero, nothing, dark' defining the state of night and the emergence of the new moon (NANA) after the sun had set.

During the ancient year in PHASE ONE and mother centrality the moon associated with female menstruation was the major time keeper. The twenty-eight days of the lunar cycle had been broken up into two equal balanced fourteen day segments. One fourteen day segment waxed toward the full moon and light in the midnight sky pushing back the chaotic terrors of the carnivore night. The other fourteen day phase dealt with the waning of the new moon until it completely disappeared from the night sky leaving the creatures of the savannah in total predatory darkness. In Wolof 'chaos' and 'nothingness' is nen (NANA). For the Egyptians nu, nun (NANA) meant 'chaos' in sink with the cyclical, predictable nightly disappearance of the moon. It is also the hieroglyph for water as the sun sank out of sight into its horizontal watery grave and the SHAPE shifting new moon waned its way out of the sky plunging the Earth below into total darkness. For the early Semites Nu and Nun (NANA) were represented by the fish as the Mother of the Sea.

In Persian Quanun (KANANA) was the 'law giver'. Since it had been perceived that the moon (NANA) activated the menstrual bloody flow out of female bodies, the same activity extended to the body of Mother Earth. It was Her lava, her menstrual blood out of Her volcanic cone (KANA) that erupted across Her surFACE creating the blanket of land. In PHASE ONE truth was based on the natural law of experience and not on theoretical speculation of the mind. It was lava that defined what was not only real but defined the basic tenets of natural law. The (V) and (W) are interchangeable.

The ancient Akkadian Goddess Ninsun (NANAsana) knew all knowledge and founded the dynasty of Ur. SOUNDS the same as the Tuareg Al Kahina, the mother mystic warrior, the free woman. In Arabic to be 'free born' was to be defined by the nose (NASA). To be 'free born' meant that you were the one who chose your mate in PHASE ONE by smelling them and nuzzling (NASA-) them with the nose (NASA) and not the other way around in PHASE THREE. Many of the Polynesian tribes and the Eskimos rub noses as a kind of a kiss. What they are doing is smelling their nuzzler (NASA-). In Sanskrit to 'kiss' is nins (NANASA) contining in its linguistic folds both the kiss as a nuzzling by the nose (NASA) and the time of the kissing as occurring by the light of the silvery moon (NANA). In India out of PHASE TWO Nanda (NANADA) Devi was defined as the 'Mountain Mother' who gave birth to the river Ganges. After the shift into male centrality in PHASE THREE the male God Vishnu gave birth to the River Ganges out of his left toe. The Sumerian 'Birth Goddess' was Ninti (NANATA) also called 'the lady of life' and the 'lady of the rib'. This was way before Adam entered the scene and pulled the suppliant Eve out of his rib. For the Dahomey NANA Buluku was the moon and the sun. The first woman and man emerged from them. The moon as nana surfaces in all the above beatific configurations.

The double *negation* associated with the moon (NANA) surfaces in another set of dyads. This time we are moving into male centrality and the passage of time dictated by the sun. In PHASE ONE it took ten lunar months to gestate a baby out of the mothers disTENded belly. When you move into male centrality in PHASE THREE and time reckoned by the sun, the duration required for a baby to gestate in the mothers womb becomes nine (NANA) irregular months. In Spanish the name of a small child is nino (NANA). The German nein (NANA) for 'no' exposes us to another clue. For the birth of a baby is also a double *negation*. One *negation* (NA) deals with the separation of the mother from the fetus after nine (NANA) months. The other *negation* (NA) dealt with the separation of the fetus from the mother saying nein (NANA) to remaining in her womb. In Wolof 'to be little' is neew (NAWA) looking suspiciously like the English word for new (NAWA) or emergence (NA) out of the watery (WA) womb of the mother.

On the body of Mother Earth the name for 'morning' in Spanish is manana. Mother Earth (MA) giving birth to the next morning, to tomorrow having its beginning with the moon (NANA). For ancient mothers their beginning dealt with the setting of the sun and the onset of night.

Closer to home it is also a name of the Greek 'aunt' nanna (NANA) and the Latin nonna (NANA). As the sister, and niece (NASA) she was also in PHASE THREE the nun (NANA) an aunt or sister to the nursing children. Like dairy farmers keep their cows pregnant in order for them to constantly produce milk, so it may have been among the ancient mother's a similar practice keeping the nieces (NASA) pregnant in order to provide a steady supply of milk. Once removed it is also the name of another provider of milk, the ubiquitous nanny (NANA) goat and the mares that the nursing mothers followed on their semi yearly migrations across the savannah for an extra supply of milk.

In Chequa nunu (NANA) is the name for milk. It is N'yu N'yu (NAYA NAYA) as cow's milk for the Japanese. Since the N SOUND deals with *negation* then the *negation* deals with light, aya in Persian as light and aya as dawn in Assyrian. Then we are in the arms of night and the milky moon (NANA) in the starry sky who has *negated* the power of the sun and its light. It SOUNDS like the milking of cows was done at night.

Most of the activities associated with the moon dealt with beginnings, milk and birthing. There was another aspect to the moon for it represented the night sky and the apparent death of the sun as it disappeared into the body of Mother Earth making room for the moon to emerge on its own journey. In Sanskrit nasa means 'end', the blood (SA) no longer coursing through the body, *negating* (NA) its possibility to sustain life. It also has links with the activity of the nose (NASA). For the nose (NASA) withdrew its sniffing canine like passage across the vault of air ferreting its way to its ultimate terminus (taramaNASA). In Latin finis (faNASA) means 'end'. A 'burial place' in Latin is funus (faNASA). Both establish links with the English funeral (FANArala). In Greek necis (NASAsa) means 'death'. The 'final, last and end' in Lithuanian is galinis (galaNASA) having links with the moon Luna (LANA) and its nocturnal terminus (taramaNASA). For the Wolof the 'last breath' is naw (NAWA) and it deals with the *negation* (NA) of life and light as the sun sinks into the entombing waters (WA) on the Western horizontal rim. It is new (NAWA) to its nocturnal passage but no longer above the body of Mother Earth.

Antecedents to the letter N out of the Middle East after the linguistic break erased much of the ancient knowledge out of female centrality. In some of the languages the angular SHAPE of the nose remains but its origins out of the SHAPE of the nose as seen in profile on the mothers face in PHASE ONE disappears into prehistory.

The time of the LINGUISTIC BREAK must have been preceded by some kind of cataclysm associated with water. It might have been the massive universal flood that so many of the ancient myths recount. Perhaps it was a tsunami that obliterated traces of the ancient mother based civilizations. It might have been the time of a climactic change as the rain poured down from the sky obliterating everything in sight. The changes might have occurred even before the prehistoric verdant Sahara was so abundantly green. For much of what emerges on the linguistic landscape all around the Mediterranean basin defining the letter N of negation after the LINGUISTIC BREAK in PHASE THREE seems to deal with some aspect of a watery cataclysm. The water may be represented as water itself or it may deal with a fish, or a cobra. It may deal with the SHAPE of the fin or a snout on a fish or snake poking up to the surFACE when the world was surrounded by water.

In Phoenician the SHAPE of the angular nose surfaces associated with NUN (NANA) for 'fish'. It does the same for the Egyptians as nun (NANA) for 'water' and the hieroglyph of a 'cobra'. The same linguistic construct surfaces in Semitic as NUN (NANA) for the 'fish' represented singularly by the cobra. In North Semitic only the 'cobra' surfaces for the letter N. The NANA dyad represents a double *negation* either dealing with the moon, Nana in Uruk and Greek or for the milk providing nanny (NANA) goat. It can also go in the direction of the two titties containing the nipples on the mother's body that provide the 'two in one' scenario and with milk. As a double *negation* it can emerge defining an aspect of water as the reflective surface of life. The reflection establishes the first *negation* (NA). Its association with death establishes the second *negation* (NA). In Greek the angle of NU looks like the nose but the actual definition associating it with the proboscis has been left behind. The only links with the actual nose itself seems to surface in Slavonic and the aspect of breathing with the letter N represented by the SHAPE of the letter H of the breath and with exHAlation. In Cretan Linear B NU may contain in its picture the two crescents of the moon rising and setting above the surFACE of Mother Earth and below Her skin. In association with the monthly passage of the moon is the flow of menstrual blood. In Cretan Linear B, NE looks like the pubis but slanted to the SHAPE of the maritime trident. The water again. The same association surfaces with the Cypriotic NO in the SHAPE of the empty buttocks. The rest of the letters go in their own directions no longer apparently related to the nose of smelling, the *negation* of edible food and *negation* itself, of breathing, beginnings and ends and the process of knowledge and recognition.

What began in PHASE ONE during female centrality and the SHAPE of the letters emerging out of the organs on the mother's face and the surFACE of Mother Earth seems to have disappeared into the bin of history emerging in PHASE THREE and male centrality as unrelated symbols, some dealing with the many aspects of water.

THE LETTER L

The letter L, voiced alveolar lateral consonant

The *tongue* is an angle that LIES on the floor of the oral cavity and tells LIES. It belongs to the mothers mouth in stage one.

SOUND; Flapping LALA of LAllation and Lullaby

SHAPE; The angle of the *tongue* assisting in the liquefying of food and of pushing both food and the SOUND of language out of the mouth. As lengua associated with language it defines the tongue in Latin

MOTHER's body; angles of movement, legs, lids, lips, labial folds (vulvic lips), elbows

MOTHER EARTH; angles of movement, into and out of Her body; sun, moon, birds, lava, Luna, plants, lady of the land

CONCEPT; Angular movement, up and down, in and out, sideways, diagonally.

The letter L in stage one comes out of the angular SHAPE of the *tongue* (lengua in Latin) lying on the floor of the oral cavity making the flapping LALA SOUND of lallation (singing), liquefying food, milling it into smaller pieces for it to slide effortlessly down the gullet. It also helps in the creation of smaller pieces as SOUND to emerge into specific segmented meaning. In PHASE THREE it emerged to define the two thin lips on the human face coming together to create the human mouth. Since the angular SHAPE of the two lips are thin, then we have wandered off the continent of Africa in PHASE ONE into the regions of the Middle East, Southern Asia and Europe in PHASES TWO and THREE.

On the body of the individual mother out of PHASE ONE in Africa the lips are either symbolized by the letter B of the bulbous mouth seen in profile or the labial folds, the two angles coming together on the bottom of the trunk that form the mons veneris. On the body of Mother Earth the letter L comes to represent many angles dealing with the SHAPE of movement out of Her vertical or lateral surFACE; emergence of the heavenly bodies and birds out of Her flat horizontal rim, growth of plants at a vertical angle out of Her ground of being, growth of branches out of trees, emergence of wings out of bird's bodies.

The SHAPE of movement began its life out of the angular SHAPE of the *tongue* in the mother's mouth darting in and out creating the concept of movement itself. In English the suffix (-LY) at the end of words deals with the extension of movement itself (slowLY, gentLY, manLY, terribLY). In Sanskrit the (LI) phoneme also defines movement and surfaces in the name for the penis as the LIngum defining movement up and down.

The LAtin name for the *tongue* is lengua (LANAGA). It shares its roots with the English word for language (LANAGA-). It expanded to include the body of Mother Earth with the help of the snake (IS NAKA) pushing her volcanic eruption up to the surFACE as land (LANADA), for land is the 'gift of' (DA) (LANA). How? Somehow the moon Luna (LANA) in Latin makes its entrance here. The dyad (NAGA) in lengua (LANAga) and language (LANAga-) is one of the most ancient names for the snake (NAKA, NAGA) out of the Harrapan culture. The (K) and (G) are interchangeable. The *tongue* in the oral cavity of the mouth, in the dark chambers within the skull had been likened in PHASE ONE to the moon in the mysterious dark nocturnal cavity under the surFACE of Mother Earth. As individual mothers with their snake like *tongues* (taNAGA) pushed food out of their lubricating lips for their hungry brood, so Mother Earth with the help of the snake (IS NAKA) had been linguistically perceived to push one of Her creations, the SHAPE shifting nocturnal (NAKA-) moon up to the surFACE to be reborn at twilight.

In PHASE ONE it was the snake (IS NAKA) SHAPED like the *tongue* in the oral cavity behind the lips that guided the heavenly bodies like the moon up to the light. With a shift into male centrality in PHASE TWO ferrymen and psychopomps co-opted the role of the celestial guides.

The SHAPE of the moon's emergence out of the dark night into the light up in the sky in Latin is Luna (LANA). Beginning with the anlaut (L) Luna goes back to PHASE ONE when the body of Mother Earth was perceived to be a flat round surFACE and the moon (Luna) emerged out of Her horizontal side, rim or maw at a right angle, like a *tongue* pushing the moon (Luna) up to Her surFACE, forcing it to face its nocturnal (NAKA-) demise. As the *tongue* (TANAGA) pushed food out of the individual mother's mouth, be she bird, wild dog or human, so the perceived *tongue* (TANAGA) on the body of Mother Earth pushed the moon, Luna up to Her surFACE to do its job of bringing Light to Her creatures below.

It wasn't only the moon that was shoved up to the surFACE of Mother Earth by the ever ready *tongue* (taNAGA). The sun followed the same trajectory.

SECTION THREE

As the Spanish sol (IS HALA) the sun also emerged at an angle out of the circular flat horizontal surFACE of Mother Earth filling the patient belly of air with the blessing of Light and Life. The Light of the moon as Luna and the Light of the sun as the Spanish sol (IS HALA) both deal with the *tongue* SHAPED like the snake doing its job of not only guiding but pushing the celestial bodies up to the Light. The ubiquitous role of the snake (IS NAKA) as the guide of both the sun and the moon being pushed up to the surFACE have been encoded in the angular SHAPE of emergence in the letter (L).

It becomes apparent that the L or the LA SOUND and SHAPE of the mother's *tongue* became so associated with mothers that LA for the Maya defined 'that which existed forever'. For the Middle Easterners in PHASE THREE it was the male RA 'that which existed forever'. The LA 'that existed forever' in PHASE ONE like the letter M, it became associated with LAdies of the LAnd the world over.

Out of the mother's lallating organ the LA is defined as an 'echoic' SOUND. In SWAHILI LA means 'to eat' covering both bases of SOUND and liquidification of food. When food had been ejected from the mouth by the *tongue* because it is not appropriate to eat, you not only have the N SOUND of negation but the LA SOUND as 'no' in Swahili, and 'not' in Akkadian and Arabic and LO as 'not' in Hebrew. Related to the female as mother in Spanish LA defines the female, In Hawaiian LA'I LA'I has been defined as the 'first woman'. For the Aztecs the mother of Quetzalcoatl was called LA. In Sanskrit LA is Mother Earth, In Hawaiian echoes of a distant past out of PHASE ONE surface in LA as the sun and LALA as the heat of the sun reflecting the repetitive angle of the sun's emergence pushed up to the surFACE by the ever ready *tongue* at dawn. It also establishes the at one relationship between Mother Earth and the sun. LA'A also in Hawaiian as 'sacred and holy' is not only the heat of the sun but the lavic terrain (AA), the body of Mother Earth as the single unit of creation and maintenance out of PHASE ONE.

The 'echoic' LA SOUND moves into the actual repetitive dyad of LALA. In Swahili LALA means 'to lie down'. In Wolof lal (LALA) means 'bed' the place where you lie down. In Bemba LALA means not only to lie down but 'to go to bed'. It establishes direction, similar to the Hebrew LA which deals with 'to' or 'to the'. The direction it establishes in Swahili is LAteral, having linguistic links with the SOUND and SHAPE of the *tongue* that lies LAterally upon the floor of the oral cavity behind the two Labial folds.

In Bemba lalila (LALALA), thrice blessed, means 'to lie in' or 'to sit on eggs'. To 'lie in' deals with the last stages of pregnancy and it shares its tryad with a mother bird, a hen, who while sitting on her eggs tucks them under her breast and softly clucking as if to fill them with comfort she warms them and gently cooks them into being.

The LALA dyad dealing with direction, as an angle off the main stem, surfaces in Hawaiian establishing a branch or a limb. LALA as a branch or a 'limb' in Hawaiian emerges out of the trunk, like a *tongue* emerges out of the hole in the throat, like the sun, moon and birds emerge out of the perceived horizontal hole out of the edge on the body of Mother Earth, like a limb emerges out of the trunk of the body.

In Hawaiian LALA can also mean 'diagonal' or 'slanted' dealing with the direction that some branches take as they sprout diagonally out of the mother plant. A pLAnt becomes one of the definitions of the pLAnet.

For the Bugotu of the South Pacific Islands lali (LALA) is the 'buttress of a tree', the diagonal roots spreading down and under the waters below, anchoring the majestic growth of a tree to the watery body of Mother Earth. In Hebrew lulav (LALAVA) is 'palm (paLAma) branch', the angular SHAPE (LA) that branches off a palm tree emerging out of the trunk on either side, the LA of the angle repeated.

Like lava pouring out of the body of Mother Earth leaves (LAVA-) Her body, like leaves (LAVA-) sprout out of branches and then leave (LAVA-) them to fall in the fall (faLALA), like limbs poke out of trees, like trees emerge out of the body of Mother Earth, like appendages sprout out of the trunk, like the *tongue* sticks out of the throat, they all deal with the SHAPE of movement, to emerge at an angle out of their primary maternal source.

In Sumerian lul (LALA) means 'to lie' and among the American Indians in the tribe of Quechua llu llu (LALA) also means 'to lie', both can go in two directions. One direction being similar to the Swahili LALA to 'lie down' and the Bemba LALA 'to go to bed', or it can go in the direction out of PHASE ONE dealing directly with the *tongue*. When it represents the *tongue* it deals with the *tongue* lying on the floor of the oral cavity and not telling the truth. For when all is said and done; The *tongue* is an angle that LIES on the floor of the oral cavity and tells LIES.

In Latin lengua (LANAGA) means either *tongue* or in English language (LANAGA-). Lingo (LANAGA) and slang (IS LANAGA) in English fall into a similar category. The second dyad (NAGA) deals with the snake (IS NAKA, NAGA) the (K) and (G) are interchangeable. As the snake (IS NAKA) with its forked tongue ensconced in both the *tongue* (taNAGA) and language (laNAGA-) the duality of lying comes into play in the doer and the result.

For the Bugotu leuleu (LALA) expands to embrace 'mocking'. Not only is mockery done with a snappy *tongue* but it also deals with an alternate universe of making fun of, of put downs, fantasy and intimidation.

On the open savannahs, the sweaty human migrators may have focused their hopes on the comforting shade of the distant baobab tree, lalo (LALA). The lalo (LALA) or baobab tree not only emerged at an angle out of the surFACE of Mother Earth but its branches sprouted in an angular circle surrounding the top of the tree trunk like an erratic hat.

Not to leave behind the *tongue* in its primary function of creating meaningful SOUND, for the Bugotu in South Pacific lua (LALA) means 'to emit SOUND'. In Basque lelo (LALA) is a 'chorus, or refrain' made by the lallating lengua and expands to embrace 'the fool', (LALA-land comes to mind). For the Bemba -lila (LALA) means to make 'SOUND', 'lament' and 'mourn'. To ululate (HALALATA) in English also means to 'wail' and to 'howl'. To 'cry' and 'to roar' in Swahili is lia (LAYA). In Persian aya is light and in Assyrian aya is dawn. The Swahili lia (LAYA) may deal with the racket made by the birds and all the creatures of the savannah and jungle crying and roaring to wake the sun up at dawn and to bless them with its light.

In Greek to talk is lalein (LALANA), containing in its linguistic overlapping coils not only the (LALA) dyad created by the *tongue* but also the Latin Luna (LANA) of the moon. The moon perceived to be in the oral cavity under the surFACE of Mother Earth in PHASE ONE had been likened to be like the *tongue* in the oral cavity of the individual mother's mouth. In Bemba lulimi (LALAMA) is both '*tongue*' and 'language'. It is the (MA) of the mother that holds the lallating (LALA-) *tongue* in her mouth. In Arabic 'language' is kalaam (KALAMA), associating it with the English call (KALA), made by the mother (MA) in one direction and the birds (KA) in another. In Wolof lammin (LAMANA) is the '*tongue*'. Here the English moon (MANA) enters the picture establishing the same hidden *tongue* in the oral cavity concept as the Latin Luna (LANA).

Within the Old Irish word hullabaloo (HALABALA) there lies hidden the English word syllable (IS HALABALA) emerging with its own secret, hiding in its linguistic coils the Latin name for the lips as labios (LABASA). The lips (LAPA) in turn hide the *tongue* within the oral cavity that create meaningful SOUND. The (B) and (P) are interchangeable.

In English hello (HALALA) is 'a greeting'. In Hawaiian alelo or elelo (HALALA) deals with the '*tongue*' and 'language' that also work in concert to create the 'greeting'. The SHAPE of the hole (HALA) on the face makes the

(LALA) SOUND of language. In South Africa the word ulliloo (HALALA) goes back to PHASE ONE and means a 'song of joyous welcome'. To 'rejoice' in Bugotu is lealeaa (LALA). In English the word for 'rapturous singing' is alleluja (HALALAYA), with the aya dyad of light and dawn.

Again we are dealing with the welcome or the hailing (HALA-) out of the hole (HALA) on all of the radiant faces of Mother Earth's creatures giving thanks to the birthing hole (HALA) on Her flat circular horizontal rim out of which the sun emerged on Her surFACE bringing with it warmth, Light, Life and an end to the perilous dark night.

For Greeks in PHASE THREE their 'battle cry' was alala (HALALA), or hello (HALALA) on another level. The Akkadians had a deity connected with 'noise making' called Alalu (HALALA). The howling deity probably made a lot of noise saying hello (HALALA) to the sun at dawn. In Polish chalas (HALASA) deals with 'noise'. In Swahili to 'make noise' is kelele (KALALA), back to the call (KALALA) of the birds noisily returning to their nests. It seems more benign in PHASE THREE than k'lala (KALALA) that in Hebrew means 'a curse'. A 'curse' is a spell, it is something that is created by the *tongue* (LALA), it is in its own way a call (KALALA) for intercession from a higher power. For the Bemba -lila (-LALA) means to make 'SOUND', 'lament', 'mourn'. To ululate (HALALATA) in English also means to 'wail' and to 'howl'.

In one direction the SHAPE of the letter (K) deals with an open beak of a bird cackling, cooing, chirping it's way across the belly of air. In Persian the name for stork is lak lak (LAKA LAKA) the white feathered messenger of hope that semiannually returned to bear its young in the lakes (LAKA) and lagoons (LAgana) of the flooded African savannah. Its arrival in the fall in Africa at the time that herbivore mothers gave birth to their foals, became associated with birth, the bringing of babies and the concept of smallness.

In Europe and the Western world the fairy tales of the stork bringing babies still echo in children's literature. The fact that a stork stood on one leg as it hypnotized the water below, feeds into what subsequently emerged as the symbol for the one legged maimed, crippled smithy and shepherd in PHASE THREE.

The various holes (HALA) on the mother's body were subject to a great deal of scrutiny. Some of the holes had flaps that covered them. Others did not. The *tongue* hid behind the cover of the two lips that when closed created the mouth and when opened created the door of passage for SOUND and lubricated food. There were holes that created the cavities for the eyes. They had lids (LADA) that covered them. Then there were the ears, they were permanently open to the reception of SOUND. The nose had two holes that secretly held the breath and the promise of life.

On the upper part of mother's trunk there were the holes of the nipples that periodically flowed with milk. Specific intermittent processes dealing with birthing opened the holes in the nipples and milk flowed from them. At other times it was as if there was an invisible flap that stopped the flow and hid the contents within.

Further down the trunk of the mother there emerged the second major hole on her body, wrapped and enclosed by her two angles that met and formed the labial lips that hid the mysterious process of creation behind them. The only thing that peeked out from between those two angular lips was the tip of the beak of the clitoris. The two lower lips, the mons veneris, the two angles covered the entrance to the inner sanctum. As the lips on the mother's face covered the oral cavity hiding the *tongue* so the lower lips of the vulva, or mons veneris hid the clitoris and the passage to the creation of life. The SHAPE of the two lips creating the vulva is reminiscent to the SHAPE of the two lips that create the volcanic cone on the body of Mother Earth.

Not to digress but to expand. At first glance, the lily (LALA) is a flower. There are many kinds of lilies but there is only one that expresses a specific aspect related to the female body. That prize goes to the Calla (KALA) lily (LALA) representing more than what meets the eye. For the calyx (KALAKASA) of the Calla (KALA) lily looks suspiciously not only like the SHAPE of the female vulva but embraces the SHAPE of the clitoris (KALA-) emerging from its base. It is the symbolic vulvic cleft (KALA-) the hole (HALA), the calyx (KALAKASA) on the bottom of her trunk that creates the possibility of life. It is in the mother's body that the coagulated blood (SA) within her that creates a solid baby out of her coos (KASA) when the noisy birds (KA) return to their nesting sites among the great African lakes (LAKA and the Okobongo River Delta.

The Calla lily (LALA) is also called the Easter lily having ancient symbolic PHASE ONE links with the female vulva as the beginner of life creation. In PHASE THREE having lost its ancient provenance out of the female vulva, the Calla, Easter lily (LALA) of the double crescents enclosing the coagulating processes within, adorns the altars of the Roman Catholic Church ushering in a different beginning, the beginning of resurrection and with Jesus, the promise of immortality. As East is the beginning of a new day, so Easter evolved to begin not only a new year, but forever.

The white Calla lily as the ultimate expression of perfection and beauty is a subtle symbol of lunar seduction. In Basque a lily (LALA) is lili (LALA) and liluration (LALA-) means to 'dazzle' and to 'seduce'. I don't think that they had the Calla lily in mind. But the Basque have ancient linguistic links with mother centrality in PHASE ONE and the worship of a specific area on the female body extending to the body of Mother Earth as the creators of life.

The white color of the Calla lily has ancient links not only with the color of the moon in the night sky but with the color of milk after the time of birthing. As the white moon rose out of the circular flat side of Mother Earth, out of Her horizontal hole at Her rim, so the milk also emerged out of the two holes on the upper trunk of the individual mother's body out of the two angles that protruded from her chest.

In Greek mythology in PHASE TWO, the breasts of the Goddess Hera (HARA), the belly of air (HARA) above Her (HARA) surFACE holding her new born son (RA), sprouted with flowing white milk that erupted as lilies when they hit the ground. On one level down the line as male centrality began to take over in PHASE TWO they created the Milky Way *away* and *above* the body of Mother Earth, on another in PHASE ONE creating 'the white lilies of the field' still aligned the process with the body of Mother Earth.

In Chinese ling (LANAGA) means 'magical power'. The first overlapping dyad as (LANA) may have links with the Latin Luna (LANA), the moon, that which emerges (NA) at an angle (LA) out of the body of Mother Earth. The second dyad (NAGA) is the ancient metaphor for the Kundalini energy and the guide of the sun and the moon was the snake (IS NAKA,NAGA). The letters (K) and (G) are interchangeable.

It was the 'magical power 'of the moon guided by the snake through the body of Mother Earth to rise into the dark sky awakening young girls to the 'magical power' of menstruation, menarche and readiness for motherhood. Hermes performed the same function for the Greeks. It was the time of 'seduction' and 'bedazzlement' that the white seductive lilies of the field came to symbolize.

Ling (LANAGA) as the Chinese 'magical power' also goes into the direction of SOUND. For the Chinese 'magical power' as ling (LANAGA) showers us with the realizatioin that it has links with the Latin lengua (LANAGA) dealing with language and speech. Here we are dealing with words as spells, curses having a life of their own to mystify and to create their own 'magical power'. Like the breath as the spirit of life floated upon the sacred air, the Tibetan 'intermediate state', so words also used the air as a vehicle of passage.

Section Three

In Latin spirare means to breathe. Close enough to spirit.

In PHASE THREE the Chinese 'magical power' of ling (LANAGA) originally associated with the moon (LANA), milk, the snake (IS NAKA) and language (LANAGA-) in Sanskrit became the lingum (LANAGA-). The SHAPE of the penis associating it with the SHAPE of the snake (IS NAKA) like *tongue* may have been visually similar but the linguistic origins have been more recent.

The Chinese 'magical power' of ling in PHASE ONE out of the moon, language and the snake shifted in PHASE THREE from the centrality of the mother to the centrality of the father. The gala of the galaxy as the spilling of the mother's milk across the starry night sky shifted in Sanskrit with male role in paternity becoming realized to represent the Semones (IS HAMANA) or the stars splattered across the night sky as male semen, (IS HAMANA) out of his 'magical power', his lingum. A penis in this case became associated with the serpentine movement of the angle of the *tongue* (taNAGA) that went up and down in the oral cavity. It was also understood that the lingum, or the penis also went up and down on the male body. It became an extended angle when it went up during an erection and came down when it relaxed, reflecting the flapping activity of the *tongue*. It harkens back to a similar concept of the Hebrew abib (HABABA), the ear of corn erect on a corn stalk. For the Hebrews the abib, the erect ear of corn never flopped down, it stayed eternally erect. In Hebrew AB or BABA defined the father.

The Sumero-Babylonian Goddess Lilith (LALATA) belongs here as representing an aspect of the lilies (LALA) of the field. As the first wife of the Biblical Adam she decided to forgo her future as his partner and stayed like Mother Earth the eternal virgin.

Since all the processes, qualities and functions that were expressed through the bodies of individual mothers extended to the body of Mother Earth, then She too had a *tongue* hidden in her horizontal maw that pushed the heavenly bodies up to the surFACE, the sun at dawn and the moon at twilight. The SHAPE of that emergence of the sun and the moon out of the horizontal hole on the body of Mother Earth became the angle of ASCENT encoded in the letter (L) as the sun soared into the sky at dawn and the moon peeked its way up to the surFACE at twilight.

In Hebrew ala (HALA) means 'to ascend'. In Latin on the body of a bird, the 'wing' is also called ala (HALA) or that which emerges at a right angle out of an avian body and ASCENDS into the belly of air above the body of Mother Earth. In Hebrew al (HALA) is the 'upper part' and alt (HALATA) deals with 'height'. Alt (HALATA) turns into altar (HALATA-), the highest plateau on the top of a mountain. It was on the highest part of the mountain, at the PHASE THREE altar that an ALTeration of young boys took place. In PHASE ONE the first born son was castrated (altered) as the eunuch uncle to protect his mother's and his sister's children. Because the birthing breath of the mother in the last stages of labor bestowed such great power of leadership, healing, prophesy and creativity upon the laboring mother, men who were not privy to the birthing breath of the mother's began to pursue that experience through ritual. In this case the ritual was castration.

For the Greeks the priests of the sun God Apollo castrated young boys and buried their severed penises under the ALTar of ALTeration. It was as far as they could go up into the sky on top of the mountains without leaving the body of Mother Earth behind. The Hebrew bris (BARAsa) as the act of circumcision follows a similar trajectory, for the bris has links with debris (daBARAsa), or that which is discarded. That which had been discarded had been some aspect of the male genital structure.

The SHAPE of the angle of the sun's emergence out of the Eastern horizontal rim on the body of Mother Earth encoded in the letter (L) with the letter A(ah) of the mother becomes Al (HALA) of the highest Hebrew deity as Alohim, (him who is not only the (O) of the sun but the highest Al (HALA) the Spanish sol (IS HALA). Alohim (HALAHAMA) contains in his actual linguistic structure three overlapping dyads. (HALA), (LAHA) and (HAMA) and therein lies the coded tale.

(HALA) is the most ancient name for the sun out of PHASE ONE. It surfaces in Spanish as the sol (IS HALA). The (LA) is the angular SHAPE of the emergence of the sun out of the flat circular Eastern horizontal surFACE of Mother Earth. The place where the sol (IS HALA) makes its angular (LA) emergence is the belly of air (HA) above Her body.(LAHA) is the reflection of the sol (IS HALA) above the surFACE of Mother Earth to exist hidden from view below Her surFACE to become HALA/LAHA. In the African tribe of Wolof that which is 'hidden' is loh (LAHA) and it deals with the sol (IS HALA) that is hidden (LAHA) from sight during the night hours. Also on the body of Mother Earth as She creates land out of Her deep dark hidden volcanic recesses within Her body that mysterious process of emergence up to the surFACE is actually called lahar (LAHARA).(HAMA) deals with an ancient aspect of the sun as the bloody disc that on its way to being swallowed by the watery grave on the Western rim of Mother Earth creates a bloody spectacle as it seems to be swallowed by Her masticating maw creating a bloody passage for the sun to float through, under Her skin within Her intestines to get to the other side and to be reborn at dawn. Blood in Greek is ema (HAMA) giving its name to one of the aspects of the ancient sun.

Alohim (HALAHAMA) the Hebrew God in PHASE THREE has a variety of concepts locked in his name; the sun above Mother Earths surFACE (HALA), the sun below Her surFACE (LAHA) and the sun actively making its way through the bloody (HAMA) corridors of the dark night to be reborn at dawn. Alohim has ancient linguistic antecedents that harken back to PHASE ONE and mother centrality.

The LA/AL (LALA) as the repetition of Mother Earth the LA of the land became the reflected AL/LA as the Allat (HALATA), up in the sky the Islamic moon Goddess of milk with her abundant titties (TA) of the individual mother and the tetons (TA), the snow capped mountains on the body of Mother Earth. With the addition of the letter (H) on the end of Allat dealing with space, Allat in PHASE THREE became the Islamic God Allah (HALAHA). (HALA/LAHA) moves his way into space above the body of Mother Earth as the emerging solar deity above Her surFACE and as loh (LAHA) the Wolof word for 'hidden' under Her surFACE.

As the aqueous body of the pLAnet above, reflected Her reality in the standing marshes below becoming associated with males, so the subsequent names of male Gods reflected the names of the ancient Goddesses. The LA of the watery pLAnet, as Her LAkes and LAgoons, pLAces where pLAnts burst upon Her surFACE, becomes reflected by the AL of the father (LA/AL) reaching up to the sky as far *away* and *above* the actual body of Mother Earth as the emerging male base of power can get to create their own sense of 'source'. Their first reflected SHAPE of 'source' *away* and *above* the body of Mother Earth after they left the top of the mountains behind is not only the AL (HALA) of the sun, sol (IS HALA) in Spanish and eelyos (HALASA) of the sun in Greek. Further down the line in PHASE THREE as the sun loses some of its magic, the male 'source' turns to the hidden mind of a Father God and the male definition of reality out of the left hemispheric fear driven space of reason, theoretical speculation and fantasy.

There occurs a linguistic break in the SHAPE of the letters. There must have been a great cataclysm on that beleaguered continent of Africa that all but erased the source of human language out of the individual mother's face and the surFACE of Mother Earth.

The angle remains but the angle no longer deals with the *tongue* in the mother's mouth or the angular SHAPE of the emergence of the heavenly bodies out of the circular flat horizontal side of Mother Earth. The angle that surfaces after the linguistic break is the neutral leg (LAGA), still dealing with the anlaut of the letter (L) but moving down the human body to define a plethora of customs dealing with the mutilation of one leg. As in PHASE ONE the mutilation of young boys dealt with the removal of their genitalia, so in PHASE THREE the mutilation of young men dealt wit the mutilation of one leg. They were probably the same first born sons who were not only eunuchized but had been also crippled. It was they who limping across the Earth began to ask the question of WHY of their enslaved and peripheral state leading to the letter Q of questing and a search for the father.

The moon had in PHASE ONE originally been associated with menstruation and the product of that menstruation the baby who needed milk out of the round white disc floating above them that defined their LActic source. In PHASE THREE becoming settled in agrarian warring societies after the linguistic break the lunar disc became the SHAPE shifting fourteen cycled crescent, the scythe of death as shepherding of lambs and goats and metallurgy emerged with the crippled smithy at the forge of the sun and the one legged herdsman leaning on his staff.

Limiting (LAMA-) it to the letter (L) associated with the angle of the leg, explains how the following Middle Eastern words evolved to express the concept of crippling and lameness (LAMA-) in English. Semitic LAMEd= goad or cane, Phoenician LAMEd=whip, Hebrew LAMEth= ox goad, Babylon LAMAshtu=sacred crook, Philistine LAMEdh=ox goad.

A variety of possibilities emerge out of those clarifying words. An ox (HAKASA) is a castrated bull as a result of the hackig (HAKA-) and balancing out with the coos (KASA) of the mothers. He became the steer who as a docile creature steered (IS TARA-) the plow down the terrain (TARA-). You needed a variety of objects to encourage the docile ox to do its job. To that end the ox goad and whip came into play.

When you are one legged, you need some sort of support. To that end the cane emerged as a useful tool. Then we move into who became the priesthood of the future and the Babylonian LAMAshtu as the 'sacred crook' plunges vociferously into contemporary popes and priests who lean on their shepherds crooks as they pontificate about sacred hidden secrets that have to be obeyed at one's peril. Then there are the Tibetan LAMIseries where the celibate monks succumbing to ritual, pursue the birthing breath of the mother's.

In Polish there is a word that fits into this picture and has hidden implications. It is kaleka (KALAKA) and it deals with being a cripple. Coming (KA) and going (KA), it deals with balance. It was perceived that when a young boy was castrated and his violence was neutralized he often became balanced. The word lib (LABA) for castration and maiming has links with Libra with her balanced scales and LIBerty. He was cut free LIBerated from his violence by the lance of balance

The (KA) at the beginning and end of kaleka (KALAKA) deals with smallness and has links with the coming and going of birds clacking (KALAKA) their way across the sky semiannually like clock (KALAKA) work. The coming and going of birds twice a year soaring their way to the great lakes (LAKA) coincided with the time of the great migrations across the savannahs of Africa in March and September which became the beginning of the year in Hebrew and Roman calendars. It was also the time when young boys were castrated and altered.

The Hebrew word for 'curse' as K'LALA (KALALA) may have ancient associations with the call (KALALA) that the birds made as they semiannually soared across the sky heading toward the spread of lake (LAKA) water, or it may have links with the limb as LALA in Hawaiian. A limb (LAMABA) is that when compromised creates a limp (LAMAPA). The (BA) in limb (LAMABA) deals with a noun and the two physical legs. The (PA) in limp (LAMAPA) deals with passage (PA) and a verb, an activity. The (BA) is voiced. The (PA) is unvoiced. As the time of passage it worked on two levels. One dealt with the coming and going of the birds toward the lakes (LAKA). The other dealt with the passage of young boys into their changed state of becoming crippled and altered into a state of peaceful eunuchs. In Hawaiian LAKA means tame, gentle, domesticated. Had it been the passage of the birds across the sky toward the lakes (LAKA) teeming with fish and insects that became associated with the pacification of young boys? Also in kaleka (KALAKA) the (KA) deals with smallness associated with the SHAPE of a birds beak and the concept of massive egg laying leading to the concept of smallness.

For the Hindus Mother Kali (KALA) deals with life and death wearing a garland of skulls. She not only represents the passage of time emerging into calendars (KALA-) but with her *tongue* sticking out reflects the fact that she ate time, represented by the swallowing of the sun and the moon at the end of their journeys as they sank back into the side (IS HADA) of Her body in the Western horizontal rim. She also has her foot on Siva a male person who looks like the castrated docile eunuch.

The letter (L) as the angle of emergence or movement, be it of a body or of SOUND had its origins out of the organ that made the SOUND of lallation, the *tongue* (taNAGA) in the mother's mouth that had been likened to the SHAPE of a snake (IS NAKA). On the body of Mother Earth it dealt with the SHAPE of emergence of the heavenly bodies and birds out of Her flat circular horizontal side and of the many angles of emergence out of Her other creations.

After one of the great cataclysms that befell the African continent and after a dextral shift into male centrality in PHASE THREE there is a massive change in the perception dealing with the letter L. There exists an enormous linguistic break that no longer reflects the ancient migrations but a development into territorial agrarian societies and the need of those societies.

The letter (L) has been no longer associated with the *tongue* or the snake or the SHAPE of emergence of the heavenly bodies and birds. It begins to deal with an angle of movement but the angle of movement it deals with it the angle of the *leg* in stage three and has links with mutilatioin, maiming and castration.

In PHASE THREE after the linguistic break and a movement into sedentary societies in the Middle East the angle encoded in the letter (L) became associated with territoriality, agriculture and the tilling of the land. What also became encoded is the lengths that owners of the land resorted to keep their male workers from leaving their flocks, their forges and their farms. What also becomes apparent that in so many of the words have in them the English dyad lame (LAMA). In Old English lame is actually Lama. The castration of first born sons goes back to PHASE ONE and the rule of the mothers. The leg mutilation surfaces as male centrality overran the linguistic scene in PHASE TWO.

THE LETTER B

as two in one it emerges out of stage one and stage three.
The letter B is a voiced *bilabial* stop, plosive labial consonant.

SOUND; Babble of a baby, two lips approximated.

SHAPE; Both blbous lips seen in profile on the stem of the I.

MOTHER'S body; Breasts buttox, brain, brazos, arms in Spanish, Labials lips in Latin, buzia lips in Polish.

MOTHER EARTH; Birth and death of the sun, birth and death of all life, back and forth of ancient migrations, bio of life, bud of flower, birds emerging and departing twice a year,

CONCEPT; 'TWO IN ONE' *bilabial*, balance, breath, birth, baby, both, body

Section Three

(two sides), boy, brat (two genders), brother.

It becomes apparent that in both the Western Alphabet and the Finnish Aakkoset that the letter A (ah) came first. As the Alpha, the SHAPE of the triangular calderic cone of creation on the body of Mother Earth began it all, by belching, volcanic regurgitating, defecating, menstruating land up to Her surFACE. With land the possibility of beginnings took form.

In the Finnish Aakkoset, the A(ah) of the body of Mother Earth as Her calderic (KA-) cone (KA-) is repeated. Her job of blasting land across Her surFACE was a repetitive activity as She created Herself out of Herself. The double AA construct is followed by the double KK construct.

The Western Alphabet also begins with the letter A, as the Alpha (HALAFA) of beginnings, letting us know that it is telling us only half (HALAFA) of the story. It is followed by the letter B, that is constructed out of the two bulbous loops (lips), the *bilabials* superimposed on the stem of the I. Its SHAPE originally came out of the two lips of the mother as seen in profile in stage one. Since the lips are full, it becomes apparent that the letter B came out of a group of mothers who had full lips and the origins of the letter B point to Africa.

The letter B in the Western Alphabet follows the letter A to become (AB). In Etruscan, Greek and Slavonic in PHASE ONE the letter B emerges intact as the SHAPE of the two lips as seen in profile on the mothers face. In Hebrew and Arabic it looks like a mother's pregnant belly. In the languages that have come down to us in PHASE THREE the letter B in Egyptian, Old Indian, Hebrew (beth), Phoenician (beth) all deal with some aspect of enclosure or house. House is casa (KASA) in Spanish having links with the mother's coos (KASA) as the house (HASA) of creation. The (K) and (H) are interchangeable.

In Moabite, North Semitic, Irish, Western Greek, Slavonic and Phoenician the letter B looks like a grub. A grub is an insect baby. What we are dealing with here is the beehive, as the house with a grub or baby in it. The hexagonal SHAPE of the larval cell surfaces in many other emerging concepts. As the metaphor for the singular, overwhelming maternal expression of existence defined by the queen bee, it became a metaphor for the body of Mother Earth. In English the words for BEing, BEginning, BEgetting, all come out of the egg laying queen BEe.

Part of the bee hive was above the ground. The other part of the bee hive was situated below the ground. Together they symbolized the ancient observation of how the sun moved in an arc across the belly of air upon the body of Mother Earth, creating part of the house of existence ABOVE Her surFACE.

They were not all that sure of the SHAPE of passage of the sun within the body of Mother Earth, so they came up with the angles of descent and ascent on both sides in time creating a square, a box, or a house and in Greek named it the ETA.

The beehive was not only the metaphoric SHAPE of passage of the sun above and through the body of Mother Earth, it was also the place that oozed with the gift of sweetness from the sun (IS HANA), or honey (HANA). What the beehive represented was the SHAPE of the ancient matriarchial house, with the queen bee laying her endless grubs or babies and had been associated with the tribes of Amazons, cum Tuareg Berbers who inhabited much of North Africa, Southern Europe and South Western Asia. Since the Amazons were not too happy to have violent heterosexual males around and used them only to have children, the Linear B symbol for MA looks very much like the nuptial flight of the queen bee impaling the drone below her.

In this construct, in the Western Alphabets that have come down to us, the letter B, following the letter A (ah), establishes its links not only with migrating birds (B) but with the bee the industrious, prolific, single focused insect.

In Greek in PHASE THREE the SHAPE of the beehive as ETA where the hidden queen bee labored in darkness consisted of a symbolic arc on top and a box, or house underneath. The arc on top remained as the creative source of Mother Earth and the box on the bottom of ETA became the symbolic male four sided square.

There must have been some overlapping between the two alphabets, for the word bird also begins with the anlaut of B. Like the bee, birds were also creatures of the air, of the 'intermediate state' as the Bardo defined by the Tibetans also extending to deal with the 'two in one' (BA) passage of the sun (RA) rising and setting, creating day and night.

What the letter B establishes in its SHAPE and SOUND is that which came after the letter A (ah), that which was next, that which followed her and that which expanded into the concept of 'two in one', or both. Mother Earth and the females of the specie represented by the letter A(ah) came first. Their babies not only sequentially came after her, but actually physically followed her. They were no longer part of her body. They were individual segmented perambulating selves codified by the side view leg of the Egyptians on their temple walls.

In Egyptian the letter B is represented by the angle of a leg. It also expands to define the SHAPE of Egyptian figures parading across the temple walls, their bodies twisted forward, but their legs always walking to the side.

It seems that the Egyptians understood that human life existed as a passage toward the Western horizontal side of Mother Earth where they fell off into eternity. Human beings as upright bi-pedal creatures came into their own. Who also followed the females, cum mothers were the heterosexual males watching and fighting other males and the protective eunchs for their opportunity to mate.

In Hebrew the phoneme BA means 'what came next, or what came after.' It could mean one of three things. It could deal with the BA of the baby, or it could deal with the male as the emerging father, the BA in Maya. On the body of Mother Earth it could deal with the 'two in one' concept and what came after life dealing with death. In Egyptian the phoneme BA, is also one of the seven souls that is given to the baby at birth.

A baby of any mother was perceived to be a creature whose body was made up of two identical sides. It seemed as if one side reflected the other. It contained within its physical structure the concept of 'two in 'one', or both. One side reflected the other side perfectly. It was as if there was a line of demarcation, a mirror down the center halving the creature in twain.

The same perception expanded to include the body of Mother Earth. She apparently didn't stand up. She lay on Her side. Her primary function, like the function of a queen bee, was to lay eggs, and to endlessly give birth, Her lava in the creation of land becoming the slave (IS LAVA) to creative reproduction.

Existence ABove Her surFACE dealt with life. Ove of abOVE, has links with ovum, the egg, as the potential beginning of life. Ove (HAVA) goes into another direction, for to lay an egg was to have (HAVA) the possibility of having a baby. (VA) deals with the area on the mother's body, the vulva out of which life emerged. The area into which it emerged was the belly of air (HA) above the surFACE. On the body of Mother Earth, life emerged out of Her volcanic cone (VA) the metaphoric vulva on Her body. Existence BElow Her surFACE was the other half, the reality of death reflected in the standing waters.

The phoneme BA in Egyptian also stands for the number eight (8) as it does in Chinese. We are dealing here with linguistic puns that cross over time and space. Ancient burial places were situated in such a way that the sun setting in the horizontal West always seemed to disappear into the reflected surFACE of the standing waters. As the sun began its descent into the watery grave reflected in the waters below, it looked like the letter eight (8). At this point in human perception in PHASE ONE Mother Earth ate the sun, swallowed it into Her great maw (MAWA) it deals with Mother Earth (MA) as water (WA). The 'two in one' concept emerges here, for the sun disappears from its life ABove the plane into its life BElow the plane. It establishes the continuum 'AS ABOVE SO BELOW'. Death was part of life. Life was part of death. You had to die to be 'born again'. When you were 'born again' your destiny was to die.

As Mother Earth lay on Her side to lay Her endless eggs of creation, so the SHAPE of the letter B also plunked onto the ground to become the SHAPE of infinity. Infinity was a closed system based on two circles reflecting each other sideways. The Alpha of beginnings not only began the journey into life, it also began the reflected journey into death. Both journeys were perceived to be equally important. What followed life A(ah), what came after, what was next was death, encoded in the BA of the Hebrews.

The existence of life represented by the letter A, ABove the surface, became associated with motherhood on all levels. The existence of death BElow the surface became associated with transformation, with the eunuchized priesthood and in time with transformed males. The letter (B) dealt with the reflected disc of the sun, the BA as the number eight of the Egyptians and Chinese. The setting sun became the symbol of rebirth and reincarnation. No matter what happened, it always rose at dawn.

The underworld which the sun had to pass through after it set became the domain of the eunuchized male priesthood who originally followed their sisters assisting the clan mothers during the rites of burial. They became the OTHER, not the M OTHER. The M associated with motherhood was denied them. The OTHER not the M OTHER became associated with 'that which came after, came next', (BA of the Hebrews), not only the baby as the OTHER, the eunuchized older brOTHER as the OTHER, but the undefined males in general after being defined as one more, became defined as the OTHER. The O that became associated with maleness, surfaces here. The BR OTHER was also not the M OTHER. The phonemic construct also includes the English word another (A NOT HER) and also deals with anyone else, not the mother. In PHASE ONE it was only the mother who had been defined. That definition emerged out of her capacity to produce babies, the SHAPES of the organs on her face that assured linguistic survival for the baby and the cones of creation or the mountains on the body of Mother Earth.

As in PHASE TWO male role in specific procreation was becoming known, in Maya the father is BA, the one who came after, or followed the A(ah) of the mother. In Africa, the Swahili name for father is BABA as it is in Hebrew. On the other side of the world in China the name for father is also

BABA. In India the name for the transformed male who could be a father is also BABA. The European Italians call father BABBO. The Chinese came up with an eminently inclusive name for parenting, BABAMAMA, BABA for the father, MAMA for the mother.

In Eastern Europe and Russia an old crone, the wise old grandmother (who wore the crown), the BABA not only knew the words of power, (they floated on the air like the blessed breath) but through the transformation of her blood during birthing and menapause into wisdom, and areas beyond wisdom, straddled both worlds. She had a foot in both sides of the great divide. She still had links with the world of the living through her physical body. She also had links with the nether world through the transformation of her blood into the SAga of SAgacity. The Egyptians called SA, the 'wise blood' of the mother. In India, sages, males who transformed their bodies into states of suspended bliss and peace, have also been known as BABA.

Following this train of thought there emerges the linguistic construct of ABBA. In the word ABBA there exists the perception of reflection AB/BA. The phoneme AB is reflected by the phoneme BA. It echoes linguistically in its phonemic construct the physical reality of the two sides of the body reflecting each other. On the body of Mother Earth it dealt with existence ABove the plane in life, reflected in the waters at the horizon line as the BA of existence BElow the horizon line in death.

Because the knowledge of specific paternity surfaced at different times in different places, in PHASE ONE the birth of a baby boy defied definition. He obviously had a body like the other baby girls. Except in the area of the pubis he didn't have a hole, he had what looked like the inTESTines growing on the outside. He had what became defined as a penis and TESTicles. Along the way he was defined not only as the other, not like the mother, the O of the empty womb, the neutral I, of one more, but also by the concept of 'two in one'. In English a male child is called a boy (BAYA). His name begins with the anlaut B. As the 'two in one' concept at this particular time took hold male children were considered physically androgynous at birth, having both a female body and male genitalia.

The ancient homosexually disposed Greeks thought so highly of the penis that they likened it to an air plant or ORCHID. The orchid flowered beautifully, had no roots in the body of Mother Earth and received its sustenance from the air. When it burst into magnificent bloom it lived its life anchored to the tree and was essentially a parasite (PARASATA) like a priest (PARASATA). It was perceived that a penis was to a female body like an ORCHID was to a tree. Another name for penis in Greek, along with the pleasure giving phallus, is ORCHIS, the beautiful parasitic air plant.

Within the dyad of boy (BAYA) there exists a series of clues. The letter B deals with duality, with 'two in one' of the androgynous male child. Since AYA deals with light in Persian and dawn in Assyrian, then the first born little boy was destined to become the guide of the sun on its journey of rebirth. To protect his sisters children, after he became a eunuch (HANAKA), turning into an uncle (HANAKALA), he became not only the protector, but the watcher, the male head of the family. Following his mother and sisters in all the activities over which they officiated as priestesses, he as the priest dealt with the reflected underground realms within darkened caves.

Second and subsequent sons were pushed out of the female clan at puberty when hormones activated their violence and were left adrift to compete in the mating game with other males and to become the warriors and rulers above ground. The firstborn eunuchized sons became closely allied with the mothers. The subsequent second and third sons became allied with the circling peripheral males. In PHASE THREE as male role in paternity was becoming known and sky Gods *away* and *above* the body of Mother Earth emerged as the male 'source' of creation taking to the sky completing the cycle of death (the sun setting) and resurrection (the sun rising). As the rising sun, with its gift of light, he replaced the ubiquitous snake as the guide and savior of the sun becoming the actual savior of light. 'HE IS RISEN' goes back much earlier than Christianity.

The ABBA or AB/BA construct of the phoneme AB being reflected by the phoneme BA may also deal with the 'two in one' concept associated with the ancient migrations, following the herds in one direction and then turning back, creating a reflection in the pattern of movement back and forth across the savannahs of Africa and the ancient Sahara Desert.

In Persian the AB of the rain as AB/BA that as water fell from the sky was followed by the BA of the drought. The Hebrew BA as 'what came after' or 'what was next', surfaces here also dealing with the twice yearly monsoons.

The letter A(ah) as the cone of creation bursting forth with land (AA lavic terrain in Hawaii), was also associated with the fans of water that as geysers shot up into the air and upon their descent created many of the waters on the body of Mother Earth, (AA a river in Latvia). Mother Earth created Herself out of Herself on many levels.

In Sumer the letter A(ah) stood for water. In Persian AB means water. For some, the volcanic mountains were perceived to come first, (the Alpha of beginnings dealt with the calderic cone of creation giving its SHAPE to the letter A(ah). What followed the triangular peaks of the mountains and emerged from them, was cascading waterfalls of flowing water, the Persian AB.

In this case A (ah) as water falling from the sky and being flushed from the mountains came first dealing with the ancient migrations and the coming of rain. In Sanskrit ABda is 'water giving' or 'rainy season'. (DA) deals with 'gift of' AB is the life giving water. After the drought, with the savannahs parched and dry from the broiling equatorial sun, when the rains came, it must have seemed like a gift from the belly of air ABove them, a gift from their great nurturing Mother Earth. One of the words for the belly is ABdomen, the dome (DAMA), the distended belly of air that hovered over the body of Mother Earth and out of which seasonally the blessed water poured down from the sky.

In Syriac AB is the last month of summer. In Arabic AB is the month of August. The A(ah) of the mother came first. The B of the baby followed her in the foaling, sexually driven sixth month of August.

Due to massive climactic changes on the continent of Africa the separation of the migrating herds in the seventh month of September was preceded by foaling in the sixth month of August resulting in a sexual frenzy of post partum mating if you counted from March when the ancient migratory march began. Six (IS HAKASA) and sex (IS HAKASA) both have the same ancient dyadic construct. (HAKA) deals with hacking, splitting in half. (KASA) deals with the coos (KASA), the area where the split occurred, or the creation of the 'two in one' scenario occurring on a variety of levels. When foals split off the bodies of the herbivore mares and fell to the ground at the end of the summer in August, the beginning of the fall season, they created a minute reflection of the mother.

On the body of Mother Earth when the rains announced their presence in the far distance, the ancient migrators turned their way back home. It was also the time when in November the body of the human mother with the hole on the bottom of her trunk, her coos (KASA), was rendered in half with the birth of a baby creating a new member, when she too was hacked apart separating into two pieces. It seemed to them that when a mother, any mother gave birth, part of her broke apart from her body. It was as if she broke into two distinct pieces. For the herbivore mares one larger piece remained standing while the other smaller piece steaming in the sun temporarily lay struggling on the ground. It was a time of rampant sexuality for the herbivores in August (six, sex) with a similar construct as (sun, son), only the vowels change. The consonants stay constant.

August as AB in Syriac and Persian had been the beginning times of the herbivore sexuality, of the butting of male heads and the butting of the female buttox. In Hebrew ABib is an ear of corn. An ear of corn usually matures at the end of summer about the time of August. On the upright corn stalk, an ear of corn looks suspiciously like an erect penis, the symbol of rutting, bellowing and rampant sexual activity. In Arabic, ABBA means, to 'pack up'. It could have its links with the ancient migrations moving in one direction, then reflecting the movement by turning around. When you traveled, even in those ancient times, there were things that you had to gather together, to 'pack up' on the journey. Or it could mean something much more prosaic. To 'pack up' could also mean that the father (BA) packed up the mother (AB) with his penis during copulation. In Minoan Linear B the symbol for KO is and again looks suspiciously like the SHAPE of the penis packing up the circle of the vulva, establishing ancient links with COpulation, COhabitation and COitus.

The Egyptian God AMON aside, creating the universe every night by masturbating, you needed two people to fornicate. You needed a COuple (KA-). Kiokio (KAKA) is fornication in the South Pacific Islands of the Bugotu tribes. The use of the K SOUND associated with the coos (KASA) and beaks of birds begins to enter the picture.

Pkak (PAKAKA) in Hebrew means cork stopper. The female vagina has often symbolically been likened to a bottle. The cork stopper packed up the entrance to the bottle, ie vagina. The Hebrew pkak (PAKAKA) may have been the cock (KAKA) that did the 'packing'. In Polish ptak (PATAKA) means bird. Only the second consonant seems to have changed.

In Egyptian ABtu was the fish of Isis swallowing the penis of Osiris every night in the Western sky in ABydos, the city on the Western banks of the river Nile. Its a poetical way of saying that the sun as it sank in the West, at the time that this perception evolved, not only COpulated with the body of Mother Earth but met his demise in Her Western waters as She swallowed him. Echoes of the drone meeting his death at the hands of the queen bee. Since there was no real knowledge where the sun went once it sank in the West, they called the place on the body of Mother Earth, the AByss. The AByss still existed in life upon the body of Mother Earth as a place of passage. Originally it had not been linked with chaos or nothingness.

In Numidian the letter B is represented by two symbols, a dot and a square.

The dot deals either with the mothers period at the end, or with the baby in the belly of the mother. The square takes us to PHASE THREE becoming associated with males and as male role in specific pro-creation was becoming known, with the father, as co-genitor. As a square it falls into the category of a four sided house.

AB for the Egyptians was the 'heart-soul', the dancing heart, beating out the rhythm of life, one of the most important souls that came with the baby at birth. On the body of Mother Earth the A(ah) dealt with the cone of creation. The letter B symbolizing the concept of 'two in one', dealt with the body of Mother Earth and with the bio of life. On the more prosaic physical level, it was the mother A(ah), carrying what came after her or followed her, the baby, B, within her belly, under her beating heart, floating in its watery cacoon, that established the ancient AB construct.

In Bengali ABar means 'again' and deals with the repetitive passage of the sun (RA) rising and setting ABove the body of Mother Earth. In Lithuanian ABu means both. It was in the belly, the ABdomen of the individual mother, that the blood, the spot, the period within began to COagulate to create a baby. An ancient European name for the vulva is ABricot and has links with the apricot, the oval juicy SHAPE that has often been associated with the SHAPE of the clitoris. The (B) and (P) are interchangeable. In Lithuanian ABipus means both sides and could have been an early word dealing with the two sides of existence.

For the ancient mother-centered belief systems there was a place within Her body, a cave under the shrine called the ABaton (HABATANA) where people incubated, reconnected with the Kundalini energies of Mother Earth to free themselves of their physical, psychological and spiritual burdens which remained as entrenched habits (HABATA) created through the filter of their panic stricken infancy. ABaton (HABATANA) has the same phonemic construction as habit (HABATA). The ABaton (HABATANA) has the NA on the end of it. NA deals with 'emergence upon the surface', or 'the negation of a former state'. Was it the emergence of fears that had been dealt with? Were fears transformed and negated? Were they flushed to the surface through the ministrations of a wise woman, the ancient houris, the spiritual whisperer who was at one (ATONE), with the energies of Mother Earth? In Egyptian, one of the seven souls given at birth to a baby was Khaibit, (HABATA), or the shadow. The shadow stalks a human creature on the outside, as infantile panic stricken habit (HABATA) stalks the creature on the inside. What it meant was that the decisions turned into habits, internalized in human beings as a result of their helpless, panic-stricken infancy, could be faced and could be transformed. The fear of death, human beings greatest fear could be faced. They could be healed only by entering the great womb of Mother Earth, (delphos of the Greeks), while still alive, and facing their awesome fear alone, in a dark cave under the shrine of the Goddess, helped by a holy woman, the houris, as the oracle of Delphi.

To worship in Swahili is ABudu. In Lithuanian ABu means both. The Swahili word for worship as ABudu is the 'gift of' (DA) of Abu who is established as having a dual purpose or both, having linguistic links with the Lithuanian Abu meaning both. Since we have both the A(ah) of the mother and the B of the baby as the AB or what she had created we are dealing with the worship in PHASE ONE of not only the individual mother but the Maternal context of Mother Earth.

In Amharic the metaphoric snake, the guide of the sun, moon and soul on their journey of transformation, had been called ABad. Both words contain within them the (DA), or 'gift of' the AB. It repeats their links with the body of Mother Earth A(ah), and the B of duality or 'two in one' represented by life and death. In PHASE THREE the Hebrew ABad meant 'to perish and to be cursed'. The ABaton, or the cave of transformation, became redefined as the ABaddon, or the 'bottomless pit' that in time became further redefined as Hell as males shifted into the violent, sexually unrelenting left hemisphere. The Biblical snake also lost its symbolic status to become the bearer of horrific tidings and the cause of human expulsion from the Garden of Eden. What the snake represented had been the transformative knowledge of the electro magnetic Kundalini energy that only mothers experienced at the time of birthing. Adam was not ready to receive it, so both he and Eve had to be expelled from paradise.

The nude human body, especially of the pleasure bearing body of the female, became redefined as defiled. Not only the female body became defiled but all physical activity and human body parts had to be hidden from view. The processes inherent in the creative natural aspects dealing with Mother Earth in PHASE THREE had to be jetissoned and defined as evil. The metaphoric snake symbol of the electro magnetic Kundalini energy identified with the ancient knowledge of ecstasy and transformation slithered underground forever. With the redefinition of the metaphoric snake came the loss of the ancient knowledge of healing, ecstatic transformation and conscious rebirth. The Greeks took it one step further and created Apollo, the homosexual sun God, rising from his underground caverns, *away* and *above* the body of Mother Earth, the killer of his twin sister, the healing Goddess Artemis, with the many bee grubs, symbols of Mother Earth hanging upon her body. With her was put to death the multi faceted layers of knowledge of the ancient mothers.

In Africa the great Mother was Mother Earth, defined by the SHAPE of Her cone of creation, the volcanic crater on Her body, made explicit by the SHAPE of the letter A(ah). Many of the ancient tribes in South West Africa, those that came after Her as Her BAbies, have names beginning with the letter B. In the language of Bemba, the phoneme ABA or BA stands for 'they', or 'them', the off spring on the body of Mother Earth. It expands to include the people of; Bantu, Bavenda, Bapedi, Basuto, Bakongo, Bachama, Bambara, Baranga, Batta, Bambala, Banda, Bakuba, Baluba, Babua, Botswana, Bushongo, Bechuana Bauleto, to name just a few.

Then in PHASE TWO depending upon when the knowledge of specific paternity entered the picture, the letter B as BA, became associated with the name of the father as co-genitor who came after her. In Amharic, BA means 'with'. It could either deal 'with' the baby, or 'with' the father. The baby was 'with' the mother, in her belly, or the father was 'with' the mother, during copulation. In Hebrew BA meaning 'what came next', or 'what came after', may be associated with BA the one who came, or arrived, and could deal either with the baby, or has possible linkage with 'coming' itself, the orgasm that had been associated with birthing.

The ARRIVAL of a baby meant the coming of a new RIVAL, the one who supplanted the still suckling baby at the breast. As human females shifted from seasonal to lunar then year round sexual receptivity and closely spaced offspring, the still suckling baby was pushed aside, replaced at the breast. Here we have one of the roots of the seeds of rage, of the awesome burden of sibling rivalry and of stultifying jealousy.

In PHASE THREE Cain (KANA), the first born Biblical son, killed his younger brother ABel, who may have replaced him prematurely at the breast. The Biblical legend may have nothing to do with the evolution of agrarian societies out of the more primitive migrating ones. Since Cain was also called 'the limping one', he must have been part of the eunuchized crippled smithies, who as priests of the underworld dealt with the rites at the forge of the setting sun. It may have been that Cain (KANA), represented the victory of the eunuchized priesthood over the AB of the ancient Mother love, the heart soul of the Egyptians. It may also signal the emergence of the priesthood as the power base separate from their role as side participants in the rites of the dead in the underground caverns, to emerge into the temples above the body of Mother Earth. The first born eunuchized Cain not only killed his rival and brother ABel, but his much larger competitor, the heart soul of the Egyptians (AB) and the power base of the ancient mothers. This story deals with the eunuch priesthood at the center fighting for supremacy with the heterosexual males who circled the periphery.

After PHASE ONE a bit of a change took place. The mother as A(ah) came first. The mother, as Mother Earth was not only land, She was also water. That was a given. In Persian the link may exist establishing the change from the body of the mother as the singular source, based on the SA or 'wise blood' of the mother of the Egyptians. The 'wise blood' of the mother knew all by itself how to coagulate within the belly and how to make a baby. Then the change occurred in PHASE THREE to the singular source, out of the body of the father through masturbation and the passing of water (semen). The Egyptian God Amun, or AMMON (HAMANA) who nocturnally masturbated all of existence into being, gives us a clue for it has the same ancient construct as semen (IS HAMANA). In Greek HAMA means 'together with' and mano (MANA) is 'hand' in Spanish. There emerged the realization that not only masturbation brought forth a baby out of the mother but semen also performed the same function out of the father (the Numidian box, four sided square with the dot in it defining the letter B surfaces here). They didn't seem to take the next step that the semen needed the female body to create life. Ergo the female body had to be covered, shrouded, veiled to disguise the fact that her body distended with new life, that she could be seen as the apparent parent.

In PHASES TWO and THREE the water dealing with the individual female body and the body of Mother Earth became redefined as the AB of Persian water coming out of the male penis, the semen that became the singular physical creator of life. There emerges AB as father in Arabic. In Amharic AB defines the forefather, or elder. In Ethiopian, Coptic, Hebrew, Amharic and Arabic ABa, ABu or ABba became the names for the father. For the Hebrews, the father of the ancient tribe of Israel became Abraham (ABrahama).

For the Maori who left Africa fifty thousand years before settling in New Zealand, their word for the intestines that the sun had to pass through within the nocturnal body of Mother Earth was MAHARA. Using the process of reflection that was used to establish male deities and male source in PHASE TWO and THREE, the MAHARA reflected becomes becomes rahama (MAHARA/RAHAMA). With the addition of the Hebrew AB of the father

Section Three

Ab (RAHAMA) surfaces as a much more ancient deity than the Middle East would have us believe. Not only that, but dealing with the Maori intestines establishes the fact that there was an ancient source out of Mother centrality as far back as fifty thousand years ago that considered Mother Earth as having intestines under Her surFACE through which the sun had to travel to be reborn at dawn.

The symbol for the Greek Goddess Athene reflects a variety of major ancient perceptions. The triangle on top is the volcanic cone of creation, the Alpha of beginnings. The cross underneath splits into two possible directions. One still deals with the body of Mother Earth and the passage of the sun and moon horizontally across Her belly of air and the passage the birds vertically upon the same belly creating the cross that became symbolized by the letter KA in Linear B. The other perception may deal with the individual female. The cross or X=KS (KASA) could be the coos (KASA) on her body out of which life also emanates. The X and the cross(+) had been interchangeable in Early Greek.

The Goddesses and their names beginning with the anlaut A, came first. They were followed by the names of Gods that began with the anlaut of B. The source for ancient Hebrew Gods surfaces in the word Ba'al, as the name for 'husband'. It seems that if mothers could be associated with the Goddesses representing the many aspects of Mother Earth beginning with the letter A, then the husbands could be associated with the emerging Gods of their creation, following the mother with the letter B; Baal Hammon of Carthage, Baal Sapon of the Caanonites, Bellephoron of the Greeks, Bassareus of Lydia, Baal Peor of Phoenicia, Baal Rimmon Babylonian storm God, Baal Berith Caanonite city, (berit is circumcision in Hebrew), Baal Gad Semitic name for Pan, Baal Hadad of the Caanonites, Baal-Zebub of the Philistines, Bala Rama Vedic brother of Krishna, Behemoth of the Bible, Bacchus of the Greeks, Brahma of India, Balder God of the Scandinavians, Bog Slavic God and river, Buddha Sanskrit.

In Amharic Bal means husband. In Hebrew Ba'al also means, the husband. In Hebrew Baal Mum (MAMA) is the name for the invalid or cripple and deals with the practice of not only eunuchizing the firstborn sons, but also of maiming (MAMA-) them. What this ancient set of dyads tells us is that the husband, or the original head of the family, was the eunuchized uncle. The practice of the uncle as head of the family still exists in many tribal societies around the world and has its roots in the firstborn son being castrated to protect his mothers and sisters children from rape and kidnapping and to become the head of the family. It seems that the Baal concept as husband and then God, came out of the time when male role in specific procreation was as yet unknown for it has links with the castrated firstborn son.

After the linguistic break and a shift away from the face of the Mother, the echo of the babble of the baby surfaces in the baby as a grub, as a larve out of the bee hive. It begins to look like the SHAPE of a lower case vowel associating it with the bee as the metaphor for Mother Earth. The grub SHAPE emerges in Moabite to the left, Western Greek to the left, North Semitic to the left, Irish and Slavonic to the right. In the Moabite, Western Greek, and North Semitic the grub looks like the number nine and may deal with male centrality in PHASE THREE and the solar reckoning of gestational time. The Irish and Slavonic the grub facing to the right looks like the number six dealing with August as the sixth month of the ancient migratory trek when the herbivore mares gave birth to their calves (grubs) and the birds returned to their nesting sites. For the Greeks eta becomes the SHAPE of the bee hive, the actual home of the bee.

With the evolution of the square as a male symbol in PHASE THREE, the four sided house came into being. Early huts built by women were round SHAPED. The Phoenician BETH as house straddles both symbols, the name of the house and the SHAPE of the grub, if a bit stylized. The square house as BETH surfaces in Hebrew, and a bit fancy in Egyptian with a door and an alcove in the corner. Old Indian stays with a plain square. In Numidian the square gets a dot or period within it. Part of the Numidian stays with the symbology of the mother's with a circle with a dot or period in it. The circle of the mother's belly also surfaces in the Hebrew curved abdomen facing to the left. In Arabian the curved belly faces in both directions. Since the pregnant curve out of Arabic and Hebrew may also have meant the phases of the crescent moon also coming and going.

In Arabian there is also the SHAPE of a menhir or a dolman, the square with no bottom, the PI SHAPE and the heh (HAHA) of the birthing breath of the Hebrew mothers before the shift into male centrality occurred in PHASE THREE. The Egyptian foot or leg facing to the left as the Egyptian B gives pause. Could the birth of a fetus becoming an upright bipedal human being is that what all those pictures on temple walls with their feet facing in one direction and their bodies straining in another are trying to tell us? To be human is to become separate from the beasts. What supposedly separates us is bipedal locomotion.

THE LETTER P
A VOICELESS BILABIAL STOP

SOUND; Plosion of air out of the top lip

SHAPE; The top lip seen in profile

MOTHER'S body; top lip, fingers, palce, Polish, feet, paws, pads, pieds

MOTHER EARTH; fire, fuego, palic,

CONCEPT; *Passage*, serial order, linear movement through, (P) became (F) in Anglo Saxon and German. (B), (V), (F) are often interchangeable.

The SOUND of the voiceless letter (P) has links with the voiced letter (B) made in the same area of the mouth. The letter (B) deals with both sides of the mouth, the 'two in one concept'. The letter (P) deals primarily with the top lip, its SHAPE deals with the top part of the letter (B) on the edge as the plosive SOUND carried by a rush of air exploding out of the mouth. Having links with the letter (V) it may deal with the vocal cords as they give vent to the air that escapes through the top lip.

It may have its roots in running as the air exploded out of the mouth and the feet carried the heavy breather past its predatory doom. Or it may have dealt with fighting itself as the fingers of the hand fought off the attacker accompanied by the heavy breathing of the attacker and the prey. It primarily has roots in movement, be it the *passage* of air out of the mouth, the foraging of fingers or the patter of paws. It may also deal with the heavy breathing dealing with the last stages of sexual activity.

The letter (P) deals with *passage*; *passage* of linear uninterrupted air out of the mouth in heavy breathing , *passage* of running feet one after another across the body of Mother Earth, *passage* of fingers across the skin, *passage* of urine out of the lower hole, *passage* of the baby out of the mothers body, help in the *passage* across with the cane, *passage* of life itself as the boomerang of constant returns. It emerges into the expansive concept of that which lies next to, or *passes* beside. The activity of *passage* is the major factor encoded in the letter (P) and the special movement defines it.

Everything that occurred on and out of the body of Mother Earth were Her smaller creations. She gave birth to everything. They were all small segmented reflections on Her surFACE. Her extensions in the creation of smaller reflections out of their bodies on the mat of matter were the individual mothers, Her surrogates or daughters. Not only creatures were Her creations but also the sun, moon, clouds and even the fog that rose across Her valleys at dawn and *passed* across Her surFACE were Her off spring . In Chinese PA defines the 'daughter' of Mother Earth. who as Her surrogate played a role in mutual creation. It was the time in PHASE ONE that the sun (RA) also rose to create the fog that rose in the Eastern sky. In Polish PARA is the name for the fog, mist or steam that *passed* across the surFACE of Mother Earth at dawn. It hugged Her valleys and hills as it rose into the heavens upon the thermal wings of the sun.

In Persian PA defines the 'foot' or 'leg' the movement or *passage* through, based on the use of the feet. In Latin pied (PADA) defines the feet. (DA) is 'the gift of' the PA or 'leg' of *passage*. In Sanskrit PADA is also the 'leg' or 'foot' dealing with the (DA) 'gift of *passage*'. In Polish the dyad pada defines a movement of 'falling down' which is what the feet do when they pound their way across the ground. Also in Polish PO deals with 'that which came after' dealing with serial movement, one foot after another.

The concept of movement and *passage* includes other carnivore animals and their PAws reflecting the SHAPE of the top lip as they cover the ground. It is to the PAws of carnivore creatures, especially the lioness Pride that we owe our word for Power (PAWA-). No only did the carnivore mother sMOTHER her prey but she held it fast with her PAws. On the body of Mother Earth Her power (PAWARA) dealt with the *passage* (PA) of the sun (RA) across Her waters (WA).

The movement through also deals with human fingers. PAws were to four legged creatures as hands and fingers were to humans. In Polish PAlec (PALASA) is the dyad for finger, the four or five poles (PALA-) that straddle the hand. Also in Polish the word for fire is palic (PALAJA). There in hangs another tale.

It was universally understood that the fingers of the hand brought pleasure (PALASARA), through touching and caressing, through gently moving the digital pads (PADA-) across the skin. Mothers massaged their babies. The massage of the mother is the message of love shared with her child. Sexual partners massaged their beloved. Primates looking for pests gently touch the skin of their family members.

The Polish word for fingers as palce (PALASA) obviously has ancient links not only with the word for pleasure (PALASARA) palases (PALASA) but with the Greek word for the penis or phallus (PALASA) or (FALASA). The

SOUNDS of (P) and (F) are interchangeable. The (RE), or (RA) on the end of the word pleasuRE, deals with the male sun God of the Egyptians, as the doer and helper of Mother Earth. The phallus was considered to be an extra finger on the male body that pleasured their partners. Shades of masturbation. At the time that these activities became codified, it was perceived that sexuality for men dealt with the release of pRessure. Sensuality for ladies dealt with the activation of pLeasure.

It was in the 'abominable' pleasure palaces (PALASA), that women, the ancient houris, cum prostitutes, or holy women, had a variety of functions, one of them was to teach men how to pleasure their partners. As men learned to pleasure women, they also learned how to expand their own pleasure and to release the built up pressure in their bodies, the 'must' or 'rut' of their African animal male relatives.

In the words pleasure (PALASARA) and pressure (PARASARA) there exist some telling clues. In the word pleasure (PA (LA) SARA) of sensuality, there exists the phoneme (LA), which is associated with the female as the LAllating, LAdy of the Land. For the Maya who left the African continent in PHASE ONE after one of the many cataclysms, defines (LA) associated with the body of Mother Earth as 'that which existed forever'.

In the word pressure (PA(RA)SARA) of male sexuality, in the same place, there is the phoneme (RA), establishing links with the Egyptian male sun god (RA) as the doer. For the Middle Easterners in PHASE THREE it was (RA) as the male sun was 'that which existed forever'. Our ancient maternal ancestors understood better than contemporary humans have done the role of sensual sexuality used as pleasure, satisfaction and stress reduction, not only as an aspect of power and procreative control. Shades of the Bonobo.

In the Greek word phallus, as either (PALASA) or (FALASA), you have FALA, which in Polish means wave. A wave is that which goes up and down, not unlike the phallus (FALASA). Ending with the phoneme (SA), one of the perceptions was that the penis when it became erect filled up with blood. (The SA, of sanguine, means both bloody and hopeful). The ancient humans obviously had a sense of humor. The phoneme (SA) was also associated with the spiral of air. As these perceptions evolved the phallus at the time of its upward trajectory was perceived to have been blown up not only with blood but with air, like an inflated derma. It established its links with the Greek hubris, becoming defined as lechery, pride and penile erection. Having its roots in what was perceived to be the ancient air filled phallus, dealing not only with going up and down and being used as an extra digit, but also evolving into the endearing quality associated with hubris.

Also in Polish, the linguistic construct of the fingers as palce (PALASA) expands to include the body of Mother Earth. For palic (PALASA) in Polish means, 'to burn'. It has links with both the volcanic cone of creation, and the time of the blazing eruption, when Mother Earth spasmed, orgasmed, and blasted Herself up to the surFACE, as Her fingers of fire rose and then caressed Her skin in the creation of land. It also dealt with the flaming fingers of fire that like the stiletto rays of the sun helped to pierce a break through the fabric of dawn in the Eastern sky and then raced across Her surFACE, caressing Her body with the light and the warmth of a new day. Fingers, fire, pleasure, pleasure palaces and the male phallus share similar ancient perceptions.

The SHAPE of air exploding out of the open mouth defining the letter (P) of the specific top lip surfaces in Egyptian and Arabic. In Cypriotic the symbol for PA deals with inhalation and exhalation and the *PAssage* of air. Moving down her body the letter (P) as an anlaut for *passage* deals with the 'leg' or 'foot' in Persian, Greek and Cypriotic. Also in Greek the PH of the PHallus halves the circle of the mother as he hacks her in half. The (G) and (C) in Etruscan for the letter (P) comes out of the same construct as the circle around the skull that ends at the center of the human face in the SHAPE of the open mouth.

That same construct became established on the body of Mother Earth at the rim around Her flat round horizontal surFACE that also had to have a mouth out of which the heavenly bodies and birds could have their being. The letter (P) may stand for *passage* through of air out of the top lip but the (C) and (G) establish the open mouth as the place of Creation and Generation. At a very ancient time in PHASE ONE, regurgitation of food had been likened to a kind of *passage*.

The most repetitive SHAPE that emerges associated with the letter (P) of passage deals with the SHAPE of a crutch in Phoenician, North Semitic, perhaps Etruscan, Hebrew, Greek, the PO of Cypriotic, Roman and Lycian. We are in PHASE TWO and the male centered territory of leg mutilation to keep the shepherds tending to their sheep and the blacksmiths remaining at the forge of the sun.

For the ancient Dogon tribe of Africa another wrinkle enters the collage. Their letter (P) comes with a slightly different but related provenance. For their letter (P) is SHAPED like a drumstick and looks like a crutch. Its definition establishes the fact that the drum stick was used in the circumcision ceremony for drumming and dancing, initiating the passage of young boys

Section Three

into manhood. The name Dogon (DAGANA) is the (DA) 'gift of' (GANA) and (GANA) gyno (GANA) in Greek defines the 'woman'. For it was understood that the Kundalini energy of ecstasy rose up from the maternal body of Mother Earth. We are in the territory of ancient castration and the birthing breath of the mother as the source of ecstasy, leadership, prophecy, healing and knowledge.

When males began to understand the power inherent in the birthing breath of the mother, they through a variety of ritual in PHASE TWO also gave birth to the trance state often becoming the shaman of the tribe. For the Dogon, the ritual consisted of dancing to the transformative response of repetitive drumming and dancing. The fact that it occurred at the time that young boys were circumcised goes back to the ancient activity of castration. For circumcision in PHASE TWO became a symbolic ritual of castration while maintaining the male essence having links with the power inherent in the first born eunuchized son out of PHASE ONE. The drum stick looks suspiciously like a crutch.

In Chinese PI created a circle of two serpents representing day and night which became the redefined Yin and Yang. The two symbols spinning together in space went through many convolutions. The most ancient in PHASE ONE dealt with both the Yin and the Yang representing two aspects of the sun above the plane as the female YIN (HAYANA) and the male sun under the surFACE of Mother Earth as the Yang (HA(YA)NAGA). It also dealt with motherhood as the (Y) SHAPE of the pubic anlaut establishes. The Yin was the mother-son unit above in life. The Yang was the mother-son unit below in death. Both systems had been considered to have been equally real

With the Yang (HA(YA)NAGA) you already have the snake (IS NAKA, NAGA) as part of the picture. Since the Yang (HA(YA)NAGA) contains within its inguistic coils the name of the eunuch (HANAKA) and that in Chinese becomes the catrated male is YANG E (HA(YA)NAGA) then we are with the mother sun combine above the plane and Her mother eunuch son combine below the plane as one unit of creation. For it was necessary for the snake (IS NAKA) to guide the soul through the underground portals of death.

The second definition of the Yin and Yang still in PHASE ONE dealt with the body of Mother Earth as the 'source' of the two aspects spinning together in space. It dealt with the observable fact that Mother Earth regurgitated or gave birth to the sun in the East and swallowed the sun in the West. The Yin became the solar disc above the plane and Yang (HANAGA) stayed as the solar disc under the plane, guided by the metaphoric snake (IS NAKA) traveling through the nocturnal body of Mother Earth.

The third definition dealt with male role in specific procreation becoming known in PHASE TWO the spinning circle was no longer singularly female and mother based. The Yin stayed female but the Yang became male. That is the perception that became accepted in PHASE THREE.

But that in not the end of the story. As massive catastrophic climactic changes on the continent of Africa and male centrality overran the global scene in PHASE THREE male Gods took flight into the open heavens *away* and *above* the body of Mother Earth. The ubiquitous snake representing the Kundalini energy replacing the sun also took flight grew feathers like a bird to help him soar above the body of Mother Earth in the 'intermediate state' of air becoming the feathered serpent, the KU KUL KAN of Central and South America.

In Greek the place of passage as PI not only defines the circumference of a circle but looks suspiciously like a dolman or a menhir, the two massive vertical stones with a lentil on top that defy explanation but look like a place of some kind of mysterious *passage*. The PI in Greek also resembles the crutch which begins do deal with castration, mutilation and the trance state.

The Hebrew huh (HAHA) apparently associated with the birthing breath of the panting mother is SHAPED like a dolman or a menhir with two upright pillars with a lentil straddling them creating a place of passage as in Stonehenge. The passage was through the body of Mother Earth, through Her Kundalini electro magnetic shakti or prana in order to emerge transformed. That is why Christ on the cross with His last words intoned "Ele, Eli why hast thou forgotten me?" He learned in His last moments on Earth that transformation came through the Mothers body not through the fathers mind.

THE LETTER W

An aphthong, an unvoiced consonant.

As a double you (UU) it evolved with a different provenance containing a double dip under the surface.

SOUND; expelled woo breath of weeping, woe, wonder, why, what

SHAPE; the *lower lip*, mirror of the top lip on the mother's face MOTHER'S body; watery womb of woman

MOTHER EARTH ; reflective, mirroring surFACE of water

CONCEPT; reflection, mirroring, swallowing, seven (is even)

Section Three

W-The letter W is the SHAPE of the *lower lip*, perceived as a reflection of the letter M of the top lip on the mother's face, with the horizontal line of the mouth as the line joining and separating them. The SHAPE of the letter (W) contains a double construction. It echoes within its structure the 'two in one' concept. It may originally have been made out of the repeated double (UU) vowel construct dipping under the surFACE of Mother Earth but with the emergence of the chisel and angular lines made by the chisel on stone in Cuneiform to confuse the issue further, it became associated with the singular letter (V).

The SOUND associated with the SHAPE of the letter (W) as either the double (UU) or (V), is the *lower lip* puckered up to create the woo as the wails of woe and wonder and the asking of why became associated with grief and sadness.

On the body of Mother Earth the SOUND of woe metaphorically made by the *lower lip* became associated with quietly standing pools of water into which the sun sank every night and died to its light. It was perceived that the sun was chewed into small pieces leaving a gory stain in the Western sea to be sWALLowed by the body of Mother Earth at the Western WALL of water, into Her mysterious maw, to WALLow slowly in the gory waters until the metaphoric snake, The Kundalini energy appeared to guide it through the underground entrails of the great Mother, to be coagulated and transformed and to be reborn at dawn.

The reality created in the reflective surFACE of water had been perceived to be once removed. It was a reflection, not the real thing. It was not the actual referent but like a NAME, a watery reflection of the referent reality that was above the surFACE. To that end the letter (W) came into play. As a reflection of what was above defined by the letter (M), the letter (W) came to define the reflected NAME of things, the Who, What, When, Which, Where, Wither. Reality was the real THING. Once you named something, or it became reflected in the standing waters you had to use the mind to name it. You had to THINK up a name. The THING uses a voiced (G) of beGetting at the end of the dyad standing for what is real. The THINK uses an unvoiced (K) at the end for it is once removed, not physically real but a reflection based on the activity of the mind.

It was the reflected picture in water that created an alternate reality that accompanied the naming of non physical things created by the mind and imagination. It comes out of the same context as the Goddess 'water drawer' that had been so grossly misinterpreted. She did not throw a bucket into a well and 'drew' the water up to the top. It was Mother Earth who 'drew' or painted an alternate reflected reality on the surFACE of Her standing 'waters'.

The mountains at the edge, at the rim of Mother Earths flat round surFACE that were reflected or 'drawn' in the standing 'waters' below. (SOUNDS like drown). The SHAPE of the mountain peaks on the edge of the flat circular rim on the surFACE of Mother Earth were like the mouths on the face of the individual mother. The mouth like SHAPE of the mountain peaks on the edge expanding to become the letter (M) dealt with the SHAPE that came to be mirrored in Her reflective watery depths as the letter (W).

Existence above the surFACE of Mother Earth dealt with life and its maintenance (MA). The 'drawn' reality in the reflected waters (WA) dealt with the watery womb of death to which the human soul had become attached. Passage across some sort of dangerous water of reeds of a river after death claimed the body is a constant in many of the mythologies of the world. It probably had its origins out of the ancient African migrations and the passage across crocodile infested rivers of death on their way to the 'promised land' of the verdant savannahs.

The concept locked in the letter (W) deals not only with water but with the metaphorical reflective surface of death and the accompanying puckered up trembling, *lower lip* of grief. That grief had been expressed primarily for the loss of the sun's rays at twilight and the perilous dangers locked in the dark predatory night.

The second major grief emerged out of males asking WHY of their peripheral state. The heterosexual males grieved that no baby issued forth from their bodies, that they had a permanently empty belly. The other WHY dealt with the castrated eunuchs, the smiths and herdsmen who not only became castrated but in PHASE TWO had their one leg mutilated in the service of the emerging metallurgic and herding no longer migrating societies.

In PHASE ONE the SHAPE of the letter (W) of the reflected *lower lip* on the face of the mother joined the top lip creating the possibility of humming that said yes to life and the acceptability of the presented food. Closed, it held the contents in place. Within the cavity of the mouth the dead food was chewed, milled, ground into smaller moistened pieces so that it could be swallowed to make its life supporting journey down the gullet and not be allowed to wallow in the mouth before it descended into the belly.

The SHAPE of the letter (W) as the double (UU) became associated with the creation of life in the individual mother's body. She was the one (U). The fetus was another (U). Together they created the double (UU). The mother became defined as the WOMB of WOMAN, containing within her belly the 'hidden' WATERY sac of fetal survival. The letter (V) surfaces here also for it is within the watery vagina and vulva that life has its beginnings as a via of passage.

In Arabic wa stands for 'and' (repetitive procreation), as wa'a in 'awake' it has to deal with a baby making its first SOUND at birth. In Swahili wa means 'to be' associating it with water either as the placental sac or water on the body of Mother Earth. In Polish way up there in the cold Northern reaches of Europe the letter (W) pronounced as a (V) simply means 'in' the mothers body. The (V) nd (W) have often become interchangeable.

In North Africa a wadi (WADA) is a dry via of passage for an intermittent rush, or gift (DA) of water (WA). Similar word surfaces in wood (WADA). It too is (DA) 'the gift of' water (WA), as is weed (WADA). How about wade (WADA)? All need the gift of water to survive. In Polish vodka (VADAKA) is the small (KA) of water, woda (VADA). Here the (V) and (W) are obviously interchangeable. Mother Earth also turned to Her watery effulgence out of her horizontal rim as rain poured down from the sky. It made HER and all of Her creations WET establishing an ancient linguistic concept of weather (WET HER) or HER becoming WET.

On the surFACE of Mother Earth the reflected quality of WATER also created a variety of concepts. One was to feed into the evolution of the number seven (IS EVEN or HAVANA). It was in the reflective surFACE of the quietly standing pools of water, on the expansive marshes and great lakes of the Rift Valley and the Okavongo River Delta in Africa that the concept of evenness (HAVANA-) came into being. The physical reality above as life on the body of Mother Earth was evenly (HAVANA-) reflected as the metaphor for death in the standing waters on Her surFACE.

Thunder in the far distance alerted the elephants to start the ancient semi-annual migrations. Monsoon waters gushed from the sky creating pools of standing waters and raging rivers that our humanoid and human ancestors had to pass following the herds of the wildebeest and zebra to get to the verdant grass of the 'promised land' on the other side. Those waters were filled not only with hungry waiting crocodiles but also with angry territorial hippopotamus. The concept of passing a river of death to get to the 'promised land' in the distance surfaces in mythologies all around the world.

In PHASE ONE it evolved into the concept of 'rebirth' as the verdant grass filled the hungry migrating bellies with new life. In PHASES TWO and THREE it became an imaginative 'spiritual' journey sourced by the mind. For the Hebrews it was the River Jordan. For the Greeks it was the Acheron and the Styx. For the Romans it was the Cocytos. The Chinese called it HO-T-SU. For the Japanese it was the Sanzunokawa. For Gilgamesh, the curious prince of Sumer it was the River Kur. His great contribution was that he debunked the ancient belief in reincarnation, that the human soul (IS HALA) followed the same journey of rebirth as did the solar (IS HALA-) disc through the body of Mother Earth. It threw the ancient Middle Eastern world into chaos and helped to forge some of the nails that began to lock the ancient systems of mother centrality and the worship of Mother Earth as 'source' into a coffin of oblivion.

The ancient migrations also fed into the number seven (IS EVEN). The ancient year in PHASE ONE had been primarily based on the constant predictable passage of the thirteen phases of the moon that worked in concert with the passage of blood out of female bodies. The ancient migrations began in March or early April at the time of the Spring Equinox and the accompanying estral orgy, with the trekkers traveling six months to the 'promised land' of grass in the verdant savannah. The herbivore mares gave birth to their foals and in the seventh (IS HAVANA-) month, halving the thirteen month lunar year into two even (HAVANA) sections journeyed back to their beloved mountains.

The celestial bodies were perceived to sink into the waters on the edge of the Western wall into the waiting mountainous mouths, the holes on the edge of the flat circular surFACE of Mother Earth. Ancient burial sites were situated in such a way that as the sun sank in the Western waters it could be reflected in the waters below. They were usually situated on the West side of the standing reflective still waters of a river or lake. It was on the Western side of the waters that the sun died to its light, so the human soul accompanying the journey of the sun, sol (IS HALA) in Spanish also had to be buried on the Westren side of standing waters.

The letter (W) of the *lower lip* dealt with the SOUND of wailing, of the holding of wakes, of the (OO) or (UU) at the watery Western wall of passage where the sun disappeared back into the body of Mother Earth, dying to is light, saying no to life, being killed outright, dragging the cloak of nocturnal (NAKA-) darkness in its wake embarking on a journey guided by the ubiquitous snake (IS NAKA) through the body of Mother Earth. It was on those darkening shores that the eunuchized priesthood with the crippled smithies and herdsmen beat their chests, wailed their grief, not only at the loss of the blessed light of the sun, which was bad enough, but began to wail WHY

Section Three

of their often enslaved and peripheral state hammering out the theological speculations that exist to this day.

The battle involving the individual mother and the body of Mother Earth began in earnest in PHASES TWO and THREE as on the one hand heterosexual males began to discern their roles in specific paternity (the begats of the Bible) and on the other hand the eunuchized priesthood also began to ask WHY, and to question their peripheral state. The limping hobbling around his forge smithy has a long and recurrent history surfacing in many mythologies of the world. The most virulent contemporary literary classic deals with the obsessive one legged Captain Ahab in 'Moby Dick' doing battle with the Kundalini energy, the dreaded white whale, Mother Earth in her most powerful and gigantic aspect as the monster of the watery deep, ie death, echoing the Babylonian Tiamat. They kill each other creating their own prophecy as males not only abuse and vilify women but desecrate the sacred body of Mother Earth. It is a disquieting tale fortelling the future as men do war against all that motherhood represents. The mutilated smithy surfaces more benignly in a television series 'Gunsmoke' as Chester the limping smithy.

The WAR that bears witness to the battle between emerging males and the ancient mothers moved onto a larger metaphorical stage. It embraced the whole planet as it established a reflection of the battles in PHASES TWO and THREE between the emerging male powers and the ancient entrenched mothers on the plane below.

As males became aware of their role in paternity and fatherhood they needed to create their own process and definition of 'source' *away* from the body of Mother Earth.

Searching for a 'source' *away* and *above* the body of Mother Earth males already had links with the sun, at times the moon, and the stars. Their battles with female centrality became likened to the battle that the sun had to fight every night as it followed its nose into the horizontal hole in the Western wall of watery death. Mother Earth swallowed the sun every night, killed it to the rays of its light, ate it, made it disappear. That's how males felt what had been happening to them at the time of female centrality in PHASE ONE. The sun became their apt metaphor. As EL (HALA) or AL HALA) it had already established its links with the solar (IS HALA-) disc. What males needed was something much more aggressive and violent, more in keeping with the rape that was happening to the females and their children that needed the first son to be castrated to protect the family. They turned to the Egyptian Ra, the sun God who emerged as raging, roaring fire out of the bowels of Mother Earth after She swallowed him at twilight into the gory Western waters, transforming himself as he passed through Her intestines, erupting as lavic blood out of Her volcanic vents.

The (WA) of the waters on the body of Mother Earth plus the Ra of the resistant sun created the dyad of WAR (WARA) reflecting the battle that was occurring between mothers (MA) and the emerging fathers (RA) on the Earthly plane below. It was at the time in PHASE TWO that this dyad of WAR (WARA) linguistically surfaced on the planet and the world (WARA(LA)DA) became defined by it. The concept that it was the watery mouth of Mother Earth that swallowed the sun in the West surfaces in Polish as WARga (WARAga) defining the *lower(laWARA) lip*. It had been perceived that words had been created by the *lower lip* on the face of the mother. Water (WA(TA)RA) contains in its inguistic structure the possibility of violence and war as it swallows the sun and declares with words the activity of WAR.

It became apparent to our ancient ancestors that the process inHERent in life dealt with the hunt and to be hunted, eat and be eaten became the reality. The bigger creature ate the smaller creature and so on down into an orgy of stalking and killing. If you wanted to stay alive you killed any creature that could sustain you. A war (WARA) existed on the Earthly plane between all creatures. No one was spared. The body of Mother Earth in PHASE TWO became defined by it in the name of the emerging world (WARA(LA)DA)). To hunt (HANA-) dealt with the sun (IS HANA). It was perceived that Mother Earth hunted the sun as it made its way across the sky following its naïve nose until it fell afoul of the hole on the edge either among the mountainous mouths or the standing bodies of Western WAter.

It was originally Mother Earth, the lady (LADA) of the land that understood and accepted the activity of mass murder of Her creatures coming and going as an aspect of survival as the dyads in world (WARALADA) proclaim.

Then with male centrality gaining ground in PHASE TWO and with men beginning to define their centrality and power bases based on explanations, justifications and 'reason' they deleted the lady (LADA) of the land off the name of Her world (WARALADA) it became theirs emerging as the Written WORD (WARADA), the (DA) as the 'gift of 'WAR (WARA). Hidden in its linguistic folds is the reflection of death in the waters below as they had been reflected on the lower (LA*WARA) lip* of the mothers, the WARga as the *lower lip* in Polish.

So it came to be that 'IN THE BEGINNING WAS THE WORD', defining a new mental reality taking root in the left hemisphere of the male brain no longer based on the balanced feelings, trance states and intuition of the mothers. The word (WARADA) was the (DA) 'gift of' war (WARA) as human males following the example set by the violent North Congo male chimps, humanity's closest cousins not only fought for territory, control, power and survival but for the sport of it as the reality of universal war against all creatures and the body of Mother Earth beset the worsening (WARA-) human condition.

The word became a tool for war. Because words carried such weight being associated with that which like the breath floated upon the air as the Bardo of the Tibetan ' intermediate state', the air was considered to be sacred. Therefore words also emerged as being sacred and available only to the cogniscenti. They took on a life of their own as spells and objects of secrecy and WOnder. The concept of worship (WARA-) of the word entered the picture.

Out of that linguistic context the sWORD became a tool of war as did a reWARD of looting after the killing was done. Originally a WARD of the emerging state was a captured slave who did all of the work (WARAKA). Within that linguistic construct you have not only (KA) as work being the small war (WARA KA) but (RAKA) the Polish reka (RAKA) or hand of face to face combat with the sWORD. It was also perceived that worry (WARA) was to be at war with yourself. Someone must have thought that war was a weird (WARADA) condition as they longed for the days of mother centrality and a relatively predictable peaceful world.

The LINGUISTIC BREAK surfaces with the letter (W) of the *lower lip* no longer reflecting the (M) of the top lip and on the body of Mother Earth associated with water. It becomes apparent that we are straddling a new PHASE TWO male reality dealing with sedentary societies and the emergence of herding and metallurgy. What surfaces in Phoenician, Egyptian and Semitic is the hook or the support pole for the maimed shepherds and blacksmiths who had to lean on their staffs. What also surfaces is the woo SOUND of weeping and wailing as a result of inflicted pain. A similar concept surfaces under the letters L, F, Y, and V. The Greek Woo as epsilon is a fancy way of symbolizing the support pole or hook. The Etruscan W as a F or V also has links with the furka, a fork, hook or crutch as does digamma of the Egyptians Set, the ass headed god of the setting sun was sacrificed on a furka, a fork or a crutch. He had to go through the symbolic mule, ride upon the metaphoric ass, the buttocks on the mother's body, go through the mysterious process of transformation within her, to become 'born again', a hybrid. Christ was crucified on a cross like wooden rood. As the redefinitions solidified in PHASE THREE, the limping shepherd leaning on his staff became the redefined gentle caretaker of human souls establishing his ancient links with the eunuchized avuncular uncle out of a distant PHASE ONE.

THE LETTER V

A VOICED LABIO-DENTAL FRICATIVE

SOUND; voiced V (VEE), friction of air against bottom lip

SHAPE; angle of creation, via of passage

MOTHER'S body; vulva, vagina, vocal cords, vision

MOTHER EARTH; *vias*, volcanoes, *vents*, valleys, lava, live, hive

CONCEPT; hinged valve of the *via* of passage

V-The letter V as via (VAYA) or vent (VANATA) in some languages is often interchangeable with the letter W (WAYA). In Polish woda as water is pronounced voda. In Persian both words contain the passage of the aya of light. The letter V as the apparent angle had been considered to belong to the ancient mothers. The letter W had links with the surFACE and body of Mother Earth as the waves upon Her watery surFACE, a magnificent *via* of passage.

The letter V as an angle comes out of the SHAPE of many organs on the indiVidual mothers surface and body. To begin with the face or head of the indiVidual mother the letter V (VAYA) as an angle began its life out of the two orbs, the eyes (AYAS) that sat laterally on either side of the nose. The angle comes out of the perception that the pupil of the eye had been the actual angle of the letter V lying on its side and as Vision spread out to create the central and peripheral capacity to see. The SHAPE of the letter V lying on its side acted as a Vehicle for the unrelenting mass of images that made their home in the brain, specifically in the left hemisphere. Perceptively lower than the mothers face, the neck makes its appearance. The internal Vocal chords, although not apparently Visible on the outside created the angled SHAPE within the throat that dealt with SOUND, with Vomiting or regurgitation. When the Vocal chords parted they created a *via* of passage for food, Vomit, SOUND and the supporting breath that gave birth to life. When they rested together, they created the equal (=) sign of closure. It was also the place at the pharynx that a dam had been created with the Vocal chords acting like a guard at the gate that kept the contents in and the inVaders out. The word Vomit (VAMATA) establishes its links with the vent (VA) of the mouth (MATA) of the mother (MATA-).

The most apparent V on the indiVidual mother's body which often defined her is the triangled outside SHAPE of the Vulva and the intuited internal SHAPE of the Vagina, the *vias* of passage for the emergence of living creaturers on her surface. The vulva (VALAVA) acted like a valve (VALAVA) of constant returning and the returning was of life itself. Vagina (VAJANA) has links with the Greek gyno (JANA) for woman and the giant jenie (JANA) that when it rubbed the bottle it brought forth three wishes. The bottle or pot with its long neck and bulbous bottom had been likened to the Vagina and the oVary (HAVA-). It was the ovary (HAVA-) that established the gift of having (HAVA-). In this case the perception had been that it wasn't the liver that had been the seat of coagulated blood creating the baby but it was the SHAPE of the metaphorical pot or bottle that gave birth to a liVing creature.

In the word indiVidual there hides linguistic links with the word for diVision. When a mother gave birth, created a liVing creature she rendered herself in twain. She diVided herself into two apparently diVerse pieces becoming her and her offspring. That's where the word deVision comes in. That is where the words apparent for the parent had their beginnings. It was the mother with her distended belly that had been considered to be the apparent parent. At this time when these concepts were being codified in PHASE ONE male role in specific procreation had been unknown.

On the body of Mother Earth the *vias* of passage are the triangular SHAPED Volcanoes, that when reflected in the waters below create the diamond SHAPE that surfaces in the Maya and others. There had been *vias* of passage for the bloody magmic laVa that turned into land, caping the land with fire and blasting Her way through tubular Vents beneath Her surFACE. The Valleys etching their way across Her skin were the *vias* of passage for the rains that churned into raging riVers and turned the parched saVannas into marshy swamplands. She created the air aboVe Her surFACE, oVer Her creations out of Her sissing Vents. The CONCEPT expressed through the angled letter V is the SHAPE of the *vias* that acted as the vehicles of creation.

THE LETTER F

A LABIO DENTAL VOICELESS FRICATIVE

SOUND; unvoiced V, friction of air against bottom lip

SHAPE; splayed out fingers

MOTHER EARTH; first fan of four or five fingers of fire at dawn,

CONCEPT; fingers of creation manifested by the rays of the sun

The SHAPE of the letter F deals with the splayed out fingers associated with the human hand and as rays of the flaming sun extending to the body of Mother Earth. The SOUND encoded in the letter F deals with the FH, or PH SOUND made by the air escaping or being pushed out of the top lip of the partially closed mouth.

It shares that SOUND of air escaping out of the fissures and vents, the cracks and breaks out of the surFACE on the body of Mother Earth, out of Her many top lips of creation. Carried upon that escaping air on Her surFACE out of Her planetary mouths the fingers become the helping hands that as the four or five fingers of fire, like flaming stilettos pierced through the darkness of night and as rays of light fought their way up to the surFACE creating a passage for the sun to be born out of Her opening at Her Eastern horizontal rim.

On the other side of the body of Mother Earth the same fingers of fire as rays of light disappeared out of sight back into Her body, dying to their light creating the perils of the dark night. The letter F establishes the fingers as the helping hands of Mother Earth expressed through the activity of the sun rising at dawn into a new life pushed to the surFACE by the ever ready fingers of fire and pulled back down into the Western blood splattered watery abyss at twilight. The five fingers including the V SHAPE created by the opposable thumb represented the helping hands of the sun and the V the Latin number five, the upper part of number X halved laterally or ten in Roman. The four fingers without the opposable thumb of holding became the male number dealing with four. In PHASE ONE Males had not been involved in the maintenance and holding of children.

In Swahili FA means 'to die'. In Persian FADA means 'sacrifice'. The 'gift of' (DA) death of (FA), the rays of the sun as the fingers of fire being snuffed out. In Arabic FANA means annihalation and non-being, the sun lost to its

Section Three

light. (NA) deals with the 'negation of a former state'. In Chinese FU is the symbol of reversal'.

FA also deals with the concept of 'less than' as the fingers of fire disappear off the Western rim, the sun FAdes, FAlls, off the body of Mother Earth, into Her cravassic FAult on Her Western side FAiling Her creatures with the promise of light giving up as Fatigue makes Her descend into the Frightening abyss.

The CONCEPT out of the letter F deals with the fingers as the rays of the sun, the helpers of Mother Earth in the birth and death of Her most important assistant and helper, the sun. For Atunkhamen in PHASE THREE the Egyptian pharaoh (FA-) created the sun as the singular God dealing with the solar disc as the monotheistic concept of the helping hands (HANAda) of Mother Earth. He and it didn't last long. Shinto (IS HANAta) as the 'gift of' (DA) the sun (IS HANA) in Japan establishes the sun (IS HANA) as their major deity.

In Latin Fa means 'to speak'. Words at some times and some places were not considered to be the real thing. They were the products of the mind and like opinions were creatures of the air. Pinion is a 'birds wing' and the vowel O became one of the male symbols. Not only the words shared the fate of fantasy but phonetics (FANA-) and phonemes (FANA-) also emerged as phony (FANA). The FA phoneme not only gave us the FAn of FAntasy, that which emerged out of the FA of FAbricating, but also the realization that we are in male centrality in PHASE THREE for FA also defines the FAther. In PHASE TWO as male role in specific procreation was becoming known the FAT HER was the one who made HER FAT

In PHASE THREE with the evolution of male power and redefinition the father became the speaker, the holder of the word, the creator of FAtum in Latin 'that which had been spoken', and FAte 'that which had been spoken by the Gods'. Since the male God rose into the heavens and 'hid' from sight, tomes of phantastic (FANA-) writings had to be used to create His reality. That which is real does not need to be repeated over and over. It is self evident. In Spanish FE surfaces as FAith. FAntasy as the FAith of the FAthers sourced by the imagination as FAlasehood redefined the emerging PHASE THREE world. To that linguistic buffet can be added FAbles, FAbrications and adult FAiry tales. The baby was no longer the coagulated blood of the mother. It became the Fetus (FATASA) sourced by the seminal waters of the father the one who made her FAT.

In Greek the word Phantasia (FANA-) SOUNDS like the English word fantasy (FANA) but means 'that which is made visible'. When something is made visible it means that once it had been hidden. It was the FANTASY as the FAith of the FAthers that had been perceived to be hidden. In PHASE THREE as the redefinitions proliferated the FAntasy revealed the FAith of the fathers that became the universal FAte of the mothers.

The number four (FARA) as the triangle of the mother plus one more shares its linguistic links with the Egyptian FAther as the pharaoh (FARA-) to the crowd of his followers, as did the Feuhrer (FARA-) of the Nazis. The Greek PH verbal construct also surfaces in the word phallus (FALASA) for penis.

After the shift at the time of the LINGUISTIC BREAK the association of the letter F to the body of the individual mother and to the surFACE and body of Mother Earth become occluded as the redefinitions tried to find their source. The letter F as the First Fan of the Four or Five Fingers of Flaming Fire that like Flashing stilettos Fought their way through the rim on the edge of the body of Mother Earth to break through First at dawn and to be swallowed back Fast into Her bloody waters in the West. In Etruscan and Roman the SHAPE of the letter F as emerging out of the SHAPE of the rays of the sun Fanning out at dawn say little about their source out of the face and body of the individual mother or the surFACE of Mother Earth. The Greek Digamma surfaces with the SHAPE of the letter F but in PHASE THREE already in male centrality defines it as a furka or fork associated with the limping shepherd and smith. In Semitic the hook or furka is called a WAW. Also for the Greeks the SOUND of the letter F was W (ff) made in the same area of the mouth.

The syllable FA is the FOURTH note on the musical scale. What does surface in Phoenician, Egyptian, Semitic and Sinai is the hook, crutch or furka that had been associated with the limping smith and shepherd. As the horned viper in Egyptian and Greek it deals with the Forked tongue of the snake that bears witness to the SHAPE of crutch or furka. The SHAPE of the furka (FARAKA) gave birth to the English fork (FARAKA). The small (KA) fingers (FA) of the sun (RA).

In Cypriotic the only recognizable relationship to the Female body surfaces in the symbol for Fava and Fava is a bean. The bean to the life of a plant is like the SHAPE of the FEtus is to a FEmale body. The curve underneath the Female buttox establishes the perception that something is trying to push its way up to the surface. The (Fa) in Fava are the Fingers of Fire that try to Flush the promise of life up to the surFACE out of the vent (VA-) on the body of Mother Earth or the vulva (VA-) on the body of the individual mother. In Cypriotic FO looks like plants also trying to make that same compelling

Fight. As the SHAPE of the letter (T) the phoneme FO also established its relationship to the surface or TOP. In Etruscan the letter F facing to the left comes out of writing having been done by the left Fingers of the PHASE ONE mothers and their castrated First born Facilitators. As the number Five became associated with the maintaining capacity of the mother's with their two hands working in concert so without the opposable thumb of work and maintenance the number Four became in PHASE THREE a male number and symbol.

THE LETTER D

A VOICED ALVEOLAR STOP.

SOUND; voiced letter T, tip of tongue against the top teeth

SHAPE; circle halved vertically, dome like container

MOTHER'S body; dent (teeth), abDOMEn, dome of skull, fist

MOTHER EARTH; dirt

CONCEPT; (DA) 'the gift of'

D-The letter D deals with the SHAPE out of which gifts occur; of busy fingers (dactyls), helping hands, of distended bellies as abDOMEns on the bodies of individual mothers before they gave birth, of the 'wise blood' of the mother that coagulated to present the present of life, of the two Dugs on her trunk that swelled with the promise of milk, of the Dome of the skull that gave birth to meaning. On the body of Mother Earth with Her gifts of light as the helping hands of Her celestial sun and with the gifts of rain water to quicken Her parched savannah for Her foraging creatures, all had been necessary to maintain life.

The letter D with its distended belly facing to the right as the anlaut for so many words, deals with 'giving' and 'doing' on a variety of levels. In English 'to do' is obvious. Past tense of 'to do' is 'did' (DADA). In Persian DA means 'do'. In Sanskrit 'to do' is also DHA. 'To do' with the two hands in Persian is DO. In Greek 'two' is DI. In Latin 'two is' DUO. In Polish 'two' is DWA, including water (W) as a reflective surface. In Latin and Italian DO is 'give'. In Spanish, Polish and Latin DA or DAR means 'to give'. In Sanskrit DA means 'She who bestows'. In Hebrew DAA was the 'bird of prey' a 'vulture', the one that dispatched the carrion to early absorption within the body of Mother Earth. The sooner you were reabsorbed, the sooner you could be reborn and bestowed with the 'gift of' new life. When you were reborn you said 'yes' to your new life. In Swahili N DAYA (NADAYA) means 'yes', as the sun said yes to a new day and the soul said yes to a new life. (AYA) means light in Persian and dawn in Assyrian. (NA) deals with emergence on the surface' or 'the negation of a former state', dealing with the rising of the sun and the emergence of the soul into a new life.

The same concept surfaces in the Chinese YIN (YANA or (HAYANA), as the female essence of daylight that also said 'yes' to life. To 'die (DAYA)' is the 'gift of' (D), of death. Death was considered to be the movement through darkness into the light, aya in Persian. Same construct surfaces in day (DAYA) as the 'gift of' (D) of aya, of light itself, carried by the sun that had spent the night in darkness within the body of Mother Earth. Dye (DAYA) is the 'gift of' (D), of color. It was the brilliant, blazing color of the rising sun at dawn that created the wonder leading to the howling of monkeys, the singing and the clapping of hands in awakened humanity.

Dry (DARAYA) is 'the gift of' (D) the rays (RAYA) and the heat of the scorching sun. In Spanish dar (DARA) means 'to give'. It could mean with the open hand, or with the pregnant belly. What becomes apparent here is that we are dealing linguistically with the body of Mother Earth. The open helping hands that flowed with life and light, as the rays of the sun, became the singular solar deity for Atun, considered the first monotheistic solar deity of Egypt. The rays of light emerged as the helping hands in the creation and maintenance of life upon Her body. The RA phoneme deals with the sun. In Persian dar (DARA) means 'to hold'. In Sanskrit the dar (DARA) of 'holding' comes out of PHASE TWO where the bossy male sun Ra as the solar disc held the body of Mother Earth as the volcanic cone under him. The activity of 'holding' as the potential carrier of the 'gift of', surfaces in Persian as dast (DASATA) for 'hand'. Dactyls (DAKA-) are fingers. In Greek deka (DAKA) is ten, not only as the 'gift of' (DA) creation of smaller (KA) aspects off the body of Mother Earth, but the ten deals with the concept of 'holding' with the ten fingers, tenere (TANA-), in Latin.

In Sanskrit Daksa (DAKASA) is the God of the Hand, 'gift of (DA) the coos (KASA). The Sanskrit name of Daksa, as the God of the Hand may deal with masturbation, the same activity that defined the Egyptian supreme God Amun (HAMANA) of the nocturnal sun, who masturbated existence into being every night. Both of them Daksa of the Hindus and Amun of the Egyptians, believed that the massaging of the clitoris during the birthing process producing repetitive orgasmic spasms, assisted in the bringing forth of a baby. So in PHASE THREE they created Gods who masturbated not only to bring forth a baby, but one better, to bring forth all of existence into being.

A little confusion enters the picture here as the redefinitions proliferate in PHASE TWO. Are we dealing with the ten fingers of the hand, the daksa (DAKASA) or with the female coos (KASA), the holders of the baby for ten lunar months of gestation. Also in Sanskrit dasa is the 'gift of' (DA) the 'blood' SA. In Old Iranian dasa is the name for ten. It would seem that the 'gift of' (D) of (SA), is the gift of blood for the ten lunar moths of gestation as it coagulates within the pregnant mother and solidifies into a baby. Sa for the Egyptians was the 'wise blood of the mother' that knew how to coagulate for ten lunar months within the mothers body to create a baby. In Persian the name for the 'hand' is dast (DASATA). In Lithuanian 'ten' of the ten fingers, or ten lunar months is desimi (DASAMA).

The CONCEPT of 'the gift of' associated with (D) deals either with the 'gift of (D) the ten fingers of the hand, or 'the gift of' the ten lunar months of gestation dealing with the mothers 'blood' that produced a baby, or the 'gift of' the sun as the 'bloody' offering of Mother Earth. The possibility of the 'blood' as the 'gift of' surfaces also in Swahili, as damu (DAMA). In English dam (DAMA) is a 'female'. In Spanish, as in Polish dama is a 'lady'.

The word dam (DAMA) also means something that is 'blocked up'. When the blood was blocked or dammed (DAMA-) up within a woman's body for ten lunar months the dam broke and she gave birth becoming a mother. In Wolof 'to break' is defined by the word damm (DAMA). It was believed that the coagulated dammed up blood in a woman's body had to break free to give birth to a baby. In Hebrew dam (DAMA) splays out from 'blood' to 'juice', 'sap' and 'red wine'. Dama in Hebrew means 'to be like', 'to resemble', 'to make like'. Only the mother can make one that 'is like her', 'resembles her', or is 'made like her'. In Polish the meaning takes a more basic turn. For in Polish dupa (DAPA) is the dyad for the ass. It surfaces in English as duplicate (DAPA-) or that which is repeated over and over, like a baby out of a mother's body. (DA) is the 'gift of' and (PA) deals with passage. It is similar to the Hebrew dama.

In the word demi (DAMA) the mother creates a 'smaller half' of herself. When the 'smaller half' grew up and she was a girl, as deme (DAMA), she became a ruler. Before she became the dame (DAMA), the mistress of the land, she was a damsel (DAMA-). In Greek demos (DAMASA) means 'people'. It was people who the damsel, deme and dama created out of her wise blood (SA). As she grew up she set up her own home, dom (DAMA) in

519

Polish. In Latin domus (DAMASA) is the name for 'house'. In Spanish the name for 'house' is casa (KASA), the 'gift of' holding of the family. It is the same linguistic construct as coos (KASA) performing the same if slightly more narrow function of containment. The demos (DAMA-) as the common Greek people gave birth to the name of democracy (DAMA-) out of the right hemispheric perception of the mother and not out of the left hemispheric dictatorship of the father.

The redefinitions begin to proliferate. In Hebrew Adam was made out of the mother's blood, but its not that simple. For adam (HADAMA) also means 'land' or 'ground'. As adamdam in Hebrew it means 'reddish'. Was Adam fashioned out of the reddish African clay of Mother Earth as the first man? Or was he fashioned out of the body of a personal mother in whose body the blood was dammed up for ten lunar months as she created him. He obviously emerged out of PHASE ONE when the male role in specific paternity was unknown.

In PHASE THREE to be 'damNed' (DAMA-) was to have been cursed by God. Did it apply only to women? Apparently it did. DamNing comes out of the dyad associated with the mothers as 'dam', 'dama', 'deme', the makers of babies out of their dammed up blood. Leaving the mother behind in PHASE ONE, in PHASE THREE only males, the father and the mind of God of the left hemispheric and right handed brain emerged as the singular tri parted source of creation. One of the names for the emerging new God had been and still is Dominus having linguistic links with the mother.

The repetition of phonemes surfaces here. Dad (DADA) in Hebrew means 'breast', or 'teat' (TATA). The two breasts, as dugs (DAGA-) are the 'double' 'gifts of' milk, the titties (TATA-). The (T) and (D) are interchangeable. In Hindi dudh (DADA) means 'milk'. In Persian dadan (DADANA) means 'to give', possibly out of the breasts as milk for (NA) deals with 'emergence on the surface'. The udder (haDADAra), as the other (haDAra) set of hanging teats on a herbivore mother, is also a giver of milk.

On the West Coast of Africa the God of Nature already in PHASE THREE was called DADA. The wandering Gypsies out of the Indus Valley called their father DAD or DADO (DADA). A current name for the father in English is DAD (DADA). The white seminal fluid that like milk flowed out of male penises defined them also as the 'givers' and creators of life. In PHASE THREE they became the sole contributors. The ancient mothers decried the redefinitions. They called the new male perceptions of their emerging centrality as a dud (DADA). The above ground gangs of roving band of brothers fought

Section Three

their way around the closely knit female clans. They used their fists to establish primacy. A fist is a daddle (DADA-), used not unlike a paddle.

One of the emerging male symbols in PHASE TWO was the square. From the square it became a more substantial object. It became a cube. A cube is a dado (DADA), and Orthodox Jews wear them as the tefilah on their heads and upper left arm when they pray. The Muslims went for something bigger and during their haj pray around the Kabba, a cube (KABA) in the desert.

The process of castration and circumcision surfaces here. Lopped off means dodded (DA-). Dodded (DADA-) also means hornless applying to bulls. Hornless is a euphemism for castration. In Hebrew dakka (DAKA) meant 'castration'. The 'gift of' (D), KA or Mother Earth making smaller aspects. A dod (DADA) was a process that made the top rounded. The rounding of the head of the penis originally in PHASE ONE dealt with castration and then in PHASE TWO circumcision, for dodded (DADA) means 'lopped off'. The dud (DADA) as a 'counterfeit thing', became a hybrid, a transformed male, a eunuch, no longer male and not quite female. In his gorgeous vestments, swaying before the altars of the setting sun, the dude (DADA) of old of the underground eunuch priesthood became the 'fastidious dresser'.

In Greek legend Daedalus (DADA-) having many creative gifts, become arrogant landing in jail, used his son Icarus to forge some wings out of left over feathers and wax, he had him fly too close to the sun and the son plunged into the sea. It establishes the battle between the father and the son. In this case the father of the son wins. This occurs in PHASE TWO with the emerging male role in paternity not only surfaces here, but the father gets rid of the son by making Mother Earth as water absorb him. The tale of the Biblical Abraham and Isaac and the sacrifice of the son surfaces here.

Shunting off to a different track, the 'gift of' (DI), of 'DIrection' is an 'erection'. A dildo (DA(LA)DA) is the 'gift of' the DADA, the angle of (LA) in the center, to pleasures the lady (LA-). The phoneme L has been associated with angles, of the tongue generally, the SHAPE of the sun's emergence in the East and on the male body as the erect penis.

The (-D-ED) on the end of English words deals with past tense, with what has been 'done or depicted'. In mind (MANADA) it is the 'gift of' (DA) holding (MA) and releasing (NA) of images, thought and meaning (MANA-). It is also associated with the 'gift of' (DA) the hands, manos in Spanish. In Hebrew da means 'to know', to say yes to wisdom, the house 'dom' In Polish of the 'wise'. In Russian da means 'yes'. To find (FANADA) deals with 'the gift of' (DA) of the fan (FANA), the SHAPE of the outstretched four fingers (FANA-)

that search out things. To fend (FANADA) off, is to create the 'the gift of' (DA) protection with the fan (FANA) of the fingers (FANA-).

In the word kind (KANADA) it establishes the (DA) as the 'gift of' the kin (KANA), the kindness as the 'gift of' protection, shared by relatives sharing the same skin (IS KANA).

To rend (RANADA) is to separate the fat from the meat. (DA) as the 'gift of' feeds into the process of rendering. In Polish one of the meanings of rana is 'wound'. To 'rend' (RANADA) is to create 'the gift of' the 'wound'. Practically only a wounded or sacrificial beast could be killed or rendered. In PHASE TWO as the possibility of a supreme male deity entered the scene, the name of God (GADA) established (DA) 'the gift of' begetting (GA-gha). In Polish the word gada surfaces as the 'prattler' the internal voice over within the mind that ceaselessly admonished the poor over evolved left hemispherically human creature with an endless litany, not only with rationalizations, explanations, judgments, corrections and orders, but with often erratic violent guidance (GADA-) to smite everything in sight.

It becomes apparent that the consonants stay relatively constant but the vowels do a SHAPE shifting dance all their own. The general concept that evolved into the letter D deals with 'the gift of', the fingers, the hands, the breasts, Her belly, the blood and emanations out of the body of Mother Earth, as sun and water. The SOUND encoded in the letter D has no apparent links to it's original SHAPE except that it uses the dome of the skull as its resonating chamber.

After the dextral shift into male centrality and the LINGUISTIC BREAK in PHASE THREE the hand out of stage three associated with the process of giving encoded in the letter D surfaces only in Egyptian. It establishes the concept that 'giving' dealt with the opening of a door in Phoenician, Hebrew and Egyptian. An open door is also an open fist, the fingers extended revealing the 'gift' that is given. In Etruscan the belly facing to the left as a template for the letter (D) dealing with the distended abdomen out of stage three establishes 'the gift of' life out of the individual mother. As a grub in Irish it also establishes the 'gift of' beginnings.

That opening as a (DA) 'gift of' also emerges out of the body of Mother Earth as the Greek delta (DALATA) the (DA) gift of water and fertile deposits of land. It is also the daleth (DALATA) or door in Hebrew and Phoenician. It was as if Mother Earth opened a door into Her body out of which the 'gift of' (DA) water and fertile land emerged like an angle (LA) out of Her tip, top (TA).

In Hebrew the SHAPE of the number seven pointing to the left establishes the '(DA) 'gift of' death (DATA). It deals with the SHAPE of the fall of the sun off the Western horizontal tip (TA) or side of Mother Earth into either, the swallowing waters, the toothy mouth, or the ultimate nihilistic abyss. The SHAPE of the door in Hebrew as a box deals with the tefilah, the gift of transformation and d'avening that Orthodox and Hassidic Jews practiced when they prayed. They wore the box or tefilah on their upper arm and forehead and prayed into the opening that dealt with an experience of God.

In Slavonic the letter D looks suspiciously like an anvil, the place where the maimed hobbling smith created tools and weapons out of metals (MATA-), 'gifts' out of the body of the Great Mother (MATA-) Earth.

(KS) (KASA) of the mother's coos (KASA) on the bottom of her buttox, with triad of creation on top, establishing the fact that the great Mother was Mother Earth as creatress, maintainer and destroyer. The phoneme DE also means 'away from'. When a gift is given it is taken 'away from' its source, be it the individual mother or the body of Mother Earth.

THE LETTER T

A VOICELESS ALVEOLAR STOP

SOUND; unvoiced letter D, tip of tongue against top teeth

SHAPE; arrow, pole with cross bar, tongue, tip, top, tail end

MOTHER'S body; tongue, titties, toes, teeth

MOTHER EARTH; tetons, Tara, tor, trees, transformation

CONCEPT; end run on tip, top, two, three, truth, tale, trance

T- The letter T deals with the tip, top or edge. Clues surface in words such as tongue that emerges out of the throat and has its end run on the floor of the oral cavity in stage one, the teeth that sprout out of the edge of the gums also out of stage one, the toes that create the end run at the tip of the feet in stage three, the tail that is always at the back end, the tip top of an animal's body.

The letter T in PHASE ONE dealt with that which came at the end, or the edge, like a tale that like a bell had to be tolled at the tail end of an exciting activity. On the individual mothers body it dealt with her titties that like milk-filled arrows pointed to the baby. On the body of Mother Earth it dealt with all of Her creations, all the things that She made out of Her vast terrain; these, those, they, them, that, all the its, even trees, that emerged out of Her body. All things that could be pointed to or touched with the tip of the finger. The concept that emerges out of the letter T deals with movement from inside to outside, with tenderly touching, pointing out individual creations or things with the piercing arrow SHAPE of emergence on the tip, top, edge or surFACE on the body of Mother Earth. It also deals with what that emergence defines; the uni-verse, truth, the numbers two and three of -teens and the role of trees.

The dyad TARA is not only an ancient linguistic construct dealing with the surFACE and body of Mother Earth Her terrain (TARA-) made out of the tar (TARA) that creates the tor (TARA), the terra (TARA) firma upon which all terrestrial (TARA-) creatures can have their being. In PHASE ONE Tara is also the name of an ancient Mother Earth Goddess representing the surFACE and body of Mother Earth from Ireland across the Middle East and Southern Asia.

As the uni-verse and one unit of creation the TARA dyad emerges out of early PHASE ONE when the surFACE of Mother (maTARA) Earth, Her tip, top (TA) and the sun (RA) worked as one collaborative balanced unit. Out of that perception the concept of truth (TARATA) came into being. Ancient truth dealt with that which came back up to the surFACE of Mother Earth out of Her majestic intuitive throat (TARATA) as the law of the land deals with the ratio (RATA) of a circular passage of all that died and their constant return (RATA-) back up to Her surFACE. She spoke to Her creations in a thousand different ways to help them to survive. It was natural law that held sway, not as in PHASE THREE the pronouncements made by emerging mostly hidden male sky Gods.

Mother Earth regurgitated the sun (RA) at dawn in the Eastern sky out of Her pregnant belly and then Her throat (TARATA) creating the terrain (TARA-) upon which Mother Nature could speak and write Her laws. Since the overlapping dyads truth (TARATA) and throat (TARATA) come from exactly the same linguistic roots it must have been that truth telling out of the throat was native to humanitys ancient mothers in PHASE ONE. With the asking of WHY of male periphery in PHASE TWO and the answers to that WHY as theoretical speculation, that lying came into being.

THE ANSWER TO WHY IS ALWAYS A LIE.

In both the words for throat (TARATA) and truth (TARATA) the second dyad is (RATA) and (RATA) deals with the ratio (RATA) of a circle, its return (RATA-) back up to the surFACE of Mother Earth as the circular journey of the sun, the law out of of lava and the planet of emerging plants.

The concept of three (TARA) must have very ancient roots for it goes back not only to the SHAPE of the triangular volcanic cone on the body of Mother Earth and the reflected hairy pubis on the individual mother's body but into the tryad (TARAda) dealing with trees (TARA). Because trees existed within the envelope of air that surrounded the body of Mother Earth in the air as one of the 'intermediate states' between the body of Mother Earth and the sun, because air was associated with the living breath they were both considered to be sacred. It had also been perceived that trees pulled the circulating water up just inside of their trunks up from the body of Mother Earth. Since water had also been considered as a conductor of electricity they knew that it had been the electro magnetic Kundalini energy coming up from the body of Mother Earth that united the electro magnetic energy with the sacred air above Her. Throughout the ancient world ttrees had been worshipped. They also understood that the spiral spin that fused the body of Mother Earth with the sun working in concert out of the uni-verse concept. In Greek that spiral spin within the tree was called atractos (haTARAkatasa) a word for the 'spindle'. The tree with its fan of roots (RATA) under the ground within the body of Mother Earth and its fan of branches spreading across the sun lit sky acted like a bridge of passage using the trunk (TARAnaka) as a metaphoric unifying 'spindle' to weave the web of fate.

It also surfaces with the number three (TARA) not only as the triad of trees as roots, trunk and branches but for a much more ancient concept dealing with Mother Earth as the triad (TARA-) of existence; creatress, maintainer and destroyer, a concept that extended to most of the ancient specific Goddesses that came to personify Her. The ancient triad originally out of the volcanic cone SHAPE out of the body of Mother Earth and the reflected pubic triangle out of the body of the individual mother in PHASE THREE morphed into the trinity (TARA-) dealing with the Hebrew Star of David, Father, Son and Holy Ghost in Christianity and the Krishna, Vishnu and Siva triad in Hinduism.

The body of Mother Earth as the law of the land also contained not only the (TARA) dyad that defined Her terrain (TARA-) but also other maintaining aspects. Upon Her snowy summits She flowed with tetonic milk. It was the Tetons (TATANASA) that reflected the titties (TATASA) on the individual mother's body or the other udders on the bodies of Her surrogates. On the individual mother's body the titties (TATASA) filled with milk pointing like arrows toward the mouth of the baby creating all the magical passionate bonding love that followed. The repetitive dyad of (TATA) deal with the SHAPE of the firm pointed titties of a young mother with her first baby. (TANA) in Tetons (taTANAta) expresses the concept of 'holding' tenere (TANAra) in Latin. It have had its origin out of the ten (TANA) fingers that did the holding out of stage three. Or in may move to the body of the individual human mother counting the ten (TANA) months of lunar gestation that she held the fetus within her body out of stage three. The dyad ten (TANA) out of either the ten fingers or ten months of gestation moved into the emotional state of tenderness (TANA-) the (DA) 'gift of' the ten (TANA) fingers that tended tenderly. It is also the Tatoo (TATA) that covers the skin with accompanying tenderness.

With the tips of the fingers of both hands touching they created a tent (TANAta) like SHAPE that became a symbolic sign of hemispheric fusion and transformation. It also reflected the most ancient Mother based house of creation the three sided tent echoing the most majestic SHAPE of creation on the body of Mother Earth Her three sided volcanic cone that gave birth to the letter A(ah) and alpha as the creation of land on Her surFACE.

After a great cataclysm and the loss of many of the original concepts locked in the capital letters that survived as the Western Alphabet after the LINGUISTIC BREAK, the only SHAPES that are reminiscent of the TIP of anything are the TI of Linear B, the triangular SHAPE that survived in the tent and the teepee, the Old Indian symbol on its side. Out of Mesopotamia it also emerges as TI and is associated with an 'arrow' and 'to give'. The tips of the fingers of the hand do the giving. The TE in Linear B throws it back to the Phoenician symbol for X as the sun working in concert with the body of Mother Earth, born at one tip in the East passing overhead, and setting on the other side in the West, the other tip on Her body, dissecting the three parted body of Mother Earth to make its appearance on Her surFACE. In Polish TA deals with the finger pointing to specific things; (to, tamto, this, that etc. same activity in Chinese for the TA symbol but a more personal pointing to he, she, it.

The letter T as the Arabic, Phoenician, Egyptian hieroglyph cross seems to have links with the letter X, but it may deal with the daily passage of the sun from East to West and the birds from North to South semiannually across the body of Mother Earth. The Greek TAU seems like a movement up to the lateral surface of a singular vertical object. Same in Old Indian. The Cypriotic TA in and out, deals with inhalation and exhalation of the breath. Together they form the letter H which deals with the air as breath.

Section Three

The Egyptian hieroglyph T as a curve across a flat surFACE defining a 'loaf' of BREAD reeks with creative thinking. As the sun rose in the East on one tip or side of Mother Earth to create the SHAPE of the belly of air above Her surFACE to help maintain Her creatures, so the 'loaf' of bread also rose with the yEAST to create a similar SHAPE as the belly of life's maintenance on a more mundane level. The Y in YEAST deals with the female pubis, the maker of the loaf of bread. A loaf (LAFA) and life (LAFA) share the same linguistic links. (LA) is the SHAPE of the sun's emergence out of the Eastern tip of Mother Earth. (FA) deals with Her solar rays as the five solar fingers of fire that flamed across the Eastern firmament at Her tip, to create the belly of passage across Her top.

After the shift into male centrality in PHASE THREE anything that questioned the newly cognizant Middle Easterners of their emerging role in paternity had to be demoted, especially the bloated body of the pregnant mother. The abdominal curve on her belly, the solar curve above the belly of Mother Earth *AND* the risen 'loaf of bread' had to be flattened down. To that end the matzoh (MATA-) bread had to be delivered of its yeast to become the leavened 'flat' bread not only of the Hebrews but of the whole Middle East. The ancient PHASE ONE memory that life emerged out of the mother's body not out of the mind of God had to be dealt with on all levels. The Arabian burkas forced on women to hide their swelling bellies followed the same perception.

THE LETTER S

A VOICELESS ALVEOLAR GROOVED FRICATIVE

SOUND; siss or hiss

SHAPE; two broken circles, one above, one below the line, snake

MOTHER'S body; no specific SHAPE, menstrual blood (SA)

MOTHER EARTH; spiral spin, hurricanes, tornadoes, lavic blood (SA)

CONCEPT; internal hidden movement of existence, 'isness', 'being', 'is' in English, 'est' in Latin, 'es' and 'esta' in Spanish, 'jest' in Polish

The Sissing Sister at the Cistern

The letter S-The SOUND associated with the letter S has no corresponding SHAPE that creates it either out of the individual mothers face in stage one, or her body in stage three. The SOUND associated with the letter S in stage one is of sissing out of the human mouth made by the front and sides of the tongue wedged up against the palate with the air being pushed through.

The letter S establishes its SOUND conjointly with the body of Mother Earth, the sissing and hissing at Her vents and fissures, out of Her many creative mouths, Mother Earth breathing AND creating the air above Her surFACE in Her belly of air. It is the SOUND of 'isness', the dual activity of breathing, of inspiration and of expiration. It is the intuited and perceived SHAPE, if not the SOUND of spiral spins, of hurricanes, tornadoes and whirlpools, of the hidden internal engine of helical solar magmic life that as lavic blood creates external movement.

As the movement that animates life, it is also associated with the pulsation of blood (SA) hidden under the skin within both the individual mother's body and the magmic cum lavic blood (SA) of Mother Earth. As the SASA dyad it emerges to define the process associated with the activation of the Kundalini energy in both the individual mother (SA) and the expansive body of Mother Earth, the other (SA). The double (SASA) exists at the end of mothers names; mistreSS, laSS, priesteSS,

GoddeSS, actress, etc. It is also the SHAPE of the spiral spin closed off at one end breaking off the open ended helical coil of existence associated with the solar wind, to create individual specific forms of life.

At the beginning of mostly English words the (SA) syllable is an empnatic and stands for it is. To get to the original meaning of the subsequent (SA) syllable at the beginning of mostly English words has to be removed Skin (IS KIN) or (KANA). At the ends of mostly English words the letter (S) or (ES) stands for plurality, as in skins. The (S) deals with blood (SA) as the maker of plural agents.

Since the metaphoric ubiquitous snake out of prehistoric times in PHASE ONE became the guide of the sun helping it to find its way back up to the surFACE, at one with Mother Earth along with the bee and goose became one of Her major creature symbols of existence. The slithering, sinuous, seductive, sissing serpent or snake, dragon, Leviathan even worm became Her greatest mythological metaphors in, out, above and under Her body, followed by the equally soaring, sissing swans and the symbols of truth, Her equally ubiquitous geese.

The sissing Phrygian Serpent God SAbazius (IS HABASASA) representing the ancient 'snake people' became the companion of the great Mother of the Gods, ie Mother Earth. The Nessians (NASASANA) had also been considered as the 'snake people' they expanded into the South Pacific as PolyneSSians (-NASASANA), and MelaneSSians (-NASASANA-).

Section Three

Out of Egypt SA associated with the Goddess Isis (HASASA) represented not only the 'wise blood' of the Mother but the 'spirit of intelligence'. The Greeks took it up with the definition for 'knowledge' as gnosis (ganaSASA). Could the Minoan Cretan KnoSSos (-NASASASA) be far behind? The (G) and (K) are interchangeable. The (IS) plus (IS) of Isis reiterates the concept of the dual activity of 'isness' out of the individual mother's menstrual blood (SA) and the lavic blood (SA) of Mother Earth. Also out of Egypt the great Goddess SAis (IS HASASA) linguistically carries in her name both the (SA) of the mother's 'wise blood and (IS) the concept of 'isness' out of the body of Mother Earth. Both phonemes surface linguistically in English holding on to their original concepts. It was the Goddess SAis who proclaimed in PHASE ONE 'I am all that was, all that is and all that is to come' which in PHASE THREE as the redefinitions proliferated into male centrality all that had been mother sourced had to be destroyed the saying became attributed to the Hebrew God Jehovah.

At the beginning of words the SOUND of the letter S becomes an emphatic and establishes the concept of 'it is' associated with the coursing 'hidden' movement of blood that travels under the skin. On the body of Mother Earth the dyad for skin (IS KANA) defines the skin as the source of the kin (KANA), or all those creatures who emerged out of the prolific body of Mother Earth, Her cone (KANA) of creation and were therefore related to each other.

Her volcanic cone (KANA) of creation with the lavic blood of potential spewing forth out of Her volcanic craters and vents brought forth the possibility of life upon Her surFACE. As the lavic stream of planetary menstrual magmic blood hardened into land upon Her plain it created Her skin (IS KANA), the place where all of Her related kin (KANA) could have their being. The (KA) deals with the creation of 'smaller aspects as all that Mother Earth created was considered to be smaller than She was. (NA) deals with either 'emergence on the surFACE' or 'a change from a former state' dealing with the 'hidden' magma emerging upon Her surFACE, slithering down Her flanks as lava and coagulating into land. In Kenya (KANAya) the volcano with volcanic tubes on the West side of the Great Rift called Mount Susswei (IS HASASAwaya) had been recognized as one of the magical creative lavic sources out of the body of Mother Earth.

The SA phoneme surfaces in Swahili as the number seven. It deals with the ancient migrations in PHASE ONE when after the foaling time in the verdant savannahs in the sixth lunar month of their circular trek, in the seventh month the herbivore mares came into estrus, passed blood (SA) and were mounted to bear their foals at the time of the Spring Equinox at the foot of their beloved mountains.

In Sanskrit SA is not only 'seven' harkening back to the ancient African migrations to the verdant savannahs but also 'snake', 'air' and 'bird'. SA as movement through the vehicle of 'air' bears a great resemblance to the Bardo (BARA-) dyad of the Tibetans defining the 'intermediate state' of which the Breath (BARATA) as 'air' takes up residence, Bird (BARADA) as the creature that uses the 'air' as a vehicle of passage, and the 'snake' as the 'feathered serpent' had been believed to guide the sun back up to the surFACE of Mother Earth to travel through that 'intermediate state' of air. The Egyptian Goddess Sais had been depicted as a 'bird' also traveling through that 'intermediate state' of air between the surFACE of Mother Earth and the belly of sky above Her. All of these perceptions emerged out of the first born eunuchized son, the balanced brat (BARATA) or brother (BARATA-). In PHASE ONE he was no longer fully male and still not the hoped for female who also existed in that 'intermediate state'. The (T) and (D) are interchangeable.

Because menstrual blood (SA) of the individual human mother was governed by the cycles of the moon and the moon was the major ruler of time in PHASE ONE, in Swahili SAA deals with either 'hour' or 'time' as does the Arabic SA'A also defining both 'hour' and the present 'moment'. It was the present 'moment' of experience that defined reality. 'Now' or the present 'moment' in Swahili is SASA establishing the dyad that came to define a score of emerging perceptions defining both mothers. The menstrual blood of the individual human mother (SA) and the movement inherent in the spiral spin and lavic blood (SA) out of the body of Mother Earth defined that a miracle of creation had taken place in the 'hidden' recesses within both of their bodies creating the repetitive SASA dyad.

In PHASE ONE way before the accursed clitorectomies held sway in PHASE THREE, at the time of giving birth, a mother went through a very specific experience that defined her with the honored SASA dyad at the end of her name; GoddeSS (GadaSASA), princess (paranaSASA), mistress (masataraSASA), hostess (hasataSASA) , etc. In Swahili uzazi (haSASA) defines 'childbirth' and sisi (IS haSASA) as 'we' and 'us' expands to embrace the whole tribe that both the individual mother's blood (SA) and the lavic blood (SA) of Mother Earth had a hand in creating.

In PHASE TWO moving into the redefinitions in PHASE THREE the Syrian, cum Hebrew Azazel (HaSASAla) as the 'Lords Messinger' dealt with the moon as the original ancient deity that announced the coming of the female menstrual period, was the 'Lords Messinger' creating the flow of the potential mother's blood that coagulated inside of her to create the baby. Azazel (HaSASAla) shed his own blood and took on the sins of the world. It SOUNDS like the subsequent Hebrew goat sent out into the desert performing the same task ridding himself of the accursed menstrual blood visited upon menstruating women.

Before male role in procreation was becaming known in PHASE TWO blood had been considered as the singular creative source of life. It also dealt with Azazel (haSASAla) being a subversive angel (HANAGALA) still in touch with the ancient mothers. His original name as an angel (HANAGALA) harkens back to the first born son and eunuch uncle (HANAKALA) (The (G) and (K) are interchangeable. The castrated eunuchs had been considered to be the original angels. Some not castrated at birth with the Kundalini energy alive in them created the much feard Biblical giants (HANAGALA).

For the Egyptians Amasis (hamaSASA) dealt with 'the moon is born' establishing its links with the passage of blood (SA) out of the individual mother's body and its own birth out of the lavic blood (SA) of Mother Earth. The (HAMA) establishes it's links with the Greek blood as ema (HAMA). In Wolof SA defines the concept of intimate possessiveness, for it means 'your' and 'your' blood on all levels created the product of 'your' or the mothers creative labors.

One of the most obvious and recurrent creatures associated with the letter S is the SHAPE of the metaphoric snake representing the electro magnetic Kundalini energy. It existed both within the body of Mother Earth as the guide of the sun back up to the surFACE and in the human body as the electro magnetic Kundalini energy the source of ecstasy and power. At the base of the spine clandestinely coiled, secretive and mysterious lay what became defined as the SHAPE of a double serpent or snake, a coil of the electro magnetic Kundalini energy. In the last stages of labor as the birthing mother accelerated her breath and began to pant, with her bellowing breath she blew into action this magical source of power. As it exploded within her it carried upon her accelerated birthing breath not only ecstasy but an entrance into a state of trance that burned out her pain and moved her to fall in love with the product of her labors. She as all mothers became a fearless protector of her baby, but that wasn't all.

As the last stages of labor gathered her in their coils, she not only panted hard and fast but intensely focused to get the large headed fetus out of her narrow hipped body. That intense focusing fused together the two hemispheres of her brain across the corpus callosum creating not only a state of trance but the *balance* of power that made her not only fearless, but a leader, healer, prophet and the original female shaman as either SHE man or (IS HAMANA) linking it to the human race (HAMANA) and not pushing it into the realm of gods or extra terrestrials. The movement into fearless motherhood out of her coagulated blood became the first SA and surfaces among the Tuareg Berbers as the 'free woman', the mother warrior, the Al Kahina. Further down the line into modern Basque the ladama became redefined as a 'lady witch'. It is an ancient word in PHASE ONE based not only singularly on the (ah) SOUND but containing in its folds the dam (DAMA) of the mother's dammed up or coagulated blood and the (LA) linking her with the pLAnet or Mother Earth. As holy women in PHASE THREE of ancient wisdom the witches were clitorectomized, summarily burned at the stake and have been vilified to this day. Since the shift into male centrality in PHASE THREE and the over evolution of the left hemisphere of the human brain dealing with linear power, greed and control, shamanism associated with the mothers powers had to be discarded and destroyed for there is no rational way that the emerging male power bases in PHASES TWO and THREE could control and exploit the powerful state of trance it had to be defined not only as the devil, the gift of (DA) evil but demonic.

In PHASE ONE with female centrality and the definition of reality out of the experience of the mothers, the birthing breath and the powerful gifts that it endowed upon the birthing mother was defined by her as something that was, MY STORY (MA IS TARA). In PHASE TWO as males began to redefine their reality, because they did not go through the process of birthing they defined the process of birthing as a MYSTERY (MASATARA). In PHASE THREE as left hemispheric male concepts became further pushed away from reality, the mother's personal story, cum emerging mystery became associated with the suspect MISTIC (MASATAKA), someone shrouded in the mists of time irrational and generally rejected by the left hemispheric simplistic rational male brain. The only way to get rid of the power inherent in the clitoral birthing breath of the mother was to remove it. Also in PHASE THREE as clitorectomies entered the scene MISERY without the (T) at the center of the word replaced the MYS(T)ERY of the ancient mothers. The (T) also deals with that which exists on the tip, top or surface of the vulva as does the victimized clitoris. To that end MA'S STORY of the mother became replaced by PA'S STORY of the pastor and the emerging male dominated monotheistic patriarchal religions that came to dominate the world in PHASE THREE.

Clitorectomies are still performed on girls all around the Mediterranean world, in North Africa and Southern Asia.

Whatever happened to the individual mother expanded to include the expansive body of Mother Earth. It was believed that both the individual mother and the body of Mother Earth shared the same energy of creation out of their internal 'hidden' movement and blood. On the body of Mother Earth the same 'hidden' internal workings under Her surFACE created the life above Her surFACE. Within Her underground recesses there flowed a stream of creation that was the source of the Kundalini energy. It rose out of Her Fiery depths entering the human body through the soles of the feet while standing and through the anus while sitting. For the birthing mother it entered her body naturally awakening into ecstatic state of trance blasted into habit erasing flames of the birthing breath.

Since all that Her surrogates experienced was also shared by the all encompassing body of Mother Earth, the pulsating heart carrying the blood through the mother's body was wise enough to know how to coagulate to create the baby inside, as the lavic blood pouring across the skin of Mother Earth knew how to coagulate outside to create land.

The dam created in the dama, or mother of the backed up menstrual blood created an internal 'hidden' dammed up space for the blood to do its job of coagulation and transformation from a bloody liquid to a solid baby. The (DA) in dama is the 'gift of' and (MA) stands for the 'mother'. So the dammed up blood (SA) in both the individual mother and the lavic blood (SA) on the body of Mother Earth shared their 'gift of' creation of their many offspring out of the 'hidden' internal blood coursing through both their veins. In Hebrew dam (DAMA) is blood. Close in Swahili damu (DAMA) also stands for blood. In Persian the dammed up blood within a mother's body was caught by a 'snare' or another dam (DAMA). Since the coagulated blood creating the baby sat next to the bloody liver it was perceived that the baby was the (DA) 'gift of' the liver, or to this day to bring forth a baby is to DELIVER it.

In Hebrew the baby in a mother's belly as a 'hidden secret' is also sod (IS HADA), defining also Her maintaining 'breasts' which goes into both directions as the (DA) 'gift of' (SA) the coagulating and maintaining blood out of the individual mother's body, or the sod (IS HADA) is the ground of being of Mother Earth, out of which everything emerged. It was out of the 'hidden' dark, lightless recesses within both the bodies of the individual mother and the all encompassing body of Mother Earth that all of creation came into being.

In PHASE THREE as all source of creation out of the individual mother's body and the body of Mother Earth was being obliterated and redefined, the dark space within both of their bellies of creation became redefined by the concept of darkness and doom (DAMA). In PHASE THREE the 'hidden one' in space became the emerging male father God Jehovah (JAHAVA). In Polish chowa (HAVA) means 'hidden'.

Out of the Egyptian SA as the 'wise blood' of the mother on all levels emerged the French SAng for blood, the Spanish SAngre and the Latin SAnguis. At the end of English words the letter S establishes the concept of plurality. It is the mother's blood on both levels that creates the one more, the 'and', the 'add', the reflection of both mother's. As (-ISH) the letter S at the end of words deals with 'one that is like', as in brackISH. Not to be left out (-IST) defines 'the one who is' as in artIST.

The original natural PHASE ONE stage three definitions of the volcanic fires within the body of Mother Earth under Her surFACE in Polish is zar (IS HARA). Hara is 'belly' in both Hebrew and Japanese. In Maori as maHARA it deals with the 'intestines.

In Greek the A (ah) as Alpha of the triangular SHAPE of the volcanic cone of Mother Earth in PHASE TWO led the other letters across the page to end in the male symbol of O (oh) of Omega. The Western Alphabet also begins with the letter A (ah) related to the mother as Alpha and ends with the letter Z (zee) to give the father his due. How did that happen? Mother's blood on both levels ABOVE the plane created life' Out of the individual mother's body her blood coagulated and created the baby inside her belly, the first SA. On the body of Mother Earth Her lavic menstrual flows had been considered to be Her creation of reality above Her surFACE as she deposited magma creating land the second SA.

As male role in specific procreation was becoming known in PHASE TWO they took over the realms UNDER the plane of Mother Earth, the 'hidden' reality as seen in the reflective surFACE of water. Above the reflective line was the realm of the mother's, below the aquatic line was the realm of the emerging fathers. The eunuch sons at the center and the gang of brothers on the periphery created a shaky truce as they began the shift into male centrality, subsequent control and unlimited power.

The unvoiced SA of the mother's blood creating life above the surFACE out of both the individual mothers belly and the 'hidden underground intestinal belly of Mother Earth, embraced the male role in specific procreation in PHASE TWO with the creation of the Z (zee) voiced SOUND ending the

Western alphabet as the male Omega ended that O (oh) SOUND in the Greek alphabet. It echoes the same concept as thinG and thinK. The voiced (G) in thinG deals with a *real* physical object. The unvoiced (K) in thinK deals with an *image* housed in the brain.

To that end the role of redefinition took center stage. In Polish zar (IS HARA) deals with the boiling, fulminating fires cooking within the body of Mother Earth as the 'hidden' magma UNDER Her surFACE. Zar (IS HARA) Her volcanic belly of creation begins with the voiced letter Z (zee), so we are in a transitional stage in PHASE TWO still with the body of Mother Earth but using the male Z (zee) as the linguistic source of the fires. Male role in procreation below the surFACE of Mother Earth was becoming established. What is also dragged in the wake of that establishment is the role of males out of PHASE ONE, when they failed to be defined as a co-creative source. Since only the HIStorical record dealing with males survives in PHASE THREE the concept of zar (IS HARA) harkens back to the definition dealing with women. For zar as (IS HARA) is the belly of creation. In Hebrew harah (HARA) deals with pregnancy in the individual mother's body and har (HARA) deals with the mountain on the Eastern side of a body of water out of which Mother Earth birthed or regurgitated the sun to travel through Her belly of air (HARA). For the Japanese hara also means belly as in hara kiri or disembowelment. Related to the belly are the coils of gut that made their home in the belly. For the Maori who left Africa fifty thousand years before, after one of the major cataclysms to settle in New Zealand, maHARA is the name for their 'intestines'. It only means that the concepts dealing with the flat circular body of Mother Earth and Her underground maze as a reflection of an individual mother existed at least fifty thousand years before, as did the language that bears the same linguistic burden.

The concept of zero (IS HARA) originally dealt with an empty female belly (HARA). It meant that the female was not pregnant. Her belly (HARA) was empty. In PHASE THREE Oriental traders used a dot to signify zero. A dot is a spot, or a period at the end, which meant that the female was menstruating and that her belly (HARA) was devoid of life, becoming defined by the zero (IS HARA) of emptiness. When writing with the right hand entered the scene in PHASE THREE, the period at the end dealt with ending a thought. In PHASE ONE as a period at the end of a human female buttocks it dealt with the ending of the promise of life. Originally SAnguine dealt not only with 'bloody' but with 'hopeful'.

The zero (IS HARA) of the empty belly became associated with maleness on both levels, the protective eunuch brothers inside the human family and the violent predatory heterosexual gang of brothers circling the periphery. In PHASE ONE all males had been defined as carrying a permanently empty belly before their role in procreation in PHASE THREE had become known. The harah (HARA) of Hebrew pregnancy and the zero (IS HARA) of the empty belly (HARA) led to many bizarre customs as males tried to mutilate themselves hoping to create a female body in which a baby would take root. The ancient mother's helped them in that quest when they castrated the first born sons to act as protectors of their subsequent children. That act led to many unanticipated problems.

As males began to understand their role in procreation and the ramifications of that discovery their source of creation had to emerge from somewhere. Since they had a permanently empty belly, then to fill that belly their source had to come out of what was BEFORE or the space of emptiness that preceded it. It couldn't have a physical SHAPE. That had been taken by the THINGs created by the mothers. It had to come out of THINKing, the ideas adrift in the mind. The *'word made flesh'* phenomenon enters here. The word (think) made flesh (thing) spreads its linguistic net. Except that it is backwards. For the thing, the physical object came first and the word defining the thing using the process of thought ie to think, came after.

As an idea floats upon the vehicle of air, so does an opinion. The anlaut of the male O (oh) of opinion deals with pinion and a pinion is a bird's wing. The bird's wing uses the air upon which to make its ascent into space, as does an idea. Idea (HADA) houses another clue. Rational thought came to be worshipped as something given exclusively to human males out of the 'hidden' mind of their emerging God. An idea (HADA) is the (DA) 'gift of' air (HA) on one level. On another level it is related to deus (DASA) another name for God. The (DA) remains as the 'gift of' and (SA) surfaces as the creative blood of the mother. Add the idea (HADA) and deus (DASA) together and lo and behold there surfaces Hadassah (HADASA) a Hebrew women's organization. Whence? Early Hebrew mothers in PHASE ONE were not only the creators of the physical universe of specific things, ie babies, but were also the thinkers. They were privy to the birthing breath that led to mysticism, courage, unconditional love, leadership, healing and all those mysterious qualities that helped in the survival of the specie. It was in the Hebrew Bible that Jehovah intoned' Ye shall bear your children in pain.' Was there a time that Hebrew mothers bore their children with pleasure? Was the origin of clitorectomies a result of that admonition?

In PHASE THREE the Hebrew God Jehovah because He had no physical area through which He could have His domain, claimed to Himself the concept inherent in the 'hidden' source of creation within the 'hidden' mysterious individual mothers belly and the even more mysterious 'hidden' belly of Mother Earth. In PHASE TWO the Hebrew priests came up with the CONCEPT of 'hidden' dealing with Jehovah (JAHAVA) as having no physical apparent substance. Jehovah (JAHAVA) has links with the Polish word for 'hidden' as chowa (HAVA). The Muslims took the idea one step further and not only is Allah 'hidden' but PHYSICAL reproductions of Him, associating Him with the physical body of Mother Earth on any level, are verboten.

The Muslim Allah (HALAHA) has links with the sun, a transitional deity before the 'hidden' mind of God held sway over the expanding North African desert. Allah (HALAHA) is a composite of two dyads dealing with the sun which was a transitional male deity in PHASE TWO. One is Al (HALA) that surfaces in Greek as the sun eelyos (HALASA) and Helios (HALA-) the solar God above the surFACE of Mother Earth. The (SA) at the end of both eelyos (HALASA) and Helios (HALASA) establishes the God as having links with the lavic blood (SA) of Mother Earth. The second dyad (LAHA) establishes its linguistic links with the African Wolof tribe representing the 'hidden' nocturnal sun as loh (LAHA) under the surFACE of Mother Earth. Allah (HALAHA) emerges as representing the ancient sun becoming a male deity *away* from the body of Mother Earth in its dual aspect as rising (AL) and setting (LOH). Many separation myths around the world document that separation.

Back to the voiced Z (zee) and the 'hidden' male underworld that it came to represent. The PHASE ONE zar (IS HARA) in Polish of Mother Earth and Her boiling volcanic caldera represented the 'hidden' source of all creation out of Her belly (HARA). In Ethiopian in PHASE TWO Zer (IS HARA), or Zar (IS HARA) as the male 'Lord of the Underworld' establishes his reflected, up side down domain 'hidden' under the skin of Mother Earth within Her magnificent ever creative belly (HARA). For the Egyptians the Lord of Death was Seker (IS HAKARA). Not too far afield, the Babylonian Messinger of the Moon, a phallic deity was Zaqar (IS HAKARA). The zero (IS HARA) of the empty belly fuses with the square (IS KARA or HARA), a male symbol that becomes Zaquar (IS HAKARA). The (KA) in the middle deals with smallness. The smallness defines the small belly either as a baby in the individual mother's belly or the thought of 'source' in the mind of the emerging male father.

As the SA represented source out of the blood of all of the mothers creations, so ZA staying closer to home came to represent source out of the male essence. The penis in PHASES TWO and THREE after going through so many linguistic permutations came into its own. The SHAPE of the erect penis was likened to a hook (HAKA) sharing its perception in Hebrew with the abib (HABABA), the direction of an erection of a ripened corn on a stalk, the ab and baba defining the father.

For the Hebrews a dagger is zakara (IS HAKARA). It may very well have links with the expanding and declining SHAPE of the crescent moon waxing and waning, the scythe, bringing forth blood periodically, every twenty eight days out of female bodies. When blood emerged out of the bodies of the mothers it announced to the assemblage that the female was menstruating and that her belly (HARA) was empty, defined by the zero (IS HARA). The letter S for the Etruscans SAKARA (IS HAKARA) was not only a snake but a square with four boxes within it. Four became a male symbol. For the Basque the penis is zakila (IS HAKALA). In Arabic the penis is zeker (IS HAKARA). For the Hebrews the name for virility is zakara (IS HAKARA). For masculine sex and pederasty it is zakhar (IS KARA or HARA). It expands to include male erection as zeekpah (IS HAKAPA). The (PA) at the end deals with PAssage and not a permanent condition. In Polish way up North a similar linguistic construct surfaces for the hacking ax as siekiera (IS HAKARA). The (KA) in the center of these words deals with the small hacker and not the crescent moon up in the sky that was considered to be the large hacker with time as the scythe.

Its ironic that the penis, virility, masculine sex, the crescent scythe and the ax all contain in their linguistic folds the process of *hack*ing apart. In PHASE ONE and stage one, the hook (HAKA) on the carnivore mothers snout was the lower mandible that not only sMOTHERED her prey, clutched it with her paws of power, but hacked it free from its life. It is a long convoluted linguistic journey that takes its hacking quality from the hungry mother lion to the crescent moon and the male penis.

Even though males began to understand their role in specific procreation in PHASES TWO and THREE they still did not understand HOW to gain the mysterious ecstatic birthing breath of the mothers and the powers inHERent in that singular experience. They did not give birth. That experience had been denied them. They had a zero (IS HARA) a permanently empty belly. But they became aware of a condition that was experienced by the castrated animals and their first born eunuch brothers. They not only became docile but some gained powers that transcended their former heterosexual condition. They became defined by a condition out of Tibet called the Bardo

Section Three

(BARA-) which defined an 'intermediate state'. The (RA) deals with the sun and the (BA) deals with the 'two in one' concept with the passage of the sun back and forth daily through that 'intermediate state' of air between the body of Mother Earth and the belly of air above Her surFACE. The first born castrated eunuch sons were no longer masculine and not really feminine and a name was given to their neither nor and 'intermediate state', the bar (BARA) that extended to the castrated brother (BARA-), the Polish brat (BARAT) also for brother and endless examples that had been considered to represent the 'intermediate state' such as birds (BARA-) that flew through that 'intermediate state' if air, I'bur (haBARA), another Hebrew (HABARA) word for pregnancy. A fetus in the mothers belly was in that 'intemediate state' of non-being and being. A bear (BARA) while hiBERnating was also in that 'intermediate state'. The brain (BARA-) had been considered a fickle companion as thoughts flitted through it. Many other dyads based on the Tibetan Bardo (BARA-) concept expand their linguistic reach around the world; Berbers, Britain, Barcelona, Barbadoes, Burma, etc.

It also became apparent to the heterosexual circling males on the periphery of the migrating herds that the powers of the birthing breath of the mothers and the castrated eunuch brothers created a trance like 'intermediate state' that had been likened to that Tibetan definition. It was the power inherent in that state that the rejected at puberty brothers yearned for. Somehow they too without losing their genitalia had to find a way to experience it. To that end in PHASE TWO with the shift into the left hemisphere of the brain and right (RATA) handedness there began the story of male ritual (RATA-). They became aware that a variety of means activated the trance state within them. Drumming on hollow logs to communicate must have put them into a trance like ecstasy as did drugs, alcoholic beverages, beer (BARA) any spirits, twirling, sex, dancing, fasting in caves, meditation, chanting, humming, running. Then to defuse the habits of a panic stricken infancy they realized that they had to clean themselves out and shed all the negative habits that held them in a circle of fear, the Augean stables come to mind, as the two coursing rivers of manure had to be cleaned out as do all the quests that males embarked on to find their way into that ancient mystical breath of the mothers that brought with it not only great power but courage and the capacity of leadership.

The males that set out on that quest to find the birthing breath of the mothers mystical trance not only went through the process of TRANSFORMATION but gained courage and 'knowledge', gnosis (ganaSASA) in Greek and Knossos (kanaSASA) in Minoan Crete, in the process gaining the SASA dyad of the mothers at the end of their names. Through their quests documented in the Illiad and Odyssey of the Greeks and many other legends around the world they internalized the energy of the birthing breath carried by the individual mothers blood (SA) and the Kundalini energy up from the volcanic body of Mother Earth (SA). The ancient mythologies give up their names as Mo'asses (MASASA) the founder of Persia and the precursor to the Biblical Moses (MASASA). The Egyptian Ramses (RAMASASA), the Greek God Zeus (IS HASA) or SASA) joins the list as does Jesus (JASASA). For the Greeks there were Theseus (TASASA) and Perseus (PARASASA). Then there is the Syrian Azazel, (HASASALA) or Aziz (HASASA) 'the Lords Messinger' that like the Greek Hermes bore witness whether the individual mother was pregnant or not, whether blood flowed from her body encoding both the menstruating female and shedding its light into the darkened corners of the night.

The 'ancient ones' of Colorado were called the Anasazi (HANASASA) also related to the sun (IS HANA). In Egyptian amasis (HAMASASA) deals with 'the moon is born' out of the body of Mother Earth, Her bloody nocturnal creation. In Greek ema (HAMA) is blood. A horse enters the picture in Hebrew as sus (SASA or IS HASA) as in Lithuanian does the cloud debesus (DABASASA) and zasis (IS HASASA) the sissing goose.

The SASA dyad originally associated with the birthing breath of the mother as she engaged her serpentine Kundalini blood of creation (SA) and the Kundalini energy out of the body of Mother Earth (SA) leading to a trance like state of transformation shared her condition with her castrated eunuch first born son. He as the priest stood at her side hailing the rising sun and wailing at its demise.

The castrated first born eunuch son then became the shaman, healer, psychic, prophet and often leader. Not to be left out the heterosexual peripheral males used ritual and a system of quests to awaken the Kundalini energy within them in the process becoming transformed and acquiring the SASA dyad at the end of their names. The battles between the violent heterosexual band of brothers above the body of Mother Earth and the protective eunuch priesthood in Her underground caves splatter across the pages of mankind's history. It is a battle that rages to this day 'hidden' as a fight for the superior 'straight' dominant left hemispheric male and the hate for the balanced internalized before birth brain of the gay (GAYA) man.

The simplest way to understand the meaning inherent in the letter S and the many hidden ramifications that it establishes as the concept of isness deals with the following two words exist (hakaSASAta) and exit (hakaSAta). To exist was to be hacked (HAKA-) free from death. To exit was to be hacked (HAKA-) free from life. The concept of hacking done by the lower mandible or jaw out of PHASE ONE and stage one covers many bases. The letter S in exiSt deals with life above the plane upon the body of Mother Earth and the birthing body of the individual mother. To make an exit you lose one of the S's, the S related to the blood of the individual mother is lost but not the S associated with the lavic blood of Mother Earth. For it had been perceived that the creature would be reborn, would be reincarnated. Because in PHASE ONE our ancient relatives believed TO HAVE BEEN BORN WAS TO HAVE BECOME IMMORTAL. In Bugotu the word for exit is watta (WATA). It was in the briny WATERY (WATA-) deep that the sun made its exit as it plunged, or was swallowed by the ever waiting Western horizontal maw of Mother Earth.

Not to straddle, but to leap over linguistic fences in both Phoenician and Hebrew, SHIN (IS HANA) emerges as the symbol for the letter S defining other concepts but hiding in its linguistic coils the dyad for the sun (IS HANA). As SAN (IS HANA) in Chinese it stands for the three lateral lines defining the movement of the sun (IS HANA) *above, upon and below* the body of Mother Earth. A similar structure emerges in the Chinese SHEN (IS HANA) dealing with the sun (IS HANA) defining the electrical energy that rises up from the body of Mother Earth in a double meandering pattern. SOUNDS like the Kundalini. The Tantrists defined the Kundalini energy within the human body rising up along the spine in a double entwining pattern symbolized by the snake. As a metaphoric healing power it surfaces in the Greek medical symbol of the balanced Caduceus (KADASASA) also composed of two winding mother snakes with the two wings of the male birds on top of the stem. For the Egyptians the double entwining emerges as the hank (HANAka).

In both the Phoenician and Hebrew SHIN (IS HANA), again jumping over linguistic fences not only deals with the sun (IS HANA) but with the place on the human body where the Kundalini solar based energy after being burned clean in the oven of Mother Earth, entered the heel or the shin (IS HANA). For the Greeks Achilies was drained of his power when he became wounded on his shin (IS HANA).

The SHAPE of the snake surfaces in Hebrew as the SHIN (IS HANA) or the solar energy entering the heels in the SHAPE of the serpentine solar guide. In Semitic it surfaces as SAMEKH (IS HAMAKA) with the ema (HAMA) of the Greek name for blood. In Polish zamek (IS HAMAKA) is a castle. Etruscan S as the snake becomes SAKARA (IS HA(KA)RA) dealing with the small (KA) out of the belly (HARA) of either the individual mother or the belly of Mother Earth. Based on the A (ah) SOUND it may be the oldest. The Greek SIGMA (IS HA(GA)MA) also shares the blood of both mothers as (HAMA), with the (GA) of begetting similar to the Etruscan SAKARA (IS HA(KA)RA). The (G) and (K) are interchangeable. For the Chinese SHE (IS HA) deals with the air (HARA) as the 'intermediate state 'of passage defining the metaphoric snake as the solar guide. SHE is also a name associated with 'mounds of Earth'. Since both the snake and mounds of Earth occur throughout most of the cultures of the world their relationship may not only be very ancient out of PHASE ONE but it also may have hidden mysterious related faculties.

If the SHAPE of the Kundalini energy exploding upward through the human body was perceived to be in the SHAPE of a winding double snake, then that same energy rising out of the body of Mother Earth must have been perceived to also emerge in a double serpentine coil. It may explain not only the whirling hurricanes, dust devils and whirlpools but all those cave drawings on the rock overhangs in the Sahara with the double pattern of helical spins with bird wings on top of the stem. The double meandering pattern of the recently discovered DNA molecule echoes the ancient perception of the Kundalini coiling snake.

THE LETTER C

AN ALVEOLAR VOICELESS GROOVED FRICATIVE

SOUND; Double SOUND, C (see) of seeing, C(kh) cough of death

SHAPE; Mother's body, C of hiss, C(kh) back palate

MOTHER EARTH; the letter S above and below Her plane, cave

CONCEPT; Existence as a double reality of life and death

THE C (see) OF SEEING AND C (kh) the COUGH OF DEATH

The SOUND associated with the letter C, (see) and the SOUND associated with the letter C, (kh), create a double reality associated with life and death embracing the total story encoded in the letter S of isness or 'existence'. They both emerge out of the same apparent origins out of the SHAPE of the letter S. The letter S straddles the plane, straddles the surFACE, the ground of being of Mother Earth. The letter S of 'existence' deals with a double reality. It has to be cut in half, halved horizontally, creating the two C's, the one

Section Three

made in front of the mouth sissing C (see) working in concert with the eyes to see. On the surFACE of Mother Earth it is the breath of air hissing out of Her volcanic vents defining life above the plane. The C (kh) the cough of death filibrating deeper out of Her throat emanating out of Her deep internal sources of creation (KARATANA), Her internal caves (KAVA-) and cavities (KAVATA-).

The top half of the truncated letter S as the letter C (see), deals with light and life, with breathable sissing, hissing air, escaping from the volcanic vents and from the break in Mother Earth's circular horizontal crack. With the emergence of the sun at dawn and the rays of the sun acting like stiletto fingers of light piercing the fabric of dawn creating the break through which the rays of the sun could soar into the heavens bathing the surFACE of Mother Earth with the caress of light and with the process of seeing (C-ing) supporting the existence of life above Her plane.

Upon Her watery surFACE Her reflective seas (Cs) acted like enormous eyes that relentlessly gazed at the vault of the changing sky. In Polish oko (HAKA) reflecting the dual balance on the face in stage one defines the eye. In Africa the Okabongo (HAKA-) River Delta floods the patiently waiting savanna with a placid spread of water that like a seeing eye of the sea reflecting reality, mirrors the sky. On the other side of the world in Georgia of the 'New World' the Okeefenokee (HAKA-) Swamp shares in that majestic activity as does the Lake Okeechobee (HAKA-) in Florida, Lake Okonee in Georgia. Then there surfaces the OKAnagan Lake in Canada. How far back were these places named and by whom?

As the eye on a creatures face hacks (HAKA-) reality in half, the reality on the outside and the image on the inside, so the same process was believed to occur on the surFACE of Mother Earth's reflective seas.

The bottom half of the letter S reflects life equally in the process of death. As the sun halved the sky and then at the equator halved it into equal day and night, so the cycle of life and death in PHASE ONE had been perceived to be of equal duration. Time had been reckoned by the cycles of the moon and the eve of evening establishes that ancient even perception. It also deals with the reflective quality of water that creates an even balance between what is real above and what is reflected as an image on the surFACE waters. Observing the perfect reflection of life above the surFACE the perception evolved that 'look is even' which morphed into the number seven (IS EVEN) and Havana.

The truncated bottom half of the letter S of 'existence' dealing with death gives birth to a different source of SOUND, the C (kh) (KAHA) as the cough

(KAHA) of death fillibrating the vocal cords and pushing the breath on its way out of the deeply hidden thoracic and oral cavity.

The reality that humanity lived in PHASE ONE was perceived to be that of a flat maternal surFACE and body that existed as a circle that ended at the horizontal rim all around them. For the heavenly bodies to make their entrances and exits out of that horizontal circular sweep on the circular surFACE of Mother Earth ending at the horizon line all around them, there had to exist a break in the integrity of that horizontal sweep. The circle around them had to have an opening. Like the face of an individual mother, who had a horizontal slit on her face creating the mouth, the maternal surFACE of Mother Earth also had to acquire a slit, a break in the circular integrity of the horizon line. For the circle around them also represented the surFACE, the face, the head on the body of Mother Earth. She had to acquire a mouth, a break in that circle for Her to eat the heavenly bodies, swallow them on the Western side and then in the East either regurgitate them back up to Her surFACE, like birds and wild dogs were observed to do, defecate them, or give birth to them. At different times different processes came into play.

That break in the integrity of the circle (O), ending at the horizon line around them in stage one, emerged initially out of the SHAPE of the vowel (O) of the individual mother's open mouth extending to the surFACE of Mother Earth in stage three swallowing the sun in the Western waters. Then, as they with grief gazed at the suns descending reflection, it moved into the SHAPE of the number eight (8), the vowel (O) of the open mouth reflected in Her standing waters that at twilight ATE the heavenly bodies.

As an emerging concept the vowel (O) reflecting itself and the break on the circular side of Mother Earth emerged with the SHAPE of the letter S with the two sides open, two broken circles but facing in opposite directions. Facing to the left, the top part of the letter Ƨ of seeing, (C-) dealing with life above the surFACE became associated with the ancient mothers. The bottom part facing to the right dealing with death became associated with the emerging fathers and the eunuch priesthood. This linguistic construct emerged out of PHASE TWO as male role in specific paternity was becoming known. It also surfaces in the Chinese Yin Yang. Originally in PHASE ONE the Yin Yang dealt with the sun above and below the body of Mother Earth. The Yin was the sun as the female aspect saying yes above the plane in sunlight. The Yang (HA(YA)NAGA) was the reflected castrated male sun under the mantle of Mother Earth saying no at the loss of light and the beginning of night. As male role in specific paternity was becoming known and the growth of power of the emerging eunuch priesthood, it became redefined as the Yin female and the Yang male fused within an S SHAPED circle of creation spinning together through space.

The top part of the letter S halved horizontally, as the SHAPE of the broken circle encoded in the letter C (see), deals with 'existence' above the body of Mother Earth in daylight. It deals with light and how light figures in the capacity of what can be seen, what can be observed by the opening sheltered by the lids of the eye ball of C-ing.

The bottom part of the horizontally halved letter S, as the activity of the other broken circle is the activity of creation occurring below and within the cavernous body of Mother Earth. The SHAPE of the letter C(kh) deals with all of the cups of internal hidden creative containment (KANATA-) especially of the individual mothers cunt (KANATA).

On the human body it deals with the cavities of creation, of the eye cavity that holds the eye ball and creates the possibility of seeing, of the aural cavity that contains the cochlea and creates the possibility of hearing, of the oral cavity that contains the tongue and creates the possibility of licking, lallation and food regurgitation, of the thoracic cavity that creates SOUND and the possibility of communication, the belly cavity that contains the liver, uterus, and intestines, out of which all sorts of creations come into being; fetus, feces, urine and blood. On the body of Mother Earth it deals with all the creative cavities that hold on to the dead waiting to be reborn as the potential hidden within Her, before they emerge into segments of creative creations above Her surFACE out of the; cup, crater, caldera, cleft, couldron, cave, crevasse, volcanic cone, culvert and crack.

The SOUND encoded in the letter C(kh) (KAHA) is the cough (KAHA) of death, the last breath fillibrating the vocal cords on its way out of the oral cavity to become at one with the corpse, cadaver, carapace, crypt, canopic jar, catacombs, the many and varied containers of death, not unlike the catastrophe and cataclysm that often accompanies the exit.

Out of the vowel O of the open mouth, into the SHAPE of the O of the solar disc reflected in Her vast seas to become the number eight (8), emerges the SHAPE of the mouth of Mother Earth that ATE the celestial bodies at the horizon line. Out of that SHAPE of the number eight (8) into the SHAPE encoded into the letter S of 'existence' with the two broken circles one on top of the other and then the letter S halved horizontally to become the C of see-ing above ground and the C (kh) of containment (KANATA-) in the cunt (KANATA) below ground. The number eight (8) laid on its side becomes the SHAPE in the eye of seeing (C-ing). It emerges down the line in PHASE THREE as a concept, as the sign of infinity. To see was to become immortal. The ancients believed that to have been born was to have become immortal.

After the LINGUISTIC BREAK and the African catastrophes that must have preceded it, the only SHAPE that surfaces with any repetitive clarity in the following alphabets is the SHAPE of an angle. It evolved out of the PHASE TWO chiseling of the triangular wedge SHAPED Cuneiform. Making alphabetic curves with a metal or stone wedge would have been impossible. The North African Tuareg, cum Berbers used the angle that preceded the C SHAPE of the letter S of 'existence' as the 'interchangeable birthing vowels' that are used to this day. As the Egyptian boomerang the C angle symbolizes the process of life going in one direction, the C (see) of seeing above the surFACE and then after going through the C (kh) of the death rattle coming back up from underneath the surFACE of Mother Earth.

The SHAPE of the letter C as (KH) (KAHA), the broken circle, the bottom half of the letter S, under the surFACE of Mother Earth during its stay in death, waiting to be reborn is a symbol for the process of reinCArnation.

In North Semitic, Etruscan, Phoenician and even Greek, the angle looks like a number seven (7). One of the perceptions dealing with the number seven is that in PHASE ONE it was the number for separation in September during the ancient migrations. The ancient mothers following the herbivore herds for an alternate milk supply traveled by the lunar calendar of thirteen months. Moving six months in one direction, then in September, the seventh month, if you count March as the beginning of the march as the first month, mating, then separating and moving in the other direction.

The number seven (7) expanded to include other SHAPES of separation and ultimately settling for death. It is the SHAPE of the descent of the sun off the body of Mother Earth as it was swallowed, killed to its light by the open maw of the Western waters encoded in the bottom half of the letter S as the C(kh) the cough of death.

On the level of humanity it also became associated with the actual cough (KAHA) of death as the air fillibrated the vocal chords on its last exit out of the dying body. In the East the sun rose into the sky encoded in the SHAPE of the vertical angle of ascent associated with the open mouth of Mother Earth with Her tongue pushing the solar disc up to the surFACE, symbolized by the letter L (lengua as tongue in Latin). In the Western sea at the Equator of even day and even night, the sun after passing through the vault of air sank out of sight in the vertical angle of descent encoded in the number seven (7) both in Hebrew and in English. The even day and even night became reflected in the two even broken circles one above and one below encoded in the letter S.

The Phoenician C as the symbol for camel or gimel, seems to deal with the angular SHAPE of the hump on a camels back. It seems that a camel could go without water for long stretches of time as it carried the weary travelers across the burning sands of the Gobi, Kalahari and then the Sahara deserts. It used the fatty curve on its back to survive as the hump slowly shrank out of sight. Some kind of metaphor resides here.

There is a development after the LINGUISTIC BREAK that surfaces in the Middle East with the use of the crutch which is also symbolized by an angle. With the development of herding and metallurgy we are no longer in PHASE ONE and the ancient migrations of the mothers. Herding of domesticated animals deals with husbandry and with shepherds. To keep them at the flock they were not only castrated but uniformly crippled as were the blacksmiths at the forge. Castration put to death their male essence. Their crutches not only look suspiciously like the number seven of death but more like the angle that held up their mutilated bodies. In PHASE THREE after the shift into male centrality and a total redefinition of even practical objects, the shepherds crook became the symbol of royalty for powerful male rulers and the staff of religious power for the eunuch priesthood. It exists to this day.

THE LETTER K

A VOICELESS ALVEOLAR STOP

SOUND; multilayered cacophonic bird song

SHAPE; birds open beak, the letter X (KS) of buttox halved vertically,

MOTHER'S body; in stage one the letter X (KS) (KASA) of the buttox or coos (KASA), in stage one (KH) cough (KAHA) of death,

MOTHER EARTH; KAKA creating smaller aspects, (KHU) ending, death, burial ground

CONCEPT; beginning and end, appearance and disappearance, small aspects, separation, transformation, the SOUND has been associated with bird coos and the female coos out of the X halved vertically, The SHAPE has been associated not only with a birds beak seen in profile but with with the female buttox holding the coos (KASA) and the creative emergence out of creature bodies and the body of Mother Earth (KAKA).

The letter K has no organs on the individual mother's face that can lay claim to creating it other than the air escaping out of the thoracic cavity in stage one. The primary SOUND that is associated with the letter K out of stage five deals with the noisy coos made by birds. On the more closely related human level in stage one it is associated with the cough (KAHA) of death. On the level of individual mothers the more apparent source of beginning and joy is the SOUND made by women that related the coos (KASA) of bird song to their coos (KASA) and their primary source of pleasure their clitoris (kleitor) in Greek. Often the SOUNDS made by birds with their open beaks and the SOUNDS created deeper in their oral cavities become intermingled. The cooing, clacking, clucking, calling, cawing SOUNDS made by birds have been internally created within the oral CAvity in a bird's head C(kh) and externally expelled by a bird's open beak (K) and is onomatopoeic. This led to a great deal of linguistic confusion.

There are Latin scholars who to this day still agonize over the pronunciation of Cicero, whether it is Cicero as in sissy, or Kikero as in kicker. The problem goes even further back for the Celts in the British Isles as either the Celts (C (see) or Kelts as in (KA).

There existed an ancient association and affectionate appreciation between human beings and especially the birds. Out of a specific line in linguistic evolution human beings began to understand their need to expand their communication. They became aware that birds had and still have an almost unlimited multitude of SOUNDS at their disposal. Birds along with bugs may be the oldest denizens of our world going back to the dinosaurs, honing their communicative skills along the way. Creating specific SOUNDS to get their message across they cooed, gooed, chirped, clucked, cawed, hissed, whistled, coughed, moaned, cried, gurgled, hacked, whooped, whined, sang, screeched, snorted, hummed, chortled, cheeped, squealed, and even squeaked. Mocking birds can not only express themselves through their own song but they can mimic the songs of any other birds and the alarms of cars and fire engines. Parrots can learn to mimic not only human SOUNDS but have been known to hold conversations.

No SOUND is beyond their capacity to reproduce. It separated them from other creatures who were limited to one, two and sometimes three SOUNDS with which to communicate. Cows mooed, sheep and goats baad, cats purred, mewed and hissed, lions moaned and roared, snakes hissed, horses whinnied and snorted, dogs barked and growled, hyenas laughed, whales wailed, otters squealed, apes screeched and howled, shrimps created popping SOUNDS, dolphins whistled and that is only part of the story. As far as they had been able to ascertain the fish in their mysterious waters reflecting death, like death stayed relatively silent. The birds on the other hand filled the African sky with their multi-phonic cacophony (KAKAfana) of SOUND.

It becomes apparent that the letter K establishes its source out of bird SOUND and has ancient links not only with the body of the female and her coos, but with the body of Mother Earth. Further clues exist in the Finnish word for alphabet, which comes up as AAKKOSET. For the Finnish AAKKOSET runs on a parallel track with the Western Alphabet. The A for the mother as Mother Earth and the A of the female of the specie becoming the other A, morphing into the double AA construct define what came first. The Egyptian Mother Goddess of creation and truth as MAAT establishes the example of the AA repeated.

In the Finnish AAKKOSET (HAKA-) that which came second after the AA, represented by the letters KK, dealt with the SOUNDS made by the beaks of birds. They didn't deal with the Alpha and Beta, as B of the babble SOUNDS associated with the baby, or the B of the father, as following the mother. They dealt with the importance of birds as coming second right after the body of Mother Earth, representing the SHAPE of an open birds beak as the original SHAPE that fed into the letter K or KK.

In the language of Bemba in Zambia of South Africa, there is a greeting that is shared only by women and that greeting is KUKU that is considered to be a chuckle. In the Solomon Islands of the South Pacific of the Bugotu people, almost on the other side of the world, the same word for chuckle is also KUKU. For the Swahili a chicken or a hen is KUKU. The Basque also call their coocoo bird KUKU. It establishes the fact that these diverse people had links and appreciation of the SOUNDS made by birds and that the KUKU SOUND had been used and associated with women. Who knows, it may have been a secret greeting. In the Cameroons of West Africa there is a tribe called KUKU. Could this have been the place in Africa where the K SOUNDS associated with birds have their origins? Could it have splayed out from that particular center?

In the Solomon Islands the word for ancestor or descendent in Bugotu was Kukua (KAKA). In Africa there is a tribe called the Kikyu (KAKAYA). They considered themselves to be the people of light. (AYA) is light in Persian. They did not establish themselves directly out of the body of Mother Earth and have their tribal name begin with the letter A or B. They established their links directly with the arrival and departure of birds and the SOUNDS that they made, not unlike the AAKKOSET of the Phoenicians (FANASA-) who may have ended up as the Finnish (FANASA) people of Northern Europe.

The concept spreads across the globe like the rays of the sun spread across the Eastern sky at dawn. For K begins the journey not only originating the K SOUNDS made by birds but how those SOUNDS became associated with women and with the body of Mother Earth in PHASE ONE. Not only does the Finnish Alphabet as AAKKOSET, establish links with the birds through the letter KK (KAKA) repeated, but they expand to define AKKA (HAKAKA), that in Finnish means 'old woman'. The clues become more specific, for not only do they come out of the 'old woman' in Finnish, but they specifically come out of her mouth. In Finnish, the opening of the mouth is AUKKO (HAKAKA). The area where SOUND is hacked (HAKA-) into meaningful comprehensible pieces. The fact that on the other side of the world KOU is mouth in Chinese, only intensifies the quest for a single common source of language and that leads us to Africa. What the Finnish Alphabet as AAKKOSET tells us is that comprehensible SOUNDS as communicative speech, came out of the mouths of 'old women' as they imitated the SOUNDS of birds.

It was the crones, the grandmothers (wearers of the crowns), who codified the SOUNDS of the K family and they fashioned them on the SOUNDS made by the multi-phonic cacophony (KAKA-) of birds. In Hebrew one who 'imitates', is KHEEK (KAKA or (KAHAKA). Since the SOUND of 'imitating' has links with birds through the KK construct, then that which was imitated came out of the deep recesses of the oral cavity and palate. In Hebrew the name for palate, the plate that supports the roof of the mouth is called KHEKH (KAKA or KAHAKAHA), the place that creates repetitive SOUND. The KH (KAHA) SOUND in stage one emerged out as the last cough (KAHA) of the death rattle and is also onomatopoeic.

It goes even further back into PHASE ONE of mother centrality. There was an ancestral Goddess of AKKAD (HAKADA) who as a wise old woman, grandmother and midwife, was the 'water drawer' who brought Gods out of the primal deep. In Greek she was AKKA, ACCA, ACCO (HAKA) who was given the title, 'she who fashions'. To fashion is to create. The ultimate creatress was Mother Earth. She had been perceived to fashion all that existed. To 'draw water' was not necessarily to float a bladder and bring up a liquid. What it originally meant is that Mother Earth as the Goddess AKKA 'drew', sketched a picture upon the reflective surfaces of standing water out of which the metaphoric Goddesses emerged in PHASE ONE and then created the subsequent gods in PHASES TWO and THREE.

As males began to create their own gods and the search for the father, they appropriated the birds as their symbolic source. Not only did birds use the 'intermediate strate' of the sacred air as their vehicle of passage, the KU KUL KAN the feathered Serpent of the Maya but feather(FATARA) and father (FATARA) have very ancient linguistic links.

For the Lapps and Finns she was MADER-AKKA, who created humanity. The Romans, ever ready to copy anything Greek, called her ACCA LARENTIA, mother of Lares, the left handed ancestral maternal spirits, who 'drew' male rulers out of the same primal deep. As the creatress of male Gods who had been represented by the reflective surFACE of the waters, she 'drew' Remus and Romulus out of the Tiber to found the city of Rome. She also drew Sargon out of the Tigris. As the pharaohs daughter in Egypt, she drew Moses out of the Nile. The triad 'drew' (DARAWA) contains in its linguistic folds (DA) the 'gift of' the sun (RA) reflected in the standing waters (WA).

In Central America there was a Goddess called ACAT (HAKATA), or AKNA (HAKANA). In Egypt she was known as the midwife HECATE (HAKATA) or HEQ (HAKA), the wise old woman, the grandmother who knew the HEKAU, (HAKA) or the mother's 'words of power.' The 'words of power', were segmented SOUNDS of communication that could be strung like beads upon the currents of air to create meaning. Could it be that those ancient 'words of power' were nothing more than the SOUNDS based on the communicative ability of birds, whose SOUNDS were originally mimicked exclusively by older women, the wise old grandmothers. They through their oral traditions repeated their ancient tales and became associated not only with them, but with the rites of death over which they originally officiated?

In all of these names; ACCA, AKKA, HEKAE, HEQ (HAKA), there is a common linguistic ancestor, and that ancestor is HAKA. HAKA deals with hacking (HAKA-), with cutting apart into segments. Originally it dealt with the lower jaw in stage one, the hook (HAKA) on the skull of a carnivore mother who hacked her prey into digestible pieces. In the human family it dealt with the hacking of SOUND using the jaw, the same mandibular hook (HAKA) on the bottom of her face that hacked (HAKA-) into recognizable syllabic segments that held meaning.

The Goddess AKKAD (HAKADA) as the 'water drawer' may have more expansive interpretations. It may mean that she, as one of the personifications of Mother Earth, drew, sketched pictures on the surFACE of Her waters that reflected the reality above. It was out of that reflected reality of life above

Her surFACE, that death below Her surFACE could release new life to spring into being. Half of existence as life was above Her surFACE. The other half, just as important was death below Her surFACE creating an even balance. In Amharic the dyad for 'equal or peer' is ACCA (HAKA). The (AC) is reflected by the (CA) creating the balance. It was the standing waters on the water filled savannahs that created the illusion of reflected equality (HAKA-). In Latin the word for water is aqua (HAKA), the hacker (HAKA-) of reality into two equal (HAKA-) halves. The reality reflected in the quietly standing spread of waters below, was perceived to be equal to the reflected reality above the surFACE of Mother Earth. The Central American Goddess AKNA (HAKANA) bears a striking resemblance for the word 'window' in Polish as okno (HAKANA). A 'window' is what separates two sides of reality with a reflective surface, like water does on the body of Mother Earth. It hacks (HAKA) the physical reality on the body of Mother Earth represented by the cone (KANA) of creation and Her very skin (IS KANA) into two areas, existence above Her surFACE in life and existence below Her skin in death. The Polish okno (HAKANA) hides in its linguistic folds the word for eye, oko (HAKA) breaking reality into two equal halves, one the image on the inside and the other, the perceived reality on the outside.

The whole family of SOUNDS related to the letter K came out of the SOUND and the SHAPE of a bird's beak and are onomatopoeic. The two alphabets, Western and Finnish cross lines, share ancient sources, give rise to speculations that can be more than conjectural. The origins are more than startling, for they deal with perceptions that have not only been ignored but suppressed to such a degree, that what is needed is more than a linguistic backhoe to unEarth them. For the SOUND locked in the letter K that came out of the SHAPE of an open beak of a bird, is also most anciently related to that rarely mentioned part, the tip of an organ that barely peeps out of the bottom folds on the female body, the Greek KLEITOR, or clitoris.

An island sticks out of the ocean cradled by the waves, like a nose sticks out of the human face cradled by the cheek flaps. A snout sticks out of the skull of a creature like an island sticks out of the ocean. A beak sticks out of the bird's head often surrounded by a cascade of feathers that on some birds looks like a nose, or on the female body it looks like the clitoris, surrounded by a halo of hair.

What is it that sticks out of the female body, not necessarily the nose on her face, (for that had been taken by the letter N), hidden from the back by the folds of the cheeks encoded in the letter X and the cloak-like labia majora from the front, obviously the nose like tip of the clitoris. For the clitoris on the female body must have been much larger in the past and must have stuck out past the hairy vulvic folds that enshrined it, like the folds of the cheeks on the face were once perceived to enshrine the protuberant nose.

The letter A as with the place of beginnings on the female body in so many of the ancient Alphabets or Aakkosets, gives us a clue.

It is curious that the hands, once the humanoid creature became fully bi-pedal and upright, fall right at the level of the human genitalia. Humanoid beings must have appreciated the pleasure of masturbation and of its stress releasing satisfaction, long before they emerged into their tormented PHASE HREE rape filled sexuality. Human beings must have appreciated their bodies and realized that the greatest source of satisfaction and joy lay at their fingertips. There may have been a double process at work here. The area of the damp genitalia with hair around it, (like trees along a river), could have harbored itchy bacteria or microscopic varmints. Since due to bi-pedal locomotion the tips of the fingers hung right there, what would have stopped our ancient ancestors from scratching that 'forbidden' itchy zone. Ironically the word to scratch (IS KARAJA), contains within it the same linguistic construct as crotch (KARAJA). Linguistically speaking, scratching did not deal with any itchy skin, or a specifically itchy scalp. No matter what arguments notwithstanding, it dealt with the itchy crotch. The scratching that went on to relieve the physical itching, leading to relief and pleasure, extended to relieve the psychological, emotional and even sexual itching. The growth of fear and stress in the vulnerable human creature obviously needed some form of relief. Masturbation must have provided that outlet. If it wasn't the case, then why have so many of the patriarchal religions in PHASE THREE, who demean and condemn the physical universe, have relegated the pleasure of the human body and the specific female body to the back seat and rail vehemently against both? To scratch (IS KARAJA) and crotch (KARAJA) contain in them the small (KA) and the second dyad (RAJA) which deals with Middle Eastern royalty. Was masturbation relegated only to the rulers? When did that happen?

Our nearest Simian relatives, the Bonobo chimpanzees of the South Congo River basin in Africa, have sex every time their paths cross, all kinds of sex, with all kinds of partners, apparently to defuse tension. Discrimination is not one of their high points. Its their way of saying hello, I'm OK, you're OK, let's get on with it. The Bonobo found a different way of dealing with potential pent up violence.

The male chimpanzees studied by Jane Goodall in the North Congo River basin in Africa, released their stored up territorial rage and violence by organizing, stalking and killing males that had formed other groups and mutilating them by removing their genitals and thorax. They not only killed them but made sure that they cold not reproduce and communicate. They resorted to war, to establish their power and territoriality. Since the chimpanzees are our nearest cousins sharing ninety nine per cent of their genes with us, then the 'killer gene' attributed to mankind cannot be summarily dismissed. How does the angle of the female clitoris, the volcanic cone on the body of Mother Earth, the beak of a bird, and the letter K become related? The clues exist in ALL of the languages of the world establishing the fact that not only are the volcanic cones, the clitoris, the beaks of birds and the letter K related, but that language began in Africa and spread out around the globe. For it is not only with the SOUNDS made by their beaks that we have to deal with but with the semiannual migration of birds North and South, on the African continent. For it is in that movement that we begin to see an ancient SOUND based puzzle taking SHAPE.

That which must have defined women, other than their periods and child bearing, that came out of the same area of their bodies, and gave them their greatest pleasure, must have been the small clitoral beak like structure that when scratched and rubbed, brought them to orgasm and sent them into paeans of ecstatic joy. It was that beak like protuberance, hidden partially by the folds of skin, that reminded them of the beak that stuck out of the face of a bird, not any bird, but one that had a halo of feathers that reminded them of the hair that surrounded the labia majora, around the clitoris.

In the Zoa tribe of South America, in the rain forest of the Amazonian basin, the women wear a halo of down like white feathers around their faces. When the mothers give birth, the men, of this very peaceful tribe of people, also glue a halo of white feathers around their faces. It doesn't go as far as the couvade of some tribes, where men were put in bed to share the birth pangs of the birthing mother. They shared in the act of birthing, by gluing feathers around their faces.

In Polish the word for beak, is dziob (JABA) and has links with the activity of the beak in English. The beak jabs (JABA). Also in Polish the familiar and playful word for clitoris is dziobek (JABAKA) and means 'little beak' (BAKA). The phoneme (KA) in Polish defines the diminutive at the ends of words associated with female nouns. What the beak (BAKA) establishes in its phonemic dyadic construct, is the concept of duality, the 'two in one' locked

Section Three

in the SHAPE of the letter B (out of the two lips seen in profile on the mothers face, creating the babble of communication), the two halves of a beak creating the unit of a single bill in one direction and two sides of the female vulvic clitoris from another.

The SHAPE of the letter K is based on the SHAPE of the open beak (BAKA) of a bird. KA deals with smaller aspects that emerge out of the female body and the body of Mother Earth. Accompanied by other vowels it often deals with the 'concept' of making things smaller. It expresses a similar concept that exists in the word, to speak (IS PAKA). For to speak (IS PAKA) deals with poking (PAKA-) the ear drum. For the beak (BAKA) of a bird creates SOUND and speaks (IS PAKA) as it pokes (PAKA) around the ground and picks (PAKA) up bugs and seeds. The mother hen, possessor of the beak, clucks and alerts her brood to what food is edible and by scratching around, where to find it. (PA) deals with passage and (KA) deals with Mother Earth as the creator of smaller units out of Herself. The voiced SOUND encoded in (BA) deals with a physical entity. The unvoiced SOUND of (PA) deals with an activity, or even a concept. Voiced and unvoiced SOUNDS often follow that pattern. The physical universe and actual objects are often represented by voiced SOUNDS. Concepts or activities are more often than not represented by unvoiced SOUNDS, the thinG, thinK phenomenon.

In the search after food, chickens come to mind as pecking and poking the ground as they cluck and scratch, sharing their knowledge with their chicks. Air borne birds peck and poke at the barks of trees. Shore birds poke at the sand. Insect eaters poke at the air. The beak as it speaks, like the voice, also pokes the eardrums with SOUND. Mother Earth is the greatest Ear to her needy children. She hears every word that is sent upon the wind. If the intent is clear enough, She even answers.

The passage of birds semiannually North South across the African sky emerged as a CAlendar, a time keeping process that in time emerged as the SHAPE of the swastika. The birds shared the vault of air as their vehicle of passage with the sun and the moon. But they went in different directions. The sun and the moon moved laterally across the sky from East to West, creating a great arc in that inverted bowl of the heavens, establishing an implied line of separation, the halving of the great vault of air into two sections.

Then the birds entered the picture. The migrating fowl came and went out of the body of Mother Earth at the Southern and Northern horizons, at the beginning of their own ancient seasonal migrations. But they didn't pass laterally from East to West. The semi annual migration of birds moved vertically, longitudinally from North to South, creating a cross across the ancient pathways created by the sun and the moon. The SHAPE of that cross, contained in the circular horizon rim in Cretan Minoan Linear B, is represented by the SOUND of KA. Since KA came out of SOUNDS made by the open beaks of birds, therefore the KA SHAPE and SOUND in Linear B, has its origins in the migratory passage of birds.

In the South African language of Bemba, 'to migrate' is KUKA (KAKA) and is reminiscent of the trumpet blasts of arrival that hailed the return of the birds with the cackling, cawing, clucking SOUNDS that accompanied them as they passed overhead.

In Amharic the word for longitude is kerros (KARASA). It deals with the activity and direction cleaved by the passage of birds across (HAKARASA) the belly of air. (HAKA) deals with hacking, or cutting into two parts). With their longitudinal crossing, they halved the great vault of the sky into two sides. The migratory crossing, as the Amharic word for longitude kerros (KARASA) tells us, has ancient links not only with the SHAPE of the cross (KARASA), but also where that crossing occurred in that great belly of air above the surFACE of Mother Earth. The Hebrew word for belly or abdomen dealing with the belly of air above the surFACE of Mother Earth is keres (KARASA). Also in Hebrew keres (KARASA), is another word for the swastika. What you have here is the SHAPE of that criss-crossing up in the belly of air above the body of Mother Earth in which birds played a part. They formed half of the equation created daily by the sun and monthly by the moon in one direction and their semiannual coming and going in another. Together they created the cross across the belly of air above the body of Mother Earth symbolized by the swastika as a celestial time clock.

The ancient symbol of passage made by the birds and the heavenly bodies became incorporated by the Nazis turning to the right of the fathers as a link to a much more 'noble', Aryan past. Actually, the swastika had little to do with the Aryans. Its links go much further back to the passage of birds vertically, and the sun and moon laterally, across the continent of Africa.

The sun in its daily rising and setting, delineated the passage of time as an equal distribution of light and darkness at the equator. The moon with its repetitive four phases, delineated the passage of weeks and months. Women with their menstrual cycles based on the passage of the moon, became associated with the thirteen month lunar CAlendar. In Polish CZAS is a word that means both the female period and time. It comes out of the association with the four phases of the moon that coincided with the flow of blood (SA)

Section Three

out of female bodies. The (CZ) SOUND pronounced as (CH), deals with the coming and going of birds. The birds with their semi annual coming and going were one of the earliest means that delineated the two African seasons.

In Sanskrit the word for time is KA and is linked with the seasonal coming and going of birds. The Hindu Goddess KALI, is the Goddess of Creation and Destruction. In her most basic ancient aspect she represents the calendar (KALA-) of time. With her bloody tongue sticking out she kills and swallows the sun every night, the solar time keeper. It is the movement of time that spares no living thing, not even the sun that Mother Kali represents as the bloody personification of life and death. Time is the only constant.

The activity associated with the crisscrossing of the sun, moon and birds, the passengers of the air, was considered like a never ending caress (KARASA) to the abdominal vault of air above the body of Mother Earth. It may SOUND poetic, but that was the ancient perception and attitude that emerging human beings had to their beloved planetary nest. Keres (KARASA), as 'belly or abdomen' in Hebrew, deals with the belly of air above Her surFACE. The SHAPE of the passage of the heavenly travelers across the belly of air, was believed to be reflected below Her surFACE, in the watery womb of re-creation. Both movements, the crisscrossing above in the belly of air above Her surFACE and the intuited crisscrossing below in the reflective womb of re-creation, was ALSO symbolized by the SHAPE of the cross (KARASA).

The emergence of the passengers of the air above Her surFACE and their descent below Her surFACE, dealt with the SHAPES of the angles of emergence and descent. Above Her surface, the angle of emergence, (the vertical movement up, of sun, moon and birds) from the body of Mother Earth, was encoded into the SHAPE of the letter L, of LIfe, LIght and of movement. (LI is movement in Sanskrit). The angle of descent (the vertical movement down of sun, moon and birds) into the body of Mother Earth, was encoded into the SHAPE of the number seven, the KH (KAHA), or the cough (KAHA) of death of the Hebrews. Both the cross and the angles of ascent and descent also fed into the SHAPE of the swastika. On the ends of the arms of the cross in the East is the SHAPE of the letter L, and in the West with the death of the sun the SHAPE is encoded in the number seven. Same concept is expressed through the KH (KAHA) of the Hebrews with the cough (KAHA) of death that as the SHAPE of the number seven established for the sun both the time of separation and the time of death.

In PHASE THREE as the redefinitions proliferated the 'FALL' of the heavenly bodies and birds, off the edge into the horizontal body of Mother Earth, became redefined as the 'FALL OF MAN' in PHASE THREE and with it all the admonitions that the descent implied, resulting in damnation, guilt and shame. As you fell, if you went deep enough beneath Her surFACE, you reached the burning fires of everlasting Christian hell. Twisting, turning, mist of the mister.

In Greek KHOROS (KARASA) is 'dance'. Movement across the sky was not only a caressing, but a dance of the sun, moon and of the birds accompanying their pavan with a chorus (KARASA) of song. SOUND traveling upon the wind, caressed the air, as the fan SHAPE of the spread fingers of light caressed the body of Mother Earth at dawn. The word dance (DANASA) is the gift of (DA) the nose (NASA). They all circled each other, danced around each other, based on the sense of smell, led by the nose. The males circled the females in heat. The sun, moon and birds circled the body of Mother Earth. Out of contemporary scientific discovery the moon circles the Earth, the Earth circles the sun and the electron circles the nucleon. Can physical chemistry be based on the sense of smell?

The circle is the round ground, the flat plane that was perceived to be the body of Mother Earth. If you stood at the center and looked around, the land ending at the horizon line created an equidistant circle as far as the eye (I) could see. Wherever you went, the circle went with you. You were always at the center of it.

The body of Mother Earth always surrounded you, always held you at the center in Her great belly of air above Her surFACE. That SHAPE of the cross, created by the migratory patterns of the birds began to feed into many evolving concepts. For not only did the birds create a vertical passage across the sky from North to South, but they seemed to precipitate the rain and the beginning of two major human rites of passage. One was in the spring, at the time when estral herbivore females reddened their flanks with blood, when males butted heads with other males and then proceeded to butt buttocks with the receptive females. The other time was in the fall, when herbivore mothers gave birth to their young. These two movements fell at the times when the stirring of the ancient migrations of the herbivore herds began across the plains of Africa. The bird migrations, coming and going, coincided with these two events and originally reckoned the seasonal passage of time.

After they noisily greeted each other, found their nesting sites, sometimes in isolated nests, and at others times in extended avian cities, laid their eggs, fed and regurgitated food for their fledgling brood, at the end of their stay with the savannah turning to dust, they too felt the pull to move. In great swirls, often obscuring the sun they sailed into the heavens and disappeared back into the body of Mother Earth, at what was considered to be the darkness in the Northern sky and the Southern fareaches.

The heavens held light out of three directions. One was where the pale disc of the newly born sun rose low in the Eastern sky. Another was when the parching, broiling tropical sun rose to its highest point in the Southern sky, casting few shadows below. The third was when the blazing setting sun, still holding on to its light, tired from its journey across that distended belly of air, sailed into the Western horizon, into the waiting bosom of Mother Earth, to die to its light and to the warmth of day.

The sun never sailed through the Northern reaches of the sky where it was always cold and dark. The KHU (KAHA) of the Egyptians with the anlaut of the letter K, defines the SHAPE of the lotus and delineates the process. The left arm of the lotus is the West. The center arm of the lotus is the South. The right arm of the lotus is the East. The Northern reaches are represented by the stem or trunk of the lotus, emerging out of the darkness below. The darkness below was not only the nether reaches within the body of Mother Earth where it was always dark, but it also dealt with the Northern reaches of the sky through which the sun never sailed and where it never shone. The internal darkness within the body of Mother Earth became associated with the darkness in the Northern sky and the darkness of the night sky. In all three cases it was perceived that a death had occurred and it was the death of the sun. When after one of the great cataclysms the Maya ventured across the great oceans to settle a new continent, they took that fear of the suns demise with them. Their need to sacrifice every human slave, servant or captive was to send a river of blood for the sun to sail through the under ground intestines on its way to be reborn.

For the Greeks, the Goddess Keres (KARASA) was associated with the dog faced furies and the underworld of death, the womb of re-creation, the belly under the surFACE of Mother Earth. The same Goddess, Ceres (KARASA) of the Romans, not only ruled the underworld but was also accompanied by canines or kurs (KARASA). There was an ancient belief that the sooner you were reabsorbed back into the body of Mother Earth as digested CAnine feces, the sooner you could be reborn. CArrion eaters of all sorts filled the bill. Cats, vultures, hyenas, jackals and especially dogs, were considered to be the companions of the Goddess and assistants in the process of re-creation within the body of Mother Earth. They sCAvenged and dispatched the fallen corpses, leaving their defecation to be readily absorbed and sent on its journey of transformative rebirth.

In Northern Europe the Valkyres (VALAKARASA) performed the same function. They were considered to be sacred bitches, she wolves, female psychopomps, Nekhbet vultures, who facilitated in the passage of corpses, ie fallen heroes on their journeys of transformation.

THE CROSS (KARASA), OF CHRIST. The anlaut in the name of Christ did not come out of the C (see) or CH SOUND of birds chirping their way into new life. The CH of Christ came out of the KH SOUND of death and rebirth, and then the subsequent more expansive movement into transformative immortality. The cross, created by the sun and moon moving vertically across the sky and the birds moving longitudinally back and forth across the continent of Africa, became appropriated in PHASE THREE by the emerging Christian religion as the subsequent symbol of Christ. His sacrifice was to hang upon the cross, uniting the body of Mother Earth and the sky, (which had emerged as the domain of the Father). The overhead passage of the heavenly bodies and the birds united the belly of air with the body of Mother Earth. Early Christian crosses bear a marked resemblance to the Cretan, Minoan Linear B symbol for the phoneme KA associated with the SOUNDS made by the beaks of birds. Leaving behind the circle, the ground of being, the circular plane on the body of Mother Earth, it emerged simply as the cross, the major symbol of male based Christianity. The transformed male Christ (KARASA-) was related to both crystals (KARASA-) and specifically to the metamorphic transformative stage of the chrysalis (KARASA-) of flying insects.

In Europe trees emerged to represent the same concept of unity between the body of Mother Earth and the belly of air above Her. It may be one of the reasons why the Druids worshipped them. They were a living metaphor of a greater and more comprehensive concept. The SHAPE of a tree with its fan of branches shooting up into the heavens and its fan of roots creeping deep into the Earth had been perceived to be in the SHAPE of a spindle. Originally it dealt with the three parted unity that was Mother Earth; the belly of air above Her surFACE, the womb of re-creation below Her surFACE and the round ground of being upon Her surFACE.

The roots dug deep into the body of Mother Earth. The branches fanned out into the heavens. The trunk united what was above and what was below, acting as a vehicle of passage for the energies that attracted the energies of the sky (sun and moon), to the body of Mother Earth. With male role in specific paternity becoming known in PHASE TWO the attraction shifted to the mind of the Father in the heavens toward the body of the Mother in the Earth. It was a period where there was a short lived balance of shared power between the sexes. In Greek the word for spindle that united the body of Mother Earth with the Father God in the sky is ATRACTOS, having links with a celestial ATTRACTION.

The SHAPE of the tree as the spindle, or the Greek ATRACTOS, extended to embrace the SHAPE of the apple core. As the centrality of the Mother was shoved aside and obliterated, as Her ancient power became hidden underground, in PHASES TWO and THREE the apple core became one of Her hidden symbols as was the Bemba female greeting of KUKU. Halved vertically, with its *five* pits exposed it became the numerical symbol of the ancient mothers. Originally it was all one, a complete singular unit, which embraced Mother Earth, the sun and the moon. Then it became two, Mother Earth and the belly of air above Her. Then it became three, Mother Earth, the belly of air above Her, and the womb of re-creation below Her. Then with male role in specific paternity becoming known, it became four, out of the four phases of the moon which sailed through the nether portals of night and was officiated over by the eunuchized male priesthood.

With the obliteration of female centrality based on the worship of the Mother, the apple core with its five hidden seeds became Her secret symbol. Mother right went underground with the number five, the apple, Avalon, the Court of King Arthur with its round table, all dealing with the balanced, cooperative worship of the triparted aspect Mother Earth. It surfaced in Romanticism and was quashed as heresy, replacing the more extensive horrific practice of European witch burning by the Christian mobs and the practice of clitorectomies in North Africa, Southern Asia and the Middle East. In PHASE THREE to round out the picture of redefinitions the pentagon (five triangles) became redefined as part of satanism, devil worship, the black mass and wanton sexuality. The ancient sources out of female experience locked in the ancient phonemes, still poke their way through the miasma of male redefinitions.

For the sun and the moon, the time of their departure and death, was in the West where they fell off the edge at a right angle, were swallowed by the great maw, fell into the encircling arms, settled into the waiting bosom, penetrated the vigilant vagina (you can take your pick depending on when you chanced on the going ancient perception). For the birds, the same process of cyclical death occurred when they disappeared into the body of Mother Earth in the far reaches of the Northern sky. They too died to the light of their life in the North, not unlike the sun and the moon had died to their light and life in the West. As the sun and moon began their transformative journey of rebirth through the body of Mother Earth after they disappeared in the West, so the birds too began their transformative journey through the body of Mother Earth, after they disappeared in the North.

It was a wonder and a mystery to our ancient ancestors as to what happened to the sun and the moon after they slowly slid out of sight and pulled their light down after them. It was no less of a wonder what happened to the flocks of migrating birds when they too disappeared back into the body of Mother Earth, taking their endless chatter with them, leaving the heavens empty and silent. They pondered and came up with what probably seemed to them very reasonable conclusions. Like the sun and moon disappeared in the Western sky, back into the body of Mother Earth to be transformed and reborn, so the birds must have followed the same pattern. They too disappeared over the rim, into the body of Mother Earth in the North. Not all of the birds left. Some like the condors and vultures remained in their territorial haunts, and like other CArrion eaters dispatched the remains (KAKA) of their prey into the realms below. Another factor emerged. Since the human spiritual essence, subsequently called the human soul, was perceived to follow the same journey as the sun and the moon, to be transformed and reborn once it died, because the birds followed the same pattern, they too must have been companions of the human soul on its journey of rebirth. Among the legends and myths that have remained in the traditions of the world, there emerges the symbolism of birds having links with the human soul after death. There emerges a curious perception that surfaces in the Tibetan word BARDO. For the Tibetans it means ' an intermediate state' and is usually associated with the Bardo the state between death and rebirth, or reincarnation. For Bardo (BARADA) is the 'gift of' (DA) the BAR, like the Christian Limbo. This gift of the BAR was not limited to reincarnation. It extended to a wide variety of ancient concepts out of PHASE ONE. It also embraced the birds (BARADA). How? Because birds existed in that 'intermediate state' of air defined by the Tibetan Bardo (BARA-), between the body of Mother Earth and the vault of the sky above. It expanded to include the I'bur (HABARA) another word for Hebrew pregnancy. A fetus existed in that 'intermediate state' between non existence and life on the surface.

One of the most ancient definitions of the 'intermediate state' dealt with the castrated eunuchs who officiated over the rites of the rising and setting sun to which the human soul had become attached. A eunuch as the first born castrated brother (BARADA) was no longer a male and not a female.

Section Three

He existed in that 'intermediate state' defined by the Tibetan Bardo (BARA-). The hiBERnating bear (BARA) also became a representation of that 'intermediate state' while it slept through the winter months. An ancient city of Ubar (HABARA) lost in time and rediscovered in the Sahara Desert sat at the crossroads of ancient trade routes and may have been named for its 'intermediate' position between other oasis.

The Phoenix (FANAKASA) an allegorical bird rising out of its own ashes, like the sun rose out of its ashes after it made its transformative journey through the immolating body of Mother Earth and then during a volcanic eruption rose out of its own ashes. Containing in its linguistic folds there surfaces the snake (IS NAKA) the symbolic form of the Kundalini energy and the mothers coos (KASA). Not to be left out the (FANA) deals with the fan (FANA) of fingers (FANA-) that had been perceived to do the actual work.

For the Toltec Indians of the 'new world' KU KUL KAN (KA KALA KANA) was the feathered serpent of light. The feathered serpent represents the Kundalini electro magnetic energy as the symbolic snake emerging from underneath the body of Mother Earth to take its place as the male sun in the sky. With the KU repeated in its name it harkens back to the KU dealing with the Hindu name for the individual mother and Mother Earth. In PHASES TWO and THREE it followed the same trajectory as the movement of the eunuchized priesthood from its power base under the ground to its power base above the ground. Since the body of Mother Earth had been taken by the ancient mothers they rose up into the sky like their distant relatives in the 'old world'. The 'old world' created a male Father God to take the place of Mother Earth. In the 'new world' they stayed with the old symbols of snake and birds and came up with the feathered serpent a convoluted combination of both. Ku Kul KAN (KA KALA KANA) not only SOUNDS like a SOUND made by a bird, but hides within its linguistic feathers many ancient clues.

(KAKA) in one direction deals with the actual SOUND made by birds. It also deals with had been perceived to defecate, the KAKA of small creations out of the body of Mother Earth. (KALA) deals with the angle of ascent from under the plane, (LA) like the sun and moon guided by the ubiquitous metaphoric snake or serpent ascended vertically up to Her surFACE. (KANA) is the skin, (IS KANA) on the body of Mother Earth, Her volcanic cone (KANA) through which all had to make their passage above into life and below into death. Like the metaphoric snake made its passage through the nether chambers of the stomach or womb to guide the rebirth of the sun, like the birds had to make their passage above Her surFACE in the belly of air to bring back life and the time of beginnings, so the skin (IS KANA) on the body of Mother Earth acted as their overwhelming unifying treadmill, or vehicle of passage.

The coming of the birds flying vertically up and down the length of the continent of Africa seemed to coincide with two human and herbivore activities. One was in the spring when herbivore mothers came into heat and the march began in March following the rains that fell in the distance creating greener pastures. The other was when the herbivore mothers dropped their foals and began their migratory march back to their ancestral homes at the foot of the mountains. Because the birds returned to their nesting grounds in Africa semi annually to lay their eggs, at the time when female animals came into heat at one end of the year and dropped their foals at the other, they became associated with the overwhelming creation of smaller replicas of themselves and of mother hood.

In Finnish the word MATKA, means 'trip'. In Polish the word MATKA, means 'mother. It was the ancient mothers who made the trip, who knew the way, who knew how to make the migratory journeys across the continent of Africa. In Egypt, the wise mother who knew 'the way' was the Goddess MAAT, the mother of wisdom and justice who weighed the soul at death against a feather. If the soul was heavier than a feather it didn't pass. Sadness and grief made the soul heavy. Sadness and grief were not a good for the ancient Egyptians and the people who preceded them. Lightness of heart and the pursuit of joy were their highest good. In PHASE THREE the pursuit of righteousness, chest beating, fear, misery and the mia culpas of guilt and shame of the Fathers in the pursuit of answers to the WHY of their empty bellies, replaced the lightness of heart of the ancient mothers. The HUM of HUMor and the LAUGH (LAFA) of LIFE (LAFA) has a place here.

It was the activities associated with rain falling out of the belly of air above the body of Mother Earth, with the processes associated with the bodies of mothers, their flow of estral blood in the spring and their birthing of calves in the fall, which precipitated the ancient migratory journeys. The showers (IS HAWARASA) in the distance showed (IS HAWADA) them how (HAWA) to get to their ultimate destination, to the grasses that came with the falling rain. The (WA) in how (HAWA) deals with the water (WA) that fell from the sky. (HA) deals with the belly of air out of which it fell upon the parched ground turning the world with the promise of greener pastures.

It was the mother that led (LADA) the ancient migrations, she as the lady (LADA), who knew the land (LA-), was the *lea*der (LADARA). The (LA) of

Section Three

leader and of lady, in this case deals with the angles of movement, the legs (LA-) that carried them across the land. (DA) deals with 'gift of'. The leader who led, was the lady, who had the gift of the angle or leg, that made the leading across the land possible. When it was discovered that the mineral lead (LADA) could show the way and always pointed North to the magnetic pole, it became named after the skill that the ancient mothers had on all levels, originally in navigating the continent of Africa and then the far reaches of the world.

It was the wise old elephant matriarch who could detect the rumbling of coming rains in the distance that also led (LADA) the ancient migrations. The word eleph (HALAFA) of elephant is close to Aleph (HALAFA) and Aleph or Alpha deals not only with beginnings but with half (HALAFA) of the journey.

Puns have a way of popping up and peppering the ancient linguistic landscape. Without them there would have been few signposts along the way. At the time that the estral blood of the herbivore females began to flow (FALAWA), many of the birds flew (FALAWA) to their nesting sites. Their flocks (FALAKA) filled (FALA-) the sky with their calls of recognition and assembly. The fowl (FALA) also emerged out of the vertical axis of the Northern sky in the fall (FALA), at the time when the foals (FALA), fell (FALA) out of the bodies of their mothers. FALA is the ubiquitous word for wave in Polish, the fingers (FA) that held the movement (LA). It means movement up and down in stage three.

With the herbivore herds it meant the migratory movement half way in one direction and then back across the continent of Africa. For the foals (FALA) it meant the movement down out of the bodies of their mothers, to fall (FALA) to the Earth and then quickly to rise to their wobbly legs, so as not to become the next meal for hungry predators. For the birds, the fowl (FALAWA) of the air, the movement up and down is not only reminiscent of flying (FALA) but at their departure, in the Fall (FALA) they seemed to fall (FALA) off the horizontal edge in the Northern reaches of the dark and lonely sky. (FA) in this case deals with fingertips, the fingers of fire, the solar rays helping the sun to be born in the Eastern sky. The fingers touching at the tips created the tent like SHAPE of a wave, the movement up and down, pushing its way to Mother Earths surFACE, like the wave on the waters moved up and down, pushing its way up to Her surFACE and then subsiding, like the estral flow within females rose to the surface and then subsided, like the foals rose to the surface out of female bodies, like the birds rose out of the body of

Mother Earth and then fell or were pulled back into Her, like the tips of the fingers, pressed into service, flushed pleasure to the surface.

The avian flocks left and faced their journey North at the time that the ancient migrations began their journeys back home to the place of their origins, leaving behind the drying savannas and the sky empty of their noisy presence. The birds also became associated with the time of leaving, departure and death. Life, nurturing and death came out of the body of Mother Earth. Life, and nurturing came out of bodies of individual mothers. Birds came to express the qualities of beginnings out of female bodies, the nurturing of the young and their disappearance back into the body of Mother Earth. In time in PHASE THREE they became male metaphoric symbols of the 'intermediate state' leaving behind their relationship with the body of Mother Earth.

The KHU (KAHA) of the Egyptians as the death rattle, symbolized by the lotus, and explained by the fact that it rose out of the mud, out of the muck below into the light above, tells only part of the story. It may very well deal with the migratory patterns of birds and their return back to life out of the dead Northern reaches, where no sun existed in the sky. The KHU (KAHA), not only symbolizes the last cough (KAHA) of death but its anlaut is the letter K. Since the letter K emerged out of the SHAPE of the birds beak, and the SHAPE of the buttox halved vertically then the KHU has its links with the departure of birds in the North, clacking their way across the sky leaving the heavens empty of their presence and the world below silent. Then it moved to express spiritual wisdom out of the top of heads of sages and gurus, the thousand petal lotus that as the Kundalini energy dealt with the light bursting within, behind the third I (eye) of the self, and a state of enlightenment. Having lost its original links with birds that arrived at the time that herbivore mares came into their estral heat, the lotus is another ancient name for the female vulva, out of which blood flowed, portending the possibility of new life. Odysseus lotus eaters, take on subtle, if different meanings, not unlike the sucre of the penis.

The flowering was not exclusive to the young girl with the flow of blood out of her body announcing that she was ready. The flowering also dealt with the phallus (FALASA) that flowered with its own flow. The SA deals with blood that engorged the penis and created an erection. The FALA deals with the movement up and down. In Polish FALA surfaces here also and means wave, that which moves up and down on the body of Mother Earth.

The flow (FALAWA) also announced the rise of sap and the flow of moisture up to the branches of deciduous trees to emerge as flowers (FALAWARA).

Section Three

As flowers announced the coming of fruit, so the rising of the menstrual flow in a young girl announced her maturity (MATARATA) and the possibility of her becoming a mother (MATARA). In the menstruating young girl it announced that the sap (SAPA) or her blood (SA) had risen. (SA) deals with blood. The (PA) deals with passage. The flower (FALAWARA) at the tip of a branch announced that the sap had risen. The sap as moisture, is represented by the (WA) of water, in the word flower (FALAWARA). The (RA) deals with the return of the sun as the doer and helper. The original menstrual flow needed no help. It responded to the periodic pull of the moon.

How do you establish the letter K as having links with the beak of a bird? If you hear the SOUND that a bird makes how do you translate it into the letter K? The answer is eminently obvious. You look to the SHAPE that made the noise associated with the SOUNDS of KA, KU, KE, KI, KO. Like the letter M came from the SHAPE of the top lip on the face of the Mother, her mouth that made the humming SOUND of assent that the food was edible, like the SHAPE of the letter N came out of the SHAPE of the nose seen in profile and made the nasal SOUND of negation as the food was being regurgitated and shoved out of the mouth as inedible, and the air moved in and out, so the SHAPE of the beak of the bird made the KA, KU, KE, KI, KO SOUNDS.

In many cases in the languages of the world, whenever there are words that begin with the anlaut of K or C pronounced as KH, X (ks) or even Q (cue), or words that have the same SOUNDS in them, what you are dealing with is their origins in the SHAPE of the beak of a bird and the SOUNDS that emanated from that beak. That concept has been made clear by the Finnish AAKKOSET as emerging out of the mouths of old women dealing with the 'holding' of meaning through the use of segmented SOUND. In the Western Alphabet it emerges as dealing with one of the concepts of 'holding', through the use of the body of Mother Earth, the female pubis, vulva or hand (KAF, KAPH). In Greek the letter K is represented by KAPPA and deals with the body of Mother Earth recreating or copying (KAPA) Herself, echoing the Hebrew concept of Kheek (KAKA) dealing with imitation.

In Meroitic Ethiopian the hieroglyph for the letter K is a bird. In Sanskrit the letter K is called KAKARA. In Basque KAKARA is to cackle and to cluck. Many of the SOUNDS associated with the birds that made them, became their actual names. In Sanskrit the word for partridge is KAKORA. The word for chicken or hen in Swahili is KUKU. There is a tribe in the Camaroons of West Africa, called KUKU. In Basque the word for the SOUND of the cookoo bird is KUKU. In Latin the name for the cuckoo bird is CUCULUS.

In Greek the name of the cuckoo bird is KOKKYX. In Sanskrit the cuckoo bird is KOKILA. In Hebrew the name of the cuckoo bird is KOKEEYAH. For the South African tribe of Bemba the word for bird is KAKA, or KAKILA. A fowl or hen is NKOKO. In Amharic a clutch of hens is ASKAKKA. To cluck in Amharic, is TANKAKKA. The TAN of TANKATTA may have links with the TEN (TANA) fingers that when joined at the tips created a tent (TANATA) or the SHAPE of a closed beak. Some birds hold their beaks up in the air as if searching for the stars. In Latin tenere (TANARA), means to hold, and it deals with the ten (TANA) fingers that do the holding. In Finnish the name of a duck is ANKAA. In Bemba the name for the chanting go hawk is KAKOSHI. In Sanskrit the crow is called KAKA and also defines cackling and contempt. In Maori the brown parrot is called KAKA. It must have made a similar SOUND. The word KAKA of the brown parrot deals with other possibilities, which will become readily apparent. KAKUTA is the name for cock (KAKA) in Sanskrit. In the Bugotu tribe of the Solomon Islands of the South Pacific, KUUKUU is the name for pigeon. In Sanskrit the SOUND that a peacock makes, is KEKA. The maker of that SOUND is KEKIN. The N in KEKIN deals with the SOUND that is made deep inside of the gullet of a peacock and is pushed up to the surface (N). In Chinese the peacock is KONGQUE. A swan in Greek is KUKNOS. A raven in Sanskrit is called KAKOLA. The green parrot of the Bugotu is called KIEKIGNEK. The Maori night owl is called KAKAPOE. In French the word for cockatoo is CACATOE. The chicken or hen in Chechen is called KOOTAM. In Polish, a chicken or hen is called KURA. For the Bugotu Islanders, the pigeon is called KAVUKU. In Sanskrit, a pigeon is called KAPOTA. The Polish rooster is called KOGUT. In English the name for the rooster is simply cock (KAKA).

Many birds were not only named by the onomatopoeic SOUNDS that they made with their open beaks that became immortalized by the letter K, but the SOUNDS themselves became codified in the languages of the world. KOKIROKO means the cock, or to crow, in Bugotu of the Solomon Islands of the South Pacific. KIKIRIKI is the onomatopoeic SOUND for cockle-doodle-do in Basque on the Iberian Peninsula in Europe. KUKURIKU is the Polish word for the crowing SOUNDS made by the exuberant cock in North Eastern Europe. KALUKULUKU is the name for turkey in the South African tribe of Bemba. Among a tribe of American Indians in California KUKSU is the 'big head' ceremony. It is a death and rebirth myth and the 'big head' is the feather headdress worn during the pageant as boys became transformed into men.

Section Three

The SOUNDS that originated out of the SHAPES of the beak of birds not only gave names to the birds that made them but also became imitated to represent an endless variety of human emotions; laughter, sadness, joy, exuberance, courtship, ownership, comfort, pride and with many of the other apparently shared feelings. Choros (KARASA) in Greek means dancing. Chorus (KARASA) in English deals with singing. Singing and dancing was an inter-joined activity. In Egypt KA is represented with the arms upraised singing and dancing, greeting the sun. The joy associated with singing and dancing was created by the birds, as they awoke just before dawn (ALFA-GIRI) in Swahili. ALFA deals with the beginning of a new day. GIRI (GARA) deals with the mountain out of which the sun rose at dawn. In Polish gora (GARA), also means mountain.

The pale glow spreading across the Eastern sky announced that the sun was coming. They all rose in a great chorus, the birds, the apes, and even humans, helping the sun to wake up from its nocturnal slumber and encouraging it to rise up into the sky. The sun is risen they cheered, it is here to light our way, to bring us warmth and to fill our lives with laughter and joy, to push back the terrors of the dark and perilous night. KA in Chinese is song. In Latin to sing is cano (KANA). In Basque to sing is cantatu (KANATATA). In Greek KHOROS (KARASA) is to dance. It was the dawning chorus (KARASA) caressing the sky at dawn that brought singing, dancing and laughter to the chilled and huddling humanity.

Laughter and joy for human beings, the howling of apes and the serenade of the avian chorus accompanied the rising of the sun at dawn. In Amharic, laughter and cackle is KAKALA. For the Bemba tribe KUKU shared by women meant to chuckle. In Bugotu to chuckle is also KUKU and KIAKUKU. To laugh in Sanskrit is KAKH and SOUNDS like a cough. Funny and amusing in Chinese is KEXIAO (KAKASAYA). (AYA) deals with light in Persian and dawn in Assyrian, and deals with the joy that the sun had risen. In Latin violent laughter is CACHINNO coming from deep within the oral CAvity.

The other side of joy and laughter also expressed by birds was sadness and grief, for the birds disappeared in the far reaches of the Northern sky, in the cold Northern tomb of darkness. They, as mourning doves made sad cooing noises that resonated in the often broken human heart. In Chinese, KU and KUQI mean to cry and to weep. KOU is mouth in Chinese, the source of all that crying. KU in Sanskrit deals with making a bad SOUND. For the Asian Indians crying must have been perceived as a bad SOUND. KAKU in Sanskrit is to cry, howl and wail. KIN, KEEN is the SOUND of lamentation and to wail in Hebrew same as KEENing in English. In Persian KIN means revenge and hatred. It was family pride in Persia that led to hatred and had to be avenged. KONO is sorrow and grief and KOKI is miserable in Bugotu. KUKOEIN in Greek is to wail and lament. In Lithuanian KAUKI is to howl, wail and hoot. KEXU (KAKASA) in Basque is to be worried and preoccupied. Also in Basque KAUKEZIA is misery and KIKLI is shy and timid. Cocytos (KAKATASA) in Latin is the stream of weeping and wailing, and is the name of the river to the nether world that had to be crossed after death.

The cries made by birds also became associated with the SOUNDS of raised voices and anger. In Swahili shouting and noise is KELELE. In Hebrew K'LALA (KALALA) is a curse, made not only by the beak of a bird but also by the angle of the tongue. Lengua in Latin, is the tongue, the angle that lies on the bottom of the oral cavity. From another direction the tongue is the angle that lies on the floor of the oral cavity and tells lies. In English, to call (KALA) is to cry out. In Ethiopia, one who acts as a mediator, makes the call is KALLU. In Greek KLEESE is the word for call. In Bugotu, KUAKUALA means to cry out. In Basque an argument or a quarrel is KALAPITA. In Sanskrit angry is KAPI and deals with Mother Earth as Her volcanic cone boiling over the top. In Polish kapi (KAPA) means to drip or boil over. KAKOS (KAKASA) in Greek is harsh SOUNDing and bad. KAKA in Sanskrit defines not only the crow, but also contempt. COCKY in English, deals with male erection, arrogance and hubris. KAWELE in Bemba are shouts and hoots of derision.

Fear also entered the picture and is expressed through the SOUNDS made by birds. KEKE in Bugotu means to cry out with fear. KIKITA is fright in Sanskrit. KIKILDU in Basque means frightened and cowed. COOEE is a SOUND made by Australian Aborigines to get attention. Mothers comforted their babies and lulled them to sleep with lullabies that also came out of the SOUNDS associated with birds. KAKALI in Sanskrit means low, sweet tone. KEHTOLAULU is lullaby in Finnish. ARRUMAKATU is to coo in Basque.

Bird SOUNDS extended to other means of communication. KIOKIDO in Bugotu means to beat a drum. For the Ashanti drumsticks of a bird were used to communicate on a drum. KABARO is drum in Amharic. In Hebrew one of the words that defines KAF is not only the hand but a spoon. A spoon SHAPED object was used as a drum stick to communicate over long distances on a drum, or more often on a hollow log. CAYO in Spanish means bone. KAKALO in Greek is also bone, the drumstick of communication. The cockle (KAKALA) shell communicated with SOUND by humming, 'holding' and then releasing the SOUNDS of the ocean. It was also used as a trumpet.

In Sanskrit KAKINI is a COwrie shell. Last but not least, a book (BAKA) like a beak (BAKA) has two sides and when opened, communicates meaning.

Stupidity and craziness were not only expressed as being a bit cuckoo, but in Basque KIAKUTU is the name of an idiot or a fool. Exhaustion in Swahili is KUUKUU, a SOUND that is often associated with chickens just before they settle down to sleep after a long day of pecking and scratching.

In Finnish the moon is KAUKAUSI (KAKASA). In Basque, KAUKEZIA (KAKASA) means misery. In Latin COCYTOS (KAKATASA) is the river of weeping and wailing that had to be crossed to get to the other side. The Caucasus (KAKASASA) Mountains in the Southern part of Europe must have played a role in the life of birds to be defined by the SOUNDS that they made. It may have come out of the observation that birds migrated back and forth across the continents, South to Africa in the fall and North to Europe in the spring. At the time of their autumnal departure they must have disappeared South over the crest of the Caucasus Mountains, alerting the huddling humanity in the European North that the time of darkness, of winter and of the gripping cold would soon descend upon them. All that they could do was wait and wonder when the sun and the birds would return to warm and light their way and noisily greet the coming of spring. That may be why the ancient Mongols faced the doors of their yurts to the South, because the coming of birds brought with them good luck.

For the African Southerners birds arrived with the promise of foals being born in the fall, of a new supply of milk and of the beginning of the journey back for migrating humanity to the foot of their beloved mountains. They left at the end of their stay and flew in great undulating waves to the far reaches in the Northern sky, where they disappeared over the CAUCASUS (KAKASASA) mountains, apparently to fall off the horizontal edge back into the body of Mother Earth. In Finnish the word for meeting, assembly or caucus (KAKASA) is KOKOUS (KAKASA) that is what the birds did as they gathered in large flocks and readied for their flight across the mountains. Also in Finnish KAAKKO (KAKA) means Southeast, which probably meant the direction that the birds disappeared after they assembled and departed.

In a North American Indian legend the birds flew Southwest in autumn to a cave at the foot of the sky with a spring in it, which was the winter home of the shades of the dead. It seemed to be a time when they took their journey to a secret, dark and distant place. The word caucus (KASASA) means a secret meeting, shielded from the eyes of the wary. In Latin CAECUS (KAKASA) means blind, invisible, concealed. The same perception out of Southern Europe was felt at the time of the new moon when the nights were plunged into total darkness. All that they could do was to wait for the moon to return. It was a time of waiting and misery, as the Basque word KAUKEZIA (KAKASA) indicates, which links it with the Finnish word for moon KAUKAUSI (KAKASA).

For the Algonquin Indians CAU CAU ASU (KAKASA) meant 'the one who advises'. Could it be that the movement of birds back and forth over the Caucasus (KAKASASA) mountains advised or alerted people to the changing of the seasons, before they migrated to the 'new world' and took the phonemes with them? It was also believed that when the birds disappeared into the Northern reaches of the sky, they settled back into the body of Mother Earth to be transformed and reborn.

In India the word for the mount of transformation is KOKKUTAPADA. Since KOKKUT is one of the names for rooster or cock (KAKA), the Polish KOGUT, then the mount of transformation may have been the place where the sun rose at dawn and the noisy rooster played a role in its awakening. The original concept of enlightenment may have had more practical origins. The Japanese word for 'space womb', dealing with a similar concept, is KOKUZO (KAKASA). The dyad KAKA deals with the SOUNDS made by birds, with the laying of eggs, and with Mother Earth making smaller aspects out of Herself. (KASA) deals with the coos (KASA), the buttox or house, casa in Spanish, of re-creation. The 'space womb' for the Japanese in PHASE TWO moved away from the body of Mother Earth, like it did in the Middle East with a Father God, who took up residence in the heavens and in Mexico with the feathered serpents covered both bases with the birds above and the snake below showing the sun the way back up to the surFACE. Male role in specific paternity was being established in PHASE TWO and with it the emergence of male symbols and a movement *away* from the body of Mother Earth. In Tierra Del Fuego CIEXAUS (KAKASASA) women originally held all of the power and they refused to listen to the men. The men killed them off and left one little girl to carry on the tribe. It was a harbinger of global things to come.

Could all of these ancient words have dealt with the appearance and disappearance of birds over the Caucasus KAKASASA) mountains signaling changes in the seasons and the strength of the rays of the returning sun? What does that say about the origins and spread of language and the durability of consonants?

In Sanskrit the plaintive cry of the cuckoo, echoing through the night, is KUHU. It is also the name for the new moon, the time of night and of total emptiness and darkness. The KH (KAHA) dealt with darkness and death. It is the dyad that is associated with the cough (KAHA) of death, the SOUND associated with the last breath fillibrating the vocal cords on its way out. In Arabic to cough is KAKH (KAKAHA). To cough in Swahili is KIKOHOZI (KAKAHASA) and has ancient echoes with the birds disappearing into the body of Mother Earth, dying to the flight of their life, over the Caucasus (KAKASASA) mountains to the North. The new moon is the time in the midnight sky when there was no moon and the mournful SOUND of the cuckoo bird, missing its nocturnal lunar companion, must have been the only SOUND that could be heard throughout the land.

The open beaks of birds of the letter K, also defined qualities that dealt with being clever, wise and intelligent as KHAKHAM (KAKAMA) in Hebrew. In Latin a braggart is called CACARE (KAKARA) and may have links with the strutting peacock in Sanskrit the KEKIN (KAKANA) making the SOUND of look at me, or KEKA (KAKA). The word coquette (KAKATA) has become associated with females but it began its life as a strutting cock (KAKA). Those betrayed by their mates have interestingly the name of birds attached to them as a cuckold (KAKALADA) or adulterer. In Basque the word KOKOLO (KAKALA) means stupid. The origins of the concept of being cuckolded, comes from the sneaky activity of birds. In Sanskrit KOOILA is a bird that lays its eggs in another bird's nest. Both the female cowbird and the female cuckoo bird lay their eggs in the nests of other birds. The SOUND of the CUCKOO was also associated with someone who was not altogether together, or a fool. The activity of laying your eggs in someone else's nest without your mate being aware of it, or being foolish about it, became associated with adultery and cuckolding.

Even the perch upon which the birds alighted became defined by the SOUNDS that birds made. In Basque the name for perch is KOKATO and SOUNDS surprisingly like the CUCKATOO in English. In Bugotu of the Solomon Islands of the South Pacific, the word for foundation is KOKOTO. A perch must have looked like the foundation for a bird. In English the name for a birdhouse is a COOP.

How did all of these qualities associated with the K SOUND out of the SHAPE of the open beak denoting the names of birds move over to become associated with the organs in and around the human face and head that made them? Imitation exists on all levels. KOO is throat in Swahili. KOU is mouth in Chinese. To vomit or to eject food out of the mouth is KU in Hebrew. To vomit alone is KI in Hebrew. Birds methodically regurgitate, or vomit food out of their beaks or mouths for their ravenous (out of raven), brood. The Sanskrit KAKU of crying and weeping came out of the KAKUD the palate, or 'the gift of' (DA), the place bearing the KAKU. In Basque to burp or to belch is KOKADA out of the same area and linguistic root. In Swahili KAAKAA is the name for the roof of the mouth. The palate in Hebrew is KHEKH. Not only is it associated with bird SOUND but the KH establishes it with the roof of the mouth through which fillibrate the SOUNDS of the death rattle. In Basque the name for the throat or pharynx is KOKORO. KIKOROMEO is larynx in Swahili. In Basque the name for the nape of the neck is KOKOT. In Greek the name for neck is KAKLAS. All of these SOUNDS even extending to deal with actual human body parts, begin with the letter K often repeated KK (KAKA), so their origins go back to the SOUNDS made by the beaks of the birds and to the palates, throats and necks that acted as their phonic vias of passage, that old women of the tribe began to incorporate as their means of communication.

CONCEPT OF SMALLER ASPECTS OF CREATION

The association that ancient human females made with the SOUNDS of birds dealt with the processes, qualities and functions that the birds possessed, the SOUNDS they made, how they reared their young, when they arrived and left, became associated with the activities of individual mothers and the body of Mother Earth.

Obviously when emergence upon the surface occurred, all female creatures pushed out of their bodies smaller, if transformed, aspects of themselves. Animal mothers produced cubs, kids, calves, foals, kittens and pups. Human mothers produced babies. Mother Earth produced not only Herself out of Herself as magma but also as lava which hardened into land, the sun and the moon out of Her side, out of Her circular surFCE at the horizon line. The SHAPE of the sun and the full moon was round. The fetus that emerged out of female bodies was not necessarily round, except for the placental sack. It came out with arms and legs flailing. It had appendages. The disc of the sun and of the full moon did not. The closest thing to the round disc of the sun and the full moon were the eggs laid by some creatures. Turtles, crocodiles, some snakes and birds laid relatively round eggs. Some, like ostriches, even laid eggs as large as a human skull. Water could be carried in them. It didn't matter. What mattered is not only did the birds lay smooth round or oval eggs, but they flew or sailed across the vault of the sky like the sun and the moon did, in the Tibetan BARDO or 'intermediate state'. Turtles and crocodiles did not, although they had other qualities to recommend them. The crocodile (KARAKADA-) became wedded to the SOUND of K, because its large jaws opened up like the beak of a bird and its young made a croaking (KARAKA-) SOUND as they became ready to break through the shells of their eggs. In Basque KOKODRILO as the crocodile associates it dimly with birds. The snake, the other part time egg layer, because of its intestinal SHAPE became relegated to assist the sun and the moon on their transformative journey through the bowels of Mother Earth. The SHAPE of the snake fit the intestines like a glove, like the skin fit the body. For the Maya KOKOATL was the water snake. ATL means water. KOKO shares its roots with the egg laying birds. Through its egg laying capacity and as a guide to the sun and moon on their transformative journeys within the body of Mother Earth, the birds joined the throng and the snake sprouted feathers. It had established its association as a guide for the sun and the moon, which expanded to include the birds, for the birds disappeared into the Northern reaches of the sky as the sun and moon had disappeared into the Western waters. For all intents and purposes guiding both the sun moon and birds through the body of Mother Earth, the lowly snake became KUKULCAN the Maya feathered serpent of light. The understanding that human beings had the processes dealing with digestion and gestation was very murky at the time that these observations were being codified. It all went in one end, went through a process of some kind of cooking (KAKA-) and change coming out the other end, as blood, urine, the fetus or feces (KAKA). Food went into the mouth, the top hole on the body, went through some kind of miraculous change and smaller aspects in different SHAPES, colors and textures then came out of the bottom holes as yellow urine and brown feces.

On the body of Mother Earth, the sun and the moon went into one hole on the horizontal side in the West and emerged out of the other hole on the other horizontal side in the East. Neat. The birds emerged out of the horizontal hole in the Northern sky, some continued on and disappeared into the horizontal hole in the Southern sky, others returned back up North.

In the language of Bemba, KUKA means to migrate. All of these emissions, feces, fetus, sun, moon, and birds were obviously smaller than the bodies of the mothers who fashioned them. Out of the bodies of birds, of mother hens (HANA), there emerged not fetuses, but round sun like eggs and that made all the difference.

A process must have existed within the female mother and the body of Mother Earth to transform the blood into a baby, and the magmic blood coursing through the body of Mother Earth into the coagulated disc of the sun and the curdled disc of the full moon. The process obviously had something to do with some kind of heat, some kind of cooking (KAKA-). When feces (KAKA) dropped or plopped from the bodies of creatures, or even human beings, steam rose from them in the tropical morning sun. Spoor (IS PARA) is more than an identifiable print. In Polish PARA is steam, the passage (PA) of the sun (RA) at dawn dispelling the banks of fog that caressed the hills and rose with the warmth of the sun into the heavens. For the Hittites there was a Goddess called KUPARA. Again in Polish PARA is steam but KUPA deals with a pile and the pile is usually feces or excrement. KUPARA the Hittite Goddess must have had links with transformation and cooking within the body of Mother Earth. When foals or calves, like feces (KAKA) dropped out of the bodies of their mothers, steam also accompanied their emergence upon the surFACE.

Eggs went through a different process. They may have emerged warm, but to hatch, for the hatchlings to emerge upon the surface, they had to go through an extra transformation. They had to be sat on by the mother hen. As she squatted above them, she had to engulf them under her heart, she had to embrace them with her very belly and the warm heat that it provided. They had to be externally cooked (KAKA-) before they pecked their way out of their shells and hatched into small replicas of the mother. In Finnish the word to peck is NOKKIA (NAKA) it has links with the snake (IS NAKA) but the double KK construct, establishes its origins out of bird SOUND.

The same process must have existed with the sun and the moon when they descended into the body of Mother Earth. To be reborn, they somehow had to go through a similar process of cooking (KAKA-) to emerge in the Eastern sky. When the sun was born at dawn, a kind of steam or fog hugged the mountains and valleys, accompanying its journey to the surFACE. When the moon rose at twilight, it was often accompanied by a misty haze. In Sanskrit mist or fog as an unknown ghostly quality is KUHI (KAHA). In the Caribbean Islands KAHU (KAHA) is the chief of evil spirits. Back in Sanskrit a rogue or a cheat is KUHA (KAHA). We are dealing here with the 'mist of the mister' in its most ancient ghostly form associated with the rites of the dead and their subterranean transformation over which the male psychopomps officiated. KH (KAHA) deals with some aspect of death in Hebrew. In Egyptian KHU (KAHA) is the lotus as the symbol of both transformation out of the murky mud and the return of the birds out of the Northern darkness associated with their departure and the death of their SOUND.

Section Three

They knew that great and awesome fires existed within the body of Mother Earth. Her calderas and craters bubbled and roiled blasting hot gas and smoke up to Her surFACE. Steam sissed and hissed out of Her vents and fissures. Steaming, boiling geysers shot up into the sky. The most ancient perception was that the body of Mother Earth under Her surFACE was like a female body with all of the internal organs, especially the intestines through which the sun, moon, birds, the soul and the snake guiding them had to pass, had to be transformed to be reborn.

Like food that was eaten became transformed into feces, as the blood that had stopped flowing coagulated and solidified into a fetus, so the splattered blood of the sun in the Western horizontal sea and the flowing milk of the moon hardened into celestial SHAPES that became the round red disc of the sun and the cheese-like whiteness of the SHAPE shifting moon.

The process that transformed food into feces, blood into fetus, magma into land, curdling into cheese, had been believed to be based on some aspect of internal cooking (KAKA-). Feces, milk, blood and fetus emerged out of the individual mothers body not only accompanied by steam, but by warmth. The sun as it emerged out of the body of Mother Earth brought not only light, but also warmth with it. Underneath the surface, whether it was within the individual mother's body, or within the body of Mother Earth, cooking (KAKA-) became the most apparent process that resulted in transformative change. That change became in time a mysterious transformation from one state into another. All things that were born, that came into existence above Her surFACE, became eventually absorbed back into Her body after they died. The sun and the moon, after making their passage through that daily cyclical return, reappeared as if born again at the time of their specific dawning. After the rains fell, grass and plants burst forth with new life upon the surFACE of the expansive savannahs. Birds announced their semi annual appearance, emerging out of the horizon line in the distance. Babies returned to the bodies of mothers to be born to a new life. The boomerang phenomenon enters here.

Everything that disappeared back into the body of Mother Earth, after some mysterious process, was in one way or another born again. They also believed in PHASE ONE that as the body was reborn into another body, into a new life, so the human essence also followed the same procedure. As a result of this ancient and universal belief, death was not a fearsome plunge into an abyss. Death was a process of change that resulted in transformative rebirth. The subsequent theories of reincarnation in PHASE ONE, as endless recycling and then immortality and as a fusion with the infinite, have their origins in those ancient belief systems. Linguistically the human soul (IS HALA) has its associative origins out of the sol (IS HALA), the Spanish word for sun. For the sun was the most profound symbol of constant rebirth, return and of being born again.

Out of Mother Earth's volcanic cone of creation her great calderic crater She not only created lava that coagulated into land upon her surFACE, she also created smaller aspects of Herself such as ash, pumice, gravel, boulders, smoke, cinders, pebbles, stones, soil, the ground itself that blasted it's way up to Her surFACE on a column of breathable air. There were periods when the volcano had been considered to be a massive vagina out of whose bloody menstrual effulgence reality came into being. There were times when the volcano was an enormous mouth that vomited land up to Her surFACE. The period that we are dealing with is when the volcano was a large anus that gave birth to feces or KAKA associating it with the coming and going of birds. The word anus (HANASA) containing two overlapping dyads (HANA) and (NASA) shouts with a major clue. For the anus (HANASA) is the birth (NASA) of the sun (IS HANA). In Latin birth is nascence (NASANASA), the repetitive quality of birthing. If the anus deals with the body of Mother Earth giving birth to the sun can the volcano be far behind giving birth to many aspects of land?

For the Hawaiians AKEKE (HAKAKA) is cinder, pebbly soil. The Chinese KI to split open and the Old English KI to burst open dealt not only in the creation of smaller aspects of Herself, but with a volcanic eruption, when Mother Earth split open the volcanic cone symbolized by the letter A, the fingertips of the helping hands closed, to become the letter H of the helping hands opened on top of air blasting it's way up to the surFACE.

In Africa for the tribe of Wolof soil and dirt are called KEKK (KAKA) making not only smaller aspects out of the body of Mother Earth as soil and dirt but those smaller aspects were named after feces (KAKA) and for some reason were linguistically associated with bird SOUNDS. In New Zealand on the other side of the great oceanic divide KAKE PUKU is the name of a maternal volcano, the maker not only of smaller aspects out of the body of Mother Earth but those smaller aspects are also feces (KAKA). PUK in Polish means to knock, to make a noise. That is what a volcanic eruption does. It makes a lot of noise. Once they blasted their way up to Her surFACE as jagged pieces of stone, pumice, and rock they fell back down upon Her and carried by molten cooling lava etched or scorched their way across Her skin creating patterns that defied explanation. It was as if the internal fires within Her body tattoed patterns upon Her skin. In Hebrew KAKA is tattoo made by Mother Earth out of Her internal cooking fires. It may explain why so many of ancient peoples out of PHASE ONE tattooed their skins. It may be to pay homage to an activity of reverential sharing in the process of creation inHERent out of the body of their great Mother Earth. Associated with the making of smaller objects related to feces (KAKA), the activity of land creation out of the volcanic cone in Polish as SKAKA means to jump. In Swedish SKAKA means to shake. KAK in Sanskrit is to tremble and shake. In Wolof to shake is YOKOKOKI covering a lot of bases. To shake and move about is KAKANU in Bugotu of the Solomon Islands. In Amharic of Ethiopia KAKA is to grind coarsely. KAKA in Basque means dirt and shit. All that jumping, shaking, trembling and grinding led to the evacuation of dirt and shit Her greatest creation of land out of the body of Mother Earth at this point in time out of Her volcanic anus.

The birds after their seasonal stay disappeared back into the body of Mother Earth in the Northern skies, they had to be somehow cooked (KAKA-) and transformed into solid flying objects. Could it be that the process of cooking (KAKA-) was originally associated with birds and the SOUNDS that they made? Or was it the other way around? Birds were cooked over hot fires to be eaten. Then why would the process of cooking (KAKA-) be associated with the SOUNDS that they made? Could it be that to cook something was to make it sacred, make it holy, have it share in the activity of transformation that was assumed to occur within the body of Mother Earth? Is that why birds became carriers of the soul and became vehicles of passage to another level after death?

To get the whole ancient picture of existence you have to weave together the warp and woof of the fabric. It all began with the mouth of the mother in stage one transforming the food from a solid fruit or meat into a masticated lubricated mass and regurgitating it for her hungry brood. Then in stage three it expanded into two processes in her body. One dealt with the transformative cooking that went on in her belly creating feces that usually emerged as a coil of solid matter out of the bottom hole on her trunk. The other process dealt with the transformative change that occurred as a result of the menstrual blood that had stopped flowing on the outside coagulating in her belly apparently cooking (KAKA-) the fetus into being. The process of cooking created a transformative change from a liquid into a solid. The feces emerged after a digested meal. The fetus emerged as a solid baby after ten lunar months of gestation.

What had been experienced by individual mothers expanded to include the body of Mother Earth. She in PHASE ONE became the most ancient fantasy created by mothers based on the shared process of motherhood. She too had to transform liquids into solids. As the solid fetus and relatively solid feces were creations of individual mothers, so that which Mother Earth created also had to go through the process of solidification.

Mother Earth created everything that existed. Plants and trees emerged out of Her surFACE. Rivers sprouted out of Her hillsides. Debris tumbled down her flanks during a volcanic eruption. Out of Her flat circular horizontal side she gave birth to the sun, moon, clouds and birds. The sun and moon usually rose in the horizontal East and after making their passage across Her belly of air were swallowed back into Her body into the horizontal maw of the Western waters. The semiannual arrival of the rain laden monsoons coincided with the arrival of the birds. The clouds usually rose in the Western horizon and swept West to East across the parched savannah. The birds flew North and South across the welcoming sky. But once the sun and moon set in the West, the monsoons became wasted in the East and the birds disappeared back into the body of Mother Earth in the North. What happened to them?

What happened to the creation of a baby out of the mothers coagulated blood was a mystery to them. What also happened to the sun, moon, clouds and birds once they set back into the body of Mother Earth was also a great mystery. They dealt with what they observed. If as a baby was created out of the flowing menstrual blood of the mother on the outside coagulating on the inside, then that same process must have happened on the body of Mother Earth. Creative myth making has an ancient history. Somehow the objects that Mother Earth created must have been created out of Her blood. But how and where?

The only magically colorful display of blood existed when at the horizontal rim the sinking sun killed to its rays of light looked as if it had been chewed into small liquid pieces reflected in the gore filled scarlet Western waters. The sun had not only to swim through that bloody sea, but also to use the bloody waters as Her sustenance.

That wasn't all. Mother Earth under Her skin had the same organs and processes that individual mothers possessed. She had a belly that transformed the liquids into solids and the sun as the bloody masticated gore splattered in the Western waters cooked its way into the solid round disc of the sun to emerge triumphant in the Eastern sky. The moon took a different route and for its whiteness emerged associated with milk.

The birds took the same transformative journey through the body of Mother Earth after they sank out of sight back into Her body in the Northern reaches. The difference between the sun, moon and clouds was that they were silent. They didn't make a peep as they found their way through the hearth and kitchen under the skin of Mother Earth. The birds on the other hand made a great racket. They became the definers of what went on under the mysterious mantle of their great Mother. As the birds disappeared under the mantle of Mother Earth they must have clacked their way through Her intestines and must have been aware of the cooking (KAKA-) that was associated with their own transformation from dying into living. The KAKA dyad may very well come from the metaphoric birds making their way through the underground intestines of Mother Earth and defining through their multi cacophonic SOUND what they experienced. Mother Earth was transforming the feces (KAKA) on one level. She was cooking (KAKA-) the pulsating liquid blood into a solid disc of the sun. As the birds cawed and clacked their way through Her intestines they also realized that some of the blood (magma) blasted its way up to the surFACE to spread out as liquid lava creating solid land. They also came to the conclusion that She kept back some of the blood to maintain Her life above the surFACE. Since they came to all those conclusions associating the body of Mother Earth with the transformative passage of birds, they went in the other direction and brought up their own creative source on their bodies, their clitoral beak, the coos (KASA) from the front and the X (KS) (KASA) of the buttox from the back. Because the birds (BARADA) flew through the air and were defined by the Tibetans 'intermediate state', the Bardo(BARADA) they emerged as not only mysterious but sacred. They like the sun and moon disappeared and then reappeared funneling into the concept of constant returns, being born again and reincarnation.

The word spirit (IS PARATA) deals with the breath, spirare in Latin. But the word spirit (IS PARATA) comes out of an even more ancient concept out of the body of Mother Earth. (PARA) in spirit (IS PARATA) out of Polish, means steam, or warm misty air that floats upon the morning breeze hugging the body of Mother Earth. (RATA) deals with return (RATARANA). To have been born again was to have had the warm breath of life return to the waiting body. The word return (RATARANA) contains in it three dyads that deal with the body of Mother Earth as the ultimate source of being born again. (RATA) deals with the ratio (RATA) or the cycle of constant returns. (TARA) deals with the terrain, the body of the planetary Mother. (RANA) deals with the emergence (NA) of the sun (RA). Again in Polish the dyad (RANA) contains in it two meanings. One RANA deals with dawn. The other (RANA) is a word for wound. It was perceived that on the body of Mother Earth, the sun rose out of the wound in the Eastern sky at dawn echoing the wounds that were being created on the bodies of individual mothers with the practice of clitorectomies.

So it came to them in one of their very early perceptions, that the body of Mother Earth was like a great big mother hen, who not only laid the eggs of the sun and the full moon but embraced them when they set back into her. She engulfed them like a great big hen, squatted on them, heated them, cooked them at Her hearth, as they made their way through Her intestines, bowels, belly, stomach, womb, gut, (you can take your pick), to emerge on the other side and be born again to their lives, to their soaring and passage through Her great belly of air above Her surFACE.

The same process had been echoed by the birds who obviously also squatted on their eggs, engulfed them under their hearts, cooked (KAKA-) them, before they too poked through their shells and took to the sky. In Hawaiian KAKALA means to be free, to take off, to be like the birds, who with their great freedom soared into the heavens and cackled (KAKALA-) their way across the sky. In the language of Bemba to squat down is MAKUNDA. In Basque the word for squatting is KUKUBILKA.

A beak is a sharp point used to break through the shell of an egg. In Swahili KEKEE (KAKA) is a boring tool, (maker of smaller aspects). In Greek AKE (HAKA) is a point. KAKUMEN in Latin is also a sharp point. In Sanskrit KAKUD means a peak or a summit. The beak of a bird pointing upward looks very much like tips of fingers touching, a tent or a mountain peak. For the Basque a hook is KAKO (KAKA). A crocodile baby has a hook on top of its upper jaw to break through its shell to be born, as do some snakes. KA deals with the making of smaller objects. Dealing with the phoneme K or KA all these words have their links with the activity associated with egg layers, snakes, crocodiles and primarily especially birds.

There are a variety of ancient myths that bear witness to that avian cooking and their emergence upon the surface whole and ready for a new life. The Phoenix or firebird, (named after the Phoenicians ?), mythologized that the bird like the penis was a symbol of immortality. It passed through fire and was reborn out of his own ashes. We are in PHASE THREE. He arose from the dead. He was transformed by the flames through which he had passed. He was cooked clean. Not only the Phoenix as the mythological bird who carried the metaphorical tale but actual flamingoes, with their pink and red feathers flaming in the sun, coming and going, appearing and disappearing from over the horizon, were the more physical manifestations of the ancient belief of reincarnation and subsequent immortality.

The Egyptians had a similar story. Their solar hero carrying the soul of the pharaoh was the hawk Horus. He also had to pass through fire to be released to immortality. There were other aspects with Horus the solar hero who as the hawk carried the soul of the pharaoh. The pharaoh not only had to pass through the fire but he also had to pass in a wooden barque through water. After passing through water, those same barques (BARA-) ascended to the air and grew wings like birds (BARA-) creations of the 'intermediate state'. This reflects the time in PHASE TWO when the priests of the nether chambers of death began to shift their perception out of the body of Mother Earth as a place of reincarnation, the endless cycle of rebirths symbolized by the sign of infinity to the stars *away* from the body of Mother Earth and open ended eternity as existing in the stars. It coincided with the time when male role in specific paternity was becoming known in PHASE TWO and RA as the Egyptian sun was becoming the major male solar deity.

The pharaoh may have been associated with the sun on one level, but he was also associated with the snake on another as the uraeus or cobra of his third eye indicates. He was also known by the soul name of BA. Now the anlaut of B of the birds, baal of husband in Hebrew and B of BA of the Egyptian soul, gives us a clue. For not only the birds had to pass through fire, or a process of cooking (KAKA-) to be reborn, but the sun, the moon, the husband, the pharaoh, and the human soul had to make the same journey. The Sanskrit baal or bali as sacrifice takes on new meanings. The tormented history of human sacrifice emerges out of convoluted interpretations of reality and the passage of the sun, moon and the birds through the nether regions within the body of Mother Earth to be cooked, transformed and be born again.

For the Romans an eagle released over the funeral pyre of an emperor representing the whole populace, was assured to carry his soul to heaven. In Latin aves, (avis is bird in Latin), ancestral spirits, ghosts and angels mean the same thing. In Central America, for the Aztec and Mayan priests the wearing of elaborate feathered outfits and calling themselves winged serpents, may have covered both bases, on their way to soul-flight and immortality. KUKULKAN was the name of their winged serpent.

Eggs came not only out of birds that flew above the surFACE of Mother Earth. They also came out of some snakes that slithered under the surFACE and through the waters on the body of Mother Earth. In PHASE THREE Christian saints ascended to heaven on the wings of white doves at the time of their Canonization (KANA-). The white dove became the symbol of peace and a symbol of their celestial deity. The only place where peace exists is after you are dead. So white doves as symbols of peace, of priests giving up the physical life turning to celibacy, of the death of the body, sacrifice of kings, elaborate preparations of the pharaohs, all have ancient links with the passage across a body of water and then the cooking (KAKA-) that was perceived to exist within the inner caverns, and then emerging as universally smaller (KA) items out of the body of Mother Earth. In PHASE THREE the immolating fires of transformative purification, out of the fantasized passage of the sun, moon and birds through the flaming body of Mother Earth embraced the human soul to make a similar journey. Except the passage was conditional. If the soul had been judged to be bad upon the planetary plane, it would never emerge up to the surFACE. It would be forever stuck in the kitchen (KAHANA) below the surFACE, in the fires of Hell within the body of Mother Earth. The good souls, like the barques of reincarnated birds, grew wings and as the feathered angles on their bodies, become the angels of light that sailed into the heavens, to rattle among the clouds for eternity. What had been left behind was the ancient knowledge of soul flight based not on bird stories as metaphors, but on the actual human spiritual experience that birds had been considered creatures of passage. Along with other female knowledge it was becoming vilified, became systematically lost, obliterated and buried. The witch hunts of recent history banged a few more nails into the coffin as not only female knowledge but female pleasure went underground. For the ancient Egyptians their great Goddess MAAT weighed the human soul at death against a feather. Birds again. If the soul was heavier than the feather it did not pass into immortality. What made the soul heavy? Sadness, grief and anger made the soul heavy. What made the soul light? Joy and laughter made the soul light. Many of the African tribes and the Arabs practice clitorectomies, to deny women their pleasure and their joy as one of their universal bases of power. The Hasidim of the Hebrews use women as reproductive beasts of burden and shave their heads as a symbolic shearing of power. Taliban of the Muslims delegate women to slavery, cover them from head to toe, so as not only to cover their faces but also to hide their distended bellies that won't show and bear witness to the lie that creation emerges out of the mind of a male God, Yahveh or Allah.

Whether you create smaller aspects out of the bodies of mammalian

Section Three

mothers, out of the bodies of herbivore mothers, out of the bodies of birds, or even the body of Mother Earth, before smaller aspects emerge, you have to have a process of separation, of bursting open which also takes the birds into consideration, as in pecking open a shell, splitting it apart. In Chinese KI is to split, a separation. In Old English KI means to burst open. In Hebrew, the process of bursting open deals with the mouth, for KI means to vomit. As the mouth separates, food bursts up to the surface is vomited up. In Finnish AUKKO (HAKA) means opening or the mouth out of which SOUND emerges. Out of Mesopotamia, KI means something that exists below the surface, ready to emerge. In Chinese, KI deals with the energy flowing up from the Earth along the YIN, or feminine meridian. In Bemba KU means out of, or from. Also from Bemba SHUKULA (IS HAKA-) means to rise from the Earth. In Chinese KUN (KANA) means the movement of the plant up from the Earth, splitting Her skin (IS KANA). In Sanskrit Ku defines Mother Earth. KUN became associated with the individual mother. KUNDA was the gift of (DA) of the Mother or the Goddess. KUNDALI dealt with movement of the Mother Earth energy of ecstasy and power. LI is movement in Sanskrit. KUNDALINI dealt with 'emergence on the surface' or a 'change from another state'. For the Bemba maKUNDA means to squat, as in either defecating or giving birth.

What is created once the split is made, are smaller aspects of the creative source. In Swahili, AKIKE (HAKAKA) or YAKIKE (HAYAKAKA) is female, the maker of smaller aspects of herself. The letter A as the anlaut glorifies the body of Mother Earth. YA glorifies the female body as the SHAPE of her pubis. In Hawaiian AKEKE (HAKAKA) means cinder or pebbly soil. Here we are dealing with the body of Mother Earth, as the great Mother throwing up cinder and pebbly soil, creating smaller aspects of Herself (haKAKA) during a volcanic eruption. In Chinese KE, is small, round things. It could deal with either pebbles or eggs. KAA in Swahili is cool embers, still dealing with the effulgence out of the body of Mother Earth, on its way to become land. AA in Hawaiian is lava, Mother Earth sourcing Herself (A) as Herself (A). KIKI in Bugotu means to be little. WAIKIKI (waKAKA) are Hawaiian Islands, small cut offs of the body of Mother Earth sticking out of the oceans, like noses out of a Her aquatic surFACE. WA of WAIKIKI deals with water. In Basque XIKI (KASAKA) means small (KA), which emerges out of the buttox halved vertically into the letter K of small creations. In Swahili K deals with a singular state and KI is the singular prefix for a noun. KAK in Chinese means each, or individual segments of the mother. KUTEN or KOTEN (KATAna)

585

is smallness in Hebrew, the cut off the whole block. KA is the sign of diminutive in Bemba of Africa. KA at the ends of feminine nouns in Polish makes them smaller; kobieta, woman, kobietKA small woman.. Of the Inca in South America EKKEKKO (HAKAKAKAKA) is a domestic God of good luck and prosperity that should be experienced forever. All statues representing him are worshipped in miniature. In Bemba KANONO (KANANA) means little things. (KANA-) depicts either the skin (IS KANA) on the individual mothers body creating the kin (KANA) or on the surFACE of Mother Earth the volcanic cone (KANA) of creation. NANA deals with the moon in Greek, the double negation. It is the moon that brings with it menstruation resulting in the creation of small little things.

In Basque K deals with plural at the ends of words the creation of smaller sequential aspects. It is the same concept as I, of one more, in Latin. Extending to S, at the ends of English words to make them plural, as another one made by the blood out of the body of the individual mother or out of the body of Mother Earth.

If KI deals with the energy of life, as the split in Chinese, as the thing under the body of Mother Earth waiting to be born up to Her surFACE, like the KI of the Hebrews which deals with vomiting up, then KID as the small young goat or child is the gift (DA) of the KI. KIDI (KADA) in Bugotu means for the first time. Each baby emerges out of the mothers womb for the first time. In Hebrew N' KUDA (NAKADA) is a dot or a period, that which also makes the KID (KADA) for the first time.

In Swahili KIDEVU (KADAva) is the chin. For it is in the chin in stage one that the original activity of chopping, chewing, chanting, and change takes place. It is the place where larger objects are milled down into smaller pieces. CHID (CHAda) in Sanskrit means to cut or divide, make into smaller pieces. Cutting and dividing is the gift (DA) of the chin (CHA-). In Sanskrit, KUD means to eat and to gorge. KUDI also in Sanskrit means body, the gift (DA) of the KU or KUD, of the mouth, or of eating. In Chinese KAU is the mouth in which all that activity of making things smaller takes place. The result of all that eating, cutting into smaller pieces, comes out of the activities associated not only with mothers but with birds for all of these words begin with the anlaut of K, which out of one perception has been established as being imitated and associated with birds and the SOUNDS that they make with their open beaks.

After the pieces of food enter the body, are chewed, milled, cut up into smaller pieces, then the tongue pushes them down into the belly, into the

Section Three

kitchen of transformation, where they were perceived to go through a process of cooking, like the birds that were perceived to be swallowed by the body of Mother Earth at the horizon line and then vomited up out of Her belly n the Eastern sky. In Bugotu KOKOILO (KAKAla) is stomach. In Sanskrit KUKSHA (KAKAsa) is belly. KUKHNE (KAKAhana) is kitchen in Chechen. KUCHNIA (KAHAna) is kitchen in Polish. CUCINA is kitchen in Italian. For the American Indians of the Southwest the original name for the KATCHINA doll is KOKO (KAKA). The KOKO (KAKA) dolls or figures have been worshipped as symbols of fertility. The most respected priests of the North were the rainmakers. It harkens back to the African savannahs when the rains came and with them came the return of the birds with their cackling (KAKALA) SOUNDS like a clock (KALAKA). Since the birds always came back when the rains fell, they became associated like the sun with the process of rebirth and being born again.

KOHTU is womb in Finnish. KOKH (KAKA) is planet in Hebrew. KUTU (KAta) is belly, womb, or heart in Bugotu. DefaCATion deals with the evacuation of feces out of the body. KUT (KAta) is manure in Persian. KETS (KAtasa)in Hebrew means end. SCATology deals with end runs. On one level it philosophically deals with death. On another it physically deals with feces. The dyad of KATA deals with cutting (KATA-) into smaller pieces and emerging on the surface on a variety of levels the KUTEN (KATA-) of smallness in Hebrew. Food is cut up within the mouth. A baby is cut or separated from the mother's body. Feces emerge and seem to be cut free from the defaCATing host. Other appropriate words beginning with the letter K of either smallness or the vehicle that creates that emergence. KEVAH (KAva-) is stomach in Hebrew. KERES (KA-) is belly, abdomen in Hebrew. CIFU (KA-) is stomach in Bemba. In Chechen KIRA (KA-) is stomach.

On the body of Mother Earth KOKH (KAKA) means planet in Hebrew the creatress of ALL smaller things that like feces emerge upon Her surFACE. In Finnish the word for womb is KOHTU (KA-) where not only smaller aspects are created but transformation into life takes place. KOOKH (KAKA) is the burial cave, where you were interred to be transformed and cooked (KAKA-) clean. KASHI (KASA) is tomb in Chechen, the coos (KASA) as the entry point where the activity within the body of Mother Earth took place. KUKSHI (KAKASA) in Sanskrit is not only the womb or belly, but it is also cavity and cavern. KSHA (KASA) in Sanskrit is one of the names of the Earth. The original coos (KASA) were the house of life. Casa (KASA) is house in Spanish. In Greek KOKKOS (KAKASA) was the bury pit and its origin according to the Oxford dictionary, is unknown. It establishes links not only with the body of Mother Earth as the original coos (KASA) but with the KAKA SOUND made by birds and the process of transformative cooking (KAKA) that went on underneath Her surFACE.

The belly of the individual mother and the internal fires within the body of Mother Earth did the cooking, the transformation into life. They were the cooks. KUKI (KAKA) is cook (KAKA) in Bemba. KOKKI (KAKA) is cook (KAKA) in Finnish. COQUIS (KAKA) is cook in Latin. CUOCO (KAKA) is to cook in Italian. KUPIKA (KApaKA) is to cook in Swahili. Before you can cook you have to pick (PAKA) the object to be cooked. Birds peck (PAKA) all around the ground, the barks of trees, the shallows, the air and then they swallow their prey. It is then that the process of digestion or internal cooking can take place. To concoct (kanaKAKAta) is to digest, in other words to cook (-KAKA-) (KATA) deals with cutting (KATA-) making smaller aspects. (KAKA) are the smaller aspects repeated as result of cooking or feces. (NAKA) deals with the metaphoric snake (IS NAKA) that guides the sun, moon, birds and soul through the body of Mother Earth, through the immolating fires to be transformed, cooked clean and reborn. (KANA) are the lea lines on the body of Mother Earth, Her lavic cone (KANA) of creation and Her skin (IS KANA) through which the creative processes above and below take place. The crater (KARATARA) is the ultimate creator(KARATARA).

The dyad (PAKA) in the Swahili word KUPIKA (KAPAKA) deals with the body of Mother Earth. When an eruption takes place the lava pours over the top. It boils over from the internal furnace, the planetary kitchen within the body of Mother Earth, it peaks (PAKA) pokes (PAKA) the air as it spreads above Her surFACE. In Polish the word KUPA (KAPA) means either just a pile, or a pile of excrement. The Swahili word KUPIKA (KAPAKA) to cook, mirrors itself (KAPA/PAKA) like GANGA (GANA/NAGA), MAGMA (MAGA/GAMA), MARA/RAMA) and gives a clue to ancient word formation out of the reflected dyads. When a word mirrors itself, linguistically it expresses itself as reflecting a change from one state to another. When something is cooked, goes through the body of Mother Earth and Her transformative fires, it changes its physical quality, but not its essence. The Indian River GANGA (GANAGA) above the surFACE as water was GANA, or the emergence upon the surFACE (NA) of begetting or going (GA). Below the surFACE it was perceived to be the snake (IS NAKA, NAGA) that guided all that died through, not only the fire, but also initially also through water. Magma (MAGAMA) establishes the same perception. Below the surFACE

Section Three

it is the holder (MA) of begetting (GA). Below the surFACE it becomes the begetter (GA) of the holder (MA) ie Mother Earth recreating Herself as all the bloody aspects of Herself.

The smaller relatively solid aspects that emerge out of the buttox are either the fetus or feces. These are not idiomatic expressions based on fashion, style or the babble of babies. They are ancient dyads that have become trivialized and pushed underground, as in PHASE THREE all bodily functions have been pushed underground. In Basque the word for excrement goes right to the source and is KAKA. Excrement in Hebrew is KAKEE (KAKA). Dung in Greek is KAKKE (KAKA). CACO (KAKA) in Latin means to defile with excrement. CACARE (KAKA-) in Latin means dung. In French, the word for evacuation is CACADS (KAKA-) and it probably didn't begin its life as a wartime activity. In Sanskrit UKKARA (HAKARA) covers many of the same bases. It means both pronunciation and evacuation. Pronunciation deals with the evacuation of SOUND out of the mouth, the top hole. Evacuation deals with the emergence of feces out of the halved buttox the bottom hole on the trunk or it could mean regurgitation or vomit also out of the top hole.

The color of feces gave its name to khaki (KAKA) as XAKA (KASAKA) in Persian. The place of emergence of the khaki colored feces is again around the area of the coos (KASA). Here again the process of reflection occurs. What happens in the area of the coos (KASA) is the emergence upon the surface of khaki colored feces as they dropped off the body were thought to be cut off. SAKA (IS HAKA) as the color of khaki XAKA (KASAKA) in Persian deals with the activity of hacking, or separation from the host. KUT is manure in Persian and also has links with the separation or cutting off the body. As feces fell off they were apparently cut off the body. In PHASE THREE as most of bodily functions were becoming systematically hidden to fall off has links with offal and the process of defacation becoming redefined not only as awful, but also dirty. Dirt was never considered filth by the ancient human beings. It was creation out of the body of Mother Earth and Her awesome body. Dirt (DARATA) was the gift (DA) of the return (RATA), out of the body of Mother Earth, back up to Her surFACE during a volcanic eruption, in the creation of land.

KINYESI (KANAYASA) is excrement in Swahili. It has an interesting construct. KANA is the skin, (IS KANA) on the body of Mother Earth out of which everything emerged and into which everything returned. AYA deals with light. YASA contains in it the SHAPE of the female pubis (YA) and the blood (SA). It may very well be that excrement in Swahili had its origins in the volcanic eruptions that spewed out of the body of Mother Earth at night when the light (AYA) of the burning fires could be seen from a great distance and her lavic blood (SA) spread across Her surFACE creating Her new skin (IS KANA).

In Greek the color red is KOKEENOS (KAKANASA) and not only deals with the color of lava, but also the color of blood. It is out of blood, that smaller aspects of the mothers buttox are created. For the Mayans, the effulgence, as an evacuation of water up to the surFACE out of the body of Mother Earth was Lake TITIKAKA. TI means moisture in Mayan. The TI repeated (TATA) may deal with titties (TATA-), one of the sources of moisture on the mothers body although KAKA takes it back to the emergence on the surFACE as smaller aspects of the Mother, water being one of Her many creations.

Then the activities of birds relating to what has come before, enters the picture again. KUS (KASA) is bird exCREMENT in Amharic. It deals with the place of evacuation out of the buttox next to the coos (KASA). Clarity was not an issue. To EXCRETE is to push out. Birds excrete lime, calcium or chalk out of their bottom holes. In Polish CREDA means chalk and has phonemic links with CRETE. In Italian CALCE is lime. In Hebrew KAV is lime. It probably has links with the body of Mother Earth as Her cave, out of which the lime may have been exCRETED. The activity of birds exCRETING lime or chalk out of the bottom holes on their bodies, and lime excreted out of the body of Mother Earth beginning with the letter K, establish ancient mutual links between female mothers, the body of Mother Earth and the SOUNDS and activities of birds. CREDO was an order, written apparently with some form of what had been called chalk. Were there great chalk mines on the island of CRETE? Was CRETE considered to be one of the ancient cradles of literary creation?

Feces and eggs were also associated with the SHAPE of their emergence, some were like beads or pebbles. Others were round, like pies. In Chinese KE means small round objects and extends to include KEKE (KAKA) for cocoa. In Hebrew KAKAO (KAKA) is cocoa. CACAO is cocoa in Italian. KAKAD is cocoa in Basque. The KAKAD establishes the cocoa as the gift (DA) of KAKA or the SHAPE of pellet like feces and droppings. The round SHAPE associating the droppings with an egg, surfaces as KOKOS that is a cocoanut in Hebrew. KOKO is also a cocoanut in Basque. In Italian a cocoanut is COCCO (KAKA). A cocoanut was not only associated with the SHAPE and emergence of feces out of the same hole on the bottom, but a cocoanut was not only SHAPED like an egg but had a similar construction inside. The pulp of a cocoanut was like the white of an egg. The center, the milky liquid was like the yolk of an egg. The shell on the outside was like the shell upon the egg of a bird. In Chinese another use of KE of small round objects is to define the shell. The cocoanut to a tree, was like an egg was to a bird. Both were smaller emanations out of the bodies of their specific maternal hosts. Both became defined by the bird SOUND and the place of emergence by the SHAPE of the letter K K.

The SHAPE of roundness coming out of cow flops, gave its name to KAK (KAKA) as biscuit in Arabic. KEK (KAKA) is cake in Amharic. In Finnish cake is KAKKU. KAKA in Old Norse was cake, round object, a disc. With the Old Norse word for disc as KAKA, we establish links not only with round cow flops but with with the round disc of the sun. For the sun and the round disc of the moon were considered to be eggs laid by the great overwhelming body of Mother Earth, the ultimate hen. In German KUKK (KAKA) is round, heap, pile of straw. KIKAR in Hebrew is a loaf of bread. It extends to include KU or KUK (KAKA) as circle itself in Greek. CAKA is wheel in Bengali. In Swahili a bracelet, the round thing worn on a wrist, neck or leg is KIKUKU (KAKAKA). In Sanskrit KIKARA (KAKARA) is the bamboo. The stem of a bamboo is hollow and could be cut into rings. Out of Africa there is a name for the 'narrow horn of birthing' and it is called KAKAKI (KAKAKA). The 'narrow horn of birthing' was the SHAPE of the vagina out of which small (KA) aspects of the mother emerged upon the surface.

THE LETTER X (KS), AS (K)
A VELAR VOICELESS STOP AND AS (S)
IS AN ALVEOLAR VOICELESS FRICATIVE GROOVE.

SOUND; X as ks (KASA) of the coos (KASA). X marks the spot, period at the end. KH as the cough of death. SA as mothers menstrual blood.

SHAPE; criss cross (KA(RA)SA), both diagonal and vertical

MOTHER'S body; oral cavity of mouth, crisscrossing at the third eye, crisscrossing of the buttox at the coos (KASA).

MOTHER EARTH; crisscrossing of sun and birds across Her belly of air.

CONCEPT; SHAPE of lifes beginning at the buttox and its terminus.

The letter X (KS) (KASA) deals with a variety of posibilities. One deals with the SHAPE of criss crossing at the third eye with the left side of the body controlled by the right hemisphere of the brain and the right side of the body controlled by the left hemisphere of the brain. It is where the Kundalini energy announces its primal ascent as light in the sixth chacra of the third eye. Another deals with the coos (KASA) associating it with the SOUNDS made by birds with their open beaks with the oral cavity (KA) behind it and the other out of stage three deals with the clitoral beak poking its way out of the female coos (KASA), labial folds or buttox. The third deals with the crisscrossing above the surFACE of Mother Earth in Her belly of air.

The saying 'X marks the spot', in PHASE ONE dealt with the 'period at the end'. In PHASE TWO as male role in specific procreation was being established in concert with the over evolution of the left hemisphere of the human brain due to the singular focused linear process of singing, speaking and writing, 'the period at the end' in PHASE THREE of left hemispheric male entrality became redefined as dealing with the end of a verbal sentence.

As the third eye of transformation it dealt with the fusion of the two hemispheres across the corpus callosum creating a balance in the brain. It had been originally experienced by the birthing breath of the mothers focusing on pushing the large headed human fetus out of their narrow hipped bodies. With it came a state of trance that brought forth the gifts of leadership, courage, bonding , healing, prophecy and shamanism.

The letter X=KS (KASA) in stage three had also been originally represented by the SHAPE of the buttocks as observed from the back where the bloody red spots of readiness could be read on the bodies of female animals.

The SHAPE of the human female vulva has been associated with the letter Y of the pubis and the side view of the letter A representing the clitoral beak and not the crisscrossing of the letter X (KS) (KASA) as part of the female symbolism. Viewed from the back the red spots on her buttox announced that she was ready for mating. Viewed from the front it became associated with her coos (KASA) and the red (RADA) spots of readiness (RADA-) that announced that she was ready (RADA-) to be mounted. In Polish the word rada means 'advice' and that is what the red spots did, they advised the ever ready (RADA-) males that the time had come when the females could be mounted.

The moon counted (KANATA-) the passage of time in concert with the female cunt (KANATA) who monthly, every twenty eight days passed blood out of her coos (KASA). In PHASE ONE she had been the countess (KANATASASA) who not only passed blood in concert with the cycles of the moon but counted (KANATA-) time and with the birthing breath of trance became the fearless mother (SA) and the surrogate of Mother Earth with the

Section Three

other (SA). In PHASE THREE with the proliferation of male redefinitions, she lost her (SASA) dyad as the countess (kanataSASA) and became the male count (KANATA) who only linguistically remained associated with the cunt (KANATA) of the mother, either that or he had been the eunuch uncle who protected her and her children.

The letter X (ks) as both a letter and number contains in its SHAPE a similar construction as the letter S dealing singularly with letters. When the letter S is halved laterally it gives birth to the C(see) of seeing on top and C(kh) of containment on the bottom.

Halved laterally the letter X as a *number* establishes the V SHAPE of the vulva above the line and an upside down SHAPE of V of the volcano below the line creating the ancient diamond SHAPE.

Both V's above and below the lateral line deal with the number five, when placed one on top of another they create the letter X emerging as the number ten in Latin. The number five establishes the five fingers of the mothers hand that do the holding. Ten is also the number of gestation, the ten lunar months of the disTENded belly out of which life issues forth.

It seems like a hidden symbol of the inverted V on the bottom as the volcano spewing forth lavic blood out of the body of Mother Earth (SA) and on top the V of the vulva on the female body also flowering with the flow of menstrual blood (SA). Both deal with creation of life out of their mutual shedding of their bloody (SA) essence.

As much of female symbology went underground after the shift into male centrality in PHASE THREE, like the plano convex bricks, the labrys, the pentagram, the apple and the letter V contains hidden implications. The two V's are like the two Hebrew triangles of the Star of David and the Masonic symbol of the the two angles superimposed on each other.

The letter X also surfaces as having been halved vertically creating the two K's facing in opposite directions, coming and going associated with the third eye and the semiannual passage of birds vertically North and South across Mother Earth's belly of air creating with their open beaks the SOUNDS of their noisy arrival and departure establishing one of the the SHAPES of the letter K.

Also in PHASE THREE as males redefined and suppressed their ancient mother defined reality they dropped off the (SASA) dyad of transformation associated with the creative blood (SA) of the individual mother and the lavic blood (SA) off the body of Mother Earth. The princess (paranaSASA) became the prince (PARANA-). The Goddess GADASASA) became the God

(GADA). The same chnges occurred to the words SHE without the (S) of the mother's blood and birthing breath became HE. The FEMALE without the (F) of the five fingers that fondly held and took care of the children became MALE. The MAN without the watery womb of WOMAN shared the same fate. HER (HARA) without the belly of creation became HE. In Polish ONA as 'her' became ON as 'he' without the A of the mother at the end. In Spanish 'she' as ELLA became the 'he' of the EL. El (HALA) dealt with the male sun, sol (IS HALA) in Spanish. The LA in ELLA dealt with the female as the LAdy of the LAnd that had to be left behind. In PHASE ONE females as mothers performed and were associated with a variety of specific functions. When males in PHASE THREE redefined themselves they kept part of the mother names but dropped off the activities and associations that had been part of the female mother context. What eventually emerged were male names without the maternal definition of source at the end.

A young girls first period at the time of her quintessence had been called menarche (MANARAJA). When she passed her first blood, she stood in line to become the subsequent not only mother but monarch (MANARAJA). The Raj (RAJA) at the end harkens back to an ancient female RUler. Among the hyena clan mothers rule and leave their matriarchy to their daughters.

In PHASE ONE the passage of blood and the promise of potential motherhood established her as the next RUler. Her RUddy (RADA-) estRUs announced that she joined the ranks of the mothers, the RUlers who marked time with the phases of the moon. To RUle does not only mean to reign. The moon was like an instrument, a RUler who measured time with the cycles of female menstruation. It pulled the blood periodically out of female bodies as it pulled the tides back and forth across the body of Mother Earth.

The Polish word rada deals with the 'gift of' (DA), the sun (RA). In this the most ancient case out of PHASE ONE the gift of the sun was the passing of seasonal estral blood out of the bodies of herbivore mothers. The shift of ancient humanoid females from seasonal sexual receptivity (estrus) to monthly lunar sexual receptivity (menstrual), to year round sexual receptivity created a mass of confusion.

The ever ready males on all levels could originally count on their noses and tongues to see if the females were in heat, ie spotted on their buttocks. Then the four legged simian creatures became upright, became bi-pedal. The male nose of the emerging humanoid creature was no longer on the level of her rump. He had to watch, to observe her rump to spot, to read (RADA) the red (RADA) spots to see if she was ready (RADA-). Menstruation or

Section Three

the bloody marks on the buttox of humanoid females did not always lead to sexual receptivity, as it did in other animals. Rape followed as unreceptive females fought off their attackers. In PHASE ONE it led to the eunuchization of the first born son to act as the uncle and protector to his sister's children. In the subsequent PHASES TWO and THREE it dealt with the subordination and the enslavement of women.

The harem (HARAMA) of overlapping dyads (HARA) and (RAMA) of the Middle East establishes its own obvious clue. (HARA) is the belly and (RAMA) is the frame (FARAMA), 'rama', in Polish. The powerful male not only enclosed his prize in his arms (HARAMA), but enslaved the bearer of the gift of life in her belly (HARA).

On the body of Mother Earth the SHAPE of the letter X dealt with the daily crisscrossing of the sun and moon laterally East and West across Her belly of air and the birds semiannually vertically North and South across the same celestial space. It created not only the cross but the swastica which had been an almost universal ancient time keeper.

When the birds arrived there was a time of great rejoicing and the time of dropping foals and mating and the beginning of new life associated with the passage of estral blood (SA). When the birds (KA) departed at the time of the Autumnal Equinox to make their way to their Northern and in some cases Southern nests there was ushered in a time of great sadness as the silence of the open sky grew empty of their noisy presence. Their appearance became associated with beginnings, with the promise of life. Their departure became associated with loss and with the promise of death.

The word exit (haKASAta) defines the state of separation as a hacking (HAKA-) apart from the reality of existence (haKASAtanasa). It also contains in its linguistic folds the dyad (KASA) and the separation from the coos (KASA) of the mother on all levels. In PHASE THREE in male based redefinitions as all of mother sourced reality became redefined as evil, in the word defining existence (hakaSATANASA) you contain the word SATAN (SATANA or IS HATANA). Similar construct happens with the word evil as the gift of (DA) of the devil. The female as mother became the vilified seductress and as the succubus (IS HAKA-), the killer of males. Lilith and Delilah come to mind.

As many catastrophes plagued the vulnerable African continent and the ancient migrants fled for their lives in all directions, many must have come to a stop and settled in what became RUssia, the land of the RUddy RUlers, the majestic women who had been recently rediscovered in sumptuous graves.

They were buried with headdresses curving forward reminiscent of the head plume of a bird. Its ironic that the RUssian flag is red, the RUby red color of blood. The RU of the RUddy color of blood remained in the Russian flag as did the name for their homeland as their *motherland*. The land of the left hemispheric Germans has been called the *fatherland*.

On the body of Mother Earth, 'soil' in Persain is defined by XAK (KASAKA) (KASA/SAKA) or (IS HAKA). It is a word that reflects itself like magma (MAGAMA) and Ganga (GANAGA). Soil is that which emerges out of a volcanic eruption as lava Her menstrual blood (SA) and reflects itself apparently as magma working its way back from under Her body to become purified, burned clean in Her internal oven to emerge as potential soil on Her surFACE.

It is the coos (KASA) on Mother Earth's body, Her gift of soil the Persian XAK (KASAKA) that establishes the possibility of land creation. Mother Earth does as all mothers do, she makes smaller replicas of Herself. The phoneme (KA) dealing with smallness associated with the coming and going of birds expresses that activity.

For the Basque who have many direct ancient linguiatic links with these SHAPES and SOUNDS koxkor (KAKASAKARA) means small. It is replete with the (KA) SOUND dealing with birds and their open beaks that arrived when all things small were being born. It announced the start of the ancient migrations and the (SA) SOUND dealing with the passage of blood out of the female coos (KASA). The (RA) at the end deals with the sun as the helper, the doer at one with Mother Earth.

Not to be left out is the Crux Ansata which is another name for the Egyptian ankh (HANAKA) one of the symbolic objects dealing with the ancient castrated first born sons who as eunuchs (HANAKA) cared for, watched over, bore witness to the human family. As uncles (HANAKALA) to their sister's children they became the benevolent eunuch protectors and as members of the 'intermediate state' sprouting bird wings they became the subsequent mythological angels (HANAGALA). Fourteen of them sat protectively on each shoulder of a newly born child. The number fourteen dealt with not only four weeks in a lunar month but the two aspects that balanced each other, the two lunar crescents waxing and waning that contained the fourteen days. The (KA) and (GA) are interchangeable.

After the LINGUISTIC BREAK it appears that the letter X and the CROSS appear interchangeably in Semitic, Etruscan and in the Sinai. Life creation out of the mother's body becomes apparent in the Cypriotic XA establishing her empty buttocks as she became the potential creatress of life out of her curved buttox that when the SHAPE became angled in Cuneiform emerging as the letter X.

On the body of Mother Earth the Cypriotic MU deals with the halving of the letter X laterally to create the V of the vulva above and the V of the reflected volcano below. The process creating the two V SHAPES as fives in Latin, deal not only the five fingers of the two hands that did the fondling but when brought together surfaced as the number ten. The number X in Latin defined not only the ten fingers that held but also the ten months of lunar gestation that held the fetus in the human mother's body. The number five also surfaces in Indian as the symbol for the letter X. In Western Greek the letter X emerges as CHI and harkens back to the movement of birds and the SOUNDS that they made filling the sky with their noisy presence.

The Etruscan cross in a box creates a double clue. One deals with the passage of the sun East West and the birds North South crisscrossing above the surFACE of Mother Earth. Had the cross been in a circle we would still have been in PHASE ONE and female centrality. But having the cross in a square puts us into PHASE THREE and male centrality. The circle and triangle in PHASE ONE had been female symbols as the square and cube in PHASE THREE became male symbols.

The volcano, vulva, the buttox and the semiannual coming of birds gave birth to the expression of creation in the verdant savannah. The departure of birds ushered in the time of silence and potential drought. Water played a major role for all of humanity. The coming monsoons brought with them not only a relief on the parched savannahs. The torrential monsoons created standing pools of reflected water and the metaphoric beginning of an alternate reality. The realty above the surFACE dealt with life and in PHASE ONE with mothers. The reflected reality below dealt with the passage into death hidden in the deep dark mysterious waters and in PHASES TWO and THREE became associated with males.

What also emerged is the fish as a symbol for the letter X with the fish as its hieroglyphic sign. For the Semites the fish had been called SEMEKH (IS HAMAKA). The symbology of the fish also goes in a variety of directions. (HAMA) is blood, ema (HAMA) Greek. Associating it with the aspects of creation the menstrual smell of blood associated with female genitalia has been likened to the smell of fish. The world wide symbol for 'The Great Mother' was the pointed oval sign of the yoni or vulva known as the vesica piscis, the 'vessel of the fish'. In China Kwan-yin often appeared as the Fish Goddess. KWAN (KA(WA)NA) deals with Mother Earth defined by Her cone (KANA) of creation halved by Her great reflective waters (WA). Yin (YANA) deals with the yoni (YANA) or vulva, the coos (KASA) on the body of Mother Earth. In PHASE ONE Yin was part of the Yin-Yang, the female sun above the body of Mother Earth and Yang the male sun under Her surFACE. With the knowledge of male role in specific procreation emerging in PHASE TWO, the Yin-Yang had been redefined as the female-male androgyny spinning through space.

The Philistine fish Goddess Atargatis attests to an ancient sensory perception. Attar is another name for fragrance, the sexual attraction based on pheromones. In Boeotia she was identified with the Goddess Artemis who wore a fish amulet over her genitals. In PHASE THREE Christianity took over the fish sign and made Christ the fisherman of men harking back to the mother as the source of smell based transformation through Her reflective waters. Islam held on to the crescent of the waxing and waning moon associated with female menstruation.

The Semitic X as the fish has been called SEMEKH (IS HAMAKA) which has a very similar SOUNDING name in Polish for castle is zamek (IS HAMAKA). In PHASE ONE it was the mother who sat on the throne in the castle. The (KA) at the end deals with the maker of small aspects and birds. The (HAMA) dyad establishes itself as the Greek name for blood, ema (HAMA). A castle (KASA-) was the coos (KASA) the casa (KASA) home (HAMA) of the mother. The place where the small (KA) individual mother passed her blood (HAMA) and ascended to her seat of power, her throne. A castle (KASA-) is also a house (HASA) and as casa (KASA) in Spanish. The (K) and (H) are interchangeable. It echoes the same concept as menarche and monarch.

In the Hebrew sacred alphabet MEM (MAMA) is the 'sea' and 'mother'. The next sacred letter is NUN (NANA), the 'fish' emerging out of the watery womb of Mother Earth. It is saying metaphorically that the fish emerged out of the reflected waters out of Her body. Nun (NANA) is a double negation. For the Greeks it deals with the moon (NANA). When it was daylight the moon existed in total darkness with the negation (NA) of light below the surFACE of Mother Earth. During the night it sailed through the other darkness, the darkness of night (NA) itself above the surFACE of Mother Earth.

ince hair had been considered immortal for on a female head it never stopped growing. The shorning of hair dealt with the establishment of powerlessness. For the Roman Catholics the nun (NANA) dealt with a celibate bald woman linking her to the bald pated powerless eunuchs. There is a link here. When a woman passed her period, her menstrual flowering on the outside indicated that she was not pregnant, that her womb was empty. There was a double negation. One dealt with the moon itself as the cause of the flow and emptiness. The other dealt with the female body as the place of the menstrual flow and the empty womb. The process became defined by the double negation of nana. The Roman Catholic nun (NANA) was also a double negation. She did pass blood in concert with the cycles of the moon, the Greek nana but she also remained empty of life, the other negation.

Jonah (JANA) spending time in the belly of a whale reeks with possibilities. The whale although a mammal, is obviously a metaphor for the largest fish in the watery body of Mother Earth. It was perceived that Mother Earth swallowed the sun in the West, ate it, declared war on it creating a bloody pool of water after it sank out of sight. It was also believed that Mother Earth regurgitated, spit the sun out of Her Eastern rim as the whale did with Jonah.

Jonah (JANA) establishes ancient links with gyno (JANA) woman in Greek. Had the sun been considered female then we are dealing with the single perception of reality out of PHASE ONE. If Jonah was female then Mother Earth gave birth to her as Her transformed daughter. She spat her out of Her watery womb to become the Hebrew hero. Convoluted links with transformation under the mantle of Mother Earth.

Jonah spending time in the belly of the whale the great fish representing Mother Earth surfaces again with Captain Ahab in Moby Dick. The limping Captain Ahab as the crippled either smithy or shepherd, in this case captain of a ship (SHE-) does battle with Mother Earth as the great white whale. In doing battle with Mother Earth the crippled captain kills Her and in the process dies himself. The Alpha and Omega surfaces here. Mother Earth as the Alpha and motherhood of life and the Omega as the big OM of the father and death. The crippled limping smitty surfaces as Chester in Gunsmoke.

THE LETTER Q

A VOICELESS VELAR STOP WITH VOWEL EXTENSIONS

SOUND; (KUE) Cough of questing with (OO) of wondering

SHAPE; open mouth, circle, zero, sun with a foot or snake tail

MOTHER'S body; puckered up mouth

MOTHER EARTH; Out of the semiannual passage of birds, sun

CONCEPT; The que of questing for answers, rationalizations as answers

The letter Q on one level is obvious, on another level it contains ominous overtones. It begins its life in PHASE ONE, stage one as the SHAPE of the puckered up mouth with the vowel LETTER of O. Then in PHASE TWO as males began to define their roles in specific procreation it expands to embrace the NUMERICAL concept of zero (IS HARA) dealing with maleness and the tragic awareness of the male empty belly (HARA) phenomenon. As males began to search for and define their creative 'source' (IS HARAsa) *away* from the body of Mother Earth, it shifted into the round disc of the sun as their primary source of creation and in PHASE THREE into the 'hidden' mind of God floating in the ethers.

There exists a relationship between the que (KUE) of questing and the que (KUE) of the Spanish why. The male quest in PHASE TWO moves into some very bizarre and not so obvious ramifications.

Young girls were defined by the cleft on their bodies and by the fact that they menstruated and grew babies in their bellies. In PHASE ONE the definition of boys was fraught with pit falls. Boy's bodies not only had a female form like the mother when they were born, but they also had an extra set of physical parts like the other males. They were considered to be two systems in one body as the anlaut of the letter B in boy illustrates. B deals with the 'two in one' definition for a boy's body had been considered to be 'two in one'. The role of male genitalia as a source of specific procreation was not even vaguely understood.

In the Greek word 'orchis' there exists a clue, for the word 'orchis' (HARAKASA) is a name for the Greek penis. It is a short stretch to the air plant named orchid (HARAKADA) that grows upon a tree. The orchid plant has no roots on the body of Mother Earth. As an air plant it exists in the tropics suspended upon the body of a tree and is uniquely beautiful. The Greeks in PHASE THREE thought that a penis was like a very beautiful and exotic flower that somehow was not attached to the body of Mother Earth. The (SA) at the end of orchis (harakaSA) deals with the infusion of blood (SA), at the time of penal erection. The orchid (harakaDA) plant contains in its linguistic coils the (DA) 'gift of' the belly (HARA). The penis as the Greek orchis (haraKASA) acknowledges not only the belly as (HARA) but the coos (KASA) of the mother as the singular and original source of creation.

Another perception enters the mythological and linguistic picture.

The emerging Hebrew and Canaanite God Adon (HADANA) had its linguistic origins out of the SHAPE of the sinking sun as it disappeared out of sight in the West, into the watery or mountainous flat side (IS HADA) of Mother Earth creating the shades (IS HADASA) of night. The SHAPE of that angular fall off the body of Mother Earth in the West became immortalized by the number seven. Seven as sheva (IS HAVA) in Hebrew means death and it originally in PHASE ONE dealt with the death of the sun. Then as Adonai (HADANA) meaning my Lord for the Hebrews, the sun became more personal. In Finnish the feeling open heart is sydan (IS HADANA). For the Greeks becoming totally male centered in PHASE THREE, the beloved God of the sun as the God of male beauty became Adonis (HADANASA), closing ranks with the beautiful orchid, orchis phenomenon. During the Romanesque period in PHASE THREE the statue of Cydippe (HADAPA) emerges as a shepherd with a pastoral staff balanced on one foot and one leg.

The letter (O) as the SHAPE of the mother's open mouth in PHASE ONE regurgitating food for her waiting hungry brood and alerting them to danger, in PHASE TWO became associated with the number zero, (O) and (IS HARA) the state of the male empty belly (HARA). Both the heterosexual brothers who had been shoved out of the family unit at puberty and the castrated first born sons as protective eunuch (HANAKA) uncles (HANAKALA) faced the despair of a permanently empty womb or belly (HARA). Not only were the first born sons castrated, but all the subsequent sons, the ones who were not pushed out of the clan at puberty, were maimed and crippled, in time in PHASES TWO and THREE with the domestication of animals and the growing knowledge of metallurgy, to act as smiths and shepherds.

The ancient unrelenting universal problem was the fact that no baby ever emerged from male bellies. The concept of the number zero (IS HARA) of the empty belly emerged out of that perception. In Arabic zero (IS HARA) is a circle with a dot in it. What it is saying is that the dot represents a period, the dot at the end. If the period is in the circle, in her belly, then the girl is menstruating and is not pregnant, her belly is empty, ergo zero (IS HARA). HARA in Japanese means 'belly'. In Hebrew it not only stands for 'belly', but for 'pregnant mountain' har (HARA). Boy children and males had a permanently empty belly. They became defined by the zero (O), of the empty womb.

The first born son in PHASE ONE was eunuchized to act as a benevolent uncle (HANAKALA) and protector to his sister's children. The subsequent sons, who did not leave the clan at puberty in PHASE TWO, were not only eunuchized, but crippled. One leg was in some way maimed. They became the one legged limping smiths and the crook leaning shepherds. The Lib of castaration and maiming enters here. The letter O moved away from its original source out of the mouth of the mother in PHASE ONE, stage one, into the zero of the empty belly and then into the round solar disc halveing the sky daily in PHASE TWO becoming the sun as the son of Mother Earth, Her first born and greatest helping hands.

The male with the zero of the permanently empty belly was often not only castrated but crippled, the lib constrct, and was given one leg, that leg became symbolized by the letter Q of the solar disc to limp across the sky, as both the male smiths and shepherds becoming lame limped on one leg across the plane. Since the sun had been guided by the snake to make its daily journey back up to the light, the trailing foot on the letter Q may very well be the tail end of the snake pushing its way across the belly of air.

For the Chinese the PI Dragon as the symbol of the universe, with the one moving foot (PI) limped across the sky. In Bemba to be crippled and lame (LAMA) is either lemana (LAMAna) or cilema (IS haLAMA) both contain the (LAMA) of lameness (LAMAnasa) dyad in their linguistic coils. The Amazonian lame (LAMA) smith Hephaestus travelled on one leg like the sun snake combine across the sky. The tail on the circle of the sun establishing the letter Q was an ancient perception that the snake like a single moving foot was guiding the sun across the sky and that the snake (IS NAKA) was associated with the castrated eunuchs (haNAKA) (HANA/NAKA) and the benevolent castrated uncles (HANAKALA) on one hand and the sun (IS HANA) on another. In Polish noga (NAGA) defines the human foot relating it to the one moving foot of the snake (IS NAKA). The (G) and (K) are interchangeable.

In Persian a stork is LAQ LAQ (LAKA LAKA), the feathered creature balancing on one leg symbolizes the one legged smithy who lost his mobility at the time of the Autumnal Equinox in the Southern Hemisphere when the birds returned to their nesting sites. The stork balancing on one leg had been related not only to the one legged smith and shepherd but to the open beaked SOUNDS that emerged as the SHAPE of the letter (K) that accompanied the return of the birds to the lakes (LAKA) of the verdant savannah, as life returned in its multifaceted majesty creating small aspects (KA) of Mother Earth (LA) on all levels.

The feathered creature balancing on one leg that arrived at the time of foaling of herbivore mares became associated with the bringing of babies in Europe and Asia in the Northern Hemisphere emerging with the anlauts of (B) as in birth and birds. Geese didn't have that honor, neither did ducks or swans, they were endowed with other metaphors to define them. The bringing of babies fell on the downy shoulders of the balancing one legged stork. It may have been that the one legged eunuchized male son was not only the benevolent uncle but also the mid wife in ancient Africa. He did assume that role at the cloistered extravagant courts of ancient China.

The Birhors of India have a headman named Naya who stands on his left leg with his right leg tucked under him like the stork. In India Naya means new. With a double (ah) SOUND within his name Naya establishes his origins as being very ancient. He also emerges as a metaphor for the body of Mother Earth and the birth of the sun as Her newly born son out of the most ancient PHASE ONE and the unity between the two of them before the separation myths entered the picture. The phoneme (NA) deals with 'the negation of a former state' or 'emergence on the surface'. (AYA) deals with light in Persian and dawn in Assyrian.

In Lithuanian kalvis (KALAVASA) defines a blacksmith. The name for a crippled person in Polish is kulawy (KALAVA). The crippled male and the blacksmith had been considered as emerging out of the same linguistic root. Out of India comes Mother Kali (KALA) in one direction as Mother Time (KALEndar) who spares no one. In another direction Mother Kali (KALA) as Mother Earth creates and kills (KALA), reabsorbing back into Her body everything that She creates. Her foot stamps down on the head of Siva (IS HAVA) of the number seven (IS HAVAna) as Her eunuchized and submissive consort. In PHASE THREE for Christianity the place of burial, the hill of death for Christ and His two miscreants was Calvary (KALAVARA) echoing ancient links with the death of the sun in the Western waters and its linguistic source out of the crippled shepherds and blacksmiths in prehistoric mother centrality.

For the Maya on the other side of the world Ku Kul Kan was the name of their feathered serpent. Once they left Africa after one of the great catastrophes that befell that stricken continent, the Mayans fused a great many metaphors together to come up with that three parted name. The feathered concept appears in the letter (K) of the open beak defining the downy bird. The serpent deals with the letter Q pushed by the one leg of the guiding snake. Ku (KA) in Hindi is Mother Earth the creatress of all things smaller than She. Kul (KALA) establishes Mother Earth as the killer (KALA-) of all that she creates. Kun (KANA) deals with Her as the creator of land out of Her volcanic cone (KANA). Ku Kul Kan covers all bases as does the feathered serpent guiding the sun to be reborn at dawn by the questing eunuch priesthood.

One of the growing and enduring torments of humanity at the time of its heritage in PHASE ONE was to pacify and find a role for their male children. There was another fact that enters the picture here. Not only were the human males apparently left out of the birthing process but at the time that the pregnant mother gave birth she was blessed with a singular and mysterious experience. Not only did she spasm a baby out of her body but as she panted hard and fast and pushed in the last stages of labor she awakened what had been lying coiled and dormant at the base of her spine what became called the Kundalini energy by the Tantrists which put her into a trance like state of ecstasy. she emerged from the experience not only as a mother but as a powerful fearless leader, a healer and often a prophet. That is why in PHASE THREE the males in North Africa, the Middle East and Southern Asia practiced the sadistic activity of clitorectomies. It didn't have anything to do with masturbation and self induced pleasure. It had to do with power. Males not only carried a permanently empty belly but also the ecstatic breath of the birthing mother's had been denied them. It was not only a total mystery to them but the mystery turned into a system of mysticism as the experience of the birthing mothers was obliterated and their power went underground surfacing only in witches who paid a heavy price for their lingering gift.

Somewhere along the way and it may have been more than fifty thousand years ago it became apparent to our ancient ancestors that there was a lack of balance in the human brain. It also became apparent to them that when young males became castrated they not only became docile and protectors of the family but many of them attained other more unique gifts that as shamans they began to share with the mothers. It seemed to them that castration led to a form of liberation from the rut, must and violence, resulting in the establishment of a balance in the human brain. The word LIB deals with castration and gives birth to LIBra with the balanced scales and LIBeration. The liberation dealt with the jettisoning of the over evolved left hemispheric linear prattling violent anguish causing bifurcated brain (Y) that dealt with fantasy and reality rationalized as ideas (HADASA). Ideas (HADASA) have their origin in the human brain. The concept of ideus (HADASA) also has links with the human mind for the human mind created the ideas (HADASA) that led to the creation of the concept of a male God dues (DASA).

In PHASE TWO as males began to grapple with their role in procreation the letter Q becomes the anlaut for many of the words that deal with males beginning to ask why (Y) and a quest for the understanding of their peripheral state. As the sun sank out of sight in the bloody maw of the Western sea, the castrated and crippled eunuchs begin to wail at the Western wall of death asking why (Y), as they began to question their sorry fate.

The original quest was how to make their bodies more like a woman's to bear babies. That only led to mutilation and the establishment of that 'intermediate state' defined by the Tibetans as the bar (BARA) that defined the Bardo, and the eunuchized, crippled brothers (BARAtara) neither female and no longer male. Castration and mutilation of their bodies didn't offer them the gift of pregnancy or a full belly. Then the quest was for the ecstatic birthing breath of the mother's that brought with it such fearless power, leadership, healing and prophecy began to fill the pages of prehistory. Drugs were used to attain that ecstatic state and to silence the unrelenting fear driven voice over brain as was alcohol, meditating, fasting, dancing, d'avening, rocking back and forth, chanting, singing, dancing, drumming , sex, whatever was available to create the total focus of the mind and not to allow the left hemisphere to continue its fear driven prattle.

That led to the great mythological quests that surface in the Sumerian Epic of Gilgamesh, the Hebrew Bible, The Indian Ramayana, Greek Homers Illiad and Odyssey, the Christian quest for the Golden Fleece or the Holy Grail, the Islamic Koran. It contains in their literary works the quest for the power inherent in the ecstatic bursting of the Kundalini, fanned by the breath of the birthing mothers as all the heroes of pre- and his story jumped on their steeds, drew their swords and smited everything in sight searching for the power and ecstasy and an answer to their peripheral plight. They came up with rationalizations that had little to do with reality. Cervantes, exposes the madness of ideas gone amuck in Don Quijote, the quixotic quester taking arms against a series of *self created fantasies*.

In Polish why (Y) is encoded in the dyad czemu (CHAMA or JAMA). For the pagan worshippers of the mother, the Moabites who were related to the Israelites, Chemush (CHAMASA or JAMASHA) related to the asking of why (Y) was one of their ancient Gods. On the Western Coast of North America there existed a tribe of Indians called Chumash (CHAMASA or (JAMASA) who were not only great navigators and traders but one of their languages bears the name of BARBARENO (BARABARA-) establishing its links with the Tibetan 'intermediate state' of bar (BARA) as one of the names for the eunuchs . How was that 'intermediate state' expressed? Were the Chumash males all castrated eunuchs? When did they make that great journey across the vast open Pacific Ocean?

In PHASE TWO extending into PHASE THREE the quest for the father took over the scene and the emergence of the total subjugation of women to prove specific paternity. There still existed the question of 'source'. Since Mother Earth had been taken by women, the emerging male power bases had to float *away* from the body of Mother Earth on feathered wings into the welcoming sky and specifically into the sun to create their male Gods in the heavens. At first males called the sun, the son of Mother Earth as their own. In PHASE TWO the separation myths began to pepper the linguistic landscape as the solar disc had to become separate from the body of Mother Earth. They had to have a father, (the one who made her fat) (fat her/her fat) as the females had a mother.

Since the baby in the mothers belly (HARA) was 'hidden' from their sight, to that end they moved further into space and into the 'hidden' mind of God way out in the ethers.

For the Egyptians amen (HAMANA) meant a pregnant belly. Also for the Egyptians their God Amun (HAMANA) 'hidden' deep within the recesses of the temple masturbated all of existence into being every night. In PHASE THREE amen became the END of a prayer in Hebrew and then Christianity. It began its life as a word for pregnancy the END of an empty womb in a mother.

The name Jehovah (JA HAVA) of the Hebrews in PHASE THREE surfaces with a salient clue. Chova (HAVA) in Polish means 'hidden'. It was at the time that the left hemisphere of the human brain was gaining in primacy and singular perception of the right hand due to the naming of things, language and then writing itself replacing the circular orientation of the ancient left handed mothers. Male 'source' based on power and control, shame, black and white definition of linear reality, more is better, became defined as emerging out of the 'hidden' mind of a male father God 'hidden' from sight in the ethers.

The physical body of Mother Earth was taken by the mother's, so they went into the sun, stars and then into the ultimate mystery of the mind defining their source as also 'hidden'. Male systems of source had to be woven from the whole cloth of ideas (I DEUS) or (HADASA). It had no links with what was real. On the basis of those ideas that began to poke their way to the surface in PHASE TWO, they began to take over the power bases and the contexts of nature that had been dominated by the mothers and their familial clans. Gods began to replace Goddesses, male eunuch priests established their domain in the underworld, dealing with the rites of the dying sun and the rites of the dead. The displaced at puberty band of brothers, became the armies that grew into territorial gangs that fell on other migrating clusters of humanity in battles above ground. Then they joined ranks and in PHASE THREE underground religious systems worshipping in caves became wedded to the above ground heterosexual armies that began to pillage the terrain, and to subjugate the already preyed upon humanity.

In the process of asking WHY (Y)) of their peripheral state the males began to bifurcate the human brain as the single focused, linear left hemisphere began its destructive journey into the future.

THE ANSWER TO WHY IS ALWAYS A LIE.

Reality had to be envisioned out of the fantasy of the fathers. If the empty male belly (HARA) was defined by zero (IS HARA), then male 'source' (IS HARAsa) came out of the area BEFORE the zero, out of the hidden abyss of space, out of the 'hidden' mind of the father God in the cosmos.

The one legged sun (SON) limping across and halving the sky pushed along by the ever present metaphoric snake surfaces in Phoenician, Etruscan, North Semitic, Greek and Roman. They all look suspiciously like the Egyptian symbol for immortality, the Ankh (HANAKA). Now the ankh (HANAKA) as the metaphoric symbol for immortality has the same ancient phonemic structure as the eunuch (HANAKA) who as the priest officiated over the rites of the dead, with the promise of reincarnation. The eunuch was also the limping shepherd and blacksmith, the castrated first born son, who was maimed to limp across the plane on one leg with his crutch, furka, or staff symbolized, not only by the letters L, F and Y but also by the letter Q.

The crook in PHASE THREE became the symbol of power for the pastors of the church. The letter (Y) also in PHASE THREE became one of the SHAPE of the crutches that propped up the crippled blacksmith. In England one of the areas of African dispersal the name of Smith (IS MATA) dealing with the ancient mother (MATA-) is very common. They asked their own questions and quested for their own answers in the wailing of why at the Western wall, the que of quests. Strange as it may seem, the letter Q with its SHAPE and SOUND reveals much more than just a circle with a tail.

THE CH SOUND

SOUND; Chirping of birds

SHAPE; The cavity represented by the letter C of the open mouth with the H of the air moving through it.

MOTHERS body; cheek, chin

MOTHER EARTH;Chirping, cheeping of birds

CONCEPT; Children, beginnings,

CH-The construct of CH. The SOUND encoded in the letters CH (CHA or JA) comes out of the SOUNDS made by young chicks (CHAKA or JAKA) chirping and cheeping with their cheeks (CHAKA or JAKA) (upper bill) and chin (CHANA or JANA) (lower bill) clacking together. It comes out of the time when the ancient migration came to their semi annual rest and the noisy birds flew back to their nesting grounds as the herbivore herds gave birth to their young. It was a time of change (CHANA- or JANA-) as CHicks emerged from their shells and newly born CHildren on all levels littered the ground. CH establishes not only CHange but the process of beginnings.

For the Chinese as an obvious choice, the SOUND of Chi is written as a Q. Therefore the Ch'i as the Chinese female soul has its links in the letter Q of male questing. As Chi and written with a Q it represented the mystical breath that filled everything between the body of Mother Earth and heaven, same as the extended definition of the Tibetan Bardo. It may have given its name to China (CHANA or JANA) and may originally have been written as Qana (KANA) relating it to the creative volcanic cone (KANA) on the body of Mother Earth. It was the creation of land out of Her magmic volcanic center that gave birth to the possibility of beginnings and life.

It also establishes its links with the eunuch priesthood with the Q of questing dealing with their peripheral state. In Swahili CHA is dawn the beginning of a new day, as the arrival of birds to their nesting sites at the time of the Autumnal Equinox established the beginning of new life on all levels. In Sanskrit choo (CHA or JA) dealt with excrement. It was at the beginning of every day that males squatted together on the edge of ditches to make doo. The anus (HANASA) had been considered to be another area where birth occurred. It was the birth on excrement as a specific anal creation out of all defecating bodies creating the KAKA dyad.

Nascence (NASANASA) means repetitive birth in Latin. It also deals out of PHASE ONE as the place out of which the sun (IS HANA) was born (NASA), the anus (HANASA) on the flat circular horizontal body of Mother Earth.

The written phoneme of CHI surfaces with many pronounciations. In English it establishes the familiar SOUND of birds CHIrping. It can also be pronounced with the bird SOUND of K (two bills clacking) as in Charisma. In Polish and Hebrew the CH is pronounced as a simple H, as in the Polish armpit pacha (PAHA) and Hebrew Chassidim as (HASADAMA). Here we become aware of the (DAMA) out of the mother and sodomy (IS HADAMA) as forbidden anal sex.

Section Three

THE LETTER G

A VOICED ALVEOLAR STOP

SOUND; Two SOUNDS, G (gh) of getting and G (jee) of generation

SHAPE; The C circle of creation with the tongue sticking out

MOTHER'S BODY; Gutteral SOUND out of the open mouth, solar plexus, anus

MOTHER EARTH: Circular rim on Her surFACE with tongue extended pushing out terrestrial beings, heavenly bodies and the birds.

CONCEPT; beginnings into creation, generation and be getting

    G-The letter G deals with two SOUNDS. One is the G (jee) of gyno Greek for woman and gna (GANA) as the divine female in Sanskrit. In Polish gna (GANA) means one who is chased. The wilderbeest of the African savannah who are led by the matriarchs are called gnu (GANA). They are often chased by carnivores and crocodiles. The other is the G (gh) of 'get'. The SHAPES of the letter G and the letter C are closely related and emerge out of the same linguistic antecedents. The letter C deals with creation and the letter G deals with generation and be-getting. Both letters in PHASE ONE stage one, originally dealt with the circle around the mothers skull that had a break in it at the front, the slit, the O of the Open mouth. It gave birth not only to regurgitated food, garganta (garaGANAta) as throat in Spanish, but also to singing and speaking out of the same area. Gana is song in Sanskrit and speech is lagein (laGANA) in Greek.

    In stage three there is the circle around the center of the trunk, the solar plexus, gonda (GANAda) the fleshy belly of creation in Sanskrit, sharing that concept with the circle around the flat round body of Mother Earth at the horizontal rim which was defined at different times as the mouth, the belly and the anus. For creation on any level to take place the circle in all three areas had to be broken, the mouth, the belly and the anus had to be opened. The letter G of begetting and generation and the letter C of visual activity (see) and the cough (kh) of death became the symbols for those activities.

    GA as gauche (GACHA) in French signifies that the anlaut of (GA-) deals with the left hand associated with the right hemisphere of the ancient mothers. In Polish from a different linguistic direction but out of the same concept smaja (IS MAYA) establishes the name for the left hand and in PHASE

THREE all the derogatory remarks associated with it. Maya surfaces as Mother Earth not only generating the name but the beGETting source as the mother of Buddha.

Harking back to PHASE ONE and the crippled shepherds and blacksmiths in Hindu ogoun (HAGANA) the name for hunters and especially blacksmiths becomes established. In Polish ogon (HAGANA) is a tail.

The letter G is the letter C with its mouth open and with the tongue sticking out pushing what exists internally up to the surface. On the body of maternal creatures the flicking tongue established bonding, licking, regurgitation and the maintenance of life. In Greek gnathos (GANAtasa) is a jaw and gnathos has links with the English gnawing (GANA-) of food. Ironically eating of food had been associated with the mother gyno (JANA) in Greek. To survive one must eat and that deals with gnawing on bones and other morsels. On the ubiquitous snake the flicking tongue smells the air. On the human body the tongue flicked out deals with the creation of meaning as the Greek lagein (laGANA) dealing with speech.

To reiterate, the SHAPE encoded in the letter G of beGETting or GEneration comes out of the SHAPE of the circular letter C of Creation with its tongue sticking out. The letter G as an anlaut establishes the G (jee) of Jenie (JANA), Jinn (JANA) or the gyno (JANA) of the female in Greek. To rub the bottle out of which a Jenie emerges on a pall of smoke has overtones with a dual creation out of two ultimate female forces; the creative volcanic body of Mother Earth and the individual body of the birthing mother. The pall of smoke emerging out of the bottle deals with the body of Mother Earth announcing Her moment of creation with the magmic lava pouring down Her flanks in the creation of land.

The SHAPE of the bulbous bottle with its long neck in PHASE ONE has been the symbol for the vagina. To rub the sacred bottle, ie vagina takes us to the activity of masturbation and the rubbing of the clitoris in order for it to spasm, orgasm and during birthing with the help of peristalsis push the large headed fetus out of the narrow hipped mother's body. To gain (GANA) a baby, to do it again (haGANA) and again (haGANA) was to increase creation out of the crease on the mothers body, the halved buttox from the back and her vulvic cleft from the front.

The Jenie (JANA) or Jinn (JANA) is always a metaphoric giant (JANA) and a giant is either the individual mother, the first giant in a baby's life, or Mother Earth, the maternal giant to all.

Jenie (JANA) and gyno (JANA) deal with the female as mother the grantor of all wishes. Mother Earth creating land and the gifts that the land promised to sustain life had been considered in that same category. In Bali Gunu Agun (-GANA HAGANA) contain a myth that Gods came out of that volcanic fire. In Sanskrit Agni (HAGANA) is the fire God. If Jenie (JANA) is Mother Earth as the fire spewing volcano in Her aspect as land, then Herman Melville in Moby Dick dealt with Mother Earth as the great white whale in Her aspect as water.

The letter G as the G (gh) of be-GETTING deals with birth and generation (JANA-) upon Her surFACE out of an internal cavity (mouth, belly, anus, pushed out by the busy snake like tongue. Other letters came to represent myriad activities ascribed to the body of Mother Earth. The letter L came to represent the SHAPE of emergence (hamaraGANAsa), the angle of the tongue pushing the heavenly bodies, especially the sun up to Her surFACE, out of Her maternal ground of being.

The SHAPE of the letter G began its life as the circle of the Open mouth of the mother in stage one becoming the letter O. Then it moved into the heavens in PHASE TWO becoming the round disc of the sun and the O descending into the reflected waters as the number eight (8), declaring that Mother Earth ate the heavenly bodies, declared war on them. Then in PHASE THREE the SHAPE of the letter S became the concept of existence above and below the plane. The two circles, one on top of the other creating the SHAPE of the letter S split horizontally became the two broken circles above as C(see) and the broken circle below as C(kh). Out of the C of seeing above the surFACE and the C (kh) the cough of death below the surFACE it covers both bases of existence encoded in the letter S. Seeing © and dying (kh) are verbs and deal with unvoiced letters. The solidity of actual females as mothers in the Greek gyno (JANA) as woman moves into the broken circle of G (jee) of generation (JANA-) with the tongue sticking out, on the body of Mother Earth pushing the heavenly bodies up to Her surFACE. It also deals with the snake guiding the sun from underneath the dark mantle of night within the body of Mother Earth pushing it out of the break at Her horizontal rim to glow with daylight above Her surFACE.

In Turkish the female out of the ancient unity, the sun pushed up at dawn giving birth to daylight is gunes (GANAsa). The sun had been perceived to do its job daily over and over again (haGANA) and again (haGANA). In Greek agein (haGANA) deals with leading, for it was the sun that led the rays of light across the newly born sky. In Japanese shogun (IS haGANA) is a leader. An ancient name for the gypsy was cygan (IS haGANA) the Indus valley serpent tribe of Harappa who led the Asiatic migrations after their dispersal after one of the great cataclysms on the continent of Africa. In Sanskrit gana is a mother created tribe.

In PHASE ONE mothers caring for vulnerable babies had to be gentle (JANA-). The gentle (JANAtala) mother as a primary caretaker became the gentile (JANA-), not a member of the Jewish tribe in PHASE TWO as specific male role in procreation was becoming known. Then in PHASE THREE the mother was left behind altogether as the source of physical creation became the inclusive genitals (JANA-) that defined gender (JANA-). The gonads (GANA-) became the male source of creation. It became even more gender neutral as the genetic gene (JANA) pool.

The GA of Mother Earth as the ultimate and sole begetter and generator surfaces in Gaea (GAYA) giving birth to Goy (GAYA) in PHASE TWO, not a Hebrew person but belonging to the 'pagan' worship of the ancient Mother Earth. A gay (GAYA) person had been the person defined as also belonging to the ancient mothers. It reflects the same reorganization of meaning that surfaces in the Yin Yang. The two circles that create the letters G and C contain in their circular SHAPES a break, an opening for Generation (JANA-), be Getting and Creation to take place covering both the individual mother and the more expansive body of Mother Earth. LET THE CIRCLE BE UNBROKEN has haunting, if curious overtones.

There are a series of aspects that deal with birth and beginning encoded in the letter G. In Chinese GAN (GANA or JANA) covers a variety of beginnings; as 'and' including 'again'(haGANA) it deals with the emergence or birth of the sun, as the concept of 'chase away' it pushes back, chases away the terrors of the dark night, In Polish dzien (JANA) is a word for day, the beginning of light. Egun (haGANA) is day in Basque.

A genius (JANASA) (JANA/NASA) establishes its links with the mother, gyno (JANA), the Greek woman. In Hebrew ga'on (GANA) is also a genius having links with the mother. What is more awesome than to bring original (haraJANAla) life up onto the surface. In PHASE THREE genius became ascribed to males with original left hemispheric technical discoveries primarily during war.

For the Hindus in PHASE THREE leaving the mother behind and establishing the God of beginnings in the elephant God Ganesh, (GANA-) no longer the matriarch elephant who hearing the vibrating thunder in the distance began the ancient migrations across the drought stricken savannah to the promised verdant land in the distance. Same linguistic presto digitations begin with Genesis (JANASASA) in the male centered Hebrew Bible with the birthing breath of the individual mother's blood as the first SA and the menstrual lavic blood of Mother Earth as the second SA, containing within their linguistic coils the inherent concept of transformation. The letter G of begetting and generation contains the same antecedents as the letter C of creation.

What survives after the LINGUISTIC BREAK may have been encoded in the triangular script of Cuneiform, for the letter C emerges as a chiseled angle in Phoenician, Egyptian, Semitic, Etruscan, Slavonic, Numidian. In Phoenician and Hebrew the camel as gimel surfaces with the name of a creature that endured the horrific heat of the emerging Sahara and created the trade routes of the ancient world moving back and forth like the sun across the shifting sands. The same concept of moving in one direction and then coming back is encoded in the throwing stick or boomerang of the Egyptians. It goes back to an ancient time when the Sahara Desert was an inland savannah with lakes and rivers and with animals that had disappeared. It also exhibits on cave overhangs women with boomerangs doing the hunting. In Lycian the SHAPE of the letter G cum C looks like the female pubis, the break at the vulvic cleft, the original source of individual life. Facing to the left, in Faliscan, the letter C (kh) harkens back to the bottom half of the letter S dealing with creation coming up from below, from within the 'hidden' source of creation of Mother Earth. The Roman letters of C, G and K cover all the possible bases of creation and generation. The letter K also includes the the concept of smallness and the open beaks of birds.

The left behind source of creation out of a female source may have its glimpses in the volcanic SHAPE on the body of Mother Earth encoded in Semitic, Greek, and Numidian and in the SHAPE of the pubis. The three lines in Numidian represent the triparted concept of creation in the body of Mother Earth; above Her surFACE, upon Her surFACE and under Her surFACE. The two periods, one above the line and the other below the line may be where the major activity occurs; one out of the individual mothers body and the other from under the body of Mother Earth. They are after all periods or spots on the end. The massive Hittite symbol looks like the two C's of creation facing each other. They may have represented the two crescents that marked time and ruled the passage of menstrual blood in women.

THE LETTER J (GEE)
AN ALVEO PALATAL FRICATIVE, SAME AS G OF GENERATION

THE LETTERS J, I, and Y come out of similar linguistic roots. JA (I am) in Polish, I (I am) in English, YO (I am) in Spanish

SOUND: J as (jee) in English , J as (yee) in Polish, J as (huh) in Spanish

SHAPE; jaw or lower mandible

MOTHER'S BODY; bottom half of her face

MOTHER EARTH; Abyss, Polish jama (yama)

CONCEPT: separation, hacking apart

J-In PHASE ONE the letter J(jee) comes out of the SHAPE of the jaw on the bottom half of the face of the mother. It needs the constricted jaw to make the SOUND of J (jee). The SHAPE of the letter J (jee) is the SHAPE of the lower mandible, the jaw, the hook (HAKA) on the bottom of the skull that moves up and down and hacks (HAKA) edible morsels into smaller pieces and hacks SOUND into meaning.

As a major tool in hunting, the jaw (JAWA) of a carnivore mother, especially the lioness, smothers her prey and as it separates it from its life, it creates a new reality. The prey becomes the source of sustaining life. It says yes to the continuation of the living. On the body of Mother Earth it is the water (WA) that acts like the jaw (JAWA) of hacking apart the reality above from the reflected reality below.

The SOUNDS associated with the letter J (gee) emerge out of two sources. One links it to the concepts of generating or separating out of the gyno (JANA) of female bodies. It is the carnivore mother that does the hunting of prey for her cubs. The other source deals with the mother as she gives birth she separates the fetus from her body. She becomes two pieces when before birth she was only one. The process of birthing was likened to the process of hacking apart associated with the jaw. In Spanish the young one, the junior (JANA-) is called a joven (HAVANA).

The other J in Polish is pronounced as a Y (yee). It becomes apparent that the SHAPE of the Y is the SHAPE of the pubis on the female body where the hacking apart in stage three occurs. This may have been and still is a reality for many African and Middle Eastern women on whom genital mutilation

SECTION THREE

has been and still is practiced. They have to be hacked (HAKA-) apart for coital penetration and for the birth of a baby.

Another hacker (HAKA-) enters the scene, for in Basque the penis as zakila (IS HAKAla) had been considered as the hacker (IS HAKAra). It harkens back to the penis in Arabic as zekker (IS HAKAra). It shares its linguistic origins with the Babylonian phallic deity Zaqar (IS HAKAra) and the Egyptian Seker (IS HAKAra), the Lord of Death. Not only the brutal birthing process in PHASES TWO and THREE led to the death of many mothers but the actual act of coital penetration after the clitoris had been excised carried with it the same dangers.

On the body of Mother Earth in stage two the SHAPE of the letter J(jee) as Her jaw had been perceived as not only the process of generation out of Her ground of being, but generation out of the lower part of Her surFACE, the part as Her lower jaw. The dip under the surFACE apparently fantastically fell down becoming the hacking jaw allowing the heavenly bodies to be eaten by Her great bloody horizontal maw in the Western abyss.

Since the same apparent process must have been associated with the activity of birthing on the other side of Her body in the East, then the separation of the sun from the body of Mother Earth must have been perceived as a hacking apart. The Polish rana as dawn and wound enters here.

There are no obvious constructs that dip under the surFACE that can be attached to the SHAPE of the jaw on the body of Mother Earth. The letter J surfaces with a series of multiple SOUNDS. In Spanish the letter J becomes pronounced as an H. Joven as the hidden 'young one', becomes pronounced as Hoven (HAVANA) the 'hidden' sun that is heaved (HAVA) into the heavens (HAVANA) at the time of birthing. For the letter H dealt with the breath of birthing air that emerged out of the fissures and vents on the body of Mother Earth out of which the sun was heaved, or born.

In Polish the letter J is pronounced as yuh associating it with the SOUND of Y and the SHAPE encoded in the female pubis (Y). It deals with the Chinese female symbol, the yin (HA(YA)NA), the Hindu yoni (HA(YA)NA), the one (HANA), the pubis on the female body, extending to the cravasse or jama (YAMA), in Polish, the cleft between two mountains, the pubis on the body of Mother Earth out of which the heavenly bodies, especially the sun were born or regurgitated. The letters J, I and Y deal with aspects of creation as separation, as being hacked apart in the process of birthing from the individual female body and the body of Mother Earth.

After the LINGUISTIC BREAK in the Middle Eastern Alphabets the letter

J as the SHAPE of the jaw, the hook (HAKA) on the lower part of the mother's skull that hacks (HAKA) food into edible morsels and SOUND into meaningful pieces disappears altogether. What surfaces dealing with the activity of hacking morsels from the prey by the mother's jaw, into putting food into the mouth done by the *hand*, in Phoenician, Egyptian and Semitic.

The SHAPE that surfaces on the body of Mother Earth is the fingers as the rays of the sun (IS HANA) piercing the pall of night to bring life and light up to the surFACE. The Egyptian hand brings it back to the human being as the eater who uses the hand to put food into the mouth. Food (FADA) is the (DA) 'gift of' the fingers (FA).

In Polish the letter J is pronounced as jot (YATA) and jad (YADA) means to eat. It is the 'gift of' (DA) the Y of the splayed fingers of the Egyptian hand. In Phoenician yad (YADA) defines the hand that puts food into the mouth. Semitic hand as yod, jod, iod (YADA) follows the same perception.

In Polish ja (YA) means "I am". ja (YA) as 'I am' in Polish says yes (YASA) to life in English, the hand that holds the food also says yes (YASA) to life. To eat was to sustain the concept of becoming, of being able to say, 'I EAT THEREFORE I AM'. This comes out of PHASE ONE when the physical universe was still mother centered and had not yet been redefined by Voltaire in PHASE THREE as the left hemispheric male side of the brain took over and it became 'I think therefore I am'. Eating comes before thinking.

It seems that the process of eating was transferred from the jaw that hacked prey into edible morsels in PHASE ONE, into the more dainty concept of the one hand putting pieces of food into the mouth in PHASE TWO. The Etruscan symbol for J as I (ONE), as either 'I am' or deals with one hand that was used for eating. In India there is a division of what hand is acceptable to be used for eating. It is the right hand of the fathers. The left hand of the mothers is the hand used to wipe the anus after defecation.

The SHAPE of the human hand in Egyptian, yod (YADA) in Semitic have links with the body of Mother Earth. In fact the SHAPE of the hand in Semitic looks like the rays of the sun emerging out of the open palm of the hand encoded in the letter F for fingers of fire. It was the hand of the rising sun that as it rose into the light of day brought not only light but the possibility of food and said yes to life. In Etruscan it surfaces as (I) one (HANA). The sun (IS HANA) was perceived to be the helping hand of Mother Earth. The setting sun in the blood drenched Western sky was not the hand that brought forth life. It brought forth the night and the death of the sun, saying no to life as the Middle Eastern killer, separator or hacker. In Cypriotic Je (JA) symbolized by the letter Z shares its origins with the male penis as the hacker.

The Persian AYA as 'light' and the Assyrian AYA as 'dawn' said yes to life and light. The SHAPE of the letter A was the two hands touching at the fingertips holding the rays of light on their way to be born out of the female pubis (YA) the fusing SHAPE of two mountains on the body of Mother Earth, massaging or masturbating the sun into existence at dawn. In Wolof 'to hand' is yot (YATA). All of these ancient mother based perceptions were lost or obliterated but the 'hands' remain out of stage three, their origins out of the mothers face and jaw obscured by the passage of time and conscious redefinitions.

THE LETTER I

A DIPHTHONG

SOUND: A (ah) and E(ee)

SHAPE: single vertical bi-pedal individual self

MOTHER'S BODY: fingers, eyes,

MOTHER EARTH: pole,

CONCEPT: one more, individual self, eye as image maker

As the most simplified linguistic construct the letter I as an extended vowel SOUND deals immediately with a concept. Like a specific name separates the thing from its background to stand alone on the landscape of the mind, so the letter I also symbolizes the individual human creature as standing alone in space on the landscape of reality. The letter I emerges as a number and the number is one. It defines the individual as the alone standing number one carrying the container of its most salient sense and that is the eye (I) of seeing, the image maker that defines the human creature.

As the individual self the number one symbolically emerged to define maleness. It became apparent that a baby boy in PHASE ONE was not a girl defined symbolically by the triangle of the mother. He had no symbol to define him. He emerged not as a girl but as one more. As one more in PHASE THREE he was added to the triangle or three sides of the mother to become the number four that emerged as the symbolic number for males. The number three remained as the symbolic number for all females. With the addition of one more as four it emerged to define all newly born male infants.

In Hebrew the four sided square is keekar (KAKARA) establishing its links with the SOUNDS made by the open beaks of birds leaving at the time of the Spring Equinox plunging the open savannah into oncoming seasonal drought and famine.

As the sun and moon made their lateral journey across the belly of air above the body of Mother Earth, the birds made their semiannual vertical journey North and South creating not only the cross but in PHASE TWO the emerging male square. A square (IS KARA) emerges as kara, or the word for punishment in Polish. It was a punishment on both levels, the loss of life supporting monsoon rains and the loss of the SOUNDS of joy that left the sky empty and silent with the departure of the birds.

In PHASE THREE the base of an Egyptian pyramid became a square with four triangles coming to a point above it. The base had been considered representing a male and the four triangles above him represented as female. It therefore emerged in North Africa and the Sahel that a man could take four wives. This was in PHASE THREE. In PHASE ONE the Zoa tribe living in the Amazon basin claimed that their distant ancestors told stories that they had to disperse from their ancient homeland after a great flood. For the Zoa the mother exists with four husbands at the center of this very peaceful jungle enclave.

In the Middle East a Sakkara (IS HAKARA) was the name of the necropolis, the place of entombment, the pyramid SHAPE that would guarantee immortality for the single, individual pharaoh. It contains in its linguistic structure the hacking (HAKA-) quality of life being hacked apart from the living.

As males began to expand on their symbolic concept of the square, it grew diametrically into a cube (KABA). The cube became in PHASE THREE a place of pilgrimage for the Muslims as the Kaaba (KABA). It also emerged as a place of passage to the Seven Sisters the starry Pleiades across the watery divide in Cuba (KABA). To this day deeply religious Jews wear a box, a tefilah when they d'aven or pray to their God.

Feeling alone, undefined and adrift in the ethers, In PHASE TWO males began to create their own source *away* from the body of Mother Earth. They already knew that Mother Earth created the sun (IS HANA) as Her son (IS HANA) who was Her major helping hand (HANADA). Their singular individual state echoed with the singular individual state of the lonely sun way up there in the open heavens. The sun (IS HANA) was the one (HANA) the lonely traveler who did its job without pause as they were wont to do. It must have been the crippled shepherds and smiths who as the emerging shamanic priesthood yearned for answers creating not only the sun as their celestial deity but also they gave birth to the letter Q (cue) based on the round circle of the sun and their questing for answers. In PHASE TWO the sun as a male deity surfaces all around the world. In Hebrew it gave birth to many of the solar heroes as Samson (IS HAMASANA), Simon (IS HAMANA). Hama deals with blood, ema (HAMA) in Greek, the bloody waters that had been perceived to emerge with the death of the sun at the Western horizontal rim when Mother Earth devoured it chomping it down into Her cavernous belly to be cooked, transformed and triumphant emerging clean and wan at dawn. The sun became the one (HANA) who in PHASE TWO became a male God away from the body of Mother Earth. He surfaces in Japan as their Shinto (IS HANATA) solar based religion.

Another concept dealing with the letter I of one more and the number one (HANA) of the sun (IS HANA) becomes apparent with the I (eye) of seeing. On the human body the eye occupies a specific area of the face, above the cheeks, below the forehead, two slits lying laterally across the face on either side of the nose with round balls within them that act as sentinels for survival. It is the primary sense of image accumulation once human beings became bipedal. The two eyes (I-) define the human creature as the individual who sees. There was also a perception that a crisscrossing occurred at some point behind the eyes. On the outside was the image. Then the outside image reflected itself upside down behind the watery orbs. Somehow it straightened itself out. Then there was another crisscrossing within the body. For the left emisphere of the brain was related to the right hand side of the body and the right hemisphere of the brain was related to the left side of the body. The crisscrossing occurred at the metaphoric third eye above the nose, and between the two actual eyes. What the third eye was perceived to do was to bring the two hemispheres of the brain together across the corpus collosum and create a balance, an evenness, an equal distribution of reason and fantasy. In some, especially birthing mothers and castrated first born sons, it created witches and shamans endowing them with ecstatic harmony, leadership, peace, healing powers and prophecy. The image maker in whose left hemisphere was stored the fear of its helplessness at birth and of a panic stricken infancy forming a lifetime habit through that filter of fear searching a way to defuse that fear. In PHASE ONE in mothers it was through the experience of the birthing breath. In men in PHASE ONE it was through castration. In PHASES TWO and THREE it was through the blessing at birth, the use of multifaceted ritual and drugs.

The fantasy of metaphoric systems being shared by individual mothers with the body of Mother Earth extends to the eyes on the body of Mother Earth surfacing out of a variety of ancient concepts. One dealt with the Persian aya as light and the Assyrian aya as dawn. They represent the eyes on the body of Mother Earth, on Her horizontal surFACE between two mountain peaks that as folded finger tips (A) cradle the sun before it was regurgitated up to Her surFACE. In aya you have the A(ah) of Mother Earth as the mountains on either side with the SHAPE of the cleft between the mountains, the pubis (Y) out of which the sun was also perceived to have been born.

The other process dealt with the eyes on the body of Mother Earth as the great seas, great bodies of water that reflected the sky above, saw it as a great arc that filled the space between the watery depths below and the spread of infinity above. Mother Earth reflected the realty above with Her watery eyes the seas that saw in the same way that it occurred on the bodies of Her creatures. The eyes of Mother Earth as the sea creaed the image above as real and the upside down reflection upon Her surFACE as that which was under Her surFACE dealing with an alternate reality and death.

The verb saw reeks with hidden implications for it not only means the past tense of seeing but it also means a rendering tool or saw that like an aqueous (HAKA-) reflection hacks (HAKA-) objects in twain.

In Polish oko (HAKA) defines the eye. Like the ocular image it hacks (HAKA) reality into two aspects, one outside ond one inside. In Africa the Okobongo (HAKA-) River Delta in Botswana creates a verdant swampy savanna and like an internal sea reflects or sees the sky. In Florida on the other side of the great watery divide the Okeechobee (HAKA-) Lake follows the same linguistic pattern as does the Okeefenokee (HAKA-) Swamp in Georgia. All deal with standing placid swampy seas that reflect or see the sky and hack (HAKA) reality in half.

The fact that the same ocular concept of hacking occurs with the seeing eyes on the body of Mother Earth on both sides of the Atlantic Ocean should give linguists a pause. Along with Havana in Cuba from the savannah (IS HAVANA) out of Africa is oko (HAKA) as eye in Polish, Maya as Mother Earth the mother of Gautama (GATAMA) Buddha and a tribe of settlers the MAYA in Central America especially in Guatamala (GATAMAla). Also the Mayaka River in Florida and Miami (MAYAma) on the Eastern coast and Canada (KANADA) as the Kunda (KANADA) of Mother Earth energy of the Hindus and many others. The sneaky snake makes its ubiquitous appearance in South America as the anakonda (HANAKANADA) (HANA NAKA KANA NADA). (HANA) is the sun (IS HANA). (NAKA) is the snake (IS

NAKA). (KANADA) taken together bears similar linguistic links with the Hindu Goddess of the Earth Kunda (KANADA) that may also have given the name of Canada. Linguistically it bears witness to the possibility that there were ancient settlements on the North American continent before the arrival of the Indians.

The letter I shares similar antecedents to the letter Y(yee) and J as (yee). In Polish I as (yee) means 'and'. It deals with birthing and the making of 'one more', out of the mother's body. The word 'and' (HANADA) is the 'gift of' (DA) the one (HANA) sun (IS HANA) and it deals with the body of Mother Earth making a succession of endless sun rises, and an endless succession of ands. And (HANADA) is also related to the hand (HANADA). For it was the hands, the rays of the sun on the body of Mother Earth as the solar fingers that helped Her in the maintenance of life. In PHASE THREE with the immersion into male centrality the sun was considered to be so important that in Egypt the God Aten was depicted as a solar disc with the rays of the sun streaming down towards the body of Mother Earth ending in open helping right hands.

On the end of Latin nouns I as (ah-ee) not only means 'one more', as in alumni but gave birth to the square as a male symbol.

Out of the body of Mother Earth, the great egg laying mother hen (HANA) gave birth to Her one (HANA) offspring, the sun (IS HANA) during the day and another one offspring, the moon, during the night. In Polynesian the moon is called hina (HANA). That which 'emerges upon the surface' (NA), into the belly of air (HA). The moon (MANA) had also been considered as Mother Earth's helping hands at night. In Spanish manos (MANA-) define the hands.

As an addendum, in PHASE ONE the mind (MANADA) had been considered as the (DA) 'gift of' the hands or manos (MANA-). In PHASE THREE with the growth of male centrality and singular reliance on the left hemisphere of the human mind, the hands, manos (MANASA) were considered the (DA) 'gift of' the mind (MANADA), or the mind was the gift of the hands. Take your pick.

The series of hands in Egyptian, Semitic and Phoenician deal with two processes; one deals with the human hand putting food into the mouth. To hand is yot (YATA) in Wolof. The other deals with the hand (HANADA) as (DA), the 'ft of' the sun (IS HANA). It survives out of PHASE ONE when the body of Mother Earth and the sun had been considered as one unit of creation. Then it echoes the perception of working together in PHASE TWO after the separation myths peppered the ancient landscape and they were both perceived to work peacefully in tandem maintaining their creations.

Everything that emerged out of the body of Mother Earth was a small aspect of Her. The dot as an iota in Greek deals with smallness on another level.

In Cypriotic the symbol for I as an X with a line above it brings it back to the individual female. The X SHAPE on the female body is the buttox, where the bloody dot of potential life marks the spot. The line emerging out of the X out of the top of the buttox is the number one (I) more of new life emerging upon the surface. In Greek an iota is a dot and surfaces under the letter J. Under the letter I the Greek iota is the I of one more, similar to the Etruscan I as the number one, standing alone. An iota is a not only a dot signifying a menstrual period but also deals with the concept of smallness. The belly was small, not pregnant when a dot or a period at her end, appeared on the female body.

THE LETTER Y
A DIPTHONG

SOUND; waa-ee

SHAPE; V on top, pole on bottom.

MOTHER'S BODY; pubis, hand, bifurcated brain

MOTHER EARTH; cleft between two mountains

CONCEPT; Why, separation on many levels

The letter Y emerges to define a host of possibilities. In PHASE ONE it had two possibilities. One dealt with the mother's body in stage three and the SHAPE of her creative organ, the pubis (Y). The other dealt with Mother Earth regurgitating, giving birth, passing the sun out of Her body between two mountains or volcanic peaks creating the (Y) SHAPE of the pubis on Her body.

As the creative organ on the individual mothers body the pubis SHAPED as a Y or trident on top had been called Ione (HAYANA) in the Middle East, also Yin (HAYANA) as the yes symbol in Chinese part of the Yin Yang. In Hindu it is the name of the vulva or Yoni (HAYANA) the one creative force in the universe. The trident in PHASE ONE has ancient links with fish, the smell associated with menstruating women and the sea as Mother Earth in Her aspect as water.

Section Three

Out of the Eastern sky the sun emerged triumphant after a night of transformative cooking within the body of Mother Earth. It may have died in the bloody Western waters dragging the pall of night behind it, as the war that was declared by the engulfing sea put it to rest. On the other side at dawn it emerged triumphant. Every night it lost the battle. Every morning at dawn it won anew.

A clue exists in the word for won (WANA). (NA) deals with either 'a change from a former state' or 'emergence on the surface'. (WA) deals with water. To win (WANA) was to emerge (NA) out of the water (WA) at dawn and only the sun could claim that passage. Dawn (DAWANA) furthers the clue. For dawn (DAWANA) is (DA) 'gift of' (WANA) or the sun having won (WANA) its battle against the cold dark night. Not to be left behind, if the color of the setting sun splintered in the horizontal bloody Western waters was bright red, then the rising sun after its meandering journey and transformative cooking beneath the surFACE of Mother Earth emerges pale and wan (WANA) in the Eastern sky.

In the Yoruba tribe in Africa a mother priestess is called Iyalode (HAYALADA) . She contains in her name not only the Aya (HAYA) of light and dawn in Persian and Assyrian but the name of the lady (LADA) of the land as her third dyad. Hidden in her linguistic folds is (YALA) dealing with the SHAPE of the sun's emergence at dawn out of Mother Earth's pubis and the pale wan color of yellow (YALA) that accompanied it.

As male centrality gained momentum in PHASE TWO the letter Y began the Wolof name of God as Yalla (YALA) not only with the female pubis but linking it to the yellow (YALA) sun at dawn. In PHASE THREE the Y of the female pubis was dropped off the Wolof name of their God Yalla and their solar deity emerged in North Africa as Allah (HALA) the original name of their solar (IS HALA-) deity.

The Hebrew God Yahweh (YHVH) not only dropped the A (ah) vowel of Mother Earth between the consonants but somehow overlooked the unholy letter (Y) as representing the female pubis. Changing it to Jehovah (JAHAVA) in PHASE THREE as the 'hidden' deity in space only re-established its links with the female body in whose belly was 'hidden' the miracle of birth. In Polish chova (HAVA) means 'hidden'. In English to carry existence into being is to have (HAVA) a baby.

On the body of Mother Earth it deals with the emergence of the sun AYA as light in Persin and dawn in Assyrian. The AYA on the body of Mother Earth reiterates the SHAPE of the EYES on the human face. With the emergence of light at dawn all could be seen. The SHAPE of that emergence at dawn was perceived to be between two mountain peaks. The two A's on either side of the (Y) of the pubis (AYA) are Her fingertips touching at the top creating the SHAPE of the mountains or volcanic cones creating the cleft between them for the emergence of the sun out of Her body at dawn or as lava out of Her volcanic interior.

In PHASE TWO the (Y) SHAPE of the pubis with a baby 'hidden' behind it on both the female body and the body of Mother Earth became an obsession of the two diverse male groups with the permanently empty bellies; the eunuch priesthood as part of the family circle and the heterosexual males pushed out at puberty, circling the periphery. The eunuch brothers and uncles were not only castrated but were also crippled in PHASES TWO and THREE to serve as shepherds and blacksmiths. They began to question their fate with the asking of (Y) or WHY.

The asking of WHY began a process which bifurcated the human brain into two diverse hemispheres that represented two different evolutionary functions. The left hemisphere controlling right handedness was perceived to have been male with the LINEAR drive of top down, exclusion, competition, secrecy, hierarchy, scheming, stalking, greed, rampant sexuality, violent power, rational single focused attention, fear and the ideal defined as real, the self created fantasy that had to be defended till death. The right hemisphere associated with left handedness had been perceived to belong to the mothers dealing with a CIRCULAR orientation of emotion, maintenance, relationships, cooperation, empathy, caring and the defense of children.

After the humanoid creature became bipedal, the next big shift was the origins of language which began with the naming of things. Surfacing as n'um (NAMA) for speech in Hebrew it defines the giving of diverse objects a name (NAMA). The hum of the mother teaching her children which fruits, berries and leaves were edible gave a name to the organ on her face that did the humming and masticating, defining the mouth (MATA) of the mother (MATA-) as the masticator and teacher. It then expanded to other organs on her face and body that were a factor in their survival, her eyes, nose, jaw, mammaries, and hands (manos in Spanish). It expanded further to include metaphorically the surFACE and body of Mother Earth. She became their beloved all encompassing mother providing for all of their needs.

It is claimed through rational scientific inquiry that most creatures have an equal distribution between left handedneass and right handedness. Studies have also declared that human beings in PHASE THREE are eighty percent right handed and twenty percent left handed. There in lies the tale. Since in PHASE ONE the circular left handedness has been ascribed to the female gender and linear right handedness to the male gender, the role of the bifurcated human mind begins to come into focus.

The naming of things separates the objects named from their natural background. It creates a separate reality floating in space of the mind based on the objects named. If enough objects become named they move into becoming stories that are stored in that separate reality to become the permanent inhabitants of the mind. When fear or trauma becomes associated with them the permanent additions of the witness bearing mind begins to explain, justify, rationalize their tenancy to help it to survive the internal fear based prattle. The fear based prattle gives the human creature no rest.

The naming of things is a process of linear image accumulation. It is in the linear left male hemisphere of the human brain that the fear based linear prattle reigns supreme.

One named object as an image follows another in a straight line. The straight line of the linear left male oriented hemisphere originally dealt with repetitive activity dealing with sexuality and power. Male sexuality is not based on cycles as it exists in the right hemisphere of the female brain. It is constant and unrelenting as the must and rut in male animals proclaims.

The naming of things must have had very positive aspects dealing with survival, for more and more objects became named. Then not only the objects were given a name but verbs entered the picture defining what the objects were capable of doing. The new system based on named objects began to take up more and more space in the left hemisphere of the human brain. The human brain began to expand to house the accumulating bank of images.

As language became more and more capable of communication the oral tradition of repeated stories based on accumulated images creating specific culture began to take form. A story (IS TARA) has two meanings. One deals with repeating an experience that occurred on the body of Mother Earth on Her terrain (TARA-). The other more recent out of PHASE THREE deals with multi levels of buildings stacked one upon the other called stories (IS TARA) like the stories (IS TARA) stacked up in the mind. As language began to take over the linear aspect of the human brain housed in the left hemisphere, it too began to expand and grow. The left hemisphere housing the linear male essence of language, power, violence and sexuality began to split away from the circular right hemisphere of emotion, compassion, caring inHERent in the mothers brain. It created the SHAPE of the (Y) of the bifurcated brain.

Since fear had been trapped and adhered to the image in the left hemisphere of the mind, every time the image popped up fear also erupted to the surface. Every time fear gripped the human creature the entrapped image also surfaced. The human creature became trapped in a circle of fear driven image and image driven fear. Fear was forbidden to the ancient males. Systems of male transformation into fearless manhood surface as universal myths. Courage was their greatest gift.

As males began the search for their own source *away* from the body of Mother Earth they had to keep their evolving perceptions a secret. They began the process of writing their secret systems down. Except for the Western Alphabet all the other alphabets are written in code available only to the cognoscenti. The scribes hidden in caves replaced the story tellers. At first they were left handed, then writing shifted to the right hand as it did in Brahman, Hebrew and Etruscan. In PHASE THREE the right hand dealing with writing became the right hand of God. It shifted from the definition of the right side of the human body into a concept of right and wrong. It was language, then writing, then a shift in to the right hand of male centrality that put the last nail into the coffin of mother centrality and female freedom.

There existed one major factor that diffused the fear in PHASE ONE and that was the birthing breath of the mother. Because of bi -pedalism and her narrow hips that facilitated walking upright, the human female had a very perilous time trying to get the large headed fetus out of her body. The fact that the fetus became smaller and smaller in order to get through the narrow birth canal made the baby helpless at birth. The head of the fetus was often too large for the vaginal opening. The birthing mother had to push hard, pant like a dog, gasp for air to help push the large headed fetus out of her body. A process lost in the mists of time and obliterated by males as mysticism and mystery, came to her aid. At the base of the spine lay coiled the Kundalini energy that the panting breath acting like a bellows activated. As it spun up the mothers spine it cradled her in an ecstatic trance like state that not only orgasmed the baby out of her body but on the wings of her ecstasy she bonded with the product of her intense labors with the ecstatic breath creating all the possibilities of love that became part of the human condition.

That may have worked for women who because of the birthing breath became the leaders, healers, and prophets but for men there was a different answer to still their prattling over evolved left hemisphere. At the side of their mothers and sisters, the eunuch priesthood often crippled and maimed began by asking (Y) WHY of their peripheral state. Their questing for an

Section Three

answer in PHASE ONE began at the WESTERN WALL where the sun sank into the sea, was sWALLowed by the hungry maw of Mother Earth. WHY did the sun die to its light? WHY did the darkness have to envelop them? In PHASE TWO as they began to associate themselves with the solitary passage of the sun alone in the sky they expanded their questions to WHY didn't their bellies produce children? WHY was the area on the female body with the SHAPE of the pubis (Y) not given to them? WHY was their belly empty and no life flowed from that area? Castration of the first born son gave them a partial answer. They became docile but no babies left their bellies. Still in PHASE ONE they turned to ritual to experience the brthing breath of the mother and the gifts that the experience endowed upon them. Then there was liQUor that stilled the quest for answers and many different drugs, from magical flowers, to mushrooms and grasses. It was the eunuch priesthood that moved first into the shamanic trance state experienced naturally by the mothers. They became the leaders, healers, prophets of the tribe. Watching them from the periphery the heterosexual males yearned for their mystical powers. They began to realize that certain activities along with spirits and drugs would send them into that ecstatic trance like state. Dancing, fasting, chanting, meditating, spinning, praying , drumming, singing, any repetitive activity done over an extended period of time brought them not only relief from the prattling over evolved left hemisphere but a relief from their fear.

The human males in whom the latent energy became activated had to defuse their negative emotions in order to enter the heavenly gates of the Kundalini energy. The Kundalini energy is neutral, rising up from the body of Mother Earth along Her LEA lines it enters the bottom of the feet or soles while standing and the anus while sitting. Males who have not risen above their power and violence locked in the third chacra use the energy as a source of control and war, the dictators, Ghengis Khan, Hitler, Stalin, Polpat, Mao, Napoleon, the list is endless. The ones who rise above their negativity into the fourth chacra of the heart become the performers, priests, pastors, sages and gurus. The battle between the eunuchs who remain in organized religion and the heterosexual males who run the secular world as presidents, kings, khans, ceos, dictators, generals, still remain locked in their horns.

Since the over evolution of the left hemisphere also created a massive shift into conservativism, rabid competition and Republicanism it also created an evolutionary addition into the human scene as mostly boys who are afflicted with autism are unable to create relationships even with help and training, repeating one activity over and over and rocking back and forth like caged animals. The end run of that evolutionary thrust is the genius savant who has tapped into the linear single focused facts and figures housed in the linear left hemisphere and is totally incapable of human relationships.

To heal the bifurcated brain the Egyptian metaphoric Ankh (HANAKA) as the ancient SHAPE of balance should be looked at as should the physical corpus collosum. The Ankh (HANAKA) establishes its links not only with balance, closing the bifurcated brain on the stem of the I into a circle of the mother but also it has linguistic links with the castrated eunuch (HANAKA). Wasn't it Isis who put together the severed pieces of Osiris her consort without his penis?

The WHY syndrome is the asking of WHY the sun sank into the waters of the Western wall dying to its light. It also asks the WHY of male periphery, WHY male bodies had a permanently empty belly, WHY had they apparently been left out of the birthing process. They also asked WHY they had to be castrated, crippled to support and protect the emerging human family and then society.

The SHAPE of the letter Y as the female pubis in PHASE ONE became associated with the male brain in PHASE TWO. The asking of WHY and the answers based on fantasy and fabrication bifurcated the male mind, split it in half. It became disconnected from itself, from the natural side of reality to dwell in theoretical speculation. The shim, as a wedge surfaces here as a balancing tool. The SHAPE of the letter Y as the asking of WHY became the symbol for the separation of the male brain on the stem of the I and a movement into the left hemispheric side of linear, exclusive thinking. There are no answers to WHY. The answers to WHY have to be made up. THE ANSWERS TO WHY ARE ALWAYS A LIE.

After the LINGUISTIC BREAK the Y as the pubis of the ancient Mothers expressing itself through the body of Mother Earth birthing Her offspring at dawn disappears from the Middle Eastern linguistic scene altogether. What surfaces is the hand (HANADA) in Hebrew. For the Phoenicians it becomes both a hand (HANADA) and a hook (HAKA), remaining as the hook (HAKA) waw for the Semites. The hand HANADA) of the sun (IS HANA) becomes a hook (HAKA) that hacks (HAKA) the sun free for the night and drags it down into a watery abyss. The waw (WAWA) as the hook (HAKA) like hand of the Semites deals with the (WA) of water coming and going, hacking (HAKA-) the sun free from the nocturnal waters (WA) in the East and hacking (HAKA-) it free from the light of day into the wall of waiting waters (WA) in the West.

The other Y SHAPES in PHASES TWO and THREE no longer represent the female pubis but as hooks (HAKA) in Phoenician, Egyptian, Semitic, Etruscan, Greek and Roman represent the crutches, the support poles of the maimed smiths toiling away at the forge of the sun creating tools and weapons of war and of limping shepherds leaning on their staffs watching their flocks at night. With the knowledge of specific paternity in PHASE THREE the WHY of their peripheral state on all levels seems to have disappeared. Also in PHASE THREE the shepherds crook became a symbol of power for the emerging monotheistic patriarchal religions.

THE LETTER R
A VOICED, ALVEOLAR SEMI VOWE

SOUND: fillibration by the tongue against top of oral cavity

SHAPE: sun on top, traingle on bottom, halved vertically

MOTHER'S BODY: none

MOTHER EARTH: circle of sun on top, cone of volcano on bottom, halved vertically

CONCEPT: emergence of male centrality and power

The letter R varies based on the time of its emergence. In some areas in PHASE TWO it deals with an equal distribution of power between the deeply ensconced mothers at one (atone) with the body of Mother Earth and the emerging fathers seeking their own power source *away* from the body of Mother Earth. The SHAPE of the letter R comes out of the SHAPE of the male circle of the sun hovering ABOVE the SHAPE of the female triangular cone of the volcano on the body of Mother Earth, halved vertically. Since metaphorically every activity upon the planet between Her creatures was echoed upon the body of Mother Earth, then the sun as the male son on top must have had its origins in the subjugation of women on the bottom. The letter R bears witness to that shift from female to male centrality as does the story of the Biblical Lilith, who checked out when Adam demanded for her to be under him not only sexually denying her control over her own pleasure but in many ways subjecting her to become his beast of burden.

In PHASE ONE, before the letter R dealing mostly with the sun came into being, it didn't surface that way. The sun (IS HANA) was a universal relative and helping hands (HANADA) of Mother Earth, at one with Her, as an extended family of women; Her grandmother, sister, aunt, niece and daughter. (HA) is the belly of air through which the sun sailed. (NA) deals with either' emergence on the surface' or 'a change from a former state'. The (DA) at the end deals with the (DA) as the 'gift of' the sun (IS HANAda). Goddesses with names associated with maternal family relatives still exist in the mythological landscape.

In PHASE ONE the sun was a consistent companion to Mother Earth, whether a family member, or in the subsequent PHASES a male son and solar deity. In the subsequent PHASES, as males realized their specific role in procreation they became not only her temporary companions but her lovers and then in PHASE THREE her domineering masters, sheiks, over lords and husbands. The process expanded to include the body of Mother Earth as Her son (IS HANA) Her close companion and helper became the sun (IS HANA) the male solar disc becoming Her master in the sky. It echoed the relationship that the individual mother had with Her first born castrated eunuch son who helped to protect the family from the marauding band of brothers on the periphery.

The eunuch (HANAKA) first born sons at the time that language was beginning to become codified settled the far reaches of the planet after a great volcanic cataclysm which dealt with the roaring (RARA-), raging (RAJA-), rumbling (RAMA-), rampaging (RAMA-) volcanic eruptions that obliterated the sun and darkened the sky. The eunuch (HANAKA) first born sons who must have been considered to be very important for they left a legacy that lies hidden in the place names across the planet; South American Inca (HANAKA), Egyptian spirit of life ankh (HANAKA), Hebrew holiday of lights Hannukah (HANAKA), Ananaki (HANANAKA) Sumerian Gods, Anglia (HANAGAla) English henges and mounds, Senegal (IS HANAGAla) stone circles, the Nagas of Harappa, Karnak (KARANAka) LEA stones in Brittany, Anak (HANAKA) Krakatoa (son of Krakatoa) Indonesian volcano, Anki (HANAKA) Sumerian Brotherhood of the Snake (IS NAKA), Angi (HANAGA) Sanskrit world, Anki (HANAKA) Sumerian Earth heaven separation myth, Enki (HANAKA) Sumerian water God, Enkidu (HANAKAda) Neanderthal friend of Gilgamesh, KAANG (KANAGA) Supreme God of African Bushmen, Seneca (IS HANAKA) North American native tribe, Sank (IS HANAKA) even in Amharic, angaffa (HANAGAfa) Amhara first born son, inike (HANAKA) Greek for victory, Anakala (HANAKAla) uncle Egyptian, English uncle (HANAKAla) avuncular protector, hunk (HANAKA) big protector, Ankassa (HANAKASA) lame in Amharic, Sanakkala (IS

Section Three

HANAKAla) cripple in Amharic, Sanga (IS HANAGA) Amharic castrated, zang (IS HANAGA) Amharic, rod or staff, Sang (IS HANAGA) weep over dead in Chinese, Inaki (HANAKA) boys name in Basque, Shang (IS HANAGA) DI Chinese God, angat (HANAGAta) entrails, intestines, gut Bugotu, HANAKA leg in Basque, ankle (HANAKALA) in English, onkia (HANAKA) angle (HANAGALA) in Lithuanian, hanko (HANAKA) Finnish fork or trident, anger (HANAGAra), hunger (HANAGAra), in English sing (IS HANAGA), sank (IS HANAKA), henki HANAKA) spirit in Finnish, kunigas (KANAGAsa) priest, Lithuanian, angel (HANAGAla), enkeli (HANAKAla) angel in Finnish, onga (HANAGA) lightning in Bugotu, shang (IS HANAGA) Chinese to be born, In Bemba -sanika (IS HANAKA) is to make light. The letters (H,K,G) are often interchangeable.

The eunuch (HANAKA) overlapping dyad defining the castrated priesthood gave birth to places, activities and names on the body of Mother Earth. It dealt with the sun (IS HANA) and the guide of the sun, the ubiquitous snake (IS NAKA) to find its way out of a major catastrophic cataclysm of the volcanic cloud of ash that obscured the sun and sent the beleaguered inhabitants of Africa into new places to inhabit. It also dealt with rape (RAPA) as the passage (PA) of the sun (RA) above and below the body of Mother Earth.

It always emerged as a pale wan solar disc on one side in the East and disappeared on the other side in the blazing bloody waters of the Western horizontal rim. As it rose at dawn into the belly of air ABOVE the surFACE of Mother Earth it brought with it light and life and a chorus of rejoicing.

For the Egyptians the name of the sun God was RA. It had both the male name of the dual aspect of the solar disc on top and the female volcanic triangle on the bottom and the A (ah) of Mother Earth as the SHAPE of the volcanic cone of creation. When it became RE of repetition as the journey of the sun was perceived to be eminently repetitive, the vowel (E) of Eviction, Emergence, or Exit up to the surFACE of Mother Earth came into being.

When the sun set at night RA represented by a hawks (HAWAKA) head swallowed by the Goddess Nut (NATA) ushered in the night (NATA) and as a metaphoric representation Mother Earth helped to establish the name of nature (NATARA). In Polish nato (NATA) means upon. Night (NATA) fell upon the cold sleeping Earth as the birds disappeared into the far reaches of the northern (NARATA-) sky. The repetitive (RAPA-) activity of rape (RAPA) not only surfaces as the passage (PA) of the sun (RA) through the body of Mother Earth but became encoded in the SHAPE of the letter R with the male solar disc on top and the female triangular cone of creation of Mother

Earth on the bottom. Beginning with the letter R rape (RAPA) in PHASE THREE is a reflection of the word para (RAPA/PARA) out of PHASE ONE.

Para in Polish deals with sensuality and the morning steam or mist hugging and caressing the valleys and hills of Mother Earth as it rose to meet the sun at dawn. The major clue to this activity and how it came to be redefined surfaces in the Polish name of both the birth of the sun in the morning as RANA and the name for wound also as RANA. How could the birth of the sun and the name for wound in Polish carry the same name? Can clitorectomies be far behind? Therein lies the tale.

In PHASE ONE when mothers defined reality, they understood the role of the blood emerging out of a girls pubis, her quintessence, becoming a monarch with her menarche, a ruler in concert with the ruling passage of the lunar clock and for all creatures at estRUs the time of the solar clock in the spring and fall. It was only in PHASE TWO and THREE when males began to define reality that they never understood the cleft on the female body and called it a wound that bled every twenty eight lunar days. The bleeding of that wound on the individual female body expanded to include the body of Mother Earth dealing with the birth of the sun out of Her horizontal rim at dawn. She too had to have a break or a wound (RANA) at Her round (RANAda) side for the sun to be born at dawn, ergo rano (RANA) as morning in Polish. Another series of words begin to make their entrance. It was at the round (RANAda) horizontal rim that the sun appeared on Her surFACE at dawn (RANA). For the sun in the morning (RANA) was the (DA) 'gift of' the wound (RANA) in Polish.

It gives birth to a series of other letters like the circle of the round horizontal rim emerging as the open (C) of creation and the open (G) of Generation, with the break in the circle allowing Mother Earth to push the heavenly bodies out of Her internal cavity up to Her surFACE with Her internal tongue.

The horizontal rim (RAMA) on the body of Mother Earth emerges out of a convoluted history. It began it's life as MARA the marine (MARA-) environment on the body of Mother Earth out of which the sun emerged pale and wan in the East and set into the bloody Western waters.

As male role in procreation was becoming known in PHASE TWO and males became heir to the realms beneath the reflected surface of water, the reflected surface of water also extended to the reflected process inherent in words. On the body of the individual mother the arms (haRAMA) of the marine (MARA-) environment became the reflected RAMA (MARA/RAMA) of the rim (RAMA) on the body of Mother Earth. The rim (RAMA) became the arms (haRAMA) of the sun that held Mother Earth and Her celestial creations, even the birds in place. In Polish a frame (FARAMA) is also called rama. In this case you have five fingers of fire (FA) that held the sun in place. You are in PHASE TWO and THREE when in Polish also the extended arms out of the shoulders emerge as ramiona (RAMANA). Also In Polish you have brama (BARAMA) which means gate. It has similar SOUNDING antecedents as Brahma (BARAMA) one of the triparted unity of the Hindu pantheon. A gate the Polish brama (baRAMA) is an opening, a wound which allowed the sun and the heavenly bodies to make their entrance upon Her surFACE. The sun was no longer the helping hands of Mother Earth. It became the male arms (haRAMA) that held Her in place once they entered Her as they held in place the struggling women whom they RAPED on the plane below. The letter R with the sun on top bears witness to that enduring activity. The RAMA dyad of male raping and rampaging activity became so popular that many of the subsequent kings, rulers and epics adopted the name; Abraham (abRA(HA)MA) of the Hebrews, RAMA as Remus and Romulus of Rome (RAMA), Ramses (RAMA-) of Egypt, Ramayana of the Hindus, Brahma (baRAMA) also of the Hindus and Buddhists.

As the herd of gentle sheep belonging to SHE or HER were associated with the nomadic migrating mothers for an alternate milk supply, with a shift into male centrality the rampaging ram (RAMA) became a male symbolic deity. The concept of R or RA emerging as a solar deity surfaces not only in Egyptian as the sun God. In Sanskrit RA defines fire, royalty and that which is exalted and high. For the Chinese RA also deals with heat and what is hot, keeping it down to Earth. Interestingly RAA standing for bad in Hebrew with the double (AA) could deal with it being associated with the dual aspect of the feminine. Or it could deal with the fact that because of their stay in Egypt as slaves they rejected everything Egyptian especially their solar deity.

For the Semites RA defined 'that which existed forever.' On the other side of the world for the Maya it was 'LA the eternal truth that existed forever.' The Semites had already moved into PHASE THREE with their solar deity *away* from the body of Mother Earth. The Maya in the New World stayed with the LA of the Lady of the Land. Another set of concepts surfaces in the words pleasure (paLAsara) and pressure (paRAsara). Pleasure (paLAsara) dealt with sensuality and women or the LAdies of the LAnd. Pressure (paRAsara) dealt with male sexuality and RA their solar deity.

When the body of Mother Earth came first, the triangle on top as in Mara or Tara or hara we are in PHASE ONE in female centrality. When the solar deity beginning with the letter R became the anlaut then we are in PHASES TWO and THREE and male centrality. Mara of the marine (MARA-) environment becomes the reflected rampaging ram (RAMA) and male deity, (MARA/RAMA). Tara as the majestic Mother Goddess of the Earth and Her terrain (TARANA) becomes the male active verb of rata (TARA/RATA) or the ratio (RATA) of the male solar journey above, upon and below the body of Mother Earth. Hara deals either with the pregnant belly and holy mountain Har (HARA) in Hebrew. One deals with the birth of a baby. The other deals with the birth or regurgitation of the sun out of two convergent mountain peaks SHAPED like a pubis on Her body.

Then there is the concept of the Tibetan Bardo (BARADA) as an 'intermediate state'. It deals with the Bardo (BARADA) or the (DA) 'gift of' the bar (BARA). It establishes the fact that they believed in reincarnation and the 'intermediate state' between death and being reborn. It is similar to the Christian limbo. As the dyad (BARA-) it splays out to define endless categories and activities dealing with the space in between. The most telling is the state of air, the breath (BARAta) that hangs suspended between the body of Mother Earth and the curve of the solar passage up in the heavens above Her. In PHASE ONE the (BARA) dyad became associated with the brats, (BARAta) the first born brothers (BARAda) who were castrated to protect the family. After their castration they were no longer male and not really female. They hung suspended in that 'intermediate state' defined by the Tibetan Bardo (BARA-). Many also in time became the shamen, the sacred angels who also floated through the clouds and defined a plethora of activities. Who also occupied that intermediate space of air above the body of Mother Earth? The birds (BARAda) who came and went semiannually at the time when the ceremonies of castration were being performed on the hapless young men. They also used the vehicle of air as their 'intermediate state' of passage.

The angels (HANAGALA) as the protective eunuch uncles (HANAKALA) became associated with birds sharing that 'intermediate space' of passage. Birds (BARADA) becoming angels surface the world over as sacred emissaries of protection. "When at night I go to sleep fourteen angels watch do-o keep' Fourteen dealt with the fourteen days that made up the two passages of the moon waxing and waning creating an even twenty-eight day lunar balance in the month. Many other words based on the (BARA) dyad expand on the same theme. A bridge (BARAja) defines an area of passage between two points. A bear (BARA) is a creature that hiBERnates, hangs suspended in a sleep like state half of the year. For the Hebrews i'bur (haBARA) as the state of

Section Three

pregnancy and conception defines the fetus as hanging suspended in a mothers belly before birth (BARAta). It extends to define the bride (BARAda) as a female, no longer a girl but not yet a mother. The (BARA) dyad surfaces the world over. It is also associated with the friend of Gilgamesh Enkidu (HANAKADA) who was hairy, squat, ate herbs and was apparently uncivilized, sort of a Neanderthal. As a brute (BARATA) he too existed in that 'intermediate state', no longer an animal but not yet as wonderful as the civilized Gilgamesh the Sumerian prince. Brut (BARATA) in French means dry and deals with the castrated eunuch priesthood. They were also the singers, the bards (BARADA) of old who sang their stories through life. There are no shortages of words that became associated with the Tibetan Bardo (BARA-) of the 'intermediate state'.

That all began in PHASE ONE with the eunuchization of the first born son. When males began to understand their specific role in procreatin and assumed power in the reflected waters below and the sky above, the reflective process created a new set of meaning in the evolving words. The (BARA) dyad became (RABA) (BARA/RABA). In PHASES TWO and THREE that (RABA) dyad became the Hebrew Rabbi (RABA) with the I of one more.

Women tried to hang on to their ancient elusive power and as the Rabbatu (RABA-) they holy ones, the Semitic Goddess priestesses they succumbed to the tide of history that was sweeping them into the abyss. The fact that i'bur (haBARA) dealing with pregnancy and conception of motherhood in Hebrew didn't save them from their sorry fate.

When the anlaut in a word begins with the R SOUND we are in PHASES TWO and THREE. Going back to the original reflected word Lar (LARA) in Etruscan deals with homeland, origins and that establishes Mother Earth as (LA) working in concert with the sun (RA). When it becomes reflected as (RALA) (LARA/RALA) it begins to define male made, God sanctified rules (RALA-) no longer associated with the moon and female menstruation but with solar based power and control.

The dyad (RANA) dealing with morning and wound in Polish before it became reflected began its life as NARA (NARA/RANA). The (NARA) dyad deals with negation found in the word nor (NARA). During the daily passage of time, night (NA-) negated the state of light supplied by the sun during the day. With the yearly passage of the sun North (NARA-) created the time of negation where no sun apparently shone in the Northern (NARA-) reaches of the sky. In Hebrew a candle is ner (NARA) and their holy candle stick with seven candles is a meNORAh) that pushes away the darkness of night and the cold of the oncoming winter.

Back to the PHASE THREE reflection, for the Egyptians ren (RANA) was the sun name, one of the seven names given to a child at birth. The sun had been perceived to emerge out of the round (RANAda) ground (gaRANAda) around (haRANAda) them out of the Polish wound (RANA) on the side of Mother Earth at dawn (RANA). The word rind (RANAda) follows a similar perception. It circles the round body of a fruit. Rain (RANA) also emerges out of the side of Mother Earth, out of Her open wound in the Western horizontal rim (RAMA). DaRANA is a Maori rainmaker.

In the latter part of PHASE ONE the castrated son became the uncle and protector to his sisters children. In PHASE TWO as male roles were becoming defined, the sun became the male son to Mother Earth, Her protector. Then he became independent of Her as Her mate and in PHASE THREE he emerged above Her as Her boss. The SOUND associated with the letter R out of the human mouth, is the fillibrating of the tongue in the frontal cavity of the mouth. On the body of Mother Earth it is associated with the raging, roaring, rampaging roar that accompanied a volcanic explosion. It was perceived that the rattling SOUND in the calderic funnel of the crater was created by the fillibrating tongue, as it pushed the lava up to Her surFACE as Mother Earth gave birth to Herself out of Herself. Like food was pushed out of the mother's mouth by the tongue, so the boiling magma was pushed up as the bloody lava that coagulated into land giving birth to the letters of generation G(jee) and begetting G (gh).

For some at some times, it was a vagina that gave vent to the sun that turned into bloody lava that then turned into solid land. At other times it was the volcanic lips that regurgitated the sun, helping it along, up to Her surFACE with the ever ready and helpful angle of the tongue. The concept that the letter R carries within it as the Egyptian RE, is the establishment of the male sun as superior to the body of Mother Earth. This was way before they knew that the world wasn't flat and that the sun did not circle around and through the body of Mother Earth.

After the LINGUISTIC BREAK, with the circle of the male sun emerging on top signifying male centrality, the letter R dealt not only with the male sun but with the human brain that named things, separated them from their natural background, created another reality based singularly on the linear left hemisphere of the human brain and in the process losing its balance and evenness. The Libra of liberty and level scales based on the asking of HOW of the ancient mothers in PHASE ONE became replaced by the WHY of male periphery in PHASE THREE.

The only symbol that establishes its links with father centrality and with the lower case (a) of the sun on top and the triangle of the mother on the bottom is the Linear B SOUND of RI. For the woman hating Manu priests in Hinduism the A (ah) SOUND that had been the mothers as alpha the beginners of life became associated with male names. Hidden in the linguistic coils the letter R in Phoenician is the head as RESH. It is also the head as RES in Egyptian and as RHO in Greek, extending to the same head SHAPE in Etruscan and Roman. In Egyptian it is also represented by the RI of the mouth in concert with the head that named things. As the fetus minnow SHAPED number nine in Egyptian, North Semitic and Etruscan it establishes it's links with the emerging solar definition of time in PHASE THREE based on the nine solar months of gestation rationalized by the fathers rather than the PHASE ONE ten lunar months of gestation of the ancient mothers. In Linear B as RU and the SHAPE of the pubis and in Cypriotic RU also as the SHAPE of the buttox, dealing with the solar and seasonal activity of mating based on the passage of estRUS or the bloody discharge out of herbivore mares. In Cypriotic RU also contains the SHAPE of a bird. For it was at the time that the birds returned to their nests when the seasonal flow of blood or estRUs emerged from the estral herbivores.

Then there is the number four which became a male number of 'one more' added to the three of the mothers. It surfaces in Phoenician as RESH, the head, Greek RHO, and Moabite. In the reflected evolving words the name of the male Rabbi contains at the end, the number of one (I) more, defining the male. As the RA in Linear B the letter looks like the sun emerging out of a cavity from under the body of Mother Earth symbolized by the three lateral lines. Also in Linear B the RE of REturn is a simplified symbol of joyful upraised arms greeting the sun at dawn. A similar concept of the solar ROad back surfaces in the Cypritic RO, the sun passing above the body of Mother Earth and then looping back under Her surFACE.

SUMMARY

It becomes apparent that there existed a civilized extensive reality before the shift into male history occurred based on rules made by the mothers which became codified in the capital letters of the Western Alphabet. It also becomes apparent that many of the capital letters of the Western Alphabet came out of the SHAPE of the organs on the face of the individual mother that made those specific codified SOUNDS. Since individual mothers were considered to be daughters of Mother Earth then as process, quality and function those same organs wedded to the SOUNDS that they had been perceived to make metaphorically extended to the surFACE and body of Mother Earth.

It was a time of very specific perceptions and conditions that existed perhaps the whole period of time that human brains were the same size as they are today and that would leave us with two hundred thousand years ago. Mother Earth had been considered to be their single source. Everthing that emerged upon Her flat round surFACE ending in a circle around them came out of the top of Her surFACE and body; plants, trees, insects, burrowing creatures and out of Her horizontal side the sun, moon, stars, clouds, even the birds. After they made their journeys through Her belly of air they became reabsorbed back into Her body.

Since specific paternity dealing with fatherhood had been unknown there were no male members to protect individual mothers and their children. Also due to many changes in sexual receptivity in the females, from seasonal to lunar, then to year round, rape, kidnapping and violence entered the scene. To protect the vulnerable familial groupings mothers castrated their first born sons to act as avuncular uncles and protectors to their subsequent children.

Also due to the movement into upright bi-pedalism, the narrow hips of the mother made birthing of the large headed human fetus a perilous activity. She had to labor, breathe hard and fast to get the large headed fetus out of her body. With the high fast panting breath acting like a bellows came the awakening of the electro-magnetic Kundalini energy of trance that lay coiled like a snake at her sacrum, the sacred area at the base of her spine. It flipped her into a state akin to a trance and on the wings of ecstasy she awakened into a transformed courageous mother, leader, healer, teacher and often prophet.

Men were not privy to the birthing breath of the mothers, they called it a mystery which evolved into mysticism. They found ritual, castration, drugs, heroic exploits, drumming, chanting, twirling, meditation, fasting, flagellation to gain the desired state of transformation.

The conditions dealing with protection of the family through the castration of the first born son expanded into the eunuch priesthood that in time circled the whole world. Names of cities, rivers, mountains, sacred places the world over have hidden in their linguistic coils the names of the eunuch priesthood, the snake, the numbers three and seven and a host of transformed males who became the subsequent 'saviors' of humanity.

Along the way there emerged another very major occurrence. The human creature as do other creatures, has two sides of the brain. One side the linear left hemisphere associated with the right hand had been perceived to belong to the males. The other side, the right hemisphere associated with the left hand had been perceived to belong to the mothers. The two sides were joined by the corpus collosum called the bridge, the ladder, the rainbow that yoked the two sides together to form a perfect balance. Balance and evenness had been considered to be a major good. But the balance became to tilt toward the left hemisphere of male *linear* thought with the beginning of naming of things separating them from their background, then with music, one note after another, then with speech one SOUND after another, then with writing itself, one word after another.

It became aaparent that along the way writing itself shifted from the left hand of the mothers to the right hand of the fathers. With that shift came linear, rational thought that left the transformative abilities of the mother behind and suppressed them. It also threw a blanket of obfuscation over the Earth sourced electro-magnetic Kundalini energy shifting its source *away* from the body of Mother Earth into the heavens and the mind of a celestial deity, or right handed God as source and religious systems of thought based on monotheistic patriarchy. With that evolution came the abuse, villificatin, enslavement of the individual mother as the source of life which extended to the abuse, exploitation of the physical body of Mother Earth.

The electro-magetic Kundalini energy rising up from the lea lines out of the body of Mother Earth had been turned up side down. With male role in specific procreation becoming known male desire to find the father entered the ancient picture. Since the body of Mother Earth had been taken by the mothers then the father had to rise above Her body, *away* from Her ground of being. First it was with the moon, then the sun emerged as their deity. In tme the stars came into their own.Ultimately it became the whole cosmos. It was apparent to them that male bodies carried a permanently empty belly and did not produce babies. They turned to the mind as their creative source and specifically the emerging linear left hemisphere of the brain to do the job. With their emerging reliance on the rational aspect of the left hemisphere of the brain the emerging priesthood took the Kundalini energy and made it their own but veiled and redefined. It was no longer out of the body of Mother Earth but out of the ethers where the male mind of God found His home. And it became redefined as Shakti of the Hindus, the Shekinah of the Hebrews and the Holy Ghost of the Christians. Underneath all those tortured rdefinitions there exists the reality that the energy of transformation rises up out of the body of Mother Earth, enters the soles of the feet while standing and the anus while sitting bringing with it a movement into the 'spiritual' state of trance.It is an energy that frees the aspiring adept into an 'intermediate state' of ecstasy, freedom from fear, the possibility of becoming a healer, prophet and shaman. It had been originally experienced by the birthing mothers. In time others through ritual joined her ranks. Becauase the state of trance could not be controlled the carriers of the gift were redefined as witches and burned at the stake. Mother healers became replaced by doctors. The left hemisphere of the rational fathers where the fear had been store emerged supreme, closing down the right hemisphere of compassion, relationship, responsibility and love of the mothers plunging the world into violence, war, irresponsible sexuality that extended to the body of Mother Earth. It is the state that the world is in today. There is no hope for the planet, Her creatures and humanity unless the violence based on power, greed and control of the fathers becomes balanced by the love and compassion of the mothers.

Section Three

CONCLUSION

How many digs have male archaeologists left untouched or even destroyed because it showed the female as the center of the social unit and the center of the religious rites, calling the statuettes of Goddesses representatives of ancient cults, not giving them the status of religions. How many sites were abandoned because deeper explorations brought forth more and more proof that the origins of humanity were based on female accomplishments and on mother based belief centers.

How much research, how many works of art, how many inventions have been ignored by males to make them powerful and to keep them in control.

In the last fifty years with more and more women becoming scholars, more and more male duplicity has been discovered. Wholesale suppression of data of female accomplishments has been uncovered. Its as if Western history had been only expressed by male writers and movie producers. No blacks and very few women, most who were wimpy and powerless took part. It's no wonder that the accumulated data of the last 6,000 years is called *his*tory (his story). It is about males, by males and for males. Up until very recently, it has left women out altogether. It has left out half of the human race, and all of its contributions. So is the glass half empty or half full? A curious question. With the women's movement, with the Kundalini energy of Mother Earth blasting through women, demanding to be heard and realized, with the movement in the sixties of Eastern religions some who embrace the Mother, we have come to know that there was a time before history, a time where our *her*itage began. There was a time when *it* was *her age*, the time before *his*tory. The word itself gives us clue. As *his* story gives us a clue what the last 6,000 years have been about male testosterone going wild with war, violence, destruction, rape, despair, depression, pollutions and destruction of the planet and the life on it, then we can see that not only a parallel line has gone along the line of this chaos but that this parallel line has been totally redefined as evil, as the seductress, as the incubus. The parallel line along this trail of horror and woe has been of women having, nurturing children and making their survival possible by discovering *herbs*, by following herds, by making tools and pots which have been defined as crafts rather than art because they had practical uses and were invented by women.

Women invented tools not men. Men invented weapons. Weapons are not tools for survival. Weapons are tools for destruction. War and destruction is a left hemispheric male game as women huddle around protecting themselves and their children.

This parallel line of women stretching back to prehistory has made humanity possible. It not only goes back to our heritage, the foundations of our own specie, but back into the roots which come through the great apes and further back through all the animals and the evolving life on the planet.

The dolphins and the whales have left us behind and may have evolved higher than human beings but because they didn't drag the panic with them we don't consider them as intelligent as mankind. The romantic poets did not anthromorphise animals and the elements, when clouds cried, and the wind wailed and Mother Earth shuddered beneath us. They not only understood the source of language out of the individual mothers face and the surFACE of Mother Earth, they also understood that all that we are stands on the foundation of all that came before us. All the characteristics thoughts, feelings, that we now express as human beings were potentials and actualites in creatures before us. They were tried over and over again in Mother Nature and if found to work were kept, if they didn't work, were discarded.

Male image driven left hemispheric fear which has dragged violence in its wake will be one of those discards of Mother Nature. It may work for a few thousands of years but in the reckoning of time that is only a momentary flash. Male contempt and the lack of reverence for the human female, for the body of Mother Earth and the Mother energy implicit in that process will bring an end to the specie. We have fouled our own nest and a creature in a fouled nest, self-destructs.

All of history and our heritage did not spring whole from the head of Zeus like Athena, or from Adams rib like Eve, it slowly rolled on. Some potentials were tried and kept, like the sharks, cocaroaches and crocodiles, others were tried and rejected only to reappear at another time in other more recent creatures. Potential is not rejected generally, it is rejected specifically by a particular specie. All potential for adaptability and survival is being constantly recycled, through different forms. Like the two hemispheres of the brain work. The two hemispheres of the brain, the two modalities, male and female, form and content, realize matter from potential.

The recycling goes on over and over again, if the potential is usable it is kept. If the potential is non-usable it goes back into the sea of possibility to be used again when circumstances warrant it to pop back up to the level of matter and reality. There are some characteristics that although no longer part of the specie pop back up, like an extra nipple on the bodies of some children, or webbing between the toes, or the stump of a vestigial tail. These are physical flashbacks that occur in our specie and manifest themselves in matter.

There are other flashbacks that occur in our specie and manifest themselves on other levels, in time, they refuse to go away. Some stand unexpectedly on the surFACE of Mother Earth as monuments, like Stonehenge, Gobkli Tepi, Machu Pichu, the caves at Malta, massive stone heads and humongous stone balls in Mexico. Pyramids that are being discovered all around the world as are stone circles and mounds.

Some of these echoes still exist as behavior pattern of healing like acupuncture, energy meridians, herbology, chakra energy, shaman visitation by spirits, etc. Others exist as superstitions unexplained aversions to the number thirteen, attraction to the number seven, black cats, walking under ladders, knocking on wood, the admonition by fathers in Poland not to kill spiders and the myths among the Amerindians that spiders created the world.

Then there is the whole area of numbers and numerology, the number seven and its repetition, the number three, the number one and 666 for the anti-Christ, then astrology and the position of the cosmic universe at the moment of our first breath. Tarot cards, glass balls, Book of Changes, the I Ching, relationships, the dealing with relationships, on the level of a forgotten modality. A throwback an echo of another time, when the potential was actual and what we consider now as quaint, mystic light headed was then part of a much more expansive and often glorious reality.

The definition as all that being silly nonsense has been made mostly by males because they not only forgot the past more quickly but they have been instrumental in obliterating it. As with the contribution of females which they have either ignored or suppressed, so they have done to all the other unexplainable data. What is unexplained is fearful so it is better either to ignore it or to deny its existence or rewrite it. The whole area of our heritage as women went into the oblivion because it exists on the level where it cannot be rationally explained by men.

What I have dealt with from the linguistic potsherds of our heritage, all those unexplained physical aspects on the planet itself and in us as psychic throwbacks, will be of a different modality that existed before this one and constantly throws itself back into our lives as portends, coincidences, as vestigial tails, as throwbacks themselves back on a physical level.

Women and children with the eunuch uncles were at the center and the band of brothers were peripheral, not the other way around. History is his story, the time when in PHASES TWO and THREE when males realized their role in specific paternity and took center stage creating not only the male BEGATS but all the chaos and mess that followed it.

In PHASE ONE there was a Garden of Eden. There was a Paradise, for when the mothers controlled the survival unit there was no need for war. It was a time before the separation of the two hemispheres of the brain and the over development of the left hemisphere, before the creation of turf and of countries resulting in the separation from Mother Earth and Her powers of healing, a time when one language was spoken by all the peoples and they not only understood each other through evolving codified words but understood the language of animals. For animals spoke to them and warned them of disasters and were often used to guide them through the passage of death.

The clues for this information exists in the languages themselves in the primitive seed words within each language and the repetition of SOUNDS on the whole planet that have similar if not identical original meaning. These SOUNDS as phonemes are the building blocks of language and as they became explicit and verbalized on the physical sensory level they stilled the intuitive inner voice, the voice of inner universal communication based on truth with all that is and with other human beings.

As the change took place and hemispheric polarity shifted and male power grew, the sham and the display of maleness could no longer exist on the inner level because that is where the fear could be detected so the inner level had to be stilled by the outer SOUND, by the noise of the spoken word and the rolling tape, the voice over that put an end of true communication. In that process symbols were created for the thing itself, symbols that reflected the image but were not the image itself. So reality became twice removed. Once seen by the eye upside down, the reflection of the real and then given a name which is another step away from the thing as it is.

Animals have SOUNDS that have practical meaning, they have body language and ritual with which they communicate. Our human communication has deep roots in our animal ancestors. Its difficult to say when actual communication becomes singularly human, for we do not dwell in the heads of animals and don't know of the processes that they go through in communicating that they also follow.

They don't need as many symbols and SOUINDS as we do, not because they have less to say but because they are less frightened than we are. They are still in touch with the cycles of life and death, so they have no need to explain them away and with rationalizations to still their fears. We use language to allay out fears, we talk to ourselves to quiet our fears and talk to others to explain them away. If we had no fears to explain away our vocabulary would be as simple as of many of the birds. Hello, how are you, nice day, you look familiar, haven't we met before, say hello to the family, have a nice trip South. Not much else is needed when you're not impressing, sizing up, stalking, manipulating, trying to better the other person because their gain in power means the loss of your own and the fear that it engenders.

Animals are mostly female oriented working out of their right side of the brain because the primary unit is still the female and child. In birds the female is usually Earth colored and camouflaged while the male is highly colored and highly vocal, both situations draw predators to him. The female and her brood blend into the woodwork and have a greater survival possibility.

SOUNDS have meaning in animals for they attach certain SOUNDS with certain situations. The chimps have screeches and gorillas have grunts. Whales wail forth their mournful song and the dolphins click their way through life. The only difference between us and the animals is that with our opposable thumb we could grasp a chisel or a brush and concretize those SOUNDS in stone so that we have a record of them and we know that they existed in prehistory. For that prehistory, that heritage has its own particular characteristics that those chiseled or brushed symbols represent. Once the SOUND passed from the actual moment that it was uttered to the papyrus or stone, it bore witness to itself and its existence.

Animals may have as complex systems of communication but they have not devised means which bear witness to their communication. As the SOUND was systemized and made linear, written in straight lines it caused the brain to flip over from the female side to the male side, for males work with linear segmentation not in a holistic rush as females do.

The process which began as sequential SOUNDS, created linear patterns in the left hemispheric male brain that was ready to receive them. For it is only through the male side of the brain that each frame, like that of a moving picture can come through. Experience, sensory input comes in a rush. The female side comes in a rush often with pleasure and ecstasy, as well as realization. The male side of the brain takes that rush and breaks it up into lines which can be fed as symbols and spat out. It is a thin focus that allows for the segmentation, the linear serialization, the looking at each frame to take place.

The rush of image based experience made the male feel panic stricken, so to survive he had to slow it down and look at each frame sequentially. It gave him a sense of control over Mother Nature, over the mother and over the female. These simple hemispheric shifts based on fear, have led us to where we are now and may be the reason why as a specie, the human race may not survive.

In the process of segmentation of separation and reordering, new molecular structures were formed, countries were formed, chemical compounds which kill living organisms were formed, and the segmentation is linear, going in a straight line. A line does not turn on itself like a cycle or spiral does. It does not have to face the product of its often destructive labors. The left hemispheric male mind never has to face the results of its actions until the results destroy the planet and cause the destruction to its inhabitants. Females by being in the experiential brain of the right hemisphere are still connected to Mother Earth by the cycles of menstruation and baby production. Because of that, women are forced to deal with responsibility. Cycles like spirals never let you off the hook. Cycles are an endless returning, going round and round but on a slightly different level every time.

A straight line shoots out into space, as a penis does, or a gun, or a missile, or a laser. What males project out from themselves in a straight line are activities that they never have to deal with, the further the better, the bigger the bang the less pieces that you have to pick up. Women are forever picking up the pieces of male linear orientation, from having babies to rebuilding societies after the male made wars have destroyed them.

What males have also done, as women bore and nurtured children, is to take each thing that women have created and made it their own. Women created tools as we see among the chimpanzees. Flo, the chimp mother using a stick to get termites out of the termite mounds and passing the information to her children, teaching them from her experience, creating transmitted culture.

Once the children knew, both male and female, then the males in their constant struggle with other males for power used the information they learned from their mothers for their own self-aggrandizement. They took tools and made them into weapons. They took herbs and the healing arts and made them into medicine and the distribution of drugs. They took intuitive compassion and morality and made it into law which furthers male games and further victimizes women and children. They took holy women, the healers and made them into houris, prostitutes whores and witches while they covered themselves with the trappings of the ancient rites to form bizarre medical practices and empty religious systems devoid of ecstasy and content.

Fear, images and the shift from the right hemisphere of the brain of the mother to the left hemisphere of the father may have had its beginning with the codification of the emerging human SOUNDS which then expanded into words.

The eyes create images. That is an obvious assumption. Then how do the linear SOUNDS picked up by the ears also create images in the brain? How does that process work? Do our ears also see? Obviously they do. The problem is that it is to the linear images that fear finds a way to attach itself. Since the process is linear and not circular, not holistic, we must realize that it has its home in the left hemisphere, the male modality of the human brain.

When and how did this happen? There are concepts that have been missing. It is not only fight or flight. It is also fright. The human creature can fight, flee but it can also freeze to the spot in fright. That has been left out of the male psychiatric mélange. Then there is another major omission based on nature and nurture. It leaves out the most important aspect of subsequent behavior and that is that the human baby is born helpless and conscious. As it takes its first breath it must be flooded with the numbing realization that it is locked in a body that doesn't work. Two major activities begin to run its life. One is to get instant attention and help. The other deals with creating its reality through the filter of panic of its helplessness. All the reality that it begins to create is through that infantile filtered panic of its helpless condition. If the images that the eyes begin to stack in its brain become associated with a traumatic experience that image doesn't flow through it gets trapped in place. The trauma activates the image. The image activates the trauma. The creature becomes locked in an unending battle with images that give it no rest. To that end the Kundalini experience came into being to flush, burn out the accumulated bank of debris based images.

It seems that theoretical speculations have surfaced and that there was a massive change in the human brain forty thousand years ago. It somehow became more outer oriented, more creative, much more rational, less relationship oriented, attached to unrelenting male sexuality and turf and more violent. Some male scientists are calling it the beginning of male genius. Explanations of Imhotep, DaVinci, Einstein, Tesla point to the difference in the way their brains dealt with the universe. They had either become totally left hemispheric or their corpus collosum joining the two hemispheres of the brain became so thin that reality and how it works became based totally on wish fulfilled answers to their periphery on fabrications, fantasy, the faith of the father, adult fairy tales and force. With the redefinitions of source out of the male left hemisphere and a 'hidden' male father God floating in the ethers creating arbitrary rules by His male priesthood came male priviledge and entitlement that exist to this day as women toil as slaves in most of the world.

CHANGES
Total freedom for women.

- Not all women want or need to be mothers. They should have the opportunity to make their own decisions how to use their bodies. Old men in long dresses should not define their lives. Massive investment should be made in safe contraception. If it doesn't work then abortions should be a matter of course.
- Prostitutes if they want to pursue the profession, should be canonized for the service that they perform and protected from male violence.
- Marriage should be redefined as legalized prostitution and not considered as such a universal good. Its only goal is to separate the young bride from her mother and to create the husband as the master.
- Women should be taught how to pleasure their bodies. Most men don't last long enough to give women orgasms and sexual satisfaction. Only about seventeen percent of women have an orgasm during coitus. It would take both sexes off the madness dealing with sexual satisfaction.
- Extended families and large homes should be encouraged so children can turn to many for their love and care.
- Upon becoming pregnant the potential mother should get total medical care and a salary for the rest of her life.
- A baby should *NEVER* be separated from the mothers body after birth for at least two years or until it walks away on its own two feet.
- A troubled mother should be helped but the baby should *always* stay with her even in jail.
- A baby should be touched and fondled by all who share the feeling of love and kindness toward it.
- Rapists and pedophiles should be castrated and the death penalty should be visited upon them.
- Pornography with children should also get the death penalty.
- Half of all laws, courts and the police should be staffed by women and run for women.
- Universal education and health care should be the heritage of all children.

CPSIA information can be obtained
at www.ICGtesting.com
Printed in the USA
LVHW091153021021
698849LV00019B/19

9 781614 937319